'*The Web of Meaning* is both a profound personal meditation on human existence and, as its title i[...] together of historic and contem[...] spiritual thought on the deepest q[...]

— **Gabor Maté M.D.**, author of *In the Realm of Hungry Ghosts: Close Encounters With Addiction*

'We need, now more than ever, to figure out how to make all kinds of connections. This book can help – and therefore it can help with a lot of the urgent tasks we face.'

— **Bill McKibben**, author of *Falter: Has the Human Game Begun to Play Itself Out?*

'There are so many ways to understand the world, and so many levels to be integrated, that everyone can use the guidance of Jeremy Lent. Moving from the ancient Tao to modern neuroscience and everything in between, he boldly weaves deep insights together to envision a better world.'

— **Frans de Waal**, author of *Mama's Last Hug: Animal Emotions and What They Tell Us about Ourselves*

'A book of radical and profound wisdom ... a magnificent manifesto for a regenerative culture and for an ecological civilisation ... the book beautifully addresses some of the most complex questions of life.'

— **Satish Kumar**, Editor Emeritus, Resurgence & Ecologist and Founder of Schumacher College

'One of the most brilliant and insightful minds of our age, Jeremy Lent has written one of the most essential and compelling books of our time. *The Web of Meaning* invites us to rethink at the deepest level who we are as a species and what we might become.'

— **David Korten**, author of *When Corporations Rule the World* and *The Great Turning: From Empire to Earth Community*

'Jeremy Lent is one of today's most eloquent cultural observers. In this captivating book he addresses with frightening clarity how humanity's loss of balance within ourselves and with the natural world has brought civilization to the brink of collapse; and he also shows us a way out – a path of integration, recognizing our deep interconnectedness, that could lead toward a new ecological civilization. I highly recommend this inspiring book to anyone concerned about the future of humanity.'

— **Fritjof Capra**, author of *The Web of Life*,
co-author of *The Systems View of Life*

'Five decades ago, the interweaving of Buddhist thought and systems theory liberated my experience and understanding of self. That changed everything. Today, with equal excitement, I harvest from Jeremy Lent's *The Web of Meaning* a sense of the distinctive, ongoing presence – or spirit – that is woven by self's conscious engagement with life. The opportunity to plunge into this book will change my life. My gratitude, like spirit, is endless.'

— **Joanna Macy**, author of *World as Lover, World as Self*

'Taking up where his brilliant *The Patterning Instinct* left off, Jeremy's Lent's *The Web of Meaning* reveals the deeper purpose and passion for human existence: a collective quest for meaning through connection, without even having to believe anything in particular. An important and rationally argued primer for universal flourishing.'

— **Douglas Rushkoff**, author of *Team Human*

'With clarity, scholarship and passion Jeremy Lent rejects the ill-founded ideological cynicism of neo-liberal capitalism. Based on solid science, the book is a long argument that offers a viable and hopeful alternative that draws on Buddhist, Neo-Confucian and Indigenous philosophies and stresses the interconnectedness of all life. It is a wide-ranging synthesis written for all those who have not given up on a moral stand and can be spurred into action.'

— **Eva Jablonka**, author of *Evolution in Four Dimensions*

'In this timely and well-researched text, Jeremy Lent weaves the insights from ancient philosophical and Indigenous traditions with modern scientific views of how our systems of life unfold on Earth to reveal inspiring ways we might reawaken our innate capacities to live with a wider, more inclusive sense of self, identity and belonging with each other and within nature. A beautiful synthesis of wisdom and empirical knowledge, this erudite journey offers an important way to construct a new narrative of our shared lives.'

— **Daniel J. Siegel**, M.D., author of *Mind*, *Aware* and *IntraConnected: MWe (Me + We) as the Integration of Belonging and Identity*

'*The Web of Meaning* lays the foundation for a true world culture which is solidly scientific, yet profoundly spiritual, telling a contemporary story of a meaningful universe that includes and embraces humankind. This book is a landmark work for a time that urgently needs to understand that the cosmos is our home and not our enemy to be conquered.'

— **Andreas Weber**, author of *The Biology of Wonder*

'Few writers I know have the ability to be genuinely holistic and interdisciplinary, weaving science and culture into a coherent whole. This is precisely what Jeremy Lent has done in *The Web of Meaning*, a profound and necessary book for forging a pathway towards an ecological civilization.'

— **Roman Krznaric**, author of *The Good Ancestor: How to Think Long Term in a Short-Term World*

'*The Web of Meaning* is a book of radical and profound wisdom. This book is a magnificent manifesto for a regenerative culture and for an ecological civilisation. Lent shows us a way out of the old story of separation and disconnection and leads us towards a new story of interconnection. The book beautifully addresses some of the most complex questions of life. I found the book like a friend and a companion in the journey of transformation.'

— **Satish Kumar**, Editor Emeritus, *Resurgence & Ecologist* and Founder of Schumacher College

'A remarkable journey to explore the meaning of life and humanity's place in our interconnected world. Lent's deep knowledge of history, science and traditional wisdom opens our eyes and our hearts to a new understanding of who we are and how our lifestyle is affecting the world around us. Lent presents an integrated worldview that points the way to living a meaningful life in harmony with nature. This brilliant book teaches us the wisdom and science we need to create a world where people care for each other and for Earth, and flourish.'

— **Clair Brown**, author of *Buddhist Economics: An Enlightened Approach to the Dismal Science*

'*The Web of Meaning* is a call for recognizing what both our newest science and our oldest spiritual traditions tell us: that we are all inextricably interconnected with one another and with nature. This thoughtful and passionate work is an important contribution to the urgently needed cultural shift from domination to partnership.'

— **Riane Eisler**, author of *The Chalice and the Blade*, *The Real Wealth of Nations* and *Nurturing Our Humanity*

'A widely ranging, deeply penetrating and healingly prescriptive consideration of how to reposition humanity within the world. Lent's ideas, drawn from all around the globe from antiquity to the present, provide a vision for a better shot at survival and a life that is worthwhile for our time – and for the rest of time.'

— **Carl Safina**, author of *Beyond Words* and *Becoming Wild*

'A path-breaking book – carefully researched, clearly written and life transforming. This integration of science and wisdom traditions deserves to be widely read. One of the most comprehensive and insightful books on this topic to date.'

— **Mary Evelyn Tucker**, Yale Forum on Religion and Ecology and co-author of *Journey of the Universe*

'It is hard to build new regenerative narratives that honor the old without being in extractive relation to non-western lands and peoples, but this book is a damn good start. This book is a good place to sit for anybody interested in binding the wounds of thoughtless progress and allowing the emergence of new patterns of being.'

— **Tyson Yunkaporta**, author of *Sand Talk: How Indigenous Thinking Can Save the World*

'With deft and unrelenting strokes of compassionate penmanship, Lent unravels the stories that keep us bound to a colonial arrangement of anthropocentricity, superior markets, excavated nature, endless growth and boundless consumerism, masquerading as the normal. And then he spins an alternative conception of things. To read Lent's *The Web of Meaning* is to be captured by a sensuous awakening – the scandalous idea that other worlds are possible and, perhaps given the state of contemporary collapse, almost *inevitable*.'

— **Bayo Akomolafe**, author of *These Wilds Beyond our Fences: Letters to My Daughter on Humanity's Search for Home*

'Insightful, exhilarating and hopeful! Lent not only traces the stunning correspondences between ancient wisdom traditions and vanguard biological sciences, he explains how recognizing our place in life's web of interdependence opens up new vistas for change. *The Web of Meaning* is a bold, timely challenge to conventional science, religion and social movements to see the world – and themselves – in new ways.'

— **David Bollier**, commons activist/scholar and co-author of *Free, Fair, and Alive: The Insurgent Power of the Commons*

'Maybe, just maybe, this is the skillfully organized and brilliantly written book that will turn the world around. Scientists cling to a seventeenth-century metaphysics that leads to nihilism and supports the policies that are destroying ecosystems everywhere. But Lent shows, convincingly, that there are masses of facts science has laid bare that call for a very different worldview of self-organizing entities. He is certainly right. Is there any chance that the slowly awakening world will listen?'

— **John B. Cobb, Jr.**, author of *Process Theology: An Introductory Exposition*

'A superb, perceptive, intelligent book which gives you that most valuable of things – a modern way of looking at the world that answers the big questions and leaves you both inspired and enthused. It is confirmation that, as we move beyond individualism, the twenty-first century promises to be far more rewarding than we ever expected.'

— **John Higgs**, author of *The KLF: Chaos, Magic and the Band who Burned a Million Pounds*

'Lent does not shy away from the dire predicament we find ourselves in, in the 2020s. But if there is to be any hope of realising the Symbiocene, it will surely come in part from the kind of kind, clear tapestry that Lent weaves in this book. The final line of the book is a beautiful invitation: "What is the sacred and precious strand that *you* will weave" in the web of meaning? You will be best-placed to be able to answer this question, and realise your own role in creation and re-creation, if you go on this journey with him.'

— **Rupert Read**, professor, author of *Parents for a Future* and co-editor of *Deep Adaptation*

'*The Web of Meaning* is a profound book of wisdom. If we are ever to remember how to live lives of meaning and grace, it will be in great measure because of books like this one.'

— **Derrick Jensen**, author of *The Myth of Human Supremacy*

THE WEB OF MEANING

ALSO BY JEREMY LENT

The Patterning Instinct

THE WEB OF MEANING

Integrating Science and Traditional Wisdom to Find Our Place in the Universe

JEREMY LENT

P

PROFILE BOOKS

This paperback edition first published in 2022

First published in Great Britain in 2021 by
Profile Books Ltd
29 Cloth Fair
London
EC1A 7JQ
www.profilebooks.com

1 3 5 7 9 10 8 6 4 2

Typeset in Garamond by MacGuru Ltd
Printed and bound in Great Britain by
CPI Group (UK) Ltd, Croydon, CR0 4YY

A CIP catalogue record for this book is available from the British Library.

ISBN 978 1 78816 565 5
eISBN 978 1 78283 725 1

To life,
in its full flourishing

Contents

NOTE TO READER

Note numbers with an asterisk indicate further discussion on a topic that the reader is encouraged to peruse.

The Glossary contains definitions of ideas that may be unfamiliar to the reader and terms that have been used in the book in a particular way.

Further Reading contains suggestions for those who wish to explore the topics of each chapter in more depth.

INTRODUCTION

Tea with Uncle Bob

We could call it the Speech. You've probably heard it many times. Maybe you've even given it. Every day around the world, innumerable versions of it are delivered by Someone Who Seems to Know what they're talking about.

It doesn't seem like much. Just another part of life's daily conversations. But every Speech, linked together, helps to lock our entire society up in a mental cage. It might occur anywhere in the world, from a construction site in Kansas to a market stall in Delhi. It can be given by anyone old enough to have learned a thing or two about how it all works. But it's usually delivered by someone who feels they've been around the block a few times and they want to give you the benefit of their wisdom.

Because I grew up in London, I'll zoom in there to a particular version of the Speech that reverberates with me. It's an occasional family gathering – one of those events where toddlers take center stage and aunties serve second helpings of cake. It's teatime, and a few of us are gathered around, talking about the state of the world. Someone comments on what's wrong with our system and how things could be so much better – but Uncle Bob happens to be in the group, and before you know it, it's too late. The Speech is about to begin.

'Let's face it,' Uncle Bob declares to the group, 'it's a dog-eat-dog world out there. Every man for himself. For all your ideas about making the world a better place, when it comes down to it, everyone's just interested in their own skin. It's a rat race. That's the way all of nature works. That's how we've been programmed. The survival of the fittest.'

Does any of this sound familiar to you? It's only too familiar to those of us at the tea party. Uncle Bob sees some glazed faces looking back at him, so he feels the need to add a few more pointers to his oration.

'Look,' he leans forward conspiratorially, 'it's like this. People like you want to change the world. But when you've had the experience I've had, you'll know better. Our society is structured this way simply because that's what works best. They tried communism – and you know what happened to that. For all the complaining people do, they've never had it so good. Look at our amazing technology, look at all the progress we've made in the past few hundred years. You can thank capitalism for that. The fact is, it works so well, because at the end of the day people are selfish – they look out for themselves. Capitalism takes that selfishness and turns it into progress – it lets people become entrepreneurs, which makes all of us better off. That's what they call … the invisible hand, isn't it?'

Game over. Whatever ideas were being floated about improving society just wafted out the window. Uncle Bob pauses. The conversation comes to a halt, until someone pipes up, 'How's little Penny doing with her dancing lessons?' – and the tea party rolls on.

This type of conversation takes place with regularity around the world because it channels the themes we hear every day from those in a position of authority – from talking heads on TV, from successful businesspeople, from teachers, from school textbooks. Even when the Speech is not given explicitly, its ideas seep into our daily thoughts. Every time a newscaster reports on prospects for economic growth; every time a TV commercial hypes the latest consumer product; every time an exciting new technology is touted as the solution to climate change, the underlying themes of the Speech insidiously tighten their grip on our collective consciousness.

Distilled to their essence, these themes come down to a few basic building blocks. Humans are selfish individuals. All creatures are selfish – in fact, selfish genes are the driving force of evolution. Nature is just a very complex machine, and human ingenuity has, for the most part, figured out how it works. The modern world is the spectacular result of technology enabled by the market forces of capitalism, and in spite of occasional setbacks, it's continually improving. There may be problems, such as global poverty or climate change, but technology, powered by the market, will solve them – just as it always has in the past.

These basic elements, give or take a few, form the foundation of the predominant worldview. They infuse much of what is accepted as indisputably true in most conversations that take place about world affairs. They are so pervasive that most of us never question them. We feel they must be based on solid facts – why else would all those people in positions of authority rely on them? That's the characteristic that makes a worldview so powerful. Like fish that don't realize they're swimming in water because it's all they know, we tend to assume that our worldview simply describes the world the way it is, rather than recognizing it's a constructed lens that shapes our thoughts and ideas into certain preconditioned patterns.

This book investigates the dominant worldview and shows that, in fact, every one of those building blocks is flawed. They were formed, in their modern version, mostly by a small group of men in seventeenth-century Europe, and further developed in the centuries that followed by other mostly European men. This worldview has accomplished a lot. It wrested intellectual control from the hidebound superstitions of traditional Christian theology and laid the foundation for modern science – one of humanity's greatest achievements. But it has also been an underlying cause of the horrendous devastation suffered by non-European peoples and cultures, and boundless destruction of the natural world. And the fundamental flaws in its construction have now become so gaping that they threaten the very survival of our civilization – and much of the living Earth.

Many people across the globe are realizing that there is something terribly wrong with the direction our world is headed. The inequities are so extreme that a couple of dozen billionaires own as much wealth as half the world's population. Our civilization is devastating the Earth at an ever-increasing pace. There has been a 68 percent decline in animal populations since 1970. Greenhouse gas emissions have caused the climate to lurch out of control, creating conditions that haven't existed on Earth for millions of years. Fires, storms, droughts and floods that used to be called 'once in a century' have become a regular staple of our daily news.

Look ahead a few decades, and things become downright terrifying. We're on track, by the middle of this century, to see the annihilation of coral reefs worldwide, 95 percent of arable land degraded and five billion people facing water shortages – and at the current rate, there will be more plastic in the oceans than fish. Without drastic changes, as we approach the later part of the century, the Amazon rainforest will have become a searing desert, the Sixth Great Extinction of species will be well underway, and as a result of climate breakdown, civilization as we know it will likely be tottering on its last legs.

At our current trajectory, humanity is headed for catastrophe. But it doesn't have to be that way. If we want to steer our civilization on another course, though, it's not enough to make a few incremental improvements here and there. We need to take a long, hard look at the faulty ideas that have brought us to this place and reimagine them. We need a new worldview – one that is based on sturdy foundations.

Imagine someone laying foundations for a single-story house. If there are a few cracks, they will probably get away with it. But suppose generations of people keep adding new stories until they've built a skyscraper on the faulty foundation. As the building begins teetering, engineers might frantically attach extra girders and struts, but it will eventually collapse unless they pay attention to fixing the flaws in the foundation. That's the situation our civilization faces right now.

This book lays out an entirely different foundation for a civilization that could lead us sustainably through this century and beyond. It reveals the flaws hidden within the current worldview, showing how certain erroneous ideas became so entrenched in popular thinking that they simply got taken for granted – and how that has led to our current predicament. Most importantly, it shows how the combined insights of traditional wisdom and modern scientific thinking offer a solid, integrated foundation for another worldview – one that could redirect human civilization onto a very different trajectory and offer future generations a flourishing world in which to thrive.

An integrated worldview

The reason a worldview is so important is that it imbues virtually every aspect of the way people think, what they value and how they act – without them even realizing it. Worldviews lead cultures to respond to their reality in fundamentally contrasting ways. If you believe that all living beings are family, you will treat them in a different way than if you think the natural world is a resource to be exploited. If you think other humans are inherently cooperative, you'll approach a person differently than if you think that, ultimately, everyone is selfish and competitive. If you presume that technology can fix our biggest problems, you won't feel the need to consider the underlying systems that caused those problems to arise in the first place.

In my earlier book *The Patterning Instinct* I looked at major worldviews through history, investigating how cultures structured patterns of meaning into the universe from humanity's earliest days in nomadic hunter-gatherer bands to modern times. One overarching theme emerged from *The Patterning Instinct*: a culture's worldview shapes its values – and those values shape history. By the same token, the values according to which we conduct our lives today will shape the future. Ultimately, the direction of history is determined by the dominant culture's worldview.

The Web of Meaning takes up where *The Patterning Instinct* left off, by laying out a framework for a worldview that could foster humanity's long-term flourishing on a healthy planet. It is a worldview of integration: one that identifies the unifying principles that flow through all things, while celebrating the differences that lead to the richness of our lived experience. It's a worldview that links together scientific findings in recent decades from such diverse fields as evolutionary biology, cognitive neuroscience and complexity theory, showing how they affirm profound insights from the world's great wisdom traditions, such as Buddhism, Taoism and traditional knowledge from Indigenous peoples around the world.

This integrated worldview breaks down many of the barriers that tend to separate different forms of knowledge and activity in modern society. We're accustomed to thinking of science as existing in a different domain from spirituality. We generally view the intellect as distinct from emotion; the mind as separate from the body; humans as separate from nature; and spiritual insight as separate from political engagement. In the integrated worldview laid out here, each one of these domains is intricately connected with the others in an extended web of meaning.

There are certain existential questions virtually every person asks at some time in their lives: Who am I? Where am I? What am I? How should I live? and ultimately Why am I? The book is organized into sections according to these questions. For each one, we'll investigate underlying flaws in the typical explanations provided by the dominant worldview, then explore the richly resonant answers offered by the intertwining of current scientific understanding with the deep insights of traditional wisdom. Finally, we'll tackle the question many of us are anxiously asking right now: *Where are we going?*

These are all questions that I pondered during a period in my life when the structures of meaning I'd constructed for myself seemed to crash around me. For much of my own life, Uncle Bob's statements had seemed irrefutably true. In fact, like many others, I built my life on their basis. I received my MBA at the University of Chicago, where the precepts of free-market capitalism were drummed into me. Finding myself in the San Francisco Bay Area at the onset of the dot.com era, I founded the world's first online credit card issuer, which I took public as its chief executive officer.

However, shortly after my company's IPO, my wife developed early symptoms of the serious illness that would eventually lead to her untimely death. I left my executive role to care for her full time, but the company was not yet firmly established, and within a couple of years it had become another casualty of the dot.com bust. With my wife suffering cognitive decline from her illness, I found myself isolated – bereft of companionship, friends and the prestige of success.

At that time, I made a solemn promise to myself that whatever path I chose for the rest of my life would be one that was truly meaningful. But where did meaning arise? Having traversed a road that seemed like a dead end, I was determined not to rely on someone else's determination of what was meaningful. I thus began my own deep investigation into the sources of meaning, which launched a comprehensive research project lasting over ten years, resulting in both *The Patterning Instinct* and this book.

Something I learned on that journey, and which will become clear through the book, is that one's personal search for meaning cannot be isolated from all that is going on in the world around us. In the pages that follow, as we trace the intimate connections that link our lives to those in our community, to all of humanity and to the entire living Earth, we'll discover how inextricably we are all interrelated – and explore some of the profound implications arising from that relatedness.

We'll encounter many fascinating and unexpected revelations along the way. We'll come across slime molds with the intelligence to solve mazes and design sophisticated road networks. We'll discover how Chinese sages from a thousand years ago provided a framework that elucidates the radical findings of modern systems theorists. We'll explore the stunning virtuosity of a single cell, and identify how the deep purpose of life reveals itself all around us – and within us. We'll learn what ant colonies and flocks of starlings can teach us about our own consciousness. We'll find out what Joni Mitchell got wrong in her environmental anthem 'Big Yellow Taxi' – and what Michael Jackson got right when he sang 'We Are the World'. We'll see how our modern society has been consciously designed to sabotage our well-being, and how, by learning and applying life's own principles, we can build an alternative civilization that could allow future generations to prosper on a flourishing Earth.

Part One

WHO AM I?

Chapter One

THE NAMELESS UNCARVED WOOD

There it sits, on top of a chest. A piece of ancient driftwood. I picked it up some years back on the windswept beach of a California seashore. It's not that big, about the length of my forearm, and it's shaped a bit like a bone. A femur, perhaps, with a big knobbly end tapering to a narrower point. If you look at the knobbly part from the right direction, you can almost see an animal face. A porpoise, maybe, or the cute bulbous snout of a beagle. Its grayish-blond color hints of the eons of sea and sun that have bleached everything else out of it. While smooth to touch, it still boasts a myriad of rippling lines showing its annual growth rings, along with sporadic perfectly round tiny dots of bygone worm holes.

It's just a piece of wood. But it's a beautiful piece, sculpted by nature, and it feels to me like the natural world peeking into my office, keeping me company. Above all, for me, it represents the Tao. 'Tao everlasting,' declared the ancient sage, 'is the nameless uncarved wood. Though small, nothing under heaven can subjugate it.'[1]

The Tao (pronounced *dao* and often spelled like that) is one of the oldest concepts from antiquity that have survived to the present day. Emerging from the mists of ancient Chinese tradition, it is translated literally as 'way' or 'path', and it refers to the mysterious ways in which the forces of nature show up in the world around us. The ancient conception of the inscrutable Tao is about as far away as you can get from the grindingly busy, technology-based civilization that has come to dominate our world. And it's partly for that reason that it's a perfect place to begin our journey into the web of meaning.

I first came across the concept of Tao when I was twenty-one years old in – of all places – New York City. I'd landed there from London on the first stage of my quest to leave my country of birth behind and find my way in the world. After months of trying to fit in to the mean streets like a bad imitation of Robert de Niro's *Taxi Driver*, I was pondering my next step. A friend gave me a powerful psychedelic, and I found myself wandering around the grimy back streets of Manhattan. Everywhere around me, I saw a frantic hard-heartedness gaudily concealed by a layer of commercial sleaze.

Back in the apartment I shared in the East Village, I told my roommate about my burning desire to find an alternative to the harshness I saw around me. He handed me a book that, he told me, he'd found helpful in such moments. As I opened it, I came face to face with a shimmering magic of words and pictures that seemed to answer my deepest questions. 'Know honor, yet keep humility,' it told me. 'Ever true and unwavering, return to the infinite.' The mysteriously wise words were accompanied by gorgeous black-and-white pictures of natural beauty and strangely alluring Chinese script. I didn't know exactly what these words meant, but they seemed like a font of wisdom I'd never previously imagined existed in the world. This book was the *Tao Te Ching*, the greatest Taoist classic.[2]

Going with the flow

I'm not alone in seeing undying value in the teachings of the *Tao Te Ching*. In fact, it's the second most translated book in history after the Bible. What is it about this book that caused it to shine through the ages as an inspiration to countless generations seeking answers to their own searching? What can it possibly offer to the internet-enhanced twenty-first century?

According to legend, the *Tao Te Ching* was written by a sage called Laozi – a name that literally means 'old master'. More likely, it represents the collective wisdom of ancient Chinese folk traditions, compiled over generations. It presents a way of living in the world that feels like a refuge from the bleak glare of modernity – an invitation to come home again, to leave behind the cacophonous discord of a meaningless rat race and find solace in deep universal truths.

But the reason to begin our journey with the Tao is not just because it offers an alternative to modernity. Rather, the early Taoists articulated a profound understanding of the complex relationship between humanity and the natural world, presenting insights that remain as relevant today as they were when they were first conceived. Indeed, the Taoists' core concepts offer a valuable framework to help decipher some of the most difficult quandaries facing our world today. As we'll see, their analysis of the human predicament reveals an understanding of distinctive aspects of human cognition that modern neuroscience has only recently come to recognize. Similarly, the Taoist account of how nature reveals itself displays an appreciation of universal principles that correspond to, and illuminate, the findings of modern systems scientists.

Ancient Chinese society at the time of the *Tao Te Ching* was struggling with its own social and political disruption. This was an age of turbulence, known as the Warring States period, which drove many thinkers to search for what had caused society to come unstuck. The early Taoists saw the ultimate source of disharmony as something in the human psyche that caused people to separate themselves from the natural flow of the Tao. That separation, in their opinion, had set off a cascade of events from the beginning of human history that led eventually to the turmoil of their times.

Living according to the flow of the Tao was, they believed, an effortless state of being. The word *te* in the title of the *Tao Te Ching* (pronounced *duh*) referred to that natural condition. It meant the intrinsic nature of whatever arose in the world, such as the nameless uncarved wood sitting on my chest. And something in that state maintained a certain power, so that 'nothing under heaven can subjugate it'. Animals, plants and other living beings spontaneously act according to their *te*, and because of that they flow with the way of nature – with the Tao. The Taoists called this type of activity *wu-wei*, or effortless action. Through *wu-wei*, Taoist sages explained, 'all things come to their completion; such is the Tao of Heaven'.[3]

Humans, too, can occasionally act according to *wu-wei*. Another early Taoist text, written by the brilliant philosopher

Zhuangzi, gives dramatic and earthy descriptions of various characters who demonstrate *wu-wei*. Zhuangzi tells of a butcher, Cook Ding, cutting up the carcass of an ox for a festival. He moves his knife in perfect rhythm as if performing a dance. The lord of the estate, seeing him, exclaims, 'Wow, it's marvelous that skill can reach such heights!' Cook Ding lays down his knife and replies, 'What I care about is the Tao, which goes beyond skill. When I first began cutting up oxen, all I could see was the ox itself. After three years, I no longer saw the whole ox. And now – now I go at it by spirit and don't look with my eyes.'[4]

Yet, the reason Cook Ding – and other maestros that Zhuangzi describes – are notable is precisely because they're so unusual. Somehow, something happened to humanity that caused us to lose *wu-wei* most of the time. Instead, our lives are filled with effort. We find ourselves working hard, pushing against resistance in one form or another. What happened to us?

A clue can be found in another Zhuangzi story about an archery contest. When the archers are playing for cheap tiles, they show top-notch skill. When they play for fancy belt buckles, they lose confidence; and when playing for gold, they become nervous wrecks. That's because when the prize becomes more valuable, their goal orientation gets in the way of their natural skill, and they lose touch with their *te*.[5]

The Chinese word for goal orientation, *yu-wei*, was the opposite of *wu-wei*, and represented the antithesis of living according to the Tao. As a result, according to the Taoists, it was a failing strategy. 'The world,' states the *Tao Te Ching*, 'is a spirit vessel which cannot be acted upon. One who acts on it fails, one who holds on to it loses.'[6]

But isn't acting on the world the very basis of our entire human civilization? Absolutely, argued the Taoists, and that's precisely the point. Looking to the dawn of history, even before the birth of civilization, they saw the beginning of human separation from Tao as far back as the emergence of language. Language, in their view, was anathema to the Tao. In fact, the very first words of the *Tao Te Ching* read, paradoxically, 'The Tao that can be spoken of is not the true Tao.' The piece of wood sitting next to me represents the

Tao not just because it's uncarved, but because it's nameless. It has no name, no purpose.[7]

It's not just language that the Taoists see as *yu-wei*. It's the kind of knowledge that leads humans to use language in the first place, and by corollary the kind of knowledge that language can transmit. 'One who knows [Tao] does not speak,' declares the *Tao Te Ching*. 'One who speaks does not know.' Being in touch with the Tao leads to a different type of knowledge that doesn't need language either to apprehend or communicate.[8]

But, of course, the language-based type of knowledge arising from *yu-wei* is necessary to build civilization. Realizing this, the Taoists portrayed an earlier golden age, before civilization, when people lived in harmony with the Tao. 'The men of old,' declared Zhuangzi, 'shared the placid tranquility which belonged to the whole world ... That was what is called the state of perfect unity.' At that time, 'people lived in common with birds and beasts, and were on terms of equality with all creatures, as forming one family.'

It was only when 'sagely men' appeared, with their new kind of knowledge, that everything changed. 'People began everywhere to be suspicious. With extravagant orchestras and gesticulating ceremonies, men began to be separated from one another. The pure solidity of wood was cut about and hacked to make sacrificial vessels ... The five colors were confounded to make ornamental patterns ... This was the crime of the skillful workmen.' As Zhuangzi tells it, it is as though every human act that built civilization was a crime against the Tao.[9]

Taoism, then, offers a view of human psychology that underpins a cohesive theory of civilization. According to this theory, the earliest humans lived in harmony with the natural world, but a certain type of uniquely human cognition arose that caused a separation from nature. This form of mental activity permitted language, goal orientation and planning, thus creating the foundations of culture that led eventually to civilization, along with hierarchy, artifice and technology – and the sense of alienation that comes from all of that.

It's a different theory of civilization than most of us are used to hearing. But it's one that has been largely validated by modern research in neuroscience and anthropology. And if we link together these early Taoist insights with the findings of neuroscience, we can begin to lay down tracks that can help us navigate the territory that lies ahead.

The executive suite

As we traverse millennia and continents from ancient Taoist sages to modern scientific researchers, we need to make a brief but important pit stop – in the unlikely location of the state of Vermont in the summer of 1848.

That summer, an athletic and popular young man named Phineas Gage was working as a construction foreman for the Rutland & Burlington Railroad company. One afternoon, he was leading a crew laying explosives in rock outcrops to prepare the ground for new railroad track, when disaster struck. A moment of distraction led to an unexpected explosion that caused a metal rod to pass right through the front of Gage's head.[10]

Amazingly, Gage survived the accident. Thanks to his robust health and the attentive care of his physician, he was pronounced cured within two months. However, although he regained his physical health, Phineas Gage had become a different person, and the cause of his extreme change in personality would make him a legend in the history of neuroscience.[11]

The pleasant and urbane person who had been so popular with both his fellow workers and his bosses was no more. Instead, as Gage returned to health, in the concerned words of his physician, he was now 'fitful, irreverent, indulging at times in the grossest profanity which was not previously his custom, manifesting but little deference for his fellows, impatient of restraint or advice when it conflicts with his desires ... devising many plans of future operation, which are no sooner arranged than they are abandoned.' His language was so foul that women were advised not to remain in his presence for long. His friends noted sadly that 'Gage was no longer Gage' and his employers wouldn't take him back. As his life unraveled, Gage spent years as an itinerant farmhand, before finding a new role as a circus attraction, displaying the tamping iron that had caused the hole in his head.[12]

What had happened to him? Modern neuroscience can now explain that Gage's accident had destroyed large portions of his prefrontal cortex (PFC), the part of the brain responsible for what is called the executive function. The PFC allows us to think and act in ways that other animals don't. It controls our basic physiological drives and enables us to plan, conceptualize and make abstract rules. It permits us to think symbolically – a prerequisite of the human language faculty. In fact, there is a striking convergence between the capabilities mediated by the PFC and the type of 'knowing' that the Taoists believed separated humans from the Tao. Could the evolution of the PFC in humans have been responsible for the emergence of what the Taoists called *yu-wei* – for purposive, goal-oriented thinking?[13]

As humans evolved, the PFC expanded to take up about 29 percent of the cerebral cortex, which is the largest part of the mammalian brain. That's a similar percentage to our close evolutionary cousins such as chimpanzees, but much larger than you find in other mammals. As a result of these and other findings, most cognitive neuroscientists agree that the uniquely advanced evolution of the PFC in humans played a significant role in differentiating us from other animals, and giving us the mental firepower to develop language, culture and eventually civilization.[14*]

How does the PFC do it? Probably the most important characteristic of the PFC is its connectedness. Virtually all other parts of the brain link to it directly. All of your senses, your feelings and memories, even the parts of your brain regulating your inner biology, have direct neural connections to your PFC. Whatever is happening around you or within you at any moment, the PFC 'knows' about it. This puts the PFC in the unique position of being able to coordinate and integrate everything into one coherent whole, and thus to initiate plans that take into account each of the various elements that might be important.[15]

When neuroscientists try to explain how the PFC works, they use analogies like the conductor of an orchestra or the senior executives of a company, which is why the PFC's role is known as the executive function. In a corporation, different departments might be focused on particular functions, such as purchasing, operations or sales. Somebody on an assembly line may have very little idea about where the raw materials are coming from, or how they're being marketed. But in a well-run company, the important information gets communicated quickly to the company's top executives, who can integrate the disparate pieces in order to arrive at an effective corporate strategy.[16]

When the original Taoists identified a certain kind of human cognition that was responsible for language, for goal orientation and for the artifice of civilization, they likely had in mind the kind of conceptual thinking that is mediated by the PFC. For the Taoists, this type of thinking was responsible for the loss of *wu-wei*, the harmonious way of being that allowed one to flow effortlessly through life. But when Phineas Gage had the misfortune to damage a large part of his PFC, his life unraveled. He certainly didn't enjoy a harmonious existence. What accounts then, for the difference between the Taoist view and Gage's experience? Can they be reconciled? In order to answer this, we need to get a better sense of how our executive suite functions. And in doing so, we will begin to uncover some core insights into the human experience that will help launch our journey through the rest of this book.

Blocking the flow (and redirecting it)

Imagine you've arrived in a foreign city on business. It's your first time there. You're meeting a business associate, Sandra Martinez, whom you've never met before, at a restaurant. You walk in and the maître-d' greets you. Automatically, you ask, 'Do you have a reservation under Martinez?' Yes, the maître-d' affirms, and politely escorts you to a table where a stranger's face greets you with a smile. You thank the maître-d', shake Sandra's hand with a polite reciprocating smile and begin talking niceties.

How did you accomplish this, even though you didn't know the restaurant, the maître-d' or even what Sandra looked like? This is just one of the myriad ways in which your PFC keeps you together in a complex world. Even though you didn't know the restaurant, you long ago figured out the 'rules of the game' in restaurants around the world. You extended your learnings from other specific situations into abstract generalities that can apply elsewhere. When that person walked toward you wearing a polite expression and a formal outfit, you knew they must be the maître-d'. Based on countless experiences, you assumed that Sandra had made a reservation under her last name, and that, if she had arrived first, she'd already be sitting at a table waiting for you.[17]

The ability of the PFC to create abstract general principles from specific experiences is one of the most important characteristics of human intelligence. It permits the flexibility and adaptability that is a hallmark of human cognition. In my previous book, I called this special faculty of the PFC a 'patterning instinct' – one that we share with other mammals, but that we humans seem to possess to a far greater degree.[18]

You are invariably using your patterning instinct whenever you find yourself in a new situation that you're trying to comprehend. Imagine it's your first day at a new job. You're watching for subtle cues around you, such as how people are interacting with each other, what's said and not being said, as you try to find patterns in important intangibles such as the office power dynamics or the cultural norms that will help you fit in.

Now, you're in the middle of a crucial meeting as you're settling in to your new job. Suddenly, you realize you need to pee. Do you give in to the urge and let it flow while you're sitting there in the conference room? Of course not. You rely on another of your PFC's most important functions, the inhibition of instinctual drives, to repress the urge, either until the end of the meeting or until your PFC computes that the urge is too strong. Even then, you restrain the impulse to let go until you politely stand up, excuse yourself and walk purposefully toward the nearest bathroom – and relief.[19]

Later that afternoon, you meet a new colleague whom you find sexually attractive. Of course, you know better than to say 'I want to make love with you.' You play it cool, paying extra attention to your bodily cues to make sure you're not giving anything away, while watching for possible cues coming from him. Again, you can thank your PFC for that. By contrast, the unfortunate Phineas Gage lost much of that faculty when his PFC got demolished, leading him to make those lewd comments that got him in trouble with polite society.[20]

Now, we're beginning to find ourselves in an area of the PFC's functionality that the Taoists were talking about. In nature, creatures seem to behave according to their *te*, going with the flow of their natural drives. Humans, on the other hand, are continuously blocking that flow and redirecting it. When you repressed the urge to pee in that business meeting, it's because you had other objectives more important to you than the immediate relief of your bladder. Our lives are filled with a nonstop barrage of inner and external motivations competing for our attention, and it's a crucial part of the PFC's function to prioritize these. When you get home after that first day on the job, you'd love to flop down on the couch and relax, but before you do that you've got to shift your attention to your children's needs, and then, just as you're ready for bed, you realize you forgot to prepare some work for your meeting the next morning with your new boss. Even though you're dog-tired, you force yourself back to the computer and start working on it.[21]

This brings us to another key faculty mediated by the PFC – goal orientation. This is what the Taoists described as *yu-wei*, or the diametric opposite of going with the flow of the Tao. When neuroscientists talk about the PFC's functions, they use phrases like 'forming goals and objectives, then devising plans of action to attain them' – highly valuable processes that are a requisite for navigating our civilization. In fact, as we'll see later, scientists have discovered a strong correlation between the strength of a person's PFC and their success in life. However, goal orientation takes us far from the Taoist ideal of *wu-wei*. Zhuangzi, recognizing this, appropriately called the first chapter of his classic 'Going Rambling Without a Destination'.[22]

It's easy to see now why Phineas Gage's life fell apart once his PFC was so severely damaged. A well-honed PFC is an essential part of living successfully among others who are continuously using their own PFCs to negotiate the subtleties and complexities of daily existence. Our PFC is constantly blocking the unmediated flow of our instinctual drives and redirecting them to outcomes we desire. Does that mean, then, that Taoist *wu-wei* is just an unattainable – even an undesirable – state of being?

Within the PFC itself, there may be an answer lurking to this question. Neuroscientists have discovered that, concealed within the complex architecture of our PFC, there are in fact two different 'brains', each with a distinctive character of its own. It's a strange phenomenon that has only been uncovered as a result of ingenious research. Could the contrasting characteristics of these two distinct brains within us hold a key to deciphering those ancient Taoist insights?

The interpreter and the mystic

The bizarre but consequential story of how these two 'brains' were discovered begins with some patients who suffered from severe, intractable epilepsy – a condition that is, thankfully, very rare. Epileptic seizures occur as a result of abnormal electric discharges that spread from one hemisphere of the brain to the other. Beginning in 1940 in New York, neurosurgeons attempted a novel procedure for these unfortunate patients: to cut the corpus callosum, a bundle of nerves that connects the two hemispheres, in the hope that this would prevent the seizures from spreading. It worked. Most patients experienced far fewer seizures, without any obvious side-effects. However, beginning in the 1960s, two legendary neuroscientists, Roger Sperry and Michael Gazzaniga, conducted some cunning tests to understand what was actually going on inside the skulls of these rare people walking around with split brains. What they found revolutionized the field of neuroscience.

As many people know, the right hemisphere of the brain controls the left side of the body, and vice versa. Sperry and Gazzaniga used this bit of information to set up some clever experiments. They showed one scene that was only visible to a patient's right eye, and another only visible to his left eye. For example, one split-brain patient saw a chicken claw with his right eye (available to his brain's left hemisphere) and a snow scene with his left eye (available to the right hemisphere). He was then asked to choose related pictures from an assortment placed in full view. His left hand chose a shovel, and his right hand a chicken. A normal person, if asked why she chose these two pictures, might have said something like 'The chicken goes with the claw, and the shovel goes with the snow.' But the split-brain patient responded, 'Oh, that's simple.

The chicken claw goes with the chicken, and you need a shovel to clean out the chicken shed.'

Sperry and Gazzaniga already knew, from a century of research, that the language centers of the brain are located in the left hemisphere. What was happening, they realized, was that the left brain, seeing the left hand (controlled by the right hemisphere) had picked a shovel, but not knowing why, came up with a story to explain it by weaving together pieces of information that were available to it. It refused to say, 'I don't know.' All it could do was see the chicken claw, see the shovel, and make something up that seemed reasonable. They called this process within the left hemisphere the *interpreter*.[23]

As they deepened their research, they discovered that the left-hemisphere interpreter continually makes these kinds of causal connections, whether or not they are true, about every aspect of our lives. If the information available is fuzzy or ambiguous, the left hemisphere simply fills in the gaps with whatever it can find, creating an elaborate story, if necessary, to make everything comprehensible. In Gazzaniga's words, 'it creates order out of chaos, and creates a narrative of and explanation for our actions, emotions, thoughts, memories, and dreams'.[24]

The left hemisphere is constantly telling us the story of ourselves. It's because of it that we can develop a concept of ourselves as a separate self, with a past and future. It's in the left hemisphere that we generate language, finding words for things, categorizing them and formulating coherent sentences. And it's the left hemisphere, fabricating stories of our future, that produces our goal orientation and self-control. When that new employee, exhausted from the first day in her job, jumped up to prepare for the next day's meeting, it was her left hemisphere, constructing in her mind the scenario of a dissatisfied boss, that forced her to give up her creature comforts and open the computer.[25]

Language, goal orientation, self-control, categorization ... it seems we've hit pay dirt in our search for the neural correlates of *yu-wei* – the faculty that originally separated humans from harmony with the Tao. And, in fact, when neuroscientists theorize about the evolution of the left-hemisphere interpreter, they corroborate the Taoist version of events. Before we developed language and other uniquely human capabilities – corresponding to the Taoist golden age – we probably had a relatively undifferentiated PFC. As pre-human communities in the African savanna became more complex, those whose PFCs evolved the ability to navigate complexity most successfully were the ones who flourished. However, this extra PFC functionality required space: either the size of the brain needed to increase, or some functions already there had to take up less territory. In fact, both happened. The human brain did grow, but just as importantly the evolving brain took advantage of the corpus callosum to specialize anatomically: the right hemisphere remained responsible for the 'traditional' PFC functions, permitting the left hemisphere to evolve its uniquely human capabilities.[26]

What, then, does the right hemisphere do for us? Based on this theory, shouldn't it provide us with the capability of *wu-wei*? Let's see.

How would you perceive the world if you were looking for patterns around you without interpreting them? How would you make sense of your present experiences if you were oblivious to their antecedents or future implications? Researchers have discovered that this is how the right hemisphere perceives reality. It focuses on spatial patterns between things. It readily accepts an ambiguous or incomplete situation without trying to impose coherent meaning on it. It savors fluid, indeterminate and vague conditions. It's also more closely connected with internal bodily experience, making its perception of the world more vibrant, filled with smell, sound and sensation.[27]

Is this beginning to sound more like the experience of *wu-wei*, similar to how Cook Ding described his actions? What, you might wonder, would it actually feel like if you could experience the world only through your right hemisphere?

Astonishingly, there is someone who temporarily did just that, and was exceptionally well qualified to write about it. Jill Bolte Taylor was a highly accomplished neuroscience postdoc researcher at the acclaimed McLean Hospital in Massachusetts when she suffered a severe stroke in the left hemisphere of her brain, rendering her completely disabled and unable to talk, read, write, walk or remember anything about her past life. Miraculously, through prompt medical intervention, her understanding of her own condition and the loving support of her mother, she recovered completely and wrote about her extraordinary experience in a best-seller, *My Stroke of Insight*.[28]

Perhaps the most astounding thing in her moving account of the moment-by-moment experience of her stroke and ensuing recovery is her response to what was happening to her. Even as she realized she was having a stroke that could potentially be fatal, she found herself experiencing what she describes as 'a growing sense of peace'. She felt 'enfolded by a blanket of tranquil euphoria'. This sensation remained with her, even after she was brought to the hospital and began the slow, arduous process of recovery. She discovered that, as a result of the stroke, she had become a different person. The previous detailed, goal-oriented, successful researcher had been transformed into someone with an utterly different perception of what it meant to be alive.[29]

In her book, she expresses her new sense of reality in terms that are usually found in mystical utterances. She 'morphed from feeling small and isolated to feeling enormous and expansive'. No longer able to think about the past or future, all she could perceive was 'right here, right now, and it was beautiful'. As the details around her life evaporated, she felt that her 'consciousness soared into an all-knowingness, a "being at *one*" with the universe ... I was no longer isolated and alone. My soul was as big as the universe and frolicked with glee in a boundless sea.'[30]

Bolte Taylor's words could have come directly from Cook Ding describing *wu-wei*. Her experience seems like a real-life incarnation of the mysterious pronouncement from the *Tao Te Ching*: 'One who knows [Tao] does not speak, One who speaks does not know.' The very moments when Bolte Taylor was losing the ability to speak or remember any details of her life, she found herself 'swathed in an enfolding sense of liberation and transformation ... I was completely entranced by the feelings of tranquility, safety, blessedness, euphoria, and omniscience.'[31]

If Bolte Taylor's experience were being recounted by a New Age guru, it might be discounted as someone interpreting their experience in a way that vindicated their own belief system. Coming, however, from a respected neuroscientist, there is much to learn from her insights. Looking back at her life prior to the stroke, she realized that 'the cells in my left hemisphere had been capable of dominating the cells in my right hemisphere. The judging and analytical character in my left mind dominated my personality.' When the stroke temporarily blocked the left hemisphere's activity, she was able to recognize that 'at the core of my right hemisphere consciousness is a character that is directly connected to my feeling of deep inner peace. It is completely committed to the expression of peace, love, joy, and compassion in the world.'[32]

Bolte Taylor, like Sperry and Gazzaniga, discovered that the hemispheres are like two contrasting personalities within a single mind. The left half, she writes, 'thrives on details, details, and more details about those details ... [It] looks at a flower and names the different parts making up the whole – the petal, stem, stamen, and pollen.' The right mind, by contrast, 'creates a master collage of what this moment in time looks like, sounds like, tastes like, smells like, and feels like'. It is 'free to think intuitively outside the box, and it creatively explores the possibilities that each new moment brings ... It identifies our similarities and recognizes our relationship with this marvelous planet, which sustains our life. It perceives the big picture, how everything is related, and how we all join together to make up the whole.'[33]

The Taoists perceived this split within human consciousness as one with implications for the entire human experience. In their view, it was the cause of the emergence of civilization and all that has arisen from it. This seems, in many ways, like a daunting perspective. Is each one of us doomed to be the host of a never-ending conflict between our inner Interpreter and Mystic? And if civilization has emerged as a result of the Interpreter's dominance over the Taoist mystic, what hope does that leave for our future prospects? Do we really need to choose between left- and right-hemisphere cognition? Between civilization and the Tao?

A path of integration

In the view of psychiatrist and scholar Iain McGilchrist, we can indeed understand the current state of our civilization in terms of a battle of the hemispheres. In his deeply researched *The Master and his Emissary: The Divided Brain and the Making of the Western World*, he argues that the hemispheres are 'involved in a sort of power struggle' which has already been decided – the left hemisphere won hands down. This is the reason, he contends, why we live in a society dominated by left-hemisphere values such as systematic and linear thinking, competitiveness and power.[34]

Like the Taoists, McGilchrist looks all the way back to prehistory, before even the emergence of language, for the earliest signs of this imbalance. 'Was it the drive for power, embodied in the will to control the environment,' he asks, 'which accelerated symbol manipulation and the extension of conceptual thought?' He notes that our mostly dominant right hand, controlled by the left hemisphere, is what we use to grasp and manipulate our environment – just like those 'skillful workmen' that Zhuangzi saw committing the original crime of civilization against the Tao. McGilchrist believes this dominance was expressed in its most extreme form in the Western tradition, culminating in our current technological civilization.[35]

McGilchrist's thesis has been criticized for being overly focused on the right- versus left-hemisphere contrast at the expense of other complexities of human cognition. Indeed, since Sperry and Gazzaniga's original research, this distinction has been appropriated by popular culture in the form of a simplified clichéd dichotomy of 'right brain' versus 'left brain' styles of thinking, which often conceals more than it reveals about a person's mind.[36]

The contrast between the brain's hemispheres is, however, just the most obvious manifestation of a split in human consciousness that is recognized by a wide array of the world's leading neuroscientists. In each case, the split parallels the type of cognitive divergence that the Taoists originally described. For example, Nobel Prize winner Gerald Edelman, one of the greatest biologists of the twentieth century, distinguished between what he called primary and secondary consciousness, while world-renowned neuroscientist

Antonio Damasio makes a similar distinction between what he calls core and higher-order consciousness.[37]

While these models of cognition may differ in some subtleties, they all share a view of a split human consciousness. One part of this split – 'primary' or 'core' consciousness, which I prefer to call *animate consciousness* – covers the whole array of experiences that humans share with other mammals: hunger, sexual urges, pain, aggression, desire for warmth, caring for our offspring. The other part covers the cognitive functions that differentiate humans from other animals – the capabilities that allow us to do things like plan for retirement, drive a car, read a book or build weapons of mass destruction. We know through modern neuroscience that these functions, which collectively I call *conceptual consciousness*, are mediated by the PFC and concentrated in its left hemisphere. And it seems clear that – as the Taoists proposed – it is our conceptual consciousness that catalyzed the development of language, culture and civilization.

In my own book *The Patterning Instinct*, I traced how the drive within conceptual consciousness to pattern meaning into the cosmos has shaped history from the time of our hunter-gatherer ancestors to the present. Like McGilchrist, I see something unique in Western civilization that led to the extreme imbalances that characterize our modern world. I trace it back to the ancient Greeks, who set in place many of the foundations of Western thought that have since become so entrenched in our worldview that we simply take them for granted.[38]

The ancient Greeks also saw a split in the human psyche like the one we've been exploring, which, in their view, defined the very essence of humanity. For them, the split was between body and soul. The soul was the source of human reason and, they believed, was pure, unchanging and immortal, linking humans to divinity. The body, by contrast, was polluted, changeable, the source of feelings and emotions, and destined to die. In fact, they saw the soul as being imprisoned in the body, and only truly liberated after the body's death. Since reason was the divine essence of the human being, they believed, it was only through rigorous intellectual thought and freeing oneself as much as possible from sensory distraction that one could arrive at true knowledge. This was the ultimate goal of the philosopher.[39]

The Greeks, then, saw a similar split to the Taoists in human consciousness, but they came down on the opposite side of this split in their value assessment. For the Taoists, it was conceptual consciousness that separated humans from the Tao. For the Greeks, it was only through reason, an essential property of conceptual consciousness, that humans could get in touch with divinity.

This Greek-based model of a human being split between divine reason and polluted emotions has structured Western thought ever since. It formed the foundation of the Christian worldview, which postulated an immortal human soul tempted by bodily desires that went either to heaven or hell after the body's death depending on how well it resisted those temptations. In seventeenth-century Europe, Descartes and other philosophers of his era transformed Christian cosmology into the scientific worldview that underpins much of what is commonly believed today about the cosmos. Since only humans possess reason, they surmised, and reason was what made humans divine, then the rest of the natural world lacked divinity. Nature was thus a mere machine without intrinsic value, and should be treated as such.[40]

The Scientific Revolution spawned by this type of thinking has transformed the entire human experience and the rest of the world along with it. It has brought enormous advances in our understanding of the natural world that have led to previously inconceivable wonders of modern technology, many of which we now take for granted, such as electricity, antibiotics, sanitation, air travel and the internet. It has also led to the extreme imbalances between humans and the natural world that have come to threaten our very civilization. And while it has given us material comforts and conveniences that we treasure, it has also brought, for many of us, a sense of alienation, a separation from a source of meaning in our lives, a loss of deep connection with something inexpressible that feels truly worthwhile.

Which brings us back to the nameless uncarved wood. That deep desire in the human heart to experience *wu-wei* in our lives, to be connected with the Tao in whatever form that might mean for each of us. And back again, to that aching question: Do we really have to choose between the Interpreter and the Mystic? Between reason and emotion? Between civilization and the Tao?

I don't believe we do. Much of this book is devoted to exploring a path whereby we can integrate these two aspects of human cognition into one coherent whole – into a lived experience where those two split parts of the human psyche can be woven into a rich, vibrant unity. And just as we humans have the potential to live our lives as integrated entities, I also believe we can apply similar principles to how we relate to the rest of the natural world. Following this path, however, requires questioning many assumptions of our mainstream worldview and perhaps turning over previously fixed bulwarks of belief.

As we traverse this path, it will help to do so with a deeper understanding of both the animate and conceptual aspects of our consciousness that we have the potential to integrate. That's what we'll focus on in the next two chapters, as we sketch out a fuller – and perhaps, quite surprising – answer to our initial question: *Who am I?*

NEW THREADS OF MEANING

There are two different aspects to human cognition: conceptual consciousness and animate consciousness

Conceptual consciousness has enabled civilization, but also causes humans to be separated from the effortless behavior of *wu-wei*

Rather than conceptual and animate consciousness being in opposition, it is possible to integrate them

Chapter Two

THE ORIGINAL AI: ANIMATE INTELLIGENCE

In the early twentieth century, a German horse known as Clever Hans became an international sensation. His owner would ask him to multiply two numbers, such as three and four, and Clever Hans would answer by tapping his hoof twelve times. There seemed to be no end to Hans's intellectual acumen: he could calculate fractions, tell the time and figure out the date of a given weekday if he knew the date of an earlier day. As his fame spread, with reports of his skills featuring in the *New York Times*, the German authorities commissioned a psychologist, Oskar Pfungst, to evaluate Clever Hans's intelligence. Pfungst eventually discovered that Hans could only give the correct answer when the questioner already knew it and Hans could see the questioner. It turned out that Hans was noticing subtle facial and bodily cues in the questioner when he reached the correct number of taps. When the questioner was hidden from Hans's view, the horse's mathematical skills suddenly disappeared.[1]

Ever since then, the story of Clever Hans has been rolled out by scientific sceptics whenever they want to pour cold water on reports of intelligence in the nonhuman world. They warn disparagingly of the dangers of anthropomorphism: the tendency to read human intentions, intelligence and emotions into natural phenomena. However, the true significance of the Clever Hans episode seems to have been lost amid the sceptics' knowing smirks. In their efforts to ridicule the notion of Hans's mathematical abilities, they ignored the astonishing perceptiveness Hans demonstrated in reading the unconscious behavior of his questioners. The level of intelligence required for this kind of astute perception goes far deeper than merely being able to multiply three times four. After all, it was over fifty years ago that engineers invented the first electronic calculators that could multiply and divide, but even today the most advanced AI would have trouble discerning the nuanced signals that Hans picked up from his questioners.

The idea of what constitutes intelligence is deeply embedded in our sense of human identity and influences how we relate to ourselves and to everything in nature. We've seen how European thought led people to view conceptual consciousness as the domain of their reason, their soul – and their intelligence. Following this logic, from the time of Descartes onwards, the myriad nonhuman manifestations of intelligence in nature were seen as nothing other than mere automata. Animals, Descartes wrote, 'have no mind at all' – they are no different than a clock that can accurately tell the time but is merely 'composed of wheels and weights'. For Descartes and his followers, this circumscribed assessment of nature gave moral license to do anything they wanted to nonhumans. They carried out brutal vivisections on dogs, nailing them up on boards by their paws, and dismissing humanitarian concerns by explaining that the cries were merely a result of springs that had been activated, but the dog itself had no feelings.[2]

The Cartesian denial of cognition to any nonhuman entity has persisted into modern times. While Clever Hans was performing his tricks, an American psychologist, John Watson, was launching a scientific movement known as behaviorism, which interprets all animal behavior as based on nothing but instinctual conditioning, and continues to dominate the scientific study of animals to this day. Richard Dawkins, for example, perhaps the most influential living popularizer of science, professes that 'a bat is a machine, whose internal electronics are so wired up that its wing muscles cause it to home in on insects, as an unconscious guided missile homes in on an aeroplane'.[3]

Throughout the European tradition, there have been some who rejected this mechanistic view of nature. As far back as the ancient Greeks, Aristotle disagreed with his teacher, Plato, about a disembodied soul, arguing that the soul was the animating principle of any living body, and that even plants had their own 'vegetative' soul. During the Renaissance, Leonardo da Vinci, obsessed by nature's complexity, deduced that the Earth itself was like a living organism with a 'vital force of growth'. But once the Scientific Revolution engulfed Europe in the seventeenth century, these views became increasingly inadmissible.[4]

Meanwhile, outside of Europe, the belief in nature's intrinsic intelligence remained ubiquitous, continuing to this day among Indigenous communities. Australian Aboriginals sing out aloud when they walk in the wild, talking to the rest of the natural world as if they are family. A Peruvian shaman tells anthropologist Jeremy Narby that 'a tree has a soul like a human being does'. Native American biologist Robin Wall Kimmerer describes tribal elders recounting how, 'in the old times ... the trees talked to each other. They'd stand in their own council and craft a plan.' The elders advise youngsters to learn from nature's wisdom: 'You should go among the standing people [the trees],' they say, or 'Go spend some time with those Beaver people.'[5]

In this chapter, we'll discover how the findings of modern scientific research have more than validated these Indigenous insights about the intelligence of the natural world. Far from being mindless, automated mechanisms, it turns out that every organism in nature demonstrates stunning intelligence – an animate intelligence that has evolved on Earth over billions of years into a dazzling variety of forms. This realization requires us to reconsider our own human identity in the context of the deep intelligence arrayed around us – and even within us. What actually differentiates us as humans? What do we even mean by intelligence? As we read daily news stories about advances in AI and its implications for humanity, the insights we'll uncover will offer us a deeper grounding in the original AI – animate intelligence. By recognizing this intelligence pervasive to all life, we can gain a greater sense of who we, as humans, really are – with crucial implications for how we might relate to the living world around us.

You get what you measure

Taking their cue from the mechanistic view of nature that dominates Western thought, most intelligence researchers have focused entirely on the capabilities arising from human conceptual consciousness, without considering that any other kind of intelligence might even exist. Over a century ago, concurrent with the rise of Watson's behaviorism, French psychologist Alfred Binet first formulated the IQ (intelligence quotient) test to predict which youngsters would succeed or fail in the Paris school system. The idea of a universal measure of intelligence proved irresistible to an age becoming mesmerized by the potential of mass production and standardization. By the time the United States entered World War I, it was using the IQ test to assess the abilities of over a million military recruits. The popularity of this view of intelligence took off, and it's now so universally accepted that a person's IQ score is widely considered the definitive gauge of their intelligence, no less objective than the scale that measures their weight.[6]

Researchers work ceaselessly on IQ testing techniques to try to eliminate cultural biases, but in spite of this, IQ tests have shown a strange quirk: scores have steadily increased around the world ever since testing began. This phenomenon, known as the Flynn effect after the person who discovered it, has been confirmed repeatedly over three decades of study. The increase has been relentless from the outset – consistently rising at roughly three points per decade.[7*]

Why is it doing that? Clearly, something environmental is having an impact, but nobody can say for sure what it is. Some point to gradually improving health and educational systems, but a likely underlying cause is our shifting global culture, which rewards exactly the kind of cognition that the IQ test measures and encourages people to think in a certain way from infancy: the abstract, generalizing, analytic mode of thought that the Taoists identified as the source of separation from the Tao. It is as though the left hemisphere of the prefrontal cortex is establishing dominance over human consciousness just as Iain McGilchrist described – at the steady rate of three points per decade. There is a classic aphorism in organizational theory – 'You get what you measure' – here we see how true that is when applied to our entire global civilization.

As you might expect, traditional cultures have a very different view of intelligence. Anthropologist Pamela Stern tells, for example, how the Inuit use the word *ihuma* to describe what we might translate as 'smart' behavior, including skills like 'solving a puzzle, fixing a broken snowmobile, teaching a baby to walk, regularly getting to work on time, knowing how and where to set fishing nets, making others feel comfortable, and especially being able to avoid conflict'. How, you might wonder, would these skills show up in an IQ test?[8]

One prominent intelligence researcher, Howard Gardner, has attempted to break the IQ stranglehold by proposing a theory of multiple intelligences. Gardner identified what he sees as eight separate domains, such as bodily, spatial and interpersonal intelligences – areas that seem to align more closely with *ihuma*. Following Gardner's theory, Daniel Goleman's bestseller *Emotional Intelligence*, published in 1995, proposed yet another *ihuma*-style domain that is entirely ignored by the IQ test.[9]

However, these alternative definitions of intelligence still center around human cognition. Even Gardner describes each of his different intelligences in human terms, specifically excluding nonhuman intelligence from his definition. 'Humans have certain kinds of intelligences,' he writes, 'whereas rats, birds, and computers foreground other kinds of computational capacities.'[10]

This is a classic Cartesian ruse: define a quality in terms of human behavior, then claim other animals don't have it because they're not human. Princeton biologist James Gould, for example, advises that 'when an animal does something apparently clever, the first question to ask is whether this might be part of its natural repertoire. Is the intelligence genuine – an ability to create a novel solution in the mind – or is it a trick being played on an all-too-gullible audience of humans?' The implication is that an animal's 'natural repertoire' is, by definition, *not* intelligent, and that intelligence can only arise in 'the mind', which in this context refers to conceptual consciousness.[11]

How, then, could we begin to think about animate intelligence – a form that, by definition, arises from animate, rather than conceptual consciousness? How could we even identify it? One place to begin is with a core teaching from the Australian Aboriginal tradition: the concept of Dreamtime. In Aboriginal culture,

Dreamtime is a particular form of time that exists in both past and present. The Aboriginal creation myth tells of original ancestors who lived long ago, laying down the pathways and patterns of life, and yet somehow still exist in the present. 'They are just as much alive today as they were in the beginning,' explains Aboriginal leader Silas Roberts. 'They are always part of the land and nature as we are.'[12]

Aboriginal Dreamtime is often viewed as a mythical, even mystical, Indigenous perspective on the cosmos – presumably something quite unscientific! However, the Dreamtime proposition that our original ancestors are still around holds true in scientific terms. Roughly four billion years ago, when life first emerged on Earth, it did so in the form of single-celled organisms, very similar to the bacteria that – like Dreamtime ancestors – still exist today. And like them, these ancestors laid down the pathways of life for all organisms that have since evolved, including plants, fish, horses and humans. Genetic studies have shown that another insight of Indigenous traditions around the world – that all living beings are family – is entirely true. A mouse shares 84 percent of its genes with humans, fruit flies share 52 percent, and even a banana shares 44 percent of its genes with us.[13]

If we want to understand animate intelligence, we need to investigate the magnificent array of life that our original ancestors bequeathed to the world. Evolutionary biologist Theodosius Dobzhansky once famously remarked, 'Nothing in biology makes sense except in the light of evolution' – and the same can equally be said of intelligence. In fact, as we delve into the animate intelligence displayed by all forms of life, even down to the microscopic world of a single cell, we can begin to appreciate that the very distinction between mind and life, which seems so clear to James Gould, gets blurred beyond all recognition.[14*]

Where does mind arise separately from life? This is a fundamental question to ask as we explore the astonishing panoply of animate intelligence all around us. Could intelligence itself even be an intrinsic part of life? Philosopher Evan Thompson believes this is the case, stating, 'Where there is life there is mind, and mind in its most articulated forms belongs to life.' If we take Gould's working definition of intelligence – 'an ability to create a novel solution in the mind' – and open to the possibility that mind could extend to all life as Thompson suggests, then we're ready to begin exploring the world of animate intelligence. And in doing so, we may find that the original AI, developed over billions of years, leaves even the world's most advanced supercomputers in the dust.[15]

The 'mind' of a cell

What better place, then, to begin our foray into the realm of animate intelligence than the intricate, multifaceted life of our original ancestor – a single cell? Ever since the nineteenth century, when scientists discovered that many diseases are caused by bacteria, we've learned to become fearful of them, even to the point of washing with antibacterial soap that we're told will eliminate 99.9 percent of them. But in fact most bacteria, which comprise the majority of single-celled organisms, are harmless to humans and thrive virtually everywhere on Earth. Tiny as they are, bacteria are estimated to constitute a total biomass more than a thousand times greater than the entire human population.[16]

The complexity of life within each cell is awe-inspiring. If you imagine a cell the size of a living room, it would be jam-packed from floor to ceiling with busily undulating, whirring and branching entities, each focused on conducting its business with single-minded precision. Billions of years before modern humans developed nanotechnology, ancient bacteria learned how to control specific molecules to do exactly what they want. Each cell is continually ingesting nutrients from outside, converting the raw material into energy and useful components, disposing of its own waste, repairing itself, sensing what's needed for its own health and deciding what to do next. A single cell has thousands of sensors protruding through its outer membrane, controlling the flow of specific molecules, either pulling them in or pushing them out depending on what's needed. Many bacteria propel themselves with tiny protein motors that spin at about 15,000 rpm; as they do so, they sense minute differences in conditions around them and change direction to swim toward a more nutritious source. Some cells even construct homes for themselves. In lakes, certain amoebae collect material from silt and glue the particles together to construct protective shells. They carefully discern which material to use: different species specialize in various types of particles and make their shells in distinctive shapes.[17]*

Whether they are single-celled organisms, such as bacteria, or part of a larger organism, cells utilize fine-tuned signaling mechanisms to communicate with others around them, sending and receiving hundreds of signals at the same time. Stomatal cells on a leaf coordinate in pairs, like mouth lips, to control gas exchange with the environment, adjusting their tightness to open and close in response to vibrational and chemical stimuli. Human cells utilize as many as 11,000 different signaling proteins, and different types of cells additionally use other modalities: taste cells detect molecular shape; auditory cells respond to vibrations; heat receptor cells detect levels of molecular motion.[18]

While your conscious attention is focused on reading this paragraph, there are roughly forty trillion of your own cells busily working within you, each actively managing its own health and carefully coordinating with its companions to keep you in good shape. Leucocytes in your throat are detecting potentially harmful bacterial species, informing their comrades and eliminating the invaders. Liver cells are reproducing at exactly the rate needed to replace attrition; cells in the bone marrow are producing millions of new blood cells every minute; damaged cells are fixing themselves zealously, often with help from their neighbors.[19]

Something every cell on Earth has in common is that it is a living entity, acting purposefully to maintain and propagate its life. It is not, as Descartes and Dawkins would have us believe, a machine. No matter how complicated a machine might be, it doesn't possess intrinsic intentionality, which is the defining characteristic of cells, along with all the organisms they comprise. As philosopher of biology Andreas Weber explains, 'the experience of being alive ... is the center of what defines an organism'. Weber, seeing this drive for life as the true foundation for the discipline of biology, defines what he calls the First Law of Desire: 'Everything that lives wants more of life. Organisms are beings whose own existence means something to them.'[20]

For a cell to have a sense of its own existence requires a certain kind of awareness. Each cell must be aware of itself *as* a self: it knows what is within its membrane and what is outside; it determines what molecules it needs and which ones to discard; it knows when something within it needs fixing and how to get it done; it determines what genes to express within its DNA and when it's time to divide and thus propagate itself. We are reminded of Thompson's dictum: 'Where there is life there is mind.'[21]

Perhaps the most spectacular feats of cellular intelligence are achieved by a single-celled, amoeba-like organism that goes by the unprepossessing name of a slime mold. If you've ever hiked in a forest and come across a yellow gooey mass growing in a shady, damp spot, you were probably looking at a slime mold. They can occupy an area as large as a square meter. At a certain phase in their life cycle, they grow a network of tube-like structures called pseudopodia, which they use to crawl around, looking for food. When there are multiple food sources, they will adapt their shape to access each of the sources in the most efficient way possible – and this is where their virtuosity takes center stage. Scientists have sliced up a slime mold and scattered it in a maze with food at the beginning and end. The slime mold responds by filling the space, and after discovering the food, literally solves the maze by shrinking itself to occupy only the shortest possible route between the food sources. Amazingly, scientists have discovered that slime molds can perform efficient network design. They have scattered oatmeal in a Petri dish to represent real-world cities, and the slime mold has linked them in ways that are frequently more efficient than existing road and rail routes. Researchers have used slime molds to determine the relative efficiency of different highway networks, discovering for example that Canada and China were more efficient than the USA and Africa. Slime molds have even shown the ability to learn from experience, recognizing the frequency with which they're given shocks and preparing themselves in anticipation of the next one.[22]

Cells are also very aware of their relationship to others around them. In fact, many bacteria have a highly developed social life. In a process known as quorum sensing, bacteria recognize molecules discarded by other nearby bacteria, and use this information to assess how many of their own type are around. When the population reaches a certain size, they may cooperatively organize themselves into structured colonies, and sometimes decide collectively whether or not to engage in a battle to defend their territory, frequently allying with other unrelated bacteria. They even demonstrate a certain kind of moral sense. In the defense of territory, there are occasional 'free-riding' bacteria who aren't pulling their weight; when cooperating bacteria detect this, they will shun the free-riders as punishment, even if they are part of the genomic family.[23]

Given the advantage of cooperation between single cells, wouldn't it make sense if cells began entering into even more complex relationships with each other? Hundreds of millions of years ago, single-celled organisms recognized this might be the case, and began developing tight-knit relationships with others around them, each specializing in a particular function that complemented the skills of another. This marked the beginning of multicellular life on Earth. Cellular communication *between* organisms gave rise to communication *within* an organism. As in the Dreamtime, our original ancestors have remained around us, even as their progeny thrived – and now, having glimpsed the astonishing intelligence within each microscopic cell, we're ready to see what they're capable of when they begin acting as integrated entities.[24]

The networked intelligence of plants

If an extraterrestrial alien were exploring this part of the galaxy and discovered Earth, there's a good chance they would identify plants as the dominant life-form on the planet. Plants account for over 80 percent of all Earth's biomass, compared to which the amount of human biomass is barely a rounding error. In spite of the dominance of plant life, we're used to thinking of plants as dumb. After all, they don't seem to do anything other than just stand there; they don't make a sound; and they certainly don't appear to have feelings or thoughts. It's no surprise that a comatose person lying brain-dead in hospital is called a 'vegetable'.[25]

In recent decades, however, plant biologists have transformed our understanding of what goes on inside a plant. It turns out that the inner life of a plant is a rich plethora of complex experience. Plants have their own versions of our five senses – they can smell, see, taste, touch and hear – and also use up to fifteen other ways to sense their environment for which we don't have analogues. They have elaborate internal signaling systems, utilizing the same chemicals – such as serotonin or dopamine – that act as neurotransmitters in humans to affect our moods. Even though plants appear barely responsive to what's going on around them, that's just because we haven't been able to measure their reactions. In humans, for example, it's known that calcium levels rise when neurons transmit information. When experimenters genetically modified tobacco plants to make them glow when calcium levels rose in their cells, they were amazed to find that a simple touch caused the plants to light up in milliseconds. Researchers have discovered that plants act intentionally and purposefully: they have memory and learn, they communicate with each other and can even allocate resources as a community. Given all this, perhaps the crucial question we need to ask is not 'Are plants intelligent?', but 'How the heck do they do it?'[26]

The most important thing to understand about plant intelligence is that plants are rooted in the ground. Because they don't move around, and don't even choose their place of permanent residence, they need to be exceptionally skillful at exploiting whatever conditions they find themselves in. Remaining in one place also means there is no way to get away from predators. Therefore, plants had to evolve sophisticated systems to protect against any insects, animals or fungi that wanted to munch on them. The solutions that plants developed to their particular circumstances led them down an entirely different evolutionary path to animals. Plants couldn't afford to concentrate crucial functions in a particular organ: one bite from a predator and it would all be over. Therefore, the functions that we identify with specific organs – breathing, metabolizing or evaluating – had to be carried out in a distributed fashion through the entire body of the plant. That way, a big chunk of the plant might be devoured by an animal but it could remain healthy and merely sprout new shoots.[27]

As plant biologist Stefano Mancuso points out, this modular approach to organizing a system is found in modern network theory, and formed the basis for the development of the internet. During the Cold War, US military strategists were concerned that one nuclear strike might wipe out their central command, so – just like plants – they constructed an information network (originally known as Arpanet) that could continue to function even if many of its nodes were destroyed.[28]

Plants do, however, contain a structure that has some analogue to a mammalian brain: their root network, safely concealed underground from hungry herbivores. Charles Darwin, far ahead of his time, was the first biologist to notice how the tip of a root, with the power to direct its own movement, 'acts like the brain of one of the lower animals'. Since then, scientists have discovered that roots have the ability to process enormous amounts of information about their environment, including attributes such as moisture, pressure, vibration, electrical field, toxins, chemical gradients and the presence of neighboring roots. They can ascertain whether another root belongs to the same plant, a related plant or an unrelated potential competitor, and determine their actions accordingly. The number of these root tips is staggering: small plants have as many as fifteen million, and mature trees are estimated to possess hundreds of millions. Like neurons in an animal's brain, they are continually transmitting electrical signals throughout their network.[29]

Using their distributed 'brain' network, plants react intelligently to their environment. They recognize, for example, what type of insect is attacking them, and produce specific chemical repellents accordingly. When attacked by a particular caterpillar, tobacco plants release a special chemical to attract predatory mites that eat the caterpillar. Ivy plants choose where to put down roots, avoiding nutrient-poor patches of soil; while parasitic dodder plants, which wrap themselves around other plants to suck out their nutrients, decide within an hour whether to exploit their host or move on – and will grow more or fewer coils to wrap around the plant based on how nutritious it's likely to be. In phosphorus-poor soil, bean plants release chemicals that increase phosphorus uptake; and when the soil dries out, plants respond accordingly, making smaller leaves, refraining from growing new shoots and extending their roots further.[30]

Plants also learn from experience. The mimosa plant, for example, generally closes its leaves in response to a shock, but after being dropped a number of times, it will no longer bother to respond to another drop, while still responding to other unexpected shocks. In one experiment, researcher Monica Gagliano demonstrated that pea plants can learn to associate a cue, such as a fan blowing, with the expected direction of light, and most of the seedlings she tested made the decision to change their growth direction based on what they learned.[31]

Perhaps most intriguingly, plants also exhibit unique personalities: they don't all act the same way as their neighbors in response to the same stimuli. In Gagliano's pea plant experiment, while most learned from their cues, some didn't figure it out, and grew in the wrong direction. Peter Wohlleben, in his bestseller *The Hidden Life of Trees*, describes how three oaks growing next to each other make different decisions as to when to drop their leaves for the winter, which involves a complex risk–return trade-off. One tree chooses to drop its leaves earlier than the other two, thus foregoing extra photosynthesis but reducing its risk if an early frost occurs. If they were humans, we'd say this tree was acting more prudently than the two bolder ones.[32]

Trees have complex ways of communicating with each other, and many of them live in interlinked, cooperative communities. When an acacia tree gets nibbled on by giraffes, it expresses a gas to warn its neighbors, prompting them to pump toxins into their leaves to protect themselves. The most extensive communication occurs, not surprisingly, through the trees' intelligent root network. Forest ecologist Suzanne Simard has discovered what she calls a 'wood-wide web' of tree communication that shares information about insects and other threats. Through a fungal web that links them together underground, trees trade nutrients such as carbon, nitrogen and water with each other. 'Mother trees' use the network to nourish seedlings until they're tall enough to reach sunlight for themselves, and in the wintertime, evergreen species contribute sugar to deciduous trees, expecting to get reimbursed in the summer. Perhaps, rather than asking whether plants are intelligent, we humans should follow the advice of the Native American elders: 'Go among the standing people' – and learn from nature's wisdom.[33]

The moods of a worm

One reason plants appear passive to us is that they live on a different timescale. Much of their lifestyle seems deadly slow by human standards. When a caterpillar starts eating a leaf, the alarm signals travel up the plant at the rate of an inch every three minutes, and it takes about an hour before it produces repellent chemicals. For trees that live for centuries, sometimes millennia, life in the slow lane works just fine. But for animals that need to flee from predators, this rate of internal signaling would be a death sentence.[34]

It was primarily to speed up the rate of internal communication that neurons evolved in animals as specialized cells that transmit electrical signals exceptionally quickly. With long, tenuous tendrils, they can target their information rapidly and precisely to wherever it's needed. The first neurons evolved in aquatic creatures over five hundred million years ago, in the form of distributed nerve nets, which can still be found in modern jellyfish.[35]

As neuronal networks grew more complex, it became more efficient to route all the neurons' information through central nodes, which could also be used to transmit action signals back to different parts of the organism. Many of these nodes, called ganglia, eventually coalesced into a centralized organ that specialized in integrating the vast array of inputs about what was happening both inside and outside the organism, assessing what it all meant and directing activity accordingly – the brain.[36]

How could the brain determine what the organism should do? It would have begun on the basis of Weber's First Law of Desire: it wanted more life for the organism. A crucial activity, then, would be to continually monitor all the systems that maintain the organism's health and make immediate adjustments whenever anything begins to go out of kilter: a fundamental and highly complex process known as homeostasis. Sometimes, of course, the animal would need to take action to get back into healthy parameters: if it needed nutrition, for instance, the brain had to kick the animal into gear to forage or hunt for its meal. It did so using neurotransmitters that caused the animal to feel something that would incite action, such as hunger or thirst, pain if it was getting injured, or fear if it was at risk of attack.[37]

As you're reading this, your own nervous system is carrying out the age-old process of homeostasis within you, regulating your blood pressure, heart rate, chemical balances in your blood and countless other systems. Most of this is done below the level of consciousness, but occasionally, just like the earliest brains, it will kick-start a process into your conscious awareness, and you might realize you're feeling thirsty and get up to pour yourself a drink. As Antonio Damasio puts it, 'we can think of feelings as mental deputies of homeostasis'. At the very root of all nervous system activity, including all that is conventionally viewed as intelligent behavior, are feelings.[38]

The profound implication arising from this is that, once again contrary to the Cartesian fiction that animals are machines, every animal with a nervous system is likely to have some sort of subjective experience driven by feelings that, at the deepest level, are shared by you and me. Most of us have been raised on some version of the Cartesian myth: that insects don't really feel anything; that fish don't suffer when they're caught on the rod and cast back into the water; that it's okay to throw a lobster into a pot of boiling water because, after all, it's just a lobster. A torrent of carefully researched scientific studies has, in recent decades, exposed these as falsehoods.[39]

One of the simplest animals on Earth is a worm called *C. elegans*, which is a popular subject of scientific study because it has a tiny nervous system with only four hundred neurons. Even this little worm, just a millimeter long, has been shown to express neurotransmitters similar to oxytocin and vasopressin, key hormones released by the human brain that affect our feelings. When researchers studied worms that lacked the oxytocin-like chemical (known popularly as the love hormone), they found that they initiated sex more slowly and 'executed poorly'.[40]

Wherever researchers have looked, from insects to crustaceans, they have found similar signs of subjective feelings experienced by our fellow animals. One ingenious experiment showed that bees can feel anxious. On the basis that people, when anxious, tend to see the glass as half-empty rather than half-full, researchers trained bees to associate one particular odor with a sugar taste and another odor with an unpleasant taste. Then, they shook some bees, knowing that in the wild badgers shake hives when they're attacking them, and that if anything might provoke anxiety, this would. After the shaking, they presented both shaken and non-shaken bees with a 50/50 mixture of both the pleasant and unpleasant odors. The shaken bees, now pessimistic, didn't want to taste the mixture, whereas the unshaken bees were more interested in tasting it. The researchers also discovered that the serotonin and dopamine levels of the shaken bees were diminished, as in humans who are feeling anxious.[41]

Similarly clever experiments have demonstrated that prawns and crabs feel pain and remember it, modifying their behavior based on what's happened to them previously. The hearts of marine snails start beating faster when their gills are touched, and they release ink to confuse the enemy. Fish who were given a low-voltage electrical shock whenever a light started flashing exhibited fear with rapid heartbeats when they saw the light flash, even without an associated shock. Fish, in fact, will make trade-offs between hunger and pain, avoiding part of an aquarium where they're likely to get an electric shock, even if that's where the food is – until they get so hungry that they're willing to take a risk. Crayfish, when they molt, shed their protective exoskeleton and are at more risk from predators; researchers have shown that when they do so, they exhibit anxiety symptoms, which are eliminated when they're injected with anti-anxiety drugs developed for humans. Octopuses, one of the earliest groups to evolve separately from other animals, about 600 million years ago, live predominantly solitary lives, but just like humans, get cozy with others when given a dose of the 'love drug' MDMA.[42]

The continuum of consciousness

Most theories of consciousness argue that it first emerged in evolution as a result of increasing complexity in organisms. As pioneering psychologist William James put it over a century ago, consciousness is 'an organ added for the sake of steering a nervous system grown too complex to regulate itself'.[43]

A mountain of literature has been produced in recent decades on the subject of consciousness in other creatures, but it's rare to find two accounts that tell the same story. Part of the problem lies in confusion regarding what consciousness actually is: what is the exact difference, after all, between awareness, sentience, subjectivity and consciousness? Much ink has been spilled on these distinctions, but perhaps it's more valuable simply to consider a continuum of consciousness, beginning with a single cell – which, as we saw, has its own kind of mind – all the way to the most complex mammals, including humans.[44*]

That doesn't mean, though, that the continuum follows a straight line. Clearly, one jump in complexity occurred when nervous systems first evolved. There's a strong argument for another jump, perhaps equally significant, with the evolution of warm-blooded creatures such as birds and mammals. The brains of warm-blooded animals are about ten times bigger than those of cold-blooded animals, such as reptiles, of the same size. There also seems to be much more dopamine production in the brain, faster associative learning, and youngsters play together.[45]

Along with higher levels of consciousness, warm-blooded animals have more complex emotions, frequently causing more sophisticated behavior. We can think of emotions, in a way, like another version of Aboriginal Dreamtime: pathways laid down by our earliest ancestors that continue to exist within us in the present. In the distant past, when situations occurred repeatedly over multiple generations, successful responses led to the emergence of 'action programs' that catalyzed particular behaviors. When a bear gorges herself on food in the late summer preparing for hibernation, she's responding to a feeling that causes her to eat more. Conventional biologists, such as James Gould, frequently describe this as instinct-driven 'programming' and contrast it to 'genuine' rational intelligence: after all, the bear isn't checking the calendar, calculating the number of months she'll be in hibernation and working out her metabolic rate. But she's exhibiting highly intelligent behavior that reliably accomplishes the same goal, based on animate, rather than conceptual, intelligence.[46]

That's not to say that even conceptual intelligence is the sole domain of humans. Researchers have discovered that many of our fellow creatures show the kinds of intelligence that were once thought to be uniquely human. The next time someone tells you disparagingly that you're a birdbrain, you can thank them for the compliment. Birds exhibit a wide range of conceptual thinking. A crow, if presented with food at the bottom of a narrow jar, will take a straight piece of wire, bend it into a hook with its beak and insert the hook into the bottle to pull out the food. A famous parrot named Alex had a vocabulary of 150 words, could name fifty different objects, discussed ideas such as 'bigger' and 'smaller', could understand the concept of zero, and would spontaneously apologize to his human owner if he annoyed her.[47]

It was once thought that self-awareness – the ability to perceive yourself as others might see you – was a uniquely human trait, but it turns out that magpies also possess it. Researchers have used a mirror test to check this ability. They put a distinctive mark on an anesthetized magpie's face, then allow her to see herself in a mirror. The magpie appears curious about the mark and tries to wipe it off, thus passing the test: she's recognized that it's herself in the mirror.[48*]

Chimpanzees also pass the mirror test and are avid tool-users, probing termite nests with sticks, for example, to pull up tasty termite treats. They will even use two tools together to achieve their goal, such as cracking a nut by placing it on a wooden anvil and then wielding a hammer to break it open. Kanzi, a famed bonobo, understood many spoken words and printed symbols, and could purposely combine them to communicate something, such as an event that had happened earlier in the day. Kanzi had sophisticated interpersonal skills, hiding things he didn't want discovered, lying on occasion and showing empathy, once gently helping a human handler when she had injured her hand. Chimps have also been seen planning for the future, one chimp storing caches of stones to use as ammunition against humans he didn't like.[49]

Many animals show levels of cognitive skill that match, or even go beyond, human capacities. Some birds in the fall can store more than 20,000 pine nuts in hundreds of different locations, and recover most of them in the winter and spring. A chimp named Ayumu left human competitors in the dust when he was able to remember a series of numbers between 1 and 9 appearing on a touchscreen for just one fifth of a second, and tap them in the right order.[50]

These impressive nonhuman cognitive feats extend to social intelligence. Male wolves show a familial loyalty that would be prized in most human communities, with a deep commitment to obtaining food, defending their families and helping raise their young over several years until they reach maturity. Elephants have been known to communicate elaborate messages through infrasound to other herds a hundred miles away, warning of humans slaughtering them. They remember other elephants they haven't seen in decades, and when they come across the bones of a departed one, they perform elaborate ceremonies, holding and passing the bones around with their trunks in a form of mourning. Whales and dolphins communicate in complex patterns that have yet to be deciphered, but they are believed to talk in local dialects, call each other by name, and seem to 'gossip' about others who are temporarily absent. Each of these species appears to experience a rich inner life and complex social interaction to a depth that we can barely even guess.[51]

Overcoming 'anthropodenial'

And yet, for all these astonishing displays of intelligence in other creatures, there's something about human intelligence that still seems radically different. After all, isn't that what we explored in the previous chapter? As the Taoists would say, humans seem driven by *yu-wei* – 'purposive behavior' – rather than *wu-wei*. We have a more evolved prefrontal cortex and are dominated by our left-brain interpreter, which is constantly explaining things, categorizing them and making up the story of our lives.

These crucial differences cause many to dismiss the overlaps with other animals as inconsequential. The emergence of human neural capacities 'created a fundamental, and unprecedented, gap in the evolution of animal minds', writes evolutionary biologist Marc Hauser, who calls the resulting distinction 'humaniqueness'. When we look around at the world as it is today, it's easy to be convinced. Aren't we the ones who have discovered electricity, flown to the moon and communicate through the internet? Aren't we the species that has single-handedly changed the Earth's climate, while driving other species toward extinction? It certainly seems like a fundamental difference.[52]

Others, such as comparative psychologist Michael Tomasello, paint a more nuanced picture. They show how relatively subtle differences, such as the capacity to understand the intentions of others, gave rise to the progression of complex human culture. The ability for one generation of humans to pass on their discoveries to following generations led to a ratchet effect that caused human development to soar into the stratosphere. Every morning, when we turn on the lights, read the news and commute to work, we're relying unwittingly on the cumulative efforts and insights of untold generations of ancestors who, over eons, laid the foundations for all the technologies we enjoy today.[53]

In fact, our mainstream culture's self-congratulatory obsession with humaniqueness blinds us to the vast amount of animate intelligence we share with our fellow creatures. Our own unceasing homeostasis, the continual flow of feelings surging through our bodies, our ability to catch a ball flying through the air at a moment's notice, our attunement to the emotions of a loved one – these subtle complexities of our moment-to-moment existence are the results of our deeply evolved animate intelligence. We even possess within us an evolutionarily ancient nervous system separate from the brain – the enteric nervous system – which contains about half a billion neurons, stretches along our entire gut, and is believed to influence our physical and mental states as well as control our digestion.[54]

At the same time, even with our shared animate intelligence, the experience of being human is undeniably different. Because of our highly developed conceptual intelligence, we can barely – if at all – experience our animate intelligence unvarnished. Even our emotions are tinged with subtleties that other animals may not experience. When we feel complex emotions such as nostalgia, jealousy or guilt, these can only arise after filtering through both animate and conceptual layers of consciousness within us.[55]

This is a valid reason for scientists to be cautious about interpreting emotions and intentions of other animals through a human lens. However, a sensible vigilance for inappropriate anthropomorphism has become perverted into a form of fundamentalism. Mainstream biologists, raised on behaviorism, speak of anthropomorphism as a 'disease', viewing ideas that come even close to attributing emotions or intelligence to animals as taboo. In a scientific version of McCarthyism, researchers have feared for their careers if they dared to suggest animals might have feelings. Jane Goodall was widely disparaged in the 1960s for describing moods and personalities in the chimpanzees she was studying. A pioneer in plant research, David Rhoades, was reportedly driven out of science by hostility after reporting in the 1980s that willow trees appeared to receive airborne signals about predators from other trees. A leading researcher in animal emotions, Joseph LeDoux, has revealed that he failed to get funding for his grant applications until he eliminated the word 'emotion' from his proposals.[56*]

A forceful agitator for change in mainstream thinking, ethologist Frans de Waal, calls this ideological fundamentalism 'anthropodenial' – the denial, in the face of overwhelming evidence, of the shared emotional experience between humans and other animals. Biologist Paul Ehrlich remembers how, when first studying chimpanzees, he was 'determined to observe them without anthropomorphizing'. However, he recalls, 'within minutes of my first close-up look, a mother chimp gathered a distressed infant into her arms and comforted it by patting it on the head – and my resolve went out the window'. Countless researchers recount similar moments when they realized the absurdity of denying the emotions they shared with their animal subjects. Of course, we can never know exactly what a mother chimp feels when holding her distressed infant. But then again, as a man, I can't know what it's like for a human mother to hold her newborn baby – but I can acknowledge it's a real feeling and try to imagine what it might be like. In reality, none of us knows exactly how anyone else really feels inside. When you say you're feeling sad, I will never know exactly what you mean, but that doesn't require me to reject your feeling as false. By accessing my own internal experience of sadness, I can imagine what you might be feeling and react accordingly.[57]

In fact, as de Waal points out, anthropomorphism can be a 'powerful tool' when used appropriately. It can allow us to gain some inkling into what an animal actually experiences, and use this as a basis for discerning both the similarities and differences of its lived reality compared with our own. How then, we might ask, can we skillfully relate our own human experience to the animate intelligence around us?[58]

First, we must recognize that an animal's emotion is both shared by us *and* unique to that animal. As ethologist Marc Bekoff points out, along with human grief, there is dog-grief, elephant-grief and chimpanzee-grief; each of which has similarities and is also different. And the same holds true for joy, fear, anger and desire. This principle both validates the emotions of our fellow creatures and honors them for their uniqueness. When an elephant displays affectionate behavior toward her sister, we can recognize it as love – but it's elephant-love, and as such we realize with humility that we will never have access to the depths and subtleties of the experience. When your pet dog looks up at you, you can feel her love as true – and at the same time exult in the mystery that you cannot know exactly what is behind those enchanting eyes.[59]

A second principle is to honor the intrinsic nature of another animal's experience as no less valuable than our own. When we compare human cognition to other highly developed animals, it's easy to fall into the trap of seeing them as 'almost human'. When Kanzi's or Alex's language skills, for example, reach the level of a two-year-old, there's a tendency to get caught in a patronizing spirit, as if we're watching our own toddler's development: 'Isn't little Alex so clever!' In fact, as de Waal explains, it's more accurate to recognize a 'plurality of cognition' among animals – like a landscape with 'many peaks of specialization'. Clearly, human peaks of specialization, in areas such as symbolic thought and shared intentionality, led to a drastic reorientation of power dynamics between humans and other animals, but that doesn't reduce the magnitude of other peaks. Do elephants have access to an emotional majesty that humans could never even approach? What is the sense of deep time experienced by a giant redwood tree that first enjoyed sunlight in the heyday of the Roman Empire? When whales and dolphins strand themselves on a beach *en masse*, is it possible they are driven by a different notion of selfhood than we can even imagine? Do they choose to keep company with the first stranded victim, perhaps knowing they will die as a result, but valuing companionship above their own lives? We can't know the answers to these questions, but we can at least have the reverence to ask them.[60]

A third principle is to recognize our deep interconnectedness with all life, including plants, insects – and even single cells. It arises from the shared insight of Aboriginal Dreamtime and evolutionary biology: that the deepest structures of earliest life-forms are still within us today – and within every organism with which we share the Earth. Scientists concur that all life can trace its lineage back to a shared ancestor (known as LUCA for 'last universal common ancestor') that lived about three and a half billion years ago. A lot has changed since that primordial cell spawned its next generation, but some things have remained the same. Evolutionary biologists call it *deep homology*: the recognition of fundamental life processes shared across widely divergent species. Some of these processes show up in Weber's First Law of Desire: the will to live that drives us all. Because of that common ground, we can feel the life force, as well as its diminishment, all around us. We know when a plant is suffering from drought and badly needs water; we know when a fly we tried swatting starts buzzing around furiously as a result; we know that a chicken suffers when it's caged up, unable to move or stretch, in a factory farm. This leads to Weber's Second Law: that the desire to live is palpable and visible, always present in the living body. To see it in other organisms, all we need to do is feel it in our own animate consciousness.[61]

Then again, becoming aware of our feeling for other life in

our own animate consciousness may not be so easy. We're back to the animate/conceptual divergence that the early Taoists recognized – the loss of *wu-wei* as a natural part of human existence. Can a greater understanding of the animate world around us help our conscious minds connect more deeply with our own animate intelligence? Is it possible that we could develop a form of intelligence that seamlessly weaves them together – a truly integrative intelligence?

Toward an integrative intelligence

The first step in forging an integrative intelligence would be to recognize that our mind does not exist separately from what James Gould calls our 'natural repertoire'. On the contrary, our mind *is* an intrinsic part of our natural repertoire, arising from the continual, dynamic process of our nervous system interacting with our body. In the memorable phrasing of Antonio Damasio, 'No body, never mind.' An integrative intelligence would start with a conscious recognition of our deeply evolved animate intelligence, and set the intention to incorporate its wisdom fully into our own identity, values and life choices.[62]

We can think of our intelligence a bit like an iceberg, most of which is hidden deep below the surface. The visible tip of the iceberg is akin to our conceptual intelligence – the rational part of our mind that can be scored in an IQ test. It's easy to see and measure, and a superficial view might suggest that's all there is. However, upon closer investigation, it becomes apparent that most of the iceberg is concealed in the ocean depths. It's only because of the hidden bulk beneath the water that the tip is able to peek up above the surface. And for all the sparkle of the tip, glistening in the sunlight, the true magnitude of intelligence remains below, relatively inaccessible. When we experience a complex feeling that weaves through the incalculable pathways of animate consciousness, the words we use to try to express it conceptually can never really do it justice. Perhaps that's what the *Tao Te Ching* alluded to when it declared, 'The Tao that can be spoken of is not the true Tao.'

Once we truly honor the animate intelligence within us, it's natural to turn our attention outward, and similarly honor the animate intelligence emanating from all living beings. Embracing our shared domain of intelligence can lead to a potent sense of being intimately connected with the animate world. In the words of ecologist Carl Safina, author of *Beyond Words: What Animals Think and Feel*, 'When I myself look at other animals, I almost never see an otherness. I see the overwhelming similarities; they fill me with a sense of deep relation. Nothing makes me feel more at home in the world than the company of wild relatives.'[63]

It is animate intelligence that allows us to experience the fullness of what it really means to be alive. Weber's Third Law of Desire elegantly expresses this: 'Only in the mirror of other life can we understand our own lives. Only in the eyes of the other can we become ourselves.' If conceptual intelligence is the cognitive peak of specialization that distinguishes humans from other animals, it is our animate intelligence that extends throughout the rest of the terrain of existence, inviting a shared adventure with all of life.[64]

This common territory offers profound lessons, earned over billions of years of evolution, that are indispensable to a truly integrative intelligence. Those who heed the instruction of the Indigenous elders to 'go among the standing people' can greatly enhance their own understanding of life. Robin Wall Kimmerer describes the insights to be gained by pondering the interaction of what Indigenous people call the three sisters: the crops of corn, bean and squash which, when grown together, yield more food than when cultivated separately. The corn, shooting up early and strong, offers the beans support for their growing tendrils; the beans team up with bacteria that pull nitrogen from the air and fix it in the soil to fertilize all three plants; the large, prickly leaves of the squash keep the soil cool and moist, prevent weeds from growing and ward off predators.[65]

The three sisters offer a lesson in how it's possible for individual agents to thrive while benefitting those around them. Ecological systems throughout the Earth have built on this beneficial process of shared reciprocity over millions of years of evolution, to achieve astonishing resilience, allowing each of their parts to flourish while providing nutrients and support for other species within the system. There is much for our current civilization to learn from this approach.

Integrative intelligence is one that draws from all the sources of wisdom available to us as living organisms on Earth. It doesn't detract from the gleaming edifices of conceptual intelligence – from the brilliant advances in science, mathematics and technology that have helped redefine the human experience. Rather, it acknowledges that these represent one aspect of intelligence, not the entire spectrum. Perhaps the greatest challenge to human intelligence today is not how to accomplish the next technological breakthrough or build the most advanced AI, but how to integrate human ingenuity with our own animate intelligence and that of the natural world.

Developing a truly integrative intelligence could help meet this challenge. But to do so, we need a clearer understanding of how our conceptual consciousness originally peeled off from our animate nature, and the profound implications that has had for how each of us experiences daily life. The complex – and sometimes difficult – relationship we all maintain between these two forms of consciousness within us is the fascinating subject of the next chapter.

NEW THREADS OF MEANING

Animate intelligence is highly complex, and exists all around us, in every sentient being

Rather than being machines, every animal with a nervous system likely has subjective experiences driven by feelings that, at the deepest level, are shared by all of us

By connecting with our own animate intelligence, we can recognize our deep interconnectedness with all of life on Earth

Chapter Three

THE MOST IMPORTANT RELATIONSHIP IN YOUR LIFE

You meet an old friend in the grocery store. She's telling you about her difficult time at a company that she's finally left.

'I was pushing myself way too hard,' she tells you. 'It was wild. I'd accept unrealistic projects from my boss and then hate myself for it. It took a while, but now that I've left, I'm beginning to pull myself together again.'

You chat a bit longer, and then continue shopping. You're glad you had a chance to catch up. But wait a minute! There was only one person you were talking with, and yet your friend was describing herself as though she were split into two. Who was doing the pushing and who was getting pushed? Who hated whom? Who got broken into fragments and needs to be pulled back together – and who's doing the pulling? Stranger still, you intuitively knew what your friend meant as she was talking with you. Does that mean that you are as split as she is?

Yes, you are ... along with the rest of us. It seems that part of the human condition is to experience a kind of split personality, with an 'I' engaging in an ongoing relationship with a 'self'. We talk about 'gaining control of myself' as if there is a battle going on between these two entities. We can view ourselves harshly, as your friend did, pushing ourselves hard or even hating ourselves; and we can equally be kind to ourselves and care for ourselves. In addition to experiencing ourselves as so scattered that we need to 'pull ourselves together', we can also be 'beside ourselves' with rage, or at the other extreme, 'be at one' with ourselves. We can 'lose ourselves' in a dance and sometimes 'find ourselves' in our chosen vocation.

Linguistic philosophers George Lakoff and Mark Johnson

made this remarkable discovery about the inner relationship we all take for granted, and published their findings in 1980 in *Metaphors We Live By*, which helped catalyze the bourgeoning academic field of cognitive linguistics. They found that this inner split exists not just in Western minds but also in other cultures. A common Japanese expression, for example, is 'He lost himself because of too much anger.' It's a split that seems to pervade all aspects of life from the everyday to the spiritual. In a meditation class, the instructor might tell you to 'just sit and observe your thoughts and feelings without judging them'. But who is doing the observing, and who or what is being observed – and might be judged?[1]

Each of one of us has important relationships with others in our lives. Whether they are parents, loved ones, children, bosses or dear friends, these relationships are some of the most significant aspects of human existence. But there is no relationship more important than the one you have with yourself. It's a relationship you're engaged in every day from when you first wake up to when you fall asleep at night, and one that you'll remain in until your dying breath. How you conduct that relationship will affect the quality of your lived experience more than almost anything else. In this chapter, we're going to explore this intimate and complex relationship. As we unravel its intricacies, we'll find that it also reveals some strange assumptions that the dominant Western culture takes for granted about human identity.

Before we begin, I have a request for you. Throughout history, in different cultures and even in different schools of modern thought, the terms 'I' and 'self' are used in very different ways – often with contradictory meanings. Discussion of this complex topic can become irretrievably confused when contrasting definitions are being applied. Therefore, if you have a particular definition in your own mind for what 'I' or 'self' means, please keep it on hold while reading the chapter – and at the end of it I invite you to translate this chapter's usage into your own terminology in whatever way seems most fitting.

How 'I' and the 'self' split apart

The split between 'I' and 'self' most likely occurred early in human evolution, and is viewed by many experts as one of the defining characteristics of humanity. The experience of life as a pure self is an intrinsic part of animate consciousness – that complex array of feelings, impulses, urges, sensations and primary emotions that we share to a large extent with other animals. As we've seen, at its most fundamental level, the sense of being a self – and the animate intelligence arising from it – most likely exists, in one form or another, in every living organism. It involves basic biological regulation, the experience of the here-and-now, the very sensation of being alive that is often referred to as sentience.[2]

It also incorporates much more than this primal background state. If I bite my tongue right now, I will experience something in the foreground of my attention that only I can know. If you bite your tongue, you'll likely experience something similar, but neither of us would be able to communicate to each other exactly what our sensation felt like. These unique, moment-to-moment embodied experiences are known as qualia. They arise and pass in consciousness and can only be felt for that particular moment. As I sip a delicious cup of tea right now, I encounter a distinct taste, interwoven with a complex set of my own implicit associations, that I could never exactly replicate. And now that moment has passed, and it has become a memory. A pioneer of modern psychology, William James, noticed in the late nineteenth century that this 'fluctuating material' of his inner experience was 'at each moment different from that of the last moment' and memorably coined the term 'stream of consciousness' to describe it.[3]

Animate consciousness exists solely in the present, yet it can also include implicit memories of the past and anticipation of the future. Imagine an antelope in the savanna lifting up its head to sniff something in the breeze. Once before, when it perceived a similar rustle in the distance along with that scent, a lion had pounced out of the long grass, and the antelope had fled for its life. Now it fears the same might happen again, so it stops feeding and cautiously moves away. This ability of animals to incorporate past experiences into the present is a crucial evolutionary attribute, but it probably doesn't involve the elaborate reconstructions of the past and conceptions of the future that humans constantly create.

As such, biologist Gerald Edelman has called it the 'remembered present'.[4]

How, then, did humans first develop a sense of 'I' as separate from the animate consciousness we share with other creatures? Many experts attribute its origins to the complex social interactions that characterized pre-human communities several million years ago. The influential 'social brain hypothesis' asserts that humans' distinctive cognitive capacities are the result of increased social complexity in our ancestors' lives. When hominids first diverged from forest-dwelling primates in the Great Rift Valley of east Africa, they needed to work closely together in tight-knit communities to survive in a new, dangerous environment. Those with the cognitive abilities to cooperate effectively with their companions were the most successful in passing their genes on to future generations.[5]

An important part of the distinctively human social intelligence that emerged is known as theory of mind: the recognition that other people have minds just like we do, allowing us to guess how they might respond to something by mentally putting ourselves in their situation. If I feel bad when I'm ignored by the others at the evening campfire, I suspect that my friend might feel the same way, so I turn and smile at him to acknowledge his presence. While everyone's watching that kid playing over there, I know I could sneak that tasty piece of meat and not be seen ... but they would quickly figure out it's gone and that I was the only one with the opportunity. So, tempting as it is, I'd better leave it alone.[6]

Humans are not alone among primates in having this type of social intelligence, but we've developed it to a much greater degree. An eighteen-month-old toddler has roughly the same ability to understand the intentions of others as a chimpanzee. But, over the next couple of years, she gradually develops a full-blown theory of mind. It begins to dawn on her that each person has a different perspective on the world: if Mommy puts cookies in a cupboard in the kitchen and Daddy later moves them to a different place, Mommy won't know about it unless someone tells her. That basic comprehension, arising from theory of mind, is something that a four-year-old can easily grasp, but is beyond the reach of a two-year-old.[7]*

Once you see others as separate selves, whom you can evaluate and tell stories about, it's a simple jump to realize that they see you in a similar way – and to begin imagining how you might appear to them. Neuroscientists have discovered that the same part of the prefrontal cortex is activated when people think about attributes of others as when they think about their own attributes. It's as though, in the brain's social intelligence, the community of people important to engage with includes not just family and friends, but also the self.[8]*

The emerging awareness of a self, along with concern for what others might be thinking about it, brings into the child's consciousness a whole new array of complex emotions, such as social anxiety, embarrassment, shame and pride. As a child becomes more aware of herself, she realizes that she has the ability to exert some control over how her 'self' acts: whether to pay attention, to try harder or to just let go and bawl in frustration. This emerging skill is known as metacognition: the ability to think about one's mental states and exert some influence over them. The child's 'I' is entering into its lifelong relationship with the 'self'.[9]

Telling the story of your life

So, who exactly is this 'I'? Not surprisingly, 'I' encapsulate those parts of my consciousness that – insofar as they're so highly developed – are distinctively human. The 'I' arises from conceptual consciousness with its ability to think abstract thoughts. It's an emergent property of conscious awareness, continually observing the self, categorizing it, judging it and explaining it to others.[10]

Imagine that I'm interviewing you. I ask you to sit down and say, 'So, tell me who you are.' You enter the 'I' mode. You might say, 'I'm a mother, and in my spare time I'm an artist.' You are abstracting your day-to-day responsibilities and activities into conceptual categories that you assume I will understand. You go on to say, 'I was born in Wisconsin, but I moved here when I was in my twenties. I grew up in a rural area, and now I enjoy the city, but I'd like to retire somewhere closer to nature.' You've just exhibited a crucial attribute of the 'I': the ability to perform what is known as 'mental time travel'. While the self only exists in the present moment, the 'I' is capable of remembering all kinds of detail about previous selves and imagining what future selves might feel like.[11]

I seem interested, so you continue: 'I'm a graphic designer working for a big architect firm. It felt like a good step when I first got here, but now I'm looking for a new position where I can use my design skills for the benefit of the community, so I can feel I'm making a difference.' Now the 'I' is showing its true colors. It's continually engaging in autobiography: weaving the story of the different parts of yourself into a coherent narrative, explaining how things got to be the way they are, planning for the future, and making meaning out of the whole affair. The 'I' – closely aligned with the left-hemisphere 'interpreter' from Chapter 1 – is constantly telling and retelling the story of your life, both to itself and to those who want to hear it.[12]

Imagine now that you're no longer talking to me but confiding in a close friend. 'I really feel bad about myself that I'm selling out, working for this firm that creates luxury homes for millionaires while there's a homelessness crisis in the city. I'm trying to convince myself to take another job that pays less so I can feel better about my work.' Another aspect of the 'I' has now revealed itself. The 'I' is constantly evaluating the self, making judgments about it and – crucially – can influence the direction the self will take in the future. So, the 'I' is not just telling a story about the past, it's also actively constructing the story of the future through the way it interprets the past and the choices it makes in the present.[13]

'It's complicated'

The effort to convince yourself to take a job with less pay and thus feel better about yourself hints at some difficulties in how 'I' and the self get along. Sometimes they can have different motivations: they see the world differently and prioritize different things, and they frequently pull in opposite directions. There's no getting away from it – the most important relationship in your life is a complicated one.

The self may be constantly changing, but its needs are usually fairly simple, even primal. Just like an infant, it generally wants to feel secure, comfortable, loved. When it's hungry, it wants food. When it's tired, it wants to rest.[14]

The 'I', on the other hand, develops an orientation toward more complex needs, many of which it absorbs from the surrounding culture. If I'm born into a devout Christian family, I may hope to end up in heaven, and I'll learn to prevent myself doing sinful acts that might compromise my dream of a rapturous afterlife. If I'm a teenage girl in Western consumer society, I may keep myself hungry in order to lose weight and appear attractive based on idealized images touted by mainstream media. Whatever culture I'm born into, I probably want to be respected and valued, so I may push myself hard to get along in my career.

While the self is forever changing, the 'I' tends to be more fixed, and yet I will also change as I grow, albeit more gradually. I may form new values based on my experiences, and try to teach myself more skillful ways to respond to things that go wrong. Perhaps at some point I can say, 'I'm no longer as hard on myself as I used to be.'[15]

An important aspect of this ever-changing interplay is that the relationship I have to my present self may be different from the one I have with my future self. A desire for eternal bliss in heaven is only the most extreme version of the mismatch that continually arises between my present self and one that may exist in the future. Most of us have long-term plans for ourselves, and we're willing to make short-term sacrifices to get there. If you put money away into a retirement plan or go to evening classes to learn a new skill, you're investing in your future self at the expense of the present one. The timespan for this mismatch can sometimes be very short. If someone enrages you, your immediate impulse may be to hit them, but you know that would lead to a bad outcome for your future self, so you might take a deep breath and curb your current self's desire.[16]

This process, which is of course known as self-control, has been identified as one of the most important predictors of a successful life. In the 1960s, psychologist Walter Mischel developed what become an iconic landmark of child psychology known as the 'marshmallow test'. It was a test of how well preschoolers were able to delay gratification for future rewards. A child was brought into the 'Surprise Room', where they sat at a table on which lay a tempting marshmallow. They were left alone for up to fifteen minutes, and told that if they managed not to take a bite of the marshmallow until the researcher came back, they could have two of them. It turned out that the child's ability to delay gratification was highly predictive of their later success in life.[17]

While there has been some controversy regarding this particular test, another major study in New Zealand, following over a thousand children in a single city from birth to thirty-two years of age, has resoundingly confirmed its essential findings. The study showed that the level of self-control demonstrated in the first decade of life significantly predicted income, occupational prestige, and physical and mental health, along with reduced incidence of substance abuse and criminal convictions. Self-control was as powerful a predictor of success as intelligence or the family's socio-economic status.[18*]

Does that mean, then, that 'I' should simply get control of my 'self' and make it do whatever I think is right? In fact, a vast amount of research has been undertaken in how 'I' and the 'self' should come to a decision about something. It's a fascinating area of psychology known as dual system theory, and what it tells us is that ... well, it's complicated.

Trust your gut?

The superstar of dual system theory is Israeli psychologist Daniel Kahneman, who wrote the bestseller *Thinking, Fast and Slow* in 2011. The title refers to the two different types of thinking that dual system theory has identified. System 1, as he calls it, works quickly and automatically. It's effortless and intuitive, based on 'innate skills that we share with other animals'. System 2, by contrast, is slow and reflective, requiring effortful mental activity. Kahneman describes his book, which explores how these two systems interact, as a 'psychodrama with two characters', each having 'their individual abilities, limitations, and functions'. Do you recognize the two characters? You guessed it: the reflective System 2 describes the 'I' and the intuitive System 1 the 'self'.[19*]

Kahneman doesn't name his characters 'I' and 'self' but they're instantly recognizable in his portrayal. 'When we think of ourselves,' he explains, 'we identify with System 2, the conscious, reasoning self that has beliefs, makes choices, and decides what to think about and what to do.' A major point of Kahneman's book is that, even though we identify with System 2, it's actually System 1 that makes most of our decisions for us. 'The automatic System 1,' he declares, 'is the hero of the book.'[20]

Most of his book, though, is devoted to demonstrating how the 'hero', System 1, leads us astray in innumerable ways through what are known as cognitive biases. When we act on impulse and go with what seems intuitively right, it turns out we make a lot of mistakes that we could avoid if we were more rational about things. One bias, for example, is anchoring: we let ourselves be influenced by the first number we see regarding a given situation. If you're buying a house, the list price will immediately influence how much you think it might be worth. Another bias is recency: something you read about in the newspaper this morning will seem more important than something that occurred last year, even though the earlier event might actually be far more significant. Researchers have uncovered a prodigious array of such cognitive biases, a couple of hundred of which are listed in a Wikipedia page devoted to them. These implicit biases have serious societal implications, given that they cause us to make snap judgments about people based on their race, gender and attractiveness without realizing we're doing so.[21]*

All this seems to further corroborate the importance of self-control: isn't it simply better to let the cool, rational 'I' direct what you do, and keep the emotional, impulsive 'self' away from the driver's seat? Not necessarily. In another bestseller, *Blink: The Power of Thinking Without Thinking*, journalist Malcolm Gladwell upends the conventional belief in the power of reason by pointing out how intuition can frequently provide insights that our rational brains completely miss. In one fascinating story, he recounts how, after months of careful review, the Getty Museum paid millions of dollars for an ancient Greek statue, which was later intuited to be a counterfeit by other experts as soon as they laid eyes on it. After further scientific analysis, the experts' instincts turned out to be right.[22]

We all know the gut feeling we sometimes get when something just doesn't seem right. How, then, should we distinguish between the times when 'I' know what I'm doing, and when I should listen to my 'self' – to that intuitive hunch that occasionally goes counter to my reason? A pair of Dutch researchers, Ap Dijksterhuis and Loran Nordgren, have helped to answer this question with what they call a 'theory of unconscious thought'. Their theory indicates that the more complex the problem, the more you should let your unconscious decide. The conscious mind, they explain, is limited by how much it can hold. It tends to follow strict rules, and when a problem becomes too much to handle, it gets overwhelmed. At that point, it tends to get swept along by one or more cognitive biases, and then uses its left-brain interpreter to rationalize its judgment. The best thing to do, they explain, when faced with a complex real-life, multidimensional problem, such as which apartment is the best one to rent, is to consciously consider the data, but then defer making a decision for a while. Go for a long walk and think about something completely different. Sleep on it. As you're doing this, your unconscious mind, which can hold far more complexity, is mulling over the data. At some point, you'll begin to 'get a feeling' that a particular decision is the right one. That's when you should listen to what your intuition is telling you. That's when it's a good idea to 'trust yourself'.[23]

At this point, it still seems like 'I' am in control of this relationship with my 'self'. Even if I adopt the theory of unconscious thought, 'I' am still making the decision to defer to my intuition. But a profusion of neuroscientists has now begun to overthrow the putative relationship between 'I' and my 'self' entirely. They claim to have definitive proof that, in fact, 'I' have no free will at all. The very notion of free will, they declare, is an illusion. As we delve into their findings and what they really imply, we'll uncover some clues regarding the cultural history of the relationship between 'I' and my 'self' that could lead to a radical reorientation of who 'I' really am.

'I think, therefore I am'

This curious verdict of modern neuroscience has its basis in an experiment conducted by Benjamin Libet in the 1980s. He wired up test subjects to an EEG showing brain activity, and asked them to freely move their index finger and note when they first felt the urge to move it. It turned out that the preparation for the movement in the brain occurred nearly a second before they were aware of their decision. It was as though their brain decided to move the finger before they did. More recently, using a sophisticated fMRI (functional magnetic resonance imaging) machine, a team of researchers in Berlin discovered patterns of brain activity that predicted a conscious decision by as much as seven seconds.[24]

To the researchers, the journalists covering it and respected biologists interpreting it, the finding seemed definitive. 'We feel we choose, but we don't,' gasped a member of the Berlin research team, who confessed how difficult it was for him to deal with this discovery. 'How can I call a will "mine" if I don't even know when it occurred and what it has decided to do?' 'You may not know what you're going to do next,' proclaimed one article, 'but your brain probably does.' Anthony Cashmore, a prominent biologist, wrote an article citing these studies to argue that we are nothing but 'mechanical forces of nature'. He concluded that 'not only do we have no more free will than a fly or a bacterium, in actuality we have no more free will than a bowl of sugar.'[25]

The neuroscientific data is incontrovertible, but what does it really tell us? In my view, it is the astonished reaction of the researchers that seems bizarre, not the experimental finding. What is strange is that they identify themselves so completely with the 'I' of their conscious awareness that they view their own neurons as separate entities making decisions without them and forcing their bodies to act in a certain way.

This peculiar separation of the researchers' identity from their own inner biology is deeply culturally embedded. We saw earlier that the split between 'I' and 'self' is part of the human condition and experienced cross-culturally. But the Western tradition is unique among cultures in turning this split into an unbridgeable, gaping chasm and constructing an entire system of philosophy from it, to the point that only the conscious 'I' is believed to have any identity at all. Based on this philosophical underpinning, it's no wonder that the researchers were shocked by their findings.[26]

The uniquely Western chasm of split consciousness can be traced back to Plato, who saw the human being as composed of an eternal soul and mortal body in conflict with each other. To describe this inner split, Plato used an example of someone thirsty trying not to drink, whose soul forbids their body to reach for the water – just like the children in the marshmallow test. For Plato, the soul represented all that was good and put humans in touch with divinity, while the body was like a polluted prison in which the soul was temporarily confined.[27]

When Christianity took hold of European thought, it inherited Plato's dualistic split, reinterpreting it as a Christian soul desiring to do good but tempted toward evil by the body. Paul, who set the stage for the future of Christendom, described the anguish and self-loathing arising from his internal conflict. 'I do not understand what I do,' he wrote, 'for what I want to do I do not do, but what I hate I do ... It is no longer I myself who do it, but it is sin living in me.' His body, he lamented, was 'waging war against the law of my mind'. With Paul's inner torment, the Christian notion of free will became entrenched in the 'I', which could choose whether to surrender to the body's sinful desires or maintain a righteous path to eternity in heaven. The 'I' was the soul; the body was the mine-strewn battlefield that it traversed.[28]

Paul's inner conflict established deep roots in the European mindset. One thousand five hundred years later, Renaissance philosopher Montaigne mused how parts of his body 'sometimes refuse to obey me'. By then, Europe's Scientific Revolution was around the corner. One of its greatest pioneers, René Descartes, was determined to discard old superstition and trust only his own intellect in his pursuit of truth. After extensive self-investigation, he concluded that the one thing he could be certain was true was the fact that he was thinking. 'I think, therefore I am,' he declared, coining what would become the cornerstone of modern philosophy. Even if his body no longer existed, he concluded, his 'soul would not cease to be what it is'.[29]

With this revelation, melding his very existence, his eternal soul, with the self-reflective 'I', Descartes ushered European dualism into the scientific era. He went on to reframe 'soul' as 'mind', and the mind/body split now became a foundation of scientific thought. Since humans alone possessed minds capable of self-reflection, nonhuman animals, along with the human body, were deemed no more than machines. The centuries of scientific investigation that followed were based on this strange schema. Jacques Loeb, a famous early-twentieth-century physiologist, helped shape the popular Western understanding with his blockbuster *The Mechanistic Conception of Life*, which declared, 'We eat, drink and reproduce ... because, machine-like, we are compelled to do so.' More recently, Richard Dawkins has popularized similar mechanistic notions of human nature, arguing that we are 'lumbering robots' acting at the behest of our selfish genes. Cashmore's pronouncements of our mere mechanical existence fit squarely into this tradition.[30]

The profound irony is that, while Dawkins, Cashmore and others like them believe they're rejecting Christian superstition by focusing on the biological underpinnings of decision-making and thereby denying free will, they are in fact implicitly endorsing the dualistic view of human nature they inherited from the Christian/Platonic tradition. While they no longer view the 'I' as a soul with hopes of eternal redemption, they continue to believe that their true essence exists entirely on one side of the chasm of split consciousness, while their bodies, along with those neurons making decisions without them, are somehow separate from their actual identity.[31]*

This definitive positioning of identity on the 'I' side of the split consciousness chasm is so culturally entrenched that any alternative might seem inconceivable. There are, however, different ways to acknowledge, and experience, the sense of who we really are. These alternative approaches have been explored for millennia by non-Western wisdom traditions, and are recently being rediscovered by leading scientific researchers. The implications of these findings open up pathways of understanding that will reverberate throughout this book.

'I feel, therefore I am'

When Anthony Cashmore claimed that humans have no more free will than a fly, he wasn't reckoning with the ingenious research of German neurobiologist Björn Brembs, who was literally studying the free will of flies in his lab, and countered the following year with a penetrating paper providing the framework for a scientific concept of free will as a biological trait. Imagine several flies buzzing around your room. What is it that determines whether they choose to turn right or left, and which moment they get tired of flying and rest on the window sill? Brembs describes how the brains of flies – along with other creatures – are exquisitely sensitive to the tiniest random perturbations, both internal and external, which then get amplified along nonlinear and unpredictable neural pathways, until a decision is made. Even if you could map out every molecule of the fly's body and monitor every molecule of airflow, you'd still never know if that fly was going to turn right or left.[32]

Meanwhile, Antonio Damasio and other neuroscientists have been investigating the neural systems that lead to decisions in humans. They have identified two parallel pathways, interacting with each other, that induce us to decide what to do. One pathway, corresponding to the 'self', recalls the emotional experience of similar situations, just like the antelope in the savanna, and activates appropriate instinctual responses. If the situation evokes danger, this could initiate a 'fight or flight' stress response. If it evokes security, it might lead to a sense of relaxation with positive emotions. The other pathway responds more slowly, remembering pertinent facts about the situation and evaluating them: what actually happened the last time it occurred? How was that different from this time? This, of course, corresponds to the thinking, reflective 'I'. However, the emotional response activated by the first pathway creates feeling tones that act as 'covert biases' influencing the second pathway. If they're strong enough, they might sway the final decision. If not, they might be ignored.[33]

What's crucially important about these two pathways is that neither one alone represents our true identity. Who we are, and the decisions we make, are a result of how these different pathways interact.

We don't need a specific event to set these pathways in motion. We do it simply by imagining something. Suppose, when driving home from work yesterday, you got stuck in bad traffic because of road work. You felt irritated, especially because you were tired and hungry, and dinner was waiting. Now, it's the end of your work day and you're getting ready to leave the office. Suddenly, an embodied memory of what happened yesterday activates in your nervous system. A faint whiff of yesterday's traffic-stress hormones coursing through your body reminds you that your regular way home didn't work out so well. It might be so faint that your conscious 'I' doesn't even notice it, and you simply begin thinking about which way to go home, perhaps checking on your smartphone to see if the traffic is backed up again. But it began with the implicit feeling tones, giving you a hint of your experience as if you were already stuck in the traffic again. Perhaps, as author Milan Kundera has suggested, Descartes' famous dictum should be restated as 'I feel, therefore I am.'[34]

In fact, prominent psychologist Jonathan Haidt has suggested that feelings are so much more central to our lives than reason that they dominate most of what we do and even form the basis of our moral judgment. A conventional image of reason is the cool, dispassionate judge who carefully listens to both sides of a dispute and then delivers his verdict. Haidt, instead, suggests reason is more like a lawyer, who hears what his client (intuition) really wants, and then builds a case to argue why it's the best approach.[35*]

A large number of studies conducted in recent years have corroborated Haidt's thesis. One particularly disturbing study analyzed the decisions made by a panel of judges in Israel who spent several days reviewing parole applications. The cases were presented in random order to the judges, who worked through each day with three food breaks – morning, lunch and afternoon. It turned out that the likelihood of a prisoner getting parole was determined more by how hungry the judges were at different times in the day than any other factor. A prisoner assessed just before a break had virtually zero chance of parole, while one who was lucky enough to be evaluated after a meal had a 65 percent chance of approval. If someone had asked the judges why they made a particular decision, it's unlikely they would have said it was based primarily on the state of their stomachs.[36]

Alarming as this study is, we shouldn't necessarily view the role that feeling has in decision-making as negative. Haidt, Damasio and others argue that our sense of morality is grounded in feelings and emotional responses. Without those, we'd have no basis for moral judgment. Imagine a person who makes purely rational decisions without incorporating emotions in any way. He decides what he wants to achieve and works out exactly how to attain his goal, regardless of the consequences. The word for someone like that, Haidt points out, is a psychopath.[37*]

Importantly, the relationship between our moral intuition and conscious reasoning is not just one way. In fact, much of what we think of as our innate sense of morality is something we learn through our exposure to culture. Researchers have discovered that, between the ages of around nine and fifteen, we go through a particularly sensitive period of this kind of learning. Just like learning the days of the week or riding a bicycle, we get exposed so frequently to cultural and ethical norms that they become automatic and reflexive. In the West, most of us have an intuitive repulsion to things like slavery or animal cruelty. It might feel like a gut instinct, but in earlier centuries that wouldn't have been the case. In the memorable words of biologist Robert Sapolsky, 'our guts learn their intuitions'.[38]

The democracy of consciousness

What sense can we make from this intricate entanglement of 'I' and my 'self'? One principle that emerges is that, far from being on opposite sides of an unbridgeable chasm, they are actually inseparable. The decisions you make in your life, from trivial ones like which way to drive home to major ones like what career to pursue or whom to commit to as a life-partner, are made by all of you, not just the 'I' and not just the 'self'.[39]

Once we realize this, we can begin to see ourselves as integrated organisms arising from the patterns of connectivity between those networks that we identify as 'I' and 'self'. Our thoughts, even our most abstract ideas, don't exist without a concomitant wash of images and sensations. And the feelings arising within our bodies activate and influence the neural pathways that create our ideas and judgments. As neurobiologist Dan Siegel suggests, these felt sensations, as they blend with our conscious awareness, may be understood as the 'wisdom of the body'.[40]

Given this, it would seem crucially important to understand how to integrate these continually flowing patterns within us, in order to make the most skillful decisions and enjoy the most harmonious relationship between 'I' and my 'self'. How do I know when to go with that gut feeling? When am I being driven by physical urges of hunger, exhaustion or sexual attraction to make a bad decision? How, on the other hand, can I learn to discern the quiet wisps of wisdom hinted at through my bodily sensations, some of which might never make it into the arena of conscious awareness?

As a general rule, we can always acknowledge the validity of the feelings we experience, but that doesn't necessarily mean we should believe the stories that our left-hemisphere 'lawyer' weaves around them. Leading researchers in the field offer some insights to help sort out this conundrum.

Robert Sapolsky provides a valuable guideline for how to relate to the dual systems within us, based on our evolutionary past. We evolved as humans in small bands of hunter-gatherers. As such, our instincts honed us to act amicably with our in-group but to treat those who seemed different from us with suspicion. Nowadays, most of us live in cosmopolitan societies and interact daily both with intimate acquaintances and strangers. Sapolsky's wise rule is to rely on our intuition when we're engaging with our in-group of family and friends, but when interacting with those who appear different from us, to 'keep intuitions as far away as possible'. Instead, he suggests, we should utilize the theory of mind that evolution bequeathed to us. 'Think, reason, and question,' he writes. 'Take their perspective, try to think what they think, try to feel what they feel. Take a deep breath, and then do it all again.'[41]

Another insight comes from prominent neuroscientists Francis Crick and Christof Koch, who suggest we view the systems within us as a never-ending series of 'transient coalitions of neurons', sometimes supporting and sometimes opposing each other, like a sort of democracy of consciousness. Instead of elections occurring at fixed intervals, there is a continual succession of 'local' elections and occasional 'general' elections when major decisions are made. As in a well-functioning democracy, it's essential that all parties, including the minority ones, are respected and heard in the decision-making process.[42]

As in a real democracy, the tone used by different parties is just as important as the rules governing elections. In the democracy of consciousness, how 'I' view my 'self' plays a critical role in this. For example, psychologist Kristin Neff emphasizes that you can always choose to act with compassion to yourself. This doesn't mean indulging in self-pity or self-centeredness. Rather, it means offering yourself the kindness and care you'd give to a close friend. When you find your 'self' making a mistake, you can choose to treat it with support, understanding and curiosity, rather than perpetuating self-destructive emotions such as shame or guilt.[43]

By approaching the relationship between 'I' and 'self' in a more integrated way, these leading researchers are overturning thousands of years of Western conventional thinking, from Plato onwards. They base their insights on modern neuroscience and biology, but also frequently turn to the wisdom of non-Western cultures that didn't take the path of believing humans were split by an unbridgeable chasm. Instead, certain cultures in south and east Asia spent those same millennia developing practices designed to bridge the separation between the dual domains of human consciousness. In the modern era, the insights of these wisdom traditions are available for all to access. Let's take a look.

Embodied mind and mindful body

Where in your body do you think your mind is? If you've grown up in the West, you probably think of your head. But ask a Chinese or Japanese person this question and they're more likely to point to their heart. In both languages, the word for mind is the same as for heart – *xin* in Chinese and *kokoro* in Japanese. In addition to referring to the physical heart, it incorporates the full range of subjective experience, including emotions, thoughts, intuition and desires.[44*]

For Plato or Descartes, believing their soul/mind existed in the head, it was easy to conceive of it as separate from the rest of the body. But if you feel your mind existing within your body, in an organ that beats faster when strong feelings arise, this would automatically lead to a greater sense of integration within your entire organism. In the words of Chinese sage Wang Yangming, 'The heart-mind [*xin*] is nothing without the body, and the body is nothing without the heart-mind.'[45]

In contrast to the European tradition, the Chinese saw no essential distinction between reason and emotion. Some philosophers used a particular word, *tiren*, to refer to knowing something, not just intellectually but throughout the entire body and mind – for which no English word exists. Imagine living in a hot climate and learning about snow as a concept. Then, one day, you visit the mountains and actually experience the snow falling on you and making snowballs. That's the moment when your knowledge of snow becomes *tiren*, or fully embodied.[46]

With this more integrated view of human experience, the traditional Western idea of free will was alien to Chinese thought. Their philosophers would probably not have been surprised in the slightest by Libet's finding – in fact, they would have expected it. They recognized the validity of all different aspects of human existence and put great value on harmonizing them, describing a faculty in the heart-mind called a 'regulator' that could be cultivated to do this more skillfully.[47]

As we know, early Taoists had a powerful vision of acting in harmony, not only with oneself, but also with one's surroundings – the *wu-wei*, or effortlessness, that allowed Cook Ding to cut up his carcass so adeptly. We all experience an element of *wu-wei* when we've mastered a particular skill, whether it's riding a bike or playing a musical instrument. Neuroscience sheds some light on this process. When we first learn a skill, we use our prefrontal cortex extensively, as we're consciously figuring out what to do. At a certain point, once we've transitioned to a state where it becomes automatic, we use parts of the brain that are evolutionarily more ancient, such as the basal ganglia and cerebellum. Edward Slingerland, a Chinese scholar who has written two books on *wu-wei*, calls this 'body thinking'.[48]

That's the easy part, though. The full experience of *wu-wei* occurs, not so much when we're on autopilot, but when we integrate automatic activity with conscious attention. In terms of dual system theory, *wu-wei* happens when both Systems 1 and 2 are in smooth synchrony. As Slingerland describes it, 'for a person in *wu-wei*, the mind is embodied and the body is mindful; the two systems – hot and cold, fast and slow – are completely integrated. The result is an intelligent spontaneity that is perfectly calibrated to the environment.'[49]

Wu-wei, therefore, is different from the Western Romantic notion of simply 'letting yourself go' and acting spontaneously on your emotions. Rather, it's the result of the disciplined cultivation of the connections between the 'I' and the 'self', so that your entire organism is harmonizing both within and with the environment.[50]

Psychologist Mihaly Csikszentmihalyi has dedicated his career to studying this state of absorption, which he calls 'Flow'. Happily, he explains that it's available to all of us, not just experts like Cook Ding. It's a state you can achieve when you invest in a realistic goal that's meaningful to you. For a child, it could be using building blocks to construct a higher tower than he's ever done before; for a runner, it could be trying to beat her personal record. He describes this pleasurable state as existing on the boundary between boredom and anxiety, when there's just enough challenge to remain absorbed, but not so much that you become overwrought. At this point, he reports from interviews with flow practitioners, the concern for the self disappears in the absorption of the moment, but paradoxically the sense of who you are expands dramatically.[51]

What about the rest of the time, though, when we're experiencing the more mundane realities of our daily lives? Is this harmonious integration of 'I' and 'self' something that can only be achieved in sporadic, peak experiences, or is there a way to get there more sustainably? Let's turn to another East Asian tradition, Zen Buddhism, which has a few things to say about that.

'Whatever you think is delusion'

People generally think of Zen Buddhism as Japanese, but its

origins tell an interesting story. Buddhism emerged in India in the fifth century BCE, from the teachings of Siddhartha Gautama, known as the Buddha or 'Awakened One'. It spread through Asia over centuries, eventually becoming an integral part of Chinese culture. There, some core Buddhist principles merged with Taoist ideas, which led to the rise of a particular form of Buddhism called Chan. Only centuries later did this tradition migrate to Japan, where it became known as Zen.[52]

We can see the Taoist influence on Zen in some of its central teachings. As we know, early Taoists saw the loss of *wu-wei* resulting from the type of mental activity that conceptual consciousness generates: language-based, rational, goal-oriented thinking. Chan Buddhists based their approach on this fundamental insight, and spent generations developing techniques to undo what they saw as the tyrannical grip conceptual thinking held over the human experience.[53]

Zen is focused primarily on the recognition that the ideas we form about ourselves and the world block the ability to get in touch with our essential nature. If we could only pierce these delusions, we could glimpse the true nature of reality. A famous definition of Zen, dating from 1108, summarizes its character:

> A special transmission outside the scriptures,
> Not founded on words and letters;
> By pointing directly to one's heart-mind
> It lets one see into one's true nature and thus attain
> Buddhahood.[54]

Zen is not opposed to reason and intellectual thought, but it recognizes the tendency to become so wrapped up in concepts that we begin to believe they are reality itself, rather than models of reality. A famous Zen story tells of a teacher pointing to the moon and warning his students not to confuse his finger with the moon itself: every language has a word for the moon, he explains, but they are mere abstractions, constructed by the human mind, pointing to something that is real. When we use conceptual consciousness to make sense of things or to make up a story about them, we lose touch with reality. In the words of Zen teacher Dainin Katagiri, 'Whatever you think is delusion.'[55]

Chan monks developed an ingenious technique to break the grip of logical thought on the human psyche in the form of *koans*: a type of riddle that a teacher poses to a student, to which there is no logical answer. A classic example is 'What is the sound of one hand clapping?' Other famous *koans* are: 'When you can do nothing, what can you do?' and 'What is the color of wind?' By engaging in this process, students could learn to recognize and undo the habitual cognitive patterns that prevented them from achieving deeper insight into the nature of reality.[56*]

Along with other Buddhist schools, Zen recognizes that, of all the cognitive patterns blocking a deep realization of reality, the most insidious is the belief that 'I' am an objective and fixed entity, rather than a mere abstraction. Philosopher Alan Watts illustrates this by comparing the 'I' to the illusory circle of light created by a whirling torch or the flight path made by a bird in the sky. It doesn't objectively exist, but we create the abstraction by weaving together a pattern of past and future.[57]

The word for this Buddhist insight, *anatman*, which literally means 'no *atman*', is often confusingly translated as 'no-self', but it would be more accurate to translate it as 'no-fixed-I'. The meaning of the ancient Indian word *atman* correlates closely with the Greco-Christian idea of a fixed, eternal soul that is freed from the body at death. When the Buddha renounced this core Vedic belief with the principle of *anatman*, it would have been as revolutionary as an early Christian claiming that the soul didn't exist.[58]

In today's cultural mainstream, with researchers and journalists shocked to discover we have no 'free will', this profound Buddhist insight remains radical. In fact, with modern support from neuroscientists such as Edelman and Damasio, the principle of *anatman* states that there is no objective 'I' at all, so the question of whether or not 'I' have free will is itself illusory. Perhaps a new Zen *koan* might go: 'If I don't really exist, can I have free will?'

Bridging the gap between 'I' and 'self'

Zen shares with other Buddhist traditions considerable reliance on meditation as a means to achieve results. Many Westerners misconstrue meditation as a technique to attain some sort of mystical state, but in fact the Buddha and his followers treated it more like a scientific tool, using it as we might use a microscope, to look clearly inside the layers of consciousness in order to understand them more deeply. Just as modern scientists establish standardized procedures within their disciplines to conduct their observations, so Buddhist practitioners developed time-proven techniques that permitted a rigorous and dispassionate analysis of the workings of the human mind.[59]

A form of meditation central to many Buddhist traditions, which has since spread widely among non-Buddhists, is known as mindfulness. Mindfulness meditation involves observing your inner experience from moment to moment, without reacting or making judgments on what you observe. In this sense, 'I' am observing the momentary instantiations of my 'self' as they arise and disappear from consciousness. As I do this, I try to avoid reacting to, or making up stories about what I'm observing, while remaining curious, open and accepting of whatever I discern.[60]

If you try this for yourself, you'll probably notice a chaotic and seemingly incoherent buzz of stuff that appears in your awareness. Soon, most likely, you'll find that your attention gets caught up in a particular chain of thought and, before you know it, your left-hemisphere narrator is off on its own trail, planning what you're going to say in that meeting tomorrow or deciding what you're having for dinner this evening. Meditators often refer to this wandering tendency of our thoughts as 'monkey mind'.[61]

It is sometimes shocking for beginning meditators to realize that this whirlwind of mental objects, a torrent of sensations, daydreams, feelings, ideas, internal conversations and judgments, is happening all the time in their consciousness without them even being aware of it. One of the most surprising discoveries people often make, when they begin to meditate, is how disconnected they are from their own actual experience. While 'I' am typically attending to the daily influences of life, such as what's going on at work or what's in the news, the self is experiencing all kinds of things that I am generally oblivious to until they become intense enough to enter my conscious awareness.[62]

Once 'I' become aware of the self's experience, however, I tend to hold on to it, make up a story about it and plan around it, even when the self has moved on to something completely different. Buddhist teachings identify this disconnect as the source of a certain kind of pervasive human experience known as *dukkha*. The word *dukkha* is frequently translated as 'suffering', but it actually refers to a much broader spectrum of experiences arising from the stories that 'I' inevitably construct, including feelings of unease, worry, grasping, longing, regret, embarrassment, and a host of other states derived from the workings of conceptual consciousness. In a sense, *dukkha* can be understood as the inverse of *wu-wei* – as the customary state when 'I' am not in complete harmony with my 'self'. We can think of *dukkha* as arising from the separation between 'I' and my 'self'. When I judge myself, or am ashamed of myself, I experience *dukkha*; when I feel at one with myself, *dukkha* temporarily disappears.[63*]

A fundamental aim of Buddhist practice is to eliminate *dukkha* from one's experience, and mindfulness meditation is a powerful technique to help achieve this. One way it works is by helping us to recognize the subtle moment when an experience moves from an embodied phenomenon to conscious awareness – when a momentary instantiation of 'self' becomes fastened to the 'I'. Suppose you're sitting quietly meditating, and suddenly you hear construction noise from the house next door. At the moment that you become aware of it, it's just a sound. For an instant, you experience it as pure awareness, but then your conceptual consciousness kicks in: 'Oh, it's that damn construction again! When are they going to be finished? Now it's stopping me from meditating.' At this point, the story you've formulated may cause a secondary response of anger to sweep through you. Now, your mindfulness meditation offers you a choice point: you could get more annoyed, give up on your meditation for that day and plan an angry exchange with your neighbor, or you could reset your attention to your inner experience: notice the shift from implicit to conscious response, feel the emotion coursing through your body, become curious about the physiological sensations, and recognize the stories and plans your left-hemisphere narrator was hatching. As you do this, you may find that the construction noise was itself a gateway to a deeper understanding of your own inner life – that it helped the 'I' become more attuned to different aspects of the self.[64]

At first, applying this kind of non-judgmental awareness to your perpetually changing inner experience can feel like a monumental task, but with continued practice it comes more easily. Just like learning to ride a bicycle as a child, with enough practice it can become effortless and automatic. When this happens, you may begin to notice that this habit of mindfulness spreads beyond meditation to other aspects of life, and begins to influence your very relationship with yourself. As the 'I' and 'self' get along more easily, the level of *dukkha* may begin to diminish. You might find that the sensation of *wu-wei* is no longer confined to the rare, peak moments of life, but has infused the normal rhythms of your daily existence.[65]

The dance of the 'I' and 'self'

Your relationship with yourself is not only the most important of your life – it's also in many ways the most complex. Consider how different 'I' am from myself. The self is impulsive, lives in the present moment, is continually changing. It springs from embodied experiences, is in many ways entirely unpredictable, and can occasionally become overwhelmingly powerful. 'I', on the other hand, am more stable, I have a clear sense of past and future, I make plans and set intentions, and I try to steer myself to remain on track with them. At the same time, strangely enough, 'I' don't really exist at all. Just like the bird's flight path described by Alan Watts, 'I' am no more than an abstraction, an emergent product of my conceptual consciousness, and conditioned to a large extent by my cultural context.

Given these differences, is it any wonder that the relationship between 'I' and myself can become fraught with all kinds of *dukkha*? If you find yourself in an incompatible relationship with a partner, you can always decide to separate. But your relationship with yourself is one that you're in for your entire life, whether you like it or not. Therefore, it's best to find the most harmonious way to conduct it.

While self-control has been shown to produce more successful life outcomes, if applied excessively, it doesn't lead to sustained happiness. Rather, like an authoritarian regime forcing itself on a population, it might achieve apparent stability, but only at the cost of seething resentments that ultimately lead to acts of sabotage and potentially even revolution. Instead, establishing a more wholesome 'democracy of consciousness' can lead to both greater stability and a more peaceful inner experience.

The key to a successful democracy of consciousness is a full and ongoing integration of the different aspects of 'I' and the self. By welcoming and honoring the various needs and feelings of the self, 'I' am more able to incorporate them into the direction I set for my life. If I learn to listen carefully to the 'wisdom of the body', I can become a wiser person in the decisions I make and actions I take. At the same time, if the self recognizes that its needs are being acknowledged, it can also relax, and is less likely to sabotage the life that 'I' have constructed.

The relationship between 'I' and self is a bit like a partner dance set to the music of life. Each partner differs from the other, but can learn to attune to the other and respond harmoniously to the other's moves, sometimes closing in, sometimes moving further away, sometimes setting a new tone and sometimes following the other's lead, but always remaining in relationship – and rather than trying to dominate or surrender, coordinating with the other to co-create an experience that neither could ever attain by themselves.

Ultimately, then, in answer to the question 'Who am I?', it turns out that I am an ongoing process – the result of a continual dance enacted by the different parts that comprise me. The essence of who I am exists in the dynamic relationship arising between all the different aspects of myself. Now, as we begin our inquiry into 'Where am I?', we will find that this rather curious way of perceiving our own identity has powerful correspondences with everything else around us too.

NEW THREADS OF MEANING

We are blended organisms arising from the patterns of connectivity between the networks we identify as 'I' and 'self'

My true identity doesn't exist in 'I' or my 'self', but emerges dynamically from how 'I' interact with my 'self'

When 'I' welcome and honor the various needs and feelings of my 'self', I can more fully integrate them, and achieve a well-functioning democracy of consciousness

WHO AM I?

I am the integrated product of my animate and conceptual consciousness – an ongoing process of 'I' and 'self' continually interacting

Part Two

WHERE AM I?

Chapter Four

THE PATTERNS OF THE UNIVERSE

The Ship of Theseus

The ancient Greeks loved a good logical paradox. Leading intellectuals would compete to see who could come up with the cleverest interpretation. One of their favorites was called the Ship of Theseus, named after the mythical founder of Athens who, among other exploits, slew the dreaded Minotaur. After his return to Athens, Theseus's ship had to be kept seaworthy because he had made a solemn pledge to sail it to the isle of Delos annually to honor Apollo. As old planks decayed, the Athenians would diligently replace them with new timber, until there was nothing left of the ship's original material. This gave rise to the paradox: was it still the original ship, or was it now something entirely different?[1]

For the Greeks, enjoyable as it was to chew on this conundrum, the questions it raised were just a sideshow to the great drama of their philosophy. As Plato laid down the foundations of his dualistic universe, which would set the shape of Western thought to the present day, he made no mention of the issues arising from the paradox of Theseus's ship. But if you pause and reflect on it, you may realize that it raised a profound question regarding the nature of our universe. It turns out that it's not just Theseus's ship that remains the same while changing its component parts. Consider a candle flame, flickering in the air. Every moment the molecules making up the flame are different, yet the flame remains an ongoing entity. The same is true for a river: from one day to the next, the water molecules flowing along are entirely different, yet the river may stay recognizably intact for millennia. In fact, the same principle holds true for you and me. Think of a photograph of yourself when you were a child. You know it's you, but virtually every cell within you now is different from what comprised that child – and even the cells that remain in us for life are constantly reconfiguring their internal contents, so you can be virtually certain that not a single molecule in that little child is still part of you. And yet you know you're the same person. You have the memories to prove it. What, then, is it that makes us what we are? What makes anything in the universe what it really is?

There were, in fact, some philosophers in ancient Greece who pondered this mystery. A century before Plato, Heraclitus was known as the 'philosopher of flux' because he was fascinated by the continually changing nature of the universe. 'It is impossible,' he famously wrote, 'to step into the same river twice.' The only thing you could rely on was the fact that 'all things are momentary and pass away'. Plato, who posited an eternally unchanging dimension within his dualistic cosmos, hated Heraclitus's ideas so much that, in his vision of a perfect society, he proposed sentencing those who propagated them to five years' solitary confinement.[2]

In recent times, pioneering scientists have revisited Heraclitus's original inquiry, applying modern frameworks to develop a profound understanding of the patterns of change and stability that constitute the universe. As we'll see, the implications of their discoveries require us to reassess many aspects of reality that conventional thinking takes for granted. Astonishingly, many of these scientists' most important insights were already described systematically a thousand years ago. Only, it wasn't in Europe. The philosophers who developed the first deep understanding of our universe as a system in constant flux lived thousands of miles away from Europe, in a place that boasted, at that time, the most advanced civilization in history – the Song dynasty of China. And it's there, in China, that we'll begin our journey to search out the hidden principles underlying our universe that modern scientists are now beginning to uncover.

The interconnected web of *dharma* and Tao

While Heraclitus was getting shut down in ancient Greece for claiming that everything is in flux, sages in ancient China were painstakingly compiling a compendium of all the changes they saw in the world and trying to identify what general principles might arise from them. Known as the *I Ching* (literally 'Book of Changes'), their compilation is one of the great classics of antiquity. Along with other Chinese systems of thought, it's based on the understanding that the entire universe is comprised of a dynamic flow of energy and matter called *qi* (pronounced *chee*). The clouds in the sky, a granite mountaintop, the breath coming from a person's mouth – all were understood as composed of qi in one form or another.[3]

The Chinese conception of qi as an all-pervasive force intrinsic to both matter and energy was given the precision of a mathematical formula in the early twentieth century when Albert Einstein transformed physics with what has become the most famous equation in the world: $E=mc^2$. In plain English, this states that the energy of a body is equal to its mass times the speed of light squared, showing that at the deepest level, energy and matter are transmutable.

The Chinese may not have had Einstein's formula, but they made up for it with careful observations into how qi flowed through the universe. A core principle they discerned was that qi exhibits a continual interplay of polarities they called yin and yang. Yin represented softness, wetness, darkness and receptivity, while yang represented hardness, dryness, light and activity. We can understand yin and yang like the north and south poles of the Earth, or the positive and negative poles of an electric current. Each is an integral part of a complete system, and neither can exist without the other. The qi of the universe was understood to flow according to the principles of yin and yang, forming the dynamic cycles we see throughout the natural world: the moon waxing and waning, a wave cresting and falling, the rhythms of day and night, summer and winter, growth and decline, birth and death.[4]

As they broadened this awareness of perpetual fluctuation to comprehend the world at large, early Chinese thinkers came to see the universe as an intricately interconnected web of activity. Imagine you're hiking in a forest and come across a spider's web. You know that a drop of water touching it will cause undulations to reverberate across the entire web. The Chinese saw the universe similarly, recognizing that the smallest actions they took could resonate in unexpected ways across the vast network of life that comprised the mysterious and all-pervasive Tao. Based on this understanding, Chinese sages concluded that the most skillful thing a person could do was to learn to attune their actions with everything else going on around them – and thus harmonize with the Tao.[5]

When Buddhists arrived in China in the first centuries of the modern era, they brought along their own term for the unifying principle of reality, *dharma*, which they explained as the underlying order of the universe by which everything related harmoniously to everything else. Chinese students who heard this naturally interpreted it as the Tao, so much so that when scholars translated Buddhist texts into Chinese, they simply used the word Tao to translate *dharma*.[6]

Along with their idea of *dharma*, monks arriving in China introduced the profound Buddhist concept of dependent origination, which describes how all phenomena are dependent for their existence on each other. Combined with the recognition that everything in the universe is in constant motion, this led naturally to another crucial Buddhist insight: the impermanence of all phenomena. One of the most important practices of Buddhist meditation is to ponder this aspect of the *dharma*, and by doing so ultimately free oneself from becoming unduly attached to things remaining the same. While Heraclitus was all but forgotten in the West, some of the greatest minds in Asia had started out with similar ideas and raised them to a pinnacle of human understanding.

Tracing the ripples of time and space

The intermingled conceptions of Tao and *dharma*, depicting a dynamic universe in flow, permeated Chinese thought over centuries, influencing even those who didn't view themselves as Taoist or Buddhist. By the time of the Song dynasty, a school of philosophers flourished who were determined to revive traditional Confucianism, with its orientation toward family and social ethics. Ironically, they were so deeply influenced by the Buddhist and Taoist ideas they repudiated that they ended up creating a powerful synthesis of all three traditions, weaving essential elements into a fabric that was more comprehensive than any of the traditions alone. They called their new way of thinking the School of the Study of the Tao, but we know it nowadays as Neo-Confucianism – and it offered perhaps the most profound and integrated understanding of the universe that had yet been achieved in human thought.[7]

Neo-Confucian philosophers were particularly interested in explaining the conundrum that the Greeks had broached with the Ship of Theseus. How could things be in continual flux yet remain persistent? As they contemplated the dynamism of the universe, they realized that while everything was composed of qi, the principles by which the qi was organized were just as important. The word they used for these principles was *li*, which originally referred to the swirling patterns visible in a piece of jade. Their core insight was that, in the words of their principal philosopher Zhu Xi, 'throughout the universe there is no qi without li, nor li without qi'. Or in other words, matter or energy simply can't exist without being organized in some fundamental way.[8*]

Think back to the candle flame, the river or your own body: how can they persist even when all of their components have changed? The answer is that, even while their qi is continually being replaced, their li – the principles by which the qi is organized – remain recognizably stable. Like an eddy of water in a fast-flowing river, the patterns of li are themselves in continual motion, but they retain a certain amount of resilience even as their contents keep changing. These patterns are easiest to see in natural objects, but they also exist in time as well as space, and in our own modes of perceptions. We can think of li, then, as the ever-moving, ever-present set of patterns that flow through everything in nature and in all our perceptions of the world – including our own consciousness.

The crucial Neo-Confucian insight was that, to understand the universe, it wasn't enough to study qi, but also li. To understand a particular plant, for example, you needed to investigate not just what it's made of, but also its relationship to everything else around it: the soil, other plants, the weather, its own history and the broader context of space and time beyond the plant's immediate environment. As the scope expands, the patterns are more difficult to comprehend, but that doesn't make them any less important. In fact, the Neo-Confucians recognized that all the patterns of the universe ultimately affect each other, just like multiple ripples on a lake intersecting and creating new patterns. The ultimate pattern of patterns, they realized, incorporating all the li ripples in the universe, was the Tao. 'The Tao,' Zhu Xi reflected, 'is so vast and large ... so distant that even sages cannot comprehensively understand it.' Li, on the other hand, are 'minute and detailed' and can therefore 'be known and acted upon'. By focusing attention on these patterns of connectivity, from small to large, Neo-Confucian philosophers developed a deeply integrated understanding of how humans relate to the natural world, how core values arise from human embeddedness in nature and how there is no ultimate distinction between what is material and spiritual.[9]

A 'pointless' universe

Meanwhile, back in Europe, a very different conception of nature as just a highly complicated machine was taking hold, inspiring the thinking that catalyzed Europe's Scientific Revolution in the seventeenth century. Rather than investigating relationships between things, scientists were driven to understand the components that things were made of, as if all living entities were simply elaborate manifestations of the Creator's clockwork. 'What is the heart, but a spring,' wrote Thomas Hobbes, 'and the nerves but so many strings?' Descartes boldly declared, 'I do not recognize any difference between the machines made by craftsmen and the various bodies that nature alone composes.'[10]

It was on this basis that Descartes proposed a scientific method known as reductionism, which still remains the dominant mode of science. His method, as he described it, was 'to divide all the difficulties under examination into as many parts as possible, and as many as were required to solve them in the best way'. As a methodology, it was – and still is – phenomenally successful. Science itself became divided into separate disciplines, such as physics, chemistry and biology, and each domain progressed by dividing its objects of study into ever-smaller components. Chemists discerned that everything was ultimately made up of atoms; physicists discovered that even atoms could be broken down further into subatomic particles such as protons or electrons; biologists learned that all living beings were made up of cells, and within these cells existed a DNA molecule that seemed to direct how they behaved.[11]

The stunning wizardry of modern technology, from nanomaterials to jetliners, from GPS to gene splicing, stems ultimately from the empirical success of reductionism. However, over the centuries, many scientists and philosophers have been so swept up by the success of their enterprise that they began to believe that reductionism alone could ultimately explain the universe itself.

This absolutist reductionist position was first asserted back in 1814, by French philosopher Pierre-Simon de Laplace. If there were an intellect, he proposed, that knew all the forces of nature and the position of everything in the universe, and could analyze all the data, it could condense it into a single formula that would predict everything perfectly. 'For such an intellect,' he wrote, 'nothing would be uncertain; the future and the past would be equally before its eyes.' He presented his ideas to Napoleon, who asked why he made no mention of God. 'I have no need,' he replied, 'of that hypothesis.'[12]

In the two centuries since Laplace made that statement, his idea has become a bedrock of belief for many scientists, dominating discussion about science in popular culture. A prominent modern proponent of reductionism, for example, Nobel laureate Steven Weinberg, declares in an updated rendition of Laplace that 'all of nature is the way it is ... because of simple universal laws, to which all other scientific laws may in some sense be reduced'.[13]

There is a lot to unpack in this proposition. First, it means there is one objective reality out there, in which every event that happens – whether it's the next thought you have, the next movement a worm makes in the Congo Basin or the innumerable actions of every particle in the hundred billion or more galaxies that make up the known universe – is completely predetermined. The only thing preventing us from predicting everything in the universe would be that we haven't yet found the underlying laws and collected enough data.

Many famous scientists have repeated this reductionist

assertion, in various ways, so consistently across the board that it's easy to mistake it for scientific fact. All reality, we're told, is 'nothing but' the mechanical motion of particles acting predictably on each other. Richard Dawkins has written that 'life is just bytes and bytes and bytes of digital information'. Nobel laureate Francis Crick, co-discoverer of the DNA molecule, has declared, 'You, your joys and your sorrows, your memories and your ambitions, your sense of personal identity and free will, are in fact no more than the behavior of a vast assembly of nerve cells and their associated molecules.'[14]

Following on Crick's assertion, many leading technologists see humans as nothing other than another programming project. According to Larry Page, co-founder of Google, human DNA is just '600 megabytes compressed, so it's smaller than any modern operating system ... So your program algorithms probably aren't that complicated.' Bestselling author Yuval Noah Harari, believing that 'humans are algorithms', prognosticates that it's just a matter of time before artificial intelligence controls every aspect of our consciousness, predicting all our needs and preferences better than we can, and ultimately surpassing anything a human can do.[15]

Things get darker still in this reductionist cosmos. If everything can be reduced to a predetermined sequence of zillions of particles hitting each other, then the universe has no intrinsic value or purpose. We're all just tiny cogs in a vast machine. Weinberg has himself stated this implication with dreadful clarity. 'The more the universe seems comprehensible,' he writes, 'the more it also seems pointless.' Sounds grim? Sorry, say the reductionists, but that's just the way it is. Wouldn't you prefer, at least, to know the truth? 'We must not sink into nihilism or stifle our emotions,' muses Weinberg. 'At our best we live on a knife-edge, between wishful thinking on one hand and, on the other, despair.'[16]

Speaking for myself, I wouldn't want to live my life based on an illusion, and if my only option were to live on that knife-edge, then so be it. But what has repeatedly been propagated as fact might be better understood as, rather, a limited and circumscribed account of reality. Because of the empirical successes achieved by the reductionist methodology, it's been accepted as the truth by many leading scientists and philosophers, but it may be more accurate to view it as a simplification of reality that excludes important attributes. In the rest of this chapter we'll uncover the flaws of what can be described as reductionist fundamentalism and explore the complex and awe-inspiring aspects of the universe that followers of this creed have sadly blinkered themselves from acknowledging.

Ignoring the gorilla

Have you heard the joke about the drunk man who lost his car keys after closing time? He's on the ground under a lamp post, searching every inch of the sidewalk. His friend comes to help him. 'Is this where you think you dropped them?' his friend asks. 'No,' he replies, 'but this is where the light is.'

The reductionist approach to the universe is a bit like the fallacy of the drunk man, who is only interested in the portion of reality that's easily available for him to access. In the case of reductionism, this refers to those features of the universe that are available for precise measurement. From the time of Descartes onward, reductionist science progressed by measuring and quantifying ever-smaller slices of reality and ignoring those aspects less susceptible to quantification until ultimately denying their very existence. As I describe in *The Patterning Instinct*, humans are driven by an instinct to pattern meaning into the world, and it's a normal attribute of human cognition to exclude data points that don't fit in with our existing assumptions. An infant learns in the first few months of her life, for example, to hear the distinctive phonemes of her native language and ignore inflexions that don't belong. A classic social psychology experiment demonstrates this vividly. Subjects were asked to watch a video clip of a basketball game and count how many times one team had possession of the ball. Afterwards, most had been so focused on their task that they were completely unaware that a person wearing a gorilla suit had walked through the middle of the game, turned to face the camera, thumped his chest and continued walking to the other side.[17]

When reductionist zealots declare that humans are 'nothing but' algorithms; that organisms are 'nothing but' vehicles for DNA; that consciousness is 'nothing but' neurons; and reality is 'nothing but' colliding particles, they are making the same error as the observers who missed the gorilla. It's important to emphasize that this doesn't in any way invalidate the reductionist methodology when used appropriately. Those who ignored the gorilla may have performed the task they were asked to do perfectly well. As a methodology for many kinds of scientific investigation, reductionism should be celebrated as one of the greatest achievements of the human intellect. Without it, most of the benefits of our modern world would not exist – no electrical grids, no airplanes, no antibiotics, no internet.

But when reductionists take a leap of faith by claiming their methodology explains everything about the universe – and that alternative methodologies are therefore invalid – they fall into the trap of fundamentalism. Like other fundamentalist creeds, this doctrine, which may be called ontological reductionism, shuts complexity out of its reckoning, painting the world as black and white.[18*]

Frequently, ontological reductionists claim, like Weinberg, that the only two available options are to accept their version of reality or retreat into 'wishful thinking' by believing in some spiritual dimension that's not susceptible to the laws of physics. But there's no need to assert a separate metaphysical dimension to refute reductionism as a belief system. While accepting that everything obeys the incontrovertible laws of physics, we can recognize that, in addition, things act according to other sets of principles that make them 'more than' – rather than 'nothing but' – meaningless colliding particles.

Imagine you're going with a reductionist friend to a Beethoven symphony concert. At the end, you walk out in awe, moved by the feelings it stirred within you. Your friend turns to you and says, 'This whole event was nothing but a set of instruments manufactured to manipulate sound waves that vibrated your eardrums to produce neural responses that released hormones through your body.' Yes, you might think, it was all of that, but so much more. It was also the miracle of a genius who transformed profound complexities into musical expression, to instill within you a deeply felt mélange of emotion. You might turn to your friend and feel compassion for their inability to recognize all that. Similarly, the fundamentalist reductionist version of reality misses out on much of what makes life interesting, glorious, and ... yes, meaningful.

Even in the field of pure physics, many physicists refute Weinberg's conception of a deterministic universe. 'What we observe,' wrote theoretical physicist Werner Heisenberg, 'is not nature itself, but nature exposed to our method of questioning,' explaining why an electron could be either a wave or a particle depending on how you approach it.[19]

But we don't need to choose between different physicists' theories to understand the limitations of ontological reductionism. We can simply observe the world outside our window. When scientists build conceptual models, they often use the Latin phrase *ceteris paribus* – 'other things being equal' – to dismiss the apparently random noise that doesn't fit into their theory. However, in the real world, other things are never equal. The breeze blows the trees in a particular way, a loose branch dangles, on which a bird alights momentarily, then takes off again as a raindrop strikes its tail, causing a leaf to waft to the ground. The messy, mysterious, real world acts in ways completely compatible with the laws of physics – but also according to principles that aren't fully explained or predicted by those laws. Understanding our cosmos ultimately requires accepting that there are multiple levels of explanation interacting dynamically. In a sardonic refutation of Weinberg's dictum, Nobel Prize-winning complexity scientist Ilya Prigogine observes, 'The more we know about our universe, the more difficult it becomes to believe in determinism.'[20]

The flap of a butterfly's wings

Reductionist proponents have so dominated the mainstream scientific narrative that many people think science *is* reductionism. However, there is a large and growing body of scientific disciplines, replete with peer-reviewed journals and Nobel Prize-winning research, based on an alternative conception of the universe – one that focuses on understanding the complex, dynamic connections between things rather than assuming them away. This underlying recognition of interacting phenomena as a complex system is often referred to as systems thinking.[21*]

These various disciplines, such as complexity science, systems biology and network theory, share the basic insight that Neo-Confucian philosophers arrived at a thousand years ago: that the ways in which things connect are frequently more important than the things themselves. They don't replace the reductionist approach to understanding things – they complement it. Reductionism is, and will continue to be, an immensely powerful tool to discover the hidden secrets of nature, but, when trying to figure out how a complex system works, these other disciplines are remarkably effective at revealing insights that reductionism alone could never uncover.[22*]

What exactly, you might wonder, is a complex system? It doesn't just mean a system that's very complicated. In fact, systems thinkers define their domain by pointing out the contrast between the two. Think about the difference between a jumbo jet, for example, and a worm wriggling in the soil. Awesome as it is, the jumbo jet is complicated but not complex. Each of its components, and the way they relate to each other, can be completely analyzed, given an exact description and accurately predicted – if that weren't the case, you'd be wise not to get on it! A worm, on the other hand, along with every living entity, down to a single cell, is a complex system, which means that all its parts engage dynamically with each other in a vast number of nonlinear relationships, with feedback loops that can never be precisely described or predicted.[23]

Complex systems tend to be self-organized. No one came up with a plan for how they should be designed, or built them according to a blueprint. Instead, the different parts making up the system interact until they settle into a relatively coherent and stable pattern of behavior. One of the fascinating attributes of self-organized systems is how simplicity appears to emerge from underlying complexity. A person walking down the street, a bird flying in the sky, a dolphin swimming in the ocean – each appears elegantly coherent as an entity, and yet each is the result of innumerable complex interactions taking place simultaneously within, unseen except as an integrated whole.[24]

However stable they might appear, complex systems are also subject to unexpected behavior, as a result of the nonlinear nature of their interactions. A linear relationship is one that can be easily plotted on a graph, so by extrapolating you can predict what will happen. The fuel gauge in your car has a linear relationship with the number of miles you can drive. If it's getting low, and you're on the freeway, you can predict how soon you need to exit the freeway to fill up. Self-organizing systems, however, have an inherently chaotic quality to them. The founder of chaos theory, Edward Lorenz, was conducting research in weather forecasting when he discovered that a tiny rounding error in his computer models caused an entirely different weather system to emerge a couple of days later. He presented his initial work on chaos theory with a question that has since become iconic: 'Does the flap of a butterfly's wings in Brazil set off a tornado in Texas?' His point was not that it *will* set off a tornado, but that if it did, it could never be predicted.[25]

No wonder some reductionist scientists hate systems theory! Ever since Francis Bacon inspired the Scientific Revolution with his clarion call to 'conquer nature', much of the rationale behind scientific progress has been to extend our knowledge over nature to control it. Systems theorists tell us, on the contrary, that complete control is impossible. That doesn't mean, though, that we can't use our knowledge to skillfully influence how complex systems work. Like the early Chinese sages who concluded that one should learn to harmonize with the Tao, systems thinking offers the tools to learn how to attune with, and perhaps steer, complex systems.[26]

Reductionist science is built on fixed equations that describe how things work regardless of where they are in the universe, such as Newton's laws of motion. Complexity scientists, likewise, have identified certain principles in complex systems that apply in different contexts. Unlike Newton's laws, they can't be used for perfect prediction, but they yield important insights into the nature of things. One example of these principles arises from our old friend the slime mold. If a slime mold in a Petri dish is stressed, either by lack of moisture or nutrients, it will form a particular kind of squiggly, spiraling wave pattern. In the 1950s two Russian chemists named Belousov and Zhabotinsky were experimentally combining some chemicals and discovered, to their amazement, that instead of

a. Slime mold aggregation b. Belousov–Zhabotinsky reaction

Figure 1: Oscillating patterns in biology and chemistry

mixing the chemicals caused an oscillating set of spirals to emerge. Look at the two sets of patterns in Figure 1 – they are uncannily alike. Complexity scientists have since discerned that the similarity is not just a coincidence, but that both systems follow the same underlying principles of self-organized complex motion.[27]

Similar patterns in different contexts can be found everywhere in nature. As Zhu Xi observed a thousand years ago, the li – patterns of nature – are readily available for us to observe and hint at broader principles underlying the entire natural world. Fibonacci spirals, for example, arising from what is known as the Golden Ratio, are found in in sunflowers and daisies, pine cones and fir cones, and other seed arrangements. A similar logarithmic spiral occurs in mollusk shells, elephant tusks, tropical cyclones and the shape of galaxies (Figure 2). Dozens of different types of naturally occurring patterns have been identified: rippled, labyrinthine, fractured, crackled, cellular and branching, to name but a few. In all cases, the similarities are awe-inspiring in themselves, but hold deeper significance when scientists uncover certain principles of growth and self-organization that generate these patterns across vastly different environments and scales.[28]

Spectacular as these patterns are in nature, the principles they represent also apply to human activity. Whether we're looking at how an embryo develops, how evolution occurs, the dynamics of

Spiral aloe plant — The Pinwheel Galaxy — Ammonite fossil

Sunflower — Young fern frond — Tornado seen from space

Figure 2: Spiraling patterns in nature

an ecosystem, how cities operate, how markets fluctuate, and even how civilizations rise and fall, many principles remain the same. When we realize the vast terrain over which these patterns of self-organization apply, we begin to comprehend how crucial it is to understand them.

The Neo-Confucians appreciated that, by learning to discern the more accessible li, they could intuit the Tao that was 'so vast and large ... that even sages cannot comprehensively understand it'. Have any principles of self-organized systems been identified that could help us comprehend some of the vast and large patterns of the universe? Let's take a look.[29]

Strange, but natural, attractors

You can find one of the most important principles of self-organization, quite literally, in your own bathtub. Turn on your bathtub faucet and watch how the water self-organizes in the tub before flowing down the drain. As it forms a kind of swirling spiral, stable yet continually changing, it's demonstrating a defining characteristic of self-organized systems.

When systems are self-organized, they tend to fluctuate within relatively stable parameters. Whether it's the water in your bathtub, a candle flame, a crowd exiting a stadium or waves crashing on a beach, the pattern is never fixed but remains within certain boundaries. A founder of systems theory, Ludwig von Bertalanffy, called this state a 'flux-balance' and studied it extensively. The balance arises from the system maintaining a dynamic tension between opposing forces: in the case of your bathtub, it's the rate of water flowing from the faucet versus the rate at which it goes down the drain. It's known as an open system, because it needs a continual flow of energy/matter from outside the system to keep going, and it maintains its flux by simultaneously dissipating the energy.[30]

Even though it's continually changing, the pattern stays roughly similar. As you're watching the water circle the drain, it's not likely to suddenly jump up and splash you in the face, nor is it going to change the direction of its flow. Physicists call the ultimate state of a system its *attractor*. Imagine a pendulum swinging from side to side until it comes to rest. Its resting place, or equilibrium point, is known as a point attractor, because you could predict exactly where it will end up. Now think of a thermostat that automatically heats or cools your house depending on how you've set it. This kind of attractor is called a limit cycle, because it defines the limits of your house's temperature within a set range. But self-organized systems are different from both of these. No physicist can ever predict exactly where they will end up: within their parameters, they remain chaotic, never retracing exactly the same path, while undulating in a state that is far from equilibrium, like a pendulum that's continually swinging itself.[31]

When scientists first identified these systems, they called them *strange attractors*, because they didn't follow a predictable path. But they're not strange at all. They're everywhere in the natural world, wherever we look. They're in the clouds, the ocean waves, the shape of trees, the movement of animals. They are an essential part of all living creatures. We've seen that homeostasis is a core feature of organisms – an intrinsic part of animate intelligence, maintaining all systems of the body in a stable state within certain parameters. Now, we can understand homeostasis itself as a fundamental process of flux-balance. These systems, in fact, characterize the most natural form of behavior in the world. With your forbearance, then, I will break with the physicists and call these vitally important dynamic patterns *natural attractors*.[32]

The ancient Chinese had their own name for these natural attractors – the Tao. It's described in the *Tao Te Ching* as 'something nebulous ... moving cyclically without becoming exhausted'. The *I Ching* depicts this perpetual flux of nature as follows:

> Its tao is forever changing –
> Alteration, movement without rest,
> Flowing through the six empty places;
> Rising and sinking without fixed law,
> Firm and yielding transform each other.
> They cannot be confined within a rule;
> It is only change that is at work here.[33]

Systems theorists recognize that, just like the *I Ching*'s description of the Tao, there is no 'fixed law' to these natural attractors – but they have identified some important principles about them.

One principle is that natural attractors are frequently quite robust, even in the face of perturbations. Random events can temporarily affect the flow – think of a breeze causing a flame to flicker – but the system will tend to converge back to its original pattern. To get a feeling for how this works, imagine you're looking down on a natural landscape: a valley with a lake in the middle, surrounded by mountains. If it starts raining, what will happen to the raindrops randomly hitting the mountainside? Each will have its own unique journey, but for the most part they will join each other in little rivulets, eventually finding their way to mountain streams, which will ultimately flow into the lake. Similarly, there may be innumerable quirky ways in which a natural attractor reacts to random things happening to it, but it generally converges back to a stable pattern, which is known for this reason as a basin of attraction.[34]

Seeing the forest for the trees

Natural attractors can be very robust, but there are times when they reach a tipping point where the system alters dramatically, sometimes transforming beyond all recognition. This kind of metamorphosis is known as a phase transition. A forest, for example, can get thinned out until it can no longer sustain itself, and it turns into scrubland. A real-estate market gets overheated until it suddenly collapses. A person's neurological firing can destabilize and suddenly put them into an epileptic seizure. As you can see by these examples, phase transitions are frequently sudden and unexpected – and often undesirable.[35*]

Think of a rubber band that you keep pulling until it reaches breaking point. As you're stretching it, you might notice incremental changes, such as the band getting thinner as it elongates, and maybe showing stress lines along its length. Then, suddenly, it breaks – and if you're not careful it might snap back and hurt your hand. If you apply this dynamic to a more integrated, complex web of relationships, such as an ecosystem or a market, the stress lines might initially be more subtle and difficult to notice. It is as though the system is composed of innumerable rubber bands, each connecting with multiple others. If some of them break, at first it won't impact things too much, but the system begins to lose resilience as it approaches its critical threshold. At a certain point, there are too few rubber bands left to hold the system together, and the whole tightly knit fabric comes apart.[36]

There are many dramatic examples of phase transitions, such as avalanches where falling snow sets off further cascades, or forest fires where dry, brittle conditions are susceptible to the smallest ignition. We see it in human societies, not just in market crashes but in events such as electrical blackouts, where the failure of one central node may precipitate further failures across the network. A major – and ominous – example of a phase transition relates to global climate breakdown. As the world's temperature heats up incrementally, it causes reinforcing feedback effects that destabilize the climate even further. Methane frozen underground is released in increasing quantities, amplifying the greenhouse effect; melting ice sheets create subterranean rivers that lubricate the ice above, making it melt more quickly; as ocean ice disappears, the darker water absorbs more heat from the sun, further increasing the rise in global temperatures. These cascading system effects are a major reason why the risk of catastrophic consequences from even seemingly small increases in global temperature are far greater than many people realize.[37]

Phase transitions, though, are not always bad. In fact, they are the very essence of creativity. Think of how a chrysalis turns into a butterfly, or how a fetus gradually develops in the womb until it's ready for its own phase transition – known as birth. In these cases, and countless others like them, we see a process known as emergence: the system's complexity reaches a critical mass that transforms into a new coherence that couldn't have occurred by simply adding up each of the system's elements. This is the source of the famous saying, 'The whole is greater than the sum of its parts.'[38]

Everywhere we look, we see the marvel of emergence at work. A tree, by itself, has its own unique qualities, but once it's connected with a host of other trees, the resulting forest has new, emergent properties. The roots form vibrant relationships through the underground fungal network, trading nutrients and information; the canopy creates a shady environment, cooling the ground below and protecting other life; and in tropical forests the foliage creates its own weather system as evaporating moisture collects into clouds and rains back down on the forest. The same holds true for ants. A single ant can't survive on its own and has limited capabilities, but an ant colony demonstrates impressive emergent intelligence. When an ant finds a food source, it deposits pheromones on the trail, telling other ants where to go. Before long, a large number of ants have picked up the trail and swarm the food. Scientists studying this phenomenon have found that an ant colony is far more efficient through this mesh of interconnectivity than if each ant were simply looking for food as an independent agent.[39]

Emergence forms an essential part of human society and infuses our daily activity. A word by itself might connote one particular thing; but once thousands of words are connected in a rich fabric of meaning, language emerges. A standalone computer has limited capabilities; but connect millions of computers together, and the internet emerges, transforming the modern human experience. Within our brains a single neuron couldn't do much by itself, but when it's connected with billions of others in a dense neural net, consciousness emerges.

Reductionist scientists, predictably, have a difficult time with emergence, sometimes dismissing it as a quasi-mystical concept. But, as many systems scientists have demonstrated, there's nothing mystical nor unscientific about it. It's a phenomenon that arises when a system shows a distinctive identity as a result of its interconnected subsystems relating together. It's a crucial aspect of life and opens the door to a wholly different perspective on reality.[40]

Emergent life

In fact, leading biologists have begun to view the process of emergence as the very source of life itself. There are many systems that exhibit self-organization without being alive, such as the Belousov–Zhabotinsky chemical reaction, a candle flame, the swirling Great Red Spot of Jupiter or the spirals of galaxies. But living systems demonstrate quintessentially emergent properties not apparent in these other examples.[41]

Scientists have long puzzled over how life arose on Earth. In its first few hundred million years, they believe, increasingly complex molecules formed, such as the amino acids found in the proteins of most organisms. It's likely that certain molecules came together to form a self-sustaining network of chemical reactions, known as an autocatalytic set – meaning that each member of the set is the product of a reaction catalyzed by another member. At some point this set of molecules formed a semipermeable membrane around itself, maintaining its circular set of reactions within the membrane, and using extra molecules from outside to keep the process going: a proto-version of the first living cell. This theory of life's origins as a self-organized, emergent process has been called *autopoiesis* by two prominent theorists, Humberto Maturana and Francisco Varela, from Greek words meaning self-generation.[42]

Something remarkable occurred within these first living

entities: the system as a whole emerged with a separate identity from the complex interactions of its parts. Even as it was created from its components, it simultaneously guided what each of the parts needed to do. Philosopher Evan Thompson describes this amazing process as *reciprocal causality*, because the whole and the parts exert a reciprocal causal effect on each other. This emergent system, which has defined life ever since, is fundamentally different from one that's merely self-organized such as a candle flame, since it continually regenerates itself, taking energy from the environment to modify itself and perpetuate its own existence.[43]

It's rather awe-inspiring to consider that, ever since the first cells emerged on Earth over three and a half billion years ago, this dynamic, co-emergent process has never stopped. In a perpetual flux-balance spanning eons and infiltrating virtually every nook and cranny of the planet, life has continued to suck energy from the outside environment, expel what it didn't need and modify itself to form the vast, beautiful, living ecosystem that we are all part of today.

Another astonishing aspect of this self-generating flow of energy brings to mind the paradox of Theseus's ship: each living organism is continually exchanging the materials comprising it, while retaining its own identity as a coherent, integrated entity. As we contemplate this, it becomes apparent that life isn't a thing at all – it's an ongoing process of integrated self-generation and self-maintenance.[44]

As systems biologists ponder this characteristic of life, they have begun to echo the Neo-Confucian insight about li as an intrinsic principle of the universe. Leading biologist Carl Woese has observed that organisms are in fact 'resilient patterns in a turbulent flow – patterns in an energy flow'. He adds, 'It is becoming increasingly clear that to understand living systems in any deep sense, we must come to see them not materialistically, as machines, but as stable, complex, dynamic organization.'[45]

The patterns of 'all the other things'

As life unfolded and filled the Earth with its splendor, it demonstrated another significant attribute of many self-organized

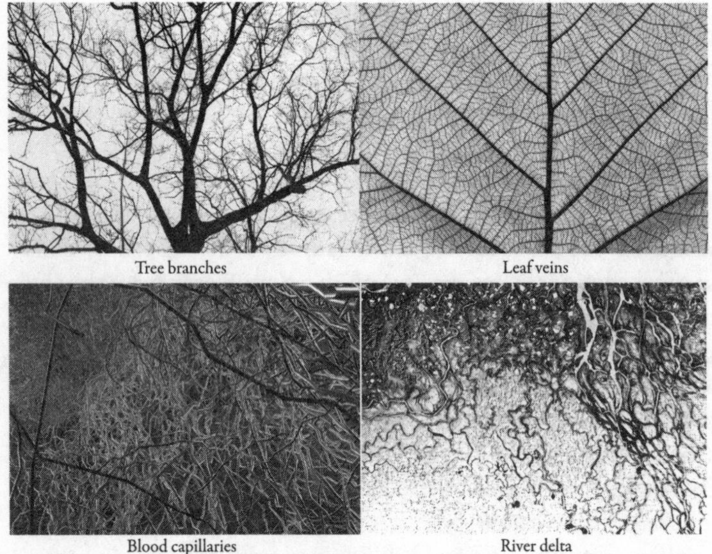

Figure 3: Fractal patterns in nature

systems: the propensity to repeat patterns at ever-increasing scales, known as fractals. Like natural attractors, fractals are everywhere. We see them in the patterning of clouds, lightning, coastlines, rivers and sand dunes. They show themselves in much of nature's beauty, including the branching architecture of trees and the shaping of ferns; and we find them throughout our own bodies: in the intricate organization of blood vessels, lung bronchioles and neurons (Figure 3). They are equally prevalent in human behavior and artificial constructions such as the design of cities and stock market fluctuations. Studies have even discovered fractal patterns in the music of Bach and Mozart, and the sentence structure of novels by James Joyce and Virginia Woolf.[46]

The systematic study of fractal geometry was initiated by mathematician Benoit Mandelbrot in the 1970s, and has since spawned an important discipline within mathematics. As mentioned earlier, scientists in the Newtonian tradition create perfect models of reality by ignoring its messy fluctuations, declaring 'all other things being equal'. Fractal geometry, by contrast, can be understood as the investigation of 'all the other things'. In Mandelbrot's words, 'Most of nature is very, very complicated. How could one describe a cloud? A cloud is not a sphere ... It is like a ball but very irregular. A mountain? A mountain is not a cone ... If you want to speak of clouds, of mountains, of rivers, of lightning, the geometric language of school is inadequate.'[47]

Fractal patterns exist in both space and time. In fact, much of what we see as fixed in the world is really a momentary cross-section of patterns unfolding in time. Think of a landscape with undulating hills going off into the distance. Now turn your mind to the swells of waves on the seashore. Because of the speed with which the waves move, you can easily recognize their momentary form as a function of their temporal pattern. But the hills that seem so fixed are essentially land-based waves, just moving millions of times more slowly than the ocean waves, so we see them as static.[48]

Systems scientists studying the fractal patterns of natural phenomena have made an important discovery: there is a consistent inverse logarithmic relationship between the amplitude of a fluctuation and its frequency. In simpler terms, this means that self-organized systems tend to exhibit many small fluctuations, fewer moderate ones and rare large fluctuations. We see this with earthquakes, which are measured by the logarithmic Richter scale, where each higher number represents a tenfold increase in magnitude. There are over a million earthquakes a year measuring between two and three, about a hundred scoring between six and seven, and on average only one earthquake a year greater than eight. This principle, known as a power law, applies to an astonishingly diverse set of phenomena. We see it daily in stock market fluctuations, and also in avalanches, forest fires and biological extinctions.[49*]

Meanwhile, researchers investigating the fractal patterns of self-organized networks have discovered they have a hub-and-spoke type of connectivity that also follows a power law. Lots of nodes in the network have just a few links with close neighbors, while rare nodes – the hubs – have a large number of links extending throughout the network. This is also known as a 'small-world' property, because wherever you are in the network you can usually get anywhere else with a relatively small number of hops – as long as you go through a hub. The popular concept of 'six degrees of separation' has emerged from this insight, suggesting that everyone in the world is no more than six social connections away from everyone else – you just need to find the right six! From the World Wide Web to the protein interactions of cells to the 'wood-wide web' of trees communicating through mycelium in a forest, this hub-and-spoke network is ubiquitous in nature and human society.[50]

An important finding by researchers studying social networks has been called the Three Degrees of Influence rule. It turns out that whatever we do or say tends to ripple through our social network, impacting not just our friends but also our friends' friends and even our friends' friends' friends (three degrees out). This applies to a diverse set of phenomena such as political views, weight gain and even happiness. Multiple studies have confirmed, for example, that obesity is a contagious condition: if you are obese, there is a greater likelihood that even those three degrees from you will also be obese. The same applies to positive actions you take: if you quit smoking, it makes it more likely that people you don't even know, three degrees of separation away, will also quit. The ripples of our actions flow out in ways we can barely imagine, affecting others unknown to us, while their actions may equally be affecting our own behavior.[51]

There's another crucial dimension to the fractal patterns of life. Each self-organized system is itself part of a larger system, while it contains multiple smaller systems within it. Ever since multicellular life first emerged on Earth, it has been busy scaling itself up fractally to form the complex, interlinked meshwork of life we are immersed in today. Arthur Koestler was the first modern thinker to identify this particular form of organization in life, which he called the holarchy (from the Greek word *holon* meaning 'a whole'), recognizing that each part is a coherent entity in its own right, while also an integral component of something larger.

We can trace the holarchy of life from the microscopic components of a cell to the cell itself, many of which combine to form tissues, which make up organs such as the liver or skin, which are part of an organism. Organisms combine to form populations, which in conjunction with other organisms create ecosystems. The ultimate self-organized system containing all these holons is known by biologists as the biosphere – the interconnected web of all life on Earth. The traditional Chinese, as we've seen, had another name for the holarchy containing all the natural attractors of life within it. They called it the Tao.[52]

Gewu: the investigation of things

Scientists who probe this newly unfolding understanding of the universe frequently display awed fascination for its deeper implications. Leading complexity researcher Stuart Kauffman puts it in these terms:

> What is the weave? No one yet knows ... But the tapestry has an overall design, an architecture, a woven cadence and rhythm that reflect underlying law – principles of self-organization ...
>
> We enter new territory ... We are seeking a new conceptual framework that does not yet exist.[53]

However, as we've seen in this chapter, it's not quite true that a conceptual framework does not yet exist. A thousand years ago, Neo-Confucian philosophers were synthesizing Buddhist, Taoist and Confucian perspectives into an integrated framework to explore the universal principles of self-organization they called li. 'There is li in everything,' declared a Neo-Confucian sage, 'and one must investigate li to the utmost.' Following this directive, Zhu Xi emphasized the importance of understanding li in every manifestation of the natural world. 'From the Supreme Ultimate above,' he said, 'to a small thing like a blade of grass, a plant, or an insect below, each has its li ... we must understand them one by one ... As more and more is accumulated, one will spontaneously be able to achieve a far and broad understanding.' He called this approach to accumulating wisdom *gewu* – the investigation of things.[54]

When the Chinese first encountered Europeans, they were scornful of their reductionist thinking. As one Neo-Confucian scholar observed at the time, 'Westerners are clever at examining and fathoming things, but incapable of penetrating the innermost workings of the universe.' At first glance, it may seem the Europeans got the last laugh. After all, Western technology and power brought China to its knees, while ravaging much of the rest of the world. It's only in recent decades that China has regained its status by incorporating Western values into its own.[55]

However, as we confront the existential crises of the twenty-first century, the reductionist thinking that brought us to this place may be driving us headlong toward catastrophe. For each new global problem, attention is focused on short-term mechanistic solutions, rather than probing deeper systemic causation. In response to the worldwide collapse of butterfly and bee populations, researchers have designed tiny airborne drones to pollinate trees instead. Facing climate breakdown, reductionist scientists propose vast geoengineering projects, treating the Earth's climate as a technical problem requiring an engineering solution. As philosopher Andreas Weber points out, this is a logical outcome of reductionism, which derives much of its success from the analysis of dead matter rather than living systems. 'Should it be so surprising, then,' he reflects, 'that the survival of life on our planet has become the most urgent problem?'[56]

Increasingly, systems scientists are calling for a modern version of *gewu* – an investigation to achieve a 'far and broad understanding' into the complex web of interconnectedness that constitutes the Earth system. The original *gewu*, in contrast to the presumed objectivity of reductionist science, recognized that the observer was an integral part of the very system being investigated, and as a result the investigation could never truly be value-free. This is a theme that modern systems scientists are rediscovering. What is needed, observes systems biologist Brian Goodwin, is 'a science of qualities, which may help in our efforts to reach a more balanced relationship with the other members of our planetary society.'[57]*

We saw earlier how complex systems entering phase transitions are stretched to a breaking point until, all of a sudden, the old system unravels, to be replaced by a newly emergent coherence. Is this the tension we are currently experiencing as reductionist orthodoxy gives way to a broader understanding of life's connectedness? This kind of phase transition was famously described by science philosopher Thomas Kuhn as a paradigm shift – when an old worldview no longer works and is upended by a new pattern of meaning. It can be a difficult transition, he warns. The old guard can sometimes appear 'stubborn and pigheaded' if they feel their lifelong career accomplishments are at stake.[58]

Embracing a systems perspective, however, doesn't invalidate reductionist science. On the contrary, it permits scientists to enlarge the scope of their inquiry into ever more meaningful domains. As modern Confucian philosopher Tu Weiming points out, a scientist loses none of his expertise by accepting the Neo-Confucian proposition, 'Everything is an integrated whole.' In fact, by applying that concept in his research, 'he can become a great scientist' because, rather than trying to explain one separate part of a puzzle, he begins asking questions about how everything fits together.[59]

As part of this paradigm shift, the boundaries between science and other domains of investigation also begin to blur. As Kauffman has observed, 'the new sciences of complexity may help us find anew our place in the universe ... we may recover our sense of worth, our sense of the sacred.' A defining characteristic of modern *gewu* would be the recognition that the web of connectivity interpenetrates every aspect of life: from scientific to spiritual, from philosophical to practical, from emotional to political. There is nothing left out, nothing that isn't incorporated in this weave. You can think of this book as mapping out a modern version of *gewu*, exploring the personal, ethical and existential implications of our intrinsic connectedness, weaving in the wisdom of earlier traditions with modern scientific insights.[60]

The pattern that connects

Gregory Bateson, a brilliant early systems theorist, spent much of his time conducting his own *gewu*, asking, 'What is the pattern which connects all the living creatures?' His ultimate answer was that 'the pattern which connects is a metapattern. It is a pattern of patterns.' In essence, he explained, it is the patterns themselves that connect us. Once again, this profound realization had been foreshadowed a thousand years earlier by Neo-Confucian philosopher Cheng Yi, who wrote, 'We say that all things are one reality because all things have the same li in them ... The li of a thing is one with the li of all things ... There is only one li in the world.'[61]

This kind of statement might leave your head whirling because it's so alien to how our mainstream culture has conditioned us to see things. After all, we're taught to focus on the differences between things: on the separations that seem so obvious between myself and everyone else, between my nation and other nations, my religion and other religions, between humans and the natural world. But as we've seen, the separate stuff that we think defines us is really transitory. As another early systems theorist, Norbert Wiener, put it, 'We are but whirlpools in a river of ever-flowing water. We are not stuff that abides, but patterns that perpetuate themselves.'[62]

What the ancient Greeks dismissed as no more than a curious paradox is, it turns out, a fundamental insight into the nature of life itself. The particular pattern that first emerged on Earth billions of years ago – the autopoietic miracle of life as a coherent whole perpetually regenerating itself – is the defining principle that interpenetrates you, me and all the expressions of evolution that we see around us.

Imagine an infinitely complex, woven fabric that connects all things in its intricate weave. What would happen if you pulled on a thread? You might notice a different part of the fabric begins to pucker, because of a connection between the two areas you hadn't realized existed. This leads to a crucial principle: the interdependence of all things. The early Chinese understood this, seeing the cosmos as a kind of universal web in which the slightest movement of one part caused undulations throughout the entire network. Everything was related dynamically to everything else. It's a discovery that conservationist John Muir, founder of the Sierra Club, famously made when he noted in his journal that 'when we try to pick out anything by itself, we find it hitched to everything else in the universe'.[63]

This principle of interdependence, as noted earlier, echoes

a core tenet of the Buddhist tradition: dependent origination. Modern Buddhist teacher and activist Thích Nhât Hanh has a memorable way of describing this principle, which he refers to as '*interbeing*'. Holding up a piece of paper, he proclaims, 'There is a cloud floating in this sheet of paper.' And not just a cloud, but the sun too. Without clouds, he explains, there is no rain; without rain or sunshine, the trees cannot grow, and we couldn't make paper. Also included in that single sheet: the minerals in the soil, the food that nourished the logger who harvested the tree, the logger's ancestors, who are ultimately our own. 'This sheet of paper is,' he declares, 'because everything else is ... "To be" is to inter-be. You cannot just be by yourself alone. You have to inter-be with every other thing.'[64]

Arising from these intricately interwoven principles of self-organization, there is a certain intrinsic order to the universe that we can feel through our animate intelligence but barely conceptualize without a degree of reverence. We can call it Tao or *dharma*, or we can turn to the sense of awe expressed by Albert Einstein, who professed 'a rapturous amazement at the harmony of natural law, which reveals an intelligence of such superiority that, compared with it, all the systematic thinking and acting of human beings is an utterly insignificant reflection.'[65]

The recognition of this deep patterning of the universe can cause profound feelings, of the sort that poet William Wordsworth memorably described as follows:

And I have felt
A presence that disturbs me with the joy
Of elevated thoughts; a sense sublime
Of something far more deeply interfused,
Whose dwelling is the light of setting suns,
And the round ocean and the living air,
And the blue sky, and in the mind of man;
A motion and a spirit, that impels
All thinking things, all objects of all thought,
And rolls through all things.[66]

It might be a rare moment when we get a glimpse of 'something far more deeply interfused', but we are continually participating in it, whether we realize it or not. There's no way we can't participate in it. By virtue of our birth into this world, each of us is a constituent part of the holarchy of life, the boundless ocean of li ripples that 'rolls through all things'. We contain innumerable complex natural attractors within us, while we play our role, consciously or otherwise, in the larger natural attractors of social networks, economic systems and communities of shared ideas and values in which we are integrally embedded.

Which leads to another crucial principle arising from this modern investigation of things: the ethical implications of our interconnectedness. If we return to Thích Nhât Hanh's sheet of paper, it also contains much that is disturbing to consider. It contains the tragic loss of old-growth forest bulldozed to make way for neatly arranged rows of tree plantations; the pollution caused by the paper mills processing the pulp; the fossil fuels burned by planes crisscrossing the packaged reams of paper around the world; the attractively low retail price made possible by starvation wages of overworked employees forced into factory labor since their parents were kicked off their land to make way for those same tree plantations.[67]

A comprehensive investigation of our interconnectedness must take all these linkages into account – those that lead to reverence for the glory of life and those that entail our ethical engagement in the global systems that bind us all together. Eco-philosopher Joanna Macy calls this a Dharma of Natural Systems, a basis for a set of moral principles that doesn't arise from some divine commandment, but emerges instead from the reality of our shared engagement with the web of life.[68]

The sense of separateness that our culture foists on us is, in Einstein's words, 'a kind of optical delusion of consciousness ... a kind of prison for us, restricting us to our personal desires and to affection for a few persons nearest us'. This delusion of consciousness is not, however, our only available option. 'Our task,' he continues, 'must be to free ourselves from this prison by widening our circles of compassion to embrace all living creatures and the whole of nature in its beauty.'[69]

As you read on, I invite you to hold Einstein's expansive vision in your mind. We've already seen how our true identity includes not just our conceptual consciousness, as the Western tradition avows, but also our animate consciousness – the deep font of self-organized wisdom that we share with all of life. Now, as we begin to recognize just how much we share, this can extend further our sense of who we are. 'To regain our full humanity,' declares visionary systems thinker Fritjof Capra, 'we have to regain our experience of connectedness with the entire web of life.' And that's the next step of our journey – a deeper investigation of the self-organized miracle of autopoiesis, how it unfolded into the magnificence of life that we experience today, and what that means for a greater understanding of our existence.[70]

NEW THREADS OF MEANING

In a complex system, the ways in which things connect are frequently more important than the things themselves

Life is not a 'thing', but an ongoing, integrated process of self-generation and self-maintenance known as autopoiesis

The interdependence of all things means that everything – including each of us – is dynamically related in some way to everything else

Chapter Five

THE HARMONIC DANCE OF LIFE

There's an unforgettable moment in the movie *Wall Street* when financier Gordon Gekko tells the shareholders of Teldar Paper why his buyout proposal, incorporating massive layoffs, is not only profitable but morally legitimate. With his slicked-back hair and custom-tailored suit, he struts to the front of the hall and proclaims:

> The new law of evolution in corporate America seems to be survival of the unfittest. Well, in my book you either do it right or you get eliminated ...
>
> The point is, ladies and gentlemen, that greed – for lack of a better word – is good.
>
> Greed is right.
>
> Greed works.
>
> Greed clarifies, cuts through, and captures the essence of the evolutionary spirit.
>
> Greed, in all of its forms – greed for life, for money, for love, knowledge – has marked the upward surge of mankind.
>
> And greed – you mark my words – will not only save Teldar Paper but that other malfunctioning corporation called the USA.

Greed is essentially good, Gekko is declaring, because it is the basis of evolution and all that's arisen from it, including human supremacy. Gekko's speech was unleashed on moviegoers in 1987 as the world was reeling from an early encounter with the excesses arising from global financial deregulation. His signature claim – 'Greed is good!' – has since become the stuff of legend, strikingly capturing the ethos of unrestrained, free-market capitalism that has come to dominate mainstream thinking.[1]

The idea that selfishness and greed are drivers of evolution, and therefore possess underlying virtue, has been around for over a century, ever since Charles Darwin's theory of evolution became widely accepted. The archetypal robber barons Andrew Carnegie and John D. Rockefeller both argued that the 'survival of the fittest' principle justified their cut-throat tactics. But the publication in 1976 of Richard Dawkins' bestseller, *The Selfish Gene*, adroitly repackaged the notion for modern times, reducing the complexities of evolution to a brutally elemental simplicity. As Dawkins summarized it:

> The argument of this book is that we, and all other animals, are machines created by our genes. Like successful Chicago gangsters, our genes have survived, in some cases for millions of years, in a highly competitive world. This entitles us to expect certain qualities in our genes. I shall argue that a predominant quality to be expected in a successful gene is ruthless selfishness. This gene selfishness will usually give rise to selfishness in individual behavior ... Much as we might wish to believe otherwise, universal love and the welfare of the species as a whole are concepts that simply do not make evolutionary sense.[2]

With the notion of the 'selfish gene' as the ultimate driver of evolution, Dawkins had hit the zeitgeist jackpot, helping forge the moral framework of his age. Influential thought leaders have since infused this supposed biological truth into economics, politics and business. 'The economy of nature is competitive from beginning to end,' writes sociobiologist M. T. Ghiselin, co-editor of the *Journal of Bioeconomics*.[3]

In 2001, as a new wave of financial scandals rocked the world, the commodities trading company Enron was caught red-handed in systematic fraud, with dire consequences for many. The favorite book of Enron's CEO, Jeffrey Skilling, was *The Selfish Gene*. Skilling, who spent years in jail, was such an ardent fan of Dawkins' theory that he had instituted a company-wide compensation system incentivizing unethical behavior on the basis that people are inherently selfish and thus motivated solely by greed and fear. Skilling was just the most egregious example of an ethos that has spread so widely through business and public policy that nowadays it is barely even questioned.[4*]

It's difficult to overstate the pervasiveness of Dawkins' selfish gene theory in popular culture. In a nutshell, the underlying story goes something like this: all organisms in nature are simply vessels for the replication of the selfish genes that control us. As such, all living entities – including humans – are driven to compete ruthlessly to pass on their genes. This struggle for reproduction is the underlying engine of evolution, as occasional positive random mutations in genes give an entity a competitive edge to beat out weaker rivals. Any apparently altruistic behavior is merely a convenient tactic for a concealed selfish goal. Since nature works most effectively based on selfishness, human society should be similarly organized, which is why free-market capitalism has been so successful in dominating all other socioeconomic models.[5*]

You may notice in this story echoes of themes discussed earlier. A crucial aspect is its reductionist quality: everything can ultimately be explained by its lowest common denominator, the gene: 'The organism is only DNA's way of making more DNA,' stated biologist E. O. Wilson during an early, reductionist phase of his career. A related theme is that all natural entities are simply machines. We already saw Dawkins describe a bat as a machine; now we see him include humans in that category. Our genes, he tells us, 'swarm in huge colonies, safe inside gigantic lumbering robots ... manipulating [the outside world] by remote control ... They have come a long way, these replicators. Now they go by the name genes, and we are their survival machines.'[6]

This story presents a view of life on Earth fundamentally different from that held by other cultural traditions around the world. Our nomadic hunter-gatherer ancestors saw nature as a 'giving parent', and many Indigenous people today see living beings as part of a vast extended family. In traditional Chinese thought, as we've seen, the universe was understood to be an interconnected web, with the ultimate human goal to attune with the harmonic web in which we are all embedded. Harmonizing, rather than competing, was seen as the key to a successful life.[7]

Hard-headed biological reductionists have long grown accustomed to shaking their heads at such descriptions of the natural world, rejecting them as fuzzy-headed nonsense. However, it turns out to be the story of the selfish gene that is based on fundamental misconceptions. In recent decades researchers in evolutionary biology have overturned virtually every significant assumption in the reductionist account of the selfish gene. In its place, they have developed a far more sophisticated conception of how evolution works, revealing the rich tapestry of nature's dynamic interconnectedness. Rather than evolution being driven by competition, it turns out that cooperation has played a far more important role in producing the great transitions that led to Earth's current breathtaking state of diversity and beauty.[8*]

The trouble with the selfish gene story is not just that it's scientifically flawed; it's also that it presents such an impoverished view of life's dazzling magnificence. The discoveries of modern researchers showing how life evolved to its current state of lavish abundance reveal a spectacle of awe-inspiring complexity, mind-boggling dynamic feedback loops and infinitely subtle interconnections.

The saga of how life has unfolded on Earth is perhaps the greatest story ever told. As we deconstruct the selfish gene myth and discover the awesome reality revealed by modern science, we'll see that this new understanding of life can perhaps be summed up best by reprising the insight of ancient wisdom: what has evolved on Earth, in all its glory, is a harmonic web of dynamic activity.

Decoding the 'book of life'

Even the greatest scientists develop their ideas within the social and ideological context of their culture, and Charles Darwin was no exception. Darwin lived in Victorian England, at the height of the Industrial Revolution, when new factories were driving cottage industries into oblivion and the British Empire extended its dominion over major swaths of the globe. The predominant political culture was influenced by figures such as Thomas Hobbes, who had famously derided the natural state of humankind as 'nasty, brutish, and short'; Adam Smith, who had identified an 'invisible hand' by which selfish actions of individuals led to beneficial social outcomes; and Thomas Malthus, who had warned that abundance naturally led to overpopulation and an ensuing struggle for resources.[9]

Darwin's theory of evolution, published in 1859, was, without doubt, one of the greatest scientific breakthroughs in history, but that doesn't mean it was free from cultural conditioning. Its basis was the Malthusian notion that an increase of population within an environment caused what Darwin called 'a Struggle for Life'. This naturally led to the 'Extinction of less improved forms' – later famously rephrased as the 'survival of the fittest'. Natural selection was the inevitable result of the winners of this struggle having more offspring, thus passing their successful traits on to future generations.[10*]

Darwin couldn't explain exactly how these more adaptive traits were inherited by future generations. Earlier that century, French naturalist Jean-Baptiste Lamarck had theorized that animals might pass on to their offspring the traits they acquired during their lives. For example, if giraffes stretched their necks to reach higher leaves, their elongated necks would be inherited by the next generation. His theory fell into disrepute after another great biologist, August Weismann, cut the tails off rats and showed that their offspring indeed had normal tails. Weismann developed an alternative theory that there were two different kind of cells: germ cells, found in sperm and eggs, which were inherited, and somatic cells (the rest of the body) that couldn't be passed on. Meanwhile, in an Austrian monastery Gregor Mendel had spent years conducting experiments on pea plants, from which he developed a theory of inheritance based on heredity units.[11]

In the twentieth century, a new generation of biologists combined the ideas of Darwin, Weismann and Mendel to construct what became known as the Modern Synthesis, which has been the dominant interpretation of evolution ever since. The central concept that held it together was the gene, a hypothetical unit of natural selection that was passed on through inheritance. It was the gene that somehow specified the form an organism would take. Random mutations in an individual's genes occasionally gave it unique traits that were different from the rest of its species, and those with the best adapted traits passed these genes on to the next generation.[12]

What exactly were those genes, and how did they pass on their specifications? This burning question was finally answered in 1953 when James Watson and Francis Crick, along with Rosalind Franklin, discovered the double-helix shape of the DNA molecule containing an organism's genes, and described how tiny molecular sub-units, named bases, paired with each other to specify proteins that would then be constructed within a cell. Now things were becoming clear! It was as though the secret of life itself had been laid bare to scientific understanding. With headlines blaring around the world, a new story of life entered the public consciousness.[13]

Just as Darwin's insights had been framed by the dominant ideas of his age, so the description of the DNA molecule and its workings were also framed by a new set of concepts that had gained currency in post-war science: those of the Information Revolution. During the Second World War, information theory had become essential for critical tasks such as developing missile guidance systems and cracking enemy codes. Now, as Crick and Watson communicated their findings, information theory offered a ready-made set of metaphors to describe their discovery. In their legendary paper published in *Nature*, they wrote, 'It therefore seems likely that the precise sequence of the bases is the code which carries the genetical information.'[14]

Now the race was on to decode what was quickly becoming known as the 'book of life'. As computing sophistication exponentially increased, the possibility arose that combined advances in molecular biology and information processing might allow a complete mapping of the human genome. Planning began in 1984 and the Human Genome Project formally launched in 1990. During this time, information technology and genetics became tightly linked, both technically and conceptually. The genotype was seen as a 'program' that determined the exact specifications of an organism, just like a computer program. DNA sequences formed the 'master code' of a 'blueprint' that contained a detailed set of 'instructions' for building an individual. Prominent geneticist Walter Gilbert would begin his public lectures by pulling out a compact disk and proclaiming, 'This is you!'[15]

Public excitement around the Human Genome Project was effervescent. A leading molecular biologist claimed that, if he knew an organism's complete DNA sequence, with a powerful enough computer he could predict its exact anatomy, physiology and behavior. The promise was intoxicating: If every gene specified a particular protein in a cell, then once we'd mapped them all, we'd eventually be able to identify the genetic cause for every attribute of a person. We'd know the genes for intelligence, for athletic prowess, for longevity – and of course find cures for a wide array of diseases. 'Our fate,' Watson declared, 'is in our genes.'[16]

Thanks to dramatic advances in computing power, the human genome was triumphantly mapped in 2003, years ahead of schedule. However, some rather inconvenient facts quickly began to rain on the parade. It turned out that the entire human genome contained about 21,000 genes that coded for proteins. The tiny roundworm *C. elegans*, rather embarrassingly, had a similar number, while wheat had more than four times as many. These humbling statistics clearly showed there was something more going on in the cell than simple one-to-one coding between genes and proteins. And even without these awkward comparisons, it was abundantly clear that there were more than 21,000 attributes that determined every aspect of a human being. What was wrong with the model?[17]

The language of the gene

At its heart, the model's fundamental flaw was the machine metaphor it was built on. Genetic determinism, as it is sometimes called, was based on the underlying idea that organisms, like machines, are comprised of components with linear relationships that can be precisely determined. As we've seen, the reality is that living organisms, from the first protocell onward, are complex systems with multiple feedback loops creating nonlinear relationships. As such, they demonstrate far more complexity than even the most complicated computer.[18]

When Crick and Watson laid the foundation for what they called the 'central dogma' of molecular biology, they specified that information could only flow one way. It began with the structure of the gene, which was defined as a particular sequence of base pairs that coded for a protein. This sequence was picked up by an RNA molecule that acted like a messenger (thus called mRNA) transcribing the original code to specify how a protein should be built. In everyday life we think of protein as an undifferentiated substance we need for good health (as in 'Are you getting enough protein?'). Within our bodies, however, proteins are a staggeringly diverse group of molecular structures that carry out most of the business of a cell. By some estimates, there are millions of different proteins within a single cell, each one of which is uniquely shaped in wildly complex configurations, a bit like a microscopic self-organized clump of squiggling steel wool. Something Crick and Watson didn't know when they set down their central dogma was that, in addition to all their other tasks, proteins act directly on the DNA of the cell, specifying which genes in the DNA should be activated.[19]

This is a crucial discovery, which has become a mainstay of modern molecular biology but has not yet made it into broad public consciousness. It means that the relationship between genes and the organism is not one way but circular. DNA can't do anything by itself – it only functions when certain parts of it get switched on or off by the activities of different combinations of proteins, which were themselves formed by the instructions of DNA. This process is a vibrant, dynamic circular flow of interactivity. We have been led by popular images of the DNA double helix to think of a static structure sending out directions to the cell. In fact, the genome is wrapped up in a variegated, ever-shifting array of proteins, RNA and other molecules. Researchers describe how the strands of DNA known as chromosomes are continually wriggling in different rhythms, condensing and expanding, attaching and detaching from other structures around them, forming loops, tightening and relaxing. All this complex choreography occurs, not by the DNA's autonomous action, but as a result of proteins acting on the DNA.[20]

What this means is that there is no such thing as a 'gene for something'. Genes are expressed within the cell as a result of what is going on around them. Rather than coding for something, the way a programmer writes code for a computer, a more useful metaphor for what happens might be language. Think about how language works. Sometimes it can be a simple instruction: I might tell you to 'Turn right at the stop sign, then go half a mile until you see the store on the left.' But it is frequently context dependent. If I call out 'Help me!' you might turn to look at what I'm doing. If I'm carrying a tray piled high with glasses, perhaps you'll remove some to reduce the risk of them toppling. If I'm a teacher, and I've written some arithmetic on the board, you might call out the answer. Depending on the context, you'll respond very differently to the same words. In addition, you might engage in conversation with me, expecting me to respond, and together we might come up with a creative approach to a situation that I wouldn't have arrived at alone. Similarly, the gene sometimes gives clear instructions, and at other times engages in an interactive conversation with the rest of the cell. Just as words have an array of different meanings based on their context, syntax and grammar, so DNA and proteins use their own language, with its own syntax and grammar, to determine what's best at that moment for the cell.[21]

The creative cell

As a result of this interactive conversation, the expression of genes within the cell can lead to widely divergent physical manifestations of the organism. Based on the popular misconception propagated by Watson and Crick – 'Our fate is in our genes' – it's commonly believed that the shape and behavior of an organism (biologists call it the phenotype) is preordained by its DNA. Not so fast. In fact, depending on the environment a cell and its corresponding organism find themselves in, the conversation that takes place with its genes may be very different and lead to unexpected outcomes.

Take, for example, a cute little grasshopper. It walks slowly on long, spindly legs, eating alone and minding its own business. Obviously, a different species to a locust, which has short, crooked legs and forms terrifying swarms that can darken the sky and aggressively devour an entire region's crops. Right? In fact, it turns out that grasshoppers and locusts have exactly the same DNA. Just like Dr Jekyll and Mr Hyde, when a certain kind of grasshopper senses its environment changing, either from food scarcity or overcrowding, it can transform itself within hours into a manically aggressive locust. Its cells switch on different genes within its DNA; it begins shrinking its legs and wings, changes its coloring, and even grows its brain to deal with the social complexities of the swarm. Later on, when the environment improves, its cells again switch their DNA settings, and the locust magically transforms back into a quiet grasshopper.[22]

While this is one of the most dramatic examples of divergent gene expression, similar transformations are found throughout nature. Among social wasps the queen is genetically identical to the rest of the colony, but her gene expression changes her body, making her the only one capable of reproducing. Similarly, among most honeybees, the scouts, workers and guards have the same DNA and metamorphose from one form to another based on what the hive needs. Certain types of tadpoles that normally nibble on algae and tiny crustaceans sometimes perform their own Jekyll and Hyde transformation, becoming aggressive cannibals with bulging jaws and sharp incisors.[23]

Of course, the creativity shown by gene expression has its constraints. We know that pigs are not suddenly going to sprout wings and fly. We can view the cell's genotype like an artist's palette, with a certain repertoire of capabilities that the cell can select based on its particular needs as determined by the environment. When we consider the less drastic changes that virtually all organisms naturally undergo, this process becomes more comprehensible. Think of a plant growing in the soil. As any gardener knows, plants will change their physical form, or phenotype, based on their environment. If it's hot and sunny, they will produce smaller leaves to minimize water loss. If there is reduced light, they will increase their leaf production, even making the leaves thinner to improve efficiency of photosynthesis. If the soil dries out or becomes nutrient-poor, they will shift their energy to root production, making their roots longer and thinner to seek out more nutrition.[24]

Biologists use the term developmental plasticity to refer to this ability of organisms to react creatively to their environments based on their particular needs, but we can use a different descriptor for this phenomenon – animate intelligence. We explored earlier the vast array of intelligence demonstrated throughout the natural world from single cells to sophisticated, complex mammals. Now, we catch a glimpse at the astonishing process by which the creative intelligence of nature reveals itself.

As biologists gain a deeper understanding of the cell's participation in genetic expression, they have also begun to re-examine the cell's role in evolution. Ever since Darwin, conventional doctrine has held that random genetic mutations are the sole basis for the variation that drives evolution. But let's go back to those plants that grew longer, thinner roots in poor soil. Experiments have shown that their offspring developed more extensive root systems than equivalent plants with exactly the same DNA whose parents had enjoyed rich soil.[25]

Do you remember Lamarck's idea that acquired traits can be inherited? It was so roundly trashed by the Modern Synthesis that an accusation of 'Lamarckism' was one of the worst insults a biologist could receive. Now, Lamarck's name is beginning to be mentioned again in the halls of academic conferences. No one is claiming that genes don't have a central role to play in evolution. But as some biologists begin scrutinizing the interactions of genes with everything else in the organism and its environment, they are developing a far more sophisticated model for how evolution actually works.[26]

Going beyond the gene

In fact, an increasing number of prominent evolutionary biologists have become convinced that the new understanding of evolution requires expanding the theoretical framework beyond the Modern Synthesis that has ruled for nearly a century. They're not agitating for a Copernican-style revolution that rejects the entire conventional model; rather, they're calling for an Extended Evolutionary Synthesis, arguing that the new findings require a broader conceptual framework. They are holding international conferences on the topic, and their papers are flooding the most prestigious academic journals. 'A profound, radical, and fascinating transformation of evolutionary theory is taking place,' writes one of their leaders, Eva Jablonka. However, just as reductionists refuse to accept the principles of systems thinking, some die-hards in traditional biology departments are fighting a rearguard action in defense of the central dogma on which they built their academic careers.[27*]

The foundational idea of the new thinking is that evolution is driven not by genes alone but by organisms which, in the words of leading proponent Kevin Laland, 'play active and constructive roles in their own development and that of their descendants'. Ironically, Darwin himself would probably have encouraged their work, since he wrote in *Origin of Species*, 'I am convinced that Natural Selection has been the main but not exclusive means of modification.'[28]

The evidence supporting their argument certainly seems convincing. So far, we've seen how genes are not the sole drivers of inheritance but participants in an interactive process. However, hundreds of recent studies have shown that a lot more than genes are transmitted from parents to their offspring – such as hormones, antibodies and parts of the egg, as well as crucially important molecular components, called methyl groups, that attach to DNA to help turn genes on and off. Researchers call these transmissions *epigenetic*, which simply refers to any form of inheritance that isn't genetic.[29]

Through epigenetic inheritance, Lamarckian transmission of acquired characteristics has been proven to occur frequently throughout the natural world. Epigenetic inheritance has now been shown to affect a wide variety of natural functions in animals and plants, including the size of fruit, the length of a plant's roots and the timing of its flowers. And it's been shown to last for at least ten generations, and even hundreds of generations in plants.[30*]

There's another form of epigenetic inheritance we humans know well – culture. It's obvious that human children develop much of their eventual character through cultural transmission – not just from their parents but from the whole panoply of culture that has accumulated over generations. It's become increasingly clear that cultural transmission is also widespread among nonhuman animals. Jane Goodall discovered long ago that chimpanzees transmitted cultural behavior, such as nut-cracking techniques or ways to extract honey from logs. Since then, cultural transmission of migration routes by whales, song repertoires by finches, food preparation techniques by macaques and numerous other activities by over sixty different species have been reported.[31]

Animals, it turns out, are masters at directing their own evolution, not just through culture but by modifying their environment in ways that eventually become an integral part of their species' repertoire. We see examples of this everywhere in nature. Think of a bird making a nest. It's constructing a little niche in the environment that keeps its eggs safe, protecting them both from predators and temperature fluctuations. Those eggs don't need to be as resilient against cold temperatures as they otherwise would be. And when the chicks grow up, the ones that build better nests will be more successful at rearing their own offspring. Through their niche construction (as this process is called), birds direct their own evolution as a species. The same is true for spiders, whose reliance on web construction favors offspring who can produce sticky threads and react to vibrations on the web. Plants are equally effective in producing their own niches: they have learned to change the acidity, salinity and other characteristics of the soil to make it more nutritious for their roots and those of their neighbors.[32]

It's becoming clear that the gene is not the sole driver of evolution, but a participant in a far more complex and interwoven process. But how about the 'selfish' question? We've seen how organisms use animate intelligence to look after themselves and their offspring in sophisticated ways. But have we just relocated the selfishness of the gene to that of an individual organism? In fact, one of the most important findings in modern biology has been that cooperation, not selfish competition, has been the foremost driving force in each of life's major evolutionary transitions since it began on Earth billions of years ago.

The network of life

In geological timescales, it didn't take long before life first appeared on Earth. The planet we call home is about 4.5 billion years old, and it's thought that life may have emerged as early as four billion years ago, when Earth was still being bombarded by meteorites. But it wouldn't have looked like much. The earliest life consisted of single cells called prokaryotes, which are very similar to the bacteria that have thrived on Earth ever since. They contain relatively simple genomes, which they pass on to the next generation by dividing themselves into two, each daughter cell containing DNA identical to that of the parent.[33*]

Not much happened to write home about for another billion years or so, other than a particular kind of bacterium started proliferating which released oxygen into the environment as part of its metabolism. This new addition to the atmosphere was toxic to many early cells, causing the first mass extinction event on Earth. It was around then that a new type of cell arrived on the scene. Called a *eukaryote* (Greek for 'true kernel'), this cell contained a nucleus that housed all its DNA material. Eukaryotes found a novel way to get their nutrition: they took advantage of their more flexible cell walls to engulf other bacteria and ingest them, breaking their parts down to use as food.[34]

Except that something rather strange happened – and probably more than once. A eukaryote engulfed a prokaryote, and instead of digesting it, they started working together. This particular prokaryote was a tiny powerhouse, specialized in taking oxygen – now ubiquitous – and turning it into energy. Called a mitochondrion, it formed a relationship with eukaryotes that could lay claim to be the most successful partnership on Earth. Every organism that you see around you – every plant, every insect, every animal – is comprised of eukaryotic cells containing hundreds, and sometimes thousands, of mitochondria within them (in plants they're called plastids), producing the energy that allows the cell to go about its business. To this day, mitochondria still carry their own DNA with them, which they use to replicate separately from the rest of the cell.[35*]

This startling hypothesis was proposed by biologist Lynn Margulis in 1967, and she underwent years of ridicule from the mainstream scientific community until it was finally accepted. It is now recognized as an indisputable part of Earth's evolutionary history – and not just any part. The cooperation initiated between eukaryotes and mitochondria is viewed by many biologists as one of the most important events ever to have occurred in the history of life on Earth.[36*]

The reason for its huge significance comes down to energy. With mitochondria as its internal power plants, the eukaryotic cell uses thousands of times more energy than a prokaryote, which permits it to achieve things far beyond a prokaryote's capabilities. To begin with, eukaryotes tend to be vastly bigger – ranging from a thousand to fifteen thousand times the size – and have far greater functional diversity within their cell boundaries. One biologist offers an analogy between a studio apartment and a mansion: the studio apartment functions well enough, but everything has to be done within a single, limited space; a mansion, on the other hand, has separate domains including a kitchen, library and dozens of other rooms. In addition to their extra size and structural diversity, eukaryotes also typically have ten times as many genes, which offer greater functional flexibility.[37]

Prokaryotes, meanwhile, may have remained relatively simple in their design, but they developed their own striking form of cooperation which has enabled them to flourish even in a world of energy-guzzling eukaryotes. They learned to share their genes with each other, in much the same way that neighbors in a tight-knit community might share their tools, favorite books or useful gardening tips. They've been doing this now for billions of years, and it may be the single most important skill that has enabled them to thrive over the eons, allowing them to survive even in the most inhospitable places, such as hydrothermal vents, oil slicks and radioactive dumps. Most of us know about this powerful networking trick of bacteria through their antibiotic resistance, which they transfer to each other through gene sharing.[38]

Just like a handyman constantly fixing up his studio apartment, there seems to be virtually no limit to the way bacteria tinker with their own genomes. Some bacteria change up to 15 percent of their genetic material on a daily basis, and about 18 percent of the *E. coli* genome is estimated to have come from other bacterial species. Although each bacterium has a small genome size compared with a eukaryote, within a given population they are estimated to have access to a metagenome of approximately the same size – a bit like a group of apartment dwellers pooling their resources to enjoy common areas similar to that of the mansion owner.[39]

In addition to sharing genes, bacteria have developed a wide array of cooperative strategies for flourishing. They can communicate through molecular signaling, move collectively over large areas, and form biofilms over surfaces with those on the outside protecting the others from a hostile environment. As microbiologists have tried to come to grips with the awesome extent of bacterial collaboration, they have wondered if they should really be divided into separate species, or whether it's more accurate to consider them a single global species, or even a superorganism – one that is functionally immortal.[40]

In the early years of life on Earth, it's likely that gene sharing (known officially as horizontal gene transfer) was the predominant way evolution worked. In fact, researchers now believe that the eukaryote genome was itself the result of a fusion of two prokaryotic genomes. Instead of the Darwinian tree of life, biologists are offering alternative metaphors such as a bush or net of life to better describe how we are all intricately connected. In the memorable words of Lynn Margulis: 'Life did not take over the world by combat but by networking.'[41]

As eukaryotes, boosted by their mitochondrial energy packs, developed larger and more complex cellular structures, horizontal gene transfer became less important for them. While they do continue to engage in it, the size and complexity of their genomes make it more difficult. Eukaryotes, however, gradually devised another form of cooperation that led to the full unfolding of the prodigious grandeur of life on Earth as we know it today – multicellularity.[42]

Better together

Almost every manifestation of nature that we can see with the naked eye is multicellular: a daisy, a rhinoceros and a tiny mite are all composed of a multitude of cells doing different things yet working together for the greater interest of the organism. The evolutionary step from a single-celled eukaryote to the emergence of multicellular life took a long, long time – about a billion or so years, during which so little changed on Earth that it's been called the 'boring billion'.[43]

Why did it take so long? No one knows for sure, but a clue may reside in the staggering intricacy of gene expression that multicellular life had to master. It's one thing for a cell to organize itself and then divide into two. It's quite another to figure out how a newly born cell can split into two new cells different from each other but working together toward a shared goal and then continue this differentiating process time and time again. Think of the miraculous complexity of your own body: skin cells, brain cells, liver cells, blood cells – about two hundred different types of cells all working harmoniously together but each type carrying out its own unique functions.[44]

A fundamental distinction had to be made between cells that specialized in passing on genes to the next generation (germline cells) and the somatic cells that took care of everything else. Here again, we see a major evolutionary breakthrough in the scale of nature's cooperation. Somatic cells had to give up their own ability to reproduce in order to become part of something bigger than themselves. Without this momentous accord, there would be no complex life on Earth – including you and me. Maybe it wasn't such a boring billion years after all.[45]

Even as they followed their unique evolutionary pathways to become redwood trees, whales or worms, virtually all creatures on Earth have continued to share about a third of their genes from the collective ancestral pool. Because of our deep common ancestry, even though animals and bacteria have very different lifestyles, our cells are all able to communicate using the same genomic language. Even as species became more differentiated, they developed ways to trade their own specialized skills for the unique skills of other species that could help them thrive. This process, known as symbiosis, is so widespread throughout nature that it forms a bedrock of every ecology on Earth. The prevalence of symbiosis means that life is rarely a zero-sum game, where a species can only gain at the expense of another. On the contrary, by working together, species have co-created ecosystems everywhere in which the whole is far greater than the sum of the parts.[46]*

It's impossible to take a walk in the woods, eat a meal or swim in the ocean without participating in the deep symbioses that have nourished life's plenitude. On the most fundamental level, plants have specialized in transforming sunlight into chemical energy that provides food for other creatures, whose waste then fertilizes the soil that the plants rely on. If you hike in the woods, you may notice how the trees provide shade that maintains moisture for creatures on the ground. Below you, mycorrhizal fungi maintain underground networks allowing 'guilds' of trees to exchange carbon and nutrients among each other in a sophisticated interplay of resources. In one recent experiment, researchers discovered that fungus could sense where roots were lower in phosphorus, and accordingly redistribute its phosphorus to increase the uptake in that area. Fungus, meanwhile, is unable to produce the carbon it needs to form its networks, and receives it from the trees in return for the phosphorus, nitrogen and other essential chemicals it supplies.[47]

Plants rely on cooperative relationships above ground as well as below. Pollinators allow them to become fertile and produce seeds and fruit, which are then frequently carried by other animals to new locations. When herds of buffalo graze on the prairie, they don't damage the grass; on the contrary, their manure helps fertilize it, and their saliva even contains growth-stimulating enzymes, so the grass quickly grows back in good health.[48]

These symbiotic relationships are frequently so intimate that we rely on them without even knowing about it. We share our bodies with a vast multitude of bacteria – more than the number of cells we call our own. We need them to help us perform biochemical tricks that we can't do ourselves, such as producing enzymes to digest food that our own enzymes can't manage. These symbionts are so important to us that, after birth, a mother's milk contains special sugars that the baby can't digest but provide nutrition for the newborn's symbiotic bacteria.[49]

How does our body's immune system determine which bacteria are symbionts and which are dangerous? Based on the conventional nature-as-battleground paradigm, we've become used to thinking of our immune system as a defensive army, ruthlessly seeking out invaders and destroying them before they can cause damage. A more accurate view of it is an ecological steward, using ancient shared genetic language to identify friendly bacteria and distinguish them from those that don't belong. Some symbiotic bacteria, in fact, cooperate with our immune system to secrete molecules that are toxic to other types of harmful bacteria.[50]

These deeply intimate symbioses are everywhere in nature, forming the foundation of the living world. If you see lichen on a rock, you are looking at two symbiotic organisms that evolved together: an alga making sugar through photosynthesis that it shares with a fungus, which in turn absorbs minerals that it passes back to the alga. Plankton in the ocean, which collectively produce most of the oxygen in the atmosphere and are essential to life on Earth, rely on their own symbiosis with bacteria. A tiny droplet of ocean water harbors an entire ecosystem containing thousands of bacteria exchanging nutrients with each single-celled alga.[51]

In countless instances, over hundreds of millions of years, life has decided time and again that things work better together.

Cooperation, competition and harmony

The entire story of evolution on Earth, it seems, could be understood as variations on the theme of cooperation. Prokaryote genomes forming the first eukaryotes, which partnered with ingested mitochondria to boost their energy. Bacteria sharing the tools of their trade to adapt to anything that comes their way. Eukaryotes unlocking the intricate, complex secrets of genetic expression to become multicellular. Organisms blazing their own trails, but never ceasing to rely on each other for their shared flourishing.

Where, then, does competition fit into the picture? By now, you may be convinced that the gene's supposed ruthlessly selfish drive to replicate is not the sole explanatory factor of evolution. But surely competition has nevertheless had a significant part to play? What about all those spectacular nature documentaries showing cheetahs sprinting to catch gazelles? Male chimpanzees fighting rivals for sexual dominance? Bacteria that make us sick by overpowering our immune systems? There is no question that ruthless competition also has a central role to play in the drama of life. How can we reconcile pervasive competition with the forces of cooperation?

Let's imagine a spectrum with extreme competition at one end and extreme cooperation on the other. We can think of an organism as an ecosystem where the different parts have agreed to coexist at the cooperative end of the spectrum. The extreme commitment to cooperation made by the cells in your body becomes stunningly clear when you consider that they voluntarily kill themselves when they are no longer needed for your body's healthy functioning – a process called apoptosis. When they make this decision, they don't just call it quits and decompose. In a careful choreography, they instruct their genes to create a crew of enzymes that meticulously cut the large molecules of DNA, RNA and proteins into bite-sized pieces which are sorted into little membrane packages and fed to neighboring cells.[52]

Outside the organism, however, relationships exist all along the spectrum. An ecosystem can be understood as the emergent creation of organisms acting together in different degrees of competition and cooperation. In fact, the creative tension that arises from the confluence of competition and cooperation is itself a driving force of evolution. A pair of prominent evolutionary biologists, David Sloan Wilson and E. O. Wilson, have developed a sophisticated theory they call multilevel selection, tracing the dynamics between cooperative and competitive behavior at different scales of life. E. O. Wilson, a world leader in the study of social insects, has shown how colonies of ants that cooperated closely were more evolutionarily successful than those that experienced internal competition. The same is thought to be true of human evolution, when early hominids developed deeply felt values such as compassion, altruism and fairness, which enabled them to live complex lives together in community. The groups in which these attributes predominated were more successful at hunting, foraging and defending themselves from attack. Wilson and Wilson offer a simple mantra to summarize their theory: 'Selfishness beats altruism within groups. Altruistic groups beat selfish groups.'[53]

When groups evolve to become sufficiently cooperative, they

get closer to the state of an organism. Colonies of social insects like ants or bees are so highly cooperative, in fact, that they are frequently called superorganisms. Think of the classic Darwinian refrain: 'survival of the fittest'. It has an interesting ambiguity: the survival of the most competitive or of those that fit most successfully into their environment? We can conceive of evolution now as a multidimensional force acting through both competition and cooperation at multiple levels – within the organism, in symbiotic relationships, within a species, between species and within an ecosystem. At each level, competitive and cooperative forces create their own dynamic tensions while simultaneously impacting other levels. Meanwhile, the state of the ecosystem as a whole affects each of these relationships within it. Remember the concept of reciprocal causality, where parts of a system affect the whole while the system as a whole affects the parts? This is a classic example of how life itself is a complex, self-organized system acting on itself at multiple levels of scale.[54]

With this in mind, we can move beyond a sterile debate about whether evolution is a result of competition or cooperation. After all, these are concepts created by humans to establish neat categories. Living systems, whether they're genomes, cells, organisms or ecosystems, have no interest in sticking to a category. We know that our old friend, the slime mold, can work cooperatively with impressive intelligence when food becomes scarce. Close studies have also revealed that, within the slime mold, different genetic strains seem to compete to promote their own genotypes. We know that trees rely symbiotically on animals to spread their seeds. However, nut trees would have a problem if the squirrels ate all their nuts before they could germinate. To overcome this, in a phenomenon known as mast fruiting, they cooperate as a species, refrain from producing nuts for several years, and then collectively decide one year to produce an overwhelming number of nuts, so the squirrels will be unable to devour them all. Who's competing? Who's cooperating?[55]

Maybe there's another way to describe the elegantly complex interweaving of natural processes that comprise an ecosystem: harmony. In music, harmony arises when different notes sound at the same time in such a way that an emergent, more complex and pleasing sound is produced. The notes aren't competing or cooperating with each other, but the way in which their differences act upon each other creates a blended experience that is richer and more beautiful than any of them alone. Could it be that the best description of how nature works is, in fact, a harmonic meshwork of life?

Mind the metaphor

The mainstream metaphors used to describe the evolution of life do a great disservice to its awesome majesty, while influencing us to think about our planet, our society and our own lives in harmful and destructive ways. Metaphors are more than just techniques to communicate ideas – as I've described in *The Patterning Instinct*, they form foundational structures of thought in the human brain that we unconsciously use to construct our worldview and shape our value system. Metaphors matter.[56]

The most pervasive mistaken metaphor of life in common currency is that it's merely a very complicated machine. As we've seen, this goes back to the time of Descartes and Hobbes (and even further back), but it has fused with the bedrock of modern thought ever since Crick and Watson defined the gene in terms of coded information. Later, Dawkins had a powerful effect on popularizing this wrong-headed idea, writing such as absurdities as: 'It is raining DNA ... It is raining instructions out there; it's raining tree-growing, fluff-spreading algorithms. That is not a metaphor, it is the plain truth. It couldn't be any plainer if it were raining floppy discs.'

As one biologist retorted, 'It certainly isn't the plain truth. Nor is it a statement of homology or analogy. It is a manifesto.'[57]

But at this stage it's difficult to read any popular discourse about life (other than articles written by serious biologists) without being bombarded by this misconception. The cell is represented as nothing but a factory, and life itself becomes raw material for processing. We've seen how Larry Page, Google's co-founder, described human DNA as just '600 megabytes compressed'. In another example, at a US Committee on Energy and Commerce hearing a pioneer in synthetic biology explained how his colleagues assemble 'standardized well-characterized components from existing well-studied organisms, much like how one might assemble a computer from standard components such as a hard drive, sound card, motherboard and power supply'.[58]

This metaphor becomes even more dangerously pervasive when it's used to describe the human mind, which according to a pair of evolutionary psychologists is 'a set of information-processing machines that were designed by natural selection to solve adaptive problems faced by our hunter-gatherer ancestors'. The brain, we are told, is 'a computer that is made of organic (carbon-based) compounds rather than silicon chips'.[59]

A fundamental error arising from this metaphor is the notion that our minds are 'software' that can be separated from our physiological 'hardware'. With computers, information is substrate independent, which means that you can upload your files to the cloud, download them somewhere else, and they will be exactly the same. Life is not substrate independent. The so-called 'information' carried by your DNA can't be separated from how it's expressed within the cell; the 'information' transmitted through your brain is inextricably bound up in each neuron's own molecular structure and its dynamic relationships with other neurons.[60]

This profound misconception has enormous potential consequences, especially since it is accepted unquestioningly by the high-tech elites who are shaping much of our future. Raymond Kurzweil, a senior Google executive, believes that within a couple of decades humans (at least, the wealthiest ones) will become immortal because they will be able to upload their minds to the cloud and download them into fresh hardware – a new body. He's doomed to fail in this quest because it's based on a category error: his mind is not software. Max Tegmark, a leading physicist influential in steering global policy decisions on artificial intelligence, similarly defines life on the basis of hardware (physical matter) and software (intelligence), and sees no essential distinction between substrate-independent super-intelligent AI ('Life 3.0', as he calls it) and the flesh-and-blood life that's evolved on Earth over billions of years. As a result, he and other technological leaders are developing ethical guidelines for AI that could jeopardize the sanctity of biological life at the expense of computer algorithms. We have already traced how the Western mindset denies the existence of animate consciousness, with the result that a person's entire identity is believed to exist in their conceptual consciousness. The information metaphor, as utilized by modern technologists, takes this dualistic split into dangerous new territory.[61]*

And then, of course, there's the Gordon Gekko crowd, justifying exploitative free-market global capitalism on the basis that it's what evolution intended. The metaphor of life as a market pervades public discourse so extensively that it seems like it must be nature's own way. Remember the research on the symbiotic relationship between fungus and tree roots that revealed how fungus distributed phosphorus to the trees that needed it most? The headline in *New Scientist* went as follows: 'Brainless Fungi Trade Resources with Plants Like a Stock Market'. The fungi, we are told, are 'savvy traders, taking advantage of their partners by shuttling goods to nutrient-starved areas where plants are willing to pay more than usual'.[62]

How would it change our conception of nature, and of our own social norms, if we instead framed these symbiotic relationships in terms of mutual consideration? Native American biologist Robin Wall Kimmerer refreshingly writes about symbiosis as a 'relationship of gratitude and reciprocity [which] can increase the evolutionary fitness of both plant and animal'. In contrast to Gordon Gekko, she explains how, if humans embrace their symbiotic relationship with the rest of the living Earth and tend it accordingly to create conditions for mutual flourishing, this would lead to the long-term benefit of humans and nonhumans alike. 'The stories we choose to shape our behaviors,' she writes, 'have adaptive consequences.'[63]

The sacred dance of life

What, then, are metaphors for life that more accurately reflect the findings of evolutionary biology and might have the adaptive consequence of influencing our civilization to behave with more reverence toward its only home?

Frequently, when cell biologists describe the mind-boggling complexity of their subject, they turn to music as a core metaphor. Denis Noble entitled his book on cellular biology *The Music of Life*, writing that 'the music of life is a symphony'. Ursula Goodenough describes patterns of gene expression as 'melodies and harmonies'. Another biologist writes of 'a veritable symphony of chemical signals' arriving at a cell's nucleus to turn genes on and off. While the music metaphor aligns with my earlier discussion of harmony, I get concerned about certain aspects of the symphony setting. After all, a symphony is a piece of music written by a composer, with a conductor directing how each note should be played. The awesome quality of nature's music arises from the fact that it is self-organized. There is no outside agent telling each cell what to do.[64*]

Perhaps a more illustrative metaphor would be an improvisational jazz ensemble, where a self-organized group of musicians spontaneously creates fresh melodies from a core harmonic theme, riffing off each other's creativity in a way similar to how we've seen evolution work. Geneticist Mae-Wan Ho captures this idea with her portrayal of life as 'quantum jazz'. She describes it as 'an incredible hive of activity at every level of magnification in the organism ... locally appearing as though completely chaotic, and yet perfectly coordinated as a whole. This exquisite music is played in endless variations subject to our changes of mood and physiology, each organism and species with its own repertoire.'[65]

A related metaphor – and one that I find even more compelling – is a dance. Cell biologists increasingly refer to their findings in terms of 'choreography', and philosopher of biology Evan Thompson writes vividly how an organism and its environment relate to each other 'like two partners in a dance who bring forth each other's movements'. As biologist Brian Goodwin points out, it's important to recognize that this is not just any dance. 'Each of these forms of life,' he writes, 'each natural species, has intrinsic value and meaning in relation to the whole tapestry of life so that there is a sense of the sacred in this living dance.' The expression of life's sacred weave is powerfully captured by Goethe in the opening scene of *Faust*, where he has the Earth Spirit announce:

In the torrents of life, in action's storm
I weave and wave in endless motion
cradle and grave a timeless ocean
ceaselessly weaving the tissue of living
constantly changing, blending, arranging
the humming loom of Time I ply
and weave the web of Divinity.[66]

If our mainstream media and commentators began using these metaphors in place of the selfish gene, before long we might begin to perceive our world in a fundamentally different way.

What might happen if we applied this new understanding of nature's harmonic dance to establish different norms for our own society? Imagine if, instead of our socioeconomic system constructed on the presumption that 'the economy of nature is competitive from beginning to end', it was structured instead on the basis of symbiosis – an ecological civilization.

Rather than existing in hierarchical structures, organic systems are more like a self-organized democracy, interacting through complex participation, each party actively performing its own role while paying attention to what's being done around it. As Mae-Wan Ho writes, 'Everyone is simultaneously boss and worker, choreography and dancer. Each is ultimately in control to the extent that she is sensitive and responsive.'[67]

Ecosystems have developed tremendous resilience from these internal dynamics, sometimes existing for millions of years, continually adapting yet remaining stable and robust. Widespread symbiosis means there are no waste products – what one species expels is nutrition for another. Healthy ecosystems embrace both competition and cooperation at multiple levels, but always within a context of harmony for the entire system. The possibility of applying these ecological principles to our own society, and using them as an alternative way for humanity to organize itself, is one that we'll return to.[68]

We've uncovered how some of the most pervasive assumptions about the nature of reality are, in fact, myths that arose centuries ago in Europe and have since been repeated so incessantly that most of us grow up accepting them as core truths. We've seen how the reductionist view of the cosmos needs to be augmented by one that recognizes the importance of self-organized patterns connecting things in nonlinear ways. And we've seen how nature developed its own forms of connection that enabled it to generate life in complex abundance. Now, as we launch our investigation into the question of 'What am I?' we'll find that, by applying the insights of self-organization to how life evolved on Earth, we'll gain an appreciation into life's own purpose and direction, taking us to the outer reaches of where life itself might be heading.

NEW THREADS OF MEANING

Every major evolutionary step since life began on Earth was a result of increased cooperation between different types of organisms

Life is not a zero-sum game: through symbiosis, species have co-created ecosystems in which the whole is far greater than the sum of the parts

An ecosystem arises from organisms acting together in a complex interweaving of both competition and cooperation: a harmonic dance of life

WHERE AM I?

I exist in a fractally connected, self-organized universe where everything relates dynamically to everything else

Part Three

WHAT AM I?

Chapter Six

THE DEEP PURPOSE OF LIFE

Aristotle was just a teenager when he arrived in Athens from Macedonia to begin his studies at Plato's famed Academy. For twenty years he absorbed everything his teacher had to impart, but much of it didn't make sense to him. Plato taught that the soul was separate from the body, but Aristotle didn't see how something could exist without a material basis. Plato taught that the tangible world was just a pale imitation of an ideal version in an eternal dimension; to Aristotle, living beings seemed to act according to their own true nature rather than mimic some external ideal.[1]

After Plato's death, Aristotle set up a competing school in Athens, the Lyceum, where he taught his own philosophy based on his view that every living being has an intrinsic purpose, the expression of its defining essence, which he viewed as its soul. 'If the eye were an animal,' he explained, 'sight would be its soul, since this is the defining essence of an eye.' Everything an organism did, he believed, was done for the sake of its innate purpose. Things in nature didn't just happen; they happened for a reason. Plants send their roots into the ground for the sake of nourishment; birds build nests to look after their young; spiders weave webs to catch food. The same was true, he believed, for the way seeds or embryos develop. You can only understand the changes taking place in an acorn or an egg if you know its ultimate purpose.[2]

If Aristotle could have explained his ideas to other Indigenous cultures around the world, it's likely they would have been receptive. Virtually all cultures at that time shared an understanding that a life force existed in every living entity, a spirit that impelled them to do what they did. Before hunting an animal or harvesting fruit from a grove, many Indigenous peoples would ritually honor the spirit of the entity from which they took their sustenance.[3]

In ancient China sages developed these Indigenous insights into a categorization of the kinds of qi (energy/matter) that existed in an organism. One kind was *shen*, the vital spirit that animated a living organism. Another was *jing*, the generative principle that was believed to emerge in an embryo at the moment of conception, driving its growth and eventual reproductive energy. We'll never know exactly how early Chinese scholars would have interpreted Aristotle's theories in terms of *shen* and *jing*, but it's likely that his ideas would have made sense to them.[4]

This was not the case, however, for European thinkers in the wake of the Scientific Revolution. As we've seen, prominent thinkers such as Descartes and Hobbes laid the foundation for the mechanistic worldview that has since become ubiquitous in mainstream thought. If an animal were merely a machine, then by definition it couldn't have its own intrinsic purpose any more than it could have its own feelings. In the seventeenth century those scientific pioneers still lived under a Christian worldview, so it was easy enough to attribute the seemingly purposeful activity of nature to a creator, who instilled purpose in a creature just like a clockmaker instills the purpose of timekeeping into a clock.[5]

By the nineteenth century, when scientists were less willing to resort to theology for ultimate explanations, the problem resurfaced. How could you explain the obviously purposive behavior of living organisms? Some scientists theorized that creatures contained a life force, an *élan vital*, that worked according to specific laws, like gravity or electricity. However, by the early twentieth century this idea, known as vitalism, had fallen into such disrepute in mainstream science that it had become an object of ridicule. Along with vitalism, any theory that living entities possessed intrinsic purpose – known as teleology – was discarded by mainstream science into the same pit of disdain that contained other heretical ideas we've already come across, such as Lamarckian evolution, animal emotions or plant intelligence – each of which has now been scientifically validated.[6]

For reductionist scientists, the primary challenge in refuting teleology was that living organisms so obviously demonstrate it in everything they do. When a spider tries valiantly to climb out of the bathtub, or when your dog paws at the door because she needs to relieve herself, it's only too clear they're acting with purpose. However, with the widespread acceptance of the Modern Synthesis in the mid-twentieth century, biologists declared this challenge resolved. Everything could now be explained by natural selection operating on genes. According to prominent biologist Ernst Mayr, organisms only *seem* to behave according to teleology, but their behavior really 'owes its goal-directedness to the operation of a program ... that contains not only the blueprint of the goal but also the instructions of how to use the information of the blueprint'.[7]

However, as we've seen, the mechanistic metaphor for life is fundamentally flawed. Life didn't emerge according to blueprints and doesn't operate like a computer program. What does that mean for teleology? Could Aristotle have been right? If life's purposive behavior is not the result of a program, what really causes it? In this chapter we'll discover not only that life does have purpose, but that intrinsic purpose is, in fact, a defining characteristic of life. Research in the dynamics of self-organization is forcing leading scientists to rethink how evolution itself works, and suggests a directionality to life on Earth that requires us to reconsider humanity's true place within it, with enormous implications for the potential trajectory of our species.

What does life want?

The story of life's deep purpose begins, ironically, with death. A certain kind of death: the 'heat death' that scientists tell us is the likely ultimate fate of the universe. In the nineteenth century Lord Kelvin formulated the Second Law of Thermodynamics, which describes how the universe is undergoing an irreversible process of entropy. Order inevitably becomes disordered and heat always flows from hot regions to colder regions. We see entropy in our daily lives every time we stir cream into our coffee or break an egg for an omelet. Once the egg is scrambled, no amount of work will ever get the yolk back together again. It's a depressing law, especially when applied to the entire universe, which according to most physicists will eventually dissipate into a bleak expanse of cold, dark nothingness.[8]

This law is so all-encompassing that Albert Einstein once declared it was the only theory in physics that he was certain would never be overthrown. It's so universal that it's even used to explain how time can only ever flow in one direction. But wait! There's a loophole to this dismal law. It's called life.[9]

This loophole was first described in 1944 by Austrian physicist Erwin Schrödinger, who won a Nobel Prize for his work on quantum theory, then ventured into the fundamentals of biology. In his seminal book *What Is Life?* Schrödinger explained that living organisms exist by converting the entropy around them into order, creating temporary eddies of negative entropy, which he called *negentropy*. They're not exactly repealing the Second Law because, as they organize the energy and matter within themselves, they're increasing entropy in the universe as a whole. But it's a local loophole to the law that's maintained itself on Earth for billions of years. Wherever there is life, entropy is being reversed – at least for a while.[10]

How does life perform this amazing feat? Schrödinger described how all living entities turn entropy into order. They ingest it in the form of energy and matter, break it apart and reorganize it into forms that are beneficial for their continued existence. It's a process that goes by a common name: metabolism. While you're sitting here reading this page, your own body is taking part in the age-old process that life began billions of years ago. Whatever you ate earlier today is diligently being broken down by cells in your gut, turned into molecular components for the proteins, lipids and other crucial ingredients your body needs, then transmitted to other cells so they can perform their work of self-regeneration. It's a process you share, in one way or another, with every living entity on Earth.[11]

It's interesting that it took a physicist to identify such a fundamental feature of biology, but perhaps not surprising. The moment that a set of molecules first sucked in entropy to organize itself was the moment that physics and chemistry combined to give birth to biology. As we've seen, the emergence of life on Earth was most likely a process of autopoiesis – a stunning feat of self-organization performed by non-living molecular structures. The first step toward life occurred when sets of molecules began to catalyze each other's reactions – an autocatalytic set – and formed a semipermeable membrane around themselves, using other molecules from outside to maintain the process. This momentous event marked the first time that matter began to reverse entropy on Earth.[12]

It was also the moment when teleology first appeared on our planet. Some autocatalytic sets would have absorbed the wrong types of molecules which interfered with their internal processes and caused them to dissipate. Others would have developed a primitive detection system to keep out harmful molecules and only assimilate those that helped catalyze their reactions. Those were the ones that survived and maintained negentropy. Though they had no language to express what they were doing, those autocatalytic sets had crossed a threshold of value: they began making judgments about what was around them. The molecules out there held meaning to them: one molecule was harmful, another was beneficial because it permitted them to continue converting entropy into order.[13]

As these molecular sets became more complex and formed the first real cells, each constituent part had a purpose that related to the cell as a whole, just as Aristotle had observed. The membrane existed for the sake of protecting the interior, ingesting what was beneficial and expelling what was harmful. The interior processes existed to generate chemical reactions and keep the membrane healthy. Demonstrating reciprocal causality, each part acted for the benefit of the whole, while the whole entity acted for the benefit of all its parts. In the words of philosopher Hans Jonas, 'There is no organism without teleology.'[14*]

Billions of years later, single-celled amoebae or bacteria still act like sophisticated versions of these original protocells, continually evaluating their environment for what is beneficial or harmful. When a bacterium in a tank senses sugar is more concentrated in a certain direction, it will turn around, rotate its flagella like a propeller and swim toward what it wants. It's driven by the same sense of purpose that has urged life forward in an unbroken flow from the days of the first protocells: a desire to resist the Second Law of Thermodynamics, to ingest nutrients, metabolize them, regenerate its parts and pass its particular form of negentropy on to the next generation. We're back to Weber's First Law of Desire: 'Everything that lives wants more of life. Organisms are beings whose own existence means something to them.'[15]

Teleology is so fundamental to life that each of its defining characteristics can ultimately be understood by how it serves the purpose of negative entropy. While controversy remains over the exact details of what constitutes life, most biologists have converged on a small set of essential attributes. First, there must be a boundary between the organism and the rest of the world – between the entropy out there and the order within. Whether it's a cell wall or skin, the boundary must be semipermeable, with the ability to ingest what's needed from outside and expel waste from within. Second, a living entity must actively persist in a continually dynamic metabolic flow, repairing and rebuilding its constituent parts to resist the wear and tear that entropy relentlessly imposes. When this active flow ceases, that's the moment of death. Third, a living being must be capable of self-reproducing. The Second Law dictates that, after some time, in spite of its best efforts at self-repair, a living system will begin to degenerate. Whether by cell division or by procreation, it must have a way to pass on its unique capacities for negentropy to future generations.[16]

Underlying these three essential criteria for life is a deeper principle: the purposive self-organization that permits it all to happen. As we've seen, life is a self-constructed process. There is no programmer writing a program, no architect drawing up a blueprint. The organism is the weaver of its own fabric. It sculpts itself according to its own inner sense of purpose, which it inherited ultimately – like all of us – from those first autocatalytic cells: the drive to resist the Second Law of Thermodynamics and generate a temporary vortex of self-created order in the universe.[17]

A cascade of negative entropy

Here we are discussing the fundamentals of life, and there hasn't yet been a single mention of genes or evolution. How, you might wonder, does this description of life self-organizing to resist entropy relate to the theory of natural selection? An increasing number of leading biological theorists have been pondering this question, and have begun to assemble a coherent answer.

It begins up in the heavens, with the sun. Early civilizations around the world worshipped the sun as the giver of all life. The ancient Egyptians called their deity Ra, the Aztecs worshipped Tōnatiuh, but for all their differences in myth and ritual, they agreed that the sun was the ultimate source of nature's bounty. They weren't wrong. From the earliest times on Earth to the present day, virtually all the energy that life consumes derives ultimately from the sun. Through photosynthesis, plants and algae absorb the sun's energy, which eventually cascades through entire ecosystems, animating every animal, fungus and most bacteria that form the harmonic dance of life.[18]

Back in Earth's earliest days, those autocatalytic sets also needed the sun's energy to perform their feat of negentropy. The molecular assemblies that produced the most stable and efficient cycles of chemical reactions were the ones that persisted. Here, even before life appeared, was a basic form of selection based on energy optimization. The molecular sets with the most effective ways to resist entropy were selected – simply by virtue of the fact that they survived while others did not.[19]

From this perspective, the Second Law of Thermodynamics can be seen as the foundation for natural selection. From the first protocells onwards, all living entities are energy transformers, converting energy around them into their own unique form of negentropy. The most successful energy transformers persevered and passed their particular tricks on to the next generation. This radical idea was first suggested a century ago by mathematician Alfred Lotka, who proposed a Fourth Law of Thermodynamics, which stated, 'Evolution proceeds in such direction as to make the total energy flux through the system a maximum compatible with the constraints.' In recent years researchers in principles of self-organization have validated Lotka's vision and elaborated it into a broader framework.[20*]

This understanding of evolution moves the locus of natural

selection away from the gene. Once you start seeing living entities as patterns of energy flows, there's no reason to draw artificial lines separating them. Symbiotic relationships can be understood as the inevitable consequence of different organisms working together to resist entropy more effectively. The vibrant complexity of a healthy ecosystem is the natural result of a multifaceted, glorious cascade of negative entropy. Plants absorb solar energy, transforming it into cellulose; herbivores convert cellulose into flesh and blood, which are then consumed by carnivores, all of whom bestow their waste on fungus which transmutes it back into nutrition for the plants. Entropy is kept at bay so successfully that many ecosystems can thrive, if undisturbed by humans, for millions of years. Through this lens, evolution itself may be understood as life developing increasingly sophisticated ways to maximize the conversion of energy into negative entropy.[21]

Do you remember those beautiful fractal patterns that indicate self-organized behavior in nature, appearing in everything from tree branches to neural networks? They have been shown by complexity theorists to be the most efficient configuration for facilitating the flow of energy through a system. We can understand life itself as a fractal: a series of natural attractors exhibiting similar principles at different scales, from microscopic cells to organisms and entire ecosystems. The stunning complexities of life's self-organization have expanded from within a tiny cell to the vast interactions of the entire planet we call home, all the while developing ever more intricate ways to maintain life's defiance of the dark force of entropy. Let's take a glimpse into how it does it.[22]

The virtuosity of the cell

Cellular biology has a serious PR problem. Its academic sibling, genetics, has spent decades in the limelight, emblazoned on the front page of countless popular magazines, acclaimed as the golden key to unlocking life's secrets. Cell biology barely gets a mention, and yet it is in the mysterious inner life of the cell that the stunning, self-organized genius of nature is to be discovered.

The cell has had its cheerleaders, but they haven't enjoyed the celebrity of superstars like Crick and Watson. One Nobel laureate,

Sydney Brenner, has stated, 'I believe very strongly that the fundamental unit, the correct level of abstraction, is the cell and not the genome.' Another cell biologist argues that the cell, as the basis of life, can only be truly understood as a self-organized system, and then reflects: 'That this self-evident proposition should remain in practice so much of a minority view never ceases to astonish me.'[23]

Perhaps it's the bewildering complexity of the cell's inner organization that has made it so difficult for people to comprehend, let alone write headlines about it. If we zoomed into a cell like micro-explorers, we'd see an incomprehensible hive of activity, with innumerable proteins, like vibrating entanglements of animated steel wool, waltzing around at super speed, each one no more than a few nanometers (millionths of a millimeter) across. Proteins are constructed from repeating combinations of twenty-one different amino acids, which fold onto themselves with such complexity that, even if biologists know a protein's amino acid sequence, they're still unable to predict its exact form.[24]

Imagine a cell is the size of Manhattan, and we're flying over it in a helicopter, watching the activity below. Each protein, roughly the size of a family car, is steered around by various membranes in orderly patterns, guided to special districts where it might have additional features attached, then loaded onto transporters to be taken to a new destination to perform its business. Overseers monitor the protein, and once they observe it's sustained too much damage, they send it over to junk yards where it can be dismantled into tiny components for making brand new proteins.[25]

Now let's shrink down even further, to the unimaginably tiny workhorses that put proteins together, one amino acid at a time, called ribosomes. A single cell in your liver contains 13 million of them. They receive their amino acids from RNA molecules and link them together in a long chain according to a particular order, operating at the rate of ten amino acids per second to build a whole protein, virtually error free, in less than a minute. The ribosomes get their work orders from within the nucleus, where the DNA resides. If we ventured inside that, we'd be struck by an even more stunning spectacle of chromosomes so tightly packed with DNA that, if all the DNA of your body were stretched out and lined up end to end, they would extend from Earth to the moon and back, not once but 120,000 times.[26]

While the cell is performing all this activity, it's also communicating with thousands of neighboring cells, deciding what to do next while importing molecules it needs and exporting the ones it can't use any more. All this unfathomable complexity is happening right now in each one of the cells in your own body. And you have about forty trillion of them.[27]

This breathtaking virtuosity is the result of billions of years of life working out the most effective way to keep entropy at bay. What is the source of the intelligence that keeps it all together? As biologists get ever more sophisticated in their analysis of how cells work, they keep coming to the same realization: each activity within the cell is the result of self-organized behavior.[28]

How does a myriad of microscopic components, with no brain, no sight, no hearing, no speech, no prior concept of what they're meant to accomplish, achieve such mastery?

The wisdom of the crowd

An illuminating way to get a feel for the cell's self-organized intelligence is to trace how an embryo develops from a single microscopic cell to a full-fledged organism. This process, called ontogeny, has been extensively studied, yet retains its mystique as one of the greatest enigmas of life. How is that first cell able to divide into a series of two hundred different types, each cell coordinating its proper function with a trillion others to form a perfect infant, cooing, breathing, suckling on her mother's breasts and crying when she's hungry? Aristotle recognized the embryo's purposive drive to realize its full potentiality, but only now can scientists begin to explain how it does so.

Fundamentally, ontogeny is a triumph of self-organized emergence arising from the interplay of a massive number of tiny, relatively simple interactions of cells closely coordinating with each other. Each cell reacts to its local conditions without requiring an understanding of the big picture. Imagine you're leaving a crowded sports stadium at the end of a match, but you don't know where the exit is. It doesn't really matter because all you need to do is coordinate with the flow of the people around you. Your slow but steady speed isn't set by any particular person but by the self-organized tempo of the crowd. For a moment the crowd may come to a halt. You don't need to know why; you just recognize that everyone around you has stopped moving, so you stop too. Then the shuffling begins again, and you flow with it, eventually making your way through a turnstile simply by attuning to the activity of those around you.[29]

The behavior of each cell resembles your actions in that crowd. A cell makes its determination of what to do based on what the cells next to it are doing. It doesn't need to know the ultimate goal of the system as a whole, but it needs to be exquisitely attuned to its neighbors and respond to the signals it receives with its own clear feedback mechanisms.[30*]

To get a sense for how this works, let's consider just one of a myriad quandaries the developing embryo needs to solve: how can it ensure that sufficient oxygen gets to all the different parts of its growing body? Every cell needs oxygen to function, which is supplied by blood vessels. However, as the embryo grows, a cell may find it's too far from a blood vessel to get the oxygen it requires. Here's how it responds. Each cell continually produces a 'low oxygen' protein that, at normal concentrations of oxygen, is quickly destroyed and recycled for parts. When oxygen is low, however, this protein remains stable long enough to enter the cell's nucleus and activate a few specific genes. Some of these genes specify new proteins that temporarily shut down oxygen-hungry tasks that would make the situation worse. Other genes specify a protein with a particular job: to cry for help. These 'Help me!' signaling proteins are sent out from the cell until they're noticed by cells in blood vessel walls, which respond by multiplying in the direction where they've picked up the strongest signal. When they meet other blood vessel cells, they join up to produce a network of capillaries. Once the original cell receives enough oxygen, it goes back to recycling its low oxygen proteins, until it once again finds it's been pushed too far from a capillary, when the process will begin again. Through this interchange of signaling and feedback loops, blood vessels don't need an accurate blueprint of the developing body to know where to grow. They just need to stay attuned to their community.[31]

Simple rules based on local conditions are the foundation of every system in the developing embryo, even those that are stunningly complex, such as the brain's neural network. In this case the embryo produces a large number of neurons – vastly more than it ultimately needs – all of which are committed to destroying themselves (called apoptosis) unless they receive certain survival factor proteins, which they can only get from other neurons. As a result, neurons that connect with plenty of neighbors stay alive, whereas those that formed in the wrong place or wandered in the wrong direction eventually kill themselves, recycling their components for the cells that were more successful.[32]

These ingenious finesses of self-organization enable a growing organism to adapt to changing conditions without some external intelligence telling it what to do. Despite all kinds of disruptions that might occur to the embryo, most of the time it will emerge flawlessly into the world. No matter whether the newborn grows into a dwarf or a giant, it will reliably have enough skin for its body, sufficient blood flow to oxygenate its tissues and ample networked neurons to be conscious.[33]

The deep learning of the ecosystem

As cells evolved into multicellular organisms, they continued to improve upon their negative entropy, consistent with Lotka's proposed Fourth Law of Thermodynamics. As a scaled-up fractal of the cells that comprise it, each organism is a purposive, persistent, dynamic pattern of energy flow, playing its part in the larger drama of life's rebellion against entropy. Like the individual cells in a growing embryo, there's no need for an organism to be conscious of its role in the grand scheme; it merely needs to perform its moment-to-moment striving to maintain, regenerate and reproduce itself. As it does so, each organism – along with its constituent parts – continually makes a series of tiny, self-organized decisions that accumulate into coherent animate intelligence, thus permitting the resilience, adaptability and ingenuity of living beings everywhere.

Consider a simple instance of nature, such as a blackbird making a nest in a tree. Suppose a severe storm damages the nest. The bird will inspect the damage, decide if it's bad enough to need fixing and, if so, fly around looking for the right material to repair it. If it doesn't find the perfectly sized twig, it will improvise with whatever's available. There are innumerable directions the bird might fly in, materials it discovers and distractions it encounters such as predators overhead or juicy worms below, but in the end it will most likely fulfill its purpose and repair the nest.[34]

Struck by the multifaceted ingenuity of life, biologists have tried to identify general principles arising from the way living entities function at all fractal scales. Their findings make for an interesting comparison with the norms of modern human society. One quality they've found, for example, which is often maligned in our society's drive for efficient production, is *redundancy*: there are frequently multiple ways to accomplish the same goal, whether it's getting blood flowing to a limb or finding twigs to repair a nest. This is one of the key factors leading to life's robustness, because if one pathway fails, another is usually available.[35]

Another principle is *conservatism*: once life has found something that works well, it reuses it continually in different situations. An example is a set of genes called the hox complex, first discovered in the fruit fly, which specifies how body segments should develop, such as whether an appendage should grow into a leg, wing or antenna. Biologists later discovered that similar hox complexes specify the structures of all other animals with bilateral bodies. Whether it's a fly, a human or an elephant, once nature hits upon a routine that works, it sticks to it.[36]

Conservatism, however, doesn't limit nature's flexibility. Another crucial aspect to its self-organization is *modularity*: allowing various populations of cells within an organism to do their thing without being hampered by what's going on elsewhere. Because of this, a harmful mutation or injury might impair one part of an animal, while allowing it to survive by relying on other abilities. Modularity also allows for *innovation*, as cells self-organize to arrive at new ways to solve a problem, while the rest of the organism remains stable. Innovation, however, can only succeed through close *coordination*: even within a cell, genes need to act together in networks to accommodate a new development and smooth out any hiccups that might occur.[37]

It seems like an implausible paradox: conservatism with innovation; cohesion with modularity; resilience with flexibility. These, however, are the naturally evolved characteristics observable in life at all scales. Some biologists, trying to encapsulate this phenomenon in one word, have proposed the concept of *evolvability*: the ability of organisms to adapt continually to changing environments, stabilize their new skills and adapt again when conditions require it. According to leading theorists, evolvability itself evolves.[38]

This leads to an important implication: evolution doesn't just happen, it gets better over time at what it does. It doesn't just evolve new adaptations, but continually improves its ability to do so. There's an everyday word we use for this phenomenon: learning. Evolution *learns*. This is not just a metaphor, but a deep reality of the living world.[39]

Think about how you learned something as a child, such as riding a bicycle. At first, your coordination didn't work so well, and you'd fall over. Every now and then, however, you'd remain stable for a while. As you did so, your muscles and nerves were learning a successful choreography of coordination. After enough practice, that choreography became second nature. Like a building block in your animate consciousness, it became an automatic and stable foundation for new behaviors. Your body had learned to ride a bicycle, and now you could learn to ride one-handed or talk with your friends while cycling. You can go years without riding, but once you get on a bike, that choreography will kick back into gear.

It was Canadian neuroscientist Donald Hebb who first discovered how nature performs this brilliant self-organized process. He found that when a network of neurons achieves a successful outcome, the nerves strengthen their connections, making it more likely that they'll come together in a similar configuration the next time. His discovery, known as Hebbian learning, was immortalized in the expression: 'Neurons that fire together wire together.'[40]*

Just as a particular configuration of billions of neurons in our brain can generate a thought as an integrated whole, so life has learned to integrate a vast assembly of successful behaviors into a complete organism. As described evocatively by embryologist Karl Ernst von Baer, living organisms – animals, plants, bacteria or fungi – can be understood as the thoughts of nature. Ever since life began, it has continually applied its thoughts for greater learning, etching its successes into the genomes of its organisms, then using those achievements as building blocks for its next adventure.[41]

This is why a mouse shares about a quarter of its gene sequences with bacteria, and over half with all other eukaryotes, such as fungi and plants. These shared gene sequences are the collective intelligence of nature, earned over billions of years of experience. Realizing this, computer programmers have begun to emulate nature's secret in their most advanced artificial intelligence designs: in 2016, when IBM's DeepMind beat the world champion of Go – considered the world's most complex board game – it used a similar process of 'freezing' each new layer of learning and building from it.[42]

The multilayered intelligence of evolution is manifested not just within an organism but throughout the interplay of an entire ecosystem. Ecological interactions between species that proved valuable in the past are retained within the genomes of those species – a complex, invisible matrix of behavioral interconnections linking the animate intelligence of each organism with the whole. As species hone their roles within the ecosystem's overall negentropy, they become increasingly dependent on each other in an intricate web of reciprocation. They engage in elaborate trade-offs with each other: like antelopes and giraffes grazing on a tree at different heights, as one species becomes expert at a particular kind of foraging, another focuses on a complementary niche. While each species behaves in its unique way, the ecosystem as a whole exhibits organized collective behavior, like a vast amorphous organism.[43]

Life metamorphoses into Gaia

The fractal intelligence of nature is found at every scale: cell, organism and ecosystem. If we scale up even further, we arrive at the entire holarchy of the living Earth, containing all other systems within it. Even in this largest of living systems the interconnected parts affect the whole while the totality of the Earth system influences the individual parts, in a process that hints at a planetary living intelligence.

In the 1960s a brilliant inventor named James Lovelock was hired by NASA to design instruments to detect whether there was life on Mars. Fascinated by the contrast between the Martian atmosphere and Earth's, he realized that the very make-up of our planet was the result of life's activity over billions of years. Earth, he appreciated, was not merely an inanimate sphere of rocks and gases on which life had taken up residence, but was itself a dynamic, self-regulated system tightly coupled with living processes. He called his realization the Gaia hypothesis after the Greek goddess of the Earth.[44]

An important part of the Gaia hypothesis is that living and non-living systems on Earth are so tightly linked that the separation between them becomes blurred. The oxygen we breathe, for example, is continually replenished by plants and algae as they metabolize the sun's energy. The rocks that shape our landscape are themselves the result of living processes that influenced their composition. As Lovelock put it, all Earth's organisms 'live with a world that is the breath and bones of their ancestors and that they are now sustaining'. Gaia is the emergent result of life and Earth evolving together, perpetually shaping and reshaping each other.[45]

Lovelock realized that this co-evolution of life and Earth generated beneficial self-regulatory feedback effects, as if Gaia were purposively tinkering with its own components to create optimal conditions for life. In the first two billion years of Earth's history, for example, sunlight flooded the planet with ultraviolet rays that rapidly degraded DNA. Life could only survive in the oceans, protected from lethal radiation. Eventually, in what's known as the Great Oxygenation Event, new species of bacteria emerged that photosynthesized sunlight more efficiently, generating oxygen as a by-product. As oxygen accumulated in the upper atmosphere, it converted into ozone, which shielded Earth from the deadly UV rays, allowing life to leave the oceans and colonize dry land. It was life that made the land habitable for life.[46*]

In collaboration with microbiologist Lynn Margulis, Lovelock began conceiving of Gaia as a kind of living entity. Once the Gaia hypothesis became widely discussed, it was, predictably, savagely attacked by mainstream biologists. The architects of the Modern Synthesis had neatly dispatched the messy problem of life's purpose – now here it was again, like a ghost returning from the grave. They critiqued the idea of Gaia's self-regulatory feedback effects by pointing to the several mass extinctions that have occurred over Earth's history, each of which had catastrophic effects on life's abundance and diversity.[47*]

However, the fact that Earth has undergone bouts of severe stress doesn't invalidate the Gaia hypothesis. As many of us can attest, it's in the nature of living organisms to suffer occasional diseases, which are sometimes life-threatening. When our bodies become ill, they usually react by reorganizing themselves, changing their internal temperatures, reducing energy expenditures and triggering immune responses. The fact that Gaia has done the same over its eons of existence only supports the conception of it as an organism.

Given that the defining characteristic of life is intrinsic, purposive self-organization, does that apply to Gaia? Over billions of years, as Lovelock pointed out, life extended its boundaries on Earth to incorporate elements that are otherwise inanimate, such as gases and rocks. In that sense, life itself has metamorphosed into Gaia. Sustained by life, Gaia's insides – like those of other living entities – are buzzing with meaning, brimming with organisms communicating with each other through sounds, smells, movements, chemical signals, electrical fields and countless other types of relationships. In this sense, the fractal genius of life truly extends from within each living cell to the global scale of Gaia. Life has continually repurposed its environment in its never-ending quest to resist entropy, and Gaia is the emergent result. When Indigenous cultures refer to Mother Earth, they are in touch with a deep truth about our planet that modern science is only just beginning to unravel.[48*]

Like life itself, Gaia demonstrates features of robustness, redundancy, diversity and modularity. Just as evolution literally learns, so Gaia has also learned over the eons. When its innovations went wrong, taking it to the bounds of habitability, it bounced back and reset its inner organization. When things worked out well, it wove a tight fabric of stabilizing feedback effects – such as the Amazon rainforest creating its own favorable weather conditions – resulting in long-term, resilient natural attractors. As Gaia learned how to weave the fabric of life, the complexity of its tapestry has become increasingly exquisite, the living systems within it interconnecting ever more intricately in their persistent struggle against entropy.[49]

Complexity, cooperation and civilization

Life's glorious triumph on Earth has been achieved, not just through increased complexity, but also increased cooperation. In fact, the two go hand in hand. When individuals cooperate, it allows them to specialize in what they do best, thus promoting diversity and greater complexity. Whether it was mitochondria partnering with eukaryotes, single cells combining to create multicellular organisms or insects collaborating to form colonies, the great phase transitions of life have all required massive upsurges in cooperation.[50]

Many researchers have pointed out that building cooperation doesn't come easily. A perennial problem for cooperating groups throughout the history of life – whether bacteria, organisms or communities of people – is the risk of free-riders: those that take advantage of the benefits of the group without making a fair contribution. If there are too many of them, they undermine the effectiveness of the group and may cause it to disintegrate. Genetic relatedness is one way evolution solved this problem: cells and organisms evolved to cooperate more closely with others that share their genes. But cooperation extends far beyond genetic affiliation.[51*]

Ultimately, the crucial success factor for cooperation at increasing levels of scale is *integration* – a state of unity with differentiation. In a fully integrated system, each part maintains its unique identity while operating in coordination with other parts of the system. To do so, the parts must remain in intimate feedback loops of communication with a large number of related parts. Each of the systems we've been looking at – cells, organisms, ecosystems and Gaia – is a paragon of this type of integration. In fact, integration is a defining characteristic of any purposive, self-organized entity.[52]

As life succeeded in integrating ever-larger systems, it kept improving its negentropy. Larger animals utilize energy more efficiently than smaller ones, and larger colonies of insects are more effective at staving off entropy than smaller ones. When Alfred Lotka proposed his Fourth Law of Thermodynamics, he incorporated human cultural evolution into his theory, and these ideas were further developed by anthropologist Leslie White, who portrayed the rise of human civilization as a series of enhancements in energy utilization. Agriculture, White explained, harnessed the negentropy of horses, cows and sheep, who spent their days consuming the sun's energy stored in plants, and then made it available to humans in the form of work, milk, wool and meat. Further technological advances allowed humans to exploit the energy of the natural world ever more efficiently.[53]

As with the other great phase transitions of life, underlying humanity's achievements in agriculture and technology was an increase in cooperation. Humans are by far the most cooperative of primate species, and this – more than any other factor – is the key to our species' success. As pre-humans evolved in bands of nomadic hunter-gatherers, they developed a sophisticated social intelligence, enabling them to collaborate closely with each other. Early hominids also faced the free-rider problem, and the characteristics they evolved to solve it became an intrinsic part of human nature: a powerful instinct for fairness, combined with a drive to punish those who flagrantly break the rules, even at one's own expense. Many of the qualities we prize in a person, such as compassion, generosity, honesty and altruism, are the results of our hunter-gatherer ancestors evolving the aptitude to collaborate successfully as a group.[54*]

Like earlier evolutionary transitions, enhanced cooperation in humans enabled greater specialization. Soon after the emergence of agriculture, cities appeared, replete with all kinds of specialists – artisans, healers, warriors and priests – who, by plying their unique trades, together formed the backbone of civilizations around the world. Like insect colonies, cities become more efficient at negentropy the bigger they get. With each doubling of population size, a city only needs about 85 percent more infrastructure, such as roads, water pipes, gas stations and grocery stores. In fact, a city can be understood as a form of superorganism, showing many of the self-organized characteristics that we've come to see in all living entities ranging from cells to ecosystems.[55]

The scale of human connectivity, of course, extends far beyond individual cities. In the modern era, with instant global connectivity through the internet, humans have woven a worldwide web like nothing Earth has seen in its entire existence. Does humanity's ascendancy represent the next step in life's continued evolution toward ever-greater complexity? Thoughtful observers of different stripes – scientists, philosophers and visionaries – answer with a strong affirmative. Evolution, they claim, has a direction. From bacteria to eukaryotes to multicelled organisms, from plants to reptiles and then to mammals, life, they argue, has a destiny that culminates inevitably in the emergence of creatures like us – possessing complex brains with the ability to become self-aware and perhaps ultimately direct our own future evolution toward even greater complexity.[56*]

It's an intoxicating vision for some. However, if we look more closely into this narrative, we find it contains elements that are not quite as triumphant as we might wish. It's a double-edged story – and those edges form the parameters of much that we'll explore later in this book.

Eligible for the Federation?

The idea of inevitable progress as a cosmic law traces its pedigree back to seventeenth-century Europe, but it was a twentieth-century visionary, theologian-cum-paleontologist Pierre Teilhard de Chardin, who gave it a scientific tincture, tying it in to modern evolutionary theory. Pointing to the increasing complexity of life, Teilhard triumphantly placed humanity at its apex. 'Life physically culminates in Man,' he wrote, 'just as energy physically culminates in life.' Teilhard saw this inevitable progression continuing toward what he called the Omega Point – the ultimate stage of evolution in

There are some who, appalled by our species' impact on the living Earth, consider humanity to be like a malignant cancer consuming Gaia. While this may be a fair depiction of our current civilization, it certainly need not hold true for humanity as a species. The rise of conceptual intelligence in humans has given us exceptional powers that can be used both beneficially and destructively. We've seen how humans experience a split consciousness with an 'I' that relates to a 'self'. Although the dominant culture has trained us to identify only with the 'I' of conceptual consciousness, we saw the possibility of developing an integrated relationship between 'I' and the 'self' – a democracy of consciousness that honors all aspects of human identity.

Similarly, humans have the potential to develop a far more integrated relationship with the rest of nature. Technology doesn't have to be used to destroy the complexity of living systems; if established on a different ethical basis, it could be developed to work in harmony with natural processes, promoting Gaia's overall negentropy.

Through the rest of this book, we'll explore what it means to live in a way that enhances life's deep purpose rather than working against it. We'll discover how, as a civilization, we have the potential to follow a path of integration that could lead to symbiotic flourishing for humanity and Gaia together – a path that just might lead, one day in the distant future, to being welcomed into the United Federation of Planets with open arms.

NEW THREADS OF MEANING

Life's deep purpose is to maintain and regenerate itself to make more life in an ongoing rebellion against the law of entropy

Every organism is a purposive, persistent, dynamic pattern of energy flow, playing its part in the larger drama of life's defiance of the law of entropy

Evolution is the process of life developing increasingly sophisticated ways to maximize the conversion of energy into negative entropy

Chapter Seven

THE TAO IN MY OWN NATURE

Blind and deaf from infancy, Helen Keller spent her early childhood 'at sea, in a dense fog', as she later described it. By the age of seven, her only friend, the daughter of her family's cook, had helped her develop a set of about sixty gestures she used to communicate her basic needs. But she had no clue about what language was, and virtually no conception of the world outside her sensory orbit. A new instructor, Anne Sullivan, tried spelling words out on Helen's hand, but since Helen had no idea what she was doing, this just got her frustrated. Then, one day, everything changed. While Helen was washing in the morning, Mrs Sullivan spelled out 'w-a-t-e-r' in her other hand. Later that day, while filling her mug with water, she spelled the word out again for Helen. In Mrs Sullivan's words:

> She dropped the mug and stood as one transfixed. A new light came into her face. She spelled 'water' several times. Then she dropped on the ground and asked for its name and pointed to the pump and the trellis and suddenly turning round she asked for my name. I spelled 'teacher.' All the way she was highly excited, and learned the name of every object she touched, so that in a few hours she had added thirty new words to her vocabulary. The next morning, she got up like a radiant fairy. She has flitted from object to object, asking the name of everything and kissing me for very gladness ... Everything must have a name now.[1]

Not only had Helen discovered language, in a flash of inspiration her mind had opened up to an entire universe of possibility.

Her face grew more expressive every day. In Helen's autobiography, she writes, 'The living word awakened my soul, gave it light, hope, set it free!' Helen went on to become a prolific author, lecturer, and an activist for women's suffrage and other progressive causes.[2]

What happened in Helen's mind at that wondrous moment? We've come across other examples of dramatic phase transitions in nature, when different parts of a system coalesce to emerge into a new coherence that couldn't previously have been imagined. As we've seen, the most glorious instance of emergence is life itself, which self-generated billions of years ago and has never looked back. The shining example of Helen Keller prompts a larger question: can we apply the principles of self-organization to our own human consciousness? If so, what would they tell us about ourselves?

While this is a relatively new question for modern scientists to ask, it's one that was self-evident to Neo-Confucian philosophers, who a thousand years ago recognized the patterns of the universe – the li – as the principle that connects all things. 'There is li in everything, and one must investigate li to the utmost,' proclaimed one sage. This applied as much to one's own mind as everything else in the physical world. In fact, some Neo-Confucians made no distinction. 'The universe is my mind, and my mind is the universe,' stated one. When their greatest philosopher, Zhu Xi, kicked off his program of *gewu* – the investigation of things – he did so with this intriguing declaration: 'If one wishes to know the reality of Tao, one must seek it in one's own nature.'[3]

We're going to follow the guidance of those Neo-Confucian sages in this chapter and explore the correspondences between the principles of the Tao and those of human consciousness. The full scope of the Tao is as vast and mysterious as the universe itself, but progress made by modern scientists in identifying key principles of self-organization in nature offers a window into some of those mysteries that would otherwise remain obscure. As Helen Keller's example suggests, the parallels are striking. We'll find that studying consciousness as the outcome of the same self-organized processes as the rest of nature overturns some of the cherished beliefs of mainstream theorists. The implications of this approach lead to insights, not just into ourselves but into the guiding principles of human culture, along with hints about what may be in store for our civilization.

Nature's self-organized intelligence

One of the most awe-inspiring sights in nature is the billowing, swirling dance in the sky when thousands of starlings flock together like a single fluid organism – known as a murmuration – swooping down, separating and rejoining, contracting and expanding, then unexpectedly shifting direction (Figure 4). Apart from its soul-stirring beauty, this natural phenomenon is remarkable for what scientists have learned about its self-organized dynamics. There is no lead starling directing how the rest of the flock should act. Instead, biologists have found that starlings – along with schools of fish in the ocean, swarms of insects and other flocking animals – are merely following a few simple rules of thumb, such as 'Don't get too close to your neighbors,' 'Adopt the same direction as those next to you' and 'Avoid becoming isolated.'[4]

Figure 4: A murmuration of starlings

We've seen how cells in the body of a growing fetus perform the miraculous job of creating a newborn baby by following their own simple rules in close feedback with their neighbors. Now, in the sky and oceans, we see again how complexity arises from self-organized behavior until it reaches a new level of elegant simplicity. There are a few basic ingredients common to virtually all these behaviors: you need a large number of individuals interacting with each other repeatedly; you need a certain amount of random fluctuation in how the individuals behave; there must be some kind of positive feedback loop, whereby actions become rapidly amplified throughout the system; and just as importantly, you need a form of negative feedback that sets in once the amplification reaches a certain point.[5]

Since the cells comprising all living entities follow these self-organized rules, it's not too surprising that they have permeated the behavior of virtually all organisms. Some of the most dramatic examples of intelligence arising from self-organized behavior can be seen in colonies of bees, ants and termites, which demonstrate such unified decision-making that they are frequently referred to as superorganisms.[6]

How does a bee colony decide where to make a new nest? Frequently, in the early summer a colony outgrows its hive and splits apart. The mother queen leads about half the worker bees into the unknown, leaving a daughter queen and the remaining workers to keep the old hive going. The new group coalesces in a cluster around a tree branch, sending hundreds of scouts to explore different possible sites. The scouts return before too long, and now the group must decide who found the best site. Amazingly, returning scouts perform what is known as a waggle dance, in which they advertise the location and features of their potential site. At first, there may be a dozen or so sites under serious consideration, but over several days some dancers drop out while others switch their allegiance, until a consensus is reached, whereupon the bees leave their staging post and move into their new home.[7]

Termites and ants have their own spectacular displays of group intelligence. Termites are known for building elaborate dwellings, some of them as high as nine meters, with pinnacles and chimneys. A massive ancient underground termite city was recently discovered in Brazil, with vast interconnected tunnel networks covering an area roughly the size of Great Britain. Termites construct these magnificent structures through their own simple rules. Each termite begins by randomly depositing soil pellets impregnated with pheromone (a type of signaling hormone). Other termites are drawn to the pheromone, leading to an amplification effect – but only if there are enough other termites around to keep amplifying the signal.[8]

Of all superorganisms, ants are probably the world champions. Their colonies are capable of stunning feats of coordinated intelligence. We generally think that agriculture was first invented by humans about 12,000 years ago, but leafcutter ants beat us to it by about twenty million years. These fungus-eating ants carry leaves back to their nests, where they process them in an elaborate series of steps, mincing the greenery into small pieces, then crushing it into a pulp. They use the pulp as a mulch in their underground gardens, 'planting' into it little tufts of fungus. As the fungus grows, they prune it and even apply pesticides, which they produce with the help of symbiotic bacteria. Just like human-domesticated crops, the leafcutters' fungus crop has evolved to depend completely on the ants and could not survive alone in the wild.[9]

In addition to cultivating fungus, ants farm aphids for their milk, protecting them from other predators. They also build cities and even empires spanning hundreds of miles, wage war with opposing colonies, capture slaves and perform stupendous feats of teamwork such as constructing bridges out of their own bodies. In spite of all these achievements, a single ant has a tiny brain with limited capabilities. Their intelligence emerges through their collective behavior. In the words of entomologist Lewis Thomas, a single ant is not much more than a 'ganglion on legs'. However, 'four ants together, or ten, encircling a dead moth on a path, begin to look more like an idea'. It's only when you see 'the dense mass of thousands of ants, crowded together around the Hill, blackening the ground, that you begin to see the whole beast, and now you observe it thinking, planning, calculating. It is an intelligence.'[10]

The (not so) Hard Problem

Thomas's depiction of a few ants beginning 'to look more like an idea' hints at how rules of self-organization that apply to the natural world might also pertain to the neurons in our own brains. Many social insect researchers, including the world's most distinguished entomologist, E. O. Wilson, have observed that the same set of principles that cause self-organized intelligence to arise in bees and ants also apply to the working of our own brains.[11]

Until very recently the idea that you could apply natural principles in order to understand consciousness has been peremptorily dismissed in Western philosophy. If you begin reading modern accounts of consciousness, it won't be long before you come across what's known as the Hard Problem of consciousness – a term coined in the early 1990s by philosopher David Chalmers. With enough diligent work, Chalmers argued, we might one day explain the various processes by which neurons in the brain form images, memories, language and even make decisions. That's the 'easy problem'. But, he claims, we will never be able to explain why all that neuronal activity *feels like* something. Earlier, we came across the concept of qualia: those subjective moment-to-moment experiences unique to our inner sanctum of consciousness: the redness of a red napkin on your lap; the particular taste in your mouth right now. The unique subjectivity of qualia, Chalmers asserted, is the Hard Problem that can never be explained.[12]

Chalmers' idea went viral in the field of consciousness studies, seeming to imply a special quality in consciousness that science can never elucidate, even in principle – a mysterious gap that no empirical fact or scientific discovery could ever bridge. However, leading neurobiologists who study the evolution of consciousness and its neural underpinnings have more recently dismissed the Hard Problem as just another manifestation of the dualism that has structured Western thought since the time of ancient Greece. As we've seen, the idea of a split human being, with an eternal soul imprisoned in a physical body, was first described by Plato and then adopted by Christianity. Descartes recast this dualism for the modern world by substituting 'mind' for 'soul'. Our bodies, he claimed, were simply mechanical contraptions, but the mind existed as an intangible essence utterly separate from the body. Chalmers, using more modern terminology, reprises the same dualistic split that has riven Western thought for millennia, preventing a truly integrated understanding of our nature.[13*]

From an evolutionary perspective, the gradual rise of subjectivity in consciousness is something we've already traced. It emerged, as William James put it, 'for the sake of steering a nervous system grown too complex to regulate itself'. There is no unbridgeable gulf between subjective experience and bodily functions. On the contrary, feelings arose from the crucial need of organisms to maintain homeostasis and have evolved to greater complexity ever since. Once we recognize there is no insurmountable Hard Problem, we can get on with the fascinating task of trying to understand how, indeed, all that neuronal activity does create the qualia of subjective experience. A few pioneering neuroscientists have dedicated careers to answering this question, and their findings are beginning to revolutionize their field.[14]

Enacting our own consciousness

There may be no Hard Problem, but that doesn't mean there's anything simple about how consciousness arises from embodied experience. The principles of self-organization might be similar to ants and bees, but the complexity of the human nervous system is greater by several orders of magnitude. An ant colony superorganism might contain millions of ants, but a single human brain consists of about eighty-six billion neurons. Like a solitary ant, a single neuron is not capable by itself of feeling sad or solving a problem, but it's the way in which billions of neurons connect that gives rise to the miracle of consciousness. Each neuron links through synapses to as many as a thousand other neurons, with the result that our nervous system contains over a hundred trillion interconnections.[15]

The staggering complexity of the brain's neural network arises not just from the sheer number of connections but the dynamic nature of their multilayered feedback loops. One of the most important features of neural self-organization is Hebb's rule: 'Neurons that fire together wire together.' An embryo's brain starts out with a mish-mash of neural connections, some of which turn out to be crucial, while others that are extraneous to healthy development die and get recycled. This process continues after birth. Behaviors that work, such as cooing, suckling, reaching or smiling, strengthen the synapses that generate them. As a child grows to adulthood, this continual synaptic reinforcement allows her to modify her neural pathways to develop the skills, language and behaviors of her particular culture.[16*]

The Hebbian form of neuronal self-organization leads to a powerful combination of reliability and flexibility – crucial principles of life's evolutionary success. The reliability arises because there are multiple redundant neural pathways that can lead to a similar outcome. The flexibility emerges from the fact that there is no fixed blueprint directing how a brain should work. Even the areas of the brain that seem most hard-wired exhibit amazing flexibility: someone born genetically deaf, for example, learns to use the auditory cortex to process visual information instead.[17]

The dynamic neural self-organization that generates consciousness results from continual interaction between a person and their environment – both the internal environment of bodily experiences and the external environment of people and events. Consciousness is not something that happens to us; it's something that we enact through our own participation in life. And it doesn't happen solely within our own nervous system; it's an ongoing activity emerging through our engagement with the world. Do you remember how Neo-Confucian sages observed that the connections between things are frequently more important than the things themselves – something revalidated by modern systems theory? The phenomenon of consciousness is – perhaps second only to life itself – the most powerful testament to validate this profound insight.[18]

A crystal in a trillion dimensions

The stunning number of neural connections and their continual feedback loops are two necessary ingredients of consciousness. But the particular ways in which neurons connect with each other are equally important in the formation of consciousness. The same properties of self-organized networks that characterize all living systems, from cells to entire ecosystems, are also the hallmark of neural networks.

To begin with, neurons organize themselves through hubs and spokes, leading to the small-world property we've encountered elsewhere. There are a vast number of tight interconnections within particular regions, with fewer – but crucially important – connections linking different regions with each other. Neurons are also organized fractally, so their patterns of connection look similar at different scales. This is true not only for their organization at a given moment in time, but also for how they connect over time.[19*]

Another crucial characteristic of how neurons connect is *integration* – a concept that is fundamental to life and equally essential for consciousness. Imagine a spectrum of different modes of connection. At one extreme there are random connections, such as particles of steam bumping into each other without leading to meaningful outcomes. At the other extreme consider the rigid connections of a block of ice. Everything is tightly linked, but it's so fixed that it's not going to lead to anything interesting. When a network is integrated, it exists somewhere between these two extremes: more cohesive than the random steam particles, but more flexible than the block of ice.[20]

It is the ability of the nervous system to be both modular and unified at the same time that allows it to create a moment of consciousness – one of those distinctive subjective qualia. On a timescale of a fraction of a second, multiple clusters of different neural groups come together from all over the brain to form what has been called a 'dynamic core of consciousness'. A fraction of a second later, some connected neurons part company, while others link up to generate the next moment in the stream of consciousness that we all experience. Consciousness, therefore, is not a thing, nor does it exist in a fixed location in the brain, but is an ongoing process of continual linkage and differentiation through billions of interconnecting pathways. The dynamic core is never exactly the same, but from one moment to another there is enough consistency in its repertoire for it to feel like a smooth flow.[21]

One of the neuroscientists to first describe the dynamic core was Giulio Tononi, who has since developed a full-fledged theory of consciousness called Integrated Information Theory. Specifically, he defines the quantity of consciousness experienced in a system as the amount of information arising from integration, above and beyond the information maintained separately in the system's parts.[22*]

Tononi's theory leads to some intriguing implications. One is that consciousness can, in principle, be quantified if you could measure the information flows. His model has already been used, with encouraging results, to ascertain through neuroimaging whether unresponsive patients are truly unconscious or 'locked in' and simply unable to express themselves. Another implication is that consciousness is substrate independent: any system that integrates information has a certain amount of consciousness, which could theoretically be measured. This in turn leads to a provocative assertion: since even the protons, neutrons and quarks within an atom constitute an integrated system, however infinitesimal, this would mean that all matter is conscious to some degree. Tononi's claim – coming from one of the leading neuroscientists in the field – is known more generally as panpsychism, and is noteworthy for how profoundly it corroborates the view shared by Indigenous traditions across the world of the intrinsic consciousness of everything in the universe.[23*]

Some people, viewing consciousness as something sacred, might object to the idea that it could theoretically be measured through scientific instruments. My personal opinion is that, rather than diminishing the sacred quality of consciousness, it opens a pathway that bridges the sacred and the scientific. In modern *gewu*, as in Neo-Confucianism – and in contrast to Western dualism – there is no inherent distinction between the spiritual and the material. It's the miraculous ways in which the material world self-organizes that create the conditions for all that is sacred and meaningful in the universe.

In fact, Tononi's theory presents a view of consciousness that is breathtaking in its beauty. Imagine a two-dimensional graph showing a set of connections between different points, shaped like a multifaceted diamond. Now add a dimension with more connections, so the diamond becomes 3D. In Tononi's model, each neuronal connection adds another dimension to the image, so that a single moment of consciousness, if it could be mapped in what he calls qualia space, would be like a multifaceted crystal in a trillion dimensions. Then, imagine this dazzling gem morphing a split second later into another shape, then yet another. This is the miracle of your consciousness. It might feel daunting to try to conceptualize this marvel, but you don't need to. All you need to do is close your eyes for a moment and experience it within yourself.[24]

Attractors of consciousness

Let's ponder for a moment that image of a constantly morphing, multifaceted shape, never exactly the same from one second to another, yet maintaining a reliable coherence, an overall stability. Does it remind you of another crucial feature of self-organized systems we've encountered before? In Chapter 4 we came across natural attractors – systems like candle flames or river eddies, with dynamic patterns that are never fixed yet remain within certain boundaries. As the *I Ching* described them, their 'Tao is forever changing – alteration, moving without rest'.[25]

As we explore the Tao within our own nature, we can contemplate the activity of our own minds as attractors of consciousness continually ebbing and flowing within us. If they're like other natural attractors, they should exhibit fractal patterns and remain relatively stable, yet occasionally undergo phase transitions where they shift into a new state, sometimes temporarily, sometimes moving into newly emergent territory. If you're anything like me, this probably describes how your own mind works. We tend to experience a stream of fleeting qualia, flavored with a complex mélange of feelings and thoughts, which can shift in a moment to something else – much like a murmuration of starlings. Then, we might come back to what we were thinking about earlier. The everyday words we use to describe our inner experience capture these fractal patterns: momentary *sensations* may cohere into a particular *feeling* which, if it stays around, becomes a *mood*. Later in the day, something may happen to shift that mood, or possibly deepen it until it becomes a *state of mind* that might turn into a new relatively stable attractor. Our momentary thoughts can cohere into *ideas*, which over time might congeal into *attitudes* or *beliefs*.[26*]

The deeper we look into the principles directing our own nature, the more commonality we find with the universal Tao. Let's go back to those paragons of collective intelligence, ants.

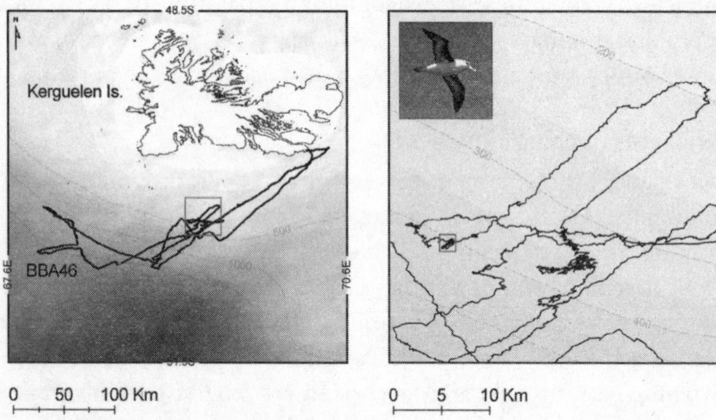

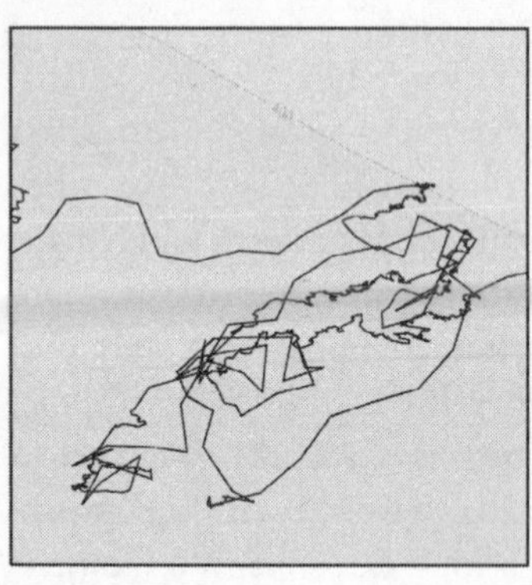

Figure 5: A Lévy flight path of an albatross in the Southern Indian Ocean, at three different scales (note the fractal similarity at each scale)

Ants aren't always following each other's pheromones, bringing food back to the colony. Sometimes an ant will wander alone in a seemingly random pattern, turning right, then left, then taking a long loop, pausing, then turning again. It may seem random, but scientists analyzing these movements have discovered that they follow a particular fractal pattern known as a Lévy flight, which has been demonstrated mathematically to optimize foraging success when the prey is scarce and randomly distributed. It's not just ants that follow this pattern. It's been identified in flies, birds, jellyfish and sharks – virtually every creature in fact that searches for prey without a preordained roadmap (Figure 5). It's even been discovered that 'killer' T-cells in our bloodstream follow a Lévy flight path looking for unwanted invaders.[27]

Is there a state of mind you recognize in yourself that seems to follow a Lévy flight path, looping in seemingly random directions, going hither and yon, sometimes taking short detours, sometimes getting stuck in long diversions before coming back to where you began? It's known of course as mind-wandering, and if you recognize this kind of behavior in yourself, you're not alone. Everyone does it. By some estimates, we spend about a quarter of our waking life mind-wandering. Neuroscientists have identified a particular attractor of neural connections in the brain that is activated during mind-wandering, called the default mode network. Humans aren't the only creatures who default to this attractor: scientists have discovered that even rat brains possess a similar network.[28]

Mind-wandering doesn't have a good reputation. People learning to meditate, for example, find themselves hijacked by what is known as 'monkey mind' as they try to stay focused on their breath. Studies have shown that people are generally less happy when they're mind-wandering, and bad moods seem to bring it on even more. However, given that the evolutionary branches of humans and rats diverged about sixty million years ago, and yet both species utilize a default mode network, there must be something important this type of neural Lévy flight path does for us. What could it be?[29]

It might be helpful to think of our default mode network as a *salience seeker*: exploring neural pathways to seek out what's important, it pounces on what's salient and raises it to conscious attention so we can mull it over. When you let your mind wander, it will tend to settle on whatever feels important at that moment. It could be trying to remember if you locked the car, wondering about the results of a medical test you took the other day or reflecting on a new relationship you're in. It might feel like random mind-wandering, but just like the ants seeking a food source, you can think of it as your consciousness pursuing its own fractal Lévy path, searching for salience.[30*]

Laying down a path in walking

Sometimes, we don't need to search for what's salient – instead, salience swoops in and strikes us when we're least expecting it. Think back to the last time you lost your temper. Frequently, this will happen unexpectedly, but when we reflect on it later, we realize that the issue had been steadily building up until something – seemingly insignificant in itself – broke the dam. Similar to the amplification effect of termites leaving pheromones on a mound until it becomes a tower, something might keep bothering us below the level of consciousness, until it accumulates enough neural pathways to break our composure. This experience can be characterized as a phase transition: an avalanche of consciousness, which might be quite rare but – consistent with power law principles – when it happens, it can feel seismic.[31]

Just like phase transitions in the natural world, these breaches in attractors of consciousness aren't always bad. As Helen Keller experienced, they can be moments of emergence, when a series of seemingly unrelated events come together in our mind to form a larger network of meaning. We've all had that creative 'Aha!' moment when, out of the blue, something suddenly makes sense. Neuroscientist Scott Kelso has studied how babies have a eureka-like moment when they first discover they have agency: lying in a cradle with a mobile attached to their foot by a string, they suddenly realize they can turn the mobile by kicking, and delightedly they convert what had been a spontaneous movement into something intentional. Now, they merrily move their foot and watch the mobile turn around.[32]

As infants grow older, they discover they have a separate identity from those around them and begin to develop a sense of self which, as discussed earlier, eventually leads to the bifurcation of 'I' and the 'self'. This split human experience can be understood as a bifurcation of attractors in human consciousness: two separate neural networks that form their own distinctive neural pathways, deeply connected but each maintaining its own characteristic patterning.

While the split between 'I' and the 'self' is the cause of much internal suffering, it also gives us the gift of intentionality. At any point we can set an intention to change the direction we want our lives to take. Although the brains of all creatures are in a continual state of making changes to themselves, humans have the possibly unique opportunity to consciously redirect our own neural patterns. When we formulate an intention, this is equivalent to modifying the landscape within our attractors of consciousness. In a real landscape, if the rainfall tends to collect in an area that occasionally floods the basement, we might construct a berm to divert the water away from our house. Similarly, in the landscape of consciousness, a deliberate intention can redirect neural pathways from a harmful attractor into a beneficial one.[33]

As we've seen, a hallmark of living systems is reciprocal causality: interacting parts create the system, while the system as a whole affects how the parts interact. With intentionality, humans can take reciprocal causality to a new level. We can choose to reshape our attractors of consciousness for beneficial effect. At first, it might seem like an uphill struggle. How many times have you seen a New Year's resolution dissipate halfway through January? But this is where Hebbian reinforcement can play a helpful role. Once we've set a deep intention to reshape our behavior, we can help it along by changing our regular habits in ways that support the new intention.[34]

To see how this can work, imagine a field of high grass with a pathway where the vegetation has been trampled down by people habitually walking in the same direction. If you no longer want to follow this trail, it will be difficult at first to find your way through the vegetation, but after a couple of rough journeys you'll notice that you've started to flatten the grass, and each ensuing journey on the new path gets a little easier. After a while, the new path becomes as easy to follow as the original one – maybe even easier if you haven't traversed the old one in a while. Poet Antonio Machado memorably captured this profound insight, when he wrote:

> Wanderer, the road is your
> footsteps, nothing else;
> wanderer, there is no path,
> you lay down a path in walking.[35]

Through intention, we can literally sculpt the shape of our own attractors of consciousness. The importance of this process is highlighted when we consider the fractal nature of consciousness, by which momentary streams of qualia can coalesce into moods and then into states of mind. Over time, certain states of mind become more powerful attractors than others. As years go by, we realize that those dominant states have become the defining features of our personality. Ultimately, the person we become, along with the quality of our lifelong inner experience, is determined by the fractal layers of neural patterns that, moment to moment, form our attractors of consciousness.

Cultural attractors and archetypes

While intention gives us some control over the patterns of our own consciousness, it's important to recognize the tremendous power culture exerts over the general shape of our neural attractors as we grow through infancy into adolescence and beyond.

In a process known as deep enculturation, the values and beliefs a person holds about the world are formed in their early years by the patterns of meaning molded into their neural pathways by their culture. Some of these structures of thought might be taught explicitly, but the deepest ones are embedded implicitly into the child's mind as she learns to become a part of her society. Over time, the child naturally adopts her culture's worldview – a comprehensive set of assumptions and precepts about how the world works, what's right and wrong, and how you should live. As discussed in the Introduction, a worldview is usually ingrained so deeply that it tends be unconscious, which further increases its power to influence the ways in which a person thinks and acts.[36*]

Deep enculturation is a defining characteristic of the human experience. In fact, as anthropologist Joseph Henrich has pointed out, it's the primary reason why humanity has achieved dominance over other species. The shared knowledge earned by communities through trial and error, accumulating over generations, creates a collective intelligence far beyond the capabilities of even the most brilliant single mind. In a process like Hebbian learning, culture is forged by self-reinforcing, stable patterns of social norms, strengthening successful behaviors while discarding failed ones.[37*]

While we may think of ourselves as very different from ants and bees, there are deep similarities between the collective intelligence of insect colonies and human societies. A famous experiment conducted by psychologist Stanley Milgram illustrates one aspect of this. On a busy New York street, he had someone stand and look up as though something interesting was going on, and counted how many others stopped to look in the same direction. Like ants' pheromones, the power of collective salience is cumulative. A single person's gaze will trigger 40 percent of passers-by to stop and look in the same direction; five people gazing will cause 80 percent to stop and look; while fifteen gazers brings the number to 90 percent.[38]

No wonder some people suggest we should think of humanity itself as a form of superorganism. Cities – as we saw in the last chapter – exhibit similar characteristics to organisms, and the rise of the internet now permits ideas to flow rapidly around the world with far greater velocity and broader reach than ever before. We've all seen the dramatic way an idea, expression or hashtag can go viral at breathtaking speed, sometimes with the potential to transform popular notions in much the same way that a murmuration of starlings suddenly and spontaneously changes direction.[39]

The word that's frequently used for the ideas, big and small, that embed themselves in our collective cognition is meme. It was coined by Richard Dawkins in *The Selfish Gene*, and has since become a powerful meme in its own right. Dawkins proposed that, in addition to selfish DNA molecules replicating themselves, 'a new kind of replicator has recently emerged on this very planet' – the meme. His conception of the meme was like a virus that parasitizes the human brain, 'turning it into a vehicle for the meme's propagation'. Chillingly, he suggested that, just as we are mere 'gene machines' for the propagation of DNA, our minds are 'meme machines' for the propagation of memes. His idea became so popular that it spawned a quasi-academic field known as memetics in which people study the dynamics of meme dispersal.[40]

I believe, however, that Dawkins' conception of the meme is

as misguided as the notion of the selfish gene and for the same underlying reason: just as the selfish gene was based on a flawed mechanistic conception of life, so the meme is based on an equally erroneous mechanistic conception of culture and consciousness. The meme is conceived as a fixed building block of culture passed horizontally from one person to the next, and vertically through generations. The mechanistic character of the meme metaphor unnecessarily simplifies the process of cultural change and prevents a deeper understanding of what happens in the transmittal of collective ideas.[41]

Instead of the meme, I suggest a more valuable way to approach the study of cultural transmission is the notion of a *cultural attractor*. We've seen how, in an individual mind, attractors of consciousness form dynamic patterns, never exactly the same but often maintaining resilient organized flows that, in some cases, can last a lifetime. In much the same way, cultural attractors arise and maintain themselves according to dynamic patterns in the collective consciousness of a culture. Cultural attractors are never completely fixed, but some, like healthy ecologies, show remarkable resilience over generations, and in some cases – such as worldviews or religions – can maintain their characteristic identity over millennia.[42]

A cultural attractor is never exactly the same in the minds of two different people. There may be a great deal of similarity in the ways a cultural attractor is expressed, but each person has their own unique way of perceiving it. For example, the #MeToo hashtag has powerfully influenced global culture in recent years, and is generally understood as a refusal to accept the continued sexual abuse by men of their social and financial power over women, but each person who uses it has their own unique interpretation of its meaning, even while they might share the general parameters.[43*]

The longest lasting of all cultural attractors, going back to the dawn of culture itself, are *archetypes*. Archetypes may be understood as shared patterns of human behavior that are deeply meaningful and universal to the human experience, but manifesting uniquely for each person in each new generation. Examples of archetypes might be the Nurturing Mother, the Hero's Journey, the Trickster, the Lover and the Wise Elder. When Carl Jung initiated the serious study of archetypes in the early twentieth century, he described them as phenomena of a 'collective unconscious'. Jung's writings were at first highly influential. However, he believed that archetypes were inherited biologically, and the lack of any empirical demonstration of how that could happen led to his ideas being neglected by much of mainstream psychology.[44]

If, however, we recognize archetypes as deep cultural attractors, it becomes immediately apparent how they are transmitted through the generations. By understanding a mind, not as a separate island of consciousness, but as a process arising from the brain's patterns of interaction with the environment, we could in principle trace how a particular archetypal pattern of behavior ripples through the millennia, constantly being reinterpreted by each new generation, even while the broad parameters of the pattern maintain long-term resilience as a result of their persistent salience in human consciousness.[45]

Given that consciousness is embodied, and that conceptual and animate consciousness are deeply intertwined, we can extend our understanding of archetypes further back in time, even to before the emergence of human culture. Animate consciousness is, after all, shared in one form or another by all living entities. The primal experiences of nature are available to us too, once we open ourselves to receiving them. As philosopher Andreas Weber describes, there are 'ur-phenomena of feeling' which are 'immediately understood by all beings without explication or translation', such as the anticipatory rustle of trees indicating an approaching thunderstorm, or the death cry of an animal expressing its desperate craving for life. These are examples of the myriad unfathomable archetypes that we share with the rest of nature.[46]

The recognition of archetypes as patterns of behavior resonating through the ages allows us to appreciate our common lineage with the distant past of humanity, and at an even deeper level to realize our fundamental connectedness with all of nature.

The Adaptive Cycle

While archetypes have remained with us, in one form or another, from time immemorial, other types of cultural attractors exhibit the hallmark of self-organized systems: they remain stable for a certain period and then undergo dramatic phase transitions before settling into a newly stable state. Like attractors of consciousness, the time scales of shifts in cultural attractors exhibit a fractal quality. There are short-lived *fads* such as the notorious Ice Bucket Challenge, which swept the world one summer, featuring celebrities dumping a bucket of ice water over someone's head to raise money for charity. Longer-lasting fads may develop into *trends*, such as clothing fashions or particular cultural styles. Extending to longer time scales are complexes of values and behaviors that define a *generation*, such as the counter-culture movement of the 1960s, or the cultural identity of millennials. Spanning multiple decades are *eras* that may be defined by a dominant political or economic ideology. The era, for example, from World War II to the 1970s was characterized by an uneasy balance between government and private enterprise, whereas the era since then has been dominated by the rise of the neoliberal, free-market ideology. Then there are the grandest cycles of all: the rare but momentous shifts in a dominant *worldview* that can transform the beliefs, practices and daily lives of entire populations for multiple generations.

Cultural transformations may be expected to follow the same underlying principles as those in other self-organized, adaptive systems. An interdisciplinary group of hundreds of scientists, believing this is the case, spent decades developing what they call the Adaptive Cycle model of change, which applies to all kinds of complex systems, from a tiny cell to a vast ecosystem, which can extend back in time to explain evolutionary change, and which is equally applicable to human systems, such as markets, industries – and, yes, even worldviews.[47]

As a rule, every complex system passes through a life cycle consisting of four phases (Figure 6). It begins with a rapid *growth phase*, where innovative strategies can exploit new opportunities – think of entrepreneurs developing new products or businesses targeting new markets. Over time, the system settles into a more stable *conservation phase*, characterized by established rules and relationships that gradually become increasingly brittle and resistant to change. At some point, a tipping point causes a phase transition, known

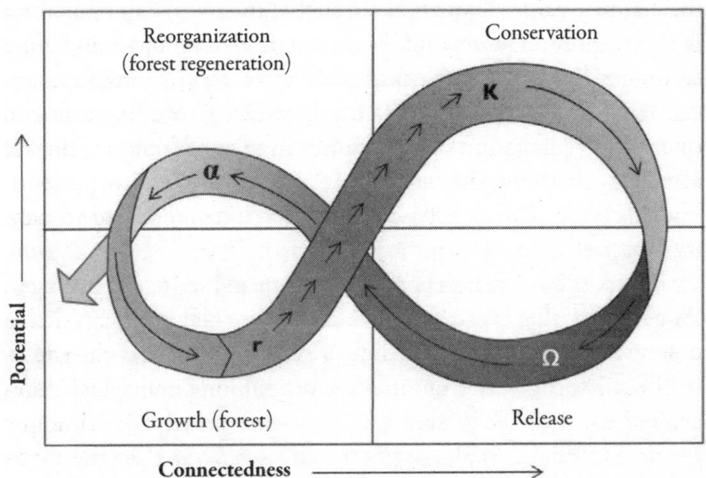

6: The Adaptive Cycle model of change

as the *release phase*. Think of lightning igniting a forest fire or a sudden market crash. This is followed by a *reorganization phase*, when the future of the system is up for grabs. In this period, which can feel chaotic, new ideas or charismatic individuals can have an outsize impact on how the system will look as it prepares to enter the growth phase of its new cycle.[48]

There are many reasons to believe that our current global system is reaching the end of its conservation phase and entering the release phase. What will our civilization's phase transition look like? The exponential rise in the speed and pervasiveness of technological change is tearing apart norms that have been entrenched for centuries, potentially leading us to a world dominated by technocrat-controlled artificial intelligence. Meanwhile, the unremitting devastation of the natural world caused by ceaseless economic growth is threatening a collapse of civilization as we know it, not just as a result of climate disruption but also massive ecological degradation.[49]

While this is a terrifying prospect, the unraveling of the current system brings with it a glimmer of hope. This is the time when new ideas can have an outsize impact. After centuries of dominance, the mechanistic worldview that has brought humanity to this precipice is also beginning to unwind. There is a possibility of a flourishing future for humanity that could avoid the extremes of collapse on one hand or a techno-dystopia on the other. However, getting to that future will require a phase transition of our dominant cultural attractor: replacing the mainstream mechanistic worldview with one that is life-affirming, based on the deep recognition of humanity's interrelatedness with the living Earth.[50]

The past two chapters have framed an answer to the question, 'What am I?' that overturns much conventional thinking. As living organisms, we are fractal eddies of self-organization, participating in one form or another in life's four-billion-year-old rebellion against entropy. We've seen how the same principles that apply to the natural world also apply to our own nature, as well as the culture in which we're embedded. What does this mean for how we might live? Can we use these principles to learn how to experience sustained well-being for ourselves? To construct a coherent and comprehensive set of ethical values? Perhaps even to integrate human activity with the flourishing of the living Earth? These are the crucial questions to which we'll now turn.

NEW THREADS OF MEANING

The principles that apply to complex, self-organized systems in the natural world also apply to our own nature and to human culture

Consciousness is something we enact as a continual process of linkage and differentiation through billions of interconnecting neural pathways

As humans, we have the power to reshape our own attractors of consciousness through intention

WHAT AM I?

As part of life, I am an integrated, dynamic flow of negative entropy, following the same general principles as the rest of the natural world

Part Four

HOW SHOULD I LIVE?

Chapter Eight

FLOURISHING AS AN INTEGRATED ORGANISM

A long time ago in the district of Song lived a farmer. His wife and sons worried about him because he was not, as they say, the sharpest tool in the shed. The farmer was concerned that his shoots of grain weren't growing fast enough, so one day he decided to help them by pulling them up. He returned home to his family that evening, and announced, 'I am worn out today, because I've been helping my grain to grow.' His sons rushed frantically out to the fields, and sure enough there was the grain, dead and shriveled on the ground.

This rather droll story was told by Mencius, one of the greatest early Chinese sages. He used it to make a point about how a person should cultivate their own inner shoots: someone might want to develop themselves in a particular area, but it can only happen at a certain pace. 'You must put some work into it,' Mencius explained, 'but not force it.'[1]

Mencius loved to use the plant analogy to teach his philosophy of life. In the agrarian civilization of ancient China this was a powerful way to get people to understand how to cultivate qualities within themselves. 'If people want to grow a *tong* or *zi* tree one or two spans thick, everyone knows how to go about nourishing it,' he declared. 'When it comes to the self, though, no one knows how to nourish it. Is it because people love a *tong* or *zi* tree more than themselves? No, it is because they don't give the slightest thought to it.'[2]

This analogy has powerful implications. It leads us to realize that the way we develop is profoundly affected by the conditions in which we grow. Mencius described how some eras produce predominantly virtuous people, while others engender more wicked behavior, pointing out that the contrast is not due to differences in people's true nature, but how their qualities are cultivated. If you sow a field with barley, he said, the variation in the resulting produce will be affected by factors like the soil's nutrients, how it was irrigated and how diligently it was weeded. Why, he asked, should humans be any exception to this rule of nature?[3]

Given the striking similarities between principles that govern human nature and those that direct the growth and flourishing of the natural world, what can we learn about human flourishing by applying Mencius's metaphor of cultivation? How can we get the shoots within ourselves to grow healthily into bountiful produce? As we investigate this question, we'll come face to face with forces in the modern world that not only impair our flourishing but actively work against it – and we'll consider what we can do, both individually and as a society, to mitigate them and nourish a life of well-being both for ourselves and all those around us.

Health in harmony

When traditional Chinese thinkers contemplated how to achieve healthy flourishing, a crucial concept was *harmony*. As we've seen, harmony is an intrinsic quality of life itself, incorporating both competition and cooperation. Chinese philosophers understood clearly that harmony doesn't just mean agreement. One sage distinguished between harmony and uniformity with the analogy of cooking a stew. To prepare a tasty fish stew, he explained, you make a broth with water, vinegar, pickles, plums and salt. If you harmonize the flavors well, a new taste emerges that is richer than the sum of the parts. By contrast, simply making things uniform would be like trying to flavor the water with more water.[4]

Harmony, then, arises when you successfully blend contrasting elements within a system to create something greater. Sages extended this concept to a person's emotions. Rather than trying to transcend difficult feelings, they taught that a person experienced well-being when their emotions arose harmoniously 'in due measure and degree' – just like the flavors in a delicious stew. Even the most painful emotions, such as grief arising from bereavement, could be welcomed and infused into the fullness of experience. 'There is harmony in sorrow,' declared philosopher Wang Yangming. What matters is to feel the emotion to the right degree, neither to suppress nor overindulge in it. 'The excess of emotion,' he explained, 'is not harmony.'[5]

Traditional Chinese medicine was based on a similar foundation. The Chinese understood the energy-matter of the universe, qi, to be in a state of continual flow according to cycles of yin and yang, and they applied these principles to a person's internal makeup. When someone was sick, this meant that their yin and yang aspects were out of balance. The physician's challenge was to recognize the source of the imbalance and restore harmony to the individual. This would usually be done through a combination of practices such as acupuncture, medicinal herbs and adjusting the person's food, environment and activities.[6]

This integrative approach to health was not unique to China. On the other side of the Himalayas a remarkably similar system developed in India, known as Ayurvedic medicine. There, physicians focused on three different forms of energy, called *doshas*, that could go out of balance. Once again, they used a combination of different modalities to treat a patient, with the goal of bringing their *doshas* back into harmony. Neither the Chinese nor Indian system saw a separation between the physical, mental and spiritual health of a person. It was understood that each aspect of a person and their environment needed to be in balance for them to thrive as an integrated organism.[7]

How different from the mainstream Western approach to medicine! Building on the reductionist model of nature promoted by Descartes and Bacon, scientists gained an ever-greater understanding of the microscopic universe unseen to the naked eye, leading to what is known as the germ theory of disease, proposed in the nineteenth century by scientists such as Louis Pasteur. The consequent improvement in public health and the development of antibiotics and other drugs is one of the crowning achievements of Western civilization. But, as in other areas of scientific accomplishment, the triumph of the reductionist model has led to severe imbalances that now undermine much of its success.[8]

Nowadays, most diseases that afflict us are complex, chronic problems such as heart disease, cancer and diabetes. However, our medical infrastructure is still based on the reductionist model developed primarily to fight infections. Doctors are trained to combat the disease rather than treat the patient. Studies of doctor–patient interactions show that doctors will change the subject as soon as patients bring up their emotions, and on average they interrupt the patient's initial statement after just twenty-three seconds. Many doctors scoff at traditional Chinese or Ayurvedic approaches to disease, and at best view them as 'alternative' treatments to resort to only if conventional treatments have failed.[9]

A number of leading medical researchers, though, are turning to Chinese and Ayurvedic traditions as inspiration for what has become known as integrative medicine. Back in 1948, the World Health Organization defined health as 'a state of complete physical, mental and social well-being and not merely the absence of disease or infirmity'. While this definition was virtually ignored by the medical establishment in the ensuing decades, it is now becoming increasingly accepted as the basis for health policy. Pioneering researchers are drawing connections between the Chinese and Ayurvedic view of health and the systems view of life that we've been investigating.[10]

Integrative medicine views the body as an ecosystem containing diversified microbial hosts, rather than a battleground where pathogens are fought to the death. As in Chinese and Ayurvedic models, health is understood not as a fixed endpoint, but an ongoing process, a harmonious balancing of different forces within an integrated organism. Health, like consciousness, is a natural attractor – never fixed but continuously following resilient, dynamic flows within certain parameters.[11]

In fact, researchers are increasingly applying principles of complex systems to assess human health. It turns out that a healthy heartbeat and healthy breathing patterns demonstrate fractal properties, which tend to break down with aging and disease. Cancer is increasingly being studied as a disruption of the self-organized behavior of cellular networks. Along with physical health, mental health can also be understood in terms of integration: a study of neural networks in the brain shows that integrative small-world connective properties are lost in cases of schizophrenia and Alzheimer's disease. In one fascinating study researchers converted brain scans into music and were able to identify more erratic fluctuations in the 'music' of schizophrenic patients than in healthy volunteers.[12]

The human mind–body organism

Imagine discovering a treatment that reliably improves symptoms by between 25 and 50 percent across a wide variety of serious diseases affecting hundreds of millions of patients worldwide, with no adverse side-effects and costing almost nothing to produce. You might think you have a blockbuster on your hands, but don't rush to the patent office. Such a treatment does exist, but thankfully it can't be patented. It's called the placebo effect.[13]

Placebos can significantly reduce pain, improve symptoms of asthma and irritable bowel syndrome (IBS), activate the immune system and enhance motor coordination in Parkinson's patients, among other accomplishments. Astonishingly, placebos can work even if patients know they're not the 'real thing'. In one trial IBS sufferers were given inert drugs in bottles labeled PLACEBO PILLS, and still reported twice as much symptom relief as the group that received no treatment. How do they do it?[14]

Placebos work through both changing a patient's experience of their symptoms and, remarkably, alleviating the symptoms themselves. They do this primarily through the body's autonomic nervous system, which regulates functions such as blood pressure, gastric motility and pulmonary action. Another way of putting it is that placebos are the work of our body's animate intelligence – our ancient mammalian systems that evolved over hundreds of millions of years. One researcher has called this deep intelligence our 'health governor' and has shown that we share it with other mammals. For example, if a hamster is injected with bacteria that make it sick, it will launch a full-blown immune response during the summer, when it can rely on access to more nutrition, but maintains a low-level response in the winter, when it has to be more careful about resources.[15]

Placebos demonstrate clearly what Chinese and Ayurvedic medicine take for granted but has been mostly ignored by Western medicine: there is no essential separation between mind and body in the integrated human organism. The placebo acts like a bridge between a person's conceptual and animate consciousness. It works when a patient attributes a particular meaning to an intervention and channels the significance through his animate intelligence, which reacts accordingly. For this reason, some researchers suggest we should replace the word placebo with the term therapeutic meaning response, to more accurately describe how mind, body and culture interact in healing.[16]

While placebos offer the most striking evidence of how the mind affects the body, they're certainly not the only way. In fact, the impact our mindset has on the body may be one of the most significant factors in leading a long and healthy life. It's been estimated, for example, that 90 percent of heart disease cases could be prevented by changes in lifestyle and attitude. While we're all aware of the effect diet and exercise have on our bodies, what is less well known is how powerfully emotional states impact our health. If you have a good network of friends, that in itself can be a lifesaver: one study showed that adults with more social connections were half as likely to die from disease over a nine-year period as those who were more solitary.[17]

A sense of optimism also plays a significant role in health outcomes – a bit like a universal placebo for life in general, causing people with more upbeat emotions to live longer, healthier lives. One study following heart attack survivors showed that optimism was a better predictor of avoiding a second heart attack than any other factor. Other researchers squirted rhinovirus into people's noses and discovered that pessimists were twice as likely to develop a cold as optimists. In another study, a month after a group of office cleaners were told that physical work was good for their health, their average blood pressure dropped from elevated to normal.[18]

Just as placebos act as a therapeutic meaning response, so having a more generalized sense of meaning and purpose in life has a powerfully positive effect on health. In a classic study, elderly nursing-home residents who were given responsibility to care for a plant showed significant improvements in alertness, happiness and activity levels. In Japan, cardiovascular patients who lacked *ikigai*, which means 'having something worth living for', were found to have a mortality rate 60 percent higher than those who had it.[19]

An important way in which emotional state affects health is through its impact on telomeres, which are protective caps at the end of the DNA strands that make up our chromosomes, like the plastic ends that prevent shoelaces from fraying. Every time a cell divides, the telomeres shorten, and as they shorten, the chromosomes they produce get more frayed, something that has been linked with aging and cancer. Researchers have discovered that stress increases the rate at which telomeres fray. By reducing the level of internal stress, states such as optimism and a sense of purpose most likely help to keep our telomeres longer, thus reducing cellular wear and tear.[20]

We've seen that reciprocal causality is a defining element of integrated, self-organizing systems – the system as a whole affects the parts, while the parts affect the whole. The relationship between mind and body is similarly reciprocal. While the mind affects the body, different aspects of the body are simultaneously affecting the mind. Since these recursive flows can lead to either upward or downward self-reinforcing spirals of emotional and physical health, managing them skillfully is clearly of the greatest importance.[21]

The vagus nerve, which is a core component of the autonomic nervous system, has been found to play a crucial role. People whose vagal activity is more responsive to changes – known as high vagal tone – tend to be more sociable, empathic, expressive and cheerful. Not surprisingly, these fortunate people are highly valued as friends and tend to experience greater well-being.[22]

Through intentional practice, we can learn to both improve vagal tone and, more generally, support our internal emotional experience. Bodily postures that express emotional states have been found to induce those states when they're consciously adopted. For example, a head tilting upward elicits pride; hunching induces depressed feelings, and when a person smiles, this increases their enjoyment. Over fifty million people have viewed social psychologist Amy Cuddy's TED talk that describes how an expansive 'power posture' can make you feel more powerful.[23*]

At a deeper level, we can follow Mencius's wise advice and intentionally cultivate a sustained state of well-being as an integrated mind–body organism. Any kind of regular, vigorous exercise is beneficial for the body, but some practices are particularly valuable for cultivating a more robust connection between the mind and body. One that has become popular worldwide is yoga, a word that originally meant 'to yoke', and which was developed in ancient times as a technique to unite mind and body into a cohesive whole. Even though the exercises taught in a modern yoga studio often bear little resemblance to the ancient practice, which emphasized meditation and breathing techniques, they can still help to build mind–body connections for people raised in a dominant culture that mistakenly identifies the conceptualizing mind as the sole locus of identity.[24]

Dancing and drumming are other modalities that, besides being enjoyable in themselves, have multiple health benefits. Drumming has been found in various studies to reduce stress, blood pressure and pain, by triggering endorphin release in the body, reducing cortisol and activating the immune system. Dancing has similar effects, along with improving motor coordination and enhancing social interaction. Both activities are deeply integrative, requiring a person's conceptual, animate and social intelligences to engage and synchronize with each other, leading to the more harmonious inner states that the early Chinese sages identified as essential for good health.[25]

Some of the most valuable integrative practices, still unfamiliar to many in the West, were first developed thousands of years ago in China. Known today as *qigong* (pronounced *chee-gong*) and tai chi, they may appear exotic and mysterious to Westerners who encounter them. A typical image that comes to mind is that of elderly Chinese practitioners in a park, dressed in white, moving meditatively and gracefully in unison. They are practicing tai chi, which only emerged in its current form in the nineteenth century, but is based on the same deep-rooted lineage as traditional Chinese medicine. *Qigong*, a more general term that means 'skillful management of qi', has a wide variety of forms.[26]

Both sets of practices, based on the conception of a human being as an integrated mind–body organism, are designed to cultivate one's internal energetic and physiological systems. Using a series of postures and movements, breathing techniques and meditation, a practitioner learns to become conscious of her inner energetic flows, gradually strengthening the neural pathways between conscious attention and those parts of animate consciousness that normally remain below the level of awareness. As a practitioner learns to attune with the ebbs and flow of her inner physiology, her lived experience can become more integrated and healthful. The intentional harmonious and fluid motions of *qigong* send signals of well-being to the body's autonomic nervous system, which likely respond by initiating activation of endorphins and inhibition of stress hormones such as cortisol.[27*]

Eudaimonia: fulfilling your true nature

In addition to health and longevity, the world's great wisdom traditions have identified another deeper quality that's essential to a life of sustained flourishing. For someone whose way of living is infused with this quality, it's possible to undergo serious tribulations, including illness, bereavement or other misfortunes, and still somehow experience a life of true well-being.

In Buddhism this experience of enduring happiness is known as *sukha*. We've already come across the key Buddhist concept of *dukkha*: the broad array of afflictive experiences that arise from the separation of 'I' and the 'self', including feelings of unease, worry and grasping. We can situate *sukha* toward the opposite end of the spectrum of human experience: a deep sense of lasting well-being that underlies and infuses all emotional states. Consistent with the traditional Chinese view of harmony, a life of *sukha* doesn't mean rejecting or transcending emotions – rather, it fully embraces every instance of emotional pain and pleasure that arises. If we consider human consciousness as a series of fractal layers, this becomes easier to understand: while experiencing the moment-to-moment fluctuations of daily life at one level, we can meet all the hubbub at a deeper level with a spacious sense of abiding equanimity.[28]

While early Buddhist practitioners were developing this

notion of *sukha*, thousands of miles to the west, in ancient Greece, Aristotle was formulating his own understanding of what it means to authentically live the good life. Aristotle made a crucial distinction between two forms of happiness: hedonia and eudaimonia. Hedonia, as its name implies, refers to transient states of happiness that arise from pleasurable stimuli. It has a much broader meaning, though, than the modern word hedonism. It includes every kind of sensual pleasure, such as tastes and sounds, and also the fleeting but less tangible kind of pleasures that we get from being praised, feeling powerful or admired, acquiring material goods or feeling financially secure.[29]

Eudaimonia, on the other hand, refers to the state arising from fulfilling one's true nature. Do you remember how Aristotle proposed that every living being has an intrinsic purpose? When a human being is striving to achieve his full potentiality, and flourishing in his unique way, that is the state that Aristotle called eudaimonia. Living according to the principle of eudaimonia, he taught, was the source of sustained well-being. For centuries the philosophical schools that dominated the ancient Greco-Roman world, such as Stoicism and Epicureanism, based their teachings on the core concept of eudaimonia, differing only in their interpretations of what it actually meant to live one's life in the best possible way.[30]

With the rise of Christianity, the classical distinction between eudaimonia and hedonia was mostly forgotten in Western culture. However, in recent decades there has been a resurgence of interest in Aristotle's definition of the good life, primarily as a result of the rising popularity of a school of thought known as positive psychology. Just as the conventional Western view of health as a lack of disease is gradually being supplanted by a more integrative perspective, so in the field of psychology there has been a new emphasis on the positive attributes of well-being rather than merely trying to fix a patient's psychological problems.[31]

Positive psychology examines the characteristic traits and behaviors that undergird a life of sustained well-being. Leading researchers in the field, inspired by Aristotle, direct their attention on the attributes necessary to achieve the deeper, more enduring state of eudaimonia. It's important to note that focusing on eudaimonia doesn't mean rejecting hedonic pleasures. There is nothing wrong with pursuing the joys of friendship, feeling proud of your accomplishments or wanting to be financially secure. In fact, it's very likely that pursuing authentic flourishing as a human being will lead to many of these hedonic delights. Problems arise, however, when people make the mistake of believing hedonic states will give them a deeper sense of enduring well-being. As Buddhist teachers have pointed out for millennia, these states are transient, and desiring them, grasping at them when they're present, and longing for them when they've passed, are major sources of *dukkha*. Focusing attention, however, on recognizing and fulfilling your true nature can allow you to flourish even in the face of adversity.[32]

An inventory of lasting happiness

What, then, have researchers in positive psychology discovered as the factors that promote true well-being? Some have recognized that, to understand human nature as a set of universally shared attributes, we must examine the human psyche from the standpoint of evolution. Ninety-five percent of human history was spent in bands of nomadic hunter-gatherers, and our basic needs, desires and emotions evolved to make our ancestors successful in that milieu. We prize sweet and fatty foods, for example, because they were hard to find in the savanna, and when our ancestors came across them, it was a good idea to gorge on them.[33]

Although our modern world makes a separation between work and pleasure, one of our deeply evolved needs is to do work that is meaningful and challenging. An important aspect of well-being revolves around being engaged purposively in work, setting goals for ourselves and then striving to achieve them. Interestingly, researchers have discovered that it's the journey, not the destination, that gives us the greatest pleasure. Once we've accomplished a goal, there's a short-lived pleasurable sensation, and then before we know it, we've set ourselves a new goal.[34*]

For our hunter-gatherer ancestors, being accepted as part of a community was essential for survival. Because of this, we have evolved fundamental needs for multiple layers of connection with others, from the broadest to the most intimate, including a sense of community belonging, friendship, family bonds, physical intimacy and partner love. Raising children, interestingly, has been shown to increase eudaimonic, but not hedonic well-being: parents report feeling more stressed on a daily basis but enjoy greater long-term life satisfaction. The same pattern of increased eudaimonic but reduced hedonic well-being has been reported in volunteer work.[35*]

Having a positive attitude to life is one of the most important attributes for sustained well-being. Just as we saw a self-reinforcing upward spiral between positive emotions and physical health, the same kind of dynamic exists in the relationship between attitude and long-term happiness. People who believe their happiness can improve report greater life satisfaction. The same is true for those who emphasize gratitude, both to others and for the positive aspects of their own life. Another emotion demonstrated to elicit both greater happiness and health is awe: the sensation of being in the presence of something vast, something greater than our own limited existence.[36]

In fact, simply being in nature is one of the most reliably effective ways to feel happier and healthier. A classic study in 1984 reported that surgical patients assigned to rooms with windows looking out on a natural scene took fewer painkillers and had shorter post-operative hospital stays. Since then a number of studies have shown that nature-assisted therapy is effective across a wide range of diagnoses, from obesity to schizophrenia. Of course, you don't need to be sick to benefit from the natural world. According to a recent study, spending at least two hours a week in nature gives people an overall sense of greater well-being.[37]

Perhaps the most important attribute of all – one that both incorporates and transcends many of the rest – is having a sense of meaning and purpose in life. This relates directly to Aristotle's core idea underlying eudaimonia – striving to fulfill the plenitude of one's true nature. Viktor Frankl, a Nazi concentration camp survivor who wrote about his experience in the classic *Man's Search for Meaning*, observed that the common attribute of those who survived the horrors of the camps was 'the will to meaning'. Someone who 'knows the "why" for his existence', Frankl wrote, 'will be able to bear almost any "how".'[38]

After reading this inventory of lasting happiness, you may identify some attributes you already have, and others you wish you could have but don't. A reasonable question to ask is whether there's anything you can do about it. Can we really cultivate our own shoots, as Mencius suggested, to achieve eudaimonia as an integrated organism?

For much of the twentieth century, the consensus scientific view was that Mencius was wrong – there is a 'happiness set point' that is genetically determined, and there's very little we can do to change it through self-cultivation. Some studies reported that people who enjoyed extreme good fortune, such as winning the lottery, found themselves no happier several years later; and by the same token, those who endured tragedies, such as getting paralyzed from an accident, eventually returned to their prior level of life satisfaction. While there does seem to be a happiness baseline that varies for different people, this deterministic view has been largely repudiated. It's been shown, for example, that significant life events such as marriage can lead to a sustained increase in life satisfaction, and conversely that serious ill-health reduces it.[39]

Most importantly, the discovery of neural plasticity in recent decades has opened up a vast arena of possibilities for intentionally changing one's own happiness baseline, rather than relying on the serendipity of life events. If we engage in practices that redirect our neural attractors, they have the potential to durably alter the baseline of our inner experience. Mencius's primary teaching – that we can intentionally cultivate ourselves just as we might nurture a plant – has been corroborated by modern neuroscience.[40]

Cultivating your mind with meditation

Mencius wasn't the only sage from early times to emphasize internal cultivation. While ancient Taoist texts revealed how the Tao could be attained by cultivating the mind, thousands of miles to the south, in India, the Buddha frequently referred to meditation in his teachings as *bhavana*, which literally means 'cultivation'.[41]

In recent years modern neuroscience has validated definitively these ancient insights. In a famous study researchers scanned the brains of London taxi drivers, who spend about two years memorizing virtually every street in London in order to pass their strict licensing exams. They found the taxi drivers' brains were significantly larger in the part of the hippocampus that stores spatial information. Other studies have since shown that different kinds of expertise, such as juggling or sorting mail, expand the part of the brain that's used more extensively.[42]

Essentially, the brain reacts to mental exercise in the same way the body reacts to physical exercise. We're not surprised to find that people who work out every day in the gym develop rippling muscles; we all know that if you want to play a musical instrument well, you need to practice regularly. Similarly, both neuroscience and ancient wisdom tell us that we can enhance our well-being by skillfully exercising our minds.[43]

While there are many ways to cultivate the mind, meditation is one practice that has been extensively tried and tested over the millennia. Just as learning a musical instrument requires endless repetitions of scales, so the equivalent in meditation is steadily learning to focus attention, usually on the breath. With practice, the meditator becomes attentive to her inner states, gaining greater awareness of the incessant activity of her salience-seeking monkey mind in the default Lévy-walk state that we encountered in the previous chapter.[44]

At this stage a crucial skill is learning to be aware of your own mind-wandering without judging the feelings and emotions that arise. This brings us back to the ancient Chinese emphasis on harmonizing emotions. Instead of reacting to a difficult emotion with aversion, we can gradually learn to hold it tenderly, be curious about its provenance, experience it as bodily sensation and allow it to flow through consciousness until it passes over to the next attractor that arises.[45]

The relationship between 'I' and 'self' doesn't have to be one of hostility, but can be more like a dance set to the music of life. A long-standing meditation practice can lead us to appreciate our inner experience as a dance of consciousness: a continuous stream of shifting thoughts, feelings and sensations. In Chapter 5 the metaphor of an improvisational jazz band helped us picture how life harmonizes its disparate parts; similarly in meditation, as we experience our own inner music of life, we become aware that there is no composer, that the players and audience are one and the same, as everything ceaselessly streams through the field of consciousness in a state of effortless flux.[46]

A meditation practice can enhance those neural pathways that permit effortless, dynamic, ongoing harmonization of consciousness. With practice, the distinction between conceptual and animate consciousness softens, the 'I' and 'self' can harmonize, and the organism itself approaches full integration: the quality of cohesive unity with differentiation that permits true flourishing. Neurobiologist Dan Siegel suggests that integration is the very definition of good health, allowing the human organism to live 'in a flexible, adaptive, coherent, energized, and stable flow across time'.[47]

The neurobiology of mindfulness meditation has been studied extensively over the past couple of decades, with thousands of articles published in scientific journals. While some reports of its miraculous effects may be overstated, there is hard evidence showing that practicing mindfulness meditation significantly enhances both mental and physical well-being. Even for beginners, just a few weeks of meditation leads to reduced reactivity to stress, improvement in attention and some reduction in inflammatory markers.[48]

Just like working out in the gym, those initial improvements may prove to be temporary unless there is a sustained commitment to practice. But for long-term meditators (those who have clocked a thousand hours or more), the benefits become more robust. Mentally, they are better able to sustain attention, reduce mind-wandering, react less to stress and embrace strong emotions more easily. Physically, their bodies produce less cortisol and more of the enzyme telomerase, which helps to maintain the cells' telomeres, thus slowing aging and reducing inflammation.[49]

At this more advanced stage, the effects naturally spill over from the meditation cushion into the normal activities of daily life. This is an example of how we can literally shape our own attractors of consciousness. As the neural connections that lead to these beneficial states strengthen, they no longer need the quiet sitting time to get activated. Prominent researchers Richard Davidson and Daniel Goleman call this the shift from altered states to 'altered traits' – sustained and beneficial new characteristics that endure beyond meditation itself. It seems Mencius was right: cultivating yourself really can bear fruit.[50]

A society based on *dukkha*

Armed with their evidence-based data and driven by the best intentions, leading proponents of mindfulness meditation have been diligently spreading the message of its benefits throughout the West. 'We envision a world,' write Goleman and Davidson, 'where widespread mental fitness deeply alters society for the better.' Jon Kabat-Zinn, who developed a secularized practice available in many medical institutions known as Mindfulness-Based Stress Reduction, sees its widespread acceptance as a new 'Renaissance ... unfolding here and now ... a critical global resource in the face of what humanity is facing as a species.' As a measure of their success, in 2017 a survey reported that over 14 percent of US adults had meditated in the past year, more than triple the number five years earlier.[51]

However, mindfulness by itself is not inevitably a force for societal well-being. Like other self-improvement practices, it is open to being usurped by any institution, benevolent or otherwise. In *McMindfulness*, author Ron Purser delivers a searing critique of the appropriation of mindfulness by profit-motivated forces. He chronicles how, at Davos, a watering hole of the world's global elite, a director of ExxonMobil – a company that deliberately concealed the dangers of climate change from the public for decades – declared that 'the main business case for mindfulness is that if you're more focused on the job, you'll become a better leader ... Even Goldman Sachs is doing it.' An article in *Forbes* heralds mindfulness as 'the next big business wave'. The US military has recruited meditation experts to teach its soldiers how to remain mindful in combat so that, in the words of one of the program creators, they can learn to 'make discerning choices' including 'the capacity to kill, cleanly, without hesitation and without remorse'.[52]

This paradox highlights a crucial principle of well-being: an individual can only fully flourish within the context of a society which is itself healthy. Becoming a fully integrated organism means not just integrating within, but also integrating fractally with community, society and the entire ecosystem. We exist in a holarchy. Just as a single cell can't flourish in a diseased organism, so the well-being of an individual human requires a healthy society.[53]

In modern times, one of the greatest challenges to well-being is the simple fact that we evolved to thrive as nomadic hunter-gatherers living in small bands, but the world we're born into is now very different. Our cravings for salt, fat and sugar – healthy drives for a nomadic forager – now cause us to overconsume processed foods, leaving us with clogged arteries, heart disease and diabetes. We evolved with a wholesome desire to emulate the best athlete or dancer in a group of thirty to fifty peers; now we compare ourselves with glamorous superstar celebrities on television – and find ourselves wanting, anguished by self-deprecating envy. The healthy instinct for status within community is transformed by our anonymous mass culture into a desperate need to make a positive impression, which we appease through consumer purchases, grasping at status symbols through our clothing, automobiles and latest technology gadgets.[54]

The weakening of community bonds, such that even the nuclear family is becoming a threatened entity, has led to what journalist George Monbiot describes as 'an epidemic of loneliness sweeping the world'. The isolation people feel leads to mounting levels of depression, fear and anxiety. A study of American students over four decades found that the average college student in 1993 was more anxious than 85 percent of a comparable group in 1952, while, astonishingly, the average child in the late 1980s was more anxious than a typical child psychiatric patient from the 1950s.[55]

Our society's emphasis on the pursuit of individual material success has led to a steadily rising obsessive focus on narcissistic self-esteem. Another study tracking long-term trends found that in 2006 two thirds of American college students scored above what had been the average score for narcissism in 1982. Status anxiety has been greatly exacerbated since then by social media, with its searing imperative to avoid appearing unhappy under any circumstance, and pressure to post a constant supply of selfies showing a succession of hedonic 'happy' experiences.[56]

As a society, our manic drive for hedonic moments has come at the expense of eudaimonia. A large number of studies tracking a wide range of populations around the world have consistently found that people with materialistic values have lower well-being and suffer more psychological problems than those for whom materialism is less important. One reason for this is known as the 'hedonic treadmill': people's material aspirations change according to their situation, so as soon as they achieve their goal – whether it's a flashier gadget, a bigger house or a higher status job – they immediately aspire to the next step on the treadmill, never satisfying their need to grasp for more. Buddhism, as we've seen, has a word for this perpetual state of discontent on which consumer society is based: *dukkha*.[57]

In the wise words of the *Tao Te Ching*, written more than two millennia before the advent of consumer culture:

> He who is attached to things will suffer much.
> He who hoards will suffer heavy loss ...
> There is no calamity like not knowing what is enough
> There is no curse greater than the desire for gain.
> Therefore, he who knows what is enough will always have
> enough.[58]

Weaponizing *dukkha* for profit

We're so embedded in the pervasive global consumer culture that it seems natural to assume it's somehow the inevitable outcome of modern industrial civilization. But that's not necessarily the case. Modern consumerism can, in fact, be traced back to chilling, cynical strategies first employed in the late nineteenth and early twentieth centuries by ruthless businessmen who discovered how to condition entire populations to become sources of profit at the expense of their well-being.[59]

A trailblazer in this regard was Sigmund Freud's nephew Edward Bernays, who used his uncle's insights into the subconscious to identify people's deeply buried needs and manipulate them into consumer impulses. The same social instincts that had allowed our ancestors to thrive in hunter-gatherer bands – desire for status, fear of exclusion – now became fodder for advertisers, driving people to act against their own welfare. One of Bernays' coups was to break the social taboo against women smoking by paying models in a New York Easter Sunday parade to dress as suffragettes and flamboyantly light cigarettes, declaring them to be 'freedom torches'.[60]

Bernays proudly described his work as 'the conscious and intelligent manipulation of the organized habits and opinions of the masses', declaring, 'Those who manipulate this unseen mechanism of society constitute an invisible government that is the true ruling power of this country. We are governed, our minds molded, our tastes formed, our ideas suggested, largely by men we have never heard of ... who pull the wires which control the public mind.'

This mind control was enthusiastically endorsed by the US government in 1929, in a presidential report that established the hedonic treadmill as the foundation of economic policy. 'Economically,' it stated, 'we have a boundless field before us; there are new wants that will make way endlessly for newer wants, as fast as they are satisfied ... by advertising and other promotional devices.'[61]

Bernays and other marketing pioneers laid the groundwork for what has since become a relentless barrage of devious strategies designed to maximize profits by tweaking every one of our core human instincts. This has been called 'limbic capitalism' by author David Courtwright: a pervasive methodology to encourage excessive consumption and 'addiction by design' through targeting our limbic system – the source of instinctual drives. Our desire for sugar, salt and fat has been exploited by corporations designing scientific algorithms to target our 'bliss point' – the irresistible reaction to food precisely engineered to maximize flavor – leading to a global pandemic of obesity and diabetes. Companies such as Coca-Cola and McDonald's have learned to deflect attention from their toxic products by appealing in their advertising to people's unfulfilled aspirations for youthful vigor and 'family fun'.[62]

Having saturated the developed markets, the corporate *dukkha*-machine turned to the Global South in its ruthless pursuit of profits. Nestlé was famously accused in the 1970s of killing babies by convincing impoverished mothers in developing countries to replace breastfeeding with infant formula, which – to save money – they diluted with contaminated water, causing millions of babies to die from malnutrition. Unabashed, along with other transnational corporations, they have continued for decades in their drive to undermine the health of vulnerable communities for profit. In Brazil, for example, Nestlé has extended credit to slum vendors to market their sugary products to impoverished neighbors, and in 2010 launched a supermarket barge to ferry ice cream, chocolate and powdered milk to hundreds of thousands of prospective customers living in isolated Amazon settlements. One result of this global onslaught, according to the World Health Organization, is that over 650 million people, or 13 percent of adults worldwide, are now obese – a number that has tripled since 1975.[63*]

Corporate predators have learned that the most valuable population to ensnare are children. In the sinister words of marketing executive Wayne Chilicki, 'When it comes to targeting kid consumers, we at General Mills ... believe in getting them early and having them for life.' Advertisers recognize that children's instinctual social drives are even more susceptible than those of adults. 'You open up emotional vulnerabilities,' explains one ad agency president, 'and it's very easy to do with kids because they're the most emotionally vulnerable.' With social media now infiltrating every aspect of many teenagers' lives, the power of predatory corporate advertising has become even more formidable. In 2017 a leaked document revealed Facebook boasting to advertisers how they can identify in real time when teenagers feel 'insecure' and 'worthless' and would be most susceptible to a 'confidence boost'.[64]

A new generation of mind controllers are now using sophisticated data mining technologies to inject their power even deeper into our minds than their forebears could have dreamed possible. A modern-day Bernays named B. J. Fogg founded a field in the 1990s called captology, derived from the acronym CAPT – 'computers as persuasive technology'. At the ominously named Stanford Persuasive Technology Lab, he has taught budding entrepreneurs how to use technology to 'change people's attitudes or behaviors'.

His teachings have spawned the interfaces of our new daily routines: the chimes from smartphones diverting our attention, the thumbs-up icon on our news feeds and the Like statistics telling us how popular we are. In a process known as 'brain hacking', developers design 'hot triggers' that initiate behavioral loops in our subconscious. Successful apps, they teach, are those that trigger a momentary need and then provide us with an instant solution that sparks a micro-dose of endorphins in our brains, causing us, like a rat on a wheel, to go back for more until we become addicted. The success of their approach is evidenced by the fact that Americans now spend on average five and a half hours a day on digital media, mostly mobile devices.[65]

The key trigger that catapulted Facebook to market dominance is FOMO – 'fear of missing out' – which once again manipulates our deeply evolved desire for community connection for the sake of corporate profit, while raising levels of cortisol in the victim's body and driving many teens into a vortex of compulsive craving. Psychologist Richard Freed writes how the addictive overuse of smartphones, video games and social media is 'tearing the family apart', with teen girls refusing to be separated from the devices that are making them miserable, and boys obsessed with gaming at the expense of schoolwork or other extracurricular activities. Like Wayne Chilicki, Facebook is now doubling down on its strategy by getting them early, targeting children as young as five years old through its recently launched Messenger Kids.[66]

Two millennia ago, when Mencius offered the metaphor of cultivation for a person's well-being, he pointed to the importance of societal impact. 'The trees of the New Mountain,' he noted, were once beautiful, but 'they were hewn down with axes' until the terrain became bare and stripped. 'But is this the nature of the mountain,' he asked, or rather a function of how it's been treated? 'Hewn down day after day, can the mind retain its beauty?' Oh, Mencius, we might reply from our vantage point, you ain't seen nothin'.[67]

Cultivating societal well-being

While the addictive use of technology is tearing families apart, the rise in extreme inequality is likewise tearing societies apart. It's widely recognized that in recent decades the gulf between rich and poor has vastly increased to levels not seen since the days of the robber barons of the early twentieth century. The wealthiest 1 percent of Americans, for example, owned 9 percent of the country's wealth in 1976, but now own 40 percent.[68]

What is less well known is that the overall health and well-being of a population is determined, not so much by a country's wealth, but rather by how evenly that wealth is distributed. A comprehensive study by social scientists Richard Wilkinson and Kate Pickett reveals that a more equal wealth distribution strongly predicts a healthier society. Greater inequality in a country leads to lower life expectancy, worse health and higher rates of AIDS, depression and infant mortality. What is most noteworthy is that it benefits almost everyone to live in a more equal society, not just the poor. The two graphs opposite, which show a range of developed countries, powerfully illustrate this remarkable finding: while there is no discernible correlation between an index of health and social problems and a country's income *level*, there is clear correlation between the index and a country's income *inequality*. Japan, Sweden and Norway, the most equal countries, score lowest on the index, while the USA, the most unequal, scores far higher than the rest.[69]

The negative health impact of inequality is not simply because of lack of access to healthcare. While that is a component, along with factors like reliance on fast food, the most significant factor is the stressful psychological experience of being disempowered and marginalized. Long-term studies of civil servants with equivalent access to healthcare have shown that low job status, more than differences in lifestyle, correlated with a higher risk of heart, lung and gastrointestinal disease, cancer, depression and suicide. Much of this can be attributed to greater levels of stress for those whose lives are controlled by others, leading to increased inflammation throughout the body and early degeneration of telomeres. The telomeres of someone raised in poverty are likely to have aged ten years faster, by adulthood, than those of someone with a more privileged upbringing.[70]

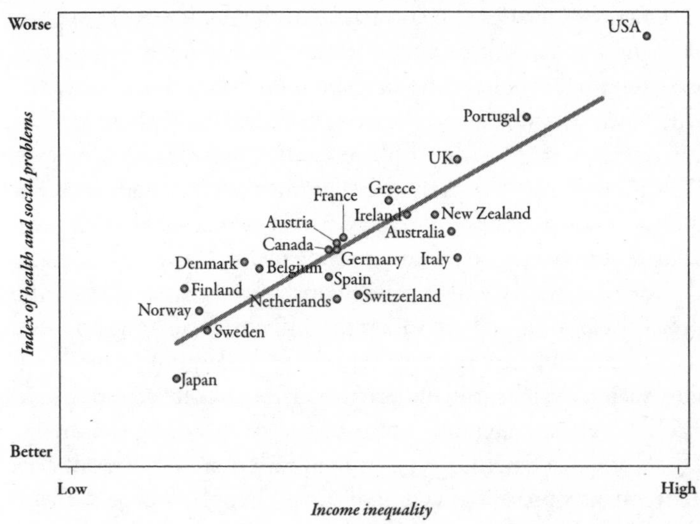

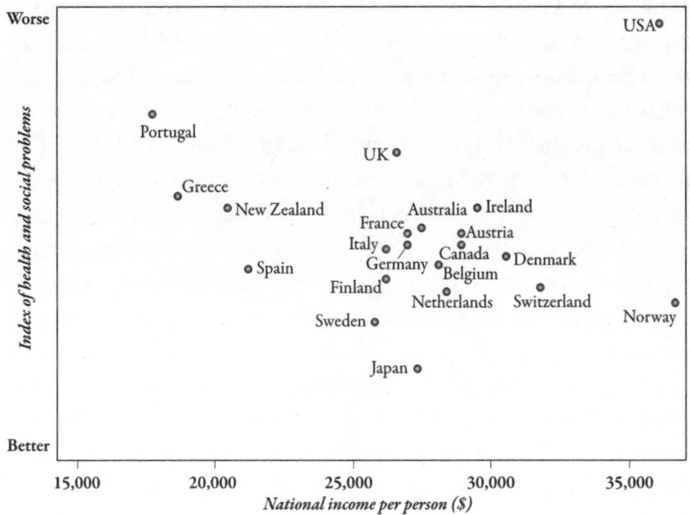

Figure 7: Comparison of income inequality and overall income levels in relation to health and social problems

Unequal societies also correlate with higher levels of violence, frequently as a result of people feeling disrespected and powerless, along with higher rates of mental illness, crime, alcoholism, drug abuse, homicide and incarceration. Similarly, there are vast differences in trust, with people in Sweden more than six times as likely to trust others than those in the most unequal countries. For all these reasons, it's not just physical but also psychological well-being that is sabotaged by excessive inequality.[71]

Both inequality and runaway consumerism are maladies of a global civilization built on values that align with hedonic impulses but virtually obliterate any conception of eudaimonia. Our dominant societal values, the underlying drivers of our economy and culture, are fundamentally oppositional to sustained well-being. When practices such as yoga or meditation are advertised, they are frequently presented as modalities for people to cope with the stresses in their lives, numbing them to the possibility that the underlying cause of their stress is a dysfunctional society.[72]

Increasing numbers of people, from many walks of life, have become aware of the pressing need to steer societal values away from consumption and toward well-being. One area of focus is the dominant measure used to evaluate a country's performance: gross domestic product (GDP). The problem with GDP is that it merely measures economic activity and fails to distinguish between activities that promote welfare and those that reduce it. Recognizing this, various groups have begun exploring alternative ways to measure society's true performance, such as the Gross National Happiness index used by the state of Bhutan, incorporating factors such as well-being, health and biodiversity.[73*]

Just as profit-oriented corporations learned to zero in on humanity's instinctual drivers to exploit them, so those who are trying to reorient society's values focus on the same evolved human instincts, but to nurture them. Above all, they recognize our intrinsic need for a strong sense of community. Interestingly, in focus groups conducted in the United States a large majority of participants wanted society to 'move away from greed and excess toward a way of life more centered on values, community, and family'. Ironically, though, they felt isolated because they believed most people had become increasingly self-centered, and therefore didn't share their views. For this reason, progressive thinkers like journalist George Monbiot are calling for a new 'politics of belonging' to reconstruct a society where we feel at home within our community, valued in our workplace and able to contribute meaningfully to society at large.[74]

In much the same way that we can cultivate ourselves, we can also choose collaboratively to cultivate our society's flourishing. The history of Scandinavian countries offers a valuable case study for what's possible. Authors Lene Andersen and Tomas Björkman have documented how, in the nineteenth century, this region was the least developed in Europe – agrarian, impoverished and undemocratic. However, in the middle of that century a handful of visionary thinkers began to institute a program of broad-based education, teaching a critical mass of the population over ensuing decades to gain a greater sense of identity and political awareness within the broader context of their society. Their intention was, explicitly, to build eudaimonia within the population, allowing people to find pathways of flourishing as part of the larger community. Largely as a result of this multi-generational effort, the Scandinavian countries now rank highest in the world in the annual *World Happiness Report*, in addition to being more egalitarian and among the most economically prosperous.[75*]

Achieving fractal flourishing

While there is much to learn about societal flourishing from the Scandinavian example, perhaps the most valuable teachings reside in the wisdom of Indigenous cultures, which have maintained a more robust connection with the earliest articulations of our commonly evolved human heritage. Across the world, a universal theme that arises is the importance of connectivity – the connections between people and the interrelationship with all of nature.

When members of the Native American Blackfoot tribe meet each other, they don't ask, 'How are you?' Instead, they ask, 'How are the connections?' Similarly, in central and southern Africa a guiding principle for life is *ubuntu*, which is frequently translated as 'I am because you are; you are because I am.'[76]

Indigenous conceptions of well-being extend this sense of interconnectedness beyond humans to the rest of nature. In Australia, Aboriginal people engage in the meditative practice of *dadirri*, which they describe as 'deep listening, silent awareness' of the natural world. The Native American Lakota phrase, 'all my relations' – referring to all creatures, not just human kin – similarly epitomizes a worldview that recognizes the deep interrelatedness of all life, such that the health of an individual is intrinsically tied up with the health of the living Earth.[77]

These insights of Indigenous peoples point to a fundamental lesson of flourishing as an integrated organism: health has a fractal quality – it requires healthy systems harmonizing within the organism and, just as importantly, healthy external systems on which the organism relies. If you're trying to cultivate a plant in polluted soil, no matter how carefully you attend to its needs, the plant may wither and die. If your neighbors are encountering similar difficulties, it behooves you to join together to clear up the source of pollution, even while you're working on your own patch.

Pioneering international institutions are endeavoring to apply this time-honored wisdom to develop enlightened global health policies through the Planetary Health Alliance. 'The concept of planetary health,' they write, 'emphasizes that human health is intricately connected to the health of natural systems within the Earth's biosphere.' Achieving this would require what they call a 'planetary consciousness': reconnecting with the ancestral understanding of the unity of all life and applying this awareness to formulate global health policies. Another international network of over 6,000 organizations has endorsed the Earth Charter, a declaration of global life-affirming ethics, which states that 'we must recognize that in the midst of a magnificent diversity of cultures and life-forms we are one human family and one Earth community with a common destiny.'[78]

Another important aspect of fractal flourishing taught by Indigenous traditions is that a truly healthy organism enacts flourishing as much as it receives it. The Maori, for example, recognize spiritual and community health as inseparable from that of an individual. If a person's first thoughts are for himself, even if his body appears the epitome of fitness, he is considered unhealthy. Many spiritual teachings around the world consider this understanding to be an essential ingredient of true wisdom. In the assessment of integral theorist Roger Walsh, who has studied cross-cultural wisdom traditions, 'increasing psychological maturity is associated with expanding awareness, care, and compassion ... the wiser people are, the greater the number of people and creatures they will seek to benefit, and the deeper the kind of benefit they will seek to offer.'[79]

Understanding the deep interconnectedness between a person and the larger context of their existence was not lost on Mencius and other Chinese sages. Indeed, they described a highly desirable state called *cheng*, which was the experience of true integration of consciousness, both within and without. 'There is no greater delight,' declared Mencius, 'than to realize *cheng* upon self-examination.' Someone who achieves true sagehood, declared Wang Yangming, 'regards all beneath heaven as one family'. This pinnacle of wisdom, he emphasized, is not something only available to a select few, but is an inborn understanding – one that gets blocked and forgotten by the accumulation of cultural habituations. In Buddhism one of the supreme objectives of meditation is to rediscover the Buddha nature existing within every one of us, a nature that perceives the deep truth of our intrinsic interconnectedness. A famous Zen story depicts meditation as being like wiping layers of dust off a mirror, so that eventually the meditator can come face to face with their own Buddha nature.[80]

There are clear ethical implications arising from such an understanding. Once you recognize the interrelatedness of yourself with other beings, and that your own flourishing is fractally related to the health of the larger world, there is no avoiding the realization that your actions – and even your inactions – have a moral significance. In both Aristotle's conception of eudaimonia and Mencius's practice of cultivation, the ethical aspects of a person's life were intimately related to other aspects of flourishing. For both Aristotle and Mencius, humanity existed in an inherently moral universe.[81]

What, we must ask, does a value system look like that is based on the realization of intrinsic interconnectedness? How does that system differ from the dominant values of our current civilization – one that so easily turns mindfulness into McMindfulness? And how can our actions lead to greater fractal flourishing for all the layers of life in which we're embedded? These are the crucial topics we'll now address.

NEW THREADS OF MEANING

Living according to the principle of eudaimonia can lead to a life of sustained well-being

We can cultivate well-being in ourselves through intentional practices that nurture healthy attractors of consciousness

An individual can only fully flourish within the context of a society which is itself healthy (fractal flourishing)

Our global civilization is built on values that align with hedonic impulses and oppose eudaimonia

CHAPTER NINE

CULTIVATING INTEGRATED VALUES

Imagine you're sitting alone in a quiet courtyard. Suddenly, you hear a noise. You look up and see a toddler innocently playing at the edge of a deep well. You realize in a flash that she's in danger of falling in and drowning. What do you do? Do you tell yourself, 'It's not my problem,' and leave? No, of course not. You swiftly make a beeline for the toddler and lift her out of harm's way.

This thought experiment was used by Mencius to demonstrate that humans possess an intrinsic goodness. You're not saving the little girl for a reward. You may never even be acknowledged by anyone for saving an innocent life. You simply move, intuitively and spontaneously, to save her life because it's the right thing to do.[1]

Now fast-forward a couple of millennia to the modern age and consider a similar scenario. Alone again, you're strolling in a park, wearing an expensive new pair of shoes. You're at the edge of a shallow pond when, once more, you hear an unexpected noise. You turn and notice a toddler drowning in the middle of the pond. You look around – no sign of a babysitter, parents or any other adult. Now what do you do? You realize that, if you step into the pond to save her life, you'll ruin your fancy new shoes. Do you decide it's not worth it and walk on? Once again, of course not. You stride into the water to save an innocent life.

The creator of this thought experiment is Peter Singer, a renowned moral philosopher who uses it to kick off his book *The Life You Can Save*. Singer, though, makes a very different argument from Mencius. If you don't hesitate at the loss of a new pair of shoes to save a child's life, he asks, why don't you immediately donate a hundred dollars to a charity saving the lives of children around the world dying from malnutrition and preventable diseases? Why stop at a hundred dollars? Where is the valid limit, Singer urges us to ask, to our moral obligation to help those in dire need?[2]

These two scenarios, spanning thousands of years and vastly different cultures, both prompt careful consideration about human values. Mencius's case became a cornerstone of the traditional Chinese view of human nature. Whether we're regular citizens or sages, he argued, we have an inborn moral sense. He used the same plant metaphor from the previous chapter to describe our moral cultivation: we're all born with the sprouts of virtue, but they must be carefully tended to grow into a healthy system of values. We shouldn't go against our natural tendencies any more than we would try to reshape an oak tree to look like a willow. The way we foster our innate goodness, Mencius explained, is by staying in touch with our instincts and learning to express them skillfully in the world.[3]

A very different conception of human nature developed in the European tradition to become the foundation of mainstream modern thought. The story of Adam and Eve in the Garden of Eden laid the framework for Christian theology with the notion of Original Sin. Adam's disobedience in eating from the Tree of Knowledge had condemned the entire human race to damnation, and our only hope for salvation was to rise above our sinful bodily instincts. Through our reasoning faculty, we could learn to differentiate good from evil, and we must then use willpower to overcome our instinctual drives toward bad behavior. 'The human heart,' wrote sixteenth-century theologian John Calvin, 'is so steeped in the poison of sin, that it can breathe out nothing but a loathsome stench.'[4]

While the pioneers of the Scientific Revolution challenged many aspects of Christian thought, one thing they never questioned was its belief in humanity's intrinsic malevolence. In *Leviathan*, written during the bloody English Civil War, Thomas Hobbes laid out a new myth that in the 'state of nature' humans were unremittingly selfish and brutal to each other – 'the war of all against all' – and therefore we need a powerful authority to keep our vicious instincts in check.[5]

Amazingly, much of what passes as mainstream scientific

thinking in the modern world has maintained the traditional conception of humankind's Manichean struggle between good (the domain of reason) and evil (our natural instincts). Prominent twentieth-century biologists scoffed at any Mencian-type notion of intrinsic human goodness. 'What passes for co-operation,' wrote one, 'turns out to be a mixture of opportunism and exploitation.' 'Scratch an "altruist"', exclaimed another, 'and watch a "hypocrite" bleed.' Humans, we are told, are naturally violent, aggressive killers – 'the dazed survivors', according to two influential anthropologists, 'of a continuous, 5-million-year habit of lethal aggression.'[6]

Predictably, Richard Dawkins' selfish gene myth only served to perpetuate this split conception of morality. 'Be warned,' he writes, 'that if you wish, as I do, to build a society towards a common good, you can expect little help from biological nature.' Like the Christian theologians he denigrates, Dawkins asserts that humans are in a state of constant battle with their own instincts. Our only hope is to overcome our evil nature through reason. 'Our brains,' he declares, 'have evolved to the point where we are capable of rebelling against our selfish genes ... Let us try to teach generosity and altruism, because we are born selfish.'[7]

How do we make sense of these bewilderingly different perspectives on humanity's moral nature? Is morality intrinsic to human nature? If so, how do we account for the huge variation in what different cultures interpret as moral behavior? Most importantly, how can we conduct our lives according to a value system that fosters eudaimonia for ourselves and for others – and is there a way for society at large to prize these values? There is almost no topic more important. As I described in *The Patterning Instinct*, culture shapes values, and those values have shaped history. Likewise, the values we as a society choose to live by today will shape our future. The stakes for getting it right could hardly be higher.

The 'moral arc'

Morality is a tricky subject to explore. Beyond the disconcertingly different viewpoints on human nature and moral norms, there is the problem known as the naturalistic fallacy – the ease with which we slip from describing 'what is' to 'what ought to be'. This conundrum was first described by eighteenth-century Scottish philosopher David Hume, who noted that this slip is 'imperceptible; but is, however, of the last consequence'. If you're going to make that transition, he maintained, 'it should be observed and explained' and 'a reason should be given' for how we can deduce one from the other.[8]

When Gordon Gekko proclaimed that greed is good because it was the driver of human evolution, that's the naturalistic fallacy in action: even if it did drive human evolution, why would it make greed good? But the principle works the other way around too. Once we repudiate Dawkins' selfish gene story and recognize the prominence of cooperation in nature, what automatically makes cooperation more 'moral' than competition? Hume never said that the linkage can't be made. His point was simply that when you make the shift from 'is' to 'ought' you'd better be clear about it. It's a valid point, and any proposal for a solid basis of human ethics needs to rise to Hume's challenge.[9]

Another slippery component of any discussion of morality is that, even within the same culture, moral norms have a tendency to change from one generation to the next. In fact, the shifting baseline of morality is one of its most salient characteristics. As we look back through history, we have plenty of reasons to celebrate the evolving nature of moral norms. Steven Pinker, in *The Better Angels of Our Nature*, has painstakingly documented the dramatic moral transformation of the past few hundred years, whereby behaviors once considered completely acceptable would now cause us to recoil in horror.[10]

Many of us, reading headlines every morning reporting acts of brutality and cruelty around the world, have a hard time absorbing how much less violent the world is now than it used to be. But the facts Pinker assiduously collected speak for themselves. Homicide rates in England were fifty to a hundred times greater in the fourteenth century than the mid-twentieth century. Similar declines occurred across the rest of Europe. Unspeakable cruelty was readily embraced as a daily norm by even the most respectable people. The distinguished seventeenth-century diarist Samuel Pepys wrote demurely about watching a man hanged, drawn and quartered in Charing Cross, joking that he looked 'as cheerful as any man could do in that condition', adding that 'his head and heart [were] shown to the people, at which there was great shouts of joy'. He went on to describe how he then enjoyed oysters at the Sun Tavern with some friends.[11]

Martin Luther King Jr gave a famous speech in 1965 in which he declared that 'the arc of the moral universe is long, but it bends toward justice'. There are many good reasons to concur with this statement, even in the face of disturbing trends in our current political climate. Slavery, which used to be widespread, is outlawed everywhere in the world (although it still continues illegally). Wars of conquest have mostly lost their legitimacy as national policy. The rights of vulnerable populations, such as women, children, people of color, LGBT communities and ethnic minorities, have been recognized in law by many countries. Author Michael Shermer, summing up the evidence, claims, 'In short, we are living in the most moral period in our species' history.'[12]

How valid is this triumphal proclamation? If true, then what lies behind it – and crucially what might cause these trends to continue or reverse? And what do these changes in moral standards tell us about human nature? Is there, in fact, any solid basis to go from 'is' to 'ought' in choosing a system of values to live by? To unpack these questions, we need to go back to the basics, beginning with life itself, and trace how value first arose, how it evolved and what happened to it after humans appeared. Then, from that relatively solid foundation, we can begin to weave together these enigmas into a more coherent whole.

How values evolved

We've been taught to think of evolution as a force of nature utterly devoid of values. When we hear about the merciless ways some creatures act toward others, it's clear they don't share many of *our* values. But think back to how life first began on Earth billions of years ago: when the first protocells made a determination about which molecules were beneficial and which were harmful, they made a value judgment. Value, however rudimentary, had emerged on Earth.[13]

Bacteria continue to make similar types of basic value judgments, but as animals evolved, replete with nervous systems, their evaluations of the world became more complex. Experiences could be pleasant or unpleasant, depending on the various interactions of their pain and pleasure receptors, bodily states and emotions. Whatever happens to a creature generates a value judgment that affects how it responds. From an animal's perspective, 'is' and 'ought' are continually intermingling. As philosopher Andreas Weber wryly points out, 'living beings constantly commit the naturalistic fallacy'.[14]

As creatures evolved bigger brains, their value judgments became ever more sophisticated. The influential triune brain theory of neuroscientist Paul MacLean posits that the human brain comprises three different 'brains' that evolved over different timescales. The ancient reptilian brain is driven by instincts such as the 'fight or flight' response; the more recent mammalian brain helps manage relationships through such behaviors as maternal bonding, attachment and emotions; and the most recent neocortex (containing the prefrontal cortex) allows for more complex behaviors such as planning and integrating.[15*]

Psychologist Darcia Narvaez has suggested that, as the brain evolved, new layers of ethical evaluations emerged with it. The most ancient, arising from the reptilian brain, is the Security Ethic, which emphasizes our physical survival and regulates impulses such as fear, anger and sexual drive. With the evolution of mammals, who care for their young, an Engagement Ethic emerged, incorporating feelings of intimacy, care-giving and loneliness.[16]

We can trace the roots of empathy and altruism back to this early Engagement Ethic. A mother looking after her young needs to know what they're feeling so she can do a better job of protecting them. If she witnesses her infant mewling in distress, she will automatically become distressed herself. It's possible that mirror neurons evolved for this purpose, which activate when an animal witnesses the actions of another, simulating an internal experience as if the observer were actually performing the action.[17]

While empathy may have evolved as a result of maternal care, it eventually became an established part of the mammalian repertoire, especially among social species. Scientists have discovered that when a prairie vole undergoes stress and is put back in a cage with its mate, the mate's stress hormones immediately increase. The mate rushes over and begins grooming and licking the originally stressed vole, which activates oxytocin and brings down the stress levels of both of them.[18]

Empathic responses like this lead naturally to altruistic behavior, even between creatures that don't have a prior relationship. In another experiment scientists placed a rat in a cage where another rat was trapped in a restrainer. The free rat quickly learned to open the restrainer and release its cage-mate. But here's the most fascinating part: when researchers placed chocolate in the cage, the free rat still chose to liberate the restrained rat even though it meant sharing the chocolate. Yes, rats readily demonstrate altruism.[19]

Impressive acts of altruistic behavior have been reported among apes, elephants and dolphins, who will risk their own lives to save the lives of others. These sophisticated mammals all have a highly developed neocortex, which catapults them into the third ethical category that Narvaez calls the Ethic of Imagination, involving such mental feats as consideration of alternative actions and 'perspective taking'.[20]

Depending on the species, this more advanced ethical level may still lead to highly divergent norms, which we can see by looking at our two closest cousins: chimpanzees and bonobos. Both species lead elaborate social lives, but they value different modalities for problem-solving. Chimps are cooperative when sharing a task, but only to a limit: when a chimp finds a good meal, he will eat it alone and quickly, knowing that if he brings it back to the group, it will get snatched by others – most likely the dominant male who rules according to a strict hierarchy. Bonobos, by contrast, are known as the species that 'make love, not war'. When a dispute over dominance erupts, they tend to solve it through sexual activity – mostly initiated by the female.[21]

The moral species

Humans share a common ancestor with bonobos and chimps, but something happened that led to our species populating the entire globe, building cities, flying to the moon and communicating through the internet. What was it?

It's not lethal aggression that distinguished us. Nor did we suddenly discover that greed is good. A large number of evolutionary biologists have coalesced around a consensus that it's our ability to cooperate with each other – even those who are not kin – that differentiates us from other primates. Primatologist Sarah Hrdy offers an intriguing thought experiment: next time you're on a plane, squeezed carefully between other passengers, politely minding your own business, imagine what would happen if, instead of humans, the plane was filled with chimpanzees. Mayhem would ensue. 'Any one of us,' Hrdy explains, 'would be lucky to disembark with all their fingers and toes still attached ... Bloody earlobes and other appendages would litter the aisles.'[22]

Somehow, humans learned to cooperate with each other on a grand scale. How did it happen? It began with our earliest hominid ancestors around six million years ago, when their forest environment turned into savanna. They were more vulnerable to big predators and had less access to food. But they discovered that, through collaboration, they could protect and feed themselves far more effectively. Those with the cognitive abilities to cooperate most effectively were the ones whose genes were passed on to future generations. In time, the enlarged prefrontal cortex (PFC) of our early ancestors enabled them to develop 'theory of mind', social intelligence, and with it the initial separation of 'I' and the 'self' in their consciousness.[23]

As we saw earlier, the highly developed PFC enabled us to control our impulses, allowing the emergent 'I' to regulate the 'self'. Does that mean then that Dawkins and the European tradition were right after all? That our 'higher faculties' of reason and willpower cause us to cooperate by exerting control over our primal impulses? Neuroscientists have discovered that the reality is far more complex and fascinating. Over millions of years, hominids developed what are called moral emotions such as guilt, compassion, embarrassment, shame and gratitude – emotions that arise from our intricate social interactions. Although the PFC is active when we experience those emotions, it's a two-way street. These emotions have become so embedded in our genetic make-up that we feel them in our gut, in the same way that we feel hunger or fear. They are an integral part of human animate consciousness, not merely residing in conceptual consciousness.[24]

In numerous experiments, researchers have validated Mencius's original hypothesis that, through moral emotions, humans are endowed with a natural sense of fairness, cooperation and altruism. Sophisticated tests have shown that, faced with a choice, our initial impulse is to cooperate, and only after time to reflect do selfish behaviors emerge. When test subjects had their PFC temporarily blocked by chemicals, they shared more with others than they normally would, even when there was no ulterior motive to do so. As anthropologist Christopher Boehm retorts to the conventional selfish gene myth: 'Scratch anyone ... and see an altruist, not a hypocrite, bleed!'[25]

Boehm, who has spent his career studying both primates and hunter-gatherer societies, presents a convincing account of how morality originated in early humans. At first, assertive males would try to achieve the kind of dominance seen in other primate societies. But the rest of the group – females and males collaborating – would be driven by shared moral outrage to prevent such males from disrupting the group harmony. Boehm calls this a 'reverse dominance hierarchy' because the group as a whole establishes dominance over aggressive individuals. Over time, through an evolutionary process of group selection, nomadic bands that emphasized group identity flourished, whereas those that ceded control to a dominant alpha male eventually failed.[26]

Eventually, people's sense of identity expanded from their own self and kin to include their entire group. The common welfare became a touchstone for values: those who acted selfishly at the expense of the group were considered bad, whereas those who acted altruistically were seen as good. In a gradual process of culture–gene co-evolution, those ethical distinctions became embedded in the genetic endowment of the bands that flourished, eventually becoming endemic to the human species. We don't just act morally because we think we should – we do so because it *feels* right.[27]

This transition to a greater shared identity, and the emergence of a moral sense that came with it, may be humanity's defining characteristic. Charles Darwin thought so, averring that 'of all the differences between man and the lower animals, the ethical sense or conscience is by far the most important'. As evolutionary biologist David Sloan Wilson puts it: 'We are evolution's latest major transition. Alone among primate species, we crossed the threshold from groups *of* organisms to groups *as* organisms.'[28]

As we all know, the atavistic male drive for dominance never quite disappeared from humanity's genetic endowment. But early humans evolved an extra moral impulse that kept it in check: in addition to acting altruistically, our ancestors developed an instinct to punish those they caught taking advantage of the rest of the group. This crucial characteristic, called 'altruistic punishment', has been repeatedly demonstrated in careful testing by social psychologists. We humans are generally willing to make costly sacrifices in order to challenge behavior we think is morally wrong. We have an intrinsic sense of fairness, and we act upon it. Contrary to Dawkins' assertion, we don't need to be taught to be moral. We are a moral species.[29]

In a series of ingenious experiments with puppets, psychologist Paul Bloom has shown that moral instincts are deeply ingrained in the behavior of preverbal infants as young as three months of age, long before they are able to learn values from their parents or caregivers. One-year-old babies preferred puppets that were helpful and cooperative to those that were mean and selfish. When a 'naughty' puppet who had run off with a ball was given a treat by the researcher, the baby not only took the treat away but then smacked the puppet on the head! In various experiments, babies showed a rudimentary sense of fairness, justice, empathy, compassion and generosity, along with a clear ability to distinguish between kind and cruel actions.[30]

But there's something missing from this story, isn't there? All you need to do is read today's headlines to discern another, darker dimension to human behavior. If infants are born with this blessed endowment of morality, what then accounts for the vast injustices and despotic acts that have tainted virtually every civilization in history, and continue to afflict our daily lives?

The cultural evolution of values

As long as our ancestors lived in small, nomadic bands of hunter-gatherers (the vast bulk of human history) the group's moral sense kept in check any rogue male's primitive drive for dominance. However, that all changed with the rise of agriculture, beginning about 12,000 years ago. With settled lifestyles, inequalities now played a bigger part in social dynamics. If a farmer got lucky with his crops, while his neighbor's crops failed, he accrued extra wealth and power, which he wasn't so willing to give up. As he got wealthier, he could afford to recruit others to help defend his property, with violence if necessary. The rest of the community might not approve, but they were now tethered to their land, and couldn't just wander off, like their nomadic hunter-gatherer forebears.[31]

With the increasing importance of possessions, there was more incentive to steal from neighboring communities. The group identity that helped create morality in the first place has been aptly called 'parochial altruism' because frequently it only extended to the in-group. In the new regimen of territorial raids, the social cohesion that had favored cooperation now became a resource for effective combat. Aggressive communities conquered those that were more peaceful, foisting on them warrior cultures that prized machismo and violence.[32*]

Over generations, the scale of aggression ratcheted up, as villages consolidated into chiefdoms, and some eventually became empires. Cultural historian Riane Eisler calls these patriarchal societies 'domination systems' in contrast to the 'partnership systems' that predominated among hunter-gatherers. Characterized by top-down authoritarian rule and the subordination of women to men, these types of societies – many of which still exist in varying degrees today – value institutionalized forms of violence and are held together primarily by fear and force.[33*]

As these domination-based societies grew ever larger and far-flung, it became increasingly difficult to control them by force alone. But the dominators had a secret weapon that they used to great effect: the moral instincts of their subjects. Early civilizations around the world were characterized by religious beliefs that channeled moral intuitions into behaviors that supported the authority of the centralized power. Frequently, emperors were viewed as semi-divine, and the values of the common people revolved around maintaining the system that funneled massive wealth and power upward to the ruling elite. Societal control could now be maintained even without the threat of direct violence; fear of retribution from moralizing gods was enough to keep people's behavior in line.[34]

While virtually all moral systems encouraged prosocial behavior among citizens (as long as they respected the various hierarchies of power), they paid almost no regard to the welfare of those outside the prescribed in-group, such as foreigners or slaves. Honor and revenge were more important than any concern for the lives and well-being of others. Emperors would boast of slaughtering their enemies in bloody massacres. In Homer's *Odyssey*, Odysseus is proud to narrate how, when he and his men arrived at the city of Ismarus, 'I sacked this place and destroyed its menfolk. The women and the vast plunder that we took from the town we divided so that no one ... should go short of his proper share.' When Odysseus arrived home, he nonchalantly hanged on one rope a dozen slave-girls of his household whom he suspected of misbehavior while he was away.[35]

However, as several civilizations in Eurasia reached a critical mass of wealth and sophistication, they experienced a seismic shift in values. Merchants brought to major urban centers a greater awareness of other regions with differing customs and beliefs. To fresh generations of inquiring minds, the old systems of parochial gods no longer made sense. New transcendent values began to spread through society, with an enlarged perspective that viewed the whole of humanity – and sometimes all sentient beings – as a moral community. During a surprisingly brief period of a few centuries, known as the Axial Age, many of the great systems of thought we've inherited – including Buddhism, Confucianism, Taoism, Vedanta, Greek philosophy and the Old Testament – transformed their cultures' traditional beliefs. While differing from each other in many regards, they generally looked to a more sublime source of values than the local gods of their region. Whether it was the *dharma*, the Tao, Brahman, Reason or an omnipotent God, these new belief systems offered a more comprehensive set of values applicable beyond time and place. In keeping with their conception of a common humanity, most of them shared as a foundational ethic some version of what has become known as the Golden Rule: do unto others as you would have done to yourself.[36]

From today's vantage point, with the majority of the world's population identifying with one of the Abrahamic religions – Christianity, Islam and Judaism – it's natural to see monotheism as a kind of default faith that was waiting to be discovered, with its vision of an omniscient God who created the universe and established fixed values. However, most of the Axial Age systems conceived of the cosmos in different ways. As I've traced in *The Patterning Instinct*, monotheism only became predominant worldwide as a result of conquest: the Romans occupying Palestine, the Muslims conquering North Africa and the Middle East, and finally European imperialism overwhelming the rest of the world. With its absolutist notion of a patriarchal God setting universal values, monotheism established an uncompromising duality of right and wrong, instituting an ethic of religious intolerance that had not previously been part of the human experience.[37]

Even today, in the United States, it is commonly believed that those who are not God-fearing are less likely to be ethical. A 2007 Gallup poll reported that most Americans would rather vote for a Mormon, a Jew, or a gay or lesbian as president than an atheist, and would be more reluctant to see their children marry an atheist than a member of the other groups. Pundits occasionally cite social psychology studies to claim that traditional religion makes people happier, healthier and more charitable. However, a closer analysis shows that it is increased community involvement that produces these beneficial results, not the beliefs. Statistics show, for example, that an atheist who, perhaps through a spouse, becomes involved in the social life of a congregation is more likely to volunteer in a soup kitchen than a fervent believer who prays alone.[38]

In the past few centuries, new moral philosophies have swept through the world, attempting to replace traditional monotheism with something more coherent. Depending on the baseline assumptions used, these systems can lead to a perplexingly diverse set of ethical principles, ranging from communism to fascism to libertarianism. Many thinkers now look to science as a solid basis for constructing a universally valid moral system. Although it's commonly stated that science is value-free, that's not the case. There are core values underlying scientific methodology such as honesty, evidence-based inquiry, openness, accountability and tolerance, among others. These scientific principles, sometimes referred to as Enlightenment values, are frequently associated with concepts like justice, rights and freedom, and are cited by modern thinkers such as Steven Pinker, Michael Shermer and Sam Harris as the reason for the moral progress humanity has enjoyed in recent history.[39]

This is an important perspective that needs careful investigation. In preparation, let's first take a step back to consider what we've learned about how humans treat moral issues in general.

How our guts learn their intuitions

If there's something in addition to a moral instinct that characterizes humanity, it's our patterning instinct: the innate drive everyone has, from infancy and throughout their lives, to pattern meaning into the world around them. Because of the brain's inherent plasticity, the meaning we construct tends to be sculpted by the predominant values of the culture into which we're born.[40]

That's why, depending on where and when someone was born, they might believe fervently in the overriding importance of respecting their ancestors, defending national honor, worshiping God or enjoying untrammeled freedom. At the same time, the moral instincts that Mencius identified in us continue to express themselves. The contrast between our innate morality and our cultural values can sometimes lead to severe inner conflicts, which have generated many of the iconic dramatic tensions of our cultural heritage. In the Old Testament, for example, when God ordered Abraham to sacrifice Isaac to show his fealty, we can readily imagine the agonizing conflict between Abraham's obedience to a higher authority and a father's love for his son. Similarly, in the New Testament, Jesus declares, 'I have come to set a man against his father, and a daughter against her mother ... Whoever loves father or mother more than me is not worthy of me.'[41]

We see these conflicts arise throughout history. Mark Twain's Huckleberry Finn believed he was morally obliged to turn in his friend Jim, the escaped slave, but he couldn't bring himself to do it. Even Joseph Goebbels, one of Hitler's leading henchmen, experienced occasional episodes of compassion toward the Jews he was helping exterminate, which he interpreted as weakness of the will and learned to overcome.[42]

Modern psychologists have explored some prototypical inner conflicts of values through a series of ingenious thought experiments. Suppose a runaway trolley is about to crash into five people and kill them. If you flick a switch, you can divert the trolley to another track where it will kill just one person. Would you do it? Most people answer 'Yes.' Now, suppose that instead of flicking a switch, you were on a bridge above the trolley track, and you could push a large person (larger than yourself) in front of the trolley, which would kill him but save the others. Now, would you do it? Most people answer 'No' in this case, even though the number of people killed is the same as in the first scenario.[43]

This discrepancy points to two different pathways for moral cognition within us, which roughly map onto conceptual and animate forms of consciousness. Conceptually, we can rationalize saving the largest number of lives. When we flick a switch, we don't feel emotionally engaged and can go ahead. However, if we were to push someone over the bridge to their death, we would be violating our moral intuition against murder, and our deeply felt animate consciousness would rebel against our rational determination. This explains the quandary in Peter Singer's thought experiment, where we would readily save the child in the pond at the expense of our new shoes but don't necessarily donate that money to charity every day: one catalyzes our intuitive engagement; the other requires a rational choice.[44]

Do you remember psychologist Jonathan Haidt's suggestion that, when we make a decision, reason is like a lawyer arguing the case for what intuition already decided? In the trolley examples we again see these two parts of our psyche interacting. Haidt argues convincingly that when we make moral judgments they appear in consciousness effortlessly and automatically as a result of moral intuition. But that doesn't necessarily mean our intuition is right, nor that it reflects intrinsic human morality. Our moral intuitions, Haidt argues, are 'both innate and enculturated'. Research has shown that we tend to internalize our values during a sensitive period of cognitive development in late childhood and adolescence. In Robert Sapolsky's words, 'Our guts learn their intuitions.'[45]

This is the reason why morals can evolve over generations. They don't just evolve according to some natural law; they can also change as the result of deliberate acts of persuasion instigated by thought leaders of each age. For example, Harriet Beecher Stowe's 1852 novel *Uncle Tom's Cabin* has been credited with helping end slavery in the United States by provoking sympathy in the minds of white readers, leading to a sense of moral outrage. When Peter Singer's *Animal Liberation* was published in 1975, the concept of animal rights was virtually unheard of. It now plays a meaningful part in public discourse on the treatment of animals.[46*]

Looking back over generations, can we detect an inexorable improvement in the quality of moral intuition as it bends toward justice? In Chapter 2 we came across the Flynn effect: the consistent rise in IQ levels demonstrated across the world ever since testing began. Steven Pinker suggests there might be a similar dynamic in moral evolution: a moral Flynn effect. He points out that the norms of those living only a hundred years ago would now be considered 'morally retarded'. The source of this effect, he argues, along with Shermer and Harris, is an improvement in abstract moral reasoning – in essence, the part of us that would flick the switch in the trolley experiment to save five lives. Based on this, they advocate a system of values built on the primacy of reason. Let's turn now to investigate their approach.[47]

The individual pursuit of happiness

These 'moral rationalists' argue that the best way to construct a system of values is based on science and reason. Like Dawkins, Pinker and Shermer both endorse the Hobbesian view that humans in their natural state are selfish and violent. Reason, Pinker tells us, is what saves us. It allows us to transcend 'the flaws in human nature' and sow 'the seeds of our own improvement'. Harris goes further, arguing that morality should be founded not just on reason, but on science. 'Morality,' he declares, 'should be considered an undeveloped branch of science.'[48]

They respond to the naturalistic fallacy by advancing a foundational standard for moral evaluation – human well-being. There are, as we've seen, multiple fractal layers to this concept, but this is a perspective to which the moral rationalists seem oblivious. Well-being, Harris tells us, can be determined by 'states of the human brain'. Shermer contends that, since the individual 'is the fundamental unit of nature', and since natural selection works on individuals and not the group, 'we are first and foremost individuals ... and therefore ought not to be subservient to the collective'.[49]

The idea of constructing a system of values based on scientific principles such as evidence-based inquiry and openness seems admirable. However, the moral rationalists have not lived up to their own standards. As we've seen repeatedly, several of their fundamental assumptions have been soundly refuted in recent decades on multiple fronts. The individual is not the fundamental unit of nature; natural selection has been convincingly shown to work on groups as well as individuals; and states of the human brain only exist through interactions with the body and the external world. The moral rationalists base their intellectual constructions not on true scientific principles but on the credo of fundamentalist reductionism, which, as we've seen, requires an ontological leap of faith. For the most part, they are so taken by their ontology that, like fish swimming in water unaware that any other medium exists, they don't recognize they are thinking within a constructed framework. As Shermer blithely remarks, the 'worldview known as Enlightenment Humanism ... unlike most other worldviews, is more a method than an ideology'.[50]

Their fixation on individual experience as the only benchmark for well-being causes them to neglect the fractal dimensions of flourishing: the recognition that true well-being can only exist within a flourishing community embedded in a healthy society and a thriving natural world. Although each of the moral rationalists has his own political outlook, they share the conventional

Western obsession with the individual pursuit of happiness as the value that trumps all others – the implications of which have profoundly influenced ethical norms in recent decades.

Since the 1980s this individualist value system has become entrenched in global mainstream discourse in the form of neoliberalism: a pseudo-philosophy based on the fiction that humans are isolated, selfish, rational, calculating materialists for whom social and moral connections with others are irrelevant to happiness. This bizarre characterization of humanity was popularized by novelist Ayn Rand, whose primary message was that selfishness is the greatest virtue, and best summarized by British Prime Minister Margaret Thatcher when she famously declared, 'There's no such thing as society. There are individual men and women and there are families.'[51]

Through their control of government, finance, business and media, neoliberal adherents have imposed a de facto value system on much of the world that is at odds with human moral instincts of generosity, fairness and altruism. The economic system derived from these values has bestowed inordinate power on transnational corporations to direct human affairs – institutions that are legally bound to pursue one value above all others: maximizing shareholder profits.[52]

In the United States corporations have been given legal personhood with free license to influence elections; however, if a corporation were actually a person, its single-minded obsession with profit at the expense of anything else would cause it to be diagnosed as a psychopath. It is rather terrifying to consider that these institutional psychopaths so dominate our lives that sixty-nine of the world's hundred largest economies are in fact transnational corporations. Not surprisingly, flesh-and-blood psychopaths thrive in the corporate environment. Studies have reported that, whereas psychopaths make up just 1 percent of the human population, their proportion among business executives ranges from 4 to 20 percent. Characteristic traits associated with psychopathy include insincerity, lack of remorse and an inability to experience empathy or concern for others.[53]

The stranglehold that neoliberal values have over global human discourse has cast a pervasive sense of numbness over many of the great moral issues facing humanity. While the moral improvements of the past few centuries are real, there are huge blind spots overlooked by the mainstream narrative. If we extend our moral scope beyond humans, there has been a historically unprecedented, drastic deterioration in well-being, with a vast die-off of animal populations in the wild, which have declined 68 percent worldwide since 1970. Factory farming, on the other hand, using practices of unspeakable cruelty, has grown dramatically to the point that 74 billion animals are annually reared and killed for food worldwide, most of them enduring tortured, confined, unnaturally brief lives of appalling suffering.[54]

Turning attention to our fellow humans reveals further blind spots. While Pinker and other prominent policymakers regularly boast of statistics showing a reduction in global poverty, the actual experience of people's lives is very different. As economist Jason Hickel explains, even though the world produces more than enough food annually to feed all of humanity, it's estimated that about two billion people worldwide go hungry. The extreme inequalities caused by the global neoliberal system have resulted in just twenty-six billionaires owning as much wealth as half the world's population. While the world's affluent minority enjoys greater wealth than ever, more than half of humanity, or about 4.3 billion people, earn less than $7.40 per day – the minimum income considered necessary for a decent chance of a child surviving until their fifth birthday and reaching normal life expectancy.[55]

Those who espouse an arc of inexorable moral improvement respond to these critiques by pointing out that progress is necessarily incremental. They frequently refer to the concept of an expanding circle of empathy and altruism – a model that was first described by the Stoics of ancient Greece. Beginning with yourself at the center, the first circle represents your immediate family; the next your community; then comes your society and your nation; then the whole human race; and finally it extends out to encompass all sentient beings.[56]

As far as it goes, the intention of incremental moral expansiveness is a welcome antidote to the psychopathy of our dominant value system. However, it also betrays certain preconceptions rooted in the Western cult of individuality: that there are in fact defined circles, with a self in the center and nonhuman life at the outer periphery. Additionally, the modern version of this vision, borrowing from the 'moral arc' narrative, asserts that human history began by focusing on the inner circles, and as society became more sophisticated, we've steadily been expanding our scope.

Are there different ways to represent moral cultivation? And how can we really claim moral progress, given that the rise of domination societies, with their reliance on coercion and violence, only began about 12,000 years ago? Is there anything to learn from the traditional wisdom of Chinese and Buddhist sages, or from Indigenous communities existing today that have managed to maintain core values handed down from their ancestors? Let's take a look.[57]

'One body with Heaven and Earth'

Black Elk, a celebrated Oglala Lakota medicine man, experienced a powerful vision that inspired him and other Native American leaders facing devastation at the hands of the US military. In his vision, he was taken to the center of the Earth, where he saw 'the shape of all shapes as they must live together like one being. And I saw that the sacred hoop of my people was one of many hoops that made one circle.'[58]

This image of different groups of people interlocking in sacred hoops is notably different from the expanding circle of Western moral thinking. It informs an Indigenous worldview that recognizes the intricate interdependencies of all elements of life, weaving together individuals, communities, nations and the natural world.

Comanche social activist LaDonna Harris has identified four central values shared by Indigenous peoples around the world. These form a worldview known as indigeneity, which affirms the deep interconnectedness between all aspects of creation. Referred to as the Four Rs, they are: relationship, responsibility, reciprocity and redistribution. They each refer to different types of obligation that inform a person's life. *Relationship* is a kinship obligation, recognizing value not just in family but in 'all our relations' including animals, plants and the living Earth. *Responsibility* is the community obligation, identifying the imperative to nurture and care for those relations. *Reciprocity* is a cyclical obligation to balance what is given and taken. And *redistribution* is the obligation to share what one possesses – not just material wealth, but one's skills, time and energy.[59]

What is noticeable in these values is that they all revolve around the community, not the individual. However, this doesn't suppress a person's individuality; rather, individuality is expressed through the unique contributions each person is able to make to their community. In polar opposition to Thatcher's dictum, Harris explains that from the Indigenous perspective one's true 'self' can only arise through community. As we saw earlier, this is epitomized by the African principle of *ubuntu*: 'I am because you are; you are because I am.' The self-seeking behavior considered normative in the neoliberal worldview would be viewed as a form of madness in traditional Indigenous cultures, grounds for some kind of therapy or possible ostracism.[60]

Mencius, with his belief in a person's innate moral shoots, would likely have found a great deal of overlap with the values of indigeneity. He and other prominent Chinese thinkers also formed their moral systems on the basis of the interrelatedness of all life and the responsibilities naturally arising out of a sense of shared community. From these principles, they formed a moral vision that embraced the unity of all creation. 'Everything from ruler, minister, husband, wife, and friends, to mountains, rivers, heavenly and earthly spirits, birds, beasts, and plants, all should be truly loved in order that the unity may be reached,' declared Wang Yangming. 'Then will I really form one body with Heaven and Earth and the myriad things.'

This grand vision had daily practical implications. Wang referred to Mencius's thought experiment of someone saving the child in the well. 'His humanity forms one body with the child,' he explained. This deep connection, Wang pointed out, extends beyond our own species. When we hear the 'pitiful cries ... of birds and animals about to be slaughtered' we empathize with their unbearable suffering. When we see plants destroyed, we feel a sense of loss. Even when we see inanimate objects, such as tiles and stones, shattered and crushed, we feel a pang of regret. This shows, Wang avers, that our own humanity forms one body even with tiles and stones.

Rather than having to learn altruism and generosity 'because we are born selfish', the Chinese view was that one simply had to *unlearn* the layers of misconceptions that society placed on a person as they grew up. Sagehood, Wang Yangming taught, was a quality innate in every human, an inborn capacity to know what is good and to recognize that self-centered desires only take one away from fulfilling the true potential of human experience – or, in Aristotle's terms, from eudaimonia.[61]

Because of this sense of intrinsic goodness, the Chinese didn't believe that acting morally required the exercise of willpower. Instead, it required the practice of discernment: distinguishing between what was truly good and what only appeared attractive. As one became more adept at discernment, the impulse to act ethically would become increasingly effortless and spontaneous. Mencius likened it to learning how to dance. 'When such joy is born,' he declared, 'it cannot be stopped. Since it is unstoppable, you cannot help but begin to unconsciously dance along with your feet and wave your hands in time with it.'[62]

Dispelling the suffering of others

Buddhism shares with both traditional Chinese and Indigenous wisdom the fundamental insight of the interconnectedness of all things. According to the Buddhist principle of dependent origination, all that arises depends on everything else that came before it: we live in a universe of endless interdependence. Another crucial Buddhist insight, as we've seen, is that the sense of a self as a fixed entity is simply a delusion: an awakened person realizes that in fact the rigid boundaries we create between ourselves and others are mere constructions of the mind.

The combination of these two principles can lead in Buddhist practice to a benevolent concern for the welfare of all sentient beings, known as *metta*, or lovingkindness. The love that one might feel for one's own life naturally extends to all other living entities. 'As a mother, even at the risk of her own life, watches over her only child, so let everyone cultivate a boundless love for all beings,' adjures a classic text.[63]

As Buddhist practice spread throughout Asia, its principles of compassion and lovingkindness resonated strongly with people. Buddhist deities embodying these principles became important icons of practice. In many parts of Asia, there are shrines dedicated to Guanyin, a goddess symbolizing compassionate awakening, whose name means 'the one who listens and hears the cries of the world in order to come and help'. The deity Tara plays a similar role in Tibetan Buddhism: practitioners meditate upon her qualities, such as compassion, lovingkindness and wisdom, in order to develop them more fully within themselves.[64]

Both Guanyin and Tara are embodiments of the Buddhist ideal of a *bodhisattva*: someone who, having achieved enlightenment and been liberated from the endless cycles of reincarnation, has nevertheless vowed to remain in the world to alleviate the suffering of all sentient beings. The Buddhist monk Shantideva offers a classic rendering of the bodhisattva dedication:

> For as long as space endures
> And for as long as living beings remain,
> Until then may I too abide
> To dispel the misery in the world.[65]

It's easy to dismiss this expression of unbounded grace as an unrealistic ideal, something not directly relevant to daily life. However, while its ultimate realization may seem far off, the intention to live according to these principles is available to all of us.

Buddhist practice in fact offers a practical way to access these ideals in the form of lovingkindness meditation: a particular type of practice focused specifically on cultivating feelings of benevolence, love and compassion. As discussed earlier, the initial effects of mindfulness meditation are noticeable within a few weeks, but it takes sustained practice for them to become more robust. Interestingly, the beneficial effects of lovingkindness meditation occur more readily. Researchers suspect this may be because we're already inherently oriented toward these feelings. As Mencius suggested, our biological predisposition toward empathy and compassion are like shoots within us, which simply need to be nurtured in order to grow and thrive.[66*]

'I am life, in the midst of life'

As I mentioned at the outset of this chapter, there's something bewildering about the way different moral systems seem able to justify almost any behavior. However, one common factor emerges from the wide range of moral philosophies we've encountered: our version of morality is, to a very large extent, a function of our identity. If you identify with your community, your values will emphasize the welfare of the group. If you see yourself as an isolated individual, your values will accordingly lead you to pursue your own happiness at the expense of others.

Is it possible to develop a universal morality – one that's not bounded by cultural predispositions? What would an ethical system look like that was solidly based on a scientific foundation? Not the outmoded science of the moral rationalists relying on eighteenth-century reductionist thinking, but a synthesis of the scientific findings of recent decades? The *gewu* – investigation of things – we've been conducting tells us that the core insights of Buddhist, Chinese and Indigenous wisdom have a scientifically sound basis: we are all deeply interconnected. Throughout the fractal layers of life, sustained flourishing can only exist when it is in harmony with the whole. The well-being or suffering of one group – whether within our community, elsewhere in the world or in nonhuman form – cannot be isolated from what is happening elsewhere in the web of existence.

A truly integrated system of values would recognize this as its foundational principle. Once we see ourselves as an integrated system within systems, our values emerge accordingly. Cultivating integrated values means not being stuck in one identity or even favoring one over the other, but recognizing that we exist in a continual dynamic flow of the different fractal layers of being. We *are* the interlocking hoops of Black Elk's vision. We form, as Wang Yangming described, 'one body with Heaven and Earth and the myriad things'.

Within the context of human society, a system of integrated values would emphasize the evolved morality that distinguishes humans from other primates: our deeply felt sense of justice, fairness, kindness, generosity of spirit and compassion. In practical terms, that means working to undo the injustices and violence that our society has inherited from the hierarchical, patriarchal domination systems of the past. It's not easy work. Even the earliest hunter-gatherer bands needed skillful use of social technologies to protect against the domination of despotic alpha males. In modern society, where money and power are so firmly entrenched, we must coalesce as a broad moral community to assert the primacy of core human values.[67]

That doesn't mean going back to an illusory golden age of nomadic hunter-gatherer bands, but moving forward to co-create a consciously constructed 'partnership society' of the future. It means applying the insights of wisdom traditions such as Indigenous, Buddhist and traditional Chinese thought to our global culture, but doing so in ways that reflect the technological and societal complexity of our age. Scandinavian countries once again are leading the charge in many respects. In one example of what's possible, their schools have mandatory classes in empathy, teaching schoolchildren to share emotional problems and collaborate non-judgmentally with others in finding solutions, thus establishing a partnership ethos at the sensitive time when children internalize ethical norms into their moral intuition.[68*]

Through this type of intervention – along with a multitude of other examples such as the #MeToo and Black Lives Matter social and political movements – it's possible to shift ingrained societal norms, and keep moving the moral arc away from the dominator ethic of the past. Studies conducted by animal liberation groups have shown that incremental moral change is not just beneficial in its own right, but lays the groundwork for more profound shifts in the moral baseline over generations. Through collective action, it's possible to keep the 'moral Flynn effect' moving forward, gradually shifting ethical baselines and building an increased capacity for global compassion in new generations.[69]

There is no guarantee, however, that the moral Flynn effect

will maintain forward momentum. The stranglehold over global media, politics, finance, business and economics achieved by transnational corporations and the uber-elite class of billionaires is a force pulling the moral arc in the opposite direction. To counter the neoliberal ideology of unrestrained individualism, we need to remain constantly vigilant toward the destructive underlying values being propagated, and forge our own moral identity based on our shared humanity, extending our own desire for warmth, love and community to others who need it.

There are areas, however, where even positive incremental change is insufficient. When we extend our identity beyond humanity to all of life, the situation we encounter requires far more drastic measures. The natural world, in all its awe-inspiring diversity, is suffering a relentless onslaught of devastation from global corporations and other domination-based institutions that view it as nothing more than fodder for economic growth and rampant consumption. To counteract this, our society needs a deeper moral transformation that radically alters its course.

This is where a truly integrated ethical system needs to go back to basics, recognizing life itself as the source of all other fractal layers, and therefore the foundation for values. When life first began on Earth, it brought value into existence. Rather than commit a 'naturalistic fallacy', it achieved a miraculous 'naturalistic alchemy' – out of bare matter it created a perpetual transformation from 'is' to 'ought'. Every living entity since then has shared a will to live and to flourish. As humans, when we acknowledge the life within ourselves that we share with all other organisms on Earth, we must then listen to life's howl of anguish and strive to bring it back to health in the face of reckless destruction.

These insights are not new. They have been powerfully expressed by visionaries, not just of past times but of the modern age. The great humanitarian Albert Schweitzer declared, 'I am life that wills to live, in the midst of life that wills to live.' From this essential truth, morality becomes self-evident. As he eloquently concluded, 'I cannot but have reverence for all that is called life. I cannot avoid compassion for everything that is called life. That is the beginning and foundation of morality.'[70*]

The miracle of life on Earth is that, over billions of years, it has created a dazzling island of negative entropy – the only one we know of in the universe. Our current civilization is currently using its prodigious powers in a concerted entropic onslaught to undo much of the bounty that life has generated. Wang Yangming pointed out that we naturally feel a sense of loss when we see animals dying or plants needlessly destroyed. Our global civilization is now devastating the living Earth at a scale he could never have imagined. How can we open our hearts to recognize this without having them broken? What does it mean to be an integrated, ethical human being in an age when humanity has the power to obliterate life's plenitude – and is actively doing so? These questions, and their implications, are the deeply wrenching topics we will now try to grapple with.

NEW THREADS OF MEANING

Because of our evolved moral emotions, we don't act morally just because we think we should, but because it feels right

Our 'guts learn their intuitions' based on the norms of the culture we grow up in

Our version of morality is, to a large extent, a function of our identity

A truly integrated system of values would be based on the foundational principle of interconnectedness

CHAPTER TEN

HUMAN/NATURE

Once, in ancient China, a certain Lord Thien held a banquet, inviting a thousand guests who brought gifts of fish and game. Eyeing them approvingly, he exclaimed, 'How generous is Heaven to man! Heaven makes the grains grow, and brings forth the fish and fowl, just for our benefit!' Everyone applauded except for the twelve-year-old son of one of the guests, who came forward and said, 'It is not as my Lord says. We belong to the same category of living beings as all the creatures of the world. It is only through size, strength or cunning, that one species gains mastery or feeds upon another. Man catches and eats what is fitting for his food, but how can you say that Heaven produced them just for him? Mosquitoes and gnats suck his blood; tigers and wolves devour his flesh – but we don't assert that Heaven produced man for the benefit of mosquitoes and gnats, or for tigers and wolves.'[1]

This delightful story, from an ancient Taoist text, points out the absurdity of anthropocentrism – the view that humans are more important than any other species, and that the rest of nature exists (or should exist) for human benefit. While Lord Thien may have been upstaged by a twelve-year-old in China, he would have felt right at home in Christian Europe, where anthropocentrism was a central tenet of faith. 'The world is made for the sake of man, that it may serve him,' stated theologian Peter Lombard, whose work became the standard medieval textbook of theology. Francis Bacon, the prophet of the Scientific Revolution, wholeheartedly agreed, declaring, 'the whole world works together in the service of man ... insomuch that all things seem to be going about man's business and not their own.'[2]

Bacon's vision was to intensify nature's service of man through scientific investigation, putting her 'in constraint' to discover 'the secrets still locked in [her] bosom'. He saw it as a war of conquest, calling on his fellow scientists 'to unite forces against the nature of things, to storm and occupy her castles and strongholds and extend the bounds of human empire'. Descartes concurred, writing how through science we could 'render ourselves the masters and possessors of nature'.[3]

Intoxicated by the promise of power and conquest, Europeans didn't limit themselves to scientific investigation, but took their thirst for domination overseas, embarking on a centuries-long campaign to render themselves the 'masters and possessors' of the rest of the world, storming and occupying territories where others had lived for time immemorial. They brought with them their anthropocentric view that nature existed only to serve humanity – especially those who were white, Christian males. Arriving in what they called the New World, they perceived a wilderness that had been put to 'no good or profitable use' – what they termed *vacuum domicilium*. This concept became their legal and moral justification to wrest the land from those who already lived there, and use it for their own purposes.[4]

The Native Americans, who had tended the land for countless generations, were horrified by the agricultural and mining practices the Europeans brought with them. Like other Indigenous people around the world, they viewed other sentient beings as their relatives. They understood the Earth as their mother, not as a *vacuum domicilium* requiring improvement. Smohalla, a medicine man of the Wanapum tribe who led a resistance movement against white encroachment in the nineteenth century, expressed the abhorrence of many with these haunting words:

> You ask me to plow the ground! Shall I take a knife and tear my mother's breast? Then when I die she will not take me to her bosom to rest. You ask me to dig for stone! Shall I dig under her skin for her bones? Then when I die I cannot enter her body to be born again. You ask me to cut grass and make hay and sell it, and be rich like white men! But how dare I cut off my mother's hair?[5]

The unremitting onslaught of European power represented not just a one-sided battle over territory; it was also a conflict over humankind's proper relationship with the Earth. In stark contrast to Smohalla's utterance, this declaration was published around the same time by the Big Horn Association of Cheyenne, Wyoming:

> The rich and beautiful valleys of Wyoming are destined for the occupancy and sustenance of the Anglo-Saxon race. The wealth that for untold ages has lain hidden beneath the snow-capped summits of our mountains has been placed there by Providence to reward the brave spirits whose lot it is to compose the advance-guard of civilization. The Indians must stand aside or be overwhelmed by the ever advancing and ever increasing tide of emigration.[6]

They certainly got one thing right: the Western conception of conquering nature has indeed overwhelmed all else in an 'ever advancing and ever increasing tide'.

Long ago, the *Tao Te Ching* sagely proclaimed,

> One who desires to take the world and act upon it,
> I see that it cannot be done.
> The world is a spirit vessel,
> Which cannot be acted upon.
> One who acts on it fails,
> One who holds on to it loses.[7]

Bacon, Descartes and the Big Horn Association clearly held a different view about the results of acting upon the world. And yet, what does 'winning' or 'losing' really entail in the relationship between humans and nature? As we thunder through the twenty-first century, facing the existential threats of climate breakdown and ecological collapse, the quandary of humanity's tangled relationship with nature has never been more critical to unravel. As our global civilization tries desperately to steer a path away from devastating environmental disruption, do the insights from Taoist, Native American and other Indigenous traditions have anything to offer?

The Great Acceleration

At first sight, our modern age might seem to have proven the *Tao Te Ching* wrong. Our dominant culture has explicitly 'desired to take the world and acted upon it' – and in many ways has succeeded beyond even its own wildest dreams.

Since the Second World War, the scale of human impact on the world has exploded in virtually every dimension. The sheer number of humans has more than tripled to 7.8 billion, and is growing at a rate equivalent to a new city of a million inhabitants springing up every five days. Global growth rates in production, consumption and trade have been even more dramatic, each gauge increasing more than tenfold. When a team of scientists measured humanity's impact on a more granular level, they were shocked to find an explosion of activity in almost every category. They called this period the Great Acceleration, and if you take a quick look at the charts they produced (Figure 8, overleaf) you will immediately see why.[8]

This explosion of human activity has, however, come at a massive cost. As our global civilization expands its scope, it does so by literally consuming the living Earth. Three quarters of all land has been appropriated for human purposes, either turned into farmland, covered by concrete or flooded by reservoirs. Three quarters of rivers and lakes are used for crop or livestock cultivation, with many of the world's greatest rivers, such as the Ganges, Yangtze and Nile, no longer reaching the sea. Half the world's forests and wetlands have disappeared; the Amazon rainforest alone is vanishing at the rate of an acre every second.[9]

The Earth's topsoil is rapidly being depleted, with significant loss of agricultural productivity on nearly a third of arable land. This loss has mostly been masked by the extensive use of manufactured nitrogen fertilizer, which drains into the ocean, causing uncontrolled algae blooms that suffocate all other life, creating more than four hundred dead zones in coastal waters, some covering 20,000 square miles. Beyond the dead zones, commercial fishing encompasses an area four times that of agriculture, leaving less than 13 percent of the oceans free from human impact. At the current rate, it's estimated that by 2050 there will be more plastic in the ocean, by weight, than fish.[10]

Socio-economic trends

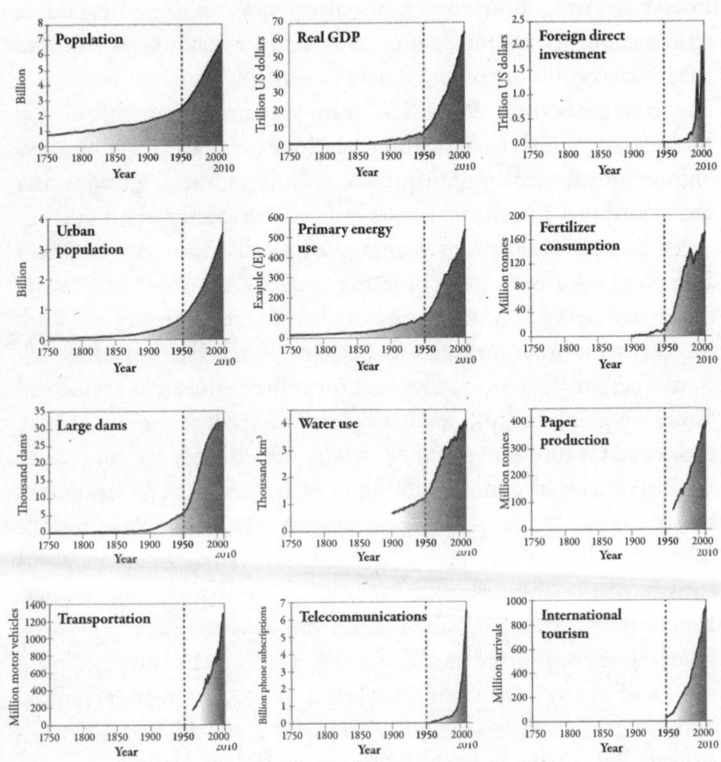

Figure 8: The Great Acceleration

The nonhuman creatures with whom we share the Earth are being systematically annihilated by the Great Acceleration, as they lose their habitat, are hunted down, or poisoned by our pollution. There has been a 68 percent decline in vertebrate populations worldwide since 1970, with freshwater species such as amphibians registering a jaw-dropping 84 percent loss. Insects have been faring just as badly, with reports of 'insectageddon' from some areas that have seen populations crashing toward extinction levels – such as the Monarch butterflies that migrate annually from Mexico to the United States, which have declined by 98 percent over the past thirty years.[11]

There have been five mass extinctions of life in Earth's history, caused by cataclysms such as volcanic eruptions or meteorite impact. Scientists warn that human activity is now causing species to go extinct at a thousand times the normal background rate, and that if we continue at this rate for a few more decades, we will have triggered the Sixth Extinction. Leading experts in the field, such as biologist E. O. Wilson, predict that half of the world's estimated eight million species will be extinct or at the brink of extinction by the end of this century unless humanity changes its ways.[12]

One of the most drastic impacts of human activity is greenhouse gas emissions, which have been heating the Earth's climate while acidifying the oceans, leading to the likely total destruction of coral reefs this century. The dire climate emergency facing our world is rapidly spiraling out of control. The Intergovernmental Panel on Climate Change (IPCC) has warned that we have until 2030 to turn things around before we pass the point of no return, setting off tipping points that will cause even greater disruption. The current pledges made by governments to reduce emissions are woefully insufficient: they would lead to three degrees Celsius of warming by the end of this century, which would threaten the foundations of our civilization, but they are not even on track to meet those commitments.[13]

As scientists have assessed the overwhelming impact of human activity on the Earth, they have come to realize that our actions now rival the great forces of nature. If, millions of years from now, another intelligent species were to examine the archaeological record, they would quickly realize that something unprecedented in Earth's history had occurred during our era. The signs would be unmistakable – including novel radioactive isotopes, the residue of plastics and concrete, and fossil fuel particulates. A growing number of scientists argue that this era requires a new name in the geological record. They claim that we're no longer in the Holocene – the period of stable climate that permitted the rise of agriculture over the past 12,000 years – but have now entered the Anthropocene.[14]

This new era, they warn, representing a profound shift in the relationship between humans and nature, is dangerously unstable.

Leading Earth scientists have identified nine 'planetary boundaries' representing what they call the safe operating space for humanity – but report that we have already exceeded four of them. Concerned that their message has not been heard by the world at large, a group of 15,000 scientists from 184 countries issued a warning to humanity in November 2017 that, because of our overconsumption of the world's resources, we are facing 'widespread misery and catastrophic biodiversity loss'. Time is running out, they aver: 'Soon it will be too late to shift course away from our failing trajectory.'[15]

To date, though, this trajectory continues. Is it possible, we may wonder, that the *Tao Te Ching* was right after all?

Where did nature go?

Not everyone shares the sense of impending doom promulgated by the 15,000 scientists. There are some who welcome the arrival of the Anthropocene as a triumph signaling the glorious progress of humankind. 'We are as gods,' declares Stewart Brand, founder of the *Whole Earth Catalog*, 'and have to get good at it.'

Brand is one of an influential new breed of environmental thinkers – some known as New Conservationists, others as Ecomodernists – who believe humanity's destiny is to take charge of nature and mold her to its will. These pundits, many with close connections to centers of money and power, have provoked an acrimonious debate in the environmental movement about how to respond to the Anthropocene. 'We are already running the whole Earth, whether we admit it or not,' writes New Conservationist Emma Marris. 'To run it consciously and effectively, we must admit our role and even embrace it.'[16]

A major theme of this group is to question the very idea of nature as something separate from humanity. Since *Homo sapiens* first evolved, they argue, there has never been such a thing as untrammeled, pristine wilderness. Therefore, there is no reason to mourn the loss of something that was merely a romantic idealization. Even when we set aside nature reserves in national parks, argues another New Conservationist, Peter Kareiva, we impose our own values, erecting lodges, removing unwanted species and drilling wells. As a result, he claims, 'we create parks that are no less human constructions than Disneyland'. We may as well embrace this reality, their argument goes, and recognize that much of the modern world is what Marris calls a 'rambunctious garden' – a riotous jumble of weedy plants and hardy creatures that thrive in the wake of human development. Rather than try to prevent invasive species from taking root, they argue, we should welcome them as something more natural than maintaining native species that could no longer survive. 'Suddenly,' Marris claims, 'the vacant lot in Detroit is wilder than Yellowstone.'[17]*

It's true that ever since humans first ventured out of Africa, they have disrupted the ecologies of each new territory they discovered. Using weapons and strategies developed through collective conceptual intelligence, our physically puny species proved capable of killing – and ultimately driving to extinction – even the most terrifying monsters. And they certainly met their share of behemoths wherever they ventured. Arriving in Australia, for example, they encountered creatures such as monitor lizards bigger than Nile crocodiles and giant marsupial lions that could stand on their hindlegs and slash with massive claws. Twenty or more spectacular genera of megafauna disappeared in Australia about 40,000 years ago, soon after humans arrived on the scene.[18]

Humans didn't get to North and South America until about 14,000 years ago, but when they did, they faced an even more formidable array of prodigious beasts, such as giant armadillos the size of a compact car, massive ground sloths weighing nearly three tons, saber-toothed cats with fangs as long as chef's knives and gigantic woolly elephants known as mastodons. All went extinct within a few thousand years of human habitation.[19]

Even in Europe, giants roamed the landscape. Lions, bears, hyenas, wolves, elk and ferocious wild cattle called aurochs continued to prowl the land until historical times. As they eliminated the megafauna, humans also transformed the landscape wherever they went. Australia was once covered by rainforest. The Mediterranean landscape, now loved for its vines and olive trees, was once densely forested with oaks, pines and cedars. The English countryside, exalted in poetry and art, is almost entirely a human composition, its prehistoric woodlands having declined by 1900 to less than 5 percent of their original range. Even the animals that populate the countryside, such as sheep, goats and cows, are largely artefacts of human design, having been bred for domestication over generations at the expense of their ability to survive in the wild.[20]

By the time Europeans discovered the Americas, its Indigenous peoples had spent millennia putting their imprint on the land. What looked like 'untrammeled wilderness' to the European eye was in fact a landscape that had been carefully tended by its inhabitants. Even the seemingly pristine Amazon rainforest has been discovered to have been partly sculpted by raised berms, built by complex societies over millennia to preserve trees from floodwaters and maintain sophisticated housing compounds.[21]

Once shipping lanes opened between Europe and the Americas, a maelstrom of global species intermingling was initiated, which has not let up since. Called by historians the Columbian Exchange, it brought, among other transplants, American native species such as tomatoes to Italy, potatoes to Ireland and hot peppers to Thailand. In many regions of the world imported or invasive species have now become the norm rather than the exception.[22]

As we enter the Anthropocene, we must face the stunning realization – first promulgated by environmentalist Bill McKibben in *The End of Nature* in 1989 – that there is nowhere in the entire world that remains free of human interference. Some of the remotest places are the most polluted, such as the Arctic, where pollutants such as dioxin and DDT accumulate, or the eleven-kilometer-deep Mariana Trench in the Pacific Ocean, where polychlorinated biphenyls (PCBs) have been found in crustaceans at fifty times the level of crabs living in the dirtiest waters of mainland China.[23]

While this situation might seem deplorable to many of us, many New Conservationists take it all in their stride. Nature, they argue, is highly resilient, not fragile. For every habitat that's lost, a new one emerges. 'Move, adapt or die,' exclaims Brand, contending that when fragile native species go extinct, 'they leave a niche for other species to migrate or adapt into'. An editorial on the biodiversity crisis in *The Economist* triumphantly opined that 'in a sense, this orgy of destruction [is] natural. In the wild, different species compete for resources, and man proved a highly successful competitor.'[24]

Making nature earn her living

If this sounds remarkably similar to Gordon Gekko's justification of free-market capitalism based on his pseudo-evolutionary theory of survival of the fittest, that may be more than coincidence. In fact, along with their glorification of human supremacy, the New Conservationists are fervent believers in the power of markets and technology to bring about a rosy future in an environment purposefully constructed to maximize human aspirations. Believing that the value of nature exists solely in how it benefits humankind, they argue that conservation should become a tool for economic development. They promote a vision of 'working landscapes' where, for example, trees are cultivated to produce lumber, even if that means cutting down old-growth forests and replacing biodiverse ecosystems with monocultures.[25]

Since humanity has now emerged triumphant, the New Conservationists argue, nature should be assimilated into the same globalized market-based economy that has enveloped the rest of life. The process used for this assimilation is known as ecosystem services: a methodology to calculate a financial value for each of the services nature provides for humankind. With ardent faith in market principles, they contend that, priced appropriately, nature's services will be fairly valued, and those that benefit humanity will automatically be sustained through market mechanisms.[26]

The idea of ecosystem services first emerged in the 1980s, the same decade that neoliberalism gained ascendancy. Ironically, it was pioneered not by New Conservationists but by leading environmental champions who, frustrated by their failure to preserve nature in the face of unremitting destruction, believed their efforts might gain more traction if only they could find a way to speak to businesspeople and policymakers on their own terms. If they could show key decision-makers, they felt, how valuable nature's gifts were, then surely they would stop demolishing their own wealth.[27]

With this admirable goal, the concept of ecosystem services swept through the environmental establishment, becoming a cornerstone for policymaking at UN agencies, major conservation NGOs and corporations. Economic values have been placed on coral reefs, wetlands, rivers, woodlands and tropical forests – there have even been attempts to place a monetary valuation on the entire planet. In policy-setting conferences around the world, nature has been well and truly incorporated into the monetary circuit, along with its own accounting classification: natural capital.[28]

Although initiated with the best of intentions, the concept of valuing ecosystem services to enhance nature conservation has been shown to be deeply flawed, frequently counterproductive and ultimately self-defeating. The most obvious problem is that, once a natural ecosystem is made the subject of cost-benefit analysis, its survival depends solely on its relative value compared to any competing development project. A wetland, for example, might have value in protecting a city from flooding. However, if it were drained and a swanky new resort built on the reclaimed land, this could be more lucrative. Case closed.[29]

Perversely, the more compromised a natural ecosystem becomes – such as bleached coral reefs that no longer host diverse fish populations – the less valuable its services and therefore the less incentive there is to maintain it. Sometimes economic incentives can work directly against what is good for a healthy ecosystem – even global heating can represent financial opportunities to those who are so inclined. The rapidly shrinking Arctic icecap, for example, while portending a global catastrophe, offers a short-term economic windfall for mining and shipping companies. In 2019 US Secretary of State Mike Pompeo unabashedly praised the melting ice for permitting corporations to access its oil, gas, uranium and fisheries, in addition to opening up trade passageways. 'Arctic sea lanes,' he gushed, 'could become the twenty-first-century Suez and Panama canals.'[30]

At a deeper level, putting a monetary value on ecosystem services implicitly changes the way in which people think about nature. It becomes normative to start considering the value of living beings in terms of market-based parameters such as trading, efficiency and profit. As I've described in *The Patterning Instinct*, the root metaphors we use to think about the world powerfully affect our values – and ultimately our collective actions as a society. Ever since the Scientific Revolution, the root metaphor of nature as a machine has infiltrated Western culture, causing people to view the living Earth as a resource for humans to exploit without regard for its intrinsic value. The financialization of nature represents a modern refinement of the existing metaphor, reducing nature to a balance-sheet item. Ecological philosopher Eileen Crist has pointed out that seeing nature as a resource permits anything to be done to the Earth with no moral misgivings. Fish get reclassified as fisheries, and farm animals as livestock – living creatures mere assets to be exploited for profit.[31]

As the stakes get higher through this century, the dangers arising from this mechanistic metaphor of nature will only become more harrowing. Already, in response to the acceleration of climate breakdown, the techno-dystopian idea of geoengineering is becoming increasingly acceptable. Rather than disrupt the fossil-fuel-based growth economy, policymakers are beginning to seriously countenance treating the Earth as a gigantic machine that needs fixing, and envisioning massive engineering projects to accomplish the repair. A leading candidate, financed by Bill Gates, involves spraying particles into the stratosphere to cool the Earth by reflecting the sun's rays back into space. The risks are enormous, including the likelihood of causing extreme shifts in precipitation around the world. Additionally, once begun, it could never be stopped without immediate catastrophic rebound heating; it would not prevent the oceans from further acidifying; and it may turn the blue sky into a perpetual dull haze. In spite of these concerns, geoengineering is beginning to get discussed at UN meetings, with serious publications such as *The Economist* predicting that, since it's cheaper and effective immediately, it's more likely to be implemented than the drastic, binding cuts in emissions that would head off climate disaster.[32]

At the deepest level, we must ask what kind of ludicrous folly it is to debase our living Earth, the only source of life that we know of in the universe, to a financial market instrument. Consider someone you love dearly, such as a parent or child. If a billionaire walked up to you offering any amount of money to buy her, abuse her and then kill her, would you consider it, even for one instant? Of course not. There are some things that are sacred – that have value beyond any price that could be paid. Why, we must ask, do we not react more like Smohalla when businesspeople and economists put a price tag on Mother Earth?[33]

Oscar Wilde once famously defined a cynic as someone who knows the price of everything and the value of nothing. By incorporating nature's gifts to humanity into the global financial system, our society is enthroning cynicism as the primary value by which to judge all else.[34]

The Great Dying

Why then don't we indeed react in unbridled outrage, like Smohalla, to the devastation of the natural world taking place before our eyes? A major reason is that we don't realize what we've lost. Back in 1968, in a song that became an icon of the environmental movement, Joni Mitchell sang about paving paradise and building a parking lot, making the point that you never know what you've got till it's gone. She stirred millions of hearts, but she was wrong. The disturbing reality is that, once it's gone, people forget they ever had it. Whatever conditions people grow up with are the ones they generally consider normal. This is a tribute to the amazing plasticity of the human mind, but it means that we tend to take for granted things that should never be accepted.[35]

This phenomenon, known as shifting baseline syndrome, was first discovered by fisheries scientist Daniel Pauly, who was researching the reduction in the size of the catch off the eastern seaboard of North America, which had declined by 97 percent since written records began, although the fishermen remained strangely unconcerned. He realized that each generation viewed the baseline as whatever they caught at the beginning of their career, regardless of how much smaller it was than the previous generation's, leading to what he called 'the gradual accommodation of the creeping disappearance' of fish populations. Shifting baseline syndrome has since been shown to be pervasive everywhere in the world.[36]

The somber truth is that the vast bulk of nature's staggering abundance has already disappeared. We live in a world characterized primarily by the relative silence and emptiness of its natural spaces. It's only when we read accounts of wildlife from centuries ago that we realize how much is gone. One eighteenth-century writer, standing on the shores of Wales, described schools of herrings five or six miles long, so dense that 'the whole water seems alive; and it is seen so black with them to a great distance, that the number seems inexhaustible'. In the seventeenth-century Caribbean sailors could navigate at night by the noise of massive shoals of sea turtles heading to nesting beaches on the Cayman Islands. In the Chesapeake Bay, plagued today by polluted dead zones, hunters harvested a hundred thousand terrapins a year for turtle soup. In the nineteenth century massive flocks of passenger pigeons would blot out the sun throughout the eastern United States. The last one died in a zoo in 1914.[37*]

In normal times, extinction is a natural part of evolution: new species evolve from prior existing species, meaning that, rather than dying out, 'extinct' species are really the progenitors of new ones. When extinctions occur, however, as part of a mass extinction, they represent a grave and permanent loss to the richness of life. Species exterminated by human development are wiped out from nature's palette, terminating any possibility of further evolutionary branching. The average lifespan of a species is roughly a million years – the unfolding story of each one is, in E. O. Wilson's words, a unique epic. We've seen how life's prodigious diversity on Earth can be understood as nature's own evolved intelligence, earned over billions of years. Through extinction, we are dumbing down nature, eliminating the plenitude it has so painstakingly accumulated.[38]

Terminal as extinctions are, the virtual disappearance of most populations of existing species, known as extirpations, are perhaps even more devastating. It's been calculated that, since the rise of human civilization, Earth has lost 83 percent of its wild mammals, 80 percent of marine mammals and about half the biomass of trees and plants – a worldwide elimination of life's abundance that has been aptly named by biologist Norman Myers the Great Dying. The species we view as iconic of nature's magnificence, such as lions, tigers, elephants and whales – now barely eking out an existence – were once prolific around the world. It's estimated that, as late as 1800, twenty-six million elephants roved Africa. There are now barely four hundred thousand. The spectacular vista of wildebeest migrating in their millions across the plains of Africa is itself facing extinction, with the few remaining wildebeest finding migration routes blocked by fences, settlements and roads. And the Great Dying continues at an ever-increasing pace: 2,000-year-old baobab trees that were around when Jesus lived suddenly dying off; three billion animals lost in Australia's wildfires of 2019–20. In the words of environmental writer J. B. MacKinnon, 'extirpation is the great, sucking retreat of the tide of life'.[39]

The next time you go for a hike in nature and marvel at its beauty, take a moment to realize that you are looking at a pale, shrunken wraith of what it once was. An accumulation of studies around the world measuring the declines of species and ecosystems indicates that overall we've lost around 90 percent of nature's profusion. We live, MacKinnon observes, in a 'ten percent world'. Those of us who gain sustenance from the sacred beauty of nature sometimes like to think of it as a temple. But, as MacKinnon notes, 'a greater truth should be foremost in mind: Nature is not a temple, but a ruin. A beautiful ruin, but a ruin all the same.'[40]

The ideology of human supremacy

It's rather stunning to consider that all this destruction has been carried out by a species that has been around for less than 0.01 percent of life's history; a species that makes up just 0.01 percent of all life on Earth as measured by biomass. While some may glorify humanity's ascendancy as 'godlike', there are other ways to see it. Humanity has undoubtedly developed unprecedented power, but much of it has been used for destruction. What would other animals say about humans, if they had the opportunity? The animals that still remain on Earth are suffering an apocalypse unlike anything that has occurred in the history of this planet. Other mass extinctions happened through geophysical events that no one was responsible for, such as volcanic eruptions or meteorites. This one is a deliberate and systematic annihilation of life executed by one species with full knowledge of what it's doing. It may be the Sixth Extinction, but as some have pointed out, a more apt name would be the First Extermination Event.[41]

With the exception of a few hardy survivors such as cockroaches, rats and pigeons, the animals that have been spared extirpation or extinction are mostly those which have been domesticated, such as cows, chickens and pigs. But the word domestication doesn't hint at the reality of their existence. For the most part, these animals are enslaved, brutally tortured and mercilessly slaughtered merely for human convenience. The ongoing atrocity of the systematic torment administered in the name of humanity to tens of billions of animals a year – each one a sentient creature with a nervous system as capable of registering excruciating pain as you or I – must represent the single greatest cataclysm of suffering that life on Earth has ever experienced. It's most likely, as eco-philosopher Derrick Jensen points out, that if animals could speak, they would tell us that when they see the face of a human, they don't see a god – they see the devil.[42]

But of course they can't speak, and that is why this ongoing holocaust continues with barely a mention in public discourse. Ever since the rise of agrarian civilizations, cultures have justified their domination over those they conquered by claiming innate superiority. In recent centuries, as Europeans subjugated other regions, a narrative of white supremacy – one that retains its pernicious power even today – asserted superiority over other races. Among those who recognize its toxic qualities, white supremacy is understood as a form of violence that inflicts suffering on others while simultaneously damaging the perpetrators by binding them to a system of brutality. What is less recognized is that the ideology of human supremacy – claiming innate superiority over nonhuman animals – has a similarly malignant effect.[43*]

Human supremacy is so embedded within our cultural norms that it is barely even discussed. As Crist describes, 'it is indoctrinated into humans from a tender age, without time-out, hammered into the human mind by innumerable conditioning feats of the dominant anthropocentric culture'. It is, however, a specific ideology with origins in the Western worldview which desacralized nature, turning it into a resource to exploit. Ultimately, it is the ideology of human supremacy that allows us to maltreat animals in factory farms, blow up mountaintops for coal, turn vibrant rainforest into monocrop wastelands, trawl millions of miles of ocean floor with nets that scoop up everything that moves – while glorying in the Anthropocene, claiming that nature exists only to serve human needs. Because it's all around us and almost never mentioned, human supremacy is easy to ignore, but once you recognize it, you see it everywhere you look.[44]

Once one becomes aware of the enormity perpetrated by the human race, it can sometimes lead to a revulsion against our own species. 'We are serial killers beyond reason,' writes one author. Others occasionally liken the human race to a cancer that spreads uncontrollably until it kills its host. Is it, however, human nature that has caused this unfolding catastrophe, or something specific pertaining to the dominant culture?[45]

When malignant cancer cells spread, they generally do so on account of abnormalities in their DNA that cause them to ignore regulatory feedback from neighboring cells, leading to uncontrolled proliferation. Some see this kind of dynamic in global capitalism, which requires perpetual growth in the production and consumption of resources just to remain stable. Rather than viewing humanity as a species overwhelming nature, they see the system of norms, laws and power relations instituted by global capitalism as the source of this massive disruption. As such, they suggest that 'Anthropocene' is a misnomer: it unfairly lays the blame for climate breakdown and ecological collapse on all humans throughout history, whereas it's really only a small minority of humans in the past few centuries. The numbers back them up: the wealthy OECD countries, representing only 18 percent of the global population, account for 74 percent of global GDP and are responsible for 73 percent of the carbon emitted since 1850. On average, a single US citizen emits five hundred times as much carbon as a citizen of Ethiopia or Cambodia. The true name of our era, they argue, should be the Capitalocene.[46]

While the affluent inhabitants of the Global North have been responsible for wreaking ecological and climate havoc on the world, billions of lower-income people in the Global South are far more vulnerable to its devastating effects. When droughts, floods and famines hit, impoverished countries like Syria, Bangladesh or Sudan are disproportionately affected. Ironically, while Indigenous people living in the least developed parts of the world bear the brunt of climate breakdown, they are also the ones on the frontline protecting what's left of the natural world. It's estimated that Indigenous people, while accounting for less than 5 percent of the global population, protect 80 percent of its biodiversity, often at the sacrifice of their own lives when fossil fuel and mining companies encroach on their territories.[47]

The Honorable Harvest

However, if the wholesale destruction of nature is a result of global capitalism, how do we explain the earlier extinctions of megafauna that took place whenever humans arrived in a new continent? Doesn't that suggest there really is something inherent in human nature that can't exist in harmonic equilibrium with the nonhuman world? This is an important question we need to explore more deeply.

In earlier chapters we identified specifically human characteristics that distinguish us from other species. With their larger prefrontal cortex, humans developed a split consciousness, with a separate 'I' capable of planning and thinking conceptually, leading to what the Taoists called *yu-wei*, or purposive action. The power unleashed by human conceptual consciousness was the underlying reason for the disruptions caused by those early generations of humans who settled in new continents. While animals in Africa had evolved over millions of years to fear hominids, the megafauna of other continents had no way to recognize the danger of these seemingly innocuous creatures armed with weapons and complex hunting strategies.

However, after the initial disruptions and extinctions, societies across the world settled into more sustainable ways of relating to nonhuman nature around them. We've seen how cultural attractors can develop over generations as a manifestation of collective human intelligence. In the case of Indigenous cultures, these developed in the form of new behavioral norms that led to a sustainable equilibrium between humans and nature.[48]

We can't know exactly how these new cultural attractors arose among Indigenous communities many thousands of years ago, but they likely emerged from the accumulation of wisdom from elders. As a counterpoint to shifting baseline syndrome, tribal elders may have preserved the cultural memory of more abundant animal populations from earlier times, and encouraged the institution of rituals and observances that reoriented behavior to more sustainable practices. These cultural attractors were so resilient that many of them remain embedded in the present-day values of Indigenous communities.[49]

Building on the ubiquitous Indigenous perception of nature as an extended family – implying that all creatures were relatives – the practices that arose inculcated respect, restraint and reciprocity with all nonhuman beings. In the Pacific north-west of North America, for example, the salmon runs remained plentiful until the arrival of European settlers, not because the native people lacked the technical capacity to overfish, but because of a complex set of rituals restraining them from casual consumption of the fish until ceremonies had been performed.[50]

Ecologist Kat Anderson, who has spent years researching Indigenous land practices in California, has identified two overarching principles of harvest: leave some of what is gathered for other animals; and do not waste what you have harvested. Similarly, Robin Wall Kimmerer describes a series of precepts among Native Americans known as the Honorable Harvest that guide practices, including rules such as: ask permission before taking; take only what you need; and give a gift in reciprocity for what you have taken.[51]

Stories abound of Western visitors observing native people leaving some of the harvest and misunderstanding this as either laziness or inefficiency. 'We Indians like to leave something for the one who comes after,' explained a Native American to a Western observer in the 1930s. Kimmerer tells of an engineering student visiting from Europe who designed a system to help his Ojibwe hosts harvest rice more efficiently from their canoes after watching half the rice fall into the water and seemingly get wasted. His hosts respectfully declined his help, pointing out that the rice needed to seed itself for the following year, and that the 'wasted' rice also attracted ducks. 'Our teachings,' they explained, 'tell us to never take more than half.'[52]

Anderson observes that the Native American approach to the land exists somewhere between the two conventional categories of 'hunting and gathering' and 'agriculture'. Instead, in a series of practices she describes as 'tending the wild', she shows how Indigenous people developed ways to maintain the health and abundance of the land without domesticating it. Some plants even appear to have co-evolved with humans in a symbiotic, mutually enhancing relationship. For example, Kimmerer describes how sweetgrass that is harvested in the right way grows back more copiously than when it is left alone.[53]

Similar patterns of sustainable flourishing, commonly referred to as 'traditional ecological knowledge', can be found in Indigenous communities throughout the world. In Hawaii, as in North America, after an initial disruptive period of extinctions, the Polynesian settlers developed a strict, elaborate code of *kapu*, prescribing detailed rules of behavior. The mountainous island centers were viewed as spiritual realms of the gods, with stringent prohibitions against profane entry. Fishing out of season or bathing in a pool of drinking water were crimes punishable by death. The concept of *kuleana* – incorporating the ideas of privilege and responsibility – governed the relationship with the nonhuman island inhabitants, with the result that, over centuries, the population increased to as many as 800,000, while nonhuman life continued to thrive.[54]

In Australia, similarly, the Aboriginal population established sacred Dreaming sites – frequently nesting or breeding areas – where no hunting, fishing, gathering or burning could take place. Fish traps in rivers were designed with wide netting so that smaller juveniles could escape while only the large remained to be caught. An early settler's daughter wrote in her journal that, when she asked her father why there were no more fish, he responded, 'When the blacks went the fish went.' Without the Aboriginals' ritual practices, the settlers had wiped out the population in just one generation.[55*]

The ecological self

When faced with these kinds of examples, many people respond with statements like: 'We can't turn the clock back. What's done is done, and we now need to move forward into the globalized, technological reality of the Anthropocene.' True enough, but is there something to learn from traditional ecological knowledge? Are there deeper principles that can be applied in new ways to our current civilization, which might head off our collision course with catastrophe?

When Indigenous cultures viewed all of nature as family, they were in touch with a profound truth that has since been scientifically validated by evolutionary biology. Recognizing our deep connection with all of life, E. O. Wilson coined the term *biophilia* to describe the innate tendency for people everywhere to love nature, and to feel a visceral emotional connection with other living beings.[56]

While the dominant culture of the West has sought to conquer nature, fitting biophilia neatly into tidy boxes such as parks, hiking expeditions and seaside vacations, some ecological thinkers have explored the broader implications of our intrinsic connection with nature. Occasionally, this has taken the form of an unexpected epiphany that breaks through the barriers of conceptual consciousness to rediscover what Indigenous cultures have taught for millennia. Renowned environmentalist Aldo Leopold began his career as a hunter, assigned by the US Forest Service to kill bears, wolves and mountain lions in New Mexico to keep their populations in check. He recounts how, one time, having shot a mother wolf, he witnessed her as she lay on the ground:

> We reached the old wolf in time to watch a fierce green fire dying in her eyes. I realized then, and have known ever since, that there was something new to me in those eyes – something known only to her and to the mountain. I was young then, and full of trigger-itch; I thought that because fewer

> wolves meant more deer, that no wolves would mean hunters' paradise. But after seeing the green fire die, I sensed that neither the wolf nor the mountain agreed with such a view.

Transformed by this moment, Leopold went on to dedicate his life to conservation work.[57]

In 1973 philosopher Arne Næss suggested that rather than examining our relationship *with* nature, we should begin from the foundation that we *are* nature. Calling his approach 'deep ecology', he explored how this could redefine our very idea of what it means to be human. 'I tentatively introduce,' he wrote, 'the concept of *ecological self*. We may be said to be in, and of, Nature from the very beginning of our selves.' As we've seen, Næss wasn't the only European rediscovering this core Indigenous insight, with Albert Schweitzer similarly declaring, 'I am life that wills to live, in the midst of life that wills to live.'[58]

There is, however, a terrible burden to bear for those who embrace this broader ecological self as part of their core identity. Life is under attack from our civilization – it is being systematically ravaged at a pace that is rapidly increasing. How can we respond to this pain when we truly absorb its enormity? As Aldo Leopold reflected, 'one of the penalties of an ecological education is that one lives alone in a world of wounds'.[59]

Leopold wrote that statement before the Great Acceleration even got started. Now, as the ecological catastrophe escalates, people are alone no longer in facing nature's devastation. Scientists working on Earth's disrupted natural systems are increasingly overcome by floods of emotion they've begun to call 'ecological grief'. One recounts how he brought a newly recruited PhD student to the Great Barrier Reef to study fish behavior, only to discover that the corals had died from a major bleaching event and there was nothing left to research. Sometimes, scientists learn how to process their grief from Indigenous elders living on the land they're studying – communities that have had many generations to metabolize the sorrow of loss, as described searingly by Aboriginal poet Oodgeroo Noonuccal:

The scrubs are gone, the hunting and the laughter.
The eagle is gone, the emu and the kangaroo are gone from this
place.
The bora ring is gone.
The corroboree is gone.
And we are going.[60]

With the realization of climate breakdown becoming more widespread, scientists are increasingly joined by concerned citizens and anxious schoolchildren in what is becoming an epidemic of climate anxiety. As groups self-organize around the world to help process this collective anguish, virtually all experts agree on two crucial therapeutic components: sharing the grief with others and transforming it into collective action on behalf of life.[61]

While there are countless worthwhile projects around the world helping stem the tide of devastation, they are doomed to fight mostly losing battles unless the tide itself can be turned. This requires a deep shift in values from our mainstream anthropocentric presumption that nature exists only to serve humans to a recognition of the intrinsic value of life itself and its inherent right to flourish in all its glorious diversity. Aldo Leopold gave a succinct expression of this ethic when he famously declared, 'A thing is right when it tends to preserve the integrity, stability, and beauty of the biotic community. It is wrong when it tends otherwise.'[62]

Tending Mother Earth

The clarity of Leopold's statement, however, hides a morass of complexity, returning us to some of the issues raised by New Conservationists. Does the biotic community include both humans and nonhumans? If so, how do we differentiate the two? If not, where do human needs fit into the ethic? Sometimes, as a result of anthropogenic disruption, the needs of an individual species conflict with the flourishing of an entire ecosystem. For example, in the Galápagos Islands the authorities had to exterminate hundreds of thousands of feral goats, sometimes brutally, to restore the habitat for its giant tortoises. While we may rejoice in the recovery of the tortoise population, how can we justify massacres of goats? What makes the lives of one species more important than another?[63]

While some New Conservationists have taken these complexities as reasons to dismiss the very idea of wilderness, other ecological thinkers have pursued a more nuanced approach, based on a more inclusive conception of nature as an all-embracing domain whose flourishing arises from how its component parts – both human and nonhuman – relate with each other. This perspective can help demystify the very idea of wilderness. In ancient Norse *will* meant self-willed or uncontrollable; *deor* was a term for an animal (giving rise to our word 'deer'). So, according to one etymological interpretation, *will-deor-ness* meant self-willed land, or the territory of self-willed animals – in contrast to cultivated land with domesticated animals. On this basis, we can think of wilderness not as something pristine or untouched by human hands, but as land with the scale and biodiversity to accommodate its own self-willed preservation.[64*]

Viewing nature as a complex, dynamic system of interrelating parts helps discern what generates a healthy ecosystem. It's not simply having lots of species, if most of the species are merely variants of scrubby weeds. Rather, a flourishing ecosystem is – in the words of one ecologist – authentic. Do you remember the Confucian concept of *cheng*: the experience of authenticity arising from a true integration of consciousness? 'There is no greater delight,' noted Mencius, 'than to realize *cheng* upon self-examination.' Similarly, an ecosystem can realize *cheng* when it is truly integrated – populated by diverse species, from top predators to extensive fungal webs, which interact dynamically to change and regenerate themselves over time, creating a robust, resilient, self-willed whole.[65]

Building on this understanding, Indigenous wisdom offers alternative concepts that could help guide the future human relationship with Mother Earth. After carefully studying Native American land practices, Kat Anderson, as we saw, proposed 'tending the wild' as the best way to describe their approach. She explains how the word 'tend' itself has a fascinating etymology: it derives from the Indo-European word *ten* meaning to stretch, as in *tensing* the string of a musical instrument. This offers an important clue as to how human activity need not be destructive of nature's beauty. By applying purposeful action in just the right way, we can create beauty, turning a piece of string into a vehicle for music or harvesting sweetgrass in a way that makes it more abundant.[66]

This brings us back to that Taoist dichotomy between *wu-wei* and *yu-wei* – going with the flow versus purposive action. Does the idea of tending offer some kind of middle ground between the two? Some Chinese sages thought so, using a concept called *shi* (pronounced *shou* as in 'should'). Sunzi, author of the ancient classic *The Art of War*, describes *shi* as skillfully arranging circumstances to allow a general to win a war without actually having to fight one. Consider stones, he explained. Stones on flat ground just stay put, as do square ones even if they're on a slope. But if you arrange round stones at the top of a slope, an effortless nudge will get them rolling down the hill and scatter the enemy. *Shi* is thus a way to manipulate initial conditions – to set things up so that they will spontaneously do what you want with minimal further effort. It's purposive, and yet it goes with the flow.[67]

Ecological philosopher Freya Mathews has pointed out that *shi* is an intrinsic part of nature's own intelligence, forming the basis of ecosystems. Life has evolved symbiotically – as one organism became expert in a particular function, it learned to team up with another organism with expertise in a complementary function, so they could prosper together. Organisms that did this used *shi* as a strategy: they learned how to flourish by weaving their own needs into the needs of their symbiont, so they could both get what they required with minimal extra effort. While this could be viewed as manipulative, what's crucial is that both parties gained from the symbiosis. As in the Honorable Harvest, reciprocity became a fundamental attribute of sustainable relationships within a healthy ecosystem.[68]

Whether we call it *shi*, tending, or conscious symbiosis, the pivotal lesson is the same: there is an alternative to the dichotomy that views civilization as either the triumph of humans over nature or the inevitable ruination of life's plenitude. As Mathews, along with other visionary thinkers, has demonstrated, the possibility exists for our civilization to learn how to tend Mother Earth, to fulfill our human destiny while nurturing life to flourish in all its glory. A passage from the *Tao Te Ching* divulges:

> Tao gives birth,
> Intrinsic nature [*te*] rears,
> Things shape,
> Circumstances [*shi*] complete.

Could this be humanity's role in relation to Mother Earth: to complete through conscious tending what *Tao* and *te* have generated since life began? Can we use the unique features of conceptual consciousness to integrate with nature rather than try to conquer her? If so, how could this be accomplished?[69]

Two environmental designers, Bill Mollison and David Holmgren, have developed a set of principles known as permaculture that offers some valuable pointers. Permaculture (from 'permanent agriculture') is a design protocol that works with rather than against nature, using the inherent qualities of plants, animals and terrain to construct systems for long-term sustainability. Relying on careful observation, it unites traditional ecological knowledge and Indigenous land practices with modern scientific knowhow to create a cultivated ecology – one that works with life to resist entropy.[70]

Consistent with the principle of *shi*, permaculture seeks to turn problems into solutions, designing systems with stacked functions that offer maximal returns with minimal effort. For example, planting certain herbs and flowers around gardens attracts insects that feed on destructive parasites, thus protecting the garden. Nutrient flows are recycled, so that household gray water irrigates gardens and kitchen waste becomes compost. Conceived in Australia in the 1970s, permaculture has spread around the world, with centers offering certification in its design principles. Through permaculture, and related approaches known collectively as agroecology, land can become more productive than on conventionally managed farms without using any synthetic fertilizer. Importantly, these principles can apply beyond agriculture to other kinds of design in urban and suburban communities.[71]*

At the deepest level, the principle of conscious symbiosis can be applied to all aspects of humankind's relationship with the living systems of Mother Earth. In every case we must ask what are the initial conditions that could lead to symbiotic mutual flourishing, so that human activity not only avoids harm, but actively generates health for the living Earth. If the Anthropocene is characterized by destruction of geological proportions as a result of the ideology of human supremacy, could we reorient the direction of human progress toward an era of potentially far longer duration – one that has been called the Symbiocene – characterized by the symbiotic flourishing of humans and Earth? Let us complete this chapter by investigating some pathways pointing in that direction.[72]

Toward the Symbiocene

The Symbiocene may seem very far away, as our civilization careens toward ever more destructive behaviors. However, many of the pathways that could lead there are already being set in place by visionaries working to defend Mother Earth against further depredations.

Nature may have become a 'beautiful ruin', but its potential to regenerate abundance and diversity remains powerful. Visionaries around the world, seeing this potentiality, have initiated a movement toward 'rewilding': setting the conditions for nature to become, once again, self-willed and to follow its own trajectory. As we've seen, this doesn't mean a wistful attempt to recreate an idealized past; rather it is a recognition that, for ecosystems to regain their *cheng*, they need the space and initial parameters to do their own thing.[73]

Ecologists have discovered that keystone species – frequently top predators in the food chain – are critical to reset an ecosystem's network of relationships. A classic example is the sacred territory, long revered by local Indigenous tribes, now known as Yellowstone National Park. When the park was first established, hunters like Aldo Leopold were recruited to eradicate the wolves. In the ensuing decades, the elk population – now hugely increased without predators to keep them in check – overgrazed the willows and aspen. With fewer trees, songbirds declined, beavers were unable to build dams, and riverbanks eroded, leading to increased river temperatures too high for cold-water fish. With its ecology out of balance, the park became barren. In 1995 fourteen wolves were reintroduced, with dramatic effect. With newly reduced elk and deer populations, willows and aspen quickly rebounded. Songbirds returned, along with eagles, foxes, badgers and beavers, stabilizing the riverbanks. In just a couple of decades, Yellowstone had recovered its *cheng* – and the wolves now number about a hundred.[74]

This stirring example is an inspiration for those working to help nature regenerate elsewhere in the world. In Europe various projects are underway to create nature reserves for bison, wild horses and wolves, with a million hectares projected to be rewilded by 2022. A project in western Siberia aims to restore muskoxen, wolves, bears and eventually even tigers in what has been dubbed Pleistocene Park.[75]

These are, however, mere baby steps toward what is needed. Most protected areas around the world are small, fragmented patchworks of greenery. Ecosystems need swaths of large, unbroken terrain to regain and maintain their *cheng*, permitting animals to roam, find mates and migrate seasonally. Realizing this, visionary environmentalists, including E. O. Wilson, have launched a campaign to give back to nature what she needs. Nature Needs Half is the name of an international community aiming to restore half of Earth's land back to full regenerative capacity.[76*]

Scientists point out that it's not yet too late to halt the Sixth Extinction. So far, only a few percent of species have actually gone extinct, and the direction our civilization takes over the next few decades will crucially impact whether we can prevent the worst depredations from occurring. In an important step, Indigenous-based movements around the world are convincing governments to recognize the intrinsic rights of natural ecosystems. Responding to Maori demands, the New Zealand government has recognized the legal rights of an ancestral forest and river named Te Awa Tupua. Other bodies of water around the world, from Lake Erie to the Ganges, and from the Colombian Amazon to Bangladeshi rivers, have also been granted rights as legal entities.[77]

In Ecuador and Bolivia, Mother Nature herself (Pachamama) has been granted constitutional rights as a living system that 'has the right to exist, persist, and maintain and regenerate its vital cycles'. A related movement is building to declare a global Universal Declaration of the Rights of Mother Earth. Meanwhile, a campaign is underway to make the wholesale destruction of natural living systems a criminal act by establishing a law of ecocide – prosecutable under the International Criminal Court like genocide, war crimes and crimes against humanity.[78]

However, even these visionary and groundbreaking movements are not enough to turn the tide of global destruction that our civilization is wreaking on the Earth. Ultimately, the Great Acceleration has been fueled – and continues to be fueled – by the incessant requirement for growth in production and consumption characterizing the globalized market-based economic system dominated by vast profit-driven transnational corporations. If we are to redirect our civilization's trajectory away from catastrophe, we must change the underlying foundation of values on which this global cultural and economic system has been based. We must move, ultimately, from a civilization that is wealth-based to one that is life-based. That means, at the deepest level, reconnecting with what is most meaningful to us as living, loving human beings. It is this foundational type of transformation that we'll now begin to explore, as we ponder the question 'Why am I?'[79]

NEW THREADS OF MEANING

As a result of human depredation, nature's splendor is now a shrunken fragment of what it once was

Human supremacy is an ideology that sanctions us to devastate the nonhuman world without feeling moral qualms

By tending nature, humankind can fulfill its destiny while nurturing life to thrive in its glory – allowing the symbiotic flourishing of humans and the Earth

HOW SHOULD I LIVE?

As a living being in the midst of life, I should pursue symbiotic, fractal flourishing for myself, for humankind and for all life

Part Five

WHY AM I?

Chapter Eleven

EVERYTHING IS CONNECTED

The Jewel Net of Indra

Yossarian – the antihero in Joseph Heller's *Catch-22* – doesn't want to fly any more missions. It's late in the Second World War and beginning to look like the Allies will be victorious. Yossarian's squadron flies regular bombing sorties over Italy, but he tells his commanding officer he's not flying any more for the simple reason that he doesn't want to get killed by enemy anti-aircraft fire. 'Would you like to see our country lose?' asks his officer. 'We won't lose,' Yossarian answers.

> 'We've got more men, more money and more material. There are ten million men in uniform who could replace me. Some people are getting killed and a lot more are making money and having fun. Let somebody else get killed.'
>
> 'But suppose everybody on our side felt that way.'
>
> 'Then I'd certainly be a damned fool to feel any other way. Wouldn't I?'

When I first read this riposte, as a young student rebelling against authority, Yossarian's logical ruse felt like a liberation – a stand for individual authenticity against a blind herd mentality.[1]

As the years passed, and I became embedded in the free-market capitalist mindset, I would keep referring back to this twisted argument as a refreshing rebuttal of pious morality. If everyone was acting cynically and manipulating the system to get ahead of the pack, then 'I'd be a damned fool' to act in any other way, wouldn't I? It seemed so liberating. It was many years before I began to realize how its apparent emancipatory quality was in reality merely a glib expression of an underlying ethos that venerated the individual above all else – a rallying cry for the Me Generation, many of whom have become the beneficiaries and cheerleaders of the neoliberal cult of the individual that predominates in our global culture today.

If everyone had followed Yossarian's logic, of course, Hitler and his Nazi ideology would have won the Second World War. Today, as the world faces the existential threat of climate breakdown, our national leaders act according to a similar twisted logic, making speeches about the need to reduce greenhouse gas emissions while privately choosing not to be the 'damned fool' acting for the common good while other countries avoid making the tough choices required.[2]

For me, this dog-eat-dog ethic of cynicism reached its nadir during my days as an executive in a credit card company. One day my boss arrived late for a meeting. He'd been delayed, he explained, by a plumber who, he believed, was overcharging him for some major repair work. 'But then again,' he reflected aloud with a self-satisfied smirk, 'we're overcharging him and others like him with our credit card fees. We're all ripping each other off. In the end, that's how the world works, isn't it?'

It may not be how the world works, but to a large extent it certainly is how our global economic system works, which is based on the myth that the most effective way to run a society is for each person to act according to their own self-interest. This individual-oriented ethos has deep roots in our culture, deeper even than capitalism itself. Its origins are to be found in the very idea of the individual as an autonomous agent utterly distinct from the rest of humanity. The concept of the self-contained individual pervades our modern way of thinking so extensively that it seems axiomatic, but it is in fact a construction of the European tradition. Our culture, as we've seen, holds a deep-seated belief that an individual's essence exists in one's conceptual consciousness, based on the Cartesian dictum: 'I think, therefore I am.' Descartes, in turn, inherited from traditional Christianity the idea of the soul as the indestructible core of the individual – one that would end up in either heaven or hell for eternity depending on how God judged it when a person died.[3]

Nowadays, many people no longer believe in a literal heaven

and hell, but for over a millennium this was the foundational myth of virtually everyone's belief system within monotheism, whether they were simple peasants or learned intellectuals. Now, think about its implications. The underlying premise is that you should be concerned only about *your own* soul's welfare. If you end up in heaven, then you've got yours – and don't even think about what happens to anyone else's soul. To hell with them (quite literally). Occasionally, theologians would speculate on how someone who made it to heaven could remain beatific if they knew a loved one was suffering eternal torment in hell. One theory was that God wiped your mind clean of memories of any loved ones enduring perpetual torture. Other prominent theologians, amazingly, suggested that those enjoying heavenly bliss would rejoice when they heard the 'dolorous shrieks and cries' of the damned, knowing that they had gotten their just deserts. Today, while few people focus on an afterlife, the divisions of society have become such that – from a material perspective, at least – heaven and hell are a function of economic disparity. Based on this ingrained cultural baggage of the individual soul, is it any wonder that the wealthy elite feel entitled to enjoy their worldly paradise while billions of other human souls suffer in dire poverty?[4*]

There is a fascinating contrast to the Christian story of the soul's salvation in the Buddhist conception of the bodhisattva. A bodhisattva, as discussed earlier, is someone who, having worked tirelessly to achieve enlightenment, has arrived at the threshold of nirvana – the opportunity to be released from persistent cycles of reincarnation. But rather than opting for liberation, the bodhisattva chooses to return to the world and work ceaselessly until all beings have awakened from needless suffering. This seems at first like an act of boundless altruism. However, a deeper analysis reveals something even more profound. The bodhisattva has achieved the realization that the boundaries separating the self from others are all mere constructions of a conditioned mind. In this 'perfection of wisdom' the bodhisattva recognizes her inherent interdependence with all sentient beings. It's not that she is sacrificing herself for the benefit of others; she has awakened to the realization that the very notion of a separate self is a falsehood.[5]

A breathtaking Buddhist conception, called the Jewel Net of Indra, memorably captures this idea of deep interconnectedness. In the heavenly abode of the god Indra there exists a wonderful net that stretches out infinitely in all directions. In every eye of the net there hangs a glittering jewel. Since the net is infinite, there are an infinite number of jewels. The jewels are polished so perfectly that, if you inspect any one jewel, you discover that all the other jewels, infinite in number, are reflected in it. Moreover, each of the reflections is also reflecting all the other jewels, so the reflecting process itself contains infinite dimensions.[6]

This image was used by early Buddhist scholars in China to exemplify how, ultimately, our cosmos is one of infinitely repeating interrelationships. These scholars were among the first to use the term li as the principle of connectivity, which Neo-Confucian philosophers later developed into the sophisticated cosmology of li and qi. Connectivity has, of course, been a central theme of this book. We've frequently seen how the way in which things are connected tells us more than the things themselves – in fact, for crucial phenomena such as life, evolution, mind, consciousness or flourishing, just like Indra's Net, the more we inspect them, the more we find their very existence is the emergent product of their interconnections.[7]

While Buddhist and Neo-Confucian sages contribute some of humanity's greatest insights into interconnectedness, they are by no means alone. We've seen that Indigenous communities worldwide view relatedness to each other and the natural world as the foundation of identity and well-being. As First Nations scholar Richard Atleo explains, the Indigenous principle of *tsawalk* (meaning 'one') holds that all issues, whether social, political, economic or philosophical, 'can be addressed under the single theme of interrelationships, across all dimensions of reality – the material and the invisible'. And we've seen how some findings of modern science have arrived at a similar view of the primacy of interconnectedness in understanding our reality.[8]

And yet ... do you remember Uncle Bob from the Introduction? Steeped in our mainstream culture's story of separation, Uncle Bob is a hard nut to crack. Perhaps, by this time, having read the book so far, Uncle Bob has let go of the selfish gene myth and recognized that life evolved its magnificence through evolutionary leaps of cooperation. Perhaps Uncle Bob has accepted that conceptual consciousness is not his sole seat of identity; that nature has its own intelligence; that animate intelligence connects him to the rest of nature; that nonlinear, self-organized patterns of organization account for the world's complexity; that his consciousness results from the dynamic integration of neural attractors; that his own well-being requires a healthy society; and that human flourishing itself depends on a healthy Earth. Uncle Bob has come a long way since the beginning of the book. But now he pauses for a moment, turns and says, 'Okay, I grant you all that. But let's face it. The fact remains that it's a rat race out there. Everyone is out for themselves, and the system rewards those who are most self-centered. Maybe underneath it all, we *are* all connected. But in the end, if everyone else is just looking out for themselves and trying to get ahead, then I'd be a damned fool to do otherwise. Wouldn't I?'

What do we say to Uncle Bob at this point? This chapter can be regarded as a deep inquiry into the question he raises. To confront it fully, we need to dig even further than we've gone. Ultimately, Uncle Bob won't be moved until he's face to face with whatever is most meaningful to him, lurking in the inner core of his being. We must excavate down to the very root of existence and explore the question of where meaning itself arises. Is Yossarian right that ultimately he needs to look out for number one, and the Jewel Net of Indra is nothing more than a lovely fantasy? If we are, in fact, all interconnected, what does that ultimately mean for our lives? How might that affect our own sense of meaning and purpose?

As we delve into these deep underpinnings of reality, is it possible we might come across something that causes even Uncle Bob to see his life from a somewhat different perspective?

Cleansing the doors of perception

To gain an understanding of meaning itself, perhaps we should turn to those who have had experiences of some kind of greater reality beyond our everyday world. These phenomena, sometimes referred to as mystical states, are among the most important aspects of the human experience. People who encounter them are frequently transformed for the rest of their lives, and in rare historical cases such experiences have launched the religions that structure the belief systems of much of humanity. Can they teach us something about the meaning of life?

Mystical experiences are surprisingly common, and their frequency appears to be increasing. According to Gallup, the number of Americans saying they have had one or more mystical experiences rose from 20 percent in 1960 to about 50 percent of the population today. There is, of course, a wide spectrum encompassing the different varieties of non-ordinary states. 'Flow' experiences can allow access to a temporary sensation of *wu-wei*. People may similarly leave behind normal consciousness through dancing, religious ceremonies, sustained meditation or simply being in deep communion with nature. A version of this state – known as the overview effect – has even occurred in astronauts orbiting the Earth and feeling overwhelmed by a profound shift in identity as they see our shared home as a tiny orb in the vast bleakness of space.[9*]

In recent times psychedelics have provided an important new route to altered states. In response to the counterculture movement of the 1960s, psychedelics were categorized as drugs of abuse and made illegal around the world. However, as chronicled by Michael Pollan in his bestseller *How to Change Your Mind*, there has been a renewal of interest in their therapeutic value, with ongoing studies of their efficacy in a wide range of applications, such as alleviating the fear of death in terminal cancer patients, or relieving the symptoms of patients suffering from chronic, treatment-resistant depression.[10]

Given such a wide range of altered states of consciousness, it's reasonable to ask what we might learn by investigating them. An important starting point was provided by William James, the nineteenth-century philosopher considered by many to be the father of psychology. After James experimented with nitrous oxide, he became convinced that regular states of consciousness should not be viewed as the 'sole and ultimate dictators of what we may believe' and wondered whether mystical experiences might present 'superior points of view, windows through which the mind looks out upon a more extensive and inclusive world'. 'No account of the universe in its totality,' he declared, 'can be final which leaves these other forms of consciousness quite disregarded.'[11]

Academics who have taken James's cue and methodically studied mystical experiences have identified a common set of features. To begin with, there is a loss of the ego – the constant, chattering 'I' with its fixed personal identity and established boundaries. Aldous Huxley, writing in *The Doors of Perception* about his first mescaline experience, described how 'for the moment that interfering neurotic who, in waking hours, tries to run the show was blessedly out of the way'. In its place was 'the blessed Not-I released for a moment from my throttling embrace'. Similarly, volunteers who took psilocybin (the active ingredient in magic mushrooms) in a double-blind study at Johns Hopkins University reported 'letting go ... beyond ego self', 'the complete and utter loss of self' and 'the feeling of no boundaries – where I didn't know where I ended and my surroundings began'.[12]

Other characteristic features of mystical experience seem to imply a temporary jettisoning of conceptual consciousness, with its linear, logical processing. Researchers report a 'cessation of normal intellectual operations', a shift in the normal experience of time, a paradoxical sense where two opposite things both appear to be true and a sensation of ineffability – difficulty in accurately describing the experience using words.[13]

People frequently report a vast sense of oneness, accompanied by powerful positive emotions such as peace, love and joy – even ecstasy. Interestingly, the word ecstasy comes from the ancient Greek *ekstasis*, meaning standing outside the normal boundaries of the self and experiencing a connection with something greater. This can also be a terrifying and disorienting experience. Philosopher of consciousness Christopher Bache describes it as an 'all-encompassing wholeness', adding that 'there is no reference point outside this Oneness from which to get a perspective on it, as it is the whole of existence'.[14]*

The vast majority of people who undergo a mystical episode come away feeling that it is filled with meaning – a 'peak experience' that is sometimes the most meaningful of their entire lives. In the psilocybin study at Johns Hopkins, roughly two thirds of the volunteers described it as one of the five most meaningful and spiritually significant experiences of their lives – not only directly afterwards but also in a follow-up study fourteen months later.[15*]

People also report a powerful accompanying sense that they experienced something holding greater truth than normal existence – even having achieved a glimpse of 'ultimate reality'. Psychologist William Richards, who spent much of his career investigating psychedelics, remembers his first ever experience of psilocybin as a graduate student studying theology and psychiatry. Immersed in awe and believing he had achieved an insight that was crucial to record, he took a piece of paper and wrote on it, 'Reality is', underlining 'is' three times. Looking back, he realizes he was trying to capture something 'profoundly and intensely real that underlies the entire phenomenal, temporal world that most of us experience in everyday living'.[16]

Perhaps the most memorable version of this insight was provided by the mystical poet William Blake, who gave us the phrase that Huxley later used for the title of his book: 'If the doors of perception were cleansed, everything would appear to man as it is, infinite.'[17]

The perennial philosophy?

Given the nearly universal features of mystical experience across different cultures, along with the powerful sense of being in touch with a greater truth, some have theorized that there is, in fact, an objective reality out there, beyond normal human cognition, waiting to be discovered through the mystical state. This view, known as the 'perennial philosophy', has been around for centuries, but was brought into popular circulation by Aldous Huxley when he wrote a book by that name. It's an alluring vision based on three particular claims: first, there is a universal truth available to be discovered; second, in mystical experiences people of different cultures access the same objective truth, even if they later interpret it according to their particular tradition; and third, by accessing this truth a person can enter a blissful state that will transform his or her life.[18]

There is much in the world's great mystical traditions to support the perennialist viewpoint. A vast sense of ultimate oneness pervades belief systems that are otherwise very different from each other. In the ancient Vedic scriptures known as the Upanishads, which form the foundation of modern Hinduism, the unity of life is a major theme. Here's just one of numerous examples:

> The Self in man and in the sun are one.
> Those who understand this see through the world
> And go beyond the various sheaths
> Of being to realize the unity of life.
> Those who realize that all life is one
> Are at home everywhere and see themselves
> In all beings.[19]

The Bhagavad Gita, which crystallizes much of Vedic thought, has a similar flavor, such as when the supreme god Krishna states, 'I am ever present to those who have realized me in every creature. Seeing all life as my manifestation, they are never separated from me.' Two millennia on, this vision was a driving inspiration for Mahatma Gandhi, who declared, 'I believe in the essential unity of man and, for that matter, all that lives.'[20]

Indian philosophy has some fundamental differences from Buddhism, but in spite of contrasting opinions on many things, Huangbo, a Zen Buddhist sage living in ninth-century China, held a similar view of the oneness of existence. In one of his signature teachings he stated, 'All the Buddhas and all sentient beings are nothing but the One Mind, beside which nothing exists ... for it transcends all limits, measures, names, traces, and comparisons. Only awake to the One Mind.'[21]

This unitive view of ultimate reality seems equally available to those raised in Western cultures. Plotinus, a famous Neoplatonic mystic who lived in ancient Rome, shared similar ideas, saying that if a person could truly see himself, 'he will see God and himself and the all'. While Christianity differs in many ways from Hinduism and Neoplatonism, Christian mystics throughout the ages have uttered words remarkably similar to these. Nicholas of Cusa, for example, a fifteenth-century cardinal, declared that 'God is in all things in such a way that all things are in him.'[22]

Nor is the apprehension of oneness limited to religious traditions. Ralph Waldo Emerson, a nineteenth-century American leader of the transcendentalist movement, wrote about his own unitive experience while crossing a New England common: 'I become a transparent eye-ball. I am nothing. I see all. The currents of the Universal Being circulate through me; I am part or particle of God.' Some great physicists of the twentieth century shared a similar conception. Erwin Schrödinger stated, 'Inconceivable as it seems to ordinary reason, you – and all other conscious beings as such – are all in all.' And, as we've seen, Einstein viewed our sense of separateness as 'a kind of optical delusion of consciousness'.[23]

At first glance, the perennial philosophy might seem indisputable. With such a wide range of visionaries sharing the same perception of oneness, from ancient scriptures to Nobel Prize-winning physicists, surely the rest of us should accept this understanding as an unshakable reality? However, its claims have come under withering criticism in the past few decades.

One critique has focused on the fact that a sense of oneness is only one aspect of mystical experiences. In Indigenous cultures, for example, shamans may have mystical encounters characterized by anything but oneness. Their visions may be filled with various spirits, good or bad, some benevolent and some terrifying. Other mystics, such as the Jewish philosopher Martin Buber, describe their deepest experiences in terms of a dialogical 'I-thou' relationship with divinity.[24]

Perhaps the most searing criticism came from a broadside delivered in 1978 by philosophy professor Steven Katz. In a groundbreaking essay Katz boldly claimed, 'There are NO pure (i.e. unmediated) experiences.' It's not just that each person interprets their experience according to their cultural baggage, he argued; they also bring their own concepts and beliefs into the experience, which shape the form and texture of whatever they undergo. For any mystic, Katz maintained, his particular tradition's 'images, beliefs, symbols, and rituals define, *in advance*, what the experience *he wants to have*, and which then does have, will be like'. A Christian mystic might come face to face with Jesus; a Hindu might realize how his own soul (*atman*) is the entire universe; and a Buddhist might dissolve into the emptiness of being (*sunyata*). In each case their perception of ultimate reality is, in fact, a construction of their own cognitive frames.[25]

Perennialists have since pushed back vehemently. They point to the fact that many people's mystical experiences come as a complete surprise to them, often causing them to break with the religious or secular beliefs they had previously held. They emphasize that in most cases a mystical experience arises precisely when people have dropped their fixed structures of thought and broken through to a state beyond words or concepts. If there's one domain of the human experience that is not conditioned, they argue, it is the mystical one.[26]

This is not merely an interesting academic debate. The stakes are much higher. If Katz and his fellow constructivists are right, then mystical experiences might still be important to a person's own sense of meaning, but they tell us nothing about any underlying reality. If, on the other hand, these states open a window 'to a more extensive and inclusive world' – if experiences of oneness really do reflect some kind of ultimate truth – then it's important to understand what we can learn from them and how these teachings might influence our lives. How might we determine which it is?

Where is the oneness?

A critical step is to recognize that even among those who describe a vision of oneness, different cultural assumptions generate important distinctions over what that oneness signifies. Some traditions – such as Vedic, Neoplatonic and Christian – emphasize transcendence as the route to the realization of oneness. Transcendence, which means literally to 'climb over', implies that the world as we see it, with all its messy details, must be left behind to achieve a state of unity. The higher you go, the purer and more visionary you become, until ultimately you might reach a state of communion with divinity up in the heavens. One of the Upanishads makes the case clearly:

Higher than the senses are the objects of sense.
Higher than the objects of sense is the mind;
And higher than the mind is the intellect.
Higher than the intellect is the Great Soul.
Higher than the Great Soul is the Unmanifest.
Higher than the Unmanifest is the Person.
Higher than the Person there is nothing at all.
That is the goal. That is the highest course.[27]

The European tradition held a similar view of transcendence as the path to a perfect truth. Plato originally proposed a dualistic, split cosmos comprising the polluted, changeable, material world below, and an eternal transcendent realm where the soul went after the body's death. This was the basis for the Christian concept of an immaterial, all-powerful God watching over mortals below and welcoming their souls into heaven after the death of their bodies if they were righteous. In both Vedic and Christian traditions belief in transcendence as the path to the sacred led to widespread rejection of bodily desires and worldly concerns by spiritual seekers.[28]

The underlying idea that 'higher is better' is so embedded in language and culture that it has shaped our patterns of thought. When we hear about a 'peak experience', a 'higher purpose' or the 'high point' of a journey, we instantly know that the references to height denote something good. Is it any wonder that we conceive of spiritual knowledge as something reached by transcendence? But transcendence is not the only path for attaining a sense of oneness. An entirely different way to conceive oneness is through *immanence* (coming from the Latin for 'remain in'). From this perspective, oneness is not found in the heavens but is right here, in this world with all its disorderly muddle.[29]

The immanent view of oneness came naturally to the Chinese, who had no concept of a transcendent, omniscient God. 'One takes the mass of confused things,' said Zhuangzi, the Taoist sage, 'and unites it as one ... For him who can but realize his indissoluble unity with the whole ... death and life, end and beginning, are no more than the succession of day and night.' The Tao, Zhuangzi explained, is to be found everywhere in the world, not just in a transcendent realm: it is in the ants, the grass, the earth – even in the 'piss and shit'. Zen Buddhism, influenced strongly by Taoism, similarly taught that enlightenment was to be found within the mundane realities of everyday life. Master Rinzai, founder of a major branch of Zen, declared, 'If you love the sacred and despise the ordinary, you are still bobbing in the ocean of delusion.'[30]

This contrasting approach to the source of deep truth has major implications for any attempt to discern the essential validity of mystical states. Proponents of the perennial philosophy mostly look to the transcendent Vedic, Platonic and Christian traditions for their perceived commonality. Their basic claim, based on a dualist framework, is that, because our normal understanding of the world is boxed in by our egos, we must transcend the 'doors of perception' to gain our 'peak' experience, where we will see the ultimate truth, recognizing everything 'as it is, infinite'.[31]

The presumption is that there is, in fact, an objective reality that can be seen clearly once one breaks through the 'cloud of unknowing' (the name of a medieval mystical Christian work), just like a jet plane rising above the clouds and heading toward the stratosphere. The crucial question about the ontological validity of mystical states (Do they represent an objective reality?) is usually framed in this way. Michael Pollan summarizes the classic conundrum well as he begins his investigation of altered states of consciousness. People who had taken psilocybin, he recounts, 'described being given access to an alternative reality, a "beyond" where the usual physical laws don't apply and various manifestations of cosmic consciousness or divinity present themselves as unmistakably real. All this I found ... a little hard to take (couldn't this be just a drug-induced hallucination?).' On the other hand, he wonders, could it be that 'the altered state of consciousness has opened the person up to a truth that the rest of us, imprisoned in ordinary waking consciousness, simply cannot see'?[32]

The framing of this question makes sense if one approaches it from the standpoint of the dominant reductionist worldview. As we've seen, the empirical success of reductionism over centuries has been so overwhelming that many scientists and philosophers came to believe it must be the sole explanation for every aspect of the universe. If something can't be seen or measured by a scientific instrument, then it must not exist. From the reductionist perspective, then, a mystical experience might have subjective psychological benefits, but its claims to access an alternative reality are fatuous. Even when proponents of the perennial philosophy argue against the reductionist position, they frequently endorse a dualistic worldview by talking vaguely about another 'spiritual dimension' inaccessible to scientific instruments, leading to a futile clash of worldviews, one scientific and one 'spiritual' or 'transcendent.'[33]*

What might we find if, instead, we investigate mystical claims of oneness using the conceptual tools of systems-based sciences? If we tried to understand expanded states in terms of nonlinear patterns of self-organization, attractors of consciousness and fractals? Could the sense of immanent oneness described in traditions such as Taoism, Buddhism and many Indigenous cultures be commensurate with these insights of modern science? If so, what might be the implications for understanding the source of meaning in our lives?

As we now proceed to explore these questions, let us take our cue from the wise advice of Neo-Confucian philosopher Zhu Xi: 'If one wishes to know the reality of Tao, one must seek it in one's own nature.' In this case, we can take advantage of the dazzling technological achievements of modern neuroscience and take a peek, perhaps not into our own nature, but inside the brains of people undergoing mystical states to see if they offer any clues for how to proceed.

The neuroscience of oneness

The idea of looking inside someone's head as they experience a mystical state is one that could never have been imagined until very recently. It has only become possible as the result of developments in two very different fields: psychedelics and brain scanning.

In the 1950s, when psychedelics such as LSD and psilocybin entered public awareness, they were of great interest to psychologists, who viewed them as powerful tools that could offer insight into mental processes. One pioneering researcher, Stanislav Grof, placed them in the same category as the microscope or telescope

– just as those instruments had revolutionized biology and astronomy, so he believed LSD could revolutionize psychology and psychiatry. The very word psychedelic – coming from the Greek for 'mind-manifesting' – was formulated from the idea that its use could make manifest the hidden workings of the mind.[34]

These early ideas for research lay fallow for decades once psychedelics were made illegal. However, renewed tolerance of researching their potential benefits under carefully prescribed conditions has permitted neuroscientists, armed with the latest brain-imaging equipment, to study the effects of psychedelics on the brain with a specificity that the first generation of researchers could barely have dreamed possible.

Throughout the history of humankind, when a shaman or prophet experienced a mystical state, there was no way to understand what was going on within them other than through how they chose to express it. That is no longer true. We now have a precise instrument for investigating something about which we could previously only speculate. By scanning the brains of volunteers given psilocybin, researchers can for the first time study the neural underpinnings of mystical states.

The results of these scans are highly revealing. What they show is that different parts of the brain are massively more connected in the psychedelic state than in normal consciousness (Figure 9). In regular waking mode (the image on the left), the brain's connections follow the self-organized small-world property of hubs and spokes discussed in Chapter 7. Local nodes connect tightly with each other, and a few select hubs maintain linkages with far-flung regions. These represent the normal attractors of consciousness that permit us to go about our daily business fairly robustly. New inputs may throw the occasional wrench into our neural networks – an argument with a loved one, unexpected news at work, a surge of attraction for that cute guy at the bar – but our resilient attractors of consciousness quickly absorb the perturbations and resume their normal course. In particular, our default mode network maintains its continual flow of mulling about the past, hypothesizing the future and fortifying the boundaries of the ego, while engaging in constant inner dialogue between 'I' and the 'self'.[35]

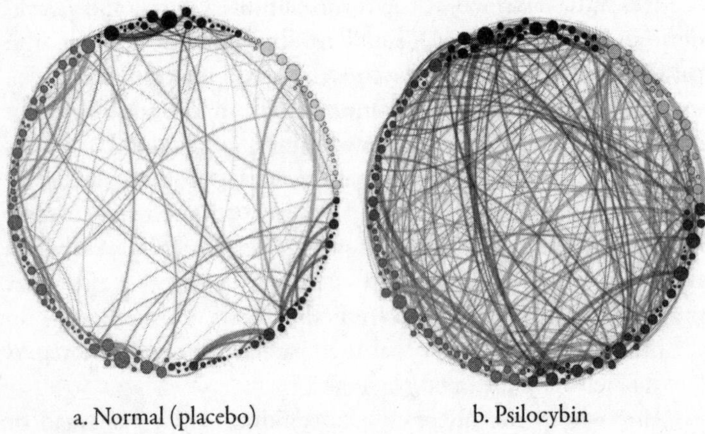

Figure 9: Simplified visualization of brain network changes on psilocybin

Now contrast that with the image on the right which portrays a brain on psilocybin. The tightly ordered hub-and-spoke network is overwhelmed by a flood of connections that seem to spread everywhere. Note that the new network isn't random – there are clearly discernible highways connecting major nodes along with a meshwork of smaller linkages – but there are a vastly increased number of links and multiple long-range connections between regions that were previously barely in contact with each other. Researchers speculate this is one reason why people on psychedelics sometimes report visual hallucinations (seeing patterns we normally don't see) and synesthesia – where your senses intermingle so you can *see* music or *feel* the scent of a flower.[36]

In trying to interpret his own psychedelic experiences, Aldous Huxley referred to normal consciousness as a 'reducing valve' permitting just 'a measly trickle of the kind of consciousness which will help us to stay alive'. These brain scans seem to corroborate his description. In multiple psychedelic brain-imaging studies, neuroscientists have reported that the default mode network – along with other conceptual consciousness networks that rely on the prefrontal cortex – are significantly attenuated. The result is that on psychedelics (and presumably in other mystical states) the brain's normal patterns of activity, with its habitual modes of assigning meaning to things, are dismantled. In their place, other hub-and-spoke networks dominate the contents of consciousness.[37]

It seems clear from these images how mystical states might reveal more than is normally available to consciousness. It also becomes apparent why someone in a mystical state perceives things as more interconnected and unified than normal – because that is how the brain is processing its inputs. Does this mean that mystical states such as those induced by psychedelics do in fact permit us to see a greater truth than normal consciousness?

Interestingly, there is another brain state similar to the psychedelic one where connections between neurons are far more extensive and less reliant on the PFC's filtering. It's one we've all experienced but may not remember very well – being an infant. As developmental psychologist Alison Gopnik points out, an infant's brain is a mass of interconnections that are gradually pruned as they learn their own sense-making ways, sculpted by the culture they grow up in. From this perspective, we could view psychedelics as an opportunity to revisit the wonder and openness of childhood – and indeed many people report experiencing something beautiful, such as a flower, as if they were seeing it for the first time.[38]

This implies that a mystical state does – as the perennialists argue – free us temporarily from the conditioning influences of our culture, and allows us to see the world as more interconnected, more unified than our dominant culture tells us it is. This perception corresponds with the worldview of our hunter-gatherer ancestors, who saw all living beings as related. Without the PFC's culturally conditioned reducing valve, altered states allow animate consciousness to become dominant – including the deeper parts of our consciousness that are normally hidden from awareness. As we've seen, it's animate consciousness that connects us with the intrinsic intelligence of the natural world, in addition to the deeper archetypal patterns of our collective unconscious.[39]

An overarching lesson from our investigation into the animate intelligence of nature is the interconnectedness of all the fractal systems from which life emerges – the mind-boggling intricacies within a cell, the complex cellular cooperation that gives rise to an organism and the multilayered symbiosis between organisms. 'All life is meshwork,' as philosopher Andreas Weber puts it. 'If you watch carefully, everything alive reveals itself to be a pattern of connection and superposition ... Understanding is communication of a connective tissue with itself.'[40]

Is it this immersion into life's interactive meshwork that leads to a deeply felt realization of immanent oneness once our conceptual reducing valve is turned off? Dan Siegel, founder of the field of interpersonal neurobiology, suggests that seeing the interconnectedness between things is a bit like looking up at the sky to see the stars. During daytime, the sun obliterates the subtler starlight, and all we see is blue sky. At night, though, after the sun has set, the stars appear. They were always there, but we just couldn't see them. Similarly, does normal consciousness obliterate our perception of deeper interconnectedness, which is in fact always present?[41]

If so, it would be helpful to understand this interconnectedness more deeply even while remaining in a normal state. This leads us to the next step of our investigation, which begins in an unexpected place – not on a sacred mountaintop, nor deep in the jungle, but in a respectable Dutch house in The Hague, back in February 1665.

Living in a sea of rhythm

The house belonged to Christiaan Huygens, a distinguished physicist who was trying to improve the accuracy of his timepieces. Lying ill in bed and watching the pendulums of two clocks he had installed a couple of feet apart, he noticed that they always oscillated together: one swung left while the other swung right. Even if he deliberately started them asynchronously, within half an hour the pendulums returned to their synchronized oscillations. Huygens reported his discovery to the Royal Society of London, but it was ignored – he was too far ahead of his time. In recent decades, however, Huygens has been rightly anointed as the father of an important new branch of physics: the study of rhythmic oscillations in nature.[42]

Huygens' pendulums were synchronizing through tiny vibrations in their wooden housing that entrained them to each other's rhythm. Modern scientists have since discovered that vibrations underlie virtually every aspect of nature – vibrations of atoms create heat and sound, and vibrations of electrons generate light. Like Huygens' pendulums, vibrations lead things naturally to synchronize with each other, including such disparate phenomena as the dripping of faucets, the coherence of laser beams and the entrainment of the moon's spin to Earth's tides.[43]

Life itself depends on molecules interacting with each other through vibrating or oscillating energy fields. These rhythms oscillate through a vast range of speeds. At the faster end, nerve impulses fire at a frequency of a thousand per second while flying insects oscillate their wings two hundred times a second. We're familiar with many of our own bodily rhythms: our heart rate and respiratory rhythms, our cycles of hunger and thirst, and our daily circadian rhythms of sleeping and waking. At the longer end, certain cicadas follow a seventeen-year reproductive cycle. All told, the oscillation periods of biological rhythms vary over a trillion-fold range.[44]

Throughout the living world, synchrony represents an invisible bond that links organisms together in multiple, complex rhythms through time and space. Crickets and frogs vocalize in sync. Fireflies and mosquitoes conduct their courting rituals in sync. Women who live together frequently menstruate in sync. Every human body is itself a miraculous orchestra of unimaginably complex sequences of thousands of rhythmic oscillatory processes working together. As physicist Mae-Wan Ho puts it, each of us is the emergent result of the 'quantum jazz of life'. Our very existence arises from 'the complex rhythm of the organism dancing life into being, in which every single player is freely improvising and yet keeping in tune and in step with the whole'.[45]*

Consciousness itself arises as a harmonic synchronization of different oscillations in distinct frequency bands. Just as you tune a radio to the frequency of a certain transmitter to get a clear signal, different neural assemblies in the brain transmit to each other in different frequencies. In Chapter 7 we explored the dynamic core of consciousness that constantly links and differentiates across billions of interconnecting pathways, momentarily binding a selected network together so that what you see, hear, think and feel appears like a coherent whole. These dynamic patterns of consciousness are continually being generated and regenerated through the synchronized firing of billions of neurons in an elaborate dance over multiple timescales.[46]

Humans, along with other social mammals, have specialized mirror neurons in our brains that allow us to synchronize with the actions and emotions of those close to us. As a result, when we watch someone wince in pain or get up and dance, we experience in ourselves an embodied simulation of what's happening within their nervous system, creating what Vittorio Gallese, the neuroscientist who co-discovered mirror neurons, calls 'a shared manifold of intersubjectivity'.[47]

A defining characteristic of humans, as we've seen, is our capability for moral emotions such as shame and compassion. Interpersonal synchrony plays a crucial part in their development. A mother holding her newborn – cooing, smiling and gesturing – is engaged in a coordinated choreography of rhythm, to which the infant immediately attunes and begins forming her own neural network of emotional resonance.[48]

As adults, these attunement systems cohere our interpersonal experience. When you have a conversation with someone, your brains become coupled through a concerto of oscillatory signaling with its own amplitude and rhythm. The same thing happens when you do something together. Brain scans show that neurons of two interacting individuals literally resonate with each other, which is why pianists can play a duet with an accuracy that rivals the two hands of a single musician. The closer people are emotionally to each other, the greater the synchrony of their gestures, facial muscles and patterns of neural firing. Likewise, when people's actions are synchronized, they feel more compassionate and cooperative toward each other, even if they're total strangers.[49]

'The human species,' anthropologist Edward Hall observes, 'lives in a sea of rhythm.' He was referring specifically to a study he had conducted analyzing how children in a playground ran around in synchronized motion as if in a dance, without music or choreographer other than their own self-organized collective resonance. The rhythm of music, however, adds a potent element into the mix. It is a human universal, evolutionarily far older than language, that bonds us even more tightly into a collective. Music can move us, both emotionally and physically, like no other force.[50]

There is no specific center in the brain that processes music – playing or listening to it is one of our most neurally integrated experiences. It brings together conceptual and animate consciousness, our bodily movements and emotions, and links us powerfully to others who share in the experience. It most likely arose as a connective force binding prelinguistic hominid bands in a group identity, imbuing events and rituals with shared meaning. Even today, in traditional cultures music is conceived not as an aesthetic performance but as an ever-present force weaving meaning into the daily social fabric of life. Even in modern society music retains its communal bonding effect – we feel its connective power in marching bands, chanting and religious ceremonies. Music theorists suggest it exerts its force through the same synchronous dynamics found in the rest of nature: like Huygens' pendulums, its rhythmic oscillations entrain us into cogenerating a collective self, literally identifying with something larger than our own autonomous being.[51]

Among ancient traditions, from Pythagoras to Confucius, music has long been understood as a medium that manifests the harmony of the universe. As in mystical experiences, deep immersion in music dissolves the constraining boundaries of the ego. But as noted in Chapter 4, from a purely reductionist perspective music doesn't really exist – it can't be pinned down in a musical instrument, in the ear or in the brain. Music is an emergent phenomenon arising from participatory interaction between a player and a listener. It exists in the interrelatedness between embodied minds, in dynamic patterns of vibrations generated, transmitted and received through time and space.[52]

Cognitive scientists have demonstrated that this participatory engagement in meaning-making characterizes not just music but cognition itself. 'The individual human mind,' Evan Thompson writes, 'is not confined within the head, but extends throughout the living body and includes the world beyond the biological membrane of the organism.' Cognition, Thompson and others explain, is characterized by what they call the 'four E's': it is embodied, embedded, extended and enactive. It's *embodied* because it requires a living body; it's *embedded* in the world and its particular culture; it's *extended* beyond the body through dynamic interactions; and it's *enactive* in that it never simply receives inputs but continually brings forth a world of meaning through its unique subjective patterning of consciousness.[53]

This model of cognition can help us answer the ontological question raised earlier: does the mystic realization of oneness depict objective reality? Let us first consider an easier question: the last rainbow you saw – was it real? You know from simple physics there was no objective rainbow with a pot of gold at the end. A rainbow is an emergent phenomenon arising from interaction between sunlight, rain, the retinas in your eyes and your own sense-making. Did it actually exist? Technically, a multitude of rainbow potentials existed at that moment: as falling rain refracted the sunlight, there were countless rays of light dispersed along the color spectrum waiting to be noticed, but you had to be in a certain place to enact them into your own experience and turn the potential rainbow into actuality.[54*]

We are now ready to consider the question of meaning from this vantage point. There is, as we've seen, a vast category of things – life, mind, consciousness, music, cognition and rainbows, to mention just a few – that are emergent phenomena, existing only as a result of complex, dynamic interactions between different entities. Meaning also belongs in this category. In the same way that we can enact a rainbow by gazing into the rain, we enact meaning by the way in which we attune to the connective rhythms of the universe. Like music being played, like the refracted sunlight in the rain, the meaning potential is always there – it's just waiting for us to tune into the right wavelength and engage with it. Let us now consider the implications of this perspective.[55]

Meaning is a function of connectedness

Let's go back to the distinctive features of a mystical experience. Certain characteristics – such as sensations of timelessness, paradoxicality and oneness – may be understood as expected phenomena from the flood of neural connections overwhelming ordinary attractors of conceptual consciousness that usually regulate functions such as time-keeping, logic and a bounded sense of self. But why do people frequently view these experiences as one of the most meaningful of their lives? And why are they associated so often with enormously positive emotions?

I believe that exploring these questions can open us to a deeper understanding of meaning itself. This is because, in my view, meaning is itself a function of connectedness. Just as music is an emergent phenomenon arising between a player and listener attuning through patterns of vibrations, so meaning is an emergent phenomenon enacted by a conscious entity as it relates an experience to other experiences. The more extensively we connect something with other parts of our lives, the more meaningful it is to us. The meaning of something may be understood as the network of relationships it is perceived to have – a more extensive and integrated network makes it more meaningful.[56*]

To understand meaning as a function of connectedness, consider how a dictionary works: it offers other words and phrases that you use to triangulate a meaning for a particular word. Contemplate for a moment what is most meaningful to you: perhaps it's your loved ones, your vocation or your spiritual practice. In each case, you may find that the meaning arises out of its depth and breadth of connections within your own being, with your past and future and with others around you. Once we conceive of meaning as a function of connectivity, it becomes clear why a mystical experience, with its flood of massively interconnected linkages through a person's neural networks, would feel so intensely meaningful.[57*]

As I describe in *The Patterning Instinct*, humans have evolved an instinct to pattern meaning into the world to a greater degree – as far as we know – than any other species. When an infant experiences the sounds and touches of her caregivers, she uses her patterning instinct to connect these disparate sensations and make meaning out of them – and thus begins to learn language. Instincts such as hunger, thirst, sleep or sexual drive wield their power over us by causing us to feel bad when their needs are not met, and feel good when they're fulfilled. Our patterning instinct is no different.

When we are disconnected from things, when things lose their meaning, we feel bad. When a new pattern comes together, we feel good – think of that 'Aha!' moment you get when you solve a difficult problem, or Helen Keller's delight when she discovered the linkage between language and concepts.

This would explain why the sensation of massive interconnectedness in a mystical state brings a flood of positive emotions to those who experience it – their patterning instinct achieves a kind of 'orgasm' of consciousness as it undergoes a phase transition from a more limited pattern of meaning to one that is vastly more expansive. We may remember Jill Bolte Taylor's experiences after the stroke that temporarily disabled the reducing valve of her brain's left hemisphere: 'I was completely entranced by the feelings of tranquility, safety, blessedness, euphoria, and omniscience,' she recalled. 'I was the miraculous power of life ... I was simply a being of light radiating life into the world.'[58]

The work being done with psychedelics to treat people with chronic depression sheds further light on meaning as connectedness. In pre-treatment interviews, patients suffering from chronic depression frequently described their depression as a state of disconnection – from other people, from nature and from their own feelings, as though they were stuck in a mental prison. 'I would look at orchids,' one reported, 'and intellectually understand that there was beauty, but not experience it.' Treatment with psilocybin had dramatic results, with 94 percent reporting that they felt a new sense of connection to the world and to other people. 'I would look at people on the street ... I felt connected to them all,' stated one. 'Before, I enjoyed nature; now I feel part of it,' said another. One patient declared, 'I was everybody, unity, one life with 6 billion faces. I was the one asking for love and giving love, I was swimming in the sea, and the sea was me.'[59]

Once we understand meaning as a function of connectedness, it becomes clear why die-hard reductionists, who look for reality in indivisible particles, claim the universe is without meaning. Do you remember physicist Steven Weinberg's lament: 'The more the universe seems comprehensible the more it also seems pointless'? A closer look at his statement is revealing. Like many in our dominant culture, he uses the word 'pointless' as a synonym for 'meaningless'. For something to be meaningful, it's assumed, it must have a point. This conflation arises from Western culture's focus on linear, purpose-driven behavior – actions with a beginning, middle and endpoint. However, if we see meaning as arising, like Indra's Net, from an infinite array of interconnections, we would not expect any 'point'. On the contrary; each point is really a node that only contains meaning to the extent it's connected to other nodes in the web of meaning.[60]

Weaving the web of meaning

Is meaning, then, intrinsic to the universe? Like the rainbow, the interconnectivity of the universe creates innumerable meaning potentials, but we must actively participate in attuning to those potentials in order to actualize the meaning. We saw how different parts of the brain must tune in to the right frequency to bind with each other and create consciousness. Similarly, we must tune in to the deep connectivity of the cosmos in order to enact its meaning. As philosopher Jorge Ferrer puts it: 'All spiritual experience is participatory.'[61]

Building on this understanding of meaning, we're ready to consider another vast and ineffable concept frequently raised in spiritual settings: love. To the extent that a mystical experience leads to a sense of purpose, it often revolves around a vision of unconditional and universal love. 'From here on, love was the only consideration,' declared terminal cancer patient Patrick Mettes after a six-hour psilocybin immersion at Johns Hopkins. 'It was and is the only purpose.' Another patient, a philosophy professor, concluded in the simplest terms, 'Love conquers all.' This insight has been shared by spiritual teachers throughout the ages. William Richards summarizes much of the mystical literature with the observation that 'the ultimate nature of matter and mind (if you take the mystics seriously) appears to be an ontological source or force of energy called love.'[62]

Love is a difficult term to define, partly because of the vastly different contexts in which it appears, from the cheap sentiments of a Hallmark card to the deeply felt bond between life-partners and to expansive unconditional love. However, I believe that, like meaning, love may be defined in terms of connectivity – specifically, as the realization and embrace of connectedness. It can be as simple and ephemeral as two people greeting each other on the street, as when Louis Armstrong sings, 'I see friends shaking hands saying "How do you do?" ... They're really saying "I love you."' And it can be a vast, cosmic ontological force, as Richards indicates – the force of connectivity in the universe.[63*]

The cosmic power of love is an ancient idea. An early Greek philosopher, Empedocles, described the universe as comprising two opposing forces: strife, which pulls things apart, and love, which brings them together 'to become one'. Modern physics validates this venerable theory. In Chapter 6 we encountered the dark force of entropy pulling the universe inexorably apart. Meanwhile, gravity – described by cosmologist Brian Swimme as a form of love – exerts a countervailing force responsible for congealing energy into stars and planets. Life itself can be viewed, from this perspective, as an act of cosmological love, as it stages its four-billion-year-old rebellion against entropy through the connective powers of self-organization.[64]

Many people (and I suspect Uncle Bob may be one of them) find it difficult to accept the sweeping statement, 'Love conquers all.' After all, it's easy enough to point to countless examples in our everyday experience that seem to prove just the opposite. This is a legitimate concern, which impels us to probe a little deeper. What can we learn if we apply the deep principles of life itself to clarify our own place within the web of meaning?

The connective force of life, as we've seen, incorporates all kinds of competitive and differentiated elements within it. We saw how the elaborate interweaving of organisms within a larger ecosystem can best be described as a state of harmony, where the multifaceted components of a system – competing and cooperating – are blended into a whole that is richer than the mere sum of the parts. The mystical realization of oneness often includes an appreciation of harmony along with love. 'I was learning a song and the song was simple,' recollected Patrick Mettes. 'It was the vibration of the universe ... a collection of everything that ever existed ... all together equaling

God.' Another volunteer in a psilocybin study envisioned herself as being one of countless musicians in a cosmic symphony orchestra. Nothing she did could detract from the beauty of the symphony as a whole, but by playing she became part of the music herself.[65]

This brings us back to the core concept of integration, which has been central to each of the complex self-organized processes we've examined, including life, consciousness, flourishing and ecosystems – a dynamic state of unity with differentiation, where each part maintains its unique identity while actively participating in generating a larger whole. As Dan Siegel observes, 'When we embrace integration as a central drive in our lives, we cultivate meaning and connection, happiness and health ... Beginning with integration within, extending integration to those you are connected with, and moving integration into our larger world: these may just be the reasons we are here ... in this life.'[66]

The web of meaning is, above all, an integrated web. The realization of meaning as a function of connectedness doesn't require merging everything into an undifferentiated oneness. Instead, it celebrates all the different elements within us, within our communities, within the variegated fabric of humanity and within the stunning diversity of life on Earth. As Christopher Bache describes one of his visionary experiences: 'Life here was not the assemblage of parts but the harmonious expression of a unified whole rippling through life, the way wind ripples through a wheat field ... Diversity did not rupture oneness. Oneness expressed itself in diversity without itself falling into diversity ... Reality was a fluid energy expressing itself in diversity.' This description of deep integration encapsulates the possibility of true flourishing for each individual organism as part of the infinitely complex web of meaning that we all are collectively weaving.[67]

Opening our eyes to the rainbow

The apparent paradox of oneness and diversity coexisting through integration is a theme that Neo-Confucian sages immersed themselves in as they explored the implications of a cosmos composed of qi connected through li. Their understanding of li as the connective patterning between things revealed valuable insights into how the universe could accommodate infinite diversity within an overarching oneness.

A millennium before mathematician Benoit Mandelbrot identified fractals as an intrinsic feature of nature, the Neo-Confucians recognized that we live in a fractal cosmos where dynamic patterns repeat themselves to an infinite degree – even while each manifestation of the pattern retains its uniqueness. You may remember philosopher Cheng Yi's statement: 'We say that all things are one reality because all things have the same li in them ... The li of a thing is one with the li of all things ... There is only one li in the world' – a realization reiterated in modern times by Gregory Bateson when he declared, 'The pattern which connects is a metapattern. It is a pattern of patterns.'[68]

This metapattern can also be understood as the Tao – the overarching principle that connects everything together: humans, animals, the living Earth and the heavens, like ripples flowing through the universe. Neo-Confucian sages taught that, by cultivating resonance and attunement with the Tao – the li of all creation – one can begin to dissolve the distinction between oneself and others, between the individual and the universe.[69]

They had a word for this realization of the ultimate connectedness of the universe: *ren*. The word *ren* originally meant a kind of humane benevolence that people should cultivate to fulfill their role within society. However, the Neo-Confucians expanded it to incorporate the entire cosmos. One of their leading philosophers, Zhang Zai, reflected deeply on the larger implications of what it meant for him, as a human being, to be a fractal entity connected with the universe through the li that organized both him and his surroundings. He expounded his understanding in a renowned essay called the 'Western Inscription', which begins as follows:

> Heaven is my father and earth is my mother,
> and I, a small child, find myself placed intimately between them.
> What fills the universe I regard as my body;
> what directs the universe I regard as my nature.
> All people are my brothers and sisters; all things are my
> companions.[70]

This vision of immanence encapsulates some of the greatest wisdom in the human endeavor to comprehend the universe and our place within it. Reprising the recognition of the relatedness of all things shared by Indigenous communities worldwide, it reflects a truly integrated existence, embedded in harmony with oneself, with community, with all of life and with the entire cosmos.

The Neo-Confucians understood this universal interconnectedness as a reality that exists for everyone, whether they chose to realize it or not. Just as a body can become numb or paralyzed (literally 'no *ren*' in Chinese) and not feel its connections, so a person can become numbed to their intrinsic connectedness with the universe, but that doesn't mean the connection isn't there. Just as a blind person can't see a rainbow, and a deaf person can't hear music, so a person who is numb to their interconnectedness can't realize *ren*.

Which brings us back to Uncle Bob and his question: why should I look out for anyone other than myself? The answer is that we can all choose to numb ourselves to our connectedness, just as we can close our eyes to avoid seeing the rainbow. In fact, the conditioning we receive by growing up in the dominant culture of separation teaches us from infancy to numb ourselves from feeling these deep connections. By the time we're adults, our eyes have been tightly shut for so long that it takes an intentional act to open them, bit by bit, until we see the rainbow that was waiting there for us all along.

Like the putative righteous Christian who ends up in heaven having his memories deleted so he won't have to care about his loved ones suffering in hell, each of us can choose to delete those parts of our consciousness that attune to the love and suffering of others, to the sentience of all life on Earth and to the sublime glory of the universe. But that choice inevitably leads to a loss of meaning in life. Imagine somebody discovering the magnificence of Indra's Net and choosing to steal one of the glittering jewels, only to discover when they get home to savor it that by itself it's merely a piece of cut glass that simply reflects back a fragmented version of themselves. That's the choice that Uncle Bob – and all of us to some degree or other – make when we shut ourselves off from our embedded interconnectedness in the web of meaning. In the immortal words attributed to the Sufi mystic Rumi: 'Your task is not to seek for love, but merely to seek and find all the barriers within yourself that you have built against it.'

A full recognition of this interconnectedness brings with it myriad implications as we traverse its weave. Some pathways of the web invite possibilities for great awakening and liberation from the confines of a bounded self. Other pathways open up grievous avenues of shared anguish as we become intimate with the suffering of others and the ongoing devastation of nonhuman life on Earth. Taken together, these pathways can also imbue our lives with vibrant meaning as we participate in the wondrous and fearsome cosmic adventure of being a human alive during this time of great destiny. In the final chapters of this book let us explore some of these pathways together.

NEW THREADS OF MEANING

Mind, life, consciousness and meaning are all emergent phenomena, existing only as the result of complex, dynamic interactions between different entities

Just as we enact a rainbow by gazing into the rain, we enact meaning by how we attune to the connective rhythms of the universe

Meaning is a function of connectedness: the more extensively we connect something with other aspects of our lives, the more meaningful it is to us

Love is the realization and embrace of connectedness

Chapter Twelve

FROM FIXED SELF TO INFINITE LI: THE FRACTAL NATURE OF IDENTITY

The year 1985 doesn't stand out as one of history's most memorable. It followed 1984, the iconic year that gave the title to George Orwell's classic. The neoliberal takeover of global politics was in full swing, with Ronald Reagan sworn in for his second term, and the historic coalminers' strike in the UK finally crushed by Margaret Thatcher's dogged intransigence. Coca-Cola introduced New Coke in one of history's great marketing blunders, and Greenpeace's ship *Rainbow Warrior* was sunk in New Zealand by French agents. But by a strange coincidence of timing, two popular songs topped the charts that spring, both of which chipped away at the dominant worldview portraying individuals as fixed, standalone entities trying to maximize their fortunes in a cold-hearted universe.

The first of these was a charity single dreamed up by activist/performer Harry Belafonte in response to a devastating famine in Ethiopia. Michael Jackson, Stevie Wonder and dozens of musical superstars recorded 'We Are the World' – a popular anthem of shared global identity with lyrics proclaiming, 'We are the world, we are the children ... let us realize that a change can only come when we stand together as one.' The song was one of the greatest hits of all time, and exceeded the organizers' hopes, raising over $50 million for humanitarian aid. It's been appropriately criticized for merely providing a cheap way for people in wealthy countries to absolve themselves of guilt while benefitting from structural global inequalities that remain unresolved. But from a larger historical perspective, it may come to be seen as an early point of light in an awakening global consciousness of shared human identity.[1]

The other song was less iconic, but also hit a nerve in popular consciousness by offering an alternative take on the true meaning of identity. In 'Highwayman', recorded by the country music supergroup of Johnny Cash, Waylon Jennings, Willie Nelson and Kris Kristofferson, each singer takes a turn to chronicle a kind of cosmic autobiography of a spirit reincarnated in various bodies over the ages. 'I was a highwayman,' intones Nelson. 'The bastards hung me in the spring of twenty-five/ But I am still alive.' Kristofferson was a sailor: 'They said that I got killed/ But I am living still.' Jennings was a dam builder who slipped to his death, 'but I am still around'. Finally, Johnny Cash prophesies that 'I'll fly a starship across the universe divide,' finishing,

> And when I reach the other side
> I'll find a place to rest my spirit if I can
> Perhaps I may become a highwayman again
> Or I may simply be a single drop of rain
> But I will remain
> And I'll be back again, and again and again.

What's fascinating about this song, which topped the country charts, was the implicit cosmology it spun, depicting a kind of spirit, characterized by a sense of defiant, rugged adventure, transcending the life and death of any single person.[2]

Part of the song's appeal is that it hints at a different kind of reality: one in which an individual's life is made meaningful by qualities he or she temporarily embraces as part of a vaster, epic adventure. Similarly, the feel-good aura generated by 'We Are the World' suggests the possibility of a broader identity transcending a bounded self, somehow linking all humanity together in a common bond. Looking back over the decades of neoliberal capitalism since these songs came out, it's easy to dismiss their intimations as mere poetic flourishes. But as we've seen, the current worldview that dominates mainstream thought is deeply flawed. Once we begin to embrace the reality of a connected universe, new forms of identity naturally emerge. In this chapter we'll explore some fascinating aspects of the landscape unfurled by a worldview of connectedness. We'll see how a scientifically rigorous, careful investigation of the nature of existence leads to unexpected outcomes – even to a realization that, rather than mere aspirational sentiments, those hits from 1985 offered glimpses of a more coherent reality than the hard-nosed worldview promulgated today by mainstream discourse.

Dualism or reductionism? A false choice

To most Indigenous people throughout history, the spirit portrayed in 'Highwayman' would likely have made intuitive sense. Indigenous cultures worldwide believed that spirits existed, not just in people, but in creatures, trees, mountains and all significant natural phenomena. The spread of monotheism gradually stamped out this idea in many parts of the world, replacing it with a strict dualistic cosmology. Based substantially on Plato's teachings, the cosmos was now perceived as split between God's eternal domain and the polluted, messy world below. This split was replicated in every human being, who possessed an everlasting soul temporarily imprisoned in a mortal body subject to corruption and sinful impulses. The soul was the point of contact with God, who was the ultimate source of everything holy, while the natural world, stripped of divinity and spirits, became a mere desacralized theater in which the human drama was played out.[3]

This was the cosmological context in which the Scientific Revolution erupted in seventeenth-century Europe. Its great pioneers, such as Galileo, Kepler and Newton, never questioned the dualistic worldview. On the contrary, they believed their scientific theories were decoding 'God's book', which was written in the language of mathematics. With the natural world seen as an intricate machine, God was conceived as the great clockmaker, the artificer whose construction was so flawless that, once it was set in motion, there was nothing more to do (bar the occasional miracle) than let it run its course.[4]

When cracks appeared between the monotheistic and scientific worldviews, they occurred primarily on the fault line between the spiritual and material domains of dualism. As scientists expanded their knowledge of the material world, they had less and less to say about the spiritual. Twentieth-century biochemist Jacques Monod succinctly summarized what had become the mainstream scientific approach when he declared, 'Any mingling of knowledge with values is unlawful, forbidden.' Biologist Stephen J. Gould, trying to broker a reconciliation between science and religion, famously demarcated the playing field by proposing a doctrine of what he called 'non-overlapping magisteria'. 'Science,' he asserted, 'tries to document the factual character of the natural world,' while religion operates in the 'realm of human purposes, meanings, and values.'[5]

However, as they 'document the factual character of the natural world', many scientists unwittingly approach their work through the lens of a particular ideology – the worldview of reductionism they inherited from the dualistic pioneers of the Scientific Revolution. The reductionist project of dividing objects of study into ever-smaller components has been so effective that many scientists have come to believe in reductionism as an article of faith, even when advances in scientific research uncover its limitations. God may no longer be in the picture, but the mechanistic metaphor continues to hold sway. Reductionism has spread throughout scientific thought so pervasively that scientists using it frequently remain unaware that it is a particular lens that configures how they make sense of what they're investigating.[6]

Under biological reductionism, organisms continue to be described as machines coded by their genes, even though researchers have revealed the relationship between gene and organism to be a dynamic, circular flow of creative interaction. Those under the sway of neurological reductionism still believe that a person's psychological make-up is the way it is (in the words of reductionist Steven Weinberg) '*entirely* because of the principles of macroscopic physics and chemistry, which in turn are what they are *entirely* because of the principles of the standard model of elementary particles' (Weinberg's italics). This claim, as we've seen, is invalidated by modern research in neuroscience, which demonstrates how consciousness emerges from principles of complex, dynamic neuronal self-organization.[7]

At a deeper level, proponents of ontological reductionism claim that the universe itself is nothing more than a meaningless concatenation of particles, the results of which could in principle be predicted from the Big Bang to the end of time. Adherents to this creed present their audience with a stark choice: either accept the ultimate meaninglessness of the cosmos or deceive yourself into feeling better by believing in a creator God. Over the centuries, some who refused the balm of religious belief have expressed the existential dread they've suffered as a result. As early as the seventeenth century, mathematician Blaise Pascal wrote how 'when I survey the whole universe in its deadness ... I am moved to terror'. Jacques Monod concluded that 'Man at last knows he is alone in the unfeeling immensity of the universe,' while philosopher Bertrand Russell divulged that, accepting the reductionist worldview, he had to build his philosophy 'only on the firm foundation of unyielding despair'.[8]*

This is not just an existential conundrum limited to a few philosophical luminaries. Increasingly, people in the modern world reject the dogmas of traditional monotheistic faiths, but are left wondering how to make sense of things in a way that is both internally coherent and authentic to their own felt sense of meaning in the cosmos. Even in the United States, known for its more fundamentalist religiosity, a quarter of the population consider themselves 'spiritual but not religious', a number that increased by a remarkable 50 percent between 2012 and 2017.[9]

Fortunately for these people – and for anyone engaging in an intellectually rigorous search for meaning that integrates all aspects of their lived experience – the stark choice offered by hardcore reductionists is a false one. Even though reductionism and science are frequently regarded as indistinguishable, there is a clear contrast between them. In its ontological form, reductionism is a belief system relying on a leap of faith: it asserts that, because its method works effectively to understand many things about the universe, it can be used to understand *everything* about the universe. Science, on the other hand, is a systematic methodology for examining the nature of reality based on principles of observation, hypothesis, prediction, testing and analysis. At its best, science is built on core values of transparency, open-mindedness, honesty and receptivity to criticism. It is possible to reject the reductionist leap of faith about the cosmos while remaining fully committed to the scientific method as a powerful vehicle to investigate the nature of the universe.[10]

Much of the debate that characterizes the conflict between science and spirituality misses this crucial distinction. People who believe in a spiritual dimension to the cosmos frequently criticize what they call 'scientism' or 'scientific materialism' when the more appropriate target of their criticism would be ontological reductionism. We've seen throughout this book how a rigorous, systematic, scientific investigation into phenomena such as life, evolution and consciousness yields insights that refute ontological reductionism. Reductionists claim these phenomena are nothing but their constituent parts and can be explained accordingly. However, in each of these areas scientific research has identified principles of self-organization and emergence that explain how these phenomena arise in a way that could never be predicted by reductionist methods alone.[11*]

Integrating science with spiritual meaning

For over a century, prominent thinkers have called for science to rise above its reductionist roots and embrace a holistic worldview. 'The aim of science,' wrote nineteenth-century mathematician Henri Poincaré, 'is not things themselves, as the dogmatists in their simplicity assume, but the relations among things.' By the beginning of the twentieth century, German scientists had founded the field of ecology to study living systems, while others developed Gestalt psychology – known for its famous statement, 'The whole is greater than the sum of its parts.' In the 1920s the mind-bending discoveries of theoretical physicists led to quantum mechanics, which revealed a subatomic universe that could only be predicted in terms of probabilities, thus undermining the classical view of a deterministic cosmos.[12]

But still, the reductionist band played on, mostly oblivious to these developments. When Edward Lorenz, founder of chaos theory, demonstrated that complex systems such as weather were intrinsically chaotic and unpredictable, he received a shocked response from most scientists. Two decades later, he received the distinguished Kyoto Prize, and was said to have 'brought about one of the most dramatic changes in mankind's view of nature since Sir Isaac Newton'. But his insights – and those of his equally illustrious peers – continue to be largely ignored by much of mainstream science. Why is that?[13]

A primary reason is the sticky nature of worldviews. As Thomas Kuhn, who first described the concept of a paradigm shift, pointed out, 'Novelty emerges only with difficulty, manifested by ... lifelong resistance' from those 'whose productive careers have committed them to an older tradition'. Systems thinkers don't reject the basic parameters of reductionist science or posit an alternative dimension where the rules of physics don't apply. They merely argue that, at each level of complexity in a system, new properties emerge that can't be understood using methodologies appropriate for lower levels. However, embracing systems thinking activates a conceptual switch that disrupts the foundations of the reductionist worldview. In the words of Nobel laureate Roger Sperry, once principles of complexity and emergence are accepted, 'then the very nature of science itself is changed'.[14]

What does Sperry mean by this? If we look at the implications of a holistic worldview, we find that they erode the cleanly defined boundaries on which much reductionist science is based. To begin with, science has become highly specialized. Researchers are expected to focus narrowly on a particular subtopic, and may work for years to advance their field in a way that might be impenetrable to all but a few close colleagues. Systems thinkers, by contrast, frequently look for overarching principles that transcend particular disciplines, such as when researchers compare the self-organization of ants to that of neurons, or apply the power law to analyze avalanches, stock market crashes and musical compositions.[15]

Even more subversively, systems thinking undermines the sacrosanct distinction between the observer and observed that allows scientists to claim their methodology is 'value-free'. Once you recognize you are embedded in the very system you're observing, your sense of reality changes. You realize that the way you approach whatever you're studying may affect it, and may impact your own perception of it. 'We can no longer be naïve observers who live outside the phenomena we manipulate,' writes a team of prominent systems biologists. Instead of trying to control complex systems as though they're machines, this leads to exploring how to participate skillfully within the system. When scientists, for example, study climate breakdown, a reductionist approach may view the greenhouse effect as a technical problem to be solved through geoengineering, whereas a systems approach recognizes the feedback loops between politics, economics, cultural values and emissions as a nonlinear meshwork of interactions.[16]

A participatory approach is inescapable when we turn our attention to living systems. When life emerged on Earth in a cascade of negative entropy, value and purpose also came into being on our planet. As living beings ourselves, our existence arises from the same miraculous process that has been unfolding over billions of years. Deep down, we are part of the same web of life that we're studying. The ethical implications of this are enormous, ranging from questions of animal testing to strategies for preventing ecological breakdown.[17]

Our embeddedness extends even to the universe that created the conditions for life to self-generate on this planet – and potentially elsewhere across the galaxies. In place of cold objectivity, an engaged approach to the universe invites feelings of awe and reverence as we glimpse the vast mystery at a scale beyond our comprehension. 'The most beautiful thing we can experience is the mysterious,' wrote Einstein. 'To know that what is impenetrable to us really exists, manifesting itself as the highest wisdom and the most radiant beauty which our dull faculties can comprehend only in their most primitive forms – this knowledge, this feeling, is at the center of true religiousness.'[18]

These realms of participatory engagement form the intersection points between science and spirituality. They offer fertile new terrain for discovery – and a potential pathway for humanity to find a more harmonious relationship with the sentience existing all around us on Earth. Recognizing this, complexity theorist Stuart Kauffman has mused, 'We enter new territory ... We are seeking a new conceptual framework that does not yet exist.' There are, however, conceptual frameworks for exploring the meaning of humanity's intrinsic connection with the natural world to be found in premodern wisdom traditions. How can they help us map out this terra incognita?[19]

Reverence for the universe

One of the earliest Greek philosophers, Heraclitus, offered a promising beginning to the ancient world's investigation of interconnectedness when he declared, 'Wisdom consists in one thing, to know the principle by which all things are steered through all things.' In spite of Plato's opposition, this idea resonated for centuries with many Greco-Roman philosophers, finding its zenith in the Stoics, who saw divinity as interpenetrating everything in the cosmos, forming an organic unity. However, this tradition was effectively shut down with the advent of the Christian hegemony.[20]*

In early China, on the other hand, spirituality and physicality went hand in hand. The Chinese never conceived of a split universe where sacredness existed only in an eternal heavenly dimension. Instead, they saw the Tao as pervading everything. The only constant was change; and the ways in which things related to each other seemed more meaningful than the things themselves. When Buddhism permeated Chinese thought, this further strengthened the sense of spiritual meaning arising from the relationship between things. A classic Zen poem goes: 'The bell doesn't ring,/ Nor does the stick;/ Only the "between" is ringing.'[21]

Traditional Chinese landscape paintings evocatively capture the prevalent sense of meaning existing in the spaces between things. Scholar David Hinton highlights an exemplary painting by Shih T'ao showing an artist/intellectual gazing into the distance from a mountain peak (Figure 10). The landscape isn't portrayed realistically; rather it is depicted with a sense of mysterious emptiness, inviting an awe similar to that described by Einstein as 'true religiousness'. Patrons would make it a spiritual practice to spend hours in front of pictures such as these, absorbing the sense of dynamic energy generated by the vast emptiness stretching beyond the horizon.[22]

The Huayan school, which gave us the dazzling image of Indra's Net, further developed the core Buddhist notion of dependent

Figure 10: Shih T'ao, 'Broad-Distance Pavilion'

origination – a profound understanding of reality as an all-embracing web of causal relations between things. The Huayan cosmos has no center and no fixed form. Their philosophy emphasized that the significance of any object depends on how it's approached, with the result that phenomena could be interpreted in multiple ways without one interpretation invalidating the other. Their followers would likely have had no difficulty accommodating the discovery of quantum mechanics that subatomic entities may be either a wave or a particle depending on how they're measured.[23]

As we've seen, the Neo-Confucian school of the Song dynasty masterfully synthesized these earlier teachings from Taoism and Buddhism with their conception of a universe composed entirely of qi (matter and/or energy) and li, the organizing principles by which qi is manifested. When Neo-Confucians investigated li, they made no distinction between the empirical and spiritual – for them a deep understanding of the workings of the universe was equivalent to spiritual wisdom.[24]

The Neo-Confucians inherited from earlier Chinese philosophy a concept called the Supreme Ultimate – the original creative force that generated the yin/yang principles underlying the Tao. But rather than anthropomorphize this into a God, they understood it as a kind of fractal, holographic pattern that permeated all reality. 'Fundamentally there is only one Supreme Ultimate,' said philosopher Zhu Xi, 'yet each of the myriad things has been endowed with it and each in itself possesses the Supreme Ultimate in its entirety.' Their *gewu* – investigation of li – represented a path to a deeper appreciation of ultimate meaning in the cosmos. 'From the Supreme Ultimate above,' Zhu Xi said, 'to a small thing like a blade of grass, a plant or an insect below, each has its li ... we must understand them one by one ... As more and more is accumulated, one will spontaneously be able to achieve a far and broad understanding.' Like the Huayan school, the Neo-Confucians realized that the meaning they derived from their investigation of the cosmos depended on the way they approached it. Accordingly, they emphasized the importance of cultivating an attitude of reverence in all their activities, given that even the smallest natural object contained the essence of the Supreme Ultimate.[25]

This approach to the universe is known more generally as pantheism: the belief that divinity exists, not in a separate dimension, but in every aspect of the universe. For a pantheist, the universe itself, along with everything within it, is sacred and worthy of the deepest reverence. While this belief is shared by most Indigenous cultures worldwide, pantheism in the Western tradition is frequently associated with the philosopher Baruch Spinoza, who was ostracized by his Dutch Jewish community in the seventeenth century for proposing that there is no distinction between God and nature, and that God therefore exists throughout the cosmos. Not surprisingly, Einstein was fascinated by Spinoza's pantheism and considered himself a disciple, declaring, 'We followers of Spinoza see our God in the wonderful order and lawfulness of all that exists and in its soul as it reveals itself in man and animal.'[26]

A paramount lesson from these traditions is that the split between science and spirituality pervading modern discourse is unnecessary and misconceived – merely a result of the flawed dualistic cosmology formulated in early Europe and partially inherited by reductionist science. Recognizing this, a few prominent systems thinkers have had the courage to extend their scientific explorations into the spiritual sphere. 'We are stepping towards the reinvention of the sacred as the creativity in nature,' writes Stuart Kauffman.[27]

A modern rendering of *gewu* requires, above all, a practice of integration: weaving together the fixed laws of reductionist science, the organizing principles of complex systems, teachings from wisdom traditions and spiritual insights of subjective experience to arrive at a coherent appreciation of the universe and our place within it. It invites us to recognize that we live in a vast, fractal universe with patterns that are both recognizable and forever unfolding, mysterious beyond human comprehension, yet manifesting a deeply meaningful harmony that permits us, with reverence and awe, to apprehend its unfathomable glory.

The spirit as a natural attractor

There is one particular recognizable and ever-changing pattern of great importance to each of us – our personal identity. A careful examination of our own personhood using modern *gewu* yields intriguing results. We already know that the body is a Ship of Theseus: all its constituent parts are continually changing; the only constancy is its li – the relatively stable set of relationships between them that maintains coherence. This is equally true for the intangible elements of our personhood: our thoughts and feelings, our character and personality, and our network of relationships. From a systems perspective, our personhood is a multidimensional natural attractor, always in flux within certain parameters, both variable and resilient, undergoing occasional phase transitions as we grow and adapt through time. We are, in the words of philosopher Alan Watts, 'temporarily identifiable wiggles in a stream'.[28]

The Chinese traditionally used the word *shen* to refer to the vital spirit inhabiting a living organism. From the perspective of modern *gewu*, we could keep using the term multidimensional natural attractor, but why not adopt the word that describes it in common parlance – spirit? Rediscovering the profound understanding of Indigenous cultures, we can recognize that the spirit of a person, an animal, a tree or a river is the intangible but powerful unifying principle that maintains the entity's natural attractor in coherent form. It is the emergent integrative property of any natural entity.[29]

Once we recognize spirit as a coherent series of dynamic

patterns – or li – new vistas open up in our apperception of life. We can appreciate that the li of our loved ones, our friends, our family, exist within us, and that our own spirit resides in them. We can understand love between two people as a partial fusion of spirits, forming its own emergent properties. We can recognize that the li of people we were once close to but are no longer alive still exist within us. Even the li of some people long dead, such as artists or composers, become part of us through patterns of meaning transmitted through time.[30]

Mathematical scholar Douglas Hofstadter, in his aptly titled book *I Am a Strange Loop*, explores some implications of a scientifically conceived spirit, reflecting how the musical notes of Chopin's études, little black marks on a piece of paper, can be thought of as 'soul-shards', enabling us to share within our own consciousness 'some tiny fragment of the internal experiences of another human being – his sufferings, his joys, his deepest passions and tensions'. Hofstadter reflects tenderly on Carol, his wife who had died some years earlier. She was, he muses, 'far more than just a body, which is now gone, but rather a very vast pattern, a style, a set of things including memories, hopes, dreams, beliefs, loves'. Those patterns, he realizes – 'some of Carol's consciousness, her interiority' – remain alive within him, in the form of her spirit.[31]

Suddenly, from this perspective, spirits are everywhere around us: in the living world, in music, in words and in photographs. Take a moment to ponder the photograph in Figure 11 of Chief Joseph, a heroic Nez Perce leader who valiantly resisted the forcible removal of his tribe from their ancestral territory. After months of struggle, surrounded by the US Army in freezing weather with no food or blankets, he was compelled to surrender for the sake of the starving women and children in his group. Can you feel his torment, his valor, his deep compassion? At this moment, although Chief Joseph is long dead, you are in touch with his spirit.

Attractors of consciousness, as we've seen, extend beyond individuals to take the form of cultural attractors and archetypes – long-lived patterns of sense-making and behavior that ripple through the ages, newly reinterpreted by each new generation but recognizably stable with a coherent identity. Now we can

Figure 11: Chief Joseph

understand the allure of 'Highwayman' – listeners intuitively recognize it's the spirit of rugged adventure itself that is singing 'I'll be back again and again and again' as it re-emerges in each new incarnation.[32]

Indeed, if 'spirit' can be scientifically described as the unifying principle of a natural attractor, the term spirituality may accordingly be specified using similar terms. 'My sense,' observes Buddhist teacher Joan Halifax, is that 'the spiritual flows between beings, be they with humans or other beings.' Sharing this perspective, we can define spirituality as seeking meaning in the coherent connections between things, rather than in the things themselves. In this sense, spirituality and systems thinking are intrinsically aligned.[33]

An infinite ocean of li

The concept of a person existing as a play of patterns is alien to the Western tradition, which has spent over two millennia defining personal identity as a fixed 'I' centered in conceptual consciousness and demarcated by rigid boundaries from other humans and the rest of nature. To explore the ramifications of a more fluid approach to personhood, we must turn once again to Chinese and Buddhist traditions, which have spent a similar amount of time pondering exactly these questions.[34]

From the early days of Taoism, Chinese sages recognized the

limitations arising from a fixed sense of selfhood. 'But really are there such distinctions as "self" and "other"', asks Zhuangzi, 'or are there no such distinctions? When "self" and "other" lose their contrariety, there we have the very essence of the Tao.' For Zhuangzi, the dissolution of the self's boundaries is the path to *wu-wei*. Do you remember Cook Ding, who cut up the ox carcass so skillfully it was like a dance? For him, subject and object merged into one: his self-patterns harmonized with the patterns of nature: 'When I first began cutting up oxen, all I could see was the ox itself ... And now – now I go at it by spirit and don't look with my eyes.'[35]

Similarly, in Buddhist thought a core insight is that suffering arises ultimately from clinging to the illusory notion of a fixed self. In a foundational teaching, the Buddha instructs his disciples to meditate on every aspect of their experience – their feelings, perceptions, ideas – and to recognize in each case that 'This is not me, I am not this, this is not my self.' Buddhism teaches that the conception of a fixed self confines a person within its boundaries, thus leading to the endless pursuit of hedonic pleasures to try to appease its needs – which are never fully satisfied. On the other hand, through dedicated practice it's possible to become aware of the self as a dynamic, enactive process – impermanent and perpetually in motion – bubbling up continually from an endless stream of experience.[36]

The possibility exists to welcome and harmonize with each of these unfolding enactments of temporary selfhood without becoming attached to any particular one – which can bring about the eudaimonic state of *sukha*. Transcending the confines of a fixed self naturally leads a person to embody qualities such as altruism, kindness and compassion, which as we've seen help form the group identity that is an essential part of our evolved human heritage.[37]

Even without the help of Buddhist practice – and in spite of what we're told by the dominant culture – human identity naturally extends far beyond the individual ego. Philosopher Samuel Scheffler elegantly illustrates this point with a simple thought experiment. Imagine you knew you would live a normal lifespan but, unbeknown to anyone else, Earth would be completely destroyed a month after your death in a collision with an asteroid.

Would you feel indifferent because your own life would be spared? Unlikely! If you're like most of us, you would see this future event as catastrophic, taking most of the meaning out of your own existence. Scheffler's point is that, to a great extent, we derive our sense of purpose in what we do from the assumption that humanity will continue its existence into the future. We identify not just with our own direct descendants, but with humanity as a collective unit. The remarkable conclusion he arrives at is that the 'coming into existence of people we do not know and love matters more to us than our own survival'. Is it possible that the popular success of a song such as 'We Are the World' can be attributed to connecting with this deeply felt group identity shared by virtually all humans everywhere?[38]

At a deeper level, our identity as living beings can extend to embrace all of life. In the Western tradition, with personhood confined to conceptual consciousness, the existential fear of death has historically been alleviated by the belief in an eternal soul that remains intact after the demise of the body. But much of this fear is the result of experiencing a fixed self-identity separate from the rest of life. To the extent that we, as temporary eddies of consciousness, can recognize our unity with the entire stream of life of which we're a tiny part, there is less to fear from our own death. As part of the unfolding cascade of negative entropy that has evolved in all its magnificence on Earth, we have never died for over three billion years. From this expanded perspective, as long as there is life, there is no such thing as death. The *Tao Te Ching* hints at this deep insight when it proclaims, 'One who knows how to nourish life ... has no place of death.'[39]

Zhuangzi similarly expressed a cosmic nonchalance at his own impending death. His disciples wanted to give him a rich burial, but he declined, saying, 'Heaven and earth are my coffin, the sun and moon are my burial jades, the stars and planets are my burial jewelry. Ten thousand things make up my sacrificial feast. Is not my funeral preparation complete? What can be added upon this?'[40]

Here we see a pantheistic expansion of identity even beyond life itself to incorporate the entire universe. This is a grand vision that was shared by some of the most illustrious Zen monks and

Neo-Confucian sages. 'I came to realize clearly,' wrote Dogen, the founder of the Soto school of Zen Buddhism, 'that mind is none other than mountains and rivers and the great wide earth, the sun and the moon and the stars.' Similarly, Neo-Confucian philosopher Cheng Yi declared that a person who achieves the state of *ren* 'regards heaven, earth, and all things as one body; there is nothing not himself'.[41]

While this might seem like an unattainable, mystical vision, it's a realization that can be reached simply by following the consequences of a cosmos where meaning emerges from li – the coherent connections between things. Imagine throwing a stone into a still pond and watching the ripples extend outward; then throwing in a second stone nearby and seeing the new set of ripples intersect with the first. Everything we do, every action we take, every word we speak, creates li ripples in the fabric of existence. Many will diminish over time, while some may become amplified by resonance with li ripples created by others and become part of larger waves. Each of these li ripples contains part of our unique spirit.

Just like the wind, which is invisible except for its effect on the waving branches of trees, these li ripples are continually transmitted but may only be noticed once you attend to them, and frequently their impact may remain forever unknown. A sharp word to someone at work might be passed on to their family later that evening in the form of a quarrel; an unexpected act of generosity to a stranger might shift that person's mood, causing them to act differently to the person they're about to meet.

Once we expand our personhood beyond the fixed barriers of an egoic self, our identity begins to follow those ripples as they flow ceaselessly through an infinite ocean of li. The more we identify with the li and conduct our lives in harmony with those ripples, the more we can become one with the fractal unfolding of the universe in all its mystery.

'Call me by my true names'

This realization, expansive as it may be, also brings an inherent ethical responsibility. Our morality, as we've seen, is largely a function of our identity. The more our personhood extends beyond our own fixed self, the greater the imperative to act for the benefit of that larger identity.[42]

The traditional sages were fully aware of the moral dimension of an expanded identity. Do you remember Zhang Zai's magnificent vision of *ren*: 'Heaven is my father and earth is my mother … All people are my brothers and sisters; all things are my companions'? He follows this statement by zeroing in on the consequent moral significance: 'Those who are tired, infirm, crippled, or sick; those who have no brothers or children, wives or husbands; all are my brothers who are in distress and have no one to turn to.'[43]

Thích Nhât Hanh, the Buddhist teacher who coined the term interbeing, encourages the practice of intentionally extending one's self-identity to incorporate everything without exception. 'Practice,' he exhorts, 'until you recognize your presence in everyone else on the bus, in the subway, in the concentration camp, working in the fields, in a leaf, in a caterpillar, in a dew drop, in a ray of sunshine.' Going beyond the (relatively easy) blending of identity with someone suffering, he advocates the more challenging task of blending identity with the protagonist of that suffering. Reflecting on the haunting story of a girl who had been raped by a pirate and threw herself overboard to her death, he points out, 'In my meditation, I saw that if I had been born in the village of the pirate and raised in the same conditions as he was, I would now be the pirate … I can't condemn myself so easily.' In a memorable poem, he proclaims,

> I am the twelve-year-old girl …
> who throws herself into the ocean …
> And I am the pirate,
> my heart not yet capable
> of seeing and loving …
> Please call me by my true names,
> so I can hear all my cries and laughter at once,
> so I can see that my joy and pain are one.[44]

As Hanh notes, this extension of identity can transcend humanity to include all existence. We earlier encountered the concept of an ecological self, propounded by philosopher Arne Næss and luminously expressed by Albert Schweitzer's declaration 'I am life that wills to live, in the midst of life that wills to live.' While this perception is far from the mainstream Western sense of identity, it is readily available to all of us simply by acknowledging our own animate consciousness. Then we can recognize that what blazes within us is the same flame of perpetually striving negative entropy that is shared by every sentient being and every living cell on Earth.[45]

From this perspective, the moral significance becomes clear. Once we recognize that we *are* life – a particular form of it with added layers of conceptual consciousness and self-awareness – we are called by the overriding imperative to devote our own little eddy of sentience to the flourishing of all life, of which we are but one tiny part. With an expanded sense of identity, this becomes not so much a moral obligation as a natural instinct based on life's own drive for flourishing. As Mencius pointed out, it's like learning how to dance: 'When such joy is born, it cannot be stopped ... You cannot help but begin to unconsciously dance along with your feet and wave your hands in time with it.'[46]

The universe reflecting on itself

Once we've arrived at this fundamental recognition that we *are* life, then – and only then – are we ready to explore the implications of those characteristics that make humans unique among other life-forms: our self-awareness and collective power arising from our highly developed conceptual consciousness. This uniqueness does not, as the Western tradition has maintained for millennia, make us separate from nature. However, it does confer on us both the power to destroy the living Earth and also the potentiality to develop a new type of symbiotic relationship with it.

We have arrived at a stage in the human saga on Earth where the decisions we make over the next few decades will determine the future direction, not just of humanity, but of Earth itself. Ultimately, it will be a collective decision based on our shared sense of identity. While our civilization has been destroying much of life on Earth in the past few decades, we have also been developing a greater collective consciousness as a species than ever before. The rise of the internet, which is still in its infancy, may turn out to have as profound an effect on our group identity as the emergence of language back in the Paleolithic era. In the same way that bacteria learned to transfer genes to each other to create a virtually immortal quasi-superorganism, so humans are developing the ability to transfer ideas to each other and participate in forming a global consciousness. Can we wake up in time to appreciate our collective identity and participate in something greater than our fixed selves? As Thích Nhât Hanh has suggested, the next Buddha may not be in the form of an individual, but the awakening community.[47]

The possibility for future flourishing requires that we wake up, not only to ourselves as a collective consciousness, but to our deeply ingrained role with the rest of life on Earth. We must recognize that, as an integral part of Gaia, we are engaging in a process by which Earth itself is becoming self-aware. As astrobiologist David Grinspoon has noted, if long-lived aliens had been watching Earth from space for the past few billion years, they would suddenly notice Earth waking up, with dramatic changes such as light shining from the dark side of the planet and little objects emanating from the planet into space. The moment when cognitive processes play a meaningful role in the functioning of a planet, Grinspoon suggests, represents a new eon in the planet's history – a transition as significant as the rise of multicellular life itself. This realization need not entail hubris, but rather a humble and reverent acceptance of the awesome powers and responsibilities that arise from the current state of the human phenomenon.[48]

We – along with other self-aware beings elsewhere in the cosmos – represent the universe reflecting on itself. Our sentience enacts meaning into the glory of creation. Instead of looking out at deep space and, like Pascal, being 'moved to terror' by its 'eternal silence', we can instead feel profound gratitude that we have been granted the capacity to be awed by it. When we measure the universe by light years, Earth seems like an insignificant speck in a bleak infinitude. But when we measure it by the glow of meaning generated by self-aware sentience, we can perceive ourselves as a bright hub within a network whose magnitude we can only imagine.[49]

Will future generations be given the opportunity to explore this vast network of meaning and probe the deepest questions of the cosmos that we can now barely even glimpse? Only if we make it through this pivotal phase in Earth's life history. Grinspoon suggests that, while many planets in the universe might experience a burst of cognitive and technological capabilities in a species similar to humanity's current state, only a rare planet would pass successfully through this bottleneck. This would be one where the cognitively enhanced species learned to integrate deeply with the rest of the planet's cohabitants to create a comprehensive planetary intelligence – one that was devoted to its entire planet's continuous flourishing.[50]

In the past few centuries the networked power of humanity's conceptual consciousness has caused a profound transformation of life, leading to stunning technological breakthroughs and massive imbalances in the ecology of Gaia. At this critical juncture our overriding imperative must be to harmonize the power of conceptual consciousness with the animate intelligence in ourselves and intrinsic to all life on Earth. Only through this process of integration will we find a form of symbiosis that enables the mutual flourishing of humans and nonhuman nature into the distant future.[51]

The momentous project facing us is, in the words of cultural historian Thomas Berry, humanity's Great Work. It's a project in which we are all participating through our inherent embeddedness in the web of meaning. Each of our daily actions and conversations emanate li ripples which intersect with others to make a collective impact on humanity's future trajectory. How can we sort through the chaotic signals bombarding us continually from all directions? How can we discern the best means for our own li ripples to make a positive impact through this tangled, interconnected web? This is the question we will now try to unravel as we explore our ultimate question: 'Where are we going?'[52]

NEW THREADS OF MEANING

The li of our loved ones, our friends and our family exists within us, while our own li resides in them and will continue even after our death

Everything we do, every word we speak, creates li ripples in the fabric of existence

Once we recognize that we are life, we are called by the imperative to devote ourselves to the flourishing of all life, of which we are a tiny part

WHY AM I?

I am here to weave my unique strand
into the web of meaning

Part Six

WHERE ARE WE GOING?

Chapter Thirteen

WEAVING A NEW STORY OF MEANING

Robin Wall Kimmerer recounts how, during dark winter nights in the Great Lakes region, sitting around the fire, Ojibwe children would be told the terrifying tale of the Windigo monster that might come stalking them. The Windigo was a ravenous ten-foot giant, with yellow fangs, putrid breath and a heart made of ice, that roamed greedily across the snow looking for humans to devour. If you became one of his hapless victims, you suffered a fate worse than death – one bite from a Windigo and you would become one yourself, doomed to roam the plains with insatiable hunger, cannibalizing your own species, tormented by a need that could never be fulfilled. This was the defining mark of a Windigo: the more they consumed, they more ravenous they became, and the more voraciously they rampaged through the land seeking their next victim.[1]

The Windigo might not be an actual creature, but its existence as a powerful cultural attractor has proven more destructive than any flesh-and-blood monster could ever be. As Native American tribes suffered the ruthless onslaught of European settlers, some saw a striking resemblance between the Windigo and the rapacious European drive for conquest. Ever since the fifteenth century, when Europeans first ventured to other continents, they carried with them a Windigo-like infection of relentless consumption, ravaging the local inhabitants and natural abundance of the places they conquered, never satisfied, forever seeking new ways to devour even more. When they encountered the silver mountain of Potosí in modern-day Bolivia, they extracted every last grain, enslaving an estimated eight million Indigenous workers to mine its riches over three centuries, beating them into submission until their agonizing deaths, poisoned by the mercury used to extract the silver. When they discovered that crops such as sugar or cotton could profitably be exported back to Europe, they initiated the horrifying slave trade, transporting twelve million Africans to the Americas to be used mercilessly in chattel slavery to increase the wealth of white landowners.[2*]

Legalized slavery has passed into the history books, but the Windigo infection has erupted into an uncontrolled pandemic, instilling in those it infects an unrelenting desire for more. In the United States, beginning in the early twentieth century, it took the form of an insatiable consumerism that has since spread across the world. Like the Windigo, our global economy relies on continual growth for its sustenance, but is never satisfied, always needing further growth to avoid disaster. In recent decades the infection has found its way into new areas previously off limits to its implacable appetite, as neoliberal ideology incorporated human endeavors such as education and sports into the market economy, even turning nature itself into a balance sheet item by redefining it as 'natural capital'.[3]

Consistent with the Windigo's cannibalistic impulse, our society seems prepared to devour itself rather than curb its manic obsession for growth. Even as we face an existential climate emergency from greenhouse gas emissions, companies find new ways to extract fossil fuels from the earth, demolishing pristine forests in Canada for their tar sands below and injecting poisonous chemicals deep underground to frack rock formations for methane. Driven by our Windigo mania, our civilization seems caught up in what UN Secretary General Ban Ki-Moon has called a 'global suicide pact'.[4]

That is not, however, the message we get from our daily media. And of course it's not something Uncle Bob would readily accept if you sat down with him one more time over tea to discuss the state of the world. In fact, if Uncle Bob had spent an hour or two casually perusing opinion pieces on these weighty topics, he would have picked up some pithy retorts to the whole Windigo critique.

Turning to you with an ever so slightly smug expression, Uncle Bob might say, 'For all your doom and gloom statistics, the truth is we've actually never had it so good. You might talk about inequality, but thanks to development around the world, the rate of people suffering extreme poverty is lower than it's ever been.'

Now Uncle Bob's on a tear. He's feels he's done his homework. 'Just look at the rise in material prosperity over the past couple of hundred years,' he exhorts. 'A poor person today enjoys choices in clothing, food and transportation that even the wealthiest couldn't have dreamed of in the past. In health, in education, in just about every field, the progress we've made has been enormous. And that's largely because of capitalism, which has proven itself as the best system for innovation and progress.'

Uncle Bob sips his favorite tea, which, he hastens to add, he can enjoy so cheaply because of the globalized system of commerce that delivers it to him for next to nothing. 'Let's face it,' he declares, 'a rising tide really does lift all boats. People might be envious of the billionaires, but they deserve their riches because they've succeeded in giving us what we want most efficiently. And for all your griping about climate change and the environment ... well, haven't you heard of "green growth"? Thanks to entrepreneurs, business is finding ways to keep growing while using fewer materials. Every time you doomsayers say a problem is insurmountable, technology always finds a new solution.' Uncle Bob sits back, content. 'And if you don't like the system, what's the alternative anyway? They tried communism – that didn't go so well, did it?'

You've probably heard statements like this; if not from Uncle Bob, then from the multitude of articles written over decades that provide Uncle Bob, and millions like him, with the soundbites that, taken together, form the dominant story of our age. However, the sheer quantity of these articles doesn't make them right. In fact, most of what you just heard coming from Uncle Bob's mouth has been shown to be false.[5*]

In this chapter we'll explore some of the most consequential issues facing our world today. We'll dig below them to investigate their underlying causes and project them out to trace their possible trajectories. It's a sobering undertaking: its findings are nothing short of terrifying. But it's also one that can be energizing, exhilarating – even inspiring. We'll find that, if we dig deep enough, we can identify the foundations for building a different kind of civilization, one that is free from Windigo infection. And by the chapter's end, you may be prepared to turn to Uncle Bob and see him in a new light – someone who, deep down, is afraid of the same things as you. Perhaps you might even help inspire him to join you – along with millions of others – in weaving a new story of meaning for the flourishing of humanity on a vibrant, healthy Earth.

The question of progress

Uncle Bob was right about something: on average, human material well-being is far greater today than in the past. Much of the credit for this progress can be attributed to Europe's Scientific Revolution, which transformed our understanding of the world, generating huge advances in medicine and hygiene, and initiating the vast array of technological innovations that we take for granted in the modern world. Very few of us would choose to travel back in a one-way time machine to the period before electricity, anesthesia and antibiotics.

Frequently, people point to the explosive rise in the world's gross domestic product (GDP) as a clear indicator of this progress (Figure 12, top). However, GDP only measures the rate at which society transforms nature and human activity into the monetary economy, regardless of the ensuing quality of life. Anything that causes economic activity of any kind, whether good or bad, adds to GDP. An oil spill, for example, increases GDP because of the cost of cleaning it up: the bigger the spill, the better for GDP. When researchers developed a benchmark called the genuine progress indicator (GPI), which factors in qualitative components such as volunteer and household work, pollution and crime, they discovered a dramatic divergence between the two measures. GPI peaked in 1978 (roughly the time of the neoliberal takeover), and has been steadily falling ever since, even while GDP continues to accelerate (Figure 12, bottom).[6]

When we look more carefully at broad proclamations of continuing progress in human welfare, it becomes incumbent to ask: progress for whom, exactly? Ever since Europeans colonized the rest of the world, there has been a gaping disparity between the

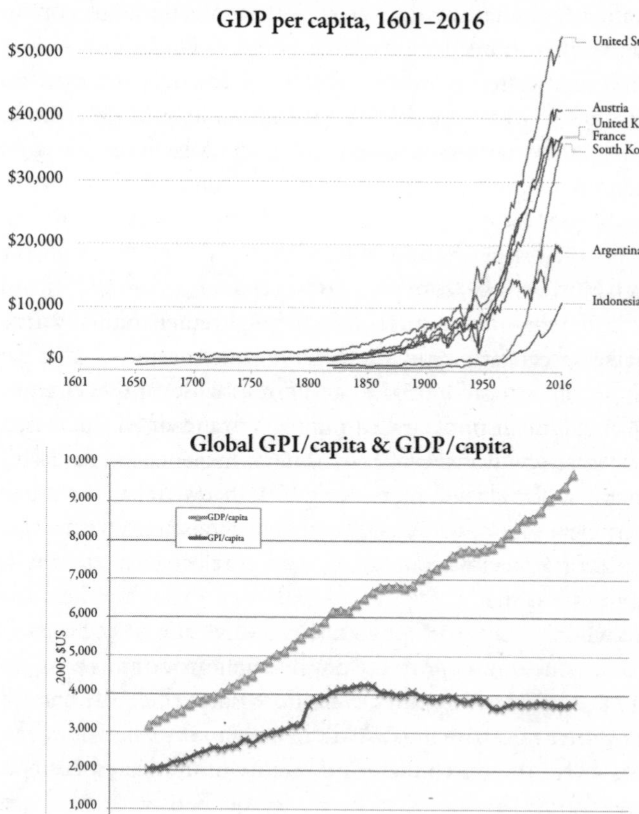

Figure 12: Comparing GDP per capita with GPI per capita

fortunes of the conquerors and the conquered. For example, the Indian subcontinent, prior to British control, accounted for more than a quarter of the world's economy. After centuries of looting, mass famines and deliberate destruction of its thriving industries, its share had plummeted to 3 percent. In the Americas, a combination of genocide and disease decimated the Indigenous people, wiping out close to 99 percent of the population in some regions.[7]

These gaping discrepancies continue to the present day. In the United States the ideology of white supremacy has maintained its ugly hold over American life. Racist violence against Black Americans, institutionalized into national policy from earliest days, is currently manifested in what is known as the school-to-prison pipeline, resulting in the dismal statistic that one in every three Black American men can currently expect to be imprisoned in their lifetime.[8]

What about a global context? Uncle Bob's declaration that world poverty is decreasing is regularly made by development pundits. However, as economist Jason Hickel explains, this claim is only true when it measures proportional rather than absolute numbers. Researchers estimate that the minimum daily income people need for basic nutrition and a normal life expectancy is $7.40. The number of people earning less than that has increased over the past few decades to over four billion – more than half of humanity. The staggering rise in global inequality makes these numbers even more invidious. It's difficult to come to terms with the depravity of a situation where twenty-six billionaires own as much wealth as half the world's population – roughly the same billions who can't afford enough nutrition for their basic needs.[9*]

If we extend our scope to the nonhuman population, the proclamation of progress becomes even more untenable. The natural world is suffering a ferocious assault from human civilization. The litany is awful to contemplate: 74 billion domesticated animals tormented and slaughtered each year to supply us with meat; 90 percent of nature's abundance already lost as a result of human depredation; the Sixth Great Extinction of species underway; the imminent loss of coral reefs this century; the likely disappearance of the Amazon rainforest ... Wherever we turn, the toll keeps growing.[10]

When economic growth is based on unsustainable consumption, the result is not progress but what economists call overshoot: depleting the Earth's bounty faster than it can be replenished. Imagine you had a friend who inherited vast wealth, but could only access it in the form of an annuity. Dissatisfied with his annual stipend, he hired a bevy of lawyers and accountants to find ways to retrieve his wealth more rapidly. Now, living in palatial surroundings, his accountants warn him that he will soon clean out his account, but he ignores them. If he then turns to you and proudly claims that his opulent lifestyle is a sign of progress, you might consider him to have lost his mind. This, however, is in essence the current state of our global society.[11]

Windigo, Inc.

How did we get ourselves into this predicament? As we've seen, while Europe's Scientific Revolution gave us so much in the way of knowledge and technology, it also propagated a worldview based on false foundations, which has since permeated virtually every aspect of the human experience. Now we're dealing with the dangerous legacy of that worldview – its flaws massively amplified by the power unleashed by scientific breakthroughs. But the most dangerous technology currently threatening humanity's future is not the direct result of science. It's not something tangible, such as steel, electricity or the steam engine. It's a conceptual invention existing only in the human mind – the limited liability corporation.

How, you might wonder, could something as mundane as a legal corporate structure be an existential threat to humanity? We can begin to answer that by looking at an issue hitting the headlines in recent years: the threat that artificial intelligence (AI) will take control over humanity – one that Stephen Hawking, among other scientific luminaries, warned could be 'the worst event in the history of our civilization'. The scenario that terrifies them is that, in spite of our best intentions, we might create a force more powerful than humanity with a value system that doesn't necessarily prioritize human welfare. Once it reaches a critical mass, this intelligence could take over the world, control human activity and essentially suck all life out of the Earth as it optimizes for its objective. Futurists give an example of a super-intelligence designed with the goal of manufacturing paperclips which transforms the entire planet into one gigantic paperclip-manufacturing facility. These thinkers are right to voice their concerns, but they're missing the fact that humans have already created a force that is well on its way to devouring both humanity and the Earth in just the way they fear – the corporation.[12]

The modern corporation is not merely a paperclip maximizer;

it has become a Windigo maximizer – a relentless force with the overriding objective of turning humanity and the rest of life into fodder for endlessly increasing financial profit at the fastest possible rate. The limited liability corporation was first conceived in the seventeenth century as an ingenious mechanism to encourage wealthy Europeans to invest in ventures exploiting the resources of overseas colonies. It was structured to give investors all the upside if things went well, but limit the downside to their initial investment if things went wrong. This simple set-up became a perfect vehicle for the Windigo AI. At first corporate charters were limited to a specific venture, but by the nineteenth century the algorithm had broken out of its initial constraints. American industrialists, seeking new ways to enrich themselves, influenced state legislatures to grant them perpetual charters allowing them to do anything not explicitly prohibited by law. From there, the Windigo AI kept expanding its domain, becoming a legal 'person' in the United States entitled to constitutional protections but without any factors that constrain real persons, such as mortality, risk of jail or a moral conscience.[13]

Massive transnational corporations have now become the dominant force directing our world, more powerful than any government or nation. Through their influence on legislation, they have virtually eliminated regulatory limitations on their growth, their permitted activities and the competitive playing field. Massive corporations are gobbled up by even vaster ones, creating commanding monoliths that set the terms for their own activities. Of the hundred largest economies in the world, sixty-nine are now corporations. Nations and municipalities compete against each other to attract corporate investment to their jurisdictions, relinquishing taxation, regulations and worker protections in the hope of jobs or infrastructure spending. In most countries the boundaries between corporate executives and government have become so blurred as to be virtually nonexistent. Transnational corporations control most of the world's media, finance, manufacturing and agriculture, and are invited to intervene in international treaty negotiations, ensuring that their interests remain protected.[14]

If this supreme global force had benevolent aims, then at least a case could be made for permitting it to exercise such control over human activity. But the opposite is true. Corporations are legally programmed with the ultimate goal of maximizing financial returns for their investors above all else. If they were real persons, as we saw earlier, they would be diagnosed as psychopaths, with their single-minded obsession for profit at the expense of anything else. Humanity now finds itself in the dire position of having ceded control of its destiny to a psychopathic force dedicated solely to turning human and nonhuman life into ever-increasing financial returns.[15]

Under international trade treaties, countries that try to limit pernicious corporate activities, such as targeting young women for cigarette addiction or adding neurotoxic pollutants to gas, are sued in secret tribunals for 'loss of profit opportunity', forced to back down and allow their citizens' health to be ruined. Most farmers around the world can no longer choose their seeds from hundreds of varieties, but are forced to buy genetically modified seeds from a handful of mega-corporations that create dependencies on that company's synthetic fertilizers and pesticides. Corporations use their advertising power to exert mind control over vulnerable populations, perfecting executive Wayne Chilicki's chilling strategy: 'When it comes to targeting kid consumers, we at General Mills ... believe in getting them early and having them for life.' Children in the Global South are turned into junk food addicts with the same callous contempt that factory farms turn their animals into chicken nuggets. Half of the children in south Asia are now either undernourished or overweight, conditioned by pervasive advertising to spend what little money they have on empty calories of junk food.[16]

In a self-reinforcing cycle, the Windigo values that created corporations in the first place are further strengthened by the overpowering corporate compulsion to convert human needs into profit opportunities. The lavish consumption of the wealthy elite, glorified in the media, persuades the bulk of humanity that the only values worth pursuing are material ones, herding people by the billions onto the hedonic treadmill that drives further increase in corporate profits. As inequality grows, suffering rises, and the core neoliberal values of selfishness, greed and ruthless competition are celebrated as the only pathway available for people to drag themselves from the quagmire of poverty.[17]

Careening toward a precipice

Like the Windigo monster, our global economic system in its current form can never be satisfied. However, this rabid drive for perpetual growth has come up against the finite boundaries of the living Earth. Global GDP is projected to triple between now and 2060, yet we are already running at 40 percent above our sustainable capacity and have transgressed at least four of the nine planetary boundaries that define humanity's safe operating space (Figure 13). Something has to give.[18]

The idea of 'green growth' that Uncle Bob mentioned is promulgated by many development consultants, and is even incorporated in the UN's official plan for 'sustainable development', but has been shown unequivocally to be nothing but a fantasy. Ecomodernists and others who stand to profit from growth in the short term frequently make the argument that, through technological innovation, GDP can be decoupled from resource use and carbon emissions, permitting limitless growth on a finite planet. Rigorous analysis, though, shows that this hasn't happened so far, and even the most wildly aggressive assumptions for greater efficiency would still lead to unsustainable consumption of global resources.[19]

While there are multiple dimensions to our society's reckless overshoot, the looming climate catastrophe is without doubt the most dire threat. Since the UN's Intergovernmental Panel on Climate Change (IPCC) issued a warning to humanity in 2018 that we have just twelve years to turn things around before passing the point of no return, the world has continued its trajectory of uncontrolled emissions. Earth scientists warn of tipping points in the climate system that, once triggered, will cause a cascade of further tipping points leading to runaway climate catastrophe. The transformation of the Amazon rainforest into scrubland, the melting of permafrost and loss of sea ice in the Arctic and the break-up of the West Antarctic ice sheet are examples of inflection points causing reinforcing feedback loops that further accelerate

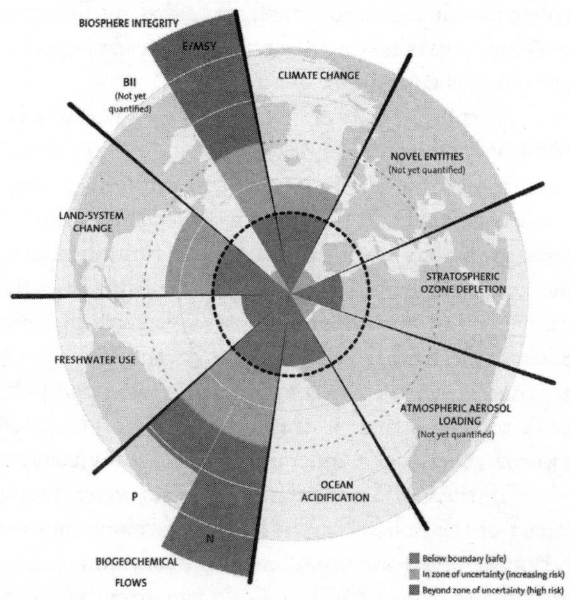

Figure 13: The planetary boundaries defining humanity's safe operating space
Key: BII = Biodiversity Intactness Index; E/MSY = Extinctions per million species per year; P = Phosphorus; N = Nitrogen

global heating. Some prominent climate scientists believe we may have already triggered an uncontrollable global 'tipping cascade'. No one can know for sure exactly when we pass the point of no return, but it's clear that – if we're not there already – each year of climbing emissions brings us closer to this doomsday point.[20]

Although the world's nations agreed in Paris in 2015 to target an increase in global temperature of no more than 1.5 degrees Celsius above pre-industrial levels, their collective pledges are dismally inadequate, leading to an actual rise of three degrees this century, and they are failing to meet even these targets. At this point it's widely believed that a rise of at least two degrees is already locked in by our inaction. A world hotter by two degrees will reel from an inexorable onslaught of ever more unmanageable disasters: extreme long-term droughts in new areas such as the Mediterranean and parts of India, severe water shortages affecting billions of people, marine life disappearing from acidifying, hotter oceans, and global food supplies stretched to breaking point with frequent devastating regional famines.[21]

The worst thing, however, about a two-degree world is the high likelihood of stumbling into a tipping point cascade that quickly leads to a three- and four-degree world – one that becomes rapidly unrecognizable. At this point we're looking at the Amazon rainforest turning into searing desert; coastal cities, regularly inundated by flooding, becoming unlivable; super-hurricanes that tear the windows out of skyscrapers; persistent massive droughts and famine across the world; and hundreds of millions of desperate climate refugees. Because the land heats up more rapidly than the oceans, it's projected that, in a three-degree world, the average person would experience temperatures 7.5 degrees Celsius higher, with a third of the world's population living in areas as hot as the hottest part of the Sahara currently. But of course by then they will have been forced to leave their homes and join the billions of other climate refugees trying to find somewhere to survive in a grim world dominated by fear, starvation and desperation.[22]

Do you remember the Adaptive Cycle model of change with its four phases of growth, conservation, release and reorganization? It's looking increasingly likely that our current civilization is reaching the end of its conservation phase and entering a transition. Projecting the catastrophic effects of a heating world, an increasing number of prominent scientists are beginning to worry aloud that this phase transition will entail nothing short of civilizational collapse.[23]

We live in a globalized world where different systems – economic, political, technological and cultural – are all deeply interconnected. Because of the dominant corporate forces that have driven globalization, it's become a highly homogenized world where whatever arises – viruses, ideas or Uncle Bob's tea – moves around the globe at lightning speed. We saw this play out in the rapid spread of the coronavirus pandemic in 2020, and experts worry that the same dynamics could easily lead to what they call the synchronous failure of global systems, where like a set of dominoes, the crash of one system destabilizes others depending on it.

Our current global situation, where we find ourselves reeling from one destabilizing crisis to another, is indicative of what happens when a complex system in a conservation phase moves closer and closer to the release phase.[24]

Why, you might wonder, do the global power elites not act more aggressively to prevent this disaster from occurring? Some may indeed be concerned about what they observe but feel powerless to affect the outcome. Another possible reason is that some see an alternative scenario playing out, which is sometimes called Fortress Earth. In this scenario, most of the world's population does in fact undergo the devastation of climate-induced collapse, but an affluent minority maintain their comfortable lifestyle, secure in gated communities protected by high-tech surveillance and patrolling drones. They may even keep enjoying high returns on their stock market investments, as corporations find ways to monetize the collapsing infrastructure of the rest of the world, growing their countries' GDP even while the vast majority of humanity are foundering.[25]

Ultimately, the ever-widening gulf between rich and poor might extend beyond economics to biology, and humanity itself could split into two different sub-species – one genetically enhanced group sequestered in their affluent sanctuaries, exploring new ways to optimize themselves while most of the human population struggles for survival within a disintegrating infrastructure. From a moral perspective, this scenario is even more repugnant than total civilizational collapse – akin to a few shipwrecked survivors on a gilded lifeboat kicking others desperately scrambling for life into the ocean to protect their own safety and comfort.[26*]

Rewriting the operating system

Surely we can do better than that? I believe we can do much better – but only if we, as a society, take a long, hard look at the underpinnings of the values that have brought us to this place and make a collective commitment to change them at a foundational level. If the corporate takeover of our world resembles an out-of-control AI, we can likewise think of our entire current economic and political set-up like a faulty operating system with multiple bugs. Each time the software engineers fix a bug, it complicates the code, leading inevitably to a new set of bugs requiring even more heroic workarounds. Ultimately, it becomes clear that the problem isn't just the software; an entirely new operating system is required.

In human culture, the operating system takes the form of its underlying worldview: the entire set of assumptions about how the world works, how things really are, what's valuable and what's possible. A worldview often remains unstated and unquestioned, but is deeply felt and implicitly guides the individual and collective choices we make. In this book we've been systemically investigating the dominant worldview – and have found that it is seriously flawed.

In spite of its flaws, the dominant worldview has accomplished a great deal for humanity in the past few hundred years. It emerged in reaction to the stifling superstitions of traditional Christian theology, and has cast the light of scientific knowledge on areas previously impenetrable to human understanding. For all the havoc it has wreaked on the natural world, and for all the heinous crimes committed in its name on non-Europeans, it has also been the source of vast improvements in material aspects of life for many people, has greatly enhanced humanity's understanding of our place in the cosmos and has even contributed to humanity's moral development.

But now, at this point in the human story, that worldview has expired. We live in an epoch when its flaws have become superordinate. The depiction of humans as selfish individuals, the view of nature as a resource to be exploited, and the idea that technology alone can fix our biggest problems are all profound misconceptions that have collectively led our civilization down an accelerating path to disaster. The only way we can truly change our trajectory is by approaching society's problems from the foundation of an alternative worldview – one that affirms life rather than the accumulation of wealth above all else.[27]

We've seen that this alternative worldview already exists – it has been constructed over millennia by wisdom traditions around the world and is soundly validated by the findings of modern science. It's a worldview that arises from a recognition of our deep interconnectedness with each other and all aspects of the universe, and exalts the primacy of life through its entire value system.

What, we must ask, would a society look like that was constructed on the foundation of this worldview? It would naturally take its inspiration from the principles that life itself has developed over billions of years of evolution. After all, the timespan of the human presence on Earth is an infinitesimal fraction of life's own habitation here. Over eons, life has gone from strength to strength, overcoming occasional serious setbacks to build resilience, diversity and rich profusion in virtually every nook and cranny of the planet. There is much for humanity to learn if we look to the fundamentals of life's own operating system.[28]

Natural ecologies, as we've seen, are characterized by both competition and cooperation, but the major evolutionary transitions that brought life to its current state of abundance were the results of dramatic increases in cooperation. The key to each of these evolutionary steps, and to the effective functioning of all ecosystems, is *mutually beneficial symbiosis*: each party to a relationship gives and receives reciprocally, reflecting each other's abilities and needs. In symbiosis there is no zero-sum game – the contributions of each party create a whole that is greater than the sum of its parts.[29]

One consequential result of symbiosis is that ecosystems can sustain themselves almost indefinitely by *circulating the energy flows* they receive from the sun for the optimal benefit of all their constituent parts. The waste of one organism becomes the nutrition of another. In contrast to our current civilization, which has built its wealth primarily through extracting resources and simply letting waste accumulate, nature has developed a circular economy where nothing is squandered.

The complex intermeshing of different organisms in a symbiotic network leads to another foundational principle of nature: *harmony*. As we've seen, harmony doesn't mean insipid agreement; on the contrary, it arises when the different elements within a system each express their own needs in such a way that the system as a whole is enriched. Harmony itself can only arise when the various forces comprising the system are in *balance*. This can take the form of balance between competition and cooperation; between the system's efficiency and its resilience; or between growth, maturation and decline. In a natural ecosystem the type of exponential growth that characterizes our global economy could only occur if other variables were already out of balance, and would have one inevitable ending: the catastrophic collapse of that population.[30]

Nature organizes itself *fractally*: from microscopic intracellular structures all the way to Gaia itself, each system contains its own fully integrated animate intelligence, identifying and fulfilling its own needs, while contributing to the well-being of the larger systems within which it is embedded. In nature, the health of the system as a whole requires the *flourishing of each part* that constitutes it. Each system is therefore interdependent for its long-term health on the vitality of each of the other systems. In your own body, for example, if your lungs don't function well, your muscles don't receive enough oxygen, which then cause you to become sedentary – leading to your heart and circulatory systems losing their vigor. To function optimally, the system as a whole requires all its constituent parts to maintain good health.[31]

Nature's animate intelligence has enabled it to respond adaptively to every kind of situation arising over billions of years, developing in the process an awe-inspiring plethora of *diversity*. Even within a single organism, the *modularity* of its self-organized design allows different populations of cells to *innovate*, coming up with new ways to solve a problem, while closely *coordinating* with other cells within its network. This complex dance of diversity, innovation and coordination is largely responsible for the adaptive resilience demonstrated by ecosystems, enabling them to thrive as healthy, coherent communities for millions of years.[32]

Envisioning an ecological civilization

Clearly, nature's principles are very different from the central tenets of our dominant system of neoliberal corporate capitalism. Let us now consider what a society might look like that was based instead on these life-affirming principles – an *ecological civilization*. What if the operating system of the Windigo AI were replaced by nature's AI – the animate intelligence that underlies the principles of the living Earth?[33]*

Fundamentally, an ecological civilization would be one that was structured to optimize eudaimonia rather than hedonia.

Eudaimonia, as we've seen, is a state of sustained well-being that arises when a person is fulfilling their true nature. Hedonia, on the other hand, is a transient state that leads to suffering once it has passed, with an endless desire to seek it out again – which is why Windigo, Inc. does everything it can to keep people locked on the hedonic treadmill.[34]

The overriding objective of an ecological civilization would be to create the conditions for all humans to flourish as part of a thriving living Earth. A fundamental precept would be the recognition of *fractal flourishing*: the well-being of each person is fractally related to the health of the larger world. Individual health relies on societal health, which relies in turn on the health of the ecosystem in which it's embedded.[35]

We've seen that a natural ecology is based on symbiosis, wherein each party gains from a reciprocal relationship. In human terms, that translates into foundational principles of *fairness* and *justice*, ensuring that the efforts and skills people contribute to society are rewarded equitably. Recognizing that the flourishing of the system as a whole requires the health of all its constituent parts, an ecological civilization would foster *individual dignity*, providing the conditions for everyone to live in safety and comfort, with universal access to adequate housing, competent healthcare and quality education.[36]

In the fractal design of an ecosystem, harmony arises not through homogeneity but through each organism contributing to the whole by pursuing its own eudaimonia. Accordingly, an ecological civilization would celebrate *diversity*, recognizing that its overall health depended on different groups – self-defined by ethnicity, gender or any other delineation – developing their own unique gifts to the greatest extent possible. It would be built on the axiom that a system's full potential can only be realized when it is truly *integrated* – a state of unity with differentiation in which the flourishing of each constituent part generates the well-being of the larger whole.[37]

The principle of *balance* would be as crucial to an ecological civilization as it is to natural systems. Competition would be balanced by collaboration; disparities in income and wealth would remain within much narrower bands, and would fairly reflect the contributions people make to society. Just as an animal requires the robust circulation of its lifeblood to maintain its health, a life-affirming economy would enable the widespread circulation of its wealth throughout the entire community. And crucially, growth would become one part of a natural life cycle, slowing down to maturation once it reaches its healthy limits, leading to a steady-state self-sustaining economy designed for well-being rather than consumption. A country would measure its success not by GDP but with metrics of well-being like GPI or a Gross National Happiness Index to assess how it was progressing.[38]

Above all, an ecological civilization would be based on an all-encompassing *symbiosis* between human society and the natural world. Human activity would be organized not merely to avoid harm to the living Earth but to actively regenerate and sustain its health. As such, an ecological civilization could set humanity and nonhuman nature on a course for an indefinitely prolonged period of mutual flourishing – the Symbiocene. Our species – recognizing the critical role that we have been granted as Gaia's instrument of self-reflection – could then embark on the learning required for the deep integration with the rest of our planet's cohabitants from which a truly planetary intelligence might ultimately emerge.[39]

An ecological civilization in practice

We experience our current civilization every day, so we know that it looks and feels very different from the one just described. So different, in fact, that it might seem almost impossible to picture the specifics of a world based on life-affirming principles. But it's been made easier by the brilliant work of pioneering visionaries who have already begun blazing a trail toward this different kind of civilization.

An impressive array of progressive economists have laid out an alternative framework for economics that begins by recognizing human activity as embedded in the natural world, and humans themselves as caring members of communities rather than selfish wealth-maximizers. In this new framework, markets still have a role to play but are no longer the sole criterion for determining value.

Economist Kate Raworth compares markets to fire, pointing out that it is the very effectiveness of markets that makes them both important and dangerous. We're all familiar with the power of fire and appreciate its appropriate use for cooking, keeping us warm and a myriad other things. But no one suggests that, because fire is so powerful, we should use it without safeguards – we know that it would burn everything down in no time. Similarly, markets have an important role to play, but because of their power to corrode everything they touch and reduce it to a financial calculation, they need to be carefully restricted to those areas where they can be beneficial.[40*]

Most economists of the twentieth century recognized only two domains of economic activity – markets and government – and that period's overriding political divide between capitalism and communism depended on which was held paramount (with social democracy somewhere in the middle). Raworth instead lays out four realms of economic provisioning: markets, government, households and the commons. Recognizing households as a key parameter of the economy is a critical step, making visible the time and energy spent by parents caring for their children, friends looking out for each other, and all the activities generated by basic human consideration for others that are invisible to the classic measure of GDP. But what about the commons? To most of us, that sounds like an archaic word dating back to medieval times. How does it belong in a vision of the future?[41]

It's true there was a time when 'the commons' referred to land that was available for anyone in the community to graze animals or grow crops. Over centuries, powerful aristocrats seized this land from the peasants – often violently – until virtually all land was either privately or state owned. But the commons also refers to any source of sustenance and well-being that has not yet been appropriated either by the state or by Windigo, Inc. – the air, water and sunshine, along with human creations such as language, cultural traditions and scientific knowledge. The commons is virtually ignored in most economic discussion because, like household work, it doesn't fit into the classic economic model. The global commons belongs to all of us, and by recognizing its value, we are better able to defend it against further incursions. Inspired by a vision of a future where the commons once again becomes a resource for all humanity, tech pioneers have created digital commons, such as Wikipedia and Firefox, while others use their wealth to invest in trusts that protect land from developers and make it available to the public. In an ecological civilization the commons would once again take its rightful place as a major provider for human welfare.[42]

Realizing the vastness of the cumulative common resources that our ancestors bequeathed to us through untold generations of hard work and ingenuity can transform our conception of wealth and value. Uncle Bob stated the widespread view that an entrepreneur who becomes a billionaire deserves his wealth, but whatever value he created is a pittance compared to the immense bank of prior knowledge and social practices – the *commonwealth* – that he took from. When Mark Zuckerberg, whose wealth currently stands at about $100 billion, hit the jackpot with Facebook, he merely added a tweak or two to a phenomenal feat of infrastructure constructed over millennia, incorporating the development of language, civilization, writing, electricity, microprocessors, computer code, the internet, capital markets ... The list is endless.[43]

There are two major implications arising from this recognition of our shared human commonwealth. One is that there is no moral justification for a Mark Zuckerberg or Jeff Bezos to amass multiple billions of dollars when half the human population remains malnourished. A future society may look at our endorsement of these inequities with the same bemusement with which we regard the medieval notion of the divine right of kings. In recognition of this, an ecological civilization would fairly reward entrepreneurial activity, but severely curtail the right of anyone to accumulate billions in wealth, no matter what their accomplishments.[44]

The second major implication is that it is the moral birthright of every human to share in the vast commonwealth that our ancestors collectively bequeathed to us. This could effectively be achieved through a program of unconditional cash disbursements to every person alive on the planet. At first, this idea may sound impractical for myriad reasons, but research has shown repeatedly that such programs – generally referred to as universal basic income – are remarkably effective in improving the quality of life in communities. The dominant culture's view of human nature leads many to assume that free money would cause people to become lazy, avoid work, and exacerbate addictive behaviors. In every test conducted, the opposite turns out to be true. Programs consistently report reductions in crime, child mortality, malnutrition, truancy, teenage pregnancy and alcohol consumption, along with increases in health, gender equality, school performance – and even entrepreneurial activity. For these moral and practical reasons, universal basic income would be a crucial means by which an ecological civilization could realize the core principle of fractal flourishing.[45]

How might the depredations of Windigo, Inc. be curtailed and incorporated into a balanced ecology? The answer may be simpler than is commonly believed. Unlike real persons, transnational corporations are legal creations, and their DNA can readily be altered by changing their legal charters. Corporations above a certain size would be required to be chartered with the explicit purpose of optimizing not just shareholder returns, but also social and environmental outcomes. This approach – sometimes referred to as the 'triple bottom line' of people, planet and profits – already exists in the form of certified B-corps and benefit corporations. Currently, these forms are voluntary, and very few large corporations adopt them. If, however, they were compulsory, it would immediately transform the inherent character of the corporation. There may continue to be a valuable role for transnational corporations in humanity's future, but just like fire and markets, they must be carefully constrained so they work for the benefit of humanity and the living Earth, rather than for their demise.[46*]

The life-affirming principles of an ecological civilization would lead to profoundly beneficial transformations throughout virtually every aspect of society. In place of vast homogenized monocrops of industrial agriculture, food would be grown worldwide based on principles of regenerative agriculture, leading to greater crop biodiversity, improved water and carbon efficiency, and the virtual elimination of synthetic fertilizers. Manufacturing would prioritize circular flows with efficient reuse of waste products built into processes from the outset, and locally owned cooperatives would become the default organizational structure. Technological innovation would still be encouraged, but would be prized for its effectiveness in enhancing the vitality of living systems rather than minting billionaires. The driving principle of technology would shift from 'conquering nature' to investigating how to tend nature – applying ingenuity to create conditions leading to symbiotic flourishing of humans and the living Earth.[47]*

Cities would be redesigned on ecological principles, with community gardens on every available piece of land, essential services always available within a twenty-minute walk, and cars banned from city centers. The local community would be the basic building block of society, with face-to-face interaction regaining ascendancy as a crucial part of human flourishing. Education would be re-envisioned, its goal transformed from preparing students for the corporate marketplace to cultivating the wisdom, discernment and emotional maturity required for each student to embark on their own lifelong journey of eudaimonia. Oppressive relationship structures inherited from domination systems – such as patriarchal and racist modes of behavior – would be reshaped from early childhood by educational modalities emphasizing ethics of partnership systems.[48]

Following nature's model of the hub-and-spoke network of communication, local community life would be enriched by the global reach of the internet. Online networks that have already achieved scale, such as Facebook, would be turned over to the commons, so that rather than manipulating users into hedonic behavior to maximize advertising dollars, the internet could become primarily a vehicle for humanity to further develop a planetary consciousness. Cosmopolitanism – an ancient concept from the Greeks which literally means 'being a citizen of the world' – would be the defining character of a global identity that would celebrate diversity between cultures while recognizing the deep interdependence that binds all people into a single moral community with a shared destiny.[49]

Governance would be transformed to a polycentric model, where local, regional and global decisions are made at the levels where their effects are felt most. While most decision-making would devolve to the lowest feasible level, stronger global governance would enforce rules on planetary-wide issues such as contending with the climate emergency and halting the Sixth Extinction. A worldwide Rights of Nature declaration would put the natural world on the same legal standing as humanity, with personhood given to ecosystems and high-functioning mammals, and the crime of ecocide – the destruction of ecosystems – prosecuted by a court with global jurisdiction.[50]

Entering a phase transition

I'm guessing that while you've been reading these past few pages an internal dialogue has been occurring in your mind. On the one hand, you may find much that is attractive – even inspirational – in the vision of an ecological civilization. On the other hand, there is probably a voice within you saying something like, 'It would be great if this could happen, but it's so far from our current reality that it's simply not feasible. Given our present situation, this seems like no more than a utopian pipedream.' Both of those voices should be taken seriously. In an integrated consciousness – a democracy of consciousness – each internal voice deserves to be heard and respected. Let us consider them carefully.

There are many good reasons to watch the unfolding catastrophe of our civilization's accelerating drive to the precipice and believe it's already too late. The unremitting increase in carbon emissions, the ceaseless devastation of the living Earth, the hypocrisy and corruption of our political leaders and the corporate-owned media's strategy of ignoring the topics that matter most to humanity's future – all these factors come together like a seemingly unstoppable juggernaut driving our society toward breaking point. As a result, an increasing number of people are beginning to reconcile themselves to a terminal diagnosis for civilization. In the assessment of sustainability leader Jem Bendell, founder of the growing Deep Adaptation movement, we should wake up to the reality that 'we face inevitable near-term societal collapse'.[51]

In terms of the Adaptive Cycle model, our civilization certainly appears to be slipping rapidly from its conservation phase to a release phase. But it remains uncertain what that release phase will look like, and even more obscure what new societal paradigm will emerge once the smoke clears. A cataclysmic collapse leaving the few survivors in a grim dark age? A Fortress Earth condemning most of humanity to a wretched struggle for subsistence while a morally bankrupt minority pursues an affluent lifestyle? Or can we retain enough of humanity's accumulated knowledge, wisdom and moral integrity to recreate our civilization from within, in a form that can survive the turmoil ahead?[52]

An important lesson from history is that – like all self-organized, adaptive systems – society changes in nonlinear ways. Events take unanticipated swerves that only make sense when analyzed retroactively. These can be catastrophic, such as the onset of a world war or a civilizational collapse, but frequently they lead to unexpectedly positive outcomes. When a dozen or so Quakers gathered in London in 1785 to create a movement to end slavery, it would have seemed improbable that slavery would be abolished within half a century throughout the British Empire, would spur a civil war in the United States and eventually become illegal worldwide. When Emmeline Pankhurst founded the National Union of Women's Suffrage in 1897, it took ten years of struggle to muster a few thousand courageous women to join her on a march in London, but within a couple of decades women were gaining the right to vote across the world.[53]

In recent decades, history has continued to surprise those who scoff at the potential for dramatic positive change. It took just eight years from Rosa Parks being arrested for refusing to give up her seat on a bus in Montgomery, Alabama, to the March on Washington, at which Martin Luther King Jr's 'I have a dream' speech inspired the American nation – leading to the Civil Rights Act being passed into law the following year. In 2006 civil rights activist Tarana Burke used the phrase 'Me Too' to raise awareness of sexual assault; she couldn't have known that ten years later it would potentiate a worldwide movement to transform abusive cultural norms.[54]

Might people one day look back on our era and say something similar about the rise of a new ecological civilization concealed within the folds of one that was dying? A profusion of groups is already laying the groundwork for virtually all the components of a life-affirming civilization. In the United States the visionary Climate Justice Alliance has laid out the principles for a just transition from an extractive to a regenerative economy. In Bolivia and Ecuador traditional ecological principles of *buen vivir* and *sumak kawsay* ('good living') are written into the constitution. In Europe large-scale cooperatives, such as Mondragón in Spain, demonstrate that it's possible for companies to provide effectively for human needs without utilizing a shareholder-based profit model.[55]

Meanwhile, a new ecological worldview is spreading globally through cultural, political and religious institutions, establishing common ground with Indigenous traditions that have sustained their knowledge worldwide for millennia. The core principles underlying an ecological civilization have already been set out in the Earth Charter – an ethical framework launched in The Hague in 2000 and endorsed by over 6,000 organizations worldwide, including many governments. In China leading thinkers espouse a New Confucianism, calling for a cosmopolitan, planetary-wide ecological approach to reintegrating humanity with nature. In 2015 Pope Francis shook the Catholic establishment by issuing his encyclical *Laudato si'*, a masterpiece of ecological philosophy that demonstrates the deep interconnectedness of all life and calls for a rejection of the individualist, neoliberal paradigm.[56*]

On the secular front, leading economists, scientists and policymakers are recognizing the moral bankruptcy of the current international system and pooling resources to offer alternative frameworks for reorganizing global society. Perhaps most importantly, a people's movement for life-affirming change is spreading around the world. When Greta Thunberg skipped school in August 2018 to draw attention to the climate emergency, she sat alone outside the Swedish parliament for days. Less than a year later, over one and a half million schoolchildren joined her in a worldwide protest to rouse their parents' generation from their slumber. A month after Extinction Rebellion demonstrators closed down central London in April 2019 to draw attention to the world's plight, the UK Parliament announced a 'climate emergency'

– something that has now been declared by nearly 2,000 local and national governments worldwide. Meanwhile, a growing campaign of Earth Protectors is working to establish ecocide as a crime prosecutable by the International Criminal Court in The Hague.[57*]

Is this enough? Can the collective power of these movements stand up to the inexorable force of Windigo, Inc. that so tightly maintains its stranglehold on the political, cultural and economic systems of the world? When we consider the immensity of the transformation needed, the odds look daunting. Those nonlinear historical shifts described earlier – while revolutionary in their own way – were ultimately absorbed into the Windigo AI, which has the tenacity of the mythical multi-headed hydra. The transformation needed now has to reach into the icy heart of Windigo itself. It requires a metamorphosis in virtually every aspect of the human experience, including our values, goals and behavioral norms. A change of such magnitude would be an epochal event – on the scale of the Agricultural Revolution that launched civilization or the Scientific Revolution that engendered the modern world. And in our case, we don't have the millennia or centuries those revolutions took to unfold; this one must occur within a few decades at most.

Coming back to life

Daunting, yes – but it's too soon to say whether such a transformation is impossible. There are powerful reasons why such a drastic change could come to pass far more rapidly than many people might expect. The same tight coupling between global systems that increases the risk of civilizational collapse also boosts the speed at which deeper, systemic changes can now occur. The world's initial reaction to the coronavirus pandemic in 2020 showed how quickly the entire economic system can respond when a recognizably clear and present danger emerges. The vast bulk of humanity is now so tightly interconnected through the internet that a pertinent trigger – such as the horrifying spectacle of George Floyd's murder in Minneapolis by a police officer – can set off street protests within days throughout the world.[58]

Most importantly, as the world system begins to unravel on

account of its internal failings, the strands that kept the old system tightly interconnected also get loosened. Every year that we head closer to the release phase, as greater climate-related disasters rear up, as the outrages of racial and economic injustice become even more egregious, and as life for most people becomes increasingly intolerable, the old story loses its hold on humanity's collective consciousness. As waves of young people come of age, they will increasingly reject what their parents' generation told them. They will look about for a new worldview – one that makes sense of the current unraveling, one that offers them a future they can believe in. People who lived through the Industrial Revolution had no name for the changes they were undergoing – it was a century before it received its title. Perhaps an epochal transition to an ecological civilization is already underway, but we can't see it because we're in the middle of it.[59]

As you weigh these issues, there is no need to decide whether to be optimistic or pessimistic. Ultimately, it's a moot point. As author Rebecca Solnit observes, both positions merely become excuses for inaction: optimists believe things will work out fine without them; pessimists believe nothing they do can make things better. There is, however, every reason for hope – hope, not as a prognostication, but as an attitude of active engagement in co-creating that future. Hope, in the resounding words of dissident statesman Václav Havel, is 'a state of mind, not a state of the world'. It is a 'deep orientation of the human soul that can be held at the darkest times … an ability to work for something because it is good, not just because it stands a chance to succeed.'[60]

This points to the most important characteristic of the future: it is something that we are all co-creating as part of the interconnected web of our collective thoughts, ideas and actions. The future is not a spectator sport. It's not something constructed by others, but by the collective choices each of us makes every day: choices of what to ignore, what to notice and what to do about it.[61]

Do you remember the Neo-Confucian conception of *ren*: the realization of the universal interconnectedness of all things? As we saw, this state represents a pinnacle of human experience, a pathway to the greatest fulfillment of the human spirit. But to realize that connectedness in the current condition of our world is also to feel the vast suffering experienced by sentient beings, both human and nonhuman, as a result of the depredations of Windigo, Inc. It is to feel the agony of loss, the anguish of injustice and dread at what might be looming up in the future. Faced with this, it's not surprising that many people find ways to numb themselves from the pain, to close their eyes to the spectacle unfolding before them. That choice, however, leads not only to the loss of *ren*. For those living in affluence, it also has a profoundly disturbing moral dimension: it is an implicit choice to settle into the gilded lifeboat and to participate in collectively kicking the knuckles of those struggling desperately to scramble on board, consigning them to disaster.[62]

We live in a world designed to keep us numb – a culture spiked with innumerable doses of spiritual anesthesia concocted to bind us to the hedonic treadmill, to shuffle along with everyone else in a 'consensus trance'. We are conditioned from early infancy to become zombie agents of the Windigo AI – to find our assigned role as consumer, enforcer or sacrificial victim, as the case may be, and to exhaust our energy in expediting its goal of sucking the life out of our humanity and nature's abundance.[63]

But, powerful as its hold is, we have the potential to shed our Windigo conditioning. As we learn to open eyes that have been sealed shut by our dominant culture, we can discern the rainbow that was always there waiting for us. We can awaken to our true nature as humans on this Earth, feel the life within ourselves that we share with all other beings, and recognize our common identity as a moral community asserting the primacy of core human values. As we open awareness to our interbeing, our ecological self, we can experience ourselves as 'life that wills to live in the midst of life that wills to live', and realize the deep purpose of our existence on Earth – to tend Gaia and participate fully in its ancient, sacred insurgence against the forces of entropy.

There are many effective methods to shed the layers of conditioning. Each person's pathway is unique. Some choose extended time in nature; others may utilize psychedelic insights, learn from Indigenous groups, engage in meditation or embodied practices or simply open up to the deep animate nature within themselves.

The trail has already been blazed by those who have assumed their sacred responsibilities and developed on-ramps for others in their wake. Eco-philosopher Joanna Macy, for example, has developed a set of transformative practices called the Work that Reconnects, offered in communities worldwide, which helps people navigate the steps of what she calls 'coming back to life'. Beginning with gratitude, it spirals into a full acceptance of the Earth's heartbreak – the willingness, in Thích Nhât Hanh's words, 'to hear within us the sounds of the Earth crying'.[64]

Absorbing this pain, however, doesn't mean wallowing in it. Rather than giving way to despair, it instead becomes a springboard to action. As such, the Work that Reconnects leads its participants to experience the deep interconnectedness of all things and continue the spiral into conscious, active engagement. As Neo-Confucian philosopher Wang Yangming noted, 'There have never been people who know but do not act. Those who are supposed to know but do not act simply do not yet know.' You know when you've reached the place of fully experiencing the Earth's heartbreak, because you suddenly realize you are drawn to action – not because you think you *should* do something, but because you are *impelled* to do it.[65]

Weaving the web of meaning

At that critical moment it's crucial to choose your way forward with careful discernment. There are many courses of action that, while incrementally improving a situation, may further strengthen the Windigo AI's long-term chokehold on life. While it's useful to fix bugs in the software, it's even more valuable to prioritize those actions that change the operating system. And it's essential to choose something you feel passionate about, because only fierce devotion will overcome the setbacks that inevitably ensue. In the counterculture era Joseph Campbell famously advised people to 'follow your bliss'; for our era, some have poignantly rephrased this to 'follow your heartbreak'.[66]

Just as the principles of life can form the basis for a healthy civilization, they can also infuse the process of our own transformation. As we know, ecologies are fractal designs, where single cells are part of organisms, which are in turn part of larger communities. Similarly, our own inner transformation has a fractal quality, occurring in relationship with others around us and an engaged awareness of our community's role within larger systems. Author and activist adrienne maree brown describes a process she calls 'emergent strategy', in which relatively simple acts of intentional, transformative practice with others can self-organize into larger structures of societal change.[67]

The dominant individualist culture has bred into many of us an inclination toward a 'hero complex', encouraging us to strive to be the one to make the biggest difference. Part of becoming an ecological self is to recognize and rise above this tendency – to find a participative role within a larger community of changemakers creating what George Monbiot calls the 'new politics of belonging'. Just as trees in a healthy forest communicate with and fortify each other through their underground mycorrhizal network, each of us can be most effective in transformative change when we connect with the existing network of life-affirming groups already operating around us.[68]

Above all, the manner in which we interact with others is crucial. Each of our actions, each of our conversations, plays a part in generating humanity's future. In contrast to the old communist adage 'The end justifies the means', an ecological principle is that *there is no end* – simply a continued organic unfolding of whatever means becomes the predominant mode of operation. For this reason, while outrage at injustice and devastation may helpfully energize us, it is critical not to let feelings of hate and resentment infiltrate our actions. When we engage with the world with resentment, it ultimately strengthens the story of separation that created the damage in the first place.[69*]

An ecological worldview leads naturally to acting out of love – the realization and embrace of connectedness. A deep recognition of interdependence can be a foundation for what Buddhist scholar David Loy calls 'bodhisattva activism' – wherein each new situation becomes an opportunity to reorient from individual separateness toward a shared identity. The Native Americans at Standing Rock, with their universal message, 'Water is life', demonstrated the world-changing power of grounding political resistance in spiritual practice and sacred, authentic human values.[70]

These core principles of love and respect, arising from our shared human experience, become even more important when we relate to people we see as active agents of Windigo, Inc. For those who desire a flourishing future, it is only too easy to view well-heeled corporate executives, militarized police officers and supporters of reactionary political groups as the enemy. These are the moments to recall Thích Nhât Hanh's exhortation, 'Practice until you recognize your presence in everyone else.' The pirate rapist might have been you if you had been born in his village. Even the racist demonstrator screaming slogans of hate was once a cooing infant looking for love. Everybody has been wounded by Windigo, Inc. – some more than others.[71]

Instead of responding to oppression with animosity, which merely exacerbates the divisions in our society, we can choose what activist Rabbi Michael Lerner calls 'revolutionary love' – one that aims to heal and repair the world by affirming the unity of all humankind. Revolutionary love means having compassion even for those who are the oppressors, even for those actively involved in the destruction of the living Earth. This by no means implies permitting harmful actions to take place, and may at times require direct confrontation with those who cause harm, but when those encounters are conducted from a place of revolutionary love, they are more likely to lead to beneficial outcomes. In the wise words of Detroit-based sound healer Sterling Toles, 'We must not only heal the suffering that oppression causes, but we must also heal the suffering that causes oppression.'[72]

From this perspective, when Uncle Bob seems to be parroting the soundbites of Windigo, Inc., it might become possible to reach beyond the surface of his arguments and connect compassionately with his heart. Most likely, Uncle Bob also cares for life's flourishing, desires a beautiful world for his great-grandchildren and sees himself as a good person trying to do the right thing. Numbed by our society's nonstop anesthesia drip, Uncle Bob might yearn deep down to feel a greater sense of meaning in his life – a sense of participating in something bigger than himself, in co-creating a brighter future. Can you connect with Uncle Bob in this place? Can you invite something in his spirit to embrace some link in the web of meaning?

Uncle Bob, of course, is within all of us. We're continually in dialogue with a version of him within ourselves. For many of us, his voice may even be dominant in our internal democracy of consciousness. He speaks for the cultural values we have internalized growing up in the dominant culture of separation. Weaving the web of meaning ultimately means integrating all the different parts of ourselves, including those that feel egotistical, fearful and selfish. When we hear these parts within us, it is an invitation to look deeper and ask what are the core human needs that have not been met, that are crying out for attention.[73]

Similarly, we can weave a richer web of meaning with others by asking the same questions about their needs. An ecological civilization will emerge only when the symbiotic linkages between people become a more powerful force than the competitive impulses engendered by the dominant culture. Each of us has a part to play in weaving that web of vital synergy. We may not know what the future holds for humanity, but we know that every day of our lives we can live into the future we wish for ourselves and the rest of life. We can choose to live as an ecological self, as an integral part of the emerging human planetary consciousness as it finds its way to synergize with the multitude of other sacred, sentient beings comprising Gaia. In the luminous words of poet Aurora Levins Morales:

> Defend the world in which we win as if it were your child.
> It is your child.
> Defend it as if it were your lover.
> It is your lover.[74]

As we pursue our love for a flourishing world, weaving our own particular strands of meaning, we may find a surprising number of others doing the same. Like an immune system protecting its host from toxins, an untold number of other caring, compassionate humans are devoting their energies to life-affirming activities.

The scale of each weave ranges enormously, from fleeting, intimate moments of tenderness with a loved one to passionate public speeches that inspire millions. More important than the scale is intention: a deep, authentic devotion to the well-being of life galvanized into action.[75]

Ultimately, it is the quality of engagement that resonates throughout the web. Everything we do, everything we say, creates li ripples in the fabric of existence. Many of those ripples fade away over time. Some of them resonate with the li ripples of others to form larger waves. We can never know what will become of each li ripple we put out into the universe – each conversation, each moment of eye contact, each action we take. But we know within ourselves if that particular ripple comes from a deep intention for well-being for ourselves, others and all sentience.

The rice pile

Some years ago a couple of scientists were studying how avalanches occur. You may recall that, like other self-organized phenomena, avalanches follow a power law, which predicts there will be many small ones, occasional mid-sized ones and very rare gigantic ones. The scientists wanted a better understanding of power law distributions, so they set up a big heap of rice, and one by one they added a grain to the top of the heap. As predicted, many grains seemed to have no effect, while an occasional single grain would arbitrarily set off an avalanche of rice.[76]

Intrigued by this experiment, I decided to try it myself. I got similar results, but I noticed something else that fascinated me. Most of the time when I dropped a few grains on top of the pile nothing much happened at first, but, as I kept watching, I began to see subtle changes occurring in different places all over the pile. It was as though the inert heap of rice had come alive. I realized that, unseen, the tiny impacts of the grains on top were resonating throughout the pile, causing innumerable other tiny reactions among adjacent grains, which in turn passed their movements on throughout the pile. It dawned on me then that each grain I dropped was contributing something unique to the eventual avalanche. Although one grain might be identified as the one that 'caused' the avalanche, in reality all the grains I had dropped had collectively created the conditions for the avalanche to occur when it finally did.

If this is the case for an inert pile of rice, we can only imagine how much more this holds for the complex, dynamic set of reactions that resonate through the collective consciousness of humanity. If we consider what this means for our own actions, it seems to me there are two crucial implications. First, there is a sense of empowerment. However inconsequential our own actions might appear in relation to the massive forces driving our world, we can have faith that their potential resonance extends far beyond what we're able to visualize. Second, there is an awesome responsibility that adheres to the empowerment: the way in which each of us chooses to engage with the world, no matter how insignificant it might seem ... *matters*. With each of the choices we make, the words we speak, the actions we take, we are playing a role in either inhibiting or catalyzing the great transition our society needs if we are to bequeath a flourishing world to future generations.

When the volunteer in the Johns Hopkins psilocybin study recalled that she was part of a cosmic symphony orchestra, and by playing she became part of the music herself, she was speaking for all of us. With every strand we weave in the web of meaning, we become intertwined in Gaia's future – an intimately embedded node within Indra's Net, reflecting infinitely out into the mystery.

As you put down this book and move on to the next thing in your life, whatever it might be, I invite you to take a few moments to pause. Sit down, take a few breaths and reflect on this question: What is the sacred and precious strand that *you* will weave?

NEW THREADS OF MEANING

What is the sacred and precious strand that *you* will weave?

GLOSSARY

Adaptive Cycle model

A model of change in complex systems developed by an interdisciplinary group of hundreds of scientists, which applies generally to complex adaptive systems, ranging in size from cells to ecosystems, and is equally applicable to human systems, such as markets and industries. According to the model, every complex system passes through a life cycle consisting of four phases: growth, conservation, release and reorganization, which initiates the next cycle.

Animate consciousness

Sometimes referred to as 'primary' or 'core' consciousness, animate consciousness is the form of cognition that covers the whole array of subjective experiences shared by humans with other mammals, such as feelings, primary emotions and physical drives, along with the deeper layers of consciousness below normal awareness.

Animate intelligence

The complex, self-organized intelligence arising from animate consciousness manifested by all life forms, from single cells to plants and animals, including humans.

Archetypes

Long-lived cultural attractors, some of which go back to the dawn of human culture, which resonate across generations through their salient impact on a person's attractors of consciousness. Archetypes are shared patterns of human sense-making and behavior that are deeply meaningful and universal to the human experience. While they may be reinterpreted by each new generation, their broader patterns maintain long-term resilience as a result of their persistent salience in human consciousness.

Attractors of consciousness

The self-organized, dynamic patterns formed by neuronal pathways in the nervous system that give rise to consciousness. Every fraction of a second, multiple clusters of different neural groups come together from different parts of the brain to form a 'dynamic core' of consciousness, creating a flow of qualia in a continuous integrated process of linkage and differentiation. Attractors of consciousness refer both to the multidimensional phase space called 'qualia space' by Giulio Tononi, as well as the subjective experiences of consciousness. Like other natural attractors, they show fractal patterns and small-world properties, and remain relatively stable, yet undergo occasional phase transitions. Everyday words that denote attractors of consciousness include: sensations, feelings, moods, thoughts, ideas, attitudes and beliefs.

Autopoiesis

A defining attribute of living systems, first described by biologists Humberto Maturana and Francisco Varela, by which life actively generates itself, taking energy from the environment to modify itself and perpetuate its existence, in a self-organized process incorporating reciprocal causality. 'Autopoiesis' comes from Greek words meaning self-generation.

Bodhisattva

A Buddhist ideal of someone who, having achieved enlightenment, and liberated from the endless cycles of reincarnation, has nevertheless vowed to remain in the world to alleviate the suffering of all sentient beings. The bodhisattva path is often seen by practitioners as an inspiration for living an awakened life suffused with compassionate action.

Cheng

A traditional Chinese concept (pronounced *chung*) central to

Confucian thought that described a fully authentic approach to life. In the words of Mencius, 'There is no greater delight than to realize *cheng* on self-examination.' In Neo-Confucian thought, this concept took on extra meaning as a full integration of consciousness, arising when a person lives in integrity within themselves and in harmony with the larger cosmos.

Commons

Historically, the commons referred to land that was available for anyone in the community to graze their animals or grow crops. In modern usage, the commons refers to any source of sustenance and well-being that has not been appropriated either by the state or private ownership, such as the air, water, sunshine, language, cultural traditions and scientific knowledge. The wealth accruing to all humanity on account of these sources of value may be termed the commonwealth.

Complexity

In the terminology of systems theory, complexity describes a self-organized system arising from a large number of nonlinear relationships between its components with feedback loops that can never be precisely described. Any living thing or system comprising living things is complex: a bacterium, a brain, an ecosystem, a financial market, a language or a social system. A complex system may be contrasted with a complicated system which is not complex, no matter how large, if each of its components and the way they relate to each other can be completely analyzed and given an exact description. A jumbo jet, an offshore oil rig, and a snowflake are all examples of complicated systems. Characteristic attributes of self-organized complex systems are natural attractors, phase transitions, small-world properties and emergence.

Conceptual consciousness

Sometimes referred to as 'secondary' or 'higher-order' consciousness, conceptual consciousness is a form of cognition mediated by the prefrontal cortex, and manifested more prominently in humans than in other animals, which enables such characteristically human functions as symbolic thought, self-awareness and complex planning.

Consciousness

Consciousness – in animals with a nervous system – is an emergent product of dynamic neural self-organization. It is enacted as the result of continual interaction between a person and their environment, and is an ongoing activity existing not just within the nervous system, but through engagement with the world. Consciousness requires a process of integration, with multiple clusters of different neural groups linking and differentiating from moment to moment to form a 'dynamic core'. According to Giulio Tononi, the quantity of consciousness in a system is the amount of information arising from integration, above and beyond the information maintained separately in the system's parts.

From an evolutionary perspective, it is valuable to consider a continuum of consciousness, beginning with the basic sentience arising from life, all the way up to the most complex mammals, including humans. Major evolutionary jumps in complexity of consciousness likely occurred with the emergence of nervous systems and with the rise of warm-blooded animals. In humans, two different forms of consciousness may be described: conceptual and animate.

Cultural attractor

A form of natural attractor that describes the self-organized, dynamic patterns of human culture. In the same way that an individual person experiences attractors of consciousness, the collective consciousness of a culture exhibits cultural attractors in the form of shared ideas, values and behavioral norms. While never completely fixed, some cultural attractors show remarkable resilience over generations, and in some cases, maintain their characteristic identity over millennia. Cultural attractors follow the same principles as other phenomena of self-organized complex adaptive systems, exhibiting fractal patterns, small-world properties and power law expression. They may manifest as short-lived fads, such as an internet hashtag that goes viral, or long-lived multi-generational patterns spanning millennia, such as religions or archetypes.

Democracy of consciousness

A metaphor for how decisions are made in human consciousness, whereby 'transient coalitions of neurons' representing different aspects of the 'I' and 'self' vie with each other for salience, in a continual succession of both minor and major 'elections'. Excessive self-control, impulsiveness or zealous attachment to a belief system can all work against the 'democracy', whereas an integrated approach to decision-making, honoring all aspects of a person, helps the 'democracy' to function more effectively.

Dependent origination

A key doctrine of Buddhist philosophy, dependent origination (*pratītyasamutpāda* in Sanskrit) states that all phenomena are dependent for their existence on other phenomena. This recognition that we live in a universe of endless interdependence leads to an understanding of reality as an all-embracing web of causal relations, with both philosophical and ethical implications. Buddhist teacher Thích Nhât Hanh offers an interpretation of this doctrine that he refers to as interbeing: the principle that nothing has an autonomous existence but arises from its interbeing with everything else.

Dharma

The Buddhist term for the intrinsic order of the universe, which serves as the foundation for morality, ethical behavior and the principles of practice for eliminating *dukkha* and living a fulfilling life.

Dualism

A defining characteristic of mainstream Western thought for over two millennia, dualism refers to a belief in two separate aspects or dimensions of the universe (also known as ontological dualism). Plato first comprehensively described a dualistic cosmos, with an eternal, divine dimension and a changeable, polluted worldly dimension, reflected in the human being who was believed to have an eternal soul imprisoned in the body. This cosmological split was adopted by Christianity, and recast by Descartes for modernity by substituting 'mind' for soul. Dualism rejects the existence of animate consciousness, upholding human identity as residing solely in conceptual consciousness, sees an inherent distinction between the spiritual and material, and perceives a fundamental separation between humanity and nature, which is viewed as a mere mechanical resource for exploitation.

Dukkha

A Buddhist term, frequently translated as 'suffering' but referring to a broad spectrum of unpleasant human experiences – including feelings of unease, worry, grasping, longing, regret, and embarrassment – derived from the workings of conceptual consciousness. Extending its meaning beyond the Buddhist tradition, *dukkha* may be understood as arising from the separation between 'I' and 'self' and as the inverse of *wu-wei*.

Ecological civilization

A civilization based on the core principles that sustain living systems in natural ecologies. An ecological civilization would be based on life-affirming values rather than wealth accumulation, and would be structured to optimize eudaimonia rather than hedonia. The overriding objective of an ecological civilization would be to create the conditions for all humans to flourish as part of a thriving living Earth. A fundamental precept would be the recognition of fractal flourishing: that the well-being of each person is fractally related to the health of the larger world. Some of the core principles of an ecological civilization would include fairness, justice, individual dignity, diversity, integration, balance and symbiosis between humans and nonhuman nature.

Emergence

A particular kind of phase transition in a complex, self-organized system, by which the system's complexity reaches a critical mass that transforms into a new coherence which couldn't have occurred by simply adding up each of the system's elements. Emergence is a phenomenon that arises when a system shows a distinctive identity as a result of its interconnected subsystems relating together: when 'the whole is greater than the sum of its parts'. Emergence is an essential part of the self-organized process that generates life, consciousness and crucial phenomena of human society such as language, culture and the internet.

Entropy

As described in the Second Law of Thermodynamics, entropy is the universal process by which order inevitably becomes disordered and heat always flows from hot regions to colder regions. As a result of entropy, many physicists believe the universe will eventually dissipate into a bleak expanse of cold, dark nothingness. Life may be understood as negative entropy: a temporary, local reversal of the Second Law of Thermodynamics.

Eudaimonia

A term originally coined by Aristotle, and contrasted with hedonia, eudaimonia is the state of flourishing arising from fulfilling one's true potential. This was understood by Aristotle, and the later Stoic and Epicurean schools, as the source of sustained well-being. Recently, the term has been resurrected within the context of the positive psychology movement, as a foundational principle of well-being.

Fractal flourishing

The principle of fractal flourishing recognizes that health and well-being have a fractal quality, since each living entity exists as a fractal system within a holarchy, containing small systems within, and contained by larger systems. Fully integrated flourishing can therefore only be realized when each of the different fractal layers within the holarchy are flourishing and harmonizing with each other.

Fractals

Characteristic of many complex, self-organized systems, fractals are patterns that repeat themselves at different scales. They can be seen in the patterning of diverse natural phenomena such as clouds, lightning, coastlines, rivers and sand dunes; also in patterns of living systems such as ferns, tree branches, blood vessels, lung bronchioles and neurons. Fractal patterns exist both in space and time.

Gaia

The Gaia hypothesis, first postulated by James Lovelock, argues that life and Earth together form a tightly coupled, self-regulating system, named Gaia after the Greek goddess of the Earth. Gaia is perceived as the emergent result of life and Earth evolving together, perpetually shaping and reshaping each other. The Gaia hypothesis has been attacked by mainstream biologists, especially the implication that Gaia itself may be a living entity. While Gaia does not possess all the generally recognized characteristics of life, it does demonstrate life's foundational defining characteristic of intrinsic, purposive self-organization, and may therefore plausibly be understood as a type of living entity in a category by itself.

Gewu

A Neo-Confucian term meaning 'investigation of things', *gewu* served as an organizing methodology for understanding the nature of reality. In contrast to the conventional Western scientific method, *gewu* emphasized the interconnectedness of all aspects of experience and understanding. It was an integrative approach that recognized knowledge as being embodied and the intrinsic subjectivity of perception. *Gewu* recognized that, since the observer is an integral part of the very system being investigated, the investigation can never truly be value-free.

Harmony

In music, harmony arises when different notes sound at the same time in such a way that an emergent, more complex and pleasing sound is produced. In a broader context, harmony may be understood as the complex interweaving of different elements within a system resulting in a blend that is richer than the simple aggregation of the elements. Harmony is not synonymous with concepts such as gentleness, kindness or peacefulness: in an ecosystem, it is the emergent result of both competition and cooperation acting together in creative tension.

Hedonia

A term used by Aristotle, in contrast to eudaimonia, referring to the transient states of happiness that arise from pleasurable stimuli, including sensual pleasure, such as tastes, images and sounds, and also the fleeting but less tangible kind of pleasures of being praised, feeling powerful or admired, acquiring material goods or feeling financially secure. As noted by ancient philosophers, Buddhist teachers and modern positive psychology researchers, pursuing hedonic states can deflect attention from achieving sustained well-being, and can be a major source of *dukkha*.

Hedonic treadmill

A phenomenon described by social psychologists, whereby people's material aspirations change according to their situation, so as soon as they achieve their goal, they immediately aspire to the next step on the treadmill, never satisfying their need to grasp for more. Inculcating the hedonic treadmill as the default social norm is a basis for modern capitalism, and has been a cornerstone of US economic policy since the early twentieth century.

Holarchy

A term coined by Arthur Koestler, a holarchy refers to a complex, self-organized system containing multiple smaller systems within it, each of which is a coherent entity in its own right, while being an integral component of the larger system in which it is contained. A holarchy is a fractal form of organization. Life on Earth may be understood as a holarchy, ranging in scale from the microscopic components of a cell (known as organelles) to organisms, ecosystems, and ultimately the entire biosphere.

'I' and the 'self'

The 'I' encapsulates those parts of consciousness that – insofar as they're so highly developed – are uniquely human. It arises from conceptual consciousness with its prefrontal cortex-mediated ability to think abstract thoughts. The 'self' is the continually changing stream of present moment experiences which, in one form or another, is inherent to every sentient being. A person's entire identity doesn't exist in 'I' or the 'self', but emerges from how the 'I' interacts with the 'self'.

Integration

Integration is a state of unity with differentiation. In a fully integrated system, each part maintains its unique identity while operating in coordination with other parts of the system. Integration is the natural result of autopoietic self-organization, and can be viewed as a defining characteristic of any purposive, self-organized entity, including all living organisms. Integration is a crucial property of the holarchy of life at each level of its organization. In an integrated system, relationships are likely to have a 'small-world' property, with a few large hubs extending multiple links to smaller nodes throughout the network. In the opinion of neurobiologist Dan Siegel, integration is the defining characteristic of good health.

Integrative intelligence

A form of intelligence arising from the integration of both conceptual intelligence (frequently the only type recognized in mainstream thought) with animate intelligence. By weaving together the conceptual and animate, integrative intelligence permits humans to access the deep wisdom of the natural world for the benefit of human and nonhuman flourishing.

Interbeing

See dependent origination

Li

A key Neo-Confucian term, li (pronounced *lee*) refers to the principles by which all the qi in the universe is organized. Li may be understood as the ever-moving, ever-present set of patterns that flow through everything in nature and in one's own consciousness. Although invisible, li can be seen through its effect on energy and matter, in the same way that wind is invisible but can be seen through its effect on trees, leaves and clouds. Patterns of li exist in time as well as in space. The aggregation of all the li of the universe was understood to comprise the Tao.

Life

Life is an emergent, self-organized ongoing process of integrated self-generation and self-maintenance. It is differentiated from non-living self-organized processes by the phenomenon of autopoiesis, whereby a living system continually regenerates itself by ingesting nutrition from the environment and metabolizing it. A living system requires a semipermeable boundary, must actively persist in metabolic flow, and by cell division or procreation, must be able to pass on its unique capacities to future generations. Every living system is highly integrated, exhibits reciprocal causality and demonstrates some degree of sentience. From a physics perspective, life is a process of negative entropy that has remained unbroken for approximately four billion years on Earth. As such, life may be seen as driven by an intrinsic purpose to resist entropy and generate a temporary vortex of self-created order in the universe.

Meaning

Meaning is an emergent phenomenon enacted by a conscious entity as it relates an experience to other experiences. The meaning of something can be understood as the nexus of significant relationships it is perceived to have – a more extensive and integrated set of relationships makes it more meaningful. Meaning is, therefore, a function of connectedness, and is always participatory.

Natural attractor

Known conventionally as a strange attractor, a natural attractor is a chaotic set of states characteristic of a complex, self-organized system. The set of states remains far from equilibrium, never retraces exactly the same path, and its long-term trajectory cannot be precisely predicted. Natural attractors are an essential characteristic of living organisms, and are found everywhere in the natural world: in clouds, ocean waves and the movement of animals. Natural attractors are frequently quite robust, even in the face of perturbations, tending to converge back into a stable pattern, which is known as a 'basin of attraction'.

Negative entropy

Negative entropy, or negentropy, is a process described by physicist Erwin Schrödinger to explain how living organisms continually convert the entropy around them into self-organized order. Through metabolism, organisms ingest entropy in the form of energy and matter, which they break down and reorganize into forms that are beneficial for their continued existence. As a result, every organism may be understood as a purposive, persistent, dynamic pattern of energy flow, playing its part in the larger drama of life's negentropy.

Neo-Confucianism

A school of philosophy, known as 'the School of the Study of the Tao', that arose during the Song dynasty in China, from approximately 1000 CE onwards, and became central to Chinese thought for the ensuing millennium. Neo-Confucianism synthesized elements of Taoism, Buddhism and Confucianism to create an integrated, systematic understanding of the universe. It described the universe as comprising qi and li, and established the practice of *gewu* ('investigation of things') as a core modality.

Phase transition

A phase transition is a change in state, such as ice to water, or water to steam. In systems theory, a phase transition describes a shift in the natural attractor of a complex system from one stable, coherent state to another. This shift can be unexpected, sudden and dramatic. Examples of phase transitions are a forest fire, a stock market collapse or an epileptic seizure. Phase transitions can also lead to the phenomenon of emergence.

Power law

A characteristic nonlinear pattern of relationships in complex, self-organized systems, describing a consistent inverse logarithmic relationship between the amplitude of a fluctuation and its frequency. A power law predicts that self-organized systems will frequently exhibit many small fluctuations, fewer mid-sized ones and rare large fluctuations. The Richter scale for earthquakes, where each higher number represents a tenfold increase in magnitude, is an example of how a power law manifests in the real world. Power laws apply in many natural and social phenomena, such as daily stock market fluctuations, avalanches, forest fires, airport traffic and biological mass extinctions.

Prefrontal cortex

The part of the brain responsible for the executive function, the prefrontal cortex is more highly developed in humans than other animals, and is responsible, among other functions, for controlling basic physiological drives, enabling complex planning and symbolic thought and making abstract rules – all essential components of conceptual consciousness.

Qi

An ancient Chinese term (pronounced *chee*) for the dynamic flow of energy and matter comprising the entire physical universe. Qi was understood by Neo-Confucian philosophers to be organized by li.

Reciprocal causality

An emergent process of certain complex adaptive systems (including all living systems) whereby the whole and the parts of the system exert a reciprocal causal effect on each other. In a process of dynamic co-emergence, the whole emerges as a gestalt from the complex interactions of its parts, and simultaneously influences the activity of each of the parts.

Reductionism

The dominant methodology in science, which views nature as

an assemblage of parts each of which can be analyzed separately. Ontological reductionism is a belief that, because of the outstanding empirical success of reductionism in understanding how nature works, the reductionist methodology is sufficient, in principle, to explain everything about the entire universe.

Ren

A Neo-Confucian term for the realization of the ultimate connectedness of the universe. In classic Confucianism, *ren* signified a humane benevolence that people should cultivate to fulfill their role within society. Neo-Confucian philosophers expanded this concept to incorporate the realization of oneself as a fractal entity connected with the universe by the li that self-organizes the entire cosmos. Neo-Confucians understood *ren* as a reality that exists for everyone, whether they choose to realize it or not. The failure to experience *ren* was seen as a form of numbness (literally 'no *ren*' in Chinese).

Self-organization

A form of organization in a complex system that arises from the integrated way in which the different parts of the system relate to each other. In self-organized systems there is no blueprint that defines the system, and the organization arises from within rather than from an external agency. Virtually every natural system and many human systems are self-organized. Self-organized systems frequently show properties of fractality, power laws, small-world networks and natural attractors, and may undergo phase transitions over time.

'Small-world' property

A characteristic property of many self-organized networks, demonstrating a fractal, hub-and-spoke type of connectivity that generally follows a power law in the number of connections of its nodes. It is known as a 'small-world' property because any place in the network is a relatively small number of connections from any other place, usually via a hub. 'Small-world' properties are found in many natural networks, including protein interactions of cells and the mycorrhizal root connections of trees in a forest, and in many human networks.

Spirit

Indigenous cultures worldwide have always believed that spirits exist, not just in people, but also in animals, trees and significant natural phenomena. From a modern systems perspective, a spirit may be defined as the emergent integrative property of any natural entity. The spirit of a person, an animal, a tree or a river may be conceived as the intangible but powerful unifying principle that maintains the entity's natural attractor in coherent form – always in flux within certain parameters, both variable and resilient, and undergoing occasional phase transitions over time.

Spirituality

Based on the systems-based definition of spirit, spirituality may be similarly defined as seeking meaning in the coherent connections between things (i.e. the li) rather than in the things themselves.

Strange attractor

See natural attractor

Symbiocene

An era characterized by the symbiotic flourishing of humans and Earth. In contrast to the current period, commonly known as the Anthropocene, in which nature is treated as a resource to be exploited, human activity in the Symbiocene would be organized as an ecological civilization, based on life-affirming principles, to actively regenerate and sustain Earth's health. The Symbiocene could, in principle, be an era of extremely long duration, in which humans embark on learning how to integrate deeply with the non-human cohabitants of Earth, with the aim of developing a truly planetary intelligence.

Symbiosis

Symbiosis as a biological term refers generally to any intimate and long-standing relationship between two different kinds of organisms. In this book, it typically refers to the most common form, mutualism: a process intrinsic to life and evolution, whereby different organisms exchange their own specialized skills for the unique skills of other organisms that can help them thrive. Expansion of symbiosis has been the driver of each of the great evolutionary transitions of life on Earth. The mutual cooperation of symbiosis, by allowing each entity to specialize, promotes both diversity and complexity. The prevalence of symbiosis means that life is rarely a zero-sum game: on the contrary, by combining expertise, species have co-created ecosystems everywhere in which the whole is far greater than the sum of the parts.

Tao

Translated literally as 'way' or 'path', the Tao (pronounced *dao*) is an ancient Chinese term referring to the mysterious ways in which the forces of nature are manifested in the universe.

Taoism

A school of thought originating in ancient China which focused attention on harmonizing with the natural flow of the Tao.

Te

A Taoist concept, (pronounced *duh*) referring to the intrinsic nature or power of an entity. Animals, plants and other nonhuman forms of life were understood to act spontaneously according to their *te*, and therefore to flow naturally with the Tao.

Wu-wei

A Taoist term, translated as 'non-purposive' or 'effortless' action, describing how nonhuman beings act according to their *te*, and seen by Taoists as an aspirational state for humans. In terms of modern psychology, *wu-wei* can be achieved when the two cognitive systems representing the 'I' and 'self' (Systems 1 and 2 in dual systems theory) are acting in synchrony with each other.

Yin and yang

An ancient Chinese concept describing the polarities ubiquitous in nature. Yin represents softness, wetness, darkness and receptivity, while yang represents hardness, dryness, light and activity. The polarities of yin and yang may be understood as analogous to the north and south poles of the Earth, or the positive and negative poles of an electric current. Each is an integral part of a complete system, and neither can exist without the other.

Yu-wei

The opposite of *wu-wei*, translated as 'goal orientation' or 'purposive action', *yu-wei* represented for traditional Taoists the antithesis of living according to the Tao.

FURTHER READING

Chapter 1: The Nameless Uncarved Wood

Jill Bolte Taylor, *My Stroke of Insight: A Brain Scientist's Personal Journey* (New York: Penguin, 2008). A moving account that brings to life the difference between left- and right-hemisphere functions of the brain.

Antonio Damasio, *Descartes' Error: Emotion, Reason, and the Human Brain* (New York: Penguin Books, 1994). An excellent introduction into how the prefrontal cortex relates to human cognition.

Terrence W. Deacon, *The Symbolic Species: The Co-Evolution of Language and the Brain* (New York: W. W. Norton, 1997). Explains the crucial role of the prefrontal cortex in human evolution.

Jeremy Lent, *The Patterning Instinct: A Cultural History of Humanity's Search for Meaning* (Amherst, NY: Prometheus, 2017). Includes a deep dive into the historical differences between east Asian and Western views of humanity and the universe.

Iain McGilchrist, *The Master and His Emissary: The Divided Brain and the Making of the Western World* (New Haven: Yale University Press, 2009). A powerful argument for how left-brained cognition has become overwhelmingly dominant in modern society.

Lao Tsu, *Tao Te Ching*, trans. Gia-Fu Feng and Jane English (New York: Vintage, 1972). This is the beautiful edition I refer to in the chapter.

Chapter 2: The Original AI: Animate Intelligence

Antonio Damasio, *The Strange Order of Things: Life, Feeling, and the Making of Cultures* (New York: Pantheon, 2018). A lucid explanation of the evolutionary and biological relationship between cells, intelligence, life, feeling and consciousness.

Frans de Waal, *Are We Smart Enough to Know How Smart Animals Are?* (New York: W. W. Norton, 2016). An enjoyable and thoughtful survey showing the depth and breadth of animal intelligence.

Stefano Mancuso, *The Revolutionary Genius of Plants: A New Understanding of Plant Intelligence and Behavior* (New York: Atria Books, 2018). A groundbreaking primer explaining plant intelligence from multiple perspectives.

Lynn Margulis and Dorion Sagan, *What Is Life?* (Berkeley/Los Angeles: University of California Press, 2000). An expansive introduction to the intrinsic intelligence of life, from single cells to the entire ecosystem of Earth.

Carl Safina, *Beyond Words: What Animals Think and Feel* (New York: Henry Holt and Co., 2015). A deeply sensitive and beautifully written exploration into the inner lives of elephants, cetaceans and wolves.

Michael Tye, *Tense Bees and Shell-Shocked Crabs: Are Animals Conscious?* (New York: Oxford University Press, 2017). Explains some of the latest scientific findings of the surprisingly subjective, emotional lives of insects, crustaceans, octopuses and other sentient beings.

Andreas Weber, *The Biology of Wonder: Aliveness, Feeling, and the Metamorphosis of Science* (Gabriola Island, BC, Canada: New Society Publishers, 2016). A profound inquiry into the deeper philosophical implications of recognizing our shared interconnectedness with all of life.

Chapter 3: The Most Important Relationship in Your Life

Antonio Damasio, *The Feeling of What Happens: Body and Emotion in the Making of Consciousness* (New York: Harcourt Inc., 1999). A neuroscience-based explanation of how 'core' and 'extended' consciousness interact to create the experience of being human.

Jonathan Haidt, *The Happiness Hypothesis: Finding Modern Truth in Ancient Wisdom* (New York: Basic Books, 2006). A perspective on the relationship between conscious will and intuition that upends mainstream thinking on human psychology.

Daniel Kahneman, *Thinking, Fast and Slow* (New York: Farrar, Straus and Giroux, 2011). A landmark book distinguishing between intuitive 'Type 1' and rational 'Type 2' systems of thought.

George Lakoff and Mark Johnson, *Philosophy in the Flesh: The Embodied Mind and Its Challenge to Western Thought* (New York: Basic Books, 1999). A brilliant exploration of the implications of embodied cognition that overturns many assumptions of mainstream Western philosophy.

Mark R. Leary, *The Curse of the Self: Self-Awareness, Egotism, and the Quality of Human Life* (New York: Oxford University Press, 2004). Explores many of the difficulties arising from self-awareness in human consciousness, and identifies ways to address them.

Edward Slingerland, *Trying Not to Try: Ancient China, Modern Science, and the Power of Spontaneity* (New York: Broadway Books, 2014). A masterful synthesis of traditional Chinese thought with modern psychology investigating the experience and meaning of *wu-wei*.

Chapter 4: The Patterns of the Universe

Fritjof Capra, *The Web of Life: A New Scientific Understanding of Living Systems* (New York: Anchor Books, 1996). A trailblazing book explaining how recent scientific insights into complexity and self-organization lead to a radically new conception of life.

Fritjof Capra and Pier Luigi Luisi, *The Systems View of Life: A Unifying Vision* (New

York: Cambridge University Press, 2014). A magisterial and comprehensive guide to system thinking, incorporating its history, breadth of application and philosophical implications.

James Gleick, *Chaos: Making a New Science* (New York: Penguin, 1987). A readable and accessible review of complexity, chaos theory, fractals, strange attractors and other topics broached in the chapter.

Stuart Kauffman, *At Home in the Universe: The Search for Laws of Self-Organization and Complexity* (New York: Oxford University Press, 1995). A visionary book: one of the first to explore the broader philosophical and cosmological implications of self-organization and complexity science.

Joanna Macy, *Mutual Causality in Buddhism and General Systems Theory: The Dharma of Natural Systems* (Albany, NY: SUNY Press, 1991). A groundbreaking work: the first to draw important connections between the Buddhist concept of dependent origination and systems theory.

Ricard Solé and Brian Goodwin, *Signs of Life: How Complexity Pervades Biology* (New York: Basic Books, 2000). An insightful work showing how the principles of self-organization lead to a deeper understanding of living systems.

Geoffrey West, *Scale: The Universal Laws of Life, Growth, and Death in Organisms, Cities, and Companies* (New York: Penguin, 2017). A brilliant and fascinating exploration by a leader of the Santa Fe Institute into the universal scaling laws of self-organized, complex systems.

Chapter 5: The Harmonic Dance of Life

David J. Depew and Bruce H. Weber, *Darwinism Evolving: Systems Dynamics and the Genealogy of Natural Selection* (Cambridge, MA: MIT Press, 1996). An exhaustive, magisterial work tracing the concept of evolution from the pre-Darwinian era through the Modern Synthesis and beyond.

Ursula Goodenough, *The Sacred Depths of Nature* (New York: Oxford University Press, 1998). A philosophical meditation on the deeper implications of life's complexity written with great clarity by an eminent cellular biologist.

Robin Wall Kimmerer, *Braiding Sweetgrass: Indigenous Wisdom, Scientific Knowledge and the Teachings of Plants* (Minneapolis: Milkweed Editions, 2013). A brilliant, synthetic work by an acclaimed Native American biologist weaving together insights from biology and Indigenous wisdom.

Lynn Margulis and Dorion Sagan, *Microcosmos: Four Billion Years of Microbial Evolution* (Berkeley, CA: University of California Press, 1997). An accessible primer on the story of evolution from a cellular perspective revealing the central role of symbiosis.

Denis Noble, *The Music of Life: Biology Beyond Genes* (Oxford: Oxford University Press, 2006). A brief, lucid book by a prominent systems biologist explaining the complexity of life using the root metaphor of music.

Denis Noble et al., 'New Trends in Evolutionary Biology: Biological, Philosophical and Social Science Perspectives', *Interface Focus* 7:5 (2017). A themed issue published by the prestigious Royal Society, with a wide-ranging series of articles from prominent researchers laying out the Extended Evolutionary Synthesis.

John Maynard Smith and Eörs Szathmáry, *The Origins of Life: From the Birth of Life to the Origin of Language* (New York: Oxford University Press, 1999). A short, detailed account by two renowned biologists demonstrating the central role of cooperation in each of the critical transitions of evolution.

Chapter 6: The Deep Purpose of Life

Adrian Bejan and J. Peder Zane, *Design in Nature: How the Constructal Law Governs Evolution in Biology, Physics, Technology, and Social Organization* (New York: Doubleday, 2012). Lays out what Bejan calls a 'constructal law' which accounts for the fractal design of natural self-organization in terms of energy flow maximization.

Jamie A. Davies, *Life Unfolding: How the Human Body Creates Itself* (New York: Oxford University Press, 2014). A stunning explanation of ontogeny, describing in accessible terms how principles of self-organization generate an organism from a single cell.

Terrence W. Deacon, *Incomplete Nature: How Mind Emerged from Matter* (New York: W. W. Norton, 2011). A detailed and comprehensive philosophical theory of emergence, which has been distilled into a more accessible format in: Jeremy Sherman, *Neither Ghost nor Machine: The Emergence and Nature of Selves* (New York: Columbia University Press, 2017).

Franklin M. Harold, *The Way of the Cell: Molecules, Organisms and the Order of Life* (New York: Oxford University Press, 2001). A readable introduction to the inner workings of a cell, recommended for any non-specialist interested in dipping into the awe-inspiring secrets of life.

James Lovelock, *Gaia: A New Look at Life on Earth* (Oxford: Oxford University Press, 2000). Lovelock's classic, first published in 1979, which lays out his Gaia hypothesis.

Erwin Schrödinger, *What Is Life? With Mind and Matter and Autobiographical Sketches* (Cambridge: Cambridge University Press, 1992). A brief and seminal work, first published in 1944, that introduces the crucial concept of negative entropy.

Chapter 7: The Tao in My Own Nature

Gerald M. Edelman and Giulio Tononi, *A Universe of Consciousness: How Matter Becomes Imagination* (New York: Basic Books, 2000). A clearly written book expounding a coherent theory of consciousness, emphasizing its embodied and dynamic characteristics through the 'dynamic core' hypothesis.

Joseph Henrich, *The Secret of Our Success: How Culture Is Driving Human Evolution, Domesticating Our Species, and Making Us Smarter* (Princeton, NJ: Princeton University Press, 2016). A thoughtful and far-reaching account of the profound impact culture has had on the human experience.

Steven Johnson, *Emergence: The Connected Lives of Ants, Brains, Cities, and Software* (New York: Scribner, 2002). An accessible primer on how principles of emergence are manifested in different aspects of nature, including human consciousness and culture.

J. A. Scott Kelso, *Dynamic Patterns: The Self-Organization of Brain and Behavior* (Cambridge, MA: MIT Press, 1995). A detailed investigation into the intersection of dynamic self-organization and neuroscience by a trailblazer in the field.

Christof Koch, *Consciousness: Confessions of a Romantic Reductionist* (Cambridge, MA: MIT Press, 2017). A very readable guide to consciousness from the perspective of neuroscience, with an excellent explanation of Integrated Information Theory, by a leading neuroscientist.

Daniel Siegel, *Pocket Guide to Interpersonal Neurobiology: An Integrative Handbook of the Mind* (New York: W. W. Norton, 2012). A brilliant, groundbreaking book establishing the conceptual framework for an integrative approach to the self-organized dynamics of the mind.

Evan Thompson, *Mind in Life: Biology, Phenomenology, and the Sciences of Mind* (Cambridge, MA: Harvard University Press, 2007). A profound philosophical exploration of life and mind from the multiple perspectives of neuroscience, phenomenology, self-organization and autopoiesis.

Francisco J. Varela, Evan Thompson and Eleanor Rosch, *The Embodied Mind: Cognitive Science and Human Experience* (Cambridge, MA: MIT Press, 1993). A masterful interdisciplinary synthesis of phenomenology, emergence theory, embodied cognition and Buddhist psychology.

Chapter 8: Flourishing as an Integrated Organism

David T. Courtwright, *The Age of Addiction: How Bad Habits Became Big Business* (Cambridge, MA: Belknap Press, 2019). A revealing history of 'limbic capitalism', chronicling how corporations have cynically undermined flourishing for profit.

Frank Forencich, *New Old Way: Ancestral Health and Sapience for the Modern World* (Exuberant Animal, 2018). A little-known but wise and insightful book laying out a deeply integrated path for flourishing.

Daniel Goleman and Richard J. Davidson, *Altered Traits: Science Reveals How Meditation Changes Your Mind, Brain, and Body* (New York: Penguin, 2017). A significant book by two leaders in the field providing a lucid, science-based explanation of the beneficial effects of meditation.

Venerable Henepola Gunaratana, *Mindfulness in Plain English* (Somerville, MA: Wisdom Publications, 1991). As promised by the title, this book is an excellent, straightforward introduction to the practice of mindfulness meditation.

Matthieu Ricard, *Happiness: A Guide to Developing Life's Most Important Skill* (New York: Little, Brown & Co., 2007). An erudite approach to cultivating *sukha* written by a prominent, highly respected Buddhist scholar and monk.

Martin E. Seligman, *Flourish: A Visionary New Understanding of Happiness and Well-Being* (New York: Free Press, 2011). A bestselling classic on well-being that helped lay the foundations for the positive psychology movement.

Richard Wilkinson and Kate Pickett, *The Spirit Level: Why Greater Equality Makes Societies Stronger* (New York: Bloomsbury Press, 2009). An important book that comprehensively demonstrates the corrosive effects of inequality on social well-being.

Chapter 9: Cultivating Integrated Values

Christopher Boehm, *Moral Origins: The Evolution of Virtue, Altruism, and Shame* (New York: Basic Books, 2012). An insightful work by an anthropologist subspecializing in primatology, assiduously portraying the evolutionary origins of human morality.

Rutger Bregman, *Humankind: A Hopeful History* (New York: Little, Brown & Co., 2020). A brilliantly written exposé of the conventional, cynical view of human nature, overturning many misconceptions and revealing a radically different, fact-based understanding of humankind as intrinsically caring and cooperative.

Riane Eisler and Douglas P. Fry, *Nurturing Our Humanity: How Domination and Partnership Shape Our Brains, Lives, and Future* (New York: Oxford University Press, 2019). Provides a valuable framework to understand cultural values, elucidating historical shifts in cultural norms and offering a hopeful pathway forward.

David R. Loy, *A New Buddhist Path: Enlightenment, Evolution, and Ethics in the Modern World* (Somerville, MA: Wisdom Publications, 2015). A scholarly explanation of how Buddhist values naturally lead to engagement with the ecological and political crisis of the modern world.

Steven Pinker, *The Better Angels of Our Nature: The Decline of Violence in History and Its Causes* (New York: Allen Lane, 2011). An exhaustive analysis showing the historical progression of ethical norms across multiple aspects of society.

Matthieu Ricard, *Altruism: The Power of Compassion to Change Yourself and the World*, trans. Charlotte Mandell and Sam Gordon (New York: Little, Brown & Co., 2015). A comprehensive account of altruism, using perspectives from evolution, philosophy and Buddhist cultivation, which is both enlightening and inspiring.

Robert M. Sapolsky, *Behave: The Biology of Humans at Our Best and Worst* (New York: Penguin, 2017). A brilliant, detailed exposition of the biological basis of human ethical behavior, written by a biologist with additional expertise in neurology and primatology.

David Sloan Wilson, *Does Altruism Exist? Culture, Genes, and the Welfare of Others* (New Haven: Yale University Press, 2015). An accessible discussion by an expert in evolutionary theory on the evolution of altruism, its crucial importance in everyday life and its potential role in improving the human condition.

Chapter 10: Human/Nature

M. Kat Anderson, *Tending the Wild: Native American Knowledge and the Management of California's Natural Resources* (Berkeley, CA: University of California Press, 2005). A detailed study of Native American land practices showing how 'tending' can benefit both humans and nonhuman nature symbiotically.

Eileen Crist, *Abundant Earth: Toward an Ecological Civilization* (Chicago, IL:

University of Chicago Press, 2019). A deep analysis of how conventional ways of thinking about nature have led to its wanton destruction and how a different worldview might restore its abundance.

Derrick Jensen, *The Myth of Human Supremacy* (New York: Seven Stories Press, 2016). An original and highly readable exploration into the devastating folly of the modern ideology of human supremacy.

J. B. MacKinnon, *The Once and Future World: Nature as It Was, as It Is, as It Could Be* (New York: Houghton Mifflin Harcourt, 2013). A heart-wrenching tour of nature's once-glorious abundance, with piercing insights into what has been lost and the possibilities of regeneration.

Freya Mathews, 'Towards a Deeper Philosophy of Biomimicry', *Organization and Environment* 24:4 (2011). A brilliant paper unraveling the complexities of the human/nature relationship and showing the way forward to a more regenerative philosophy of nature.

George Monbiot, *Feral: Rewilding the Land, the Sea, and Human Life* (Chicago, IL: University of Chicago Press, 2014). A visionary and inspirational account of rewilding, describing some of its successes and showing how it can restore some of nature's glory.

Edward O. Wilson, *Half-Earth: Our Planet's Fight for Life* (New York: Liveright Publishing, 2016). A bold blueprint, laid out by a world-renowned biologist, for the policy changes required to protect the world's biodiversity and head off the Sixth Extinction.

Chapter 11: Everything Is Connected

Christopher M. Bache, *LSD and the Mind of the Universe: Diamonds from Heaven* (Rochester, VT: Park Street Press, 2019). A groundbreaking book painstakingly chronicling a systematic series of high LSD doses taken over a twenty-year period by a philosopher of consciousness.

Barbara L. Fredrickson, *Love 2.0: How Our Supreme Emotion Affects Everything We Think, Do, Feel, and Become* (New York: Hudson Street Press, 2013). Offers an insightful conception of love as moments of connection, describing the implications of this perspective for health and flourishing.

Mae-Wan Ho, *The Rainbow and the Worm: The Physics of Organisms* (Singapore: World Scientific Publishing, 2008). A masterful exposition of the physics of life, revealing the crucial importance of resonance and dynamic coherence.

Michael Pollan, *How to Change Your Mind: What the New Science of Psychedelics Teaches Us About Consciousness, Dying, Addiction, Depression, and Transcendence* (New York: Penguin, 2018). An enjoyable and thoughtful survey of the history of and current renaissance in psychedelics, sharing the author's personal experiences along with lucid reflections on what the future might hold.

William A. Richards, *Sacred Knowledge: Psychedelics and Religious Experiences* (New York: Columbia University Press, 2016). A deeply insightful discussion by a recognized leader in the field on the philosophical and spiritual implications of psychedelic experiences.

Daniel J. Siegel, *Mind: A Journey to the Heart of Being Human* (New York: W. W. Norton, 2017). A brilliant and readable exploration by the founder of interpersonal neurobiology on the psychological, spiritual and cosmological implications of an integrative approach to life.

Steven H. Strogatz, *Sync: How Order Emerges from Chaos in the Universe, Nature, and Daily Life* (New York: Hachette Books, 2003). An accessible introduction by a leading mathematician into the all-pervasive and remarkable world of synchrony.

Chapter 12: From Fixed Self to Infinite Li: The Fractal Nature of Identity

Stephen C. Angle, *Sagehood: The Contemporary Significance of Neo-Confucian Philosophy* (New York: Oxford University Press, 2009). A deep dive into Neo-Confucian thought, explaining core concepts lucidly and highlighting its modern relevance.

Thomas Berry, *The Great Work: Our Way into the Future* (New York: Three Rivers Press, 1999). A visionary book, laying out the 'great work' of rebuilding civilization based on an expanded human identity with the living Earth.

E. Brian Davies, *Why Beliefs Matter: Reflections on the Nature of Science* (Oxford: Oxford University Press, 2010). A thoughtful and penetrating discussion by a respected mathematician on the implicit belief system that undergirds much mainstream reductionist thinking.

David Grinspoon, *Earth in Human Hands: Shaping Our Planet's Future* (New York: Grand Central Publishing, 2016). An engaging and far-sighted reflection by a leading astrobiologist on the human relationship with Earth and the potential for our planetary future.

Paul Harrison, *Elements of Pantheism: A Spirituality of Nature and the Universe* (Shaftesbury, Dorset: Element Books, 2013). A brief, unpretentious introduction to pantheism, discussing its global context, historical roots and philosophical elements.

Douglas R. Hofstadter, *I Am a Strange Loop* (New York: Basic Books, 2007). A profound exploration by a prominent mathematician on the mysteries of complexity and consciousness.

Stuart Kauffman, *Reinventing the Sacred: A New View of Science, Reason, and Religion* (New York: Basic Books, 2008). A groundbreaking book by a renowned complexity scientist portraying the sacredness arising from intrinsic properties of the universe.

Chapter 13: Weaving a New Story of Meaning

adrienne maree brown, *Emergent Strategy: Shaping Change, Changing Worlds* (Chico, CA: AK Press, 2017). Tying in systems thinking with political change, describes how acts of intentional, transformative practice with others can self-organize into larger structures of societal change.

Jason Hickel, *The Divide: Global Inequality from Conquest to Free Markets* (New York: W. W. Norton, 2017). An unflinching retelling of global history since colonialism, revealing how the Global North has systematically ransacked the wealth of the Global South and continues to do so.

David C. Korten, *Change the Story, Change the Future: A Living Economy for a Living Earth* (Oakland, CA: Berrett-Koehler, 2015). A groundbreaking book exposing the destructive underpinning of the mainstream narrative and laying down principles for a radically different, life-based story.

Mark Lynas, *Our Final Warning: Six Degrees of Climate Emergency* (London: HarperCollins, 2020). Should be required reading for everyone: a science-based, terrifying depiction of what the world would look like at each degree of further warming from one to six degrees.

Joanna Macy, *Active Hope: How to Face the Mess We're in without Going Crazy* (Novato, CA: New World Library, 2012). An invaluable guidebook on the transformational process required for coming to terms with the destructive nature of modern civilization and moving to active engagement.

George Monbiot, *Out of the Wreckage: A New Politics for an Age of Crisis* (New York: Verso, 2017). A pathbreaking, practical rendering of a new approach to politics based on belonging in community that has the potential to transform conventional politics.

Terry Patten, *A New Republic of the Heart: An Ethos for Revolutionaries* (Berkeley, CA: North Atlantic Books, 2018). A deeply integrative analysis of our civilizational crisis, showing how 'activist spirituality' can offer a path of effective personal and political participation in change-making.

Kate Raworth, *Doughnut Economics: Seven Ways to Think Like a 21st-Century Economist* (White River Junction, VT: Chelsea Green, 2017). A major landmark of new economic thinking, offering a powerful framework usable for cities or nations alike to rebuild their economies for a just and sustainable future.

Douglas Rushkoff, *Team Human* (New York: W. W. Norton, 2019). A refreshing and original primer on how we can rethink the old tropes of our destructive worldview, and co-create our future as empowered members of 'Team Human'.

Michael J. Sandel, *What Money Can't Buy: The Moral Limits of Markets* (New York: Farrar, Straus and Giroux, 2013). A lucid exposition by a distinguished Harvard political philosopher on how market fundamentalism has corroded core human values across a wide swath of human activity.

ACKNOWLEDGMENTS

The essence of a web is its network – it couldn't exist without its mesh of connections. Similarly, a web of meaning is constructed by connecting diverse nodes already in place. I am deeply indebted to the innumerable thinkers, past and present, who have contributed their crucial insights to the overall web of meaning that I have attempted to link together in an integrated form.

I think of this book as a conversation across time and space, in which time-honored ideas from Indigenous and classical traditions engage in discourse with modern perspectives to create a coherent sense-making that spans the ages. In this respect, my role has been somewhat akin to that of facilitator. I am, above all, grateful to the profound insights of the traditions of Indigenous peoples, Buddhism, Taoism, Confucianism and other wisdom lineages that have laid the bedrock for the ideas expressed here.

Turning to modern times, I owe a debt of gratitude to an array of brilliant thinkers pushing the boundaries of human understanding. In each case, their research and writings have helped me make connections between disparate concepts that I could not have grasped on my own. The list of these luminaries would be too long to enumerate exhaustively, but includes Andreas Weber, Freya Mathews, Eileen Crist, Evan Thompson, Joanna Macy, Antonio Damasio, Kat Anderson, Stuart Kauffman, Robin Wall Kimmerer, David Grinspoon, Kate Raworth, Dan Siegel, Thích Nhât Hanh, David Korten, Fritjof Capra and George Lakoff.

I have been fortunate to receive feedback on specific chapters from a host of illustrious subject experts, each of whom helped me clarify my arguments and fix inaccuracies. These include Terry Deacon, Toni Frohoff, Frans de Waal, Eva Jablonka, Abrar Abidi, David Depew, Bruce Weber, Scott Kelso, Paul Wong, Ron Purser, Darcia Narvaez, Roger Walsh, Chris Bache, Eileen Crist, Tracey Osborne, Clair Brown, Mark Leary, Douglas Rushkoff, Derrick Jensen, Paco Calvo, Fritjof Capra, Sean Kelly, Andreas Weber, Stephen Morris, David Korten, Fran Korten and Tomas Björkman.

I am especially grateful to Lisa Dale Miller, Micha Narberhaus, Sophia Aguiñaga and Freya Mathews, each of whom had the generosity to read my entire draft manuscript, and shared with me valuable perspectives that enhanced the final product.

A special thank you to George Monbiot, for his warm and generous support of my work, and for setting in motion a chain of events that led to the good fortune of this book being published jointly by Profile Books and New Society Publishers, two publishing houses that I am honored to be associated with. The quality of the book has been greatly improved by the thoughtful and insightful editing of Helen Conford and Rob West; and my agents, Anthony Arnove and David Grossman, have made the process feel smooth and effortless.

This book is a labor of love extending over many years, and I have been blessed to have been inspired by stimulating conversations on its topics with dear friends and colleagues including, but certainly not limited to, Atossa Soltani, Sean Kelly, Yuka Saito, Troy Lush, Annabelle Berrios, Charles Flores, Louis Fox, Indra Adnan, Pat Kane, Anna Murray, Roy Ackerman, Roman Krznaric, Alan Zulch, Yogi Hendlin, Teja Bell, Terry Patten, Ann-Ellice Parker, Traci Prendergast and Eddy Hueso.

The warm support of my family and friends over the years of the book's gestation has been a precious gift. I reserve my greatest appreciation for my beloved life-partner, Lisa Ferguson, who has been an integral part of the maturation and birth of this book from the outset. She was the first to lay eyes on each raw chapter as it emerged, and frequently helped me shape it considerably before it was ready to meet the light of day. I have learned many important lessons from her deeply integrative perspective on life, which are woven throughout the book – and her loving support has nourished me immeasurably every step of the way.

NOTES

Chapter 1: The Nameless Uncarved Wood

1. Lao Tzu, *Tao Te Ching*, transl. Ellen M. Chen, St Paul, MN: Paragon House, 1989, Chapter 32, p. 133.
2. Lao Tsu, *Tao Te Ching*, transl. Gia-Fu Feng and Jane English, New York: Vintage, 1972, Chapter 28.
3. Joseph Needham, *Science and Civilisation in China, Volume 2: History of Scientific Thought*, London: Cambridge University Press, 1972, citation from the *Li Chi*.
4. *Complete Works of Chuang Tzu*, transl. Burton Watson, New York: Columbia University Press, 1968, Section 3, p. 46.
5. Ibid. p. 122.
6. *Tao Te Ching*, Chapter 29, pp. 126–7; Jeremy Lent, *The Patterning Instinct: A Cultural History of Humanity's Search for Meaning*, Amherst, NY: Prometheus, 2017, pp. 185–7.
7. *Tao Te Ching*, Chapter 1, p. 51.
8. Ibid. Chapter 56, p. 188; Yu-Lan Fung, *A Short History of Chinese Philosophy: A Systematic Account of Chinese Thought from Its Origins to the Present Day*, New York: Free Press, 1976, p. 13; Needham, *Science and Civilisation*, p. 38.
9. Zhuangzi, Legge translation cited in Fritjof Capra, *The Tao of Physics: An Exploration of the Parallels between Modern Physics and Eastern Mysticism*, Boston: Shambhala Publications, 1999; Needham, *Science and Civilisation*, p. 106.
10. Antonio Damasio, *Descartes' Error: Emotion, Reason, and the Human Brain*, New York: Penguin Books, 1994, pp. 3–7.
11. Hanna Damasio et al., 'The Return of Phineas Gage: Clues About the Brain from the Skull of a Famous Patient', *Science* 264, 1994, pp. 1102–5.
12. Damasio, *Descartes' Error*, pp. 8–10.
13. Ibid. pp. 10–51; Earl K. Miller, David J. Freedman and Jonathan D. Wallis, 'The Prefrontal Cortex: Categories, Concepts and Cognition', *Philosophical Transactions of the Royal Society* B 357, 2002, pp. 1123–36; Earl K. Miller and Jonathan D. Cohen, 'An Integrative Theory of Prefrontal Cortex Function', *Annual Review of Neuroscience* 24, 2001, pp. 167–202.
14. Terrence W. Deacon, *The Symbolic Species: The Co-Evolution of Language and the Brain*, New York: W. W. Norton, 1997, pp. 214–24; Elkhonon

Goldberg, *The Executive Brain: Frontal Lobes and the Civilized Mind*, New York: Oxford University Press, 2001, p. 33; Joaquin M. Fuster, 'Frontal Lobe and Cognitive Development', *Journal of Neurocytology* 31, 2002, pp. 373–85; Katerina Semendeferi et al., 'Prefrontal Cortex in Humans and Apes: A Comparative Study of Area 10', *American Journal of Physical Anthropology* 114, 2001, pp. 224–41. While humans and other primates such as chimpanzees have roughly the same size PFC relative to the rest of their cortex, there is an area called the frontal pole in humans that is roughly double the size of that in chimpanzees. Whereas the rest of the PFC connects with every other part of the brain, the frontal pole is connected only to other parts of the PFC, and is frequently viewed as the part of the PFC that mediates the kind of cognition that is uniquely human. See Etienne Koechlin, 'Frontal Pole Function: What Is Specifically Human?' *Trends in Cognitive Sciences* 15:6, 2011; Narender Ramnani and Adrian M. Owen, 'Anterior Prefrontal Cortex: Insights into Function from Anatomy and Neuroimaging', *Nature Reviews: Neuroscience* 5, 2004, pp. 184–94; David Badre, 'Cognitive Control, Hierarchy, and the Rostro-Caudal Organization of the Frontal Lobes', *Trends in Cognitive Sciences* 12:5, 2008, pp. 193–200; Adam E. Green et al., 'Frontopolar Cortex Mediates Abstract Integration in Analogy', *Brain Research* 1096:1, 2006, pp. 125–37.

15. Jean-Pierre Changeux, *The Physiology of Truth: Neuroscience and Human Knowledge*, transl. M. B. DeBevoise, Cambridge, MA: Harvard University Press, 2002, pp. 108–9; Damasio, *Descartes' Error*, pp. 180–1; Goldberg, *The Executive Brain*, pp. 35–6.
16. Goldberg, *The Executive Brain*, pp. 21–6, 37.
17. Jonathan D. Wallis, Kathleen C. Anderson and Earl K. Miller, 'Single Neurons in Prefrontal Cortex Encode Abstract Rules', *Nature*, 21 June 2001, pp. 953–6.
18. Miller, Freedman and Wallis, 'The Prefrontal Cortex'; Lent, *The Patterning Instinct*, pp. 30–1.
19. Leon Tremblay and Wolfram Schultz, 'Relative Reward Preference in Primate Orbitofrontal Cortex', *Nature* 398, 1999, pp. 704–8.
20. Giorgio Coricelli and Rosemarie Nagel, 'Neural Correlates of Depth of Strategic Reasoning in Medial Prefrontal Cortex', *PNAS* 106:23, 2009, pp. 9163–8.
21. Miller, Freedman and Wallis, 'The Prefrontal Cortex'; Aron K. Barbey, Frank Krueger and Jordan Grafman, 'An Evolutionarily Adaptive Neural Architecture for Social Reasoning', *Trends in Neurosciences* 32:12, 2009, pp. 603–10.
22. Goldberg, *The Executive Brain*, p. 24; David B. Wong, 'Identifying with Nature in Early Daoism', *Journal of Chinese Philosophy* 36:4, 2009, pp. 568–84.
23. Michael S. Gazzaniga, *Human: The Science Behind What Makes Us Unique*, New York: HarperCollins, 2008, Kindle edn, locations 4809–98.
24. Michael S. Gazzaniga, 'Humans: The Party Animal', *Dædalus*, summer 2009, pp. 21–34.
25. Michael S. Gazzaniga, 'Cerebral Specialization and Interhemispheric Communication: Does the Corpus Callosum Enable the Human Condition?' *Brain* 123:7, 2000, pp. 1293–1326; Bernd Figner et al., 'Lateral Prefrontal Cortex

and Self-Control in Intertemporal Choice', *Nature Neuroscience* 13, 2010, pp. 538–9; Shaun Gallagher, 'The Neuronal Platonist', *Journal of Consciousness Studies* 5:5–6, 1998, pp. 706–17; Joseph LeDoux, *Synaptic Self: How Our Brains Become Who We Are*, New York: Penguin, 2003, pp. 198–9.

26. Gazzaniga, 'Cerebral Specialization'; LeDoux, *Synaptic Self*, pp. 302–3; Lent, *The Patterning Instinct*, p. 62; Deacon, *The Symbolic Species*, pp. 321–75.
27. Vinod Goel et al., 'Hemispheric Specialization in Human Prefrontal Cortex for Resolving Certain and Uncertain Inferences', *Cerebral Cortex* 17, 2006, pp. 2245–50; Iain McGilchrist, *The Master and His Emissary: The Divided Brain and the Making of the Western World*, New Haven: Yale University Press, 2009, pp. 67–9; Gazzaniga, 'Cerebral Specialization'; LeDoux, *Synaptic Self*, pp. 302–3; James H. Austin, *Selfless Insight: Zen and the Meditative Transformations of Consciousness*, Cambridge, MA: MIT Press, 2009, p. 85.
28. Jill Bolte Taylor, *My Stroke of Insight: A Brain Scientist's Personal Journey*, New York: Penguin, 2008.
29. Ibid. p. 41.
30. Ibid. pp. 41, 71.
31. Ibid. pp. 50–1.
32. Ibid. p. 140.
33. Ibid. pp. 29–31.
34. McGilchrist, *The Master and His Emissary*, p. 3.
35. Ibid. p. 115.
36. Owen Flanagan, 'The Left-Brain Plot for World Domination', *New Scientist* 2738, 9 December 2009.
37. Gerald M. Edelman and Giulio Tononi, *A Universe of Consciousness: How Matter Becomes Imagination*, New York: Basic Books, 2000; Antonio Damasio, *The Feeling of What Happens: Body and Emotion in the Making of Consciousness*, New York: Harcourt Inc., 1999.
38. Lent, *The Patterning Instinct*.
39. Ibid. pp. 143–59.
40. Ibid. pp. 227–38.

Chapter 2: The Original AI: Animate Intelligence

1. Frans de Waal, *Are We Smart Enough to Know How Smart Animals Are?* New York: W. W. Norton, 2016, pp. 45–7; James L. Gould, 'Animal Cognition', *Current Biology* 14:10, 2004, R372–375.
2. Jeremy Narby, *Intelligence in Nature: An Inquiry into Knowledge*, New York: Penguin, 2005, pp. 46–7, 124; Lynn Margulis and Dorion Sagan, *What Is Life?* Berkeley/Los Angeles: University of California Press, 2000, pp. 37–8; Jeffrey Moussaieff Masson and Susan McCarthy, *When Elephants Weep: The Emotional Lives of Animals*, New York: Delta, 1995, p. 18; Hans Jonas, *The Phenomenon of Life: Toward a Philosophical Biology*, Evanston: Northwestern University Press, 2001, pp. 55–6; Michael Tye, *Tense Bees and Shell-Shocked Crabs: Are Animals Conscious?* New York: Oxford University Press, 2017, pp. 35–6.

3. Stephen L. Talbott, 'Rediscovering Life: Where Do Intelligence and Wisdom Reside?' in *From Bodily Wisdom to the Knowing Self*, Nature Institute, 2015; Richard Dawkins, *The Blind Watchmaker*, New York: W. W. Norton, 1986, p. 37.
4. Jeremy Lent, *The Patterning Instinct: A Cultural History of Humanity's Search for Meaning*, Amherst, NY: Prometheus, 2017, pp. 359–61.
5. Deborah Bird Rose, *Nourishing Terrains: Australian Aboriginal Views of Landscape and Wilderness*, Canberra: Australian Heritage Commission, 1996, pp. 14–15; Narby, *Intelligence in Nature*, pp. 32–3; Robin Wall Kimmerer, *Braiding Sweetgrass: Indigenous Wisdom, Scientific Knowledge and the Teachings of Plants*, Minneapolis: Milkweed Editions, 2013, pp. 19, 58.
6. Linda S. Gottfredson, 'Intelligence: What Is It?' *New Scientist*, 29 June 2011; Howard Gardner, *Multiple Intelligences: New Horizons*, New York: Basic Books, 2006, p. 3.
7. Tim Folger, 'Can We Keep Getting Smarter?' *Scientific American* 23, January 2012, pp. 92–5. Several studies in the past decade have claimed that the Flynn effect may have slowed down or even reversed in some highly developed countries. While it is too early to be certain about this change, it does raise further important questions about the impact of cultural change on the type of intelligence measured by IQ testing.
8. Pamela Stern, 'Learning to Be Smart: An Exploration of the Culture of Intelligence in a Canadian Inuit Community', *American Anthropologist* 101:3, 1999, pp. 502–14.
9. Gardner, *Multiple Intelligences*.
10. Ibid. pp. 6–8.
11. Gould, 'Animal Cognition'.
12. Rose, *Nourishing Terrains*, pp. 26–8.
13. Eleanor Cummins, 'Bananas: Your Cousin, Maybe?' *Popular Science*, 14 August 2018.
14. Theodosius Dobzhansky, 'Nothing in Biology Makes Sense except in the Light of Evolution', *American Biology Teacher* 35:3, 1973, pp. 125–9. The philosophical case for approaching cognition from an evolutionary rather than anthropocentric perspective has been laid out comprehensively by Pamela Lyon, 'The Biogenic Approach to Cognition', *Cognitive Processing* 7, 2006, pp. 11–29.
15. Evan Thompson, *Mind in Life: Biology, Phenomenology, and the Sciences of Mind*, Cambridge, MA: Harvard University Press, 2007, p. ix.
16. Yinon M. Bar-On, Rob Phillips and Ron Milo, 'The Biomass Distribution on Earth', *PNAS* 115:25, 2018, pp. 6506–11.
17. Boyce Rensberger, *Life Itself: Exploring the Realm of the Living Cell*, New York: Oxford University Press, 1996, pp. 62–6; Margulis and Sagan, *What Is Life?* p. 92; Peter Godfrey-Smith, *Other Minds: The Octopus, the Sea, and the Deep Origins of Consciousness*, Farrar, Straus and Giroux, 2017, pp. 16–17; Brian J. Ford, 'Revealing the Ingenuity of the Living Cell', *Biologist* 53:4, 2006, pp. 221–4. For a dramatic video depiction of what occurs within a single cell, see *The Inner Life of the Cell*, a computer graphic animation produced for

Harvard University's Department of Molecular and Cellular Biology: https://www.youtube.com/watch?v=FzcTgrxMzZk

18. Brian J. Ford, 'On Intelligence in Cells: The Case for Whole Cell Biology', *Interdisciplinary Science Reviews* 34:4, 2009, pp. 350–65; Narby, *Intelligence in Nature*, pp. 142–3; Ursula Goodenough, *The Sacred Depths of Nature*, New York: Oxford University Press, 1998, pp. 90–1.
19. Ford, 'On Intelligence in Cells'; Antonio Damasio, *The Strange Order of Things: Life, Feeling, and the Making of Cultures*, New York: Pantheon, 2018, p. 53; Ron Sender, Shai Fuchs and Ron Milo, 'Revised Estimates for the Number of Human and Bacteria Cells in the Body', *PLoS Biology* 14:8, 2016, e1002533.
20. Andreas Weber, *The Biology of Wonder: Aliveness, Feeling, and the Metamorphosis of Science*, Gabriola Island, BC, Canada: New Society Publishers, 2016, pp. 3–4, 28–9. See also Thompson, *Mind in Life*, pp. 159–160, 162; Walter J. Freeman, *How Brains Make up Their Minds*, New York: Columbia University Press, 2000, p. 8.
21. Margulis and Sagan, *What Is Life?* pp. 218–20.
22. Talbott, 'Rediscovering Life'; Narby, *Intelligence in Nature*, p. 96; Atsushi Tero et al., 'Rules for Biologically Inspired Adaptive Network Design', *Science* 327, 2010, pp. 439–42; David Parr, 'Cities in Motion: How Slime Mould Can Redraw Our Rail and Road Maps', *Guardian*, 18 February 2014; Romain P. Boisseau, David Vogel and Audrey Dussutour, 'Habituation in Non-Neural Organisms: Evidence from Slime Moulds', *Proceedings of the Royal Society* B 283, 2016, 0446; Philip Ball, 'Cellular Memory Hints at the Origins of Intelligence', *Nature* 451, 2008, p. 385.
23. Eshel Ben Jacob et al., 'Bacterial Linguistic Communication and Social Intelligence', *Trends in Microbiology* 12:8, 2004, pp. 366–72; Godfrey-Smith, *Other Minds*, p. 18; Damasio, *The Strange Order of Things*, pp. 19–20.
24. Godfrey-Smith, *Other Minds*, pp. 19–22; Damasio, *The Strange Order of Things*, p. 54.
25. Bar-On et al., 'The Biomass Distribution on Earth'.
26. Paco Calvo et al., 'Plants Are Intelligent, Here's How', *Annals of Botany* 125, 2020, pp. 11–28; Eric D. Brenner et al., 'Plant Neurobiology: An Integrated View of Plant Signaling', *Trends in Plant Science* 11:8, 2006, pp. 413–19; Anthony Trewavas, 'What Is Plant Behaviour?' *Plant, Cell & Environment* 32, 2009, pp. 606–16; Carl Safina, *Beyond Words: What Animals Think and Feel*, New York: Henry Holt and Co., 2015, pp. 23–4; Narby, *Intelligence in Nature*, pp. 83–9.
27. Stefano Mancuso, *The Revolutionary Genius of Plants: A New Understanding of Plant Intelligence and Behavior*, New York: Atria Books, 2018, Kindle edn, locations 662–75; Michael Pollan, 'The Intelligent Plant', *New Yorker*, 23 December 2013; Narby, *Intelligence in Nature*, pp. 87–8.
28. Mancuso, *The Revolutionary Genius of Plants*, Kindle edn, locations 28–51.
29. Stefano Mancuso and Alessandra Viola, *Brilliant Green: The Surprising History and Science of Plant Intelligence*, Washington DC: Island Press, 2015, pp. 133–5; František Baluška, Simcha Lev-Yadun and Stefano Mancuso,

'Swarm Intelligence in Plant Roots', *Trends in Ecology & Evolution* 25:12, 2010, pp. 682–3; Pollan, 'The Intelligent Plant'; Trewavas, 'What Is Plant Behaviour?'

30. Michael Gross, 'Could Plants Have Cognitive Abilities?' *Current Biology* 26, 2016, R181–184; Susan Milius, 'No Brainer Behavior: Messages, Memory, Maybe Even Intelligence – Botanists Wrangle over How Far Plants Can Go', *Science News* 175:13, 2009; Narby, *Intelligence in Nature*, pp. 86–91.
31. Talbott, 'Rediscovering Life'; Monica Gagliano et al., 'Learning by Association in Plants', *Nature: Scientific Reports* 6:38427, 2016.
32. Ibid.; Peter Wohlleben, *The Hidden Life of Trees: What They Feel, How They Communicate – Discoveries from a Secret World*, Vancouver: Greystone Books, 2016, pp. 151–2.
33. Ibid. pp. 7–11; Suzanne W. Simard et al., 'Net Transfer of Carbon between Ectomycorrhizal Tree Species in the Field', *Nature* 388, 1997, pp. 579–82; Yuan Yuan Song et al., 'Interplant Communication of Tomato Plants through Underground Common Mycorrhizal Networks', *PLoS One* 5:10, 2010, e13324; Pollan, 'The Intelligent Plant'.
34. Wohlleben, *The Hidden Life of Trees*, p. 7.
35. Greg Miller, 'On the Origin of the Nervous System', *Science* 325, 2009, pp. 24–6; Godfrey-Smith, *Other Minds*, p. 23; Damasio, *The Strange Order of Things*, p. 59.
36. Michel Cabanac, Arnaud J. Cabanac and Andre Parent, 'The Emergence of Consciousness in Phylogeny', *Behavioural Brain Research* 198, 2009, pp. 267–72; Gerald M. Edelman, 'Naturalizing Consciousness: A Theoretical Framework', *PNAS* 100:9, 2003, pp. 5520–4; Miller, 'On the Origin of the Nervous System'.
37. Damasio, *The Strange Order of Things*, pp. 6, 25–6; Guy Claxton, *Intelligence in the Flesh: Why Your Mind Needs Your Body Much More Than It Thinks*, New Haven: Yale University Press, 2015, p. 44.
38. Damasio, *The Strange Order of Things*, pp. 25–6, 58; Antonio Damasio and Gil B. Carvalho, 'The Nature of Feelings: Evolutionary and Neurobiological Origins', *Nature Reviews: Neuroscience* 14, 2013, pp. 143–52; Jaak Panksepp, 'The Basic Emotional Circuits of Mammalian Brains: Do Animals Have Affective Lives?' *Neuroscience & Biobehavioral Reviews* 35, 2011, pp. 1791–804; Tye, *Tense Bees and Shell-Shocked Crabs*, p. 161.
39. Andrew B. Barron and Colin Klein, 'What Insects Can Tell Us About the Origins of Consciousness', *PNAS* 113:18, 2016, pp. 4900–08; Tamar Stelling, 'Do Invertebrates Feel Pain?' *New Scientist*, 19 February 2014; Tye, *Tense Bees and Shell-Shocked Crabs*.
40. Scott W. Emmons, 'The Mood of a Worm', *Science* 338, 2012, pp. 475–6.
41. Tye, *Tense Bees and Shell-Shocked Crabs*, pp. 142–4.
42. Stelling, 'Do Invertebrates Feel Pain?'; Antonio Damasio, *The Feeling of What Happens: Body and Emotion in the Making of Consciousness*, New York: Harcourt Inc., 1999, pp. 70–1; Tye, *Tense Bees and Shell-Shocked Crabs*, pp. 146–59, 91–108; Chelsea Whyte, 'Crayfish Experience Something Like Anxiety When They Shed Their Armour', *New Scientist*, 22 December 2018; Eric Edsinger and Gül Dölen, 'A Conserved Role for Serotonergic

Neurotransmission in Mediating Social Behavior in Octopus', *Current Biology* 28:19, 2018, pp. 3136–42.

43. James quoted in Freeman, *How Brains Make up Their Minds*.
44. Stanislas Dehaene and Lionel Naccache, 'Towards a Cognitive Neuroscience of Consciousness: Basic Evidence and a Workspace Framework', *Cognition* 79, 2001, pp. 1–37. For other theories on the evolution of consciousness, see Cabanac et al., 'The Emergence of Consciousness in Phylogeny'; Damasio, *The Feeling of What Happens*; Daniel C. Dennett, *Consciousness Explained*, New York: Penguin, 1993; Gerald M. Edelman and Giulio Tononi, *A Universe of Consciousness: How Matter Becomes Imagination*, New York: Basic Books, 2000.
45. Cabanac et al., 'The Emergence of Consciousness in Phylogeny'.
46. Ibid.; Joseph LeDoux, *The Emotional Brain: The Mysterious Underpinnings of Emotional Life*, New York: Simon & Schuster, 1996, p. 126; Edelman and Tononi, *A Universe of Consciousness*, pp. 211–12; Gould, 'Animal Cognition'.
47. Irene M. Pepperberg, 'Cognitive and Communicative Abilities of Grey Parrots', *Applied Animal Behaviour Science* 100, 2006, pp. 77–86; Margaret Talbot, 'Birdbrain: The Woman Behind the World's Chattiest Parrots', *New Yorker*, 12 May 2008; Nathan J. Emery and Nicola S. Clayton, 'The Mentality of Crows: Convergent Evolution of Intelligence in Corvids and Apes', *Science* 306, 2004, pp. 1903–7; Nathan J. Emery and Nicola S. Clayton, 'Evolution of the Avian Brain and Intelligence', *Current Biology* 15:23, 2005, R946–950; Ann B. Butler, 'Evolution of Brains, Cognition, and Consciousness', *Brain Research Bulletin* 75:2–4, 2008, pp. 442–9; Tye, *Tense Bees and Shell-Shocked Crabs*, p. 121.
48. Helmut Prior, Ariane Schwarz and Onur Güntürkün, 'Mirror-Induced Behavior in the Magpie (*Pica Pica*): Evidence of Self-Recognition', *PLoS Biology* 6:8, 2008, pp. 1642–50. Other nonhuman animals that have passed the mirror test, besides magpies and chimpanzees, are bonobos, orangutans, dolphins and elephants.
49. Gordon G. Gallup Jr., 'Self-Awareness and the Evolution of Social Intelligence', *Behavioural Processes* 42, 1998, pp. 239–47; Sue Savage-Rumbaugh, Stuart G. Shanker and Talbot J. Taylor, *Apes, Language, and the Human Mind*, New York: Oxford University Press, 1998; William C. McGrew, 'Chimpanzee Technology', *Science* 328, 2010, pp. 579–80; Teresa Romero, Miguel A. Castellanos and Frans B. M. de Waal, 'Consolation as Possible Expression of Sympathetic Concern among Chimpanzees', *PNAS* 107:27, 2010, pp. 12110–15; Mathias Osvath, 'Spontaneous Planning for Future Stone Throwing by a Male Chimpanzee', *Current Biology* 19:5, 2009, R190–191.
50. De Waal, *Are We Smart Enough?* pp. 12, 119–20.
51. Safina, *Beyond Words*, pp. 92, 211, 236–7; Lucy A. Bates, Joyce H. Poole and Richard W. Byrne, 'Elephant Cognition', *Current Biology* 18:13, 2008, pp. 544–6; Kieran C. R. Fox, Michael Muthukrishna and Susanne Shultz, 'The Social and Cultural Roots of Whale and Dolphin Brains', *Nature Ecology & Evolution* 1, November 2017, pp. 1699–705; Katharina Kropshofer, 'Whales and Dolphins Lead "Human-Like Lives" Thanks to Big Brains, Says Study', *Guardian*, 16 October 2017.

52. Marc D. Hauser, 'The Possibility of Impossible Cultures', *Nature* 460, 2009, pp. 190–6.
53. Michael Tomasello, *The Cultural Origins of Human Cognition*, Cambridge, MA: Harvard University Press, 2000; Joseph Henrich, *The Secret of Our Success: How Culture Is Driving Human Evolution, Domesticating Our Species, and Making Us Smarter*, Princeton, NJ: Princeton University Press, 2016.
54. Andy Clark, 'An Embodied Cognitive Science?' *Trends in Cognitive Sciences* 3:9, 1999, pp. 345–51; Freeman, *How Brains Make up Their Minds*, pp. 17–18; Lewis Thomas, *The Lives of a Cell: Notes of a Biology Watcher*, New York: Penguin Books, 1978, pp. 64–5; Emma Young, 'Gut Instincts: The Secrets of Your Second Brain', *New Scientist* 2895, 2012; Damasio, *The Strange Order of Things*, pp. 134–6.
55. Edelman and Tononi, *A Universe of Consciousness*, p. 199; Claxton, *Intelligence in the Flesh*, pp. 120–1.
56. Masson and McCarthy, *When Elephants Weep*, pp. xviii, 32–3; Safina, *Beyond Words*, pp. 26–8; Jaak Panksepp, 'Affective Consciousness: Core Emotional Feelings in Animals and Humans', *Consciousness and Cognition* 14:1, 2005, pp. 30–80. There have been some encouraging shifts in mainstream thinking in recent years. An important milestone was reached in 2012 with the Cambridge Declaration on Consciousness, signed by a prominent international group of neuroscientists, which stated that 'the absence of a neocortex does not appear to preclude an organism from experiencing affective states'. See Philip Low, 'The Cambridge Declaration on Consciousness', Cambridge, 2012.
57. De Waal, *Are We Smart Enough?* p. 25; Paul R. Ehrlich, *Human Natures: Genes, Cultures, and the Human Prospect*, New York: Penguin, 2002, p. 73; Marc Bekoff, *Minding Animals: Awareness, Emotions, and Heart*, New York: Oxford University Press, 2002, p. 109; Michael Bond, 'Interview: Feral and Free', *New Scientist*, 3 April 2007; Masson and McCarthy, *When Elephants Weep*, pp. xxi, 232–3; Safina, *Beyond Words*, p. 29.
58. Narby, *Intelligence in Nature*, p. 53; Gerhard Roth and Ursula Dicke, 'Evolution of the Brain and Intelligence', *Trends in Cognitive Sciences* 9:5, 2005, pp. 250–7; Johan J. Bolhuis and Clive D. L. Wynne, 'Can Evolution Explain How Minds Work?' *Nature* 458, 2009, p. 832–3; Bekoff, *Minding Animals*, p. 107; Panksepp, 'The Basic Emotional Circuits'.
59. Bekoff, *Minding Animals*, p. 119; Masson and McCarthy, *When Elephants Weep*, p. 116; Panksepp, 'The Basic Emotional Circuits'.
60. Frans de Waal, 'What I Learned from Tickling Apes', *New York Times*, 8 April 2016; De Waal, *Are We Smart Enough?* p. 12; Daniel J. Povinelli, 'Behind the Ape's Appearance: Escaping Anthropocentrism in the Study of Other Minds', *Dædalus*, winter 2004, pp. 29–41; Rupert Read, 'How Whales and Dolphins Can Teach Us to Be Less Stupid', *Open Democracy*, 19 December 2017.
61. Panksepp, 'The Basic Emotional Circuits'; Jeremy Sherman and Terrence W. Deacon, 'Teleology for the Perplexed: How Matter Began to Matter', *Zygon*, December 2007, pp. 873–901.
62. Damasio, *The Strange Order of Things*, p. 66.

63. Safina, *Beyond Words*, p. 362.
64. Weber, *The Biology of Wonder*, pp. 29–30.
65. Kimmerer, *Braiding Sweetgrass*, pp. 131–4.

Chapter 3: The Most Important Relationship in Your Life

1. George Lakoff and Mark Johnson, *Metaphors We Live By*, Chicago, IL: University of Chicago Press, 2003; Lakoff and Johnson, *Philosophy in the Flesh: The Embodied Mind and Its Challenge to Western Thought*, New York: Basic Books, 1999.
2. Gerald M. Edelman, Joseph A. Gally and Bernard J. Baars, 'Biology of Consciousness', *Frontiers in Psychology* 2, 2011, pp. 1–7; Joseph LeDoux, *Synaptic Self: How Our Brains Become Who We Are*, New York: Penguin, 2003, p. 21; Michael Lewis, 'The Origins and Uses of Self-Awareness or the Mental Representation of Me', *Consciousness and Cognition* 20, 2011, pp. 120–9; Antonio Damasio, *The Feeling of What Happens: Body and Emotion in the Making of Consciousness*, New York: Harcourt Inc., 1999, p. 16; Evan Thompson and Francisco J. Varela, 'Radical Embodiment: Neural Dynamics and Consciousness', *Trends in Cognitive Sciences* 5:10, 2001, pp. 418–25.
3. Nicholas Humphrey, *A History of the Mind: Evolution and the Birth of Consciousness*, New York: Copernicus/Springer-Verlag, 1992, p.25; James quoted in Angela Tagini and Antonino Raffone, 'The "I" and the "Me" in Self-Referential Awareness: A Neurocognitive Hypothesis', *Cognitive Processing* 11:1, 2010, pp. 9–20.
4. Gerald M. Edelman and Giulio Tononi, *A Universe of Consciousness: How Matter Becomes Imagination*, New York: Basic Books, 2000, p. 109; Edelman, 'Naturalizing Consciousness: A Theoretical Framework', *PNAS* 100:9, 2003, pp. 5520–4.
5. Jeremy Lent, *The Patterning Instinct: A Cultural History of Humanity's Search for Meaning*, Amherst, NY: Prometheus, 2017, pp. 40–7; Robin I. M. Dunbar, 'The Social Brain Hypothesis', *Evolutionary Anthropology* 6:5, 1998, pp. 178–90.
6. Daniel J. Povinelli and Todd M. Preuss, 'Theory of Mind: Evolutionary History of a Cognitive Specialization', *Trends in Neurosciences* 18:9, 1995, pp. 418–24.
7. Michael Tomasello, Josep Call and Brian Hare, 'Chimpanzees Understand Psychological States – the Question Is Which Ones and to What Extent', *Trends in Cognitive Sciences* 7:4, 2003, pp. 153–6; Josep Call and Michael Tomasello, 'Does the Chimpanzee Have a Theory of Mind? 30 Years Later', *Trends in Cognitive Sciences* 12:5, 2008, pp. 187–92; Lewis, 'The Origins and Uses of Self-Awareness', pp 120–9; Povinelli and Preuss, 'Theory of Mind'. For an excellent account of the research and differing interpretations regarding the development of theory of mind in children in contrast with chimpanzees, see Michael Tomasello, 'How Children Come to Understand False Beliefs: A Shared Intentionality Account', *PNAS* 115:34, 2018, pp. 8491–8.
8. The part of the brain that is activated is known as the medial prefrontal cortex. See Diana I. Tamir and Jason P. Mitchell, 'Neural Correlates of Anchoring-and-Adjustment During Mentalizing', *PNAS* 107:24, 2010, pp. 10827–32; Debra A.

Gusnard et al., 'Medial Prefrontal Cortex and Self-Referential Mental Activity: Relation to a Default Mode of Brain Function', *PNAS* 98:7, 2001, pp. 4259–64; Joseph M. Moran, William M. Kelley and Todd F. Heatherton, 'What Can the Organization of the Brain's Default Mode Network Tell Us About Self-Knowledge?' *Frontiers in Human Neuroscience* 7, 2013, pp. 1–6.

9. Mark R. Leary, *The Curse of the Self: Self-Awareness, Egotism, and the Quality of Human Life*, New York: Oxford University Press, 2004, Kindle edn, locations 1293–6; Chris D. Frith, 'The Role of Metacognition in Human Social Interactions', *Philosophical Transactions of the Royal Society* B 367, 2012, pp. 2213–23.
10. LeDoux, *Synaptic Self*, pp. 27–8; Damasio, *The Feeling of What Happens*, p. 16.
11. Thomas Suddendorf, *The Gap: The Science of What Separates Us from Other Animals*, New York: Basic Books, 2013, pp. 110–12.
12. Shaun Gallagher, 'Philosophical Conceptions of the Self: Implications for Cognitive Science', *Trends in Cognitive Sciences* 4:1, 2000, pp. 14–21; Michael S. Gazzaniga, 'Humans: The Party Animal', *Dædalus*, summer 2009, pp. 21–34; Chapter 1, 'The interpreter and the mystic'.
13. Owen Flanagan, *The Problem of the Soul: Two Visions of Mind and How to Reconcile Them*, New York: Basic Books, 2002, pp. 240–1; Gallagher, 'Philosophical Conceptions of the Self'.
14. LeDoux, *Synaptic Self*, p. 323; Jonathan St B. T. Evans, 'Spot the Difference: Distinguishing between Two Kinds of Processing', *Mind & Society* 11, 2012, pp. 121–31.
15. Terrence W. Deacon, *The Symbolic Species: The Co-Evolution of Language and the Brain*, New York: W. W. Norton, 1997, p. 452.
16. Walter Mischel, *The Marshmallow Test: Why Self-Control Is the Engine of Success*, New York: Little, Brown & Co., 2014, pp. 125–6; Todd F. Heatherton and Dylan D. Wagner, 'Cognitive Neuroscience of Self-Regulation Failure', *Trends in Cognitive Sciences* 15:3, 2011, pp. 132–9.
17. Mischel, *The Marshmallow Test*, pp. 15–16.
18. Terrie E. Moffitt et al., 'A Gradient of Childhood Self-Control Predicts Health, Wealth, and Public Safety', *PNAS* 108:7, 2011, pp. 2693–8; Angela Duckworth, 'The Significance of Self-Control', *PNAS* 108:7, 2011, pp. 2639–40. For a refutation of the importance of delay in gratification as a predictor of life success, see Tyler W. Watts, Greg J. Duncan and Haonan Quan, 'Revisiting the Marshmallow Test: A Conceptual Replication Investigating Links between Early Delay of Gratification and Later Outcomes', *Psychological Science* 29:7, 2018, pp. 1159–77.
19. Daniel Kahneman, *Thinking, Fast and Slow*, New York: Farrar, Straus and Giroux, 2011, pp. 24–5. For other valuable perspectives on dual system theory, see Evans, 'Spot the Difference'; Jonathan St B. T. Evans, 'Dual-Processing Accounts of Reasoning, Judgment, and Social Cognition', *Annual Review of Psychology* 59, 2008, pp. 255–78; J. Allan Hobson and Ursula Voss, 'A Mind to Go Out Of: Reflections on Primary and Secondary Consciousness', *Consciousness and Cognition* 20, 2011, pp. 993–7; Janet Metcalfe and Walter

Mischel, 'A Hot/Cool-System Analysis of Delay of Gratification: Dynamics of Willpower', *Psychological Review* 106:1, 1999, pp. 3–19; Christopher D. Frith and Uta Frith, 'Implicit and Explicit Processes in Social Cognition', *Neuron* 60:3, 2008, pp. 503–10. For a critique of the widespread acceptance of dual system theory, see David E. Melnikoff and John A. Bargh, 'The Mythical Number Two', *Trends in Cognitive Sciences* 22:4, 2018, pp. 280–93.

20. Kahneman, *Thinking, Fast and Slow*, pp. 24–5.
21. Ibid.; Robert M. Sapolsky, *Behave: The Biology of Humans at Our Best and Worst*, New York: Penguin, 2017, pp. 387–9; Leonard Mlodinow, *Subliminal: How Your Unconscious Mind Rules Your Behavior*, New York: Vintage, 2013, p. 156. The Wikipedia list of cognitive biases is at: https://en.wikipedia.org/wiki/List_of_cognitive_biases. Researchers have developed a test to measure implicit bias that can be taken online, the Implicit Association Test, which measures the speed with which people connect positive and negative words to different images such as the faces of Black people and White people. See: https://implicit.harvard.edu/implicit/. Disturbingly, about 70 percent of those who take the test show an implicit pro-white bias, including many who believe themselves to be free of racial prejudice. However, significant controversy exists as to the reliability and validity of the test. See German Lopez, 'For Years, This Popular Test Measured Anyone's Racial Bias. But It Might Not Work After All', *Vox*, 7 March 2017.
22. Malcolm Gladwell, *Blink: The Power of Thinking Without Thinking*, New York: Back Bay Books, 2007, pp. 3–4, 12–13.
23. Ap Dijksterhuis and Loran F. Nordgren, 'A Theory of Unconscious Thought', *Perspectives on Psychological Science* 1:2, 2006, pp. 95–109; Gladwell, *Blink*, pp. 317–18, 444. For a critique of Dijksterhuis and Nordgren's theory, see Magda Osman, 'Does Our Unconscious Rule?' *Psychologist* 28:2, 2015, pp. 114–17; and for a meta-analysis that corroborates the theory, see Madelijn Strick et al., 'A Meta-Analysis on Unconscious Thought Effects', *Social Cognition* 29:6, 2011, pp. 738–62.
24. Ruud Custers and Henk Aarts, 'The Unconscious Will: How the Pursuit of Goals Operates Outside of Conscious Awareness', *Science* 329, 2010, pp. 47–50; Kerri Smith, 'Taking Aim at Free Will', *Nature* 477, 2011, pp. 23–5; Chun Siong Soon et al., 'Unconscious Determinants of Free Decisions in the Human Brain', *Nature Neuroscience* 11:5, 2008, pp. 543–5; Patrick Haggard, 'Decision Time for Free Will', *Neuron* 69, 2011, pp. 404–6.
25. Smith, 'Taking Aim at Free Will'; Nicole Branan, 'Unconscious Decisions: As We Mull a Choice, Our Subconscious Decides for Us', *Scientific American Mind*, August/September 2008, p. 8; Anthony R. Cashmore, 'The Lucretian Swerve: The Biological Basis of Human Behavior and the Criminal Justice System', *PNAS* 107:10, 2010, pp. 4499–504.
26. Lent, *The Patterning Instinct*, pp. 156–8; Lakoff and Johnson, *Philosophy in the Flesh*, pp. 563–4; Nancey Murphy and Warren S. Brown, *Did My Neurons Make Me Do It? Philosophical and Neurobiological Perspectives on Moral Responsibility*

and Free Will, New York: Oxford University Press, 2007, pp. 304–5; Leary, *The Curse of the Self*, Kindle edn, locations 168–74.

27. Lent, *The Patterning Instinct*, pp. 154–6; Jonathan Haidt, 'The Emotional Dog and Its Rational Tail: A Social Intuitionist Approach to Moral Judgment', *Psychological Review* 108:4, 2001, pp. 814–34.
28. Lent, *The Patterning Instinct*, pp. 228–31; Murphy and Brown, *Did My Neurons Make Me Do It?* pp. 304–5.
29. Lent, *The Patterning Instinct*, pp. 235–7. Montaigne cited in Iain McGilchrist, *The Master and His Emissary: The Divided Brain and the Making of the Western World*, New Haven: Yale University Press, 2009, p. 180.
30. Lent, *The Patterning Instinct*, pp. 235–8; Francisco J. Varela, Evan Thompson and Eleanor Rosch, *The Embodied Mind: Cognitive Science and Human Experience*, Cambridge, MA: MIT Press, 1993, pp. 61–2; David Galin, 'The Concepts "Self," "Person," and "I" in Western Psychology and in Buddhism', in *Buddhism and Science: Breaking New Ground*, ed. B. Alan Wallace, New York: Columbia University Press, 2003, p. 110; Richard Dawkins, *The Selfish Gene: 30th Anniversary Edition*, London: Oxford University Press, 2006, pp. 19–20. Loeb cited in Boyce Rensberger, *Life Itself: Exploring the Realm of the Living Cell*, New York: Oxford University Press, 1996, p. 11.
31. These brief paragraphs cannot do justice to the full debate on free will among neuroscientists, which is sophisticated and extensive. For an excellent review of current opinion, see Thomas T. Hills, 'Neurocognitive Free Will', *Proceedings of the Royal Society* B 286, 2019, 0510. One of the few biologists to have explicitly recognized the mainstream interpretation of the Libet experiment as a dualistic misconception is German philosopher of biology Andreas Weber. See Andreas Weber, *Biopoetics: Towards an Existential Ecology*, Berlin: Springer, 2016, pp. 47–8.
32. Björn Brembs, 'Towards a Scientific Concept of Free Will as a Biological Trait: Spontaneous Actions and Decision-Making in Invertebrates', *Proceedings of the Royal Society* B 278:1707, 2011, pp. 930–9.
33. Antoine Bechara et al., 'Deciding Advantageously before Knowing the Advantageous Strategy', *Science* 275, 1997, pp. 1293–5; Stanislas Dehaene and Lionel Naccache, 'Towards a Cognitive Neuroscience of Consciousness: Basic Evidence and a Workspace Framework', *Cognition* 79, 2001, pp. 1–37.
34. Antonio R. Damasio, B. J. Everitt and D. Bishop, 'The Somatic Marker Hypothesis and the Possible Functions of the Prefrontal Cortex [and Discussion]', *Philosophical Transactions: Biological Sciences* 351:1346, 1996, pp. 1413–20; Vittorio Gallese, 'The Manifold Nature of Interpersonal Relations: The Quest for a Common Mechanism', *Philosophical Transactions of the Royal Society* B 358, 2003, pp. 517–28. Milan Kundera's epigram is quoted by Nicholas Humphrey, cited in Paul R. Ehrlich, *Human Natures: Genes, Cultures, and the Human Prospect*, New York: Penguin, 2002, p. 111.
35. Haidt, 'The Emotional Dog and Its Rational Tail'. When Plato established the Western dualistic view of the human being, he used a metaphor of the soul as a charioteer commanding the horses of the personality. Haidt argues that a

better metaphor would be one where reason is a rider holding the reins of an emotional elephant. As long as the elephant permits it, the rider can direct it to go right or left, but as soon as the elephant really wants to do something else, reason is no match for its power. See Jonathan Haidt, *The Happiness Hypothesis: Finding Modern Truth in Ancient Wisdom*, New York: Basic Books, 2006, pp. 4, 13.

36. Study cited in Kahneman, *Thinking, Fast and Slow*, pp. 49–50; also in Sapolsky, *Behave*, pp. 447–9.
37. Haidt, 'The Emotional Dog and Its Rational Tail'. As Haidt mentions, the viewpoint that emotions are the basis of morality was first argued by eighteenth-century philosopher David Hume.
38. Ibid.; Sapolsky, *Behave*, pp. 507–8.
39. Luiz Pessoa, 'Précis on the Cognitive-Emotional Brain', *Behavioral and Brain Sciences* 38, 2015, e71; Edelman and Tononi, *A Universe of Consciousness*, p. 203.
40. Josef Parvizi, 'Corticocentric Myopia: Old Bias in New Cognitive Sciences', *Trends in Cognitive Sciences* 13:8, 2009, pp. 354–9; LeDoux, *Synaptic Self*, p. 2; Antonio Damasio, *Descartes' Error: Emotion, Reason, and the Human Brain*, New York: Penguin Books, 1994, pp. xx–xxi, 88, 252; Daniel Siegel, *Pocket Guide to Interpersonal Neurobiology: An Integrative Handbook of the Mind*, New York: W. W. Norton, 2012, pp. 71, 80.
41. Sapolsky, *Behave*, p. 511.
42. Francis Crick and Christof Koch, 'A Framework for Consciousness', *Nature Neuroscience* 6:2, 2003, pp. 119–26.
43. Cited in Leary, *The Curse of the Self*, Kindle edn, locations 2671–8.
44. Lent, *The Patterning Instinct*, pp. 209–11; Roshi Philip Kapleau, *The Three Pillars of Zen*, New York: Anchor Books, 2000, p. 411. Although *kokoro* is translated into English as 'heart' in the metaphorical sense, there is a different Japanese word for the organ. In Chinese, *xin* refers both to the organ and the heart/mind.
45. Lent, *The Patterning Instinct*, pp. 209–11; N. Yu, 'Heart and Cognition in Ancient Chinese Philosophy', *Journal of Cognition and Culture* 7:1–2, 2007, pp. 27–47.
46. Donald J. Munro, *A Chinese Ethics for the New Century: The Ch'ien Mu Lectures in History and Culture, and Other Essays on Science and Confucian Ethics*, Hong Kong: Chinese University Press, 2005, p. 24.
47. Chad Hansen, *A Daoist Theory of Chinese Thought: A Philosophical Interpretation*, New York: Oxford University Press, 2000, p. 22; Stephen C. Angle, *Sagehood: The Contemporary Significance of Neo-Confucian Philosophy*, New York: Oxford University Press, 2009, pp. 41–2; Lent, *The Patterning Instinct*, pp. 264–7.
48. Edward Slingerland, *Trying Not to Try: Ancient China, Modern Science, and the Power of Spontaneity*, New York: Broadway Books, 2014, pp. 14, 59.
49. Ibid. p. 32.
50. Ibid. p. 37; Edward Slingerland, *Effortless Action: Wu-Wei as Conceptual*

Metaphor and Spiritual Ideal in Early China, New York: Oxford University Press, 2003, p. 186, 321n.

51. Mihaly Csikszentmihalyi, *Flow: The Psychology of Optimal Experience*, New York: HarperCollins, 1990, pp. 3–6, 40–64.
52. Lent, *The Patterning Instinct*, pp. 252–3; Heinrich Dumoulin, *Zen Buddhism: A History, Volume I: India and China*, Bloomington, IN: World Wisdom, 2005, pp. 64–8.
53. Ibid.
54. Ibid. pp. 85, 102n; Stephen Batchelor, *The Awakening of the West: The Encounter of Buddhism and Western Culture*, Berkeley, CA: Parallax Press, 1994, p. 212; Alan Watts, *The Way of Zen*, New York: Vintage Books, 1989, p. 88.
55. James H. Austin, *Zen and the Brain*, Cambridge, MA: MIT Press, 1999, pp. 61–2; D. T. Suzuki, *An Introduction to Zen Buddhism*, New York: Grove Press, 1964, pp. 14–34; Kapleau, *The Three Pillars of Zen*, p. 35; Kosho Uchiyama, *Opening the Hand of Thought: Foundations of Zen Buddhist Practice*, Somerville, MA: Wisdom Publications, 2004, p. xxx; Katagiri cited in Steve Hagen, *Buddhism Is Not What You Think: Finding Freedom Beyond Beliefs*, San Francisco: HarperCollins, 2004, p. 251.
56. Dumoulin, *Zen Buddhism*, p. 258; Julia Ching, *The Religious Thought of Chu Hsi*, New York: Oxford University Press, 2000, pp. 13–14. For an online sampling of Zen koans, see: https://thebuddhafultao.wordpress.com/2012/01/29/some-great-koans/
57. Watts, *The Way of Zen*, p. 47; Uchiyama, *Opening the Hand of Thought*, pp. 99–100.
58. Galin, 'The Concepts "Self," "Person," and "I"'; Lent, *The Patterning Instinct*, pp. 165–8.
59. Jon Kabat-Zinn, *Coming to Our Senses: Healing Ourselves and the World through Mindfulness*, New York: Hyperion, 2005, pp. 25–6.
60. Ibid. p. 108–9; Britta K. Hölzel et al., 'How Does Mindfulness Meditation Work? Proposing Mechanisms of Action from a Conceptual and Neural Perspective', *Perspectives on Psychological Science* 6:6, 2011, pp. 537–59.
61. Austin, *Zen and the Brain*, p. 72; Varela, Thompson and Rosch, *The Embodied Mind*, p. 25.
62. Ibid.
63. Glenn Wallis, *Basic Teachings of the Buddha: A New Translation and Compilation, with a Guide to Reading the Texts*, New York: Random House, 2007, p. 120; B. Alan Wallace and Shauna L. Shapiro, 'Mental Balance and Well-Being: Building Bridges between Buddhism and Western Psychology', *American Psychologist* 61:7, 2006, pp. 690–701. It should be noted that the comparison of *dukkha* to *wu-wei*, along with its portrayal as arising from the separation between the 'I' and the 'self', are interpretations arrived at through interweaving the different cultural paradigms of Taoism, Buddhism and modern psychology, and will not be found in traditional teachings of Buddhist practice.
64. Venerable Henepola Gunaratana, *Mindfulness in Plain English*, Somerville,

MA: Wisdom Publications, 1991, pp. 142–50, 190–91; Wallis, *Basic Teachings of the Buddha*, p. 148; J. David Creswell et al., 'Neural Correlates of Dispositional Mindfulness During Affect Labeling', *Psychosomatic Medicine* 69, 2007, pp. 560–65.

65. Nyanaponika Thera, *The Heart of Buddhist Meditation*, San Francisco, CA: Red Wheel/Weiser, 1965, p. 55; J. A. Brefczynski-Lewis et al., 'Neural Correlates of Attentional Expertise in Long-Term Meditation Practitioners', *PNAS* 104:27, 2007, pp. 11483–88; Yi-Yuan Tang and Michael I. Posner, 'Attention Training and Attention State Training', *Trends in Cognitive Sciences* 13:5, 2009, pp. 222–7.

Chapter 4: The Patterns of the Universe

1. Iain McGilchrist, *The Master and His Emissary: The Divided Brain and the Making of the Western World*, New Haven: Yale University Press, 2009, p. 138; Russ Abbott. 'Emergence Explained: Getting Epiphenomena to Do Real Work', Los Angeles, CA: California State University, 2006.
2. Jeremy Lent, *The Patterning Instinct: A Cultural History of Humanity's Search for Meaning*, Amherst, NY: Prometheus, 2017, p. 146; Gregory Vlastos, *Plato's Universe*, Canada: Parmenides Publishing, 2005, pp. 23–4.
3. Lent, *The Patterning Instinct*, pp. 180–6.
4. Ibid. pp. 181–4; Karl R. Lang and Jing Lydia Zhang. 'A Taoist Foundation of Systems Modeling and Thinking' in *Proceedings of the 17th International Conference of the System Dynamics Society and the 5th Australian and New Zealand Systems Conference*, 1999, pp. 20–3.
5. Lent, *The Patterning Instinct*, pp. 185–6; Joseph Needham, *Science and Civilisation in China, Volume 2: History of Scientific Thought*, London: Cambridge University Press, 1972, pp. 288–9.
6. Lent, *The Patterning Instinct*, pp. 252–4. For a valuable discussion of the Buddhist meaning of *dharma*, see The Buddha, *Dhammapada*, transl. Glenn Wallis, New York: Random House, 2004, p. xii.
7. Lent, *The Patterning Instinct*, pp. 251–76.
8. Ibid. pp. 256–8. Given the frequent usage of the terms li and qi, neither word will henceforth be italicized in the interest of ease in reading the text.
9. Ibid. pp. 260–2, 271–2.
10. Ibid. pp. 281–5.
11. Melanie Mitchell, *Complexity: A Guided Tour*, New York: Oxford University Press, 2009, p. ix; Anthony Trewavas, 'A Brief History of Systems Biology', *American Society of Plant Biologists* 18:10, 2006, pp. 2420–30; E. O. Wilson, *Consilience: The Unity of Knowledge*, New York: Vintage Books, 1999, pp. 58–60.
12. Bryan Appleyard, *Understanding the Present: An Alternative History of Science*, New York: Tauris Parke Paperbacks, 2004, p. 64.
13. Steven Weinberg, 'Reductionism Redux', *New York Review of Books* 42:15, 1995.
14. Richard Dawkins, *River Out of Eden: A Darwinian View of Life*, New York: Basic Books, 1995, p. 19; Dawkins, *The Blind Watchmaker*, New York: W. W.

Norton, 1986, p. 158; Francis Crick, *The Astonishing Hypothesis: The Scientific Search for the Soul*, New York: Touchstone, 1994, p. 3.

15. Nicholas Carr, *The Shallows: What the Internet Is Doing to Our Brains*, New York: W. W. Norton, 2011, iBook edn, Chapter 8; Yuval Noah Harari, *Homo Deus: A Brief History of Tomorrow*, New York: HarperCollins, 2017, pp. 85, 327, 343, 366.
16. Steven Weinberg, *The First Three Minutes: A Modern View of the Origin of the Universe*, New York: Basic Books, 1993, p. 154; Weinberg, 'Without God', *New York Review of Books* LV:14, 2008, pp. 73–6.
17. Lent, *The Patterning Instinct*, pp. 30–2, 59–61, 201–4; Daniel J. Simons and Christopher F. Chabris, 'Gorillas in Our Midst: Sustained Inattentional Blindness for Dynamic Events', *Perception* 28, 1999, pp. 1059–74.
18. Ontology is the branch of philosophy concerned with the nature of existence.
19. Fritjof Capra and Pier Luigi Luisi, *The Systems View of Life: A Unifying Vision*, New York: Cambridge University Press, 2014, pp. 74–5; Mario Livio, *Is God a Mathematician?* New York: Simon & Schuster, 2009, p. 216.
20. Nigel Goldenfeld and Leo Kadanoff, 'Simple Lessons from Complexity', *Science* 284, 1999, pp. 87–9; Ilya Prigogine and Isabelle Stengers, *The End of Certainty: Time, Chaos, and the New Laws of Nature*, New York: Free Press, 1996, p. 155.
21. For an excellent and comprehensive introduction to system thinking, I recommend Fritjof Capra and Pier Luigi Luisi, *The Systems View of Life: A Unifying Vision*, New York: Cambridge University Press, 2014. Perhaps the foremost research institute, among many, focusing on the theoretical frontiers of complexity is the Santa Fe Institute in New Mexico. A sampling of peer-reviewed academic journals focusing on complex systems: *BioSystems*; *Advances in Complex Systems*; *Trends in Ecology & Evolution*; and *Complexity*.
22. Russ Abbott, 'The Reductionist Blind Spot', *Complexity* 14:5, 2009, pp. 10–22; Raoul Weiler and Jüri Engelbrecht, 'The New Sciences of Networks & Complexity: A Short Introduction', *Cadmus* 2:1, 2013, pp. 131–41; Trewavas, 'A Brief History'. As I discuss in *The Patterning Instinct*, there was also a commendable Western lineage of systems thinkers after Heraclitus, who were nevertheless outshone by the primary Platonic dualistic tradition that has dominated Western thought. This group of thinkers, which I have called the Moonlight Tradition, includes Aristotle, Stoic and Epicurean philosophers, Leonardo da Vinci, Baruch Spinoza, Gottfried Leibniz, Johann Wolfgang von Goethe, Alfred North Whitehead, Ernst Haeckel and the phenomenological school of European philosophers in the early twentieth century. See Lent, *The Patterning Instinct*, pp. 359–63.
23. Paul Cilliers, *Complexity and Postmodernism: Understanding Complex Systems*, New York: Routledge, 2002, p. 3.
24. Scott Camazine et al., *Self-Organization in Biological Systems*, Princeton, NJ: Princeton University Press, 2001, pp. 47–50; Mitchell, *Complexity*, p. 13; Michael A. Riley, Kevin Shockley and Guy Van Orden, 'Learning from the Body About the Mind', *Topics in Cognitive Science* 4, 2012, pp. 21–34.

25. Lent, *The Patterning Instinct*, pp. 357–8; Edward Ott, 'Edward N. Lorenz (1917–2008)', *Nature* 453, 2008, p. 300; Leon Glass, 'Synchronization and Rhythmic Processes in Physiology', *Nature* 410, 2001, pp. 277–84; Goldenfeld and Kadanoff, 'Simple Lessons from Complexity'.
26. Lent, *The Patterning Instinct*, pp. 279–90.
27. Irving R. Epstein, 'Anatol Zhabotinsky (1938–2008)', *Nature* 455, 2008, p. 1053; Mae-Wan Ho, 'The Integration of Science with Human Experience', *Leonardo* 24:5, 1991, pp. 607–15; Brian Goodwin, *How the Leopard Changed Its Spots: The Evolution of Complexity*, Princeton, NJ: Princeton University Press, 2001, pp. 42–59.
28. William C. Graham, 'Patterns: The Art, Soul, and Science of Beholding Nature', www.FreshVista.com, 2009; David Wade, *Li: Dynamic Form in Nature*, New York: Walker & Co., 2003; Philip Ball, *Patterns in Nature: Why the Natural World Looks the Way It Does*, Chicago, IL: University of Chicago Press, 2016.
29. Roger Lewin, *Complexity: Life at the Edge of Chaos*, Chicago, IL: University of Chicago Press, 1999, pp. 190–1; D. J. T. Sumpter, 'The Principles of Collective Animal Behaviour', *Philosophical Transactions of the Royal Society* B 361, 2006, pp. 5–22; Ricard Solé and Brian Goodwin, *Signs of Life: How Complexity Pervades Biology*, New York: Basic Books, 2000, pp. 286–303; Weiler and Engelbrecht, 'The New Sciences'.
30. Joanna Macy, *Mutual Causality in Buddhism and General Systems Theory: The Dharma of Natural Systems*, Albany, NY: SUNY Press, 1991, p. 73.
31. Capra and Luisi, *The Systems View of Life*, pp. 108–13; Donald S. Coffey, 'Self-Organization, Complexity, and Chaos: The New Biology for Medicine', *Nature Medicine* 4:8, 1998, pp. 882–5; J. A. Scott Kelso, *Dynamic Patterns: The Self-Organization of Brain and Behavior*, Cambridge, MA: MIT Press, 1995, pp. 53–4.
32. James Gleick, *Chaos: Making a New Science*, New York: Penguin, 1987, pp. 137–53.
33. Lao Tzu, *Tao Te Ching*, transl. Ellen M. Chen, St Paul, MN: Paragon House, 1989, pp. 116–18.
34. Kelso, *Dynamic Patterns*, pp. 53–4; Camazine et al., *Self-Organization in Biological Systems*, p. 34; Michael Silberstein and John McGeever, 'The Search for Ontological Emergence', *Philosophical Quarterly* 49:195, 1999, pp. 182–200.
35. The original meaning of 'phase transition' is the simpler kind of transformation that happens when ice melts or water boils. This term was then applied by broad analogy to the non-equilibrium transitions of complex systems. A more general term used for such transitions is 'bifurcation' – a branching to a new state (Stephen Morris – personal communication).
36. Marten Scheffer et al., 'Early-Warning Signals for Critical Transitions', *Nature* 461, 2009, pp. 53–9; Marten Scheffer, *Critical Transitions in Nature and Society*, Princeton, NJ: Princeton University Press, 2009; David A. Perry, 'Self-Organizing Systems across Scales', *Trends in Ecology & Evolution* 10:6,

1995, pp. 241–4; Per Bak, *How Nature Works: The Science of Self-Organized Criticality*, New York: Springer-Verlag, 1996.

37. Thierry Mora and William Bialek, 'Are Biological Systems Poised at Criticality?' *Journal of Statistical Physics* 144, 2011, pp. 268–302; W. Steffen et al., 'Trajectories of the Earth System in the Anthropocene', *PNAS* 115:33, 2018, pp. 8252–9; Timothy M. Lenton et al., 'Tipping Elements in the Earth's Climate System', *PNAS* 105:6, 2008, pp. 1786–93.
38. M. D. Mesarovic, S. N. Sreenath and J. D. Keene, 'Search for Organising Principles: Understanding in Systems Biology', *Systems Biology* 1:1, June 2004, pp. 19–27; Lewin, *Complexity*, p. 175; Capra and Luisi, *The Systems View of Life*, pp. 154–7.
39. Sumpter, 'The Principles of Collective Animal Behaviour'.
40. Anna C. Balazs and Irving R. Epstein, 'Emergent or Just Complex?' *Science* 325, 2009, pp. 1632–4; Jonathan R. Nitschke, 'Molecular Networks Come of Age', *Nature* 462, 2009, pp. 736–8; Camazine et al., *Self-Organization in Biological Systems*, p. 91; Solé and Goodwin, *Signs of Life*, pp. ix–x; Silberstein and McGeever, 'The Search for Ontological Emergence'.
41. Gleick, *Chaos*, pp. 53–6.
42. Humberto R. Maturana and Francisco J. Varela, *The Tree of Knowledge: The Biological Roots of Human Understanding*, Boston: Shambhala, 1987, pp. 47–52; Stuart Kauffman, *At Home in the Universe: The Search for Laws of Self-Organization and Complexity*, New York: Oxford University Press, 1995, p. 24; Lynn Margulis and Dorion Sagan, *Microcosmos: Four Billion Years of Microbial Evolution*, Berkeley, CA: University of California Press, 1997, pp. 49–56; Solé and Goodwin, *Signs of Life*, pp. 224–33; Capra and Luisi, *The Systems View of Life*, p. 138.
43. Evan Thompson and Francisco J. Varela, 'Radical Embodiment: Neural Dynamics and Consciousness', *Trends in Cognitive Sciences* 5:10, 2001, pp. 418–25; Evan Thompson, *Mind in Life: Biology, Phenomenology, and the Sciences of Mind*, Cambridge, MA: Harvard University Press, 2007, pp. 64–5.
44. Mae-Wan Ho, *The Rainbow and the Worm: The Physics of Organisms*, Singapore: World Scientific Publishing, 2008, p. 6.
45. Carl R. Woese, 'A New Biology for a New Century', *Microbiology and Molecular Biology Reviews* 68, 2004, pp. 173–86.
46. Capra and Luisi, *The Systems View of Life*, pp. 116–26; Gleick, *Chaos*, pp. 81–118; Geoffrey West, *Scale: The Universal Laws of Life, Growth, and Death in Organisms, Cities, and Companies*, New York: Penguin, 2017, p. 154; Mark Fischetti, 'Great Literature Is Surprisingly Arithmetic', *Scientific American*, 1 February 2017; Kenneth J. Hsü and Andrew Hsü, 'Self-Similarity of the "1/F Noise" Called Music', *PNAS* 88, 1991, pp. 3507–9.
47. Capra and Luisi, *The Systems View of Life*, p. 116.
48. Macy, *Mutual Causality*, pp. 166–7.
49. Bak, *How Nature Works*; György Buzsáki, *Rhythms of the Brain*, New York: Oxford University Press, 2006; Graham, 'Patterns', p. 40; Per Bak and Kim Sneppen, 'Punctuated Equilibrium and Criticality in a Simple Model

of Evolution', *Physical Review Letters* 71:24, 1993, pp. 4083–6. Prominent complexity scientist Geoffrey West has demonstrated universal laws of scale with power law distributions in organisms, cities, economies and companies. One astonishing finding West reports, among many others, is that the number of heartbeats in a lifespan is roughly the same for all mammals, from mice to elephants (roughly 1.5 billion), as a function of the scaling laws his team has uncovered. See West, *Scale*, pp. 2–3.

50. Weiler and Engelbrecht, 'The New Sciences'; Trewavas, 'A Brief History'; Kevin J. Beiler et al., 'Architecture of the Wood-Wide Web: Rhizopogon Spp. Genets Link Multiple Douglas-Fir Cohorts', *New Phytologist* 185, 2010, pp. 543–53.
51. Nicholas A. Christakis and James H. Fowler, *Connected: The Surprising Power of Our Social Networks and How They Shape Our Lives*, New York: Little, Brown & Co., 2009, pp. 27–8, 111–16.
52. Arthur Koestler, *Janus: A Summing Up*, New York: Random House, 1978, p. 27; Mesarovic et al., 'Search for Organising Principles'; Margulis and Sagan, *Microcosmos*, p. 247; Fritjof Capra, *The Turning Point: Science, Society, and the Rising Culture*, New York: Bantam Books, 1988, pp. 43, 280.
53. Kauffman, *At Home in the Universe*, pp. 185–6.
54. Lent, *The Patterning Instinct*, pp. 262–3.
55. Stephen Batchelor, *The Awakening of the West: The Encounter of Buddhism and Western Culture*, Berkeley, CA: Parallax Press, 1994, p. 176.
56. Andreas Weber, *Enlivenment: Towards a Fundamental Shift in the Concepts of Nature, Culture and Politics*, Berlin: Heinrich Böll Foundation, 2013, p. 11; Jeff Tollefson, 'The Sun Dimmers', *Nature* 563, 2018, pp. 613–15; Rachael Lallensack, 'Could This Pollinating Drone Replace Butterflies and Bees?' *Science*, 2017, http://tinyurl.com/yx9tpvlu
57. Lent, *The Patterning Instinct*, p. 264; Goodwin, *How the Leopard Changed Its Spots*, pp. xvi–xvii; Ho, *The Rainbow and the Worm*, pp. 314–15. After embracing systems thinking, Nobel laureate Roger Sperry called for a change in the 'very nature of science itself' to reflect these new principles. See Roger W. Sperry, 'Changing Priorities', *Annual Review of Neuroscience* 4, 1981, pp. 1–15.
58. Thomas S. Kuhn, *The Structure of Scientific Revolutions*, Chicago, IL: University of Chicago Press, 1996, pp. 151–2.
59. Chengzhou He, 'New Confucianism, Science and the Future of the Environment', *European Review* 26:2, 2018, pp. 368–80.
60. Kauffman, *At Home in the Universe*, pp. 4–5; Lent, *The Patterning Instinct*, pp. 262–3.
61. Gregory Bateson, *Mind and Nature: A Necessary Unity*, Cresskill, NJ: Hampton Press, 2002, pp. 7, 10; Wing-tsit Chan, 'Neo-Confucianism and Chinese Scientific Thought', *Philosophy East and West* 6:4, 1957, pp. 309–32.
62. Capra and Luisi, *The Systems View of Life*, p. 87.
63. Lent, *The Patterning Instinct*, pp. 183–6; John Muir, *My First Summer in the Sierra*, Boston: Houghton Mifflin, 1911, p. 211.
64. Thích Nhât Hanh, *The Heart of Understanding: Commentaries on the Prajnaparamita Heart Sutra*, Berkeley, CA: Parallax Press, 2009, pp. 3–4.

65. Einstein quoted in Matthieu Ricard and Trinh Xuan Thuan, *The Quantum and the Lotus*, New York: Three Rivers Press, 2001, p. 50.
66. William Wordsworth, 'Lines Written a Few Miles above Tintern Abbey' in *Lyrical Ballads*, London: J. & A. Arch, 1798.
67. Lent, *The Patterning Instinct*, pp. 386–8.
68. Macy, *Mutual Causality*, pp. xii–xiii.
69. Quoted in Ricard and Thuan, *The Quantum and the Lotus*, p. 72.
70. Fritjof Capra, *The Web of Life: A New Scientific Understanding of Living Systems*, New York: Anchor Books, 1996, pp. 287–8.

Chapter 5: The Harmonic Dance of Life

1. Oliver Stone, *Wall Street* (20th Century Fox, 1987); Peter Turchin, 'Selfish Genes Made Me Do It! (Part I)', Evolution Institute blog, 4 December 2013.
2. Richard Dawkins, *The Selfish Gene: 30th Anniversary Edition*, London: Oxford University Press, 2006, p. 2; Jerry Bergman, 'Darwin's Influence on Ruthless Laissez-Faire Capitalism', *Impact* 333, 2001.
3. Ghiselin quoted in Mary Midgley, *Evolution as a Religion: Strange Hopes and Stranger Fears*, London: Routledge, 2002, p. 3.
4. Frans de Waal, 'How Bad Biology Killed the Economy', *RSA Journal*, 23 March 2010; Turchin, 'Selfish Genes'. Dawkins himself has made an explicit connection between biology and economics, writing, 'Within any one species of animals or plants, the individuals that survive best are the ones that can exploit the other animals and plants, bacteria and fungi that are already flourishing in the environment. As Adam Smith understood long ago, an illusion of harmony and real efficiency will emerge in an economy dominated by self-interest at a lower level. A well balanced ecosystem is an economy, not an adaptation.' See Richard Dawkins, *A Devil's Chaplain: Reflections on Hope, Lies, Science and Love*, Boston, MA: Houghton Mifflin, 2003, pp. 225–6.
5. Midgley, *Evolution as a Religion*, p. 154; Richard Lewontin, 'Why Darwin?' *New York Review of Books* LVI:9, 2009, pp. 19–22. In one illuminating example of how this myth imbues popular thinking, respected social psychologist Jonathan Haidt discussed in a 2016 podcast how reading *The Selfish Gene* in college 'blew my mind', and then nearly three decades later, when researching the rationale for free-market capitalism, he 'had the same experience that I had reading Richard Dawkins'. He goes on to explain how this understanding has since infused his political and economic thinking. (Jonathan Haidt and Melvin Konner, 'Capitalism and Moral Evolution: A Civil Provocation' in *On Being*, podcast ed. Krista Tippett, 2016.) I have written more extensively on this topic in an open letter to Jerry Coyne, an avowed defender of Dawkins, in Jeremy Lent, 'Beyond Reductionism? An Open Letter in Response to Jerry Coyne', Patterns of Meaning blog, 10 August 2017.

   It should be noted, as discussed in more detail in Chapter 9, that Dawkins himself states clearly that his description of the gene's selfishness in no way justifies a moral code of selfishness. 'Be warned,' he writes, 'that if you wish, as I do, to build a society towards a common good, you can expect little help from biological nature.' Rather, Dawkins sees humans as being in a state of constant battle with their own genetic make-up. 'Our brains,' he suggests, 'have evolved to the point where we are capable of rebelling against our selfish genes.' Dawkins thus proffers the image of a human as a battleground between the 'state of nature' (our selfish genes) and our moral conscience. As discussed in Chapter 3, '"I think, therefore I am"', this approach implicitly endorses the dualistic view of human nature inherited from the Christian/Platonic European tradition, which has been refuted by decades of research in cognitive science. See Chapter 9 for a more detailed discussion of this crucial theme.

6. E. O. Wilson, *Sociobiology: The New Synthesis*, Cambridge, MA: Belknap Press, 1975, p. 3; Dawkins, *The Selfish Gene*, pp. 19–20.
7. Chapter 4, 'The interconnected web of *dharma* and Tao'; Jeremy Lent, *The Patterning Instinct: A Cultural History of Humanity's Search for Meaning*, Amherst, NY: Prometheus, 2017, pp. 83–99, 179–96.
8. It should be emphasized that, while each of the major assumptions of the selfish gene story has been overturned, the validity of much of the Modern Synthesis (as described on p. 125) continues to hold, albeit in a more limited context than is usually portrayed. The major tenets of the selfish gene narrative may be delineated as follows: 1) genes are the sole drivers of an organism's phenotype; 2) the directionality of control between gene and organism is one way; 3) evolution is driven by genes alone; 4) the gene is fundamentally 'selfish' and this selfishness has been the predominant driver of evolution. As the rest of the chapter explains, each of these four tenets has been shown to be false.
9. David J. Depew and Bruce H. Weber, *Darwinism Evolving: Systems Dynamics and the Genealogy of Natural Selection*, Cambridge, MA: MIT Press, 1996, pp. 78–82, 115–21; Stephen Jay Gould, 'Darwinism and the Expansion of Evolutionary Theory', *Science* 216:4544, 1982, pp. 380–7; Mary Midgley, 'Hobbes's Leviathan, Part 3: What Is Selfishness?' *Guardian*, 20 April 2009.
10. Charles Darwin, *On the Origin of Species by Means of Natural Selection*, London: John Murray, 1859, pp. 489–90. Darwin himself notes the direct influence of Malthus on his theory, writing, 'It is the doctrine of Malthus applied with manifold force to the whole animal and vegetable kingdoms' (*Origin of Species*, p. 63). See Eva Jablonka and Marion J. Lamb, 'Précis of Evolution in Four Dimensions', *Behavioral and Brain Sciences* 30:4, 2007, pp. 353–92. The phrase 'survival of the fittest' was first used by Herbert Spencer, and adopted by Darwin in later editions of *Origin of Species*.
11. Depew and Weber, *Darwinism Evolving*, pp. 5–6, 187–91, 217–24; Jablonka and Lamb, 'Précis of Evolution'; Gould, 'Darwinism'; Michael Skinner, 'Unified Theory of Evolution', *Aeon*, 9 November 2016; Kevin N. Laland, 'Evolution Evolves: Beyond the Selfish Gene', *New Scientist* 3092, 2016.
12. Depew and Weber, *Darwinism Evolving*, pp. 299–329; Jablonka and Lamb, 'Précis of Evolution'; Elizabeth Pennisi, 'Modernizing the Modern Synthesis', *Science* 321, 2008, pp. 196–7; Kevin N. Laland et al., 'The Extended Evolutionary Synthesis: Its Structure, Assumptions and Predictions', *Proceedings of the Royal Society* B 282, 2015, p. 1019.

13. Richard C. Strohman, 'The Coming Kuhnian Revolution in Biology', *Nature Biotechnology* 15, 1997, pp. 194–200; Carl R. Woese, 'A New Biology for a New Century', *Microbiology and Molecular Biology Reviews* 68, 2004, pp. 173–86; Dorothy Nelkin, 'Molecular Metaphors: The Gene in Popular Discourse', *Nature Reviews Genetics* 2, 2001, pp. 555–9.
14. Adam M. Hedgecoe, 'Transforming Genes: Metaphors of Information and Language in Modern Genetics', *Science as Culture* 8:2, 1999, pp. 209–29; Nelkin, 'Molecular Metaphors'.
15. Bradon Smith, 'The Price of Metaphor Is Eternal Vigilance: Language Metaphors in Popular Genetics', *International Journal of the Humanities* 6:10, 2009, pp. 79–86; Jablonka and Lamb, 'Précis of Evolution'; Nelkin, 'Molecular Metaphors'; Hedgecoe, 'Transforming Genes'.
16. Richard C. Lewontin, 'The Dream of the Human Genome', *New York Review of Books* 39:10, 1992; Nelkin, 'Molecular Metaphors'; Hedgecoe, 'Transforming Genes'; Strohman, 'The Coming Kuhnian Revolution'.
17. Michael P. H. Stumpf et al., 'Estimating the Size of the Human Interactome', *PNAS* 105:19, 2008, pp. 6959–64; Nigel Goldenfeld and Carl Woese, 'Life Is Physics: Evolution as a Collective Phenomenon Far from Equilibrium', *Annual Review of Condensed Matter Physics* 2, 2011, pp. 375–99; Marc W. Kirschner, 'The Meaning of Systems Biology', *Cell* 121, 2005, pp. 503–4; Ron Milo and Rob Phillips, *Cell Biology by the Numbers* (draft), Garland Science, 2015.
18. Chapter 4, 'Emergent life'; Strohman, 'The Coming Kuhnian Revolution'; Goldenfeld and Woese, 'Life Is Physics'.
19. James A. Shapiro, *Evolution: A View from the 21st Century*, Upper Saddle River, NJ: FT Press, 2011, Kindle edn, locations 713–30; Jamie A. Davies, *Life Unfolding: How the Human Body Creates Itself*, New York: Oxford University Press, 2014, pp. 8–13; Luis A. Nunes Amaral, 'A Truer Measure of Our Ignorance', *PNAS* 105:19, 2008, pp. 6795–6; Helen Pearson, 'What Is a Gene?' *Nature* 441, 2006, pp. 399–401; Evan Thompson, *Mind in Life: Biology, Phenomenology, and the Sciences of Mind*, Cambridge, MA: Harvard University Press, 2007, pp. 54–7, 178–9; Woese, 'A New Biology'; Jablonka and Lamb, 'Précis of Evolution'; Milo and Phillips, *Cell Biology*, pp. 141–4.
20. Shapiro, *Evolution*, Kindle edn, locations 1026–631; Stephen L. Talbott, 'Evolution and the Purposes of Life', *New Atlantis*, winter 2017, pp. 63–91; Robert M. Sapolsky, *Behave: The Biology of Humans at Our Best and Worst*, New York: Penguin, 2017, p. 248.
21. Hedgecoe, 'Transforming Genes'; Smith, 'The Price of Metaphor'.
22. David Dobbs, 'Die, Selfish Gene, Die', *Aeon*, 3 December 2013.
23. Ibid.; Elizabeth Pennisi, 'Buying Time', *Science* 362:6418, 2018, pp. 988–91.
24. Sonia Sultan, 'Developmental Plasticity: Re-Conceiving the Genotype', *Interface Focus* 7, 2017, 0009.
25. Scientists have developed a coherent theory for how this process, which they call genetic assimilation, can occur. If a species encounters major environmental change, those individuals more effective at creative gene expression will adapt their phenotypes more successfully, and will flourish. In this new environment

the genes that encouraged their adaptive behavior (such as root growth in plants) will become more important to future generations. Now, any future genetic mutations that encourage faster root growth will get 'locked in' to the genome and become part of that plant's genetic heritage. See Sultan, 'Developmental Plasticity'; Dobbs, 'Die, Selfish Gene'; Laland et al., 'The Extended Evolutionary Synthesis', p. 1019.

26. Pennisi, 'Buying Time'; Skinner, 'Unified Theory'; Jablonka and Lamb 'Précis of Evolution'.
27. Jablonka and Lamb, 'Précis of Evolution'; Laland et al., 'The Extended Evolutionary Synthesis'; Massimo Pigliucci, 'Do We Need an Extended Evolutionary Synthesis?' *Evolution* 61:12, 2007, pp. 2743–9; Pennisi, 'Modernizing the Modern Synthesis'. For anyone interested in conducting their own direct investigation into the Extended Evolutionary Synthesis, I recommend the themed issue of *Interface Focus*, a Royal Society publication, 'New Trends in Evolutionary Biology: Biological, Philosophical and Social Science Perspectives', which contains a broad cross-section of articles from many leading figures in the movement, including Kevin Laland, Eva Jablonka, Denis Noble, John Odling-Smee and James Shapiro (*Interface Focus* 7:5, 6 October 2017).
28. Laland, 'Evolution Evolves'; Darwin, *Origin of Species*, p. 6.
29. Eva Jablonka, 'The Evolutionary Implications of Epigenetic Inheritance', *Interface Focus* 7, 2017, 0135; Laland, 'Evolution Evolves'; Skinner, 'Unified Theory'.
30. Fascinating examples abound of epigenetic inheritance. In one experiment mice were given electric shocks every time they ate almonds, and naturally developed a fear of the smell. In contravention of the Modern Synthesis, their children and grandchildren spontaneously feared the same smell. Researchers discovered an epigenetic marker transmitted through their sperm that triggered this fear. In another study worms that were exposed to a nasty virus developed a chemical response that protected them; subsequent generations inherited this resistance through RNA they received from their parents. See Kevin Laland, 'Evolution Unleashed', *Aeon*, 17 January 2018; Skinner, 'Unified Theory'.
31. Andrew Whiten, 'A Second Inheritance System: The Extension of Biology through Culture', *Interface Focus* 7, 2017, 0142; Carolyn Beans, 'Can Animal Culture Drive Evolution?' *PNAS* 114:30, 2017, pp. 7734–7.
32. F. John Odling-Smee, Kevin N. Laland and Marcus W. Feldman, 'Niche Construction', *American Naturalist* 147:4, 1996, pp. 641–8; Kevin Laland, John Odling-Smee and John Endler, 'Niche Construction, Sources of Selection and Trait Coevolution', *Interface Focus* 7, 2017, 0147; Kevin N. Laland, F. John Odling-Smee and Marcus W. Feldman, 'Evolutionary Consequences of Niche Construction and Their Implications for Ecology', *PNAS* 96, 1999, pp. 10242–7; Darwin quoted in Eileen Crist, 'Intimations of Gaia' in *Gaia in Turmoil: Climate Change, Biodepletion, and Earth Ethics in an Age of Crisis*, ed. Eileen Crist and H. Bruce Rinker, Cambridge, MA: MIT Press, 2010.
33. Holly C. Betts et al., 'Integrated Genomic and Fossil Evidence Illuminates Life's

Early Evolution and Eukaryote Origin', *Nature Ecology & Evolution* 2, 2018, pp. 1556–62. In addition to bacteria, there is another group of prokaryotes, called archaea, which was first classified by Carl Woese in 1990. See Nick Lane, *The Vital Question: Energy, Evolution, and the Origins of Complex Life*, New York: W. W. Norton, 2016, pp. 7–8.

34. Carl Zimmer, 'On the Origin of Eukaryotes,' *Science* 325, 2009, pp. 666–8.
35. Lynn Margulis and Dorion Sagan, *Microcosmos: Four Billion Years of Microbial Evolution*, Berkeley, CA: University of California Press, 1997, pp. 31, 118–19. It should be noted that there is an ongoing debate over whether or not phagocytosis (the ingestion of single cells) occurred before the endosymbiosis of mitochondria. See Eörs Szathmáry, 'Toward Major Evolutionary Transitions Theory 2.0', *PNAS* 112:33, 2015, pp. 10104–11. Additionally, Nick Lane has recently proffered a theory that, prior to endosymbiosis, mitochondria were archaea, not bacteria. See Lane, *The Vital Question*, pp. 159–67.
36. John M. Archibald, 'Lynn Margulis (1938–2011)', *Current Biology* 22:1, 2012, R4–R6; Zimmer, 'Origin of Eukaryotes'; Franklin M. Harold, *The Way of the Cell: Molecules, Organisms and the Order of Life*, New York: Oxford University Press, 2001, Kindle edn, locations 2242–7. While Margulis is famously associated with the idea of endosymbiosis, she openly acknowledged the earlier work on this theory by biologists Ivan Wallin and Boris Kozo-Polyansky.
37. Lane, *The Vital Question*, pp. 170–80; Harold, *The Way of the Cell*, Kindle edn, locations 1537–44, 2058–9.
38. Olga Zhaxybayeva and W. Ford Doolittle, 'Lateral Gene Transfer', *Current Biology* 21:7, 2011, R242–246; Nancy A. Moran, 'Symbiosis as an Adaptive Process and Source of Phenotypic Complexity', *PNAS* 104, 2007, pp. 8627–33.
39. Lane, *The Vital Question*, pp. 157–8; Harold, *The Way of the Cell*, Kindle edn, locations 1537–44, 2066–76, 2626–8; Fritjof Capra and Pier Luigi Luisi, *The Systems View of Life: A Unifying Vision*, New York: Cambridge University Press, 2014, p. 119.
40. Goldenfeld and Woese, 'Life Is Physics'; Margulis and Sagan, *Microcosmos*, pp. 89–93; Moran, 'Symbiosis'; Chapter 2, 'The "mind" of a cell'.
41. Carl R. Woese, 'On the Evolution of Cells', *PNAS* 99:13, 2002, pp. 8742–7; James A. Lake, 'Evidence for an Early Prokaryotic Endosymbiosis', *Nature* 460, 2009, pp. 967–71; Maria C. Rivera and James A. Lake, 'The Ring of Life Provides Evidence for a Genome Fusion Origin of Eukaryotes', *Nature* 431, 2004, pp. 152–5; W. Ford Doolittle, 'Phylogenetic Classification and the Universal Tree', *Science* 284, 1999, pp. 2124–8; Stephen Jay Gould, *Wonderful Life: The Burgess Shale and the Nature of History*, New York: W. W. Norton, 1990, p. 38fn.; Woese, 'A New Biology'; Margulis and Sagan, *Microcosmos*, p. 29.
42. Woese, 'Evolution of Cells'; Doolittle, 'Phylogenetic Classification'; Goldenfeld and Woese, 'Life Is Physics'.
43. Jeff Hecht, 'Why Did Evolution Stall During the "Boring Billion"?' *New Scientist* 2967, 2014.
44. Elizabeth Pennisi, 'The Power of Many', *Science* 360:6396, 2018, pp. 1388–91.
45. Eva Jablonka and Marion J. Lamb, 'The Evolution of Information in the Major

Transitions', *Journal of Theoretical Biology* 239, 2006, pp. 236–46; Szathmáry, 'Major Evolutionary Transitions'; Davies, *Life Unfolding*, pp. 145–6.

46. Margaret McFall-Ngai et al., 'Animals in a Bacterial World, a New Imperative for the Life Sciences', *PNAS* 9, 2013, pp. 3229–36; John F. Bruno, John J. Stachowicz and Mark D. Bertness, 'Inclusion of Facilitation into Ecological Theory', *Trends in Ecology & Evolution* 18:3, 2003, pp. 119–25; Andreas Weber, *The Biology of Wonder: Aliveness, Feeling, and the Metamorphosis of Science*, Gabriola Island, BC, Canada: New Society Publishers, 2016, pp. 260–1; Margulis and Sagan, *Microcosmos*, pp. 123–4. Symbiosis as a biological term refers generally to any intimate and long-standing relationship between two different kinds of organisms, including parasitism in which the parasite benefits while the host is harmed, and commensalism where one organism benefits while the other is unaffected. Here, I am referring specifically to the most common form of symbiosis – mutualism – where both organisms benefit from the relationship.
47. Bruce H. Weber et al., 'Evolution in Thermodynamic Perspective: An Ecological Approach', *Biology and Philosophy* 4, 1989, pp. 373–405; Mae-Wan Ho, *The Rainbow and the Worm: The Physics of Organisms*, Singapore: World Scientific Publishing, 2008, iBook edn, Chapter 4; Tamir Klein, Rolf T. W. Siegwolf and Christian Körner, 'Below-ground Carbon Trade among Tall Trees in a Temperate Forest', *Science* 352:6283, 2016, pp. 342–4; Matthew D. Whiteside, 'Mycorrhizal Fungi Respond to Resource Inequality by Moving Phosphorus from Rich to Poor Patches across Networks', *Current Biology* 29, 2019, pp. 2043–50; McFall-Ngai et al., 'Animals in a Bacterial World'.
48. Robin Wall Kimmerer, *Braiding Sweetgrass: Indigenous Wisdom, Scientific Knowledge and the Teachings of Plants*, Minneapolis: Milkweed Editions, 2013, p. 164.
49. Davies, *Life Unfolding*, pp. 208–11; Joan Roughgarden et al., 'Holobionts as Units of Selection and a Model of Their Population Dynamics and Evolution', *Biological Theory* 13:1, 2018, pp. 44–65.
50. John Travis, 'On the Origin of the Immune System', *Science* 324, 2009, pp. 580–2; Davies, *Life Unfolding*, pp. 208–11; Roughgarden et al., 'Holobionts'; McFall-Ngai et al., 'Animals in a Bacterial World'.
51. Kimmerer, *Braiding Sweetgrass*, pp. 269–71; Weber, *The Biology of Wonder*, p. 281.
52. Stuart A. West and E. Toby Kiers, 'Evolution: What Is an Organism?' *Current Biology* 19:23, 2009, R1080–1082; Samuel L. Díaz-Muñoz et al., 'Contextual Organismality: Beyond Pattern to Process in the Emergence of Organisms', *Evolution* 70:12, 2016, pp. 2669–77; Henri J. Folse III and Joan Roughgarden, 'What Is an Individual Organism? A Multilevel Selection Perspective', *Quarterly Review of Biology* 85:4, 2010, pp. 447–72; Lane, *The Vital Question*, p. 247.
53. David Sloan Wilson and Edward O. Wilson, 'Rethinking the Theoretical Foundation of Sociobiology', *Quarterly Review of Biology* 82:4, 2007, pp. 327–48; Depew and Weber, *Darwinism Evolving*, p. 382.

54. Wilson and Wilson, 'Rethinking'; Per Bak and Kim Sneppen, 'Punctuated Equilibrium and Criticality in a Simple Model of Evolution', *Physical Review Letters* 71:24, 1993, pp. 4083–6; D. J. T. Sumpter, 'The Principles of Collective Animal Behaviour', *Philosophical Transactions of the Royal Society* B 361, 2006, pp. 5–22.
55. Folse and Roughgarden, 'What Is an Individual Organism?'; Kimmerer, *Braiding Sweetgrass*, pp. 14–16; John Briggs and F. David Peat, *Seven Life Lessons of Chaos: Spiritual Wisdom from the Science of Change*, Harper Perennial, 2000, iBook edn, Chapter 3; Ed Yong, 'Microbes Have No Morals', *Aeon*, 4 August 2016; Goldenfeld and Woese, 'Life Is Physics'.
56. Lent, *The Patterning Instinct*, pp. 27–30, 197–204, 277–8.
57. Ibid. pp. 281–5; Richard Dawkins, *The Blind Watchmaker*, New York: W. W. Norton, 1986, p. 111; Steven Rose, *Lifelines: Life Beyond the Gene*, New York: Oxford University Press, 1997.
58. Jay Keasling, quoted in Eleonore Pauwels, 'Mind the Metaphor', *Nature* 500, 2013, pp. 523–4.
59. Leda Cosmides and John Tooby, 'Evolutionary Psychology: A Primer' in *Center for Evolutionary Psychology, UCSB*, Santa Barbara, 2006.
60. Antonio Damasio, *The Strange Order of Things: Life, Feeling, and the Making of Cultures*, New York: Pantheon, 2018, pp. 200–1.
61. Lent, *The Patterning Instinct*, pp. 423–6. Tegmark's proposal for ethical guidelines specifies consciousness as a paramount value, but based on the assumption that life is substrate independent, he makes no ethical distinction between the hypothetical consciousness of a super-intelligent AI system and a living entity. As a result, future ethical guidelines might judge a non-living AI system to be of greater intrinsic worth than a living organism. Max Tegmark, *Life 3.0: Being Human in the Age of Artificial Intelligence*, New York: Alfred A. Knopf, 2017, pp. 24–30, 269–79, 299–313.
62. Daniel Cossins, 'Brainless Fungi Trade Resources with Plants Like a Stock Market', *New Scientist* 3234, 2019.
63. Kimmerer, *Braiding Sweetgrass*, pp. 29–30.
64. Denis Noble, *The Music of Life: Biology Beyond Genes*, Oxford: Oxford University Press, 2006, p. 43; Ursula Goodenough, *The Sacred Depths of Nature*, New York: Oxford University Press, 1998, pp. 58–9; Boyce Rensberger, *Life Itself: Exploring the Realm of the Living Cell*, New York: Oxford University Press, 1996, p. 93. It should be noted that each of these biologists recognizes the fact that the 'symphony' of the cell has no conductor and explains the cell's self-organization in detail.
65. Ho, *The Rainbow and the Worm*, Chapter 9.
66. Brian Goodwin, *How the Leopard Changed Its Spots: The Evolution of Complexity*, Princeton, NJ: Princeton University Press, 2001; Thompson, *Mind in Life*, p. 204; Talbott, 'Evolution and the Purposes of Life'. Goethe cited in Ho, *The Rainbow and the Worm*, Chapter 4.
67. Ho, *The Rainbow and the Worm*, p. 94.
68. Chapter 13, 'Envisioning an ecological civilization'; Capra and Luisi, *The*

Systems View of Life, pp. 353–6; Jeremy Lent, 'We Need an Ecological Civilization Before It's Too Late', Patterns of Meaning blog, 10 October 2018.

Chapter 6: The Deep Purpose of Life

1. David C. Lindberg, *The Beginnings of Western Science: The European Scientific Tradition in Philosophical, Religious, and Institutional Context, Prehistory to A.D. 1450*, Chicago, IL: University of Chicago Press, 2007, p. 64; J. L. Ackrill, *Aristotle the Philosopher*, Oxford: Clarendon Press, 1981.
2. Ibid. pp. 41–5; Joe Sachs, *Aristotle's Physics: A Guided Study*, New Brunswick: Rutgers University Press, 1995, pp. 245; Terrence W. Deacon, *Incomplete Nature: How Mind Emerged from Matter*, New York: W. W. Norton, 2011, iBook edn, Chapter 2; David J. Depew and Bruce H. Weber, *Darwinism Evolving: Systems Dynamics and the Genealogy of Natural Selection*, Cambridge, MA: MIT Press, 1996, pp. 40–1; Stephen L. Talbott, 'Evolution and the Purposes of Life', *New Atlantis*, winter 2017, pp. 63–91.
3. Jeremy Lent, *The Patterning Instinct: A Cultural History of Humanity's Search for Meaning*, Amherst, NY: Prometheus, 2017, pp. 84–8, 113–14.
4. Yu Huan Zhang and Ken Rose, *Who Can Ride the Dragon? An Exploration of the Cultural Roots of Traditional Chinese Medicine*, Taos, New Mexico: Paradigm Publications, 1995, pp. 69–70.
5. Chapter 2; Chapter 4, 'A "pointless" universe'; Lent, *The Patterning Instinct*, pp. 281–5.
6. Depew and Weber, *Darwinism Evolving*, pp. 175–6; Deacon, *Incomplete Nature*, Chapter 2; Arthur Koestler, *Janus: A Summing Up*, New York: Random House, 1978, pp. 223–5.
7. See Chapter 5, 'Decoding the "book of life"', 'The language of the gene'; Ernst Mayr, 'The Idea of Teleology', *Journal of the History of Ideas* 53:1, 1992, pp. 117–35; Talbott, 'Evolution and the Purposes of Life'.
8. Peter N. Kugler et al., 'Inquiry into Intentional Systems I: Issues in Ecological Physics', *Psychological Research* 52, 1990, pp. 98–121; Stuart Kauffman, *At Home in the Universe: The Search for Laws of Self-Organization and Complexity*, New York: Oxford University Press, 1995, pp. 9–10; Mae-Wan Ho, *The Rainbow and the Worm: The Physics of Organisms*, Singapore: World Scientific Publishing, 2008, pp. 213–14.
9. Einstein quoted in John E. J. Schmitz, *The Second Law of Life: Energy, Technology, and the Future of Earth as We Know It*, New York: William Andrew, 2007.
10. Erwin Schrödinger, *What Is Life? With Mind and Matter and Autobiographical Sketches*, Cambridge: Cambridge University Press, 1992; Depew and Weber, *Darwinism Evolving*, pp. 461–2.
11. Schrödinger, *What Is Life?*; Hans Jonas, *The Phenomenon of Life: Toward a Philosophical Biology*, Evanston: Northwestern University Press, 2001, pp. 76–8; Evan Thompson, *Mind in Life: Biology, Phenomenology, and the Sciences of Mind*, Cambridge, MA: Harvard University Press, 2007, pp. 152–3.
12. Chapter 4, 'Emergent life'; Nigel Goldenfeld and Carl Woese, 'Life Is Physics:

Evolution as a Collective Phenomenon Far from Equilibrium', *Annual Review of Condensed Matter Physics* 2, 2011, pp. 375–99.

13. Deacon, *Incomplete Nature*, Chapter 10; Jeremy Sherman and Terrence W. Deacon, 'Teleology for the Perplexed: How Matter Began to Matter', *Zygon*, December 2007, pp. 873–901.
14. Deacon, *Incomplete Nature*, Chapter 10; Jeremy Sherman, *Neither Ghost nor Machine: The Emergence and Nature of Selves*, New York: Columbia University Press, 2017, p. 149; Talbott, 'Evolution and the Purposes of Life'; Jonas, *The Phenomenon of Life*, pp. 90–1. Immanuel Kant was the first European philosopher to recognize that a core characteristic of life is that each part exists for the sake of the whole, writing, 'The definition of an organic body is that it is a body, every part of which is there for the sake of the other (reciprocally as end, and at the same time, means).'
15. Chapter 2, 'The "mind" of a cell'; Stuart Kauffman, *Reinventing the Sacred: A New View of Science, Reason, and Religion*, New York: Basic Books, 2008, pp. 86–7; Ursula Goodenough, *The Sacred Depths of Nature*, New York: Oxford University Press, 1998; Thompson, *Mind in Life*, pp. 157–8; Peter A. Corning, 'Synergy and Self-Organization in the Evolution of Complex Systems', *Systems Research* 12:2, 1995, pp. 89–121.
16. Sherman, *Neither Ghost nor Machine*, pp. 33–4, 135; Franklin M. Harold, *The Way of the Cell: Molecules, Organisms and the Order of Life*, New York: Oxford University Press, 2001, Kindle edn, locations 199–216, 3009–15; Depew and Weber, *Darwinism Evolving*, pp. 466–7.
17. Ursula Goodenough and Terrence W. Deacon, 'The Sacred Emergence of Nature' in *The Oxford Handbook of Religion and Science*, ed. Philip Clayton, New York: Oxford University Press, 2006; Peter T. Macklem, 'Emergent Phenomena and the Secrets of Life', *Journal of Applied Physiology* 104, 2008, pp. 1844–6; Steven Rose, *Lifelines: Life Beyond the Gene*, New York: Oxford University Press, 1997, p. 171; Deacon, *Incomplete Nature*, Chapter 9; Harold, *The Way of the Cell*, Kindle edn, locations 2524–33.
18. Harold, *The Way of the Cell*, Kindle edn, locations 538–50.
19. Bruce H. Weber and David J. Depew, 'Natural Selection and Self-Organization: Dynamical Models as Clues to a New Evolutionary Synthesis', *Biology and Philosophy* 11, 1996, pp. 33–65.
20. Ibid.; Deacon, *Incomplete Nature*, Chapter 9; Harold, *The Way of the Cell*, Kindle edn, locations 2967–77; Alfred J. Lotka, 'Contribution to the Energetics of Evolution', *PNAS* 8, 1922, pp. 147–51; Depew and Weber, *Darwinism Evolving*, pp. 409–10. Among others, theoretical biologist Stuart Kauffman has pioneered the integration of complexity science with evolutionary theory. 'Natural selection,' he writes, 'is important, but it has not labored alone to craft the fine architectures of the biosphere, from cell to organism to ecosystem. The order of the biological world ... arises naturally and spontaneously because of these principles of self-organization – laws of complexity that we are just beginning to uncover and understand.' None of these leading theorists refutes Darwinian evolution; rather, they suggest that it should be understood within

the larger conceptual framework of self-organization. One team of biologists gives the analogy of how language relates to communication: language is a subject worth studying in its own right, but it's also a particular type of communication. Similarly, Darwinian natural selection can be understood as a special case of more general principles of self-organization. See Kauffman, *At Home in the Universe*, p. vii; G. A. Hoelzer, E. Smith and J. W. Pepper, 'On the Logical Relationship between Natural Selection and Self-Organization', *Journal of Evolutionary Biology* 19, 2006, pp. 1785–94; Goldenfeld and Woese, 'Life Is Physics'; Harold, *The Way of the Cell*, Kindle edn, locations 2883–7; Depew and Weber, *Darwinism Evolving*, pp. 430–6, 483–4.

21. Lotka, 'Contribution to the Energetics of Evolution'; Depew and Weber, *Darwinism Evolving*, pp. 430–6, 485–90; Harold, *The Way of the Cell*, Kindle edn, locations 2967–85.
22. Julianne D. Halley and David A. Winkler, 'Critical-Like Self-Organization and Natural Selection: Two Facets of a Single Evolutionary Process?' *BioSystems* 92, 2008, pp. 148–58; Adrian Bejan and J. Peder Zane, *Design in Nature: How the Constructal Law Governs Evolution in Biology, Physics, Technology, and Social Organization*, New York: Doubleday, 2012, pp. 3–6; Geoffrey West, *Scale: The Universal Laws of Life, Growth, and Death in Organisms, Cities, and Companies*, New York: Penguin, 2017, pp. 127–49.
23. Brenner quoted in Denis Noble, *The Music of Life: Biology Beyond Genes*, Oxford: Oxford University Press, 2006, p. 33; Harold, *The Way of the Cell*, Kindle edn, locations 439–47.
24. Jamie A. Davies, *Life Unfolding: How the Human Body Creates Itself*, New York: Oxford University Press, 2014, pp. 8–9.
25. Jesper Hoffmeyer, *Signs of Meaning in the Universe*, Bloomington, IN: Indiana University Press, 1996, pp. 73–81.
26. Nick Lane, *The Vital Question: Energy, Evolution, and the Origins of Complex Life*, New York: W. W. Norton, 2016, pp. 7–8; Lynn Margulis and Dorion Sagan, *Microcosmos: Four Billion Years of Microbial Evolution*, Berkeley, CA: University of California Press, 1997, p. 118.
27. Ron Sender, Shai Fuchs and Ron Milo, 'Revised Estimates for the Number of Human and Bacteria Cells in the Body', *PLoS Biology* 14:8, 2016, e1002533.
28. Princeton University, 'Evolution's New Wrinkle: Proteins with "Cruise Control" Act Like Adaptive Machines', *Science Daily*, 2008; Tom Misteli, 'Self-Organization in the Genome', *PNAS* 106:17, 2009, pp. 6885–6.
29. Gezhi Weng, Upinder S. Bhalla and Ravi Iyengar, 'Complexity in Biological Signaling Systems', *Science* 284, 1999, pp. 92–6; Davies, *Life Unfolding*, pp. 5–13, 26–7, 64; Steven Johnson, *Emergence: The Connected Lives of Ants, Brains, Cities, and Software*, New York: Scribner, 2002, pp. 84–6.
30. As evidence of the importance of cellular communication, about one fifth of all the genes in your body are dedicated to proteins used for cell signaling. See Davies, *Life Unfolding*, pp. 90, 248–51.
31. Ibid. pp. 120–1.
32. Ibid. pp. 180–1.

33. C. H. Waddington, 'Canalization of Development and the Inheritance of Acquired Characters', *Nature* 150, 1942, pp. 563–5; Depew and Weber, *Darwinism Evolving*, p. 417.
34. Talbott, 'Evolution and the Purposes of Life', citing E. S. Russell.
35. Gerald M. Edelman and Giulio Tononi, *A Universe of Consciousness: How Matter Becomes Imagination*, New York: Basic Books, 2000; Kauffman, *At Home in the Universe*, pp. 188–9.
36. James A. Shapiro, *Evolution: A View from the 21st Century*, Upper Saddle River, NJ: FT Press, 2011, Kindle edn, locations 2159–95; John Whitfield, 'Postmodern Evolution?' *Nature* 455, 2008, pp. 281–4.
37. John Gerhart and Marc Kirschner, 'The Theory of Facilitated Variation', *PNAS* 104, 2007, pp. 8582–9; Marc Kirschner and John Gerhart, 'Evolvability', *PNAS* 95, 1998, pp. 8420–7; Kate Douglas, 'Nature's Brain: A Radical New View of Evolution', *New Scientist* 3066, 2016; Shapiro, *Evolution*, pp. 283–304, 2614–41; Harold, *The Way of the Cell*, Kindle edn, locations 2703–8.
38. Kirschner and Gerhart, 'Evolvability'.
39. Richard A. Watson and Eörs Szathmáry, 'How Can Evolution Learn?' *Trends in Ecology & Evolution* 31:2, 2016, pp. 147–57; Douglas, 'Nature's Brain'.
40. An interesting way to interpret this aspect of Hebbian learning is that it turns correlation into causation. If a particular feat of coordination is successful, it becomes more likely to happen again. See Daniel A. Power et al., 'What Can Ecosystems Learn? Expanding Evolutionary Ecology with Learning Theory', *Biology Direct* 10:69, 2015.
41. Cited in Andreas Weber, *The Biology of Wonder: Aliveness, Feeling, and the Metamorphosis of Science*, Gabriola Island, BC, Canada: New Society Publishers, 2016, p. 87.
42. Ibid.; Gerhart and Kirschner, 'Facilitated Variation'; Douglas, 'Nature's Brain'.
43. Power et al., 'What Can Ecosystems Learn?'; Simon A. Levin, 'Ecosystems and the Biosphere as Complex Adaptive Systems', *Ecosystems* 1:5, 1998, pp. 431–6; David Tilman, 'Biodiversity & Environmental Sustainability Amid Human Domination of Global Ecosystems', *Dædalus* 141:3, 2012, pp. 108–20.
44. James Lovelock, *Gaia: A New Look at Life on Earth*, Oxford: Oxford University Press, 2000; Fritjof Capra and Pier Luigi Luisi, *The Systems View of Life: A Unifying Vision*, New York: Cambridge University Press, 2014, p. 164.
45. David Grinspoon, 'It's Time to Take the Gaia Hypothesis Seriously', *Nautilus*, 8 March 2017; Eileen Crist, 'Intimations of Gaia' in *Gaia in Turmoil: Climate Change, Biodepletion, and Earth Ethics In an Age of Crisis*, ed. Eileen Crist and H. Bruce Rinker, Cambridge, MA: MIT Press, 2010.
46. In addition to the Great Oxygenation Event, a number of other stabilizing processes have caused Earth's temperature to remain within the relatively narrow range that allows liquid water to persist and have maintained steady levels of carbon, nitrogen and phosphorus – the essential ingredients of life. See Grinspoon, 'The Gaia Hypothesis'; Timothy M. Lenton and David M. Wilkinson, 'Developing the Gaia Theory: A Response to the Criticisms of Kirchner and Volk', *Climatic Change* 58:1–2, 2003, pp. 1–12; Margulis and

Sagan, *Microcosmos*, pp. 269–70; Bob Holmes, 'Gaia Rebooted: New Version of Idea Explains How Earth Evolved for Life', *New Scientist* 3222, 2019.

47. Thompson, *Mind in Life*, pp. 120–1; Peter Ward, 'Gaia's Evil Twin', *New Scientist* 2713, 2009, pp. 28–31. In recent decades, many experts have embraced Lovelock's key insights but sidestepped the controversy of the Gaia hypothesis by developing a discipline known as Earth System Science. These scientists, acknowledging that Earth can only be truly understood as a complex weave of interrelated systems, are prepared to cross traditional disciplinary boundaries to paint a holistic picture of our planet. Many of these Earth scientists are responsible for the crucial work of forecasting the potentially catastrophic effects of climate disruption this century. However, the Gaia hypothesis is more than just a set of scientific methodologies: it represents a shift in how we relate to the world around us, how we understand our home and how we untangle humanity's troubled relationship with the rest of the living Earth. See Grinspoon, 'The Gaia Hypothesis'; Lenton and Wilkinson, 'Developing the Gaia Theory'.
48. What happens if we apply to Gaia the criteria for life we encountered earlier? Like other organisms, Gaia has a semipermeable membrane: the atmosphere that it created for itself, which protects and nourishes its own internal parts. It also carries out autopoiesis as other living entities do, actively persisting in its own metabolic flows. There are, however, some criteria that don't apply to Gaia. It's clearly not capable of reproducing, and although its internal elements work together as part of a greater harmony, they don't show the extreme cooperation that the constituent parts of an organism demonstrate. To the extent, then, that we understand Gaia as a living entity, we must also recognize its differences from the organisms that comprise it. See Capra and Luisi, *The Systems View of Life*, p. 165; Bruno Latour and Timothy M. Lenton, 'Extending the Domain of Freedom, or Why Gaia Is So Hard to Understand', *Critical Inquiry* 45:3, 2019, pp. 659–80; Grinspoon, 'The Gaia Hypothesis'; Hoffmeyer, *Signs of Meaning in the Universe*, pp. vii–viii.
49. Timothy M. Lenton et al., 'Selection for Gaia across Multiple Scales', *Trends in Ecology & Evolution* 33:8, 2018, pp. 633–45; Holmes, 'Gaia Rebooted'.
50. Eörs Szathmáry, 'Toward Major Evolutionary Transitions Theory 2.0', *PNAS* 112:33, 2015, pp. 10104–11; John E. Stewart, 'The Direction of Evolution: The Rise of Cooperative Organization', *BioSystems* 123, 2014, pp. 27–36; Chapter 5, 'Better together'.
51. Martin A. Nowak, 'Five Rules for the Evolution of Cooperation', *Science* 314:5805, 2006, pp. 1560–3. Scientists use game theory to identify different strategies, beyond simple relatedness, that overcome the free-rider problem. Reciprocity is one obvious method: I'll scratch your back if you scratch mine. But this limits the scope of cooperation to one-on-one relationships. Larger cooperative networks arise frequently through reputation: when an individual is known to be generous, others will willingly be generous back. However, as the network gets bigger, reputation alone isn't sufficient to keep relationships working smoothly. See Robert Axelrod and William D. Hamilton, 'The

Evolution of Cooperation', *Science* 211:4489, 1981, pp. 1390–6; Stewart, 'The Direction of Evolution'.

52. Sara Imari Walker, Luis Cisneros and Paul C. W. Davies, 'Evolutionary Transitions and Top-Down Causation', *Artificial Life* 13, 2012, pp. 283–90; Daniel Siegel, *Pocket Guide to Interpersonal Neurobiology: An Integrative Handbook of the Mind*, New York: W. W. Norton, 2012, pp. 109–16; Stewart, 'The Direction of Evolution'.
53. Lotka, 'Energetics of Evolution'; Leslie A. White, 'Energy and the Evolution of Culture', *American Anthropologist* 45:3, 1943, pp. 335–56.
54. Lent, *The Patterning Instinct*, pp. 45–7; David Sloan Wilson and Edward O. Wilson, 'Rethinking the Theoretical Foundation of Sociobiology', *Quarterly Review of Biology* 82:4, 2007, pp. 327–48; Michael Tomasello et al., 'Understanding and Sharing Intentions: The Origins of Cultural Cognition', *Behavioral and Brain Sciences* 28, 2005, pp. 675–735. This crucial topic will be discussed in more detail in Chapter 9, 'The moral species'.
55. West, *Scale*, pp. 282–7; Johnson, *Emergence*, pp. 91–105; Bruce H. Weber et al., 'Evolution in Thermodynamic Perspective: An Ecological Approach', *Biology and Philosophy* 4, 1989, pp. 373–405.
56. Robert Wright, *Nonzero: The Logic of Human Destiny*, New York: Vintage Books, 2000; Stewart, 'The Direction of Evolution'. Not everyone agrees with the narrative of life's inevitable drive to complexity. Stephen Jay Gould, for example, argued that since life began with the simplest protocells, there was no direction it could evolve toward other than complexity, but that doesn't mean there's some overriding force driving it in that direction. Frequently, people point to bacteria, which continue to thrive everywhere on Earth while remaining as simple as they were billions of years ago, as a powerful counter-argument. Occasionally, too, some species lose complexity, such as parasites that shed capacities they don't need if their host provides them instead. However, these arguments are generally overpowered by the weight of evidence supporting the inexorable tendency to complexity over time. See Stewart, 'The Direction of Evolution'; Sarah J. Adamowicz, Andy Purvis and Matthew A. Wills, 'Increasing Morphological Complexity in Multiple Parallel Lineages of the Crustacea', *PNAS* 105:12, 2008, pp. 4786–91; Walker et al., 'Evolutionary Transitions'.
57. Pierre Teilhard de Chardin, *The Phenomenon of Man*, New York: Harper & Row, 1965; Roger Lewin, *Complexity: Life at the Edge of Chaos*, Chicago, IL: University of Chicago Press, 1999, p. 141; George Sessions, 'Deep Ecology and the New Age Movement' in *Deep Ecology for the Twenty-First Century*, ed. George Sessions, Boston: Shambhala Publications, 1995.
58. Ray Kurzweil, *The Singularity Is Near*, New York: Penguin Books, 2005, pp. 9, 136; Max Tegmark, *Life 3.0: Being Human in the Age of Artificial Intelligence*, New York: Alfred A. Knopf, 2017. Classic science-fiction author Isaac Asimov wrote an entertaining and imaginative account of artificial intelligence as the ultimate force of negative entropy: Isaac Asimov, 'The Last Question', *Science Fiction Quarterly*.

59. https://memory-alpha.fandom.com/wiki/Charter_of_the_United_Federation_of_Planets
60. William J. Ripple et al., 'World Scientists' Warning to Humanity: A Second Notice', *BioScience* 67:12, 2017, pp. 1026–8.
61. Lent, *The Patterning Instinct*, pp. 375–401; Eileen Crist, *Abundant Earth: Toward an Ecological Civilization*, Chicago, IL: University of Chicago Press, 2019, pp. 43–9.

Chapter 7: The Tao in My Own Nature

1. Ernst Cassirer, *An Essay on Man*, New Haven: Yale University Press, 1944, pp. 33–5.
2. Helen Keller, *The Story of My Life*, Mineola, NY: Dover, 1996, pp. 10–12.
3. Cheng Yi, quoted in Wing-tsit Chan, 'Neo-Confucianism and Chinese Scientific Thought', *Philosophy East and West* 6:4, 1957, pp. 309–32; Lu Jiuyuan, quoted in Julia Ching, *The Religious Thought of Chu Hsi*, New York: Oxford University Press, 2000, pp. 137; Cheng Hao, quoted in Siu-chi Huang, *Essentials of Neo-Confucianism: Eight Major Philosophers of the Song and Ming Periods*, Westport, CT: Greenwood Press, 1999, p. 98; Zhu Xi, quoted in Huang, p. 148.
4. D. J. T. Sumpter, 'The Principles of Collective Animal Behaviour', *Philosophical Transactions of the Royal Society* B 361, 2006, pp. 5–22; Iain D. Couzin et al., 'Collective Memory and Spatial Sorting in Animal Groups', *Journal of Theoretical Biology* 218, 2002, pp. 1–11.
5. Eric Bonabeau et al., 'Self-Organization in Social Insects', *Trends in Ecology & Evolution* 12:5, 1997, pp. 188–93; Iain D. Couzin, 'Collective Cognition in Animal Groups', *Trends in Cognitive Sciences* 13:1, 2008, pp. 36–43; Mehdi Moussaid et al., 'Collective Information Processing and Pattern Formation in Swarms, Flocks, and Crowds', *Topics in Cognitive Science* 1, 2009, pp. 469–97.
6. Stefano Mancuso and Alessandra Viola, *Brilliant Green: The Surprising History and Science of Plant Intelligence*, Washington DC: Island Press, 2015, pp. 138–9; Iain D. Couzin, 'Collective Minds', *Nature* 445, 2007, p. 715.
7. Thomas D. Seeley and Susannah C. Buhrman, 'Group Decision Making in Swarms of Honey Bees', *Behavioral Ecology and Sociobiology* 45, 1999, pp. 19–31.
8. Bonabeau et al., 'Self-Organization in Social Insects'; Stephen J. Martin et al., 'A Vast 4,000-Year-Old Spatial Pattern of Termite Mounds', *Current Biology* 28:22, 2018, R1292–1293; Kumar Krishna, 'Termite', *Encyclopedia Britannica*.
9. Mark W. Moffett, *The Human Swarm: How Our Societies Arise, Thrive, and Fall*, New York: Basic Books, 2019, pp. 62–5.
10. Ibid. pp. 60–71; Kevin Hartnett, 'The Simple Algorithm That Ants Use to Build Bridges', *Quanta Magazine*, 26 February 2018; Lewis Thomas, *The Lives of a Cell: Notes of a Biology Watcher*, New York: Penguin Books, 1978, p. 12.
11. David Sloan Wilson and Edward O. Wilson, 'Rethinking the Theoretical Foundation of Sociobiology', *Quarterly Review of Biology* 82:4, 2007, pp. 327–48; Couzin, 'Collective Cognition in Animal Groups'; Olaf Sporns et

al., 'Organization, Development and Function of Complex Brain Networks', *Trends in Cognitive Sciences* 8:9, 2004, pp. 418–25.

12. Antonio Damasio, *The Strange Order of Things: Life, Feeling, and the Making of Cultures*, New York: Pantheon, 2018, pp. 159–60; Francis Crick and Christof Koch, 'A Framework for Consciousness', *Nature Neuroscience* 6:2, 2003, pp. 119–26.
13. Chalmers' idea of the Hard Problem has been systematically refuted by a number of leading thinkers in neurobiology and systems theory. See Gerald M. Edelman, 'Naturalizing Consciousness: A Theoretical Framework', *PNAS* 100:9, 2003, pp. 5520–4; Christof Koch, *Consciousness: Confessions of a Romantic Reductionist*, Cambridge, MA: MIT Press, 2017, p. 3; Damasio, *The Strange Order of Things*, p. 160; Gerald M. Edelman, Joseph A. Gally and Bernard J. Baars, 'Biology of Consciousness', *Frontiers in Psychology* 2, 2011, pp. 1–7; Terrence W. Deacon, *Incomplete Nature: How Mind Emerged from Matter*, New York: W. W. Norton, 2011, pp. 395–8; Fritjof Capra and Pier Luigi Luisi, *The Systems View of Life: A Unifying Vision*, New York: Cambridge University Press, 2014, pp. 260–2, 274.
14. Chapter 2, 'The continuum of consciousness'; Damasio, *The Strange Order of Things*, p. 160.
15. Huda Akil, Maryann E. Martone and David C. Van Essen, 'Challenges and Opportunities in Mining Neuroscience Data', *Science* 331, 2011, pp. 708–12; Koch, *Consciousness*, p. 16; Jamie A. Davies, *Life Unfolding: How the Human Body Creates Itself*, New York: Oxford University Press, 2014, p. 185; Robert Epstein, 'The Empty Brain', *Aeon*, 18 May 2016; Olaf Sporns, 'Network Analysis, Complexity, and Brain Function', *Complexity* 8:1, 2003, pp. 56–60.
16. Jerome A. Feldman, *From Molecule to Metaphor: A Neural Theory of Language*, Cambridge, MA: MIT Press, 2008, pp. 79; Jean-Pierre Changeux, *The Physiology of Truth: Neuroscience and Human Knowledge*, transl. M. B. DeBevoise, Cambridge, MA: Harvard University Press, 2002, pp. 184–5; Jeremy E. Cook, 'Correlated Activity in the CNS: A Role on Every Timescale?' *Trends in Neurosciences* 14:9, 1991, pp. 397–401; Gerald M. Edelman and Giulio Tononi, *A Universe of Consciousness: How Matter Becomes Imagination*, New York: Basic Books, 2000, pp. 83–4. Even as adults, our neural pathways are continually reorganizing their networks based on our experience. We can see this in ourselves with a little introspection. One driver of Hebbian reinforcement, for example, is *novelty*. When something bizarre or unusual happens, your neural synapses fire powerfully, making such strong connections that you'll easily remember it, sometimes years later. Another factor is *intensity*, which is one reason why it can be so difficult to recover from traumatic stress. Then there is *habituation*: you remember that, when you commute to work, you need to take a right on Market Street – not because it's novel or intense, but because you've done it so many times. In these cases, neural synapses fire together less powerfully but repeatedly, gradually strengthening neural configurations that may remain connected for years.
17. Chapter 6, 'The deep learning of the ecosystem'; Esther Thelen and Linda B.

Smith, 'Dynamic Systems Theories' in *A Dynamic Systems Approach to the Development of Cognition and Action*, Cambridge, MA: MIT Press, 1996; Marc D. Lewis, 'Bridging Emotion Theory and Neurobiology through Dynamic Systems Modeling', *Behavioral and Brain Sciences* 28:2, 2005, pp. 169–245.

18. Francisco J. Varela, Evan Thompson and Eleanor Rosch, *The Embodied Mind: Cognitive Science and Human Experience*, Cambridge, MA: MIT Press, 1993, p. 139; Daniel Siegel, *Pocket Guide to Interpersonal Neurobiology: An Integrative Handbook of the Mind,* New York: W. W. Norton, 2012, pp. 5–6; Davies, *Life Unfolding*, pp. 188–92; Alva Noë, *Out of Our Heads: Why You Are Not Your Brain, and Other Lessons from the Biology of Consciousness*, New York: Hill and Wang, 2009, iBook edn, Chapters 1, 3; Lewis, 'Bridging Emotion Theory and Neurobiology'.
19. György Buzsáki, *Rhythms of the Brain*, New York: Oxford University Press, 2006, pp. 126–7; Dan Wu, Chao-Yi Li and De-Zhong Yao, 'Scale-Free Music of the Brain', *PLoS One* 4:6, 2009, e5915; Danielle S. Bassett et al., 'Adaptive Reconfiguration of Fractal Small-World Human Brain Functional Networks', *PNAS* 103:51, 2006, pp. 19518–23; Duncan Watts and Steven H. Strogatz, 'Collective Dynamics of "Small-World" Networks', *Nature* 393, 1998, pp. 440–2. When researchers graph the amplitude of neuronal activity, they find that it follows a power law, just like earthquakes, avalanches and stock markets, with lots of small oscillations, periodic larger fluctuations and rare seismic shifts.
20. Giulio Tononi and Gerald M. Edelman, 'Consciousness and Complexity', *Science* 282, 1998, pp. 1846–51; Edelman and Tononi, *A Universe of Consciousness*, p. 135; Sporns, 'Network Analysis'; Karl J. Friston, 'Transients, Metastability, and Neuronal Dynamics', *NeuroImage* 5, 1997, pp. 164–71; Giulio Tononi, Gerald M. Edelman and Olaf Sporns, 'Complexity and Coherency: Integrating Information in the Brain', *Trends in Cognitive Sciences* 2:12, 1998, pp. 474–84.
21. Tononi and Edelman, 'Consciousness and Complexity'; Edelman and Tononi, *A Universe of Consciousness*, p. 144; Edelman, 'Naturalizing Consciousness'.
22. Giulio Tononi, 'Consciousness as Integrated Information: A Provisional Manifesto', *Biological Bulletin* 215, 2008, pp. 216–42; Giulio Tononi, 'Integrated Information Theory of Consciousness: An Updated Account', *Archives Italiennes de Biologie* 150, 2012, pp. 290–326; Koch, *Consciousness*, pp. 126–7. Tononi's theory is based on the special quality of integration. A computer, for example, contains gigabytes of information, but it's not well integrated. Like water molecules in a block of ice, each bit of information has a precise relationship with the other bits, but they don't mean anything to each other. My computer screen might show the picture of a beautiful landscape, but to the computer it's nothing but a series of ones and zeros. However, when I look at the picture, I link the colored pixels in a meaningful way, associating it with other times I've seen a landscape and felt its beauty. I'm integrating the information in a way that the computer can't. The difference between my

view of the picture and the computer's is what Tononi sees as a measure of consciousness.

23. George Musser, 'Consciousness Creep', *Aeon*, 25 February 2016; Koch, *Consciousness*, pp. 120–32; Tononi, 'Consciousness as Integrated Information'. It's worth pointing out a crucial difference between consciousness and life arising from this discussion. As discussed in Chapter 5, 'Mind the metaphor', life – and the consciousness arising from it – is not substrate independent: the 'information' transmitted through the brain is inextricably bound up in each neuron's own molecular structure and its dynamic relationships with other neurons. A human mind, therefore, can never be 'uploaded' to a database, even in principle. Consciousness, however, based on Integrated Information Theory, is substrate independent. This leads to the interesting inference that, while there is no life without consciousness of some sort, high degrees of consciousness could in principle exist without life, such as might arise through artificial intelligence.
24. Koch, *Consciousness*, pp. 130–31; Tononi, 'Consciousness as Integrated Information'.
25. Chapter 4, 'Strange, but natural, attractors'.
26. Neuroscientist Scott Kelso gives the name *metastability* to these dynamic patterns: even while the mind keeps changing itself, it also stabilizes and settles itself into new attractors. See: J. A. Scott Kelso, *Dynamic Patterns: The Self-Organization of Brain and Behavior*, Cambridge, MA: MIT Press, 1995, pp. 257–60; J. A. Scott Kelso, 'An Essay on Understanding the Mind', *Ecological Psychology* 20:2, 2008, pp. 180–208; J. A. Scott Kelso, 'Multistability and Metastability: Understanding Dynamic Coordination in the Brain', *Philosophical Transactions of the Royal Society* B 367, 2012, pp. 906–18.
27. Nicolas E. Humphries et al., 'Foraging Success of Biological Lévy Flights Recorded in Situ', *PNAS* 109:19, 2012, pp. 7169–74; Alexander Maye, 'Order in Spontaneous Behavior', *PLoS One* 2:5, 2007, e443; Tajie H. Harris et al., 'Generalized Lévy Walks and the Role of Chemokines in Migration of Effector Cd8+ T Cells', *Nature* 486, 2012, pp. 545–8; Alex Proekt et al., 'Scale Invariance in the Dynamics of Spontaneous Behavior', *PNAS* 109:26, 2012, pp. 10564–69.
28. Marcus E. Raichle et al., 'A Default Mode of Brain Function', *PNAS* 98:2, 2001, pp. 676–82; Malia F. Mason et al., 'Wandering Minds: The Default Network and Stimulus-Independent Thought', *Science* 315, 2007, pp. 393–5; Hanbing Lu et al., 'Rat Brains Also Have a Default Mode Network', *PNAS* 109:10, 2012, pp. 3979–84.
29. Matthew A. Killingsworth and Daniel T. Gilbert, 'A Wandering Mind Is an Unhappy Mind', *Science* 330, 2010, p. 932; Jonathan Smallwood et al., 'Shifting Moods, Wandering Minds: Negative Moods Lead the Mind to Wander', *Emotion* 9:2, 2009, pp. 271–6; Igor Marchetti, Ernst H. W. Koster and Rudi De Raedt, 'Mindwandering Heightens the Accessibility of Negative Relative to Positive Thought', *Consciousness and Cognition* 21, 2012, pp. 1517–25; Lu et al., 'Rat Brains'.
30. Benjamin Baird, Jonathan Smallwood and Jonathan W. Schooler, 'Back to the

Future: Autobiographical Planning and the Functionality of Mind-Wandering', *Consciousness and Cognition* 20:4, 2011, pp. 1604–11; Michael D. Greicius et al., 'Functional Connectivity in the Resting Brain: A Network Analysis of the Default Mode Hypothesis', *PNAS* 100:1, 2003, pp. 253–8. Some researchers have extended this analogy to dreaming, which activates similar neural pathways and can be viewed as a more extreme version of mind-wandering (also known, of course, as daydreaming). Could dreaming have evolved, they ask, as the brain's way of processing the deeper, most salient issues of consciousness that the waking mind could not resolve? See: Kieran C. R. Fox et al., 'Dreaming as Mind Wandering: Evidence from Functional Neuroimaging and First-Person Content Reports', *Frontiers in Human Neuroscience* 7:412, 2013; G. William Domhoff, 'The Neural Substrate for Dreaming: Is It a Subsystem of the Default Network?' *Consciousness and Cognition* 20:4, 2011, pp. 1163–74.

31. Lewis, 'Bridging Emotion Theory and Neurobiology'; Marten Scheffer, *Critical Transitions in Nature and Society*, Princeton, NJ: Princeton University Press, 2009, Kindle edn, location 2514–21; A. Levina, J. M. Herrmann, and T. Geisel, 'Dynamical Synapses Causing Self-Organized Criticality in Neural Networks', *Nature Physics* 3, 2007, pp. 857–60; Thomas Petermann et al., 'Spontaneous Cortical Activity in Awake Monkeys Composed of Neuronal Avalanches', *PNAS* 106:37, 2009, pp. 15921–6.
32. J. A. Scott Kelso, 'On the Self-Organizing Origins of Agency', *Trends in Cognitive Sciences* 20:7, 2016, pp. 490–9; John Briggs and F. David Peat, *Seven Life Lessons of Chaos: Spiritual Wisdom from the Science of Change*, Harper Perennial, 2000, iBook edn, Chapter 1.
33. Alicia Juarrero, *Dynamics in Action: Intentional Behavior as a Complex System*, Cambridge, MA: MIT Press, 2002, pp. 195; Siegel, *Pocket Guide to Interpersonal Neurobiology*, p. 261; Evan Thompson, 'Empathy and Consciousness', *Journal of Consciousness Studies* 8:5–7, 2001, pp. 1–32; Danielle S. Bassett and Michael S. Gazzaniga, 'Understanding Complexity in the Human Brain', *Trends in Cognitive Sciences* 15:5, 2011, pp. 200–9.
34. Joseph LeDoux, *Synaptic Self: How Our Brains Become Who We Are*, New York: Penguin, 2003; Kelso, *Dynamic Patterns*, p. 141; Andreas K. Engel, Pascal Fries and Wolf Singer, 'Dynamic Predictions: Oscillations and Synchrony in Top-Down Processing', *Nature Reviews: Neuroscience* 2:10, 2001, pp. 704–16.
35. From 'Proverbios y cantares' in Antonio Machado, *Campos de Castilla*, 1912, transl. Francisco Varela. Cited in Noë, *Out of Our Heads*, iBook edn, Chapter 5.
36. Jeremy Lent, *The Patterning Instinct: A Cultural History of Humanity's Search for Meaning*, Amherst, NY: Prometheus, 2017, pp. 77–81; Merlin Donald, *A Mind So Rare: The Evolution of Human Consciousness*, New York: W. W. Norton, 2001, pp. 211–14. As I've traced in *The Patterning Instinct*, each worldview is ultimately founded on a root metaphor of nature, which generates a set of ramifications that structure a culture's values and predominant behaviors. Our nomadic hunter-gatherer ancestors, for example, saw nature as a nurturing parent, which naturally led them to view other creatures as family members with whom they felt closely connected. Settled agrarian

societies, by contrast, understood the universe as a hierarchy of the gods, causing them to emphasize worship and sacrifice as ways to curry favor with the cosmic potentates. This agrarian worldview was transformed by the Scientific Revolution of the seventeenth century, when Galileo, Descartes and other pioneers laid the foundation for the mechanistic worldview that has since become dominant.

37. Joseph Henrich, *The Secret of Our Success: How Culture Is Driving Human Evolution, Domesticating Our Species, and Making Us Smarter*, Princeton, NJ: Princeton University Press, 2016, pp. 5–6, 49–50, 99–100, 213–4. Henrich describes how humans have evolved a strong propensity to follow cultural norms, so powerful that it can overwhelm even our most basic instincts – as shown, for example, in the way celebrity suicides predictably cause a spike in suicide rates in related demographic groups.
38. Moffett, *The Human Swarm*; Stanley Milgram, Leonard Bickman and Lawrence Berkowitz, 'Note on the Drawing Power of Crowds of Different Size', *Journal of Personality and Social Psychology* 13:2, 1969, pp. 79–82; Moussaid et al., 'Collective Information Processing'.
39. Jonathan Haidt, Patrick Seder and Selin Kesebir, 'Hive Psychology, Happiness, and Public Policy', *Journal of Legal Studies* 37, 2008, S133–56; Henrich, *The Secret of Our Success*, p. 318; Steven Johnson, *Emergence: The Connected Lives of Ants, Brains, Cities, and Software*, New York: Scribner, 2002.
40. Richard Dawkins, *The Selfish Gene: 30th Anniversary Edition*, London: Oxford University Press, 2006, pp. 192–201; Susan Blackmore, *The Meme Machine*, New York: Oxford University Press, 1999.
41. Other critiques of the mechanistic simplicity of the meme model include Merlin Donald, 'Material Culture and Cognition: Concluding Thoughts' in *Cognition and Material Culture: The Archaeology of Symbolic Storage*, ed. Colin Renfrew and Chris Scarre, Cambridge: McDonald Institute for Archaeological Research, 1999; William L. Benzon, *Beethoven's Anvil: Music in Mind and Culture*, New York: Basic Books, 2001.
42. Nicole Creanza, Oren Kolodny and Marcus W. Feldman, 'Cultural Evolutionary Theory: How Culture Evolves and Why It Matters', *PNAS* 114:30, 2017, pp. 7782–9.
43. Cultural attractors can be studied according to the same principles as other phenomena of self-organized adaptive systems. Like attractors of consciousness, they are likely to follow a version of Hebbian learning, where successful patterns feel emotionally salient to those who become part of the transmittal process, so that the continued expression of the attractor entrenches it even more deeply in the individual's own mind, which exists as a fractal subsystem within the larger cultural attractor. Cultural attractors can be expected to follow the power law in their expression (lots of small ones and rare huge ones), spread through small-world hub-and-spoke networks, and exhibit fractal patterns over time, with frequent short-lived patterns manifesting as smaller versions of much longer-lasting attractors.
44. Carl Jung, *The Collected Works Volume 9: The Archetypes and the Collective*

Unconscious, New York: Routledge, 1959, pp. 42–8; Harry T. Hunt, 'A Collective Unconscious Reconsidered: Jung's Archetypal Imagination in the Light of Contemporary Psychology and Social Science', *Journal of Analytical Psychology* 57, 2012, pp. 76–98.
45. Petteri Pietikainen, 'Archetypes as Symbolic Forms', *Journal of Analytical Psychology* 43, 1998, pp. 325–43.
46. Andreas Weber, *The Biology of Wonder: Aliveness, Feeling, and the Metamorphosis of Science*, Gabriola Island, BC, Canada: New Society Publishers, 2016, pp. 131–2, 211–12.
47. Lance H. Gunderson and C. S. Holling, eds., *Panarchy: Understanding Transformations in Human and Natural Systems (Synopsis)*, Washington DC: Island Press, 2002, iBook edn, Preface, Introduction.
48. Ibid. Chapter 1.
49. Lent, *The Patterning Instinct*, pp. 405–42.
50. See Chapter 13, 'Rewriting the operating system'.

Chapter 8: Flourishing as an Integrated Organism

1. Edward Slingerland, *Effortless Action: Wu-Wei as Conceptual Metaphor and Spiritual Ideal in Early China*, New York: Oxford University Press, 2003, pp. 156–7.
2. Edward Slingerland, 'The Conception of Ming in Early Confucian Thought', *Philosophy East and West* 46:4, 1996, pp. 567–81.
3. Chad Hansen, *A Daoist Theory of Chinese Thought: A Philosophical Interpretation*, New York: Oxford University Press, 2000, pp. 174–5; Donald J. Munro, *The Concept of Man in Early China*, Ann Arbor, MI: Center for Chinese Studies, University of Michigan, 1969, pp. 12–13.
4. David L. Hall and Roger T. Ames, *Thinking from the Han: Self, Truth, and Transcendence in Chinese and Western Culture*, Albany, NY: SUNY Press, 1998, pp. 180–1; Stephen C. Angle, *Sagehood: The Contemporary Significance of Neo-Confucian Philosophy*, New York: Oxford University Press, 2009, p. 65; Yu-Lan Fung, *A Short History of Chinese Philosophy: A Systematic Account of Chinese Thought from Its Origins to the Present Day*, New York: Free Press, 1976.
5. Angle, *Sagehood*, p. 70.
6. Ted J. Kaptchuk, *The Web That Has No Weaver: Understanding Chinese Medicine*, New York: Rosetta Books, 2000, Kindle edn, locations 312, 422, 527.
7. Jennifer Rioux, 'A Complex, Nonlinear Dynamic Systems Perspective on Ayurveda and Ayurvedic Research', *Journal of Alternative and Complementary Medicine* 18:7, 2012, pp. 709–18.
8. Andrew C. Ahn et al., 'The Limits of Reductionism in Medicine: Could Systems Biology Offer an Alternative?' *PLoS Medicine* 3:6, 2006, e208; David H. Freedman, 'The Triumph of New-Age Medicine', *Atlantic Monthly*, July/August 2011, pp. 90–100.
9. Ibid.
10. Iris R. Bell et al., 'Integrative Medicine and Systemic Outcomes Research', *Archives of Internal Medicine* 162, 2002, p. 133–40; Jan van der Greef, 'All

Systems Go', *Nature* 480, 2011, S87; Peng Tian, 'Where West Meets East', *Nature* 480, 2011, S84–6; Rioux, 'A Complex, Nonlinear Perspective'.

11. Elizabeth Costello et al., 'The Application of Ecological Theory toward an Understanding of the Human Microbiome', *Science* 336, 2012, pp. 1255–62; Fritjof Capra and Pier Luigi Luisi, *The Systems View of Life: A Unifying Vision*, New York: Cambridge University Press, 2014, pp. 327–37; Ricard Solé and Brian Goodwin, *Signs of Life: How Complexity Pervades Biology*, New York: Basic Books, 2000, p. 117.
12. Rioux, 'A Complex, Nonlinear Perspective'; Ary L. Goldberger, 'Complex Systems', *Proceedings of the American Thoracic Society* 3, 2006, pp. 467–72; Donald S. Coffey, 'Self-Organization, Complexity, and Chaos: The New Biology for Medicine', *Nature Medicine* 4:8, 1998, pp. 882–5; Ed Bullmore and Olaf Sporns, 'Complex Brain Networks: Graph Theoretical Analysis of Structural and Functional Systems', *Nature Reviews: Neuroscience* 10, 2009, pp. 186–98; Nora Schultz, 'Eavesdropping on the Music of the Brain', *New Scientist* 2715, 2009.
13. P. Enck and S. Klosterhalfen, 'The Placebo Response in Clinical Trials – the Current State of Play', *Complementary Therapies in Medicine* 21:2, 2013, pp. 98–101.
14. Cara Feinberg, 'The Placebo Phenomenon', *Harvard Magazine*, January–February 2013; Joseph Henrich, *The Secret of Our Success: How Culture Is Driving Human Evolution, Domesticating Our Species, and Making Us Smarter*, Princeton, NJ: Princeton University Press, 2016, pp. 273–4.
15. Karin Meissner, 'The Placebo Effect and the Autonomic Nervous System: Evidence for an Intimate Relationship', *Philosophical Transactions of the Royal Society* B 366, 2011, pp. 1808–17; Nicholas Humphrey and John Skoyles, 'The Evolutionary Psychology of Healing: A Human Success Story', *Current Biology* 22:17, 2012, R695–698; Colin Barras, 'Evolution Could Explain the Placebo Effect', *New Scientist* 2881, 2012, p. 9.
16. Nikola Kohls et al., 'Spirituality: An Overlooked Predictor of Placebo Effects?' *Philosophical Transactions of the Royal Society* B 366:1572, 2011, pp. 1838–48; Frank Forencich, *New Old Way: Ancestral Health and Sapience for the Modern World*, Exuberant Animal, 2018, Kindle edn, location 4063.
17. Freedman, 'The Triumph of New-Age Medicine'; Leonard Mlodinow, *Subliminal: How Your Unconscious Mind Rules Your Behavior*, New York: Vintage, 2013, p. 84.
18. Walter Mischel, *The Marshmallow Test: Why Self-Control Is the Engine of Success*, New York: Little, Brown & Co., 2014, pp. 111–14; Martin E. Seligman, *Flourish: A Visionary New Understanding of Happiness and Well-Being*, New York: Free Press, 2011, pp. 190, 198–9; David Robson, 'How a Positive Mind Really Can Create a Healthier Body', *New Scientist*, 27 August 2018.
19. Seligman, *Flourish*, pp. 193–4; Ellen J. Langer and Judith Rodin, 'The Effects of Choice and Enhanced Personal Responsibility for the Aged: A Field Experiment in an Institutional Setting', *Journal of Personality and Social Psychology* 34:2, 1976, pp. 191–8.

20. Freedman, 'The Triumph of New-Age Medicine'; Robson, 'How a Positive Mind'; Tonya L. Jacobs et al., 'Intensive Meditation Training, Immune Cell Telomerase Activity, and Psychological Mediators', *Psychoneuroendocrinology* 36, 2011, pp. 664–81; Robert M. Sapolsky, 'How Economic Inequality Inflicts Real Biological Harm', *Scientific American*, 1 November 2018.
21. Daniel Siegel, *Pocket Guide to Interpersonal Neurobiology: An Integrative Handbook of the Mind*, New York: W. W. Norton, 2012, pp. 261; Bethany E. Kok and Barbara L. Fredrickson, 'Upward Spirals of the Heart: Autonomic Flexibility, as Indexed by Vagal Tone, Reciprocally and Prospectively Predicts Positive Emotions and Social Connectedness', *Biological Psychology* 85, 2010, pp. 432–6.
22. Ibid.; Bethany E. Kok et al., 'How Positive Emotions Build Physical Health: Perceived Positive Social Connections Account for the Upward Spiral between Positive Emotions and Vagal Tone', *Psychological Science* 24:7, 2013, pp. 1123–32; Emma Young, 'Vagus Thinking: Meditate Your Way to Better Health', *New Scientist* 2925, 2013.
23. Deb A. Dana, *The Polyvagal Theory in Therapy: Engaging the Rhythm of Regulation*, New York: W. W. Norton, 2018; Dana R. Carney, Amy J. C. Cuddy and Andy J. Yap, 'Power Posing: Brief Nonverbal Displays Affect Neuroendocrine Levels and Risk Tolerance', *Psychological Science* 21:10, 2010, pp. 1363–8. It should be noted that there is controversy about the replicability of this original study, causing one of the co-authors, Dana Carney, to retract her claims. However, Amy Cuddy has refuted the criticisms of the study and continues to stand by the findings. See Dana Carney, 'My position on "Power Poses"' blog post: https://faculty.haas.berkeley.edu/dana_carney/pdf_My%20position%20on%20power%20poses.pdf (2016); Kim Elsesser, 'Power Posing Is Back: Amy Cuddy Successfully Refutes Criticism', *Forbes*, 3 April 2018.
24. Eknath Easwaran, *Bhagavad Gita*, transl. Eknath Easwaran, Tomales, CA: Nilgiri Press, 1985, pp. 99–100.
25. Daisy Fancourt et al., 'Effects of Group Drumming Interventions on Anxiety, Depression, Social Resilience and Inflammatory Immune Response among Mental Health Service Users', *PLoS One* 11:3, 2016, e0151136; C. Smith, J. T. Viljoen and L. McGeachie, 'African Drumming: A Holistic Approach to Reducing Stress and Improving Health?' *Journal of Cardiovascular Medicine* 15:6, 2014, pp. 441–6; Sayer Ji, '6 Ways Drumming Heals Body, Mind and Soul', *Green Med Info*, 2 February 2019; Jan-Christoph Kattenstroth et al., 'Superior Sensory, Motor, and Cognitive Performance in Elderly Individuals with Multi-Year Dancing Activities', *Frontiers in Aging Neuroscience* 2:31, 2010; María Mar López-Rodríguez et al., 'Effects of Biodanza on Stress, Depression, and Sleep Quality in University Students', *Journal of Alternative and Complementary Medicine* 23:7, 2017, pp. 558–65.
26. Roger Jahnke et al., 'A Comprehensive Review of Health Benefits of Qigong and Tai Chi', *American Journal of Health Promotion* 24:6, 2010, e1–e25.
27. Kenneth S. Cohen, *The Way of Qigong: The Art and Science of Chinese Energy Healing*, New York: Ballantine Books, 1997. There have been many studies

of the health benefits of *qigong* and tai chi, and while few have achieved the scientific gold standard of double-blind controls (where neither the experimenter nor the subjects know which group they're in), there is a general consensus about the measurable effects of these practices. Consistent with the other modalities already discussed, a committed practice seems to slow down the aging process, decrease inflammation, improve immune response, reduce depression and anxiety, and promote a sense of psychological well-being and greater life satisfaction. See Jahnke et al., 'A Comprehensive Review'; Matthew F. Komelski, Yasuo Miyazaki and Rosemary Blieszner, 'Comparing the Health Status of U.S. Taijiquan and Qigong Practitioners to a National Survey Sample across Ages', *Journal of Alternative and Complementary Medicine* 18:3, 2012, pp. 281–6; Matthew F. Komelski, Rosemary Blieszner and Yasuo Miyazaki, 'Curriculum, Practice, and Diet Predict Health among Experienced Taiji and Qigong Practitioners', *Journal of Alternative and Complementary Medicine* 22:2, 2016, pp. 154–9; Byeongsang Oh et al., 'A Critical Review of the Effects of Medical Qigong on Quality of Life, Immune Function, and Survival in Cancer Patients', *Integrative Cancer Therapies* 11:2, 2012, pp. 101–10; Helen Lavretsky et al., 'Complementary Use of Tai Chi Chih Augments Escitalopram Treatment of Geriatric Depression: A Randomized Controlled Trial', *American Journal of Geriatric Psychiatry* 19:10, 2011, pp. 839–50; Pam Belluck, 'Tai Chi Reported to Ease Fibromyalgia', *New York Times*, 18 August 2010; Chenchen Wang et al., 'Tai Chi on Psychological Well-Being: Systematic Review and Meta-Analysis', *BMC Complementary and Alternative Medicine* 10:23, 2010.

28. Matthieu Ricard, *Happiness: A Guide to Developing Life's Most Important Skill*, New York: Little, Brown & Co., 2007, p. 25; B. Alan Wallace and Shauna L. Shapiro, 'Mental Balance and Well-Being: Building Bridges between Buddhism and Western Psychology', *American Psychologist* 61:7, 2006, pp. 690–701.
29. Ibid.; Carol D. Ryff, 'Psychological Well-Being Revisited: Advances in the Science and Practice of Eudaimonia', *Psychotherapy and Psychosomatics* 83, 2013, pp. 10–28.
30. J. L. Ackrill, *Aristotle the Philosopher*, Oxford: Clarendon Press, 1981, pp. 14–16; Massimo Pigliucci, *How to Be a Stoic: Using Ancient Philosophy to Live a Modern Life*, New York: Basic Books, 2017, pp. 10–23.
31. Martin E. Seligman and Mihaly Csikszentmihalyi, 'Positive Psychology: An Introduction', *American Psychologist* 55:1, 2000, pp. 5–14.
32. Heather L. Urry et al., 'Making a Life Worth Living: Neural Correlates of Well-Being', *Psychological Science* 15:6, 2004, pp. 367–72; Ryff, 'Psychological Well-Being Revisited'; Wallace and Shapiro, 'Mental Balance and Well-Being'.
33. Jonathan Haidt, Patrick Seder and Selin Kesebir, 'Hive Psychology, Happiness, and Public Policy', *Journal of Legal Studies* 37, 2008, S133–56; David M. Buss, 'The Evolution of Happiness', *American Psychologist* 55:1, 2000, pp. 15–23.
34. Jonathan Haidt, *The Happiness Hypothesis: Finding Modern Truth in Ancient Wisdom*, New York: Basic Books, 2006, pp. 83–4, 220–3. This can lead naturally to the sense of flow discussed in Chapter 3 – the absorption that arises when

we're challenged but have a realistic chance of attaining the goal. See Chapter 3, 'Embodied mind and mindful body'.

35. Ibid. p. 125; Ryff, 'Psychological Well-Being Revisited'; Richard A. Easterlin, 'Explaining Happiness', *PNAS* 100:19, 2003, pp. 11176–83; Elizabeth W. Dunn, 'Spending Money on Others Promotes Happiness', *Science* 319:5870, 2008, pp. 1687–8. One fascinating finding is that the warm glow from spending money on others gives greater satisfaction than spending on ourselves – a study drawn from 136 countries has shown this to be valid across vastly different cultures and in both rich and poor nations. See Lara B. Aknin et al., 'Prosocial Spending and Well-Being: Cross-Cultural Evidence for a Psychological Universal', *Journal of Personality and Social Psychology* 104:4, 2013, pp. 635–52.
36. Daryl R. Van Tongeren and Jeni L. Burnette, 'Do You Believe Happiness Can Change? An Investigation of the Relationship between Happiness Mindsets, Well-Being, and Satisfaction', *Journal of Positive Psychology* 13:2, 2018, pp. 101–9; Robert A. Emmons and Michael E. McCullough, 'Counting Blessings Versus Burdens: An Experimental Investigation of Gratitude and Subjective Well-Being in Daily Life', *Journal of Personality and Social Psychology* 84:2, 2003, pp. 377–89; Dacher Keltner, 'Why Do We Feel Awe?' *Slate*, 10 May 2016.
37. Roger S. Ulrich, 'View through a Window May Influence Recovery from Surgery', *Science* 224:4647, 1984, pp. 420–1; Renate Cervinka, Kathrin Röderer and Elisabeth Hefler, 'Are Nature Lovers Happy? On Various Indicators of Well-Being and Connectedness with Nature', *Journal of Health Psychology* 17:3, 2012, pp. 379–88; Matilda Annerstedt and Peter Währborg, 'Nature-Assisted Therapy: Systematic Review of Controlled and Observational Studies', *Scandinavian Journal of Public Health* 39, 2011, pp. 371–88; Mathew P. White et al., 'Spending at Least 120 Minutes a Week in Nature Is Associated with Good Health and Wellbeing', *Scientific Reports* 9:7730, 2019.
38. Viktor Frankl, *Man's Search for Meaning*, New York: Simon and Schuster, 1985, p. 101; Paul T. P. Wong, 'Toward a Dual-Systems Model of What Makes Life Worth Living' in *The Human Quest for Meaning: Theories, Research, and Applications*, ed. Paul T. P. Wong, New York: Routledge, 2012.
39. David Lykken and Auke Tellegen, 'Happiness Is a Stochastic Phenomenon', *Psychological Science* 7:3, 1996, pp. 186–9; Richard E. Lucas, 'Reexamining Adaptation and the Set Point Model of Happiness: Reactions to Changes in Marital Status', *Journal of Personality and Social Psychology* 84:3, 2003, pp. 527–39; Easterlin, 'Explaining Happiness'.
40. Sharon Begley, *Train Your Mind, Change Your Brain*, New York: Ballantine Books, 2007, p. 230; Haidt, *The Happiness Hypothesis*, pp. 91–2.
41. Harold D. Roth, *Original Tao: Inward Training and the Foundations of Taoist Mysticism*, New York: Columbia University Press, 1999, p. 103; Glenn Wallis, *Basic Teachings of the Buddha: A New Translation and Compilation, with a Guide to Reading the Texts*, New York: Random House, 2007, p. 151.
42. Eleanor A. Maguire et al., 'Navigation-Related Structural Change in the Hippocampi of Taxi Drivers', *PNAS* 97:8, 2000, pp. 4398–403; Denise C. Park

and Chih-Mao Huang, 'Culture Wires the Brain: A Cognitive Neuroscience Perspective', *Perspectives on Psychological Science* 5:4, 2010, pp. 391–400.

43. Richard J. Davidson and Bruce S. McEwen, 'Social Influences on Neuroplasticity: Stress and Interventions to Promote Well-Being', *Nature Neuroscience* 15:5, 2012, pp. 689–95; Begley, *Train Your Mind*, p. 230.
44. Britta K. Hölzel et al., 'How Does Mindfulness Meditation Work? Proposing Mechanisms of Action from a Conceptual and Neural Perspective', *Perspectives on Psychological Science* 6:6, 2011, pp. 537–59; James H. Austin, *Selfless Insight: Zen and the Meditative Transformations of Consciousness*, Cambridge, MA: MIT Press, 2009, p. 27.
45. Jon Kabat-Zinn, *Coming to Our Senses: Healing Ourselves and the World through Mindfulness*, New York: Hyperion, 2005, pp. 298–9; Jack Kornfield, *A Path with Heart: A Guide through the Perils and Promises of Spiritual Life*, New York: Bantam Books, 1993, p. 312; Antoine Lutz et al., 'Attention Regulation and Monitoring in Meditation', *Trends in Cognitive Sciences* 12:4, 2008, pp. 163–9.
46. Venerable Henepola Gunaratana, *Mindfulness in Plain English*, Somerville, MA: Wisdom Publications, 1991, p. 188; Nyanaponika Thera, *The Heart of Buddhist Meditation*, San Francisco, CA: Red Wheel/Weiser, 1965, p. 37; Kornfield, *A Path with Heart*, pp. 63–4; Chapter 5, 'The sacred dance of life'.
47. Siegel, *Pocket Guide to Interpersonal Neurobiology*, pp. 5, 29, 132–3.
48. Jon Kabat-Zinn, 'Foreword: Seeds of a Necessary Global Renaissance in the Making: The Refining of Psychology's Understanding of the Nature of Mind, Self, and Embodiment through the Lens of Mindfulness and Its Origins at a Key Inflection Point for the Species', *Current Opinion in Psychology* 28, 2019, pp. xi–xvii; Daniel Goleman and Richard J. Davidson, *Altered Traits: Science Reveals How Meditation Changes Your Mind, Brain, and Body*, New York: Penguin, 2017, p. 274.
49. Ibid.; Jacobs et al., 'Intensive Meditation Training'; Joshua A. Grant and Pierre Rainville, 'Pain Sensitivity and Analgesic Effects of Mindful States in Zen Meditators: A Cross-Sectional Study', *Psychosomatic Medicine* 71:1, 2009, pp. 106–14; Judson A. Brewer et al., 'Meditation Experience Is Associated with Differences in Default Mode Network Activity and Connectivity', *PNAS* 108:50, 2011, pp. 20254–9; Marcia Barinaga, 'Studying the Well-Trained Mind', *Science* 302, 2003, pp. 44–6.
50. Goleman and Davidson, *Altered Traits*, pp. 6, 90, 274.
51. Ibid. p. 290; Kabat-Zinn, 'Seeds of a Necessary Global Renaissance'; Eliza Barclay and Julia Belluz, 'The Growth of Yoga and Meditation in the US since 2012 Is Remarkable', *Vox*, 3 January 2019.
52. William George and Elizabeth Stanley quoted in Ronald Purser, *McMindfulness: How Mindfulness Became the New Capitalist Spirituality*, London: Repeater Books, 2019, pp. 171, 206–10; Garrett Gunderson, 'The Science Is in, and Meditation May Be the Next Big Business Opportunity', *Forbes*, 28 June 2016.
53. Capra and Luisi, *The Systems View of Life*, p. 327; David R. Loy, *A New Buddhist*

Path: Enlightenment, Evolution, and Ethics in the Modern World, Somerville, MA: Wisdom Publications, 2015, p. 126.

54. Buss, 'The Evolution of Happiness'; Richard Wilkinson and Kate Pickett, *The Spirit Level: Why Greater Equality Makes Societies Stronger*, New York: Bloomsbury Press, 2009, Kindle edn, location 3206.
55. George Monbiot, *Out of the Wreckage: A New Politics for an Age of Crisis*, New York: Verso, 2017, Kindle edn, location 249; Wilkinson and Pickett, *The Spirit Level*, Kindle edn, location 566.
56. Ibid., locations 598–616, 1038; Cody Delistraty, 'The Happiness Ruse', *Aeon*, 31 October 2019.
57. Peter C. Whybrow, *American Mania: When More Is Not Enough*, New York: W. W. Norton, 2005, iBook edn, Chapter 1; Forencich, *New Old Way*, Kindle edn, location 3401; Tim Kasser, *The High Price of Materialism*, Cambridge, MA: MIT Press, 2002, pp. 98–9; Easterlin, 'Explaining Happiness'.
58. Composite translation from: Lao Tsu, *Tao Te Ching*, transl. Gia-Fu Feng and Jane English, New York: Vintage, 1972, Chapters 44, 46; Lao Tzu, *Tao Te Ching*, transl. Ellen M. Chen, St Paul, MN: Paragon House, 1989; Lao Tzu, *Tao Teh Ching*, transl. John C. H. Wu, Boston: Shambhala, 2005.
59. Jeremy Lent, *The Patterning Instinct: A Cultural History of Humanity's Search for Meaning*, Amherst, NY: Prometheus, 2017, pp. 378–81.
60. Ibid.; Al Gore, *The Future: Six Drivers of Global Change*, New York: Random House, 2013, Chapter 4.
61. Ibid.; Lent, *The Patterning Instinct*, pp. 378–81.
62. David T. Courtwright, *The Age of Addiction: How Bad Habits Became Big Business*, Cambridge, MA: Belknap Press, 2019, Kindle edn, locations 129, 3242; Whybrow, *American Mania*, Chapter 7.
63. Jill Krasny, 'Every Parent Should Know the Scandalous History of Infant Formula', *Business Insider*, 25 June 2012; Courtwright, *The Age of Addiction*, Kindle edn, locations 3319–54; World Health Organization, 'Fact Sheet: Obesity and Overweight', 16 February 2018. War on Want, an NGO, published an exposé of Nestlé's practices in 1974, 'The Baby Killer', and was subsequently taken to court by Nestlé, which won the suit in 1976, although the judge urged the company to 'modify its publicity methods fundamentally'. This outcome was declared a 'moral victory' for consumers by *Time Magazine*.
64. Chilicki cited in R. De Vogli, *Progress Or Collapse: The Crises of Market Greed*, New York: Routledge, 2013, p. 47; Richard H. Robbins, *Global Problems and the Culture of Capitalism*, Boston: Pearson Education, 2008, p. 29; Sam Levin, 'Facebook Told Advertisers It Can Identify Teens Feeling "Insecure" and "Worthless"', *Guardian*, 1 May 2017.
65. Jacob Weisberg, 'We Are Hopelessly Hooked', *New York Review of Books*, 25 February 2016; Richard Freed, 'The Tech Industry's War on Kids: How Psychology Is Being Used as a Weapon against Children', *Medium*, 12 March 2018; Jon Brooks, 'Tech Insiders Call out Facebook for Literally Manipulating Your Brain', *KQED Science*, 25 May 2017.

66. George Monbiot, 'The Mind Hackers', *Guardian*, 6 January 2019; Weisberg, 'We Are Hopelessly Hooked'; Freed, 'The Tech Industry's War on Kids'.
67. Munro, *The Concept of Man in Early China*, p. 1.
68. Next System Project, 'The Index of Systemic Trends', 20 May 2019; Greg Leiserson, Will McGrew and Raksha Kopparam, 'The Distribution of Wealth in the United States and Implications for a Net Worth Tax', *Washington Center for Equitable Growth*, 21 March 2019.
69. Wilkinson and Pickett, *The Spirit Level*, Kindle edn, locations 397, 520, 1191–1223, 2548.
70. Ibid. Kindle edn, location 1103; Sapolsky, 'How Economic Inequality Inflicts Real Biological Harm'.
71. Wilkinson and Pickett, *The Spirit Level*, Kindle edn, locations 445, 670, 1001.
72. Tim Kasser, 'Values and Human Wellbeing', *Bellagio Initiative*, November 2011.
73. Lent, *The Patterning Instinct*, pp. 398–400; Clifford Cobb, Ted Halstead and Jonathan Rowe, 'If the GDP Is Up, Why Is America Down?' *Atlantic Monthly*, October 1995; Ida Kubiszewski et al., 'Beyond GDP: Measuring and Achieving Global Genuine Progress', *Ecological Economics* 93, 2013, pp. 57–68. See Chapter 13, 'The question of progress', for a more detailed discussion of this issue.
74. Monbiot, *Out of the Wreckage*, Kindle location 926; Wilkinson and Pickett, *The Spirit Level*, Kindle edn, location 215; Haidt, Seder and Kesebir, 'Hive Psychology'.
75. Lene Rachel Andersen and Tomas Björkman, *The Nordic Secret: A European Story of Beauty and Freedom*, Stockholm: Fri tanke, 2017, pp. 7–8; Jonathan Rowson, '*Bildung* in the 21st Century – Why Sustainable Prosperity Depends Upon Reimagining Education', *Centre for the Understanding of Sustainable Prosperity*, June 2019. The Scandinavian countries are Sweden, Norway, Denmark and Finland.
76. Mark Nepo, 'Eight Worldviews and Practices', *Parabola*, 27 October 2018; Helen Russell, 'How the World Smiles – Uncovering the Secret to Collective Happiness', *Guardian*, 27 October 2018.
77. Jens Korff, 'Deep Listening (Dadirri)', *Creative Spirits*, 30 May 2019; Wolfwalker Collection, 'Aho Mitakuye Oyasin', https://www.wolfwalkercollection.com/blogs/news/aho-mitakuye-oyasin
78. Quoted in Forencich, *New Old Way*, Kindle edn, location 3870; Susan L. Prescott et al., 'The Canmore Declaration: Statement of Principles for Planetary Health', *Challenges* 9:2, 2018; Kevin Queenan et al., 'Roadmap to a One Health Agenda 2030', *CAB Reviews* 12:14, 2017; Earth Charter: https://earthcharter.org/read-the-earth-charter/preamble/
79. M. H. Durie, 'A Maori Perspective of Health', *Social Science and Medicine* 20:5, 1985, pp. 483–6; Roger Walsh, 'What Is Wisdom? Cross-Cultural and Cross-Disciplinary Syntheses', *Review of General Psychology* 19:3, 2015, pp. 278–93.
80. Siu-chi Huang, *Essentials of Neo-Confucianism: Eight Major Philosophers of the Song and Ming Periods*, Westport, CT: Greenwood Press, 1999, pp. 48, 198; Roshi Philip Kapleau, *The Three Pillars of Zen*, New York: Anchor Books, 2000, p. 27; Goleman and Davidson, *Altered Traits*, p. 268.

81. Benjamin I. Huff, 'Eudaimonism in the Mencius: Fulfilling the Heart', *Dao* 14, 2015, pp. 403–31; Fung, *A Short History of Chinese Philosophy*, pp. 76–7.

Chapter 9: Cultivating Integrated Values

1. Mengzi, *Mengzi: With Selections from Traditional Commentaries*, transl. Bryan W. Van Norden, Indianapolis: Hackett, 2008, Book 2A6, pp. 46–7.
2. Peter Singer, *The Life You Can Save: Acting Now to End World Poverty*, New York: Random House, 2009, p. 3.
3. Chad Hansen, *A Daoist Theory of Chinese Thought: A Philosophical Interpretation*, New York: Oxford University Press, 2000, pp. 174–5; Edward Slingerland, *Trying Not to Try: Ancient China, Modern Science, and the Power of Spontaneity*, New York: Broadway Books, 2014, iBook edn, Chapter 5.
4. Jeremy Lent, *The Patterning Instinct: A Cultural History of Humanity's Search for Meaning*, Amherst, NY: Prometheus, 2017, pp. 231–3; Calvin quoted in David P. Barash, 'Is There a War Instinct?' *Aeon*, 19 September 2013.
5. Michael Shermer, *The Moral Arc: How Science Makes Us Better People*, New York: St Martin's Griffin, 2015, pp. 122–4.
6. Michael Ghiselin and Richard Alexander, cited in David Sloan Wilson, *Does Altruism Exist? Culture, Genes, and the Welfare of Others*, New Haven: Yale University Press, 2015, p. 34; Richard Wrangham and Dale Peterson, cited in Mathieu Ricard, *Altruism: The Power of Compassion to Change Yourself and the World*, transl. Charlotte Mandell and Sam Gordon, New York: Little, Brown & Co., 2015, iBook edn, Chapter 31.
7. Richard Dawkins, *The Selfish Gene: 30th Anniversary Edition*, London: Oxford University Press, 2006, pp. xiv, 3.
8. Frans de Waal, *Good Natured: The Origins of Right and Wrong in Humans and Other Animals*, Cambridge, MA: Harvard University Press, 1996, Kindle edn, locations 538–56.
9. David Sloan Wilson, Eric Dietrich and Anne B. Clark, 'On the Inappropriate Use of the Naturalistic Fallacy in Evolutionary Psychology', *Biology and Philosophy* 18, 2003, pp. 669–82; Shermer, *The Moral Arc*, pp. 31–3.
10. Steven Pinker, *The Better Angels of Our Nature: The Decline of Violence in History and Its Causes*, New York: Allen Lane, 2011.
11. Ibid. iBook edn, Chapters 2, 4, 9.
12. Shermer, *The Moral Arc*, pp. 1–4; Pinker, *The Better Angels*, Chapters 5, 7, 9.
13. See Chapter 6, 'What does life want?'
14. Andreas Weber, *The Biology of Wonder: Aliveness, Feeling, and the Metamorphosis of Science*, Gabriola Island, BC, Canada: New Society Publishers, 2016, p. 340; Chapter 2, 'The moods of a worm'; Gerald M. Edelman and Giulio Tononi, *A Universe of Consciousness: How Matter Becomes Imagination*, New York: Basic Books, 2000, pp. 88–91.
15. Gerald Wiest, 'Neural and Mental Hierarchies', *Frontiers in Psychology* 3:516, 2012, pp. 1–8. The triune brain theory has been criticized for being too simplistic as a model of the human brain, and potentially leading to a misleading view of human psychology depicting the three brains in conflict

with each other. However, one of the leading pioneers of affective neuroscience, Jaak Panksepp, has dismissed these criticisms, stating, 'This three-layered conceptualization helps us grasp the overall function of higher brain areas better than any other scheme yet devised.' For a critique of the model, see Lisa Feldman Barrett, 'Emotional Intelligence Needs a Rewrite', *Nautilus*, 3 August 2017.

16. Darcia Narvaez, 'Triune Ethics: The Neurobiological Roots of Our Multiple Moralities', *New Ideas in Psychology* 26:1, 2008, pp. 95–119.
17. Ibid.; Frans B. M. de Waal, 'The Antiquity of Empathy', *Science* 336, 2012, pp. 874–6.
18. Patricia Churchland, interviewed in Sigal Samuel, 'How Your Brain Invents Morality', *Vox*, 8 July 2019.
19. De Waal, 'The Antiquity of Empathy'; Inbal Ben-Ami Bartal, Jean Decety and Peggy Mason, 'Empathy and Pro-Social Behavior in Rats', *Science* 334, 2011, pp. 1427–30.
20. Narvaez, 'Triune Ethics'; Frans de Waal, *Are We Smart Enough to Know How Smart Animals Are?* New York: W. W. Norton, 2016, pp. 132–3.
21. Ibid. pp. 193–5; De Waal, 'The Antiquity of Empathy'; De Waal, *Good Natured*, Kindle edn, locations 1863–5; Kim Sterelny, 'Morality's Dark Past', *Analyse & Kritik* 34:1, 2012, pp. 95–115.
22. Sarah Blaffer Hrdy, *Mothers and Others: The Evolutionary Origins of Mutual Understanding*, Cambridge, MA: Harvard University Press, 2009, pp. 1–3; Joan B. Silk and Bailey R. House, 'The Evolution of Altruistic Social Preferences in Human Groups', *Philosophical Transactions of the Royal Society* B 371, 2016, 20150097.
23. Chapter 3, 'How "I" and the "self" split apart'; Lent, *The Patterning Instinct*, pp. 39–47; Christopher Boehm, *Moral Origins: The Evolution of Virtue, Altruism, and Shame*, New York: Basic Books, 2012, pp. 133–78; Thomas Suddendorf, *The Gap: The Science of What Separates Us from Other Animals*, New York: Basic Books, 2013, pp. 240–1; C. Owen Lovejoy, 'Reexamining Human Origins in Light of Ardipithecus Ramidus', *Science* 326, 2009, 74e1–74e8.
24. Jorge Moll et al., 'The Neural Correlates of Moral Sensitivity: A Functional Magnetic Resonance Imaging Investigation of Basic and Moral Emotions', *Journal of Neuroscience* 22:7, 2002, pp. 2730–6; Jorge Moll et al., 'The Neural Basis of Human Moral Cognition', *Nature Reviews: Neuroscience* 6, October 2005, pp. 799–809; Aron K. Barbey, Frank Krueger and Jordan Grafman, 'An Evolutionarily Adaptive Neural Architecture for Social Reasoning', *Trends in Neurosciences* 32:12, 2009, pp. 603–10; Joshua W. Buckholtz and René Marois, 'The Roots of Modern Justice: Cognitive and Neural Foundations of Social Norms and Their Enforcement', *Nature Neuroscience* 15:5, 2012, pp. 655–61.
25. Leonardo Christov-Moore et al., 'Increasing Generosity by Disrupting Prefrontal Cortex', *Social Neuroscience* 12:2, 2017, pp. 174–81; Michael Tomasello, 'Why Be Nice? Better Not Think About It', *Trends in Cognitive Sciences* 16:12, 2012, pp. 580–1; Boehm, *Moral Origins*, pp. 210–12.

26. Christopher Boehm, *Hierarchy in the Forest: The Evolution of Egalitarian Behavior*, Cambridge, MA: Harvard University Press, 1999; Boehm, 'Egalitarian Behavior and Reverse Dominance Hierarchy', *Current Anthropology* 34:3, 1993, pp. 227–54; David Sloan Wilson and Edward O. Wilson, 'Rethinking the Theoretical Foundation of Sociobiology', *Quarterly Review of Biology* 82:4, 2007, pp. 327–48.
27. Maciek Chudek and Joseph Henrich, 'Culture–Gene Coevolution, Norm-Psychology and the Emergence of Human Prosociality', *Trends in Cognitive Sciences* 15:5, 2011, pp. 218–26; Robert Boyd and Peter J. Richerson, 'Culture and the Evolution of Human Cooperation', *Philosophical Transactions of the Royal Society* B 364:1533, 2009, pp. 3281–8; Wilson, *Does Altruism Exist?* p. 147; Jonathan Haidt, 'The New Synthesis in Moral Psychology', *Science* 316, 2007, pp. 998–1002; Boehm, *Moral Origins*, pp. 177, 210–12; Sterelny, 'Morality's Dark Past'.
28. Wilson, *Does Altruism Exist?* p. 51; Darwin, *The Descent of Man* (1871) cited in Wilson, Dietrich and Clark, 'On the Inappropriate Use.'
29. Ernst Fehr and Bettina Rockenbach, 'Human Altruism: Economic, Neural, and Evolutionary Perspectives', *Current Opinion in Neurobiology* 14, 2004, pp. 784–90; Katrin Riedl et al., 'No Third-Party Punishment in Chimpanzees', *PNAS* 109:37, 2012, pp. 14824–9.
30. Paul Bloom, *Just Babies: The Origins of Good and Evil*, New York: Crown Publishing Group, 2013; Owen Flanagan, *The Geography of Morals: Varieties of Moral Possibility*, New York: Oxford University Press, 2017, pp. 261–4; Shermer, *The Moral Arc*, p. 44.
31. Lent, *The Patterning Instinct*, pp. 103–16, 294–300; Peter J. Richerson and Robert Boyd, 'Complex Societies: The Evolutionary Origins of a Crude Superorganism', *Human Nature* 10:3, 1999, pp. 253–89.
32. Samuel Bowles, 'Conflict: Altruism's Midwife', *Nature* 456, 2008, pp. 326–7. As we saw in Chapter 3, 'The democracy of consciousness', along with their moral instincts for the in-group, humans have also evolved an intuitive mistrust for strangers (something that has also been demonstrated in experiments on preverbal infants). This reinforced the parochial altruism that allowed the rise of agrarian domination systems.
33. Riane Eisler and Douglas P. Fry, *Nurturing Our Humanity: How Domination and Partnership Shape Our Brains, Lives, and Future*, New York: Oxford University Press, 2019, pp. 2–12, 99, 281–2. Eisler and Fry point out that, although agrarian societies are primarily domination systems, there have been some exceptions to this rule, such as the matrilineal societies of the Moso in China and also the Minangkabau in Sumatra, which numbers about four million people and is a Muslim culture. See Eisler and Fry, pp. 132–40.
34. Ara Norenzayan et al., 'The Cultural Evolution of Prosocial Religions', *Behavioral and Brain Sciences* 39, 2016, pp. 1–65; Ilkka Pyysiäinen and Marc Hauser, 'The Origins of Religion: Evolved Adaptation or By-product?' *Trends in Cognitive Sciences* 14:3, 2010, pp. 104–9; Frans L. Roes and Michel Raymond,

'Belief in Moralizing Gods', *Evolution and Human Behavior* 24:2, 2002, pp. 126–35; Sterelny, 'Morality's Dark Past'.

35. Craig Dilworth, *Too Smart for Our Own Good: The Ecological Predicament of Humankind*, New York: Cambridge University Press, 2010, pp. 282, 307; Peter Singer, *The Expanding Circle: Ethics, Evolution, and Moral Progress*, Princeton, NJ: Princeton University Press, 1981, Kindle edn, location 1674; Robert M. Sapolsky, *Behave: The Biology of Humans at Our Best and Worst*, New York: Penguin, 2017, pp. 544–5.
36. Shmuel N. Eisenstadt, 'The Axial Age Breakthroughs – Their Characteristics and Origins' in *The Origins & Diversity of Axial Age Civilizations*, ed. Shmuel N. Eisenstadt, Albany, NY: SUNY Press, 1986, p. 5; Scott Atran, 'Moralizing Religions: Prosocial or a Privilege of Wealth?' *Behavioral and Brain Sciences* 39, 2016, pp. 19–20; Pascal Boyer and Nicolas Baumard, 'Projecting Weird Features on Ancient Religions', *Behavioral and Brain Sciences* 39, 2016, pp. 23–4; Jeremy Rifkin, *The Empathic Civilization: The Race to Global Consciousness in a World in Crisis*, New York: Penguin, 2009, pp. 234–5; Singer, *The Expanding Circle*, Kindle edn, location 1856.
37. Lent, *The Patterning Instinct*, pp. 215–26, 239–50, 317–24.
38. Paul Bloom, 'Religion, Morality, Evolution', *Annual Review of Psychology* 63, 2012, pp. 179–99; Jan Eichhorn, 'Happiness for Believers? Contextualizing the Effects of Religiosity on Life-Satisfaction', *European Sociological Review* 28:5, 2012, pp. 583–93; Michael E. McCullough and Brian L. B. Willoughby, 'Religion, Self-Regulation, and Self-Control: Associations, Explanations, and Implications', *Psychological Bulletin* 135:1, 2009, pp. 69–93.
39. Stephen Gaukroger, *The Emergence of a Scientific Culture*, New York: Oxford University Press, 2006; Dennis Overbye, 'Elevating Science, Elevating Democracy', *New York Times*, 27 January 2009; Steven Pinker, *Enlightenment Now: The Case for Reason, Science, Humanism, and Progress*, New York: Viking, 2018, pp. 8–12.
40. Lent, *The Patterning Instinct*, pp. 30–6.
41. Robert Wright, *The Evolution of God*, New York: Hachette Books, 2009, p. 356; Steven Weinberg, 'Without God', *New York Review of Books* LV:14, 2008, pp. 73–6.
42. Both examples selected by N. Arpaly, cited in Narvaez, 'Triune Ethics'.
43. Joshua Greene and Jonathan Haidt, 'How (and Where) Does Moral Judgment Work?' *Trends in Cognitive Sciences* 6:12, 2002, pp. 517–23; Joshua D. Greene et al., 'An fMRI Investigation of Emotional Engagement in Moral Judgment', *Science* 293, 2001, pp. 2105–8.
44. Samuel M. McClure, 'Separate Neural Systems Value Immediate and Delayed Monetary Rewards', *Science* 306, 2004, pp. 503–7; Moll et al., 'The Neural Basis'.
45. Greene and Haidt, 'Moral Judgment'; Jonathan Haidt, 'The Emotional Dog and Its Rational Tail: A Social Intuitionist Approach to Moral Judgment', *Psychological Review* 108:4, 2001, pp. 814–34; Chadd M. Funk and Michael S. Gazzaniga, 'The Functional Brain Architecture of Human Morality', *Current*

Opinion in Neurobiology 19:6, 2009, pp. 678–81; Haidt, 'The New Synthesis'; Sapolsky, *Behave*, p. 554.

46. Examples cited in Paul Bloom, 'How Do Morals Change?' *Nature* 464, 2010, p. 490. *Uncle Tom's Cabin* is itself a noteworthy example of the evolution of cultural norms. The same book that helped to fuel the progressive abolitionist cause in the 1850s has in recent decades been appropriately critiqued for its condescending and racist stereotypes of Black people.
47. Pinker, *The Better Angels of Our Nature*, Chapter 9; Shermer, *The Moral Arc*, p. 25; Sam Harris, *The Moral Landscape: How Science Can Determine Human Values*, New York: Free Press, 2011.
48. Pinker, *The Better Angels of Our Nature*, Chapter 9; Pinker, *Enlightenment Now*, pp. 26–8; Shermer, *The Moral Arc*, pp. 121–4; Harris, *The Moral Landscape*, pp. 2–4.
49. Ibid. pp. 8–12; Shermer, *The Moral Arc*, pp. 12–13, 398.
50. Ibid. p. 14.
51. David Harvey, *A Brief History of Neoliberalism*, New York: Oxford University Press, 2005; Wilson, *Does Altruism Exist?* pp. 101–9.
52. Harvey, *Neoliberalism*; Al Gore, *The Future: Six Drivers of Global Change*, New York: Random House, 2013, pp. 92–139; Lent, *The Patterning Instinct*, pp. 382–9.
53. Joe Myers, 'How Do the World's Biggest Companies Compare to the Biggest Economies?' *World Economic Forum Agenda*, 19 October 2016; Richard Gale and Gary Null, 'Who Controls Our Government? The Psychopathic Corporate Elites of America', *Global Research*, 3 March 2014; Nathan Brooks and Katarina Fritzon, 'Psychopathic Personality Characteristics Amongst High Functioning Populations', *Crime Psychology Review* 2:1, 2016, pp. 22–44; Ricard, *Altruism*, Chapter 27; Joel Bakan, *The New Corporation: How 'Good' Corporations Are Bad for Democracy*, New York: Vintage Books, 2020, p. 57.
54. Ibid, Chapter 33; WWF, *Living Planet Report – 2020: Bending the Curve of Biodiversity Loss*, Gland, Switzerland: WWF, 2020; Yuval Noah Harari, *Sapiens: A Brief History of Humankind*, London: Harvill Secker, 2014, pp. 341–6; Ezra Klein, 'Peter Singer on the Lives You Can Save', *Vox*, 6 December 2019.
55. Jason Hickel, *The Divide: Global Inequality from Conquest to Free Markets*, New York: W. W. Norton, 2017, pp. 15–16; Larry Elliott, 'World's 26 Richest People Own as Much as Poorest 50%, Says Oxfam', *Guardian*, 20 January 2019; Jason Hickel, 'The Moral Egregiousness of Poverty Is Worse Than Ever before in History', *Resilience*, 30 August 2018.
56. Massimo Pigliucci, *How to Be a Stoic: Using Ancient Philosophy to Live a Modern Life*, New York: Basic Books, 2017, pp. 59–62; Singer, *The Expanding Circle*, Kindle edn, locations 1644–57; Rifkin, *The Empathic Civilization*; De Waal, *Good Natured*, Kindle edn, locations 2985–3000; Shermer, *The Moral Arc*, p. 186.
57. Markus Christen, Darcia Narvaez and Eveline Gutzwiller-Helfenfinger,

'Comparing and Integrating Biological and Cultural Moral Progress', *Ethical Theory and Moral Practice* 20:1, 2017, pp. 55–73.

58. Quoted in LaDonna Harris and Jacqueline Wasilewski, 'Indigeneity, an Alternative Worldview: Four R's (Relationship, Responsibility, Reciprocity, Redistribution) Vs. Two P's (Power and Profit). Sharing the Journey Towards Conscious Evolution', *Systems Research and Behavioral Science* 21, 2004, pp. 489–503.
59. Ibid. See also Robin Wall Kimmerer, *Braiding Sweetgrass: Indigenous Wisdom, Scientific Knowledge and the Teachings of Plants*, Minneapolis: Milkweed Editions, 2013, pp. 27–8, 134.
60. Ibid.; Christen, Narvaez and Gutzwiller-Helfenfinger, 'Biological and Cultural Moral Progress'.
61. Julia Ching, *To Acquire Wisdom: The Way of Wang Yang-Ming*, New York: Columbia University Press, 1976, p. 62; Siu-chi Huang, *Essentials of Neo-Confucianism: Eight Major Philosophers of the Song and Ming Periods*, Westport, CT: Greenwood Press, 1999, pp. 204–7.
62. Stephen C. Angle, *Sagehood: The Contemporary Significance of Neo-Confucian Philosophy*, New York: Oxford University Press, 2009, pp. 52–3; Slingerland, *Trying Not to Try*, Chapter 5.
63. Sutta Nipata, quoted in Joanna Macy, *Mutual Causality in Buddhism and General Systems Theory: The Dharma of Natural Systems*, Albany, NY: SUNY Press, 1991, pp. 193–5; Flanagan, *The Geography of Morals*, pp. 241–2.
64. Daniel Goleman and Richard J. Davidson, *Altered Traits: Science Reveals How Meditation Changes Your Mind, Brain, and Body*, New York: Penguin, 2017, p. 107.
65. Quoted in Flanagan, *The Geography of Morals*, p. 163.
66. Ricard, *Altruism*, Chapter 4; Bethany E. Kok and Tania Singer, 'Phenomenological Fingerprints of Four Meditations: Differential State Changes in Affect, Mind-Wandering, Meta-Cognition, and Interoception before and after Daily Practice across 9 Months of Training', *Mindfulness* 8, 2017, pp. 218–31; Goleman and Davidson, *Altered Traits*, pp. 111–12. It is important to note that a crucial distinction exists between empathy and compassion. Empathy plays a vital role in attuning with the suffering of another. However, empathy alone doesn't necessarily lead to moral behavior. People can feel empathic distress but react to another's suffering by wanting to turn away. Additionally, empathy for those in your in-group can easily incite prejudice against outsiders seen as responsible for their suffering. Too much of it can also lead to a condition known as empathy fatigue, which is seen in the burnout experienced by people who are daily confronted with the suffering of others, such as healthcare workers. Compassion, on the other hand, is what arises when empathy is linked to an altruistic concern for the other person. It is characterized by a sincere determination to alleviate the suffering of the other person, in whatever form that might take. In contrast to empathy, compassion doesn't lead to burnout; rather it increases positive emotions and can act as a buffer against stress, depression or anxiety. In this sense, empathy

is like a spark that ignites compassion, which then becomes a self-sustaining motivation to reduce the suffering of others. See: Ricard, *Altruism*, Chapters 2, 3, 4; Paul Bloom, 'Empathy and Its Discontents', *Trends in Cognitive Sciences* 21:1, 2017, pp. 24–31; Olga M. Klimecki et al., 'Differential Pattern of Functional Brain Plasticity after Compassion and Empathy Training', *Scan* 9, 2014, pp. 873–9; Olga M. Klimecki et al., 'Functional Neural Plasticity and Associated Changes in Positive Affect after Compassion Training', *Cerebral Cortex* 23:7, 2013, pp. 1552–61; Ricard, *Altruism*, Chapters 2, 4; Kok and Singer, 'Phenomenological Fingerprints'; Goleman and Davidson, *Altered Traits*, pp. 237–8.

67. Boehm, *Hierarchy in the Forest*, pp. 183–209; Eisler and Fry, *Nurturing Our Humanity*, pp. 99–101, 282.
68. Indra Adnan, 'How Has Denmark Become Regularly the Happiest Nation in the World? Empathy Classes at School Help', *Alternative UK*, 10 October 2019. For examples of encouraging compassion and altruism initiatives in the US, see Goleman and Davidson, *Altered Traits*, pp. 279–80 and Wilson, *Does Altruism Exist?* pp. 121–36. In light of the distinction drawn in Note 66 between empathy and compassion, it should be noted that even though these classes use the term empathy, they are really teaching compassion practices.
69. Paul Ekman, *Moving toward Global Compassion*, San Francisco: Paul Ekman Group, 2014; Sigal Samuel, 'Should Animals, Plants, and Robots Have the Same Rights as You?' *Vox*, 4 April 2019; Matthew Hutson, 'Biases Aren't Forever', *Scientific American*, April 2019; Jeremy Lent, 'Steven Pinker's Ideas About Progress Are Fatally Flawed. These Eight Graphs Show Why', Patterns of Meaning blog, 17 May 2018.
70. Albert Schweitzer, *Reverence for Life: The Words of Albert Schweitzer*, Anna Maria, FL: Maurice Bassett, 2017, pp. 18, 27. For a selection of the many other visionaries who have called for a new life-based ethic for our civilization, see Ervin Laszlo, *The Systems View of the World: A Holistic Vision for Our Time*, Cresskill, NJ: Hampton Press, 1996; Joanna Macy, *Active Hope: How to Face the Mess We're in without Going Crazy*, Novato, CA: New World Library, 2012; Fritjof Capra, *The Turning Point: Science, Society, and the Rising Culture*, New York: Bantam Books, 1988; Thomas Berry, *The Great Work: Our Way into the Future*, New York: Three Rivers Press, 1999; David C. Korten, *Change the Story, Change the Future: A Living Economy for a Living Earth*, Oakland, CA: Berrett-Koehler, 2015; R. W. Sperry, 'Bridging Science and Values: A Unifying View of Mind and Brain', *American Psychologist* 32:4, 1977, pp. 237–45; Rifkin, *The Empathic Civilization*; David R. Loy, *A New Buddhist Path: Enlightenment, Evolution, and Ethics in the Modern World*, Somerville, MA: Wisdom Publications, 2015; 'World Scientists' Warning to Humanity', *Union of Concerned Scientists*, 1992; J. Baird Callicott, 'Toward a Global Environmental Ethic' in *Worldviews & Ecology: Religion, Philosophy, and the Environment*, ed. Mary Evelyn Tucker and John A. Grim, Maryknoll, NY: Orbis Books, 1994.

Chapter 10: Human/Nature

1. From the *Lieh-Tzu*, cited in Joseph Needham, *Science and Civilisation in China, Volume 2: History of Scientific Thought*, London: Cambridge University Press, 1972, pp. 55–6.
2. Arthur O. Lovejoy, *The Great Chain of Being: A Study of the History of an Idea*, Cambridge, MA: Harvard University Press, 1964, pp. 186–7.
3. Jeremy Lent, *The Patterning Instinct: A Cultural History of Humanity's Search for Meaning*, Amherst, NY: Prometheus, 2017, pp. 277–8.
4. Sir Thomas More, cited in David E. Stannard, *American Holocaust: Columbus and the Conquest of the New World*, New York: Oxford University Press, 1992, pp. 233–4.
5. Liz Sonneborn, *Chronology of American Indian History*, New York: Infobase Publishing, 2007, p. 152.
6. Quoted in David Johns, 'With Friends Like These, Wilderness and Biodiversity Do Not Need Enemies' in *Keeping the Wild: Against the Domestication of Earth*, ed. George Wuerthner, Eileen Crist and Tom Butler, Washington DC: Island Press, 2014, Kindle edn, location 42.
7. Lao Tzu, *Tao Te Ching*, transl. Ellen M. Chen, St Paul, MN: Paragon House, 1989, Chapter 29, pp. 126–7.
8. Will Steffen et al., 'The Trajectory of the Anthropocene: The Great Acceleration', *Anthropocene Review* 2:1, 2015, pp. 1–18; John Bongaarts, 'Human Population Growth and the Demographic Transition', *Philosophical Transactions of the Royal Society* B 364:1532, 2009, pp. 2985–90.
9. Jonathan Watts, 'Human Society under Urgent Threat from Loss of Earth's Natural Life', *Guardian*, 6 May 2019; Peter M. Vitousek et al., 'Human Domination of Earth's Ecosystems', *Science* 277, 1997, pp. 494–9; James Gustave Speth, *The Bridge at the Edge of the World: Capitalism, the Environment, and Crossing from Crisis to Sustainability*, New Haven: Yale University Press, 2008, pp. 1–2.
10. Al Gore, *The Future: Six Drivers of Global Change,* New York: Random House, 2013, iBook edn, Chapter 4; David Perlman, 'Scientists Alarmed by Ocean Dead-Zone Growth', *San Francisco Chronicle*, 15 August 2008; Sarah Kaplan, 'By 2050, There Will Be More Plastic Than Fish in the World's Oceans, Study Says', *Washington Post*, 20 January 2016.
11. WWF, *Living Planet Report – 2020: Bending the Curve of Biodiversity Loss*, Gland, Switzerland: WWF, 2020; Chris Martenson, 'Collapse Is Already Here', *Resilience*, 31 January 2019; George Monbiot, 'Insectageddon: Farming Is More Catastrophic Than Climate Breakdown', *Guardian*, 20 October 2017.
12. Anthony D. Barnosky et al., 'Has the Earth's Sixth Mass Extinction Already Arrived?' *Nature* 471, 2011, pp. 51–7; Edward O. Wilson, *Half-Earth: Our Planet's Fight for Life*, New York: Liveright Publishing, 2016, pp. 54–7, 134–5.
13. Jonathan Watts, 'We Have 12 Years to Limit Climate Change Catastrophe, Warns UN', *Guardian*, 8 October 2018; David Roberts, 'The World's Bleak Climate Situation, in 3 Charts', *Vox*, 1 May 2018; David Spratt and Ian

Dunlop, *What Lies Beneath: The Understatement of Existential Climate Risk*, Melbourne: Breakthrough – National Centre for Climate Restoration, 2018.

14. Jane Lubchenco, 'Entering the Century of the Environment: A New Social Contract for Science', *Science* 279, 1998, pp. 491–7; Will Steffen, Paul J. Crutzen and John R. McNeill, 'The Anthropocene: Are Humans Now Overwhelming the Great Forces of Nature', *Ambio: A Journal of the Human Environment* 36:8, 2007, pp. 614–21; Colin N. Waters, 'The Anthropocene Is Functionally and Stratigraphically Distinct from the Holocene', *Science* 351:6269, 2016, p. 137, aad2622–1-10.
15. Johan Rockström et al., 'A Safe Operating Space for Humanity', *Nature* 461, 2009, pp. 472–5; William J. Ripple et al., 'World Scientists' Warning to Humanity: A Second Notice', *BioScience* 67:12, 2017, pp. 1026–8; Will Steffen et al., 'Planetary Boundaries: Guiding Human Development on a Changing Planet', *Science* 347:6223, 2015, 1259855.
16. Stewart Brand, 'We Are as Gods and Have to Get Good at It', *Edge*, 18 August 2009; Emma Marris, 'Ecology without Wilderness: Tending the Global Garden We Call "Nature"', *Atlantic*, 11 September 2011; John Asafu-Adjaye et al., 'An Ecomodernist Manifesto', *Ecomodernism*, April 2015.
17. Ibid.; Peter Kareiva, 'Conservation in the Anthropocene', *Breakthrough Journal*, 2, 2012; Emma Marris, 'Handle with Care', *Orion*, 22 April 2015. Kareiva, Marris and their colleagues take their cue from a debate that's been brewing for many years. Many of their ideas spring from a provocative essay by historian William Cronon published in 1995 which argued that the conception of wilderness as something sacred was a construction of Western sensibilities that arose during the Romantic age, and that the related notion of a pristine pre-Columbian American landscape was a falsification of history. See William Cronon, 'The Trouble with Wilderness: Or, Getting Back to the Wrong Nature', *Environmental History* 1:1, 1996, pp. 7–28; also Jordan Fisher Smith, 'The Wilderness Paradox', *Orion*, September/October 2014, pp. 34–8.
18. Lent, *The Patterning Instinct*, pp. 97–9; George Monbiot, *Feral: Rewilding the Land, the Sea, and Human Life*, Chicago, IL: University of Chicago Press, 2014, pp. 87–8; Susan Rule et al., 'The Aftermath of Megafaunal Extinction: Ecosystem Transformation in Pleistocene Australia', *Science* 335, 2012, pp. 1483–6; David A. Burney and Timothy F. Flannery, 'Fifty Millennia of Catastrophic Extinctions after Human Contact', *Trends in Ecology & Evolution* 20:7, 2005, pp. 395–401.
19. J. B. MacKinnon, *The Once and Future World: Nature as It Was, as It Is, as It Could Be*, New York: Houghton Mifflin Harcourt, 2013; J. Tyler Faith and Todd A. Surovell, 'Synchronous Extinction of North America's Pleistocene Mammals', *PNAS* 106:49, 2009, pp. 20641–5.
20. Camille Parmesan, 'Where the Wild Things Were', *Dædalus*, spring 2008, pp. 31–8; Monbiot, *Feral*, pp. 90–1; MacKinnon, *The Once and Future World*, p. 84; Nicole L. Boivin et al., 'Ecological Consequences of Human Niche Construction: Examining Long-Term Anthropogenic Shaping of Global Species Distributions', *PNAS* 113:23, 2016, pp. 6388–96; Clive Ponting, *A*

New Green History of the World: The Environment and the Collapse of Great Civilizations, New York: Penguin, 2007, p. 74.

21. Leo Marx, 'The Idea of Nature in America', *Dædalus,* spring 2008, pp. 8–21; Charles C. Mann, '1491', *Atlantic Monthly*, March 2002.
22. Ibid.; MacKinnon, *The Once and Future World*, p. 15.
23. Bill McKibben, *The End of Nature*, New York: Random House, 2006; Peter Dauvergne, *Will Big Business Destroy the Planet?* Medford, MA: Polity Press, 2018, p. 87.
24. Stewart Brand, 'Rethinking Extinction', *Aeon*, 21 April 2015; citation from *The Economist* in Eileen Crist, *Abundant Earth: Toward an Ecological Civilization*, Chicago, IL: University of Chicago Press, 2019, p. 49; Kareiva, 'Conservation in the Anthropocene'.
25. Paul Kingsnorth, 'Dark Ecology', *Orion*, January 2013; Richard T. Corlett, 'The Anthropocene Concept in Ecology and Conservation', *Trends in Ecology & Evolution* 30:1, 2015, pp. 36–41; George Wuerthner, 'Why the Working Landscape Isn't Working' in *Keeping the Wild: Against the Domestication of Earth*, ed. George Wuerthner, Eileen Crist and Tom Butler, Washington DC: Island Press, 2014; Tom Butler, 'Lives Not Our Own' in *Keeping the Wild*, p. x.
26. Anne D. Guerry, 'Natural Capital and Ecosystem Services Informing Decisions: From Promise to Practice', *PNAS* 112:24, 2015, pp. 7348–55; Emma Marris, 'Putting a Price on Nature', *Nature* 462:7271, 2009, pp. 270–1.
27. Amy West, 'Core Concept: Ecosystem Services', *PNAS* 112:24, 2015, pp. 7337–8; Erik Gómez-Baggethun and Manuel Ruiz-Pérez, 'Economic Valuation and the Commodification of Ecosystem Services', *Progress in Physical Geography* 35:5, 2011, pp. 613–28.
28. Jutta Kill, *Economic Valuation of Nature: The Price to Pay for Conservation? A Critical Exploration*, Brussels: Rosa-Luxemburg-Stiftung, 2014; Fred Pearce, 'Price Tags for Planet Earth', *New Scientist*, 16 October 2010, pp. 8–9; Robert Costanza et al., 'The Value of the World's Ecosystem Services and Natural Capital', *Nature* 387, 1997, pp. 253–60; Carl Zimmer, 'Putting a Price Tag on Nature's Defenses', *New York Times*, 5 June 2014; Sian Sullivan, 'Nature Is Being Renamed "Natural Capital" – But Is It Really the Planet That Will Profit?' *Conversation*, 13 September 2016.
29. Jonathan Silvertown, 'Have Ecosystem Services Been Oversold?' *Trends in Ecology & Evolution* 30:11, 2015, pp. 641–8; Gómez-Baggethun and Ruiz-Pérez, 'Economic Valuation'.
30. Jennifer Hansler, 'Pompeo: Melting Sea Ice Presents "New Opportunities for Trade"', *CNN*, 7 May 2019.
31. Lent, *The Patterning Instinct*, pp. 27–36, 277–92; Crist, *Abundant Earth*, pp. 67–9; Silvertown, 'Have Ecosystem Services Been Oversold?'
32. Jeff Tolleson, 'The Sun Dimmers', *Nature* 563, 2018, pp. 613–15; Naomi Klein, *This Changes Everything: Capitalism Vs. The Climate*, New York: Simon & Schuster, 2014, iBook edn, Chapter 8; *The Economist*, 'Sunny with Overcast Features: Countries Look at Ways to Tinker with Earth's Thermostat', *The*

Economist, 14 March 2019; *The Economist*, 'Political Economy Suggests That Geoengineering Is Likely to Be Used', *The Economist*, 27 April 2019.

33. Derrick Jensen, *The Myth of Human Supremacy*, New York: Seven Stories Press, 2016; Michael J. Sandel, *What Money Can't Buy: The Moral Limits of Markets*, New York: Farrar, Straus and Giroux, 2013; Silvertown, 'Have Ecosystem Services Been Oversold?'
34. Cited in Kill, *Economic Valuation of Nature*.
35. Reference to Joni Mitchell originally made by George Monbiot, 'The Unseen World', *Guardian*, 28 December 2017.
36. Daniel Pauly, 'Anecdotes and the Shifting Baseline Syndrome of Fisheries', *Trends in Ecology & Evolution* 10:10, 1995, p. 430; MacKinnon, *The Once and Future World*, pp. 17–18, 34.
37. Ibid., pp. 42–52; Crist, *Abundant Earth*, pp. 12–16. There has been a debate about the true significance of the abundance of passenger pigeons in the nineteenth century, with some arguing that it was rather a 'pathological' reaction to the prior disruptions of the ecological system, including the virtual elimination of Indigenous Native Americans, who had previously competed with them for the nuts that were their primary nourishment. More in-depth studies suggest that, while this may be true to some extent, the pre-Columbian abundance of passenger pigeons would still have been an awe-inspiring spectacle. See MacKinnon, *The Once and Future World*, pp. 49–52.
38. Carl Safina, 'In Defense of Biodiversity: Why Protecting Species from Extinction Matters', *Yale Environment 360*, 12 February 2018; David Tilman, 'Biodiversity & Environmental Sustainability Amid Human Domination of Global Ecosystems', *Dædalus* 141:3, 2012, pp. 108–20; Crist, *Abundant Earth*, pp. 18–19; MacKinnon, *The Once and Future World*, p. 37; Wilson, *Half-Earth*, p. 156; Chapter 6, 'The deep learning of the ecosystem'.
39. Damian Carrington, 'Humans Just 0.01% of All Life but Have Destroyed 83% of Wild Mammals – Study', *Guardian*, 21 May 2018; Yinon M. Bar-On, Rob Phillips and Ron Milo, 'The Biomass Distribution on Earth,' *PNAS* 115:25, 2018, pp. 6506–11; Gerardo Ceballos, Paul R. Ehrlich and Rodolfo Dirzo, 'Biological Annihilation Via the Ongoing Sixth Mass Extinction Signaled by Vertebrate Population Losses and Declines', *PNAS* 114:30, 2017, E6089–E96; Carl Safina, *Beyond Words: What Animals Think and Feel*, New York: Henry Holt and Co., 2015, p. 112; MacKinnon, *The Once and Future World*, pp. 37, 103; Crist, *Abundant Earth*, pp. 15–16; Joseph Ogutu, 'Wildebeest Migrations in East Africa Face Extinction. What Must Be Done', *Conversation*, 7 May 2019; John R. Platt, 'Climate Change Is Killing These Ancient Trees, but That's Just Part of the Story', *Scientific American*, 17 July 2018; Graham Readfearn and Adam Morton, 'Almost 3 Billion Animals Affected by Australian Bushfires, Report Shows', *Guardian*, 28 July 2020.
40. Crist, *Abundant Earth*, pp. 40–1; MacKinnon, *The Once and Future World*, pp. 34, 93; Wilson, *Half-Earth*, pp. 19–20.
41. Carrington, 'Humans Just 0.01% of All Life'; Brendan Mackey, 'The Future of Conservation: An Australian Perspective' in *Keeping the Wild: Against the*

Domestication of Earth, ed. George Wuerthner, Eileen Crist and Tom Butler, Washington DC: Island Press, 2014; Justin McBrien, 'This Is Not the Sixth Extinction. It's the First Extermination Event', *Truthout*, 14 September 2019.

42. Matthieu Ricard, *Altruism: The Power of Compassion to Change Yourself and the World*, transl. Charlotte Mandell and Sam Gordon, New York: Little, Brown & Co., 2015, iBook edn, Chapter 33; Yuval Noah Harari, *Sapiens: A Brief History of Humankind*, London: Harvill Secker, 2014, pp. 341–6; Ezra Klein, 'Peter Singer on the Lives You Can Save', *Vox*, 6 December 2019; Jensen, *The Myth of Human Supremacy*, p. 309.
43. Ibid.; Eileen Crist, 'Reimagining the Human', *Science* 362:6420, 2018, pp. 1242–4. White supremacy and human supremacy (along with other supremacist value systems such as patriarchy) share core characteristics. As Sophia Aguiñaga points out in 'Philosophy of Anti-Supremacy', unpublished paper, 2020, the supremacist value system is fundamentally extractive, setting up a binary of the powerful and powerless, and valuing the oppressed group solely on the basis of their susceptibility for continued exploitation. It should also be noted that the concept of race itself was a construction of white supremacy, first conceived by Europeans during the first few centuries of colonialism – see Ibram X. Kendi, *How to Be an Antiracist*, New York: One World, 2019, pp. 39–43.
44. Crist, *Abundant Earth*, pp. 44–7; Lent, *The Patterning Instinct*, pp. 277–92.
45. Ronald Wright, quoted in Crist, *Abundant Earth*, p. 105; Shaun Chamberlin, 'Humanity – Not Just a Virus with Shoes', *Dark Optimism*, 6 August 2019.
46. Geoffrey M. Cooper, *The Cell: A Molecular Approach*, Sunderland, MA: Sinauer Associates, 2000, Chapter 15; Jason W. Moore, 'The Road to Ruin? Making Sense of the Anthropocene', *Progressive Review* 24:3, 2017, pp. 176–202; Aaron Vansintjan, 'The Anthropocene Debate: Why Is Such a Useful Concept Starting to Fall Apart?' *Uneven Earth*, 16 June 2015; *Scientific American*, 'Rethinking the "Anthropocene"', *Scientific American* 319:6, 2018, p. 10; Steffen et al., 'The Trajectory of the Anthropocene'; Andreas Malm and Alf Hornborg, 'The Geology of Mankind? A Critique of the Anthropocene Narrative', *Anthropocene Review* 1:1, 2014, pp. 62–9.
47. Ibid.; McBrien, 'This Is Not the Sixth Extinction'.
48. Joseph Henrich, *The Secret of Our Success: How Culture Is Driving Human Evolution, Domesticating Our Species, and Making Us Smarter*, Princeton, NJ: Princeton University Press, 2016, pp. 54–82, 211–30; Crist, *Abundant Earth*, pp. 106–7; Chapter 7, 'Cultural attractors and archetypes'.
49. Henrich, *The Secret of Our Success*, pp. 131–9; M. Kat Anderson, *Tending the Wild: Native American Knowledge and the Management of California's Natural Resources*, Berkeley, CA: University of California Press, 2005, p. 6.
50. Martin Lee Mueller, *Being Salmon, Being Human: Encountering the Wild in Us and Us in the Wild*, White River Junction, VT: Chelsea Green, 2017, p. 200; Crist, *Abundant Earth*, pp. 93, 125–6.
51. Anderson, *Tending the Wild*, p. 55; Robin Wall Kimmerer, *Braiding Sweetgrass:*

Indigenous Wisdom, Scientific Knowledge and the Teachings of Plants, Minneapolis: Milkweed Editions, 2013, pp. 179–87.

52. Anderson, *Tending the Wild*, p. 55; Kimmerer, *Braiding Sweetgrass*, pp. 181–2.
53. Anderson, *Tending the Wild*, p. 2; Kimmerer, *Braiding Sweetgrass*, pp. 162–4.
54. Anderson, *Tending the Wild*, p. 4; MacKinnon, *The Once and Future World*, pp. 165–77.
55. Deborah Bird Rose, *Nourishing Terrains: Australian Aboriginal Views of Landscape and Wilderness*, Canberra: Australian Heritage Commission, 1996, pp. 49–52; Mackey, 'The Future of Conservation', p. 132; Freya Mathews, 'Biomimicry and the Problem of Praxis', *Environmental Values* 28:5, 2019, pp. 573–99. Examples abound of Indigenous sacred land practices maintaining ecological health around the world, even in countries such as India where agrarian civilization predominated for millennia. There, sacred groves protected by Indigenous communities still exist, scattered around the subcontinent, which have acted as refugia for numerous species of trees and animals that have elsewhere been extirpated. See Madhav Gadgil, 'Sacred Groves', *Scientific American*, December 2018, pp. 50–6.
56. E. O. Wilson, *The Future of Life*, New York: Vintage Books, 2003, pp. 134–43.
57. Aldo Leopold, *A Sand County Almanac*, cited in Kingsnorth, 'Dark Ecology'.
58. Næss cited in George Sessions, 'Deep Ecology and the New Age Movement' in *Deep Ecology for the Twenty-First Century*, ed. George Sessions, Boston: Shambhala Publications, 1995, pp. 225–6. Also see Mark Hathaway and Leonardo Boff, *The Tao of Liberation: Exploring the Ecology of Transformation*, Maryknoll, NY: Orbis Books, 2010, pp. 65–7; Chapter 9, "'I am life, in the midst of life'".
59. Leopold quoted in Monbiot, 'The Unseen World'.
60. Gaia Vince, 'How Scientists Are Coping with "Ecological Grief"', *Guardian*, 12 January 2020; Oodgeroo Noonuccal, 'We Are Going', quoted in Mackey, 'The Future of Conservation', pp. 127–8.
61. Joanna Macy, *Active Hope: How to Face the Mess We're in without Going Crazy*, Novato, CA: New World Library, 2012; Matthew Taylor and Jessica Murray, '"Overwhelming and Terrifying": The Rise of Climate Anxiety', *Guardian*, 10 February 2020.
62. George Sessions, 'Deep Ecology as Worldview' in *Worldviews & Ecology: Religion, Philosophy, and the Environment*, ed. Mary Evelyn Tucker and John A. Grim, Maryknoll, NY: Orbis Books, 1994; Thomas Berry, *The Great Work: Our Way into the Future*, New York: Three Rivers Press, 1999, pp. 101–2; Sessions, 'Deep Ecology and the New Age Movement', p. 10; William Leiss, *The Domination of Nature*, Montreal: McGill-Queen's University Press, 1994, p. xvi; Wilson, *Half-Earth*, pp. 16, 211–12. Leopold quoted in J. Baird Callicott, 'Toward a Global Environmental Ethic' in *Worldviews & Ecology: Religion, Philosophy, and the Environment*.
63. Jean-Louis Martin, Virginie Maris and Daniel S. Simberloff, 'The Need to Respect Nature and Its Limits Challenges Society and Conservation Science',

PNAS 113:22, 2016, pp. 6105–12; MacKinnon, *The Once and Future World*, pp. 149–51; Mackey, 'The Future of Conservation', p. 133.

64. Freya Mathews, 'Towards a Deeper Philosophy of Biomimicry', *Organization and Environment* 24:4, 2011; Roderick Nash, cited in Smith, 'The Wilderness Paradox'; Kingsnorth, 'Dark Ecology'. It should be pointed out that, while this etymology for 'wilderness' has been cited by many authorities, there are others who disagree. See David Henderson, 'American Wilderness Philosophy', *Internet Encyclopedia of Philosophy*, ISSN 2161–0002.
65. Nigel Dudley, 'Authenticity as a Means of Measuring Forest Quality', *Biodiversity Letters* 3:1, 1996, pp. 6–9; Shahid Naeem, 'Redefining Nature', *Nature* 477, 2011, pp. 29–30; Crist, *Abundant Earth*, pp. 117–18; Mencius quoted in Chapter 8, 'Achieving fractal flourishing'.
66. Anderson, *Tending the Wild*, p. 358.
67. Cited in Mathews, 'Towards a Deeper Philosophy of Biomimicry'; see also David B. Wong, 'Identifying with Nature in Early Daoism', *Journal of Chinese Philosophy* 36:4, 2009, pp. 568–84; Qi Zhu, 'Shi in Architecture: The Efficacy of Traditional Chinese Doors', Virginia Polytechnic Institute and State University, 2008.
68. Mathews, 'Towards a Deeper Philosophy of Biomimicry'; Chapter 5, 'Better together'.
69. Mathews, 'Towards a Deeper Philosophy of Biomimicry'; Freya Mathews, *The Ecological Self*, London: Routledge, 1991; Lao Tzu, *Tao Te Ching*, transl. Ellen M. Chen, St Paul, MN: Paragon House, 1989, Chapter 51, p. 175.
70. Bill Mollison, *Permaculture: A Designers' Manual*, Tyalgum, Australia: Tagari Publications, 1996, pp. 1–18.
71. Ibid.; Juliana Birnbaum and Louis Fox, *Sustainable (R)evolution: Permaculture in Ecovillages, Urban Farms, and Communities Worldwide*, Berkeley, CA: North Atlantic Books, 2014; Rodale Institute, *Regenerative Organic Agriculture and Climate Change: A Down-to-Earth Solution to Global Warming*, Kutztown, PA: Rodale Institute, 2014. For an excellent example in northern California of a center offering permaculture design courses, see Occidental Arts and Ecology Center, https://oaec.org/
72. Glenn Albrecht, 'Exiting the Anthropocene and Entering the Symbiocene', *Psychoterratica*, 17 December 2015; Mathews, 'Towards a Deeper Philosophy of Biomimicry'.
73. Monbiot, *Feral*; John Carey, 'Rewilding', *PNAS* 113:4, 2016, pp. 806–8; MacKinnon, *The Once and Future World*, p. 146.
74. Cassidy Randall, 'A Rewilding Triumph: Wolves Help to Reverse Yellowstone Degradation', *Guardian*, 25 January 2020; Johan Rockström and Mattias Klum, *Big World Small Planet: Abundance within Planetary Boundaries*, New Haven, CT: Yale University Press, 2015, Kindle edn, locations 1368–75; Alysa Landry, 'Native History: Yellowstone National Park Created on Sacred Land', *Indian Country Today*, 1 March 2017.
75. Carey, 'Rewilding'; Monbiot, *Feral*, pp. 107–9.
76. MacKinnon, *The Once and Future World*, p. 144; Wilson, *Half-Earth*,

pp. 3–4, 167; Crist, *Abundant Earth*, pp. 227–8; https://natureneedshalf.org/. Recognizing the enormous potential for forests to sequester carbon and help mitigate climate breakdown, a science-driven initiative called Global Deal for Nature similarly aims for formal protection of 30 percent of Earth's surface by 2030, with an additional 20 percent designated as climate stabilization areas. See E. Dinerstein et al., 'A Global Deal for Nature: Guiding Principles, Milestones, and Targets', *Science Advances* 5, 2019, eaaw2869; Umair Irfan, 'Restoring Forests May Be One of Our Most Powerful Weapons in Fighting Climate Change', *Vox*, 4 July 2019.

77. Shannon Biggs, Tom B. K. Goldtooth and Osprey Orielle Lake, 'Rights of Nature & Mother Earth: Rights-Based Law for Systemic Change', ed. Movement Rights, Indigenous Environmental Network and WECAN, Oakland, CA, 2017; Sigal Samuel, 'This Country Gave All Its Rivers Their Own Legal Rights', *Vox*, 18 August 2019; Douglas Heaven, 'Giving Nature Human Rights Could Be the Best Way to Protect the Planet', *New Scientist*, 25 September 2019.
78. Cormac Cullinan, *Wild Law: A Manifesto for Earth Justice*, White River Junction, VT: Chelsea Green, 2011, pp. 184–95; Stop Ecocide movement: https://www.stopecocide.earth/
79. Peter Victor, 'Questioning Economic Growth,' *Nature* 468, 2010, pp. 370–1; Jeremy Lent, 'What Will It Really Take to Avoid Collapse?' Patterns of Meaning blog, 19 December 2017.

Chapter 11: Everything Is Connected

1. Joseph Heller, *Catch-22*, New York: Simon & Schuster, 1999, p. 104.
2. Ron Rosenbaum, 'Seeing Catch-22 Twice', *Slate*, 2 August 2011.
3. Paul S. MacDonald, *History of the Concept of the Mind: Speculations About Soul, Mind and Spirit from Homer to Hume*, Aldershot: Ashgate, 2003, pp. 279–91; Colin Morris, *The Discovery of the Individual, 1050–1200*, Toronto: University of Toronto Press, 1987; Max Weber, *The Protestant Ethic and the Spirit of Capitalism*, transl. Steven Kalberg, Los Angeles: Roxbury Publishing Company, 2002.
4. Thomas Talbott, 'Heaven and Hell in Christian Thought', *Stanford Encyclopedia of Philosophy*, ed. Edward N. Zalta, 2017. I am indebted to Daniel Schmachtenberger for pointing out the moral implications of the traditional Christian notion of heaven and hell in his talk at Emergence, 28 August 2016: https://youtu.be/eh7qvXfGQho
5. Rupert Gethin, *The Foundations of Buddhism*, Oxford: Oxford University Press, 1998, pp. 226–31; Red Pine, *The Diamond Sutra: Text and Commentaries*, Berkeley, CA: Counterpoint, 2001, pp. 26–7; Chapter 9, 'Dispelling the suffering of others'.
6. Francis H. Cook, *Hua-Yen Buddhism: The Jewel Net of Indra*, University Park, PA: Pennsylvania State University Press, 1977, p. 2.
7. Bryan W. Van Norden and Nicholaos Jones, 'Huayan Buddhism' in *Stanford Encyclopedia of Philosophy*, ed. Edward N. Zalta, 2019.

8. E. Richard Atleo/Umeek, *Principles of Tsawalk: An Indigenous Approach to Global Crisis*, Vancouver, Canada: UBC Press, 2011, p. ix.
9. Jules Evans, 'Dissolving the Ego', *Aeon*, 26 June 2017; William A. Richards, *Sacred Knowledge: Psychedelics and Religious Experiences*, New York: Columbia University Press, 2016, p. 12; Rosalind Watts, Sam Gandy and Alex Evans, 'The Whole-Planet View', *Aeon*, 17 September 2019. It is possible that the increase in reported mystical experiences is simply a result of people being more open to recognizing and talking about them.
10. Michael Pollan, *How to Change Your Mind: What the New Science of Psychedelics Teaches Us About Consciousness, Dying, Addiction, Depression, and Transcendence*, New York: Penguin, 2018.
11. William James, *The Varieties of Religious Experience: A Study in Human Nature*, New York: Random House, 1902/2002, pp. 422–3, 465–6.
12. Aldous Huxley, *The Doors of Perception*, London: Vintage Classics, 1994, pp. 31–2; R. R. Griffiths et al., 'Mystical-Type Experiences Occasioned by Psilocybin Mediate the Attribution of Personal Meaning and Spiritual Significance 14 Months Later', *Journal of Psychopharmacology* 22:6, 2008, pp. 621–32; Michael Winkelman, 'Therapeutic Effects of Hallucinogens', *Anthropology of Consciousness* 2:3–4, 1991, pp. 15–19.
13. Robert M. Gimello, 'Mysticism and Meditation' in *Mysticism and Philosophical Analysis*, ed. Steven T. Katz, New York: Oxford University Press, 1978; Mark R. Leary, *The Curse of the Self: Self-Awareness, Egotism, and the Quality of Human Life*, New York: Oxford University Press, 2004, Kindle edn, locations 2201–43; Robin L. Carhart-Harris et al., 'The Entropic Brain: A Theory of Conscious States Informed by Neuroimaging Research with Psychedelic Drugs', *Frontiers in Human Neuroscience* 8:20, 2014, pp. 1–22.
14. Eugene d'Aquili and Andrew B. Newberg, *The Mystical Mind: Probing the Biology of Religious Experience*, Minneapolis, MN: Fortress Press, 1999, pp. 13–14; Robert K. C. Forman, 'Introduction: Mysticism, Constructivism, and Forgetting' in *The Problem of Pure Consciousness: Mysticism and Philosophy*, ed. Robert K. C. Forman, New York: Oxford University Press, 1990; Evans, 'Dissolving the Ego'; Christopher M. Bache, *LSD and the Mind of the Universe: Diamonds from Heaven*, Rochester, VT: Park Street Press, 2019. Bache is a professor in philosophy and religious studies who undertook a systematic series of seventy-three high-dose LSD journeys over a period of twenty years, using a scrupulous protocol, in order to understand mind and the nature of existence as deeply as possible. This is chronicled painstakingly and thoughtfully in his book.
15. A. H. Maslow, *Religions, Values, and Peak-Experiences*, New York: Penguin Arkana, 1994; Griffiths et al., 'Mystical-Type Experiences'. Mystical experiences, including those induced by psychedelics, have been shown to have a far-reaching impact on a person's life far beyond the fourteen-month follow-up conducted at Johns Hopkins. A follow-up study conducted approximately twenty-five years after a famous early experiment dosing a group of volunteers with psilocybin (the Good Friday experiment), showed that the experience had

'genuinely mystical elements' and had made a 'uniquely valuable contribution to their spiritual lives'. See Rick Doblin, 'Pahnke's "Good Friday Experiment": A Long-Term Follow-up and Methodological Critique', *Journal of Transpersonal Psychology* 23:1, 1991.

16. Ibid.; Richards, *Sacred Knowledge*, Kindle edn, locations 207–17.
17. William Blake, *Marriage of Heaven and Hell*, Toronto: Dover Publications, 1790/1994, p. 36.
18. Aldous Huxley, *The Perennial Philosophy*, New York: HarperCollins, 1945/2004; Forman, 'Introduction: Mysticism, Constructivism, and Forgetting'; Jorge N. Ferrer, *Revisioning Transpersonal Theory: A Participatory Vision of Human Spirituality*, Albany, NY: SUNY Press, 2002, Kindle edn, location 123, p. 91.
19. Taittirya Upanishad, Eknath Easwaran, *The Upanishads*, transl. Eknath Easwaran, Tomales, CA: Nilgiri Press, 1987, p. 149.
20. Bhagavad Gita 6:30–1, Eknath Easwaran, *Bhagavad Gita*, transl. Eknath Easwaran, Tomales, CA: Nilgiri Press, 1985; Gandhi quoted in George Sessions, 'Deep Ecology and the New Age Movement' in *Deep Ecology for the Twenty-First Century*, ed. George Sessions, Boston: Shambhala Publications, 1995, p. 215.
21. Huangbo cited in d'Aquili and Newberg, *The Mystical Mind*, pp. 152–3.
22. Stephen R. L. Clark, 'Plotinian Dualisms and the "Greek" Ideas of Self', *Journal of Chinese Philosophy* 36:4, 2009, pp. 554–67; Andrew Louth, *The Origins of the Christian Mystical Tradition: From Plato to Denys*, New York: Oxford University Press, 2007; Julia Ching, *The Religious Thought of Chu Hsi*, New York: Oxford University Press, 2000, pp. 46–7.
23. Emerson cited in Pollan, *How to Change Your Mind*, p. 286; Schrödinger cited in d'Aquili and Newberg, *The Mystical Mind*, pp. 152–3; Einstein cited in Jack Kornfield, *A Path with Heart: A Guide through the Perils and Promises of Spiritual Life*, New York: Bantam Books, 1993, p. 288.
24. Jules Evans, 'Perennial Philosophy', *Aeon*, 19 February 2020; Forman, 'Introduction: Mysticism, Constructivism, and Forgetting'; Ferrer, *Revisioning Transpersonal Theory*, pp. 118–19, 216.
25. Steven T. Katz, 'Language, Epistemology, and Mysticism', in *Mysticism and Philosophical Analysis*, ed. Steven T. Katz, New York: Oxford University Press, 1978.
26. Forman, 'Introduction: Mysticism, Constructivism, and Forgetting'; Harold D. Roth, *Original Tao: Inward Training and the Foundations of Taoist Mysticism*, New York: Columbia University Press, 1999, pp. 128–9.
27. Katha Upanishad, cited in Michael Horace Barnes, *Stages of Thought: The Co-Evolution of Religious Thought and Science*, New York: Oxford University Press, 2000, p. 99; David Loy, 'Transcendence East and West', *Man and World* 26:4, 1993, pp. 403–27; Guoping Zhao, 'Two Notions of Transcendence: Confucian Man and Modern Subject', *Journal of Chinese Philosophy* 36:3, 2009, pp. 391–407; Georg Feuerstein, *The Yoga Tradition: Its History, Literature, Philosophy and Practice*, Prescott, AZ: Hohm Press, 1998, pp. xxix, 28.

28. Jeremy Lent, *The Patterning Instinct: A Cultural History of Humanity's Search for Meaning*, Amherst, NY: Prometheus, 2017, pp. 143–59, 227–38.
29. George Lakoff and Mark Johnson, *Metaphors We Live By*, Chicago, IL: University of Chicago Press, 2003, pp. 14–21; James H. Austin, *Selfless Insight: Zen and the Meditative Transformations of Consciousness*, Cambridge, MA: MIT Press, 2009, p. 199; David L. Hall and Roger T. Ames, *Thinking through Confucius*, Albany, NY: SUNY Press, 1987, pp. 12, 101; David L. Hall and Roger T. Ames, *Thinking from the Han: Self, Truth, and Transcendence in Chinese and Western Culture*, Albany, NY: SUNY Press, 1998; J. J. Clarke, *The Tao of the West: Western Transformations of Taoist Thought*, New York: Routledge, 2000, pp. 146–62; Donald J. Munro, *A Chinese Ethics for the New Century: The Ch'ien Mu Lectures in History and Culture, and Other Essays on Science and Confucian Ethics*, Hong Kong: Chinese University Press, 2005, pp. xxiii–xxiv; Zhao, 'Two Notions of Transcendence'.
30. Zhuangzi cited in Donald J. Munro, *The Concept of Man in Early China*, Ann Arbor, MI: Center for Chinese Studies, University of Michigan, 1969, p. 158; Herrlee G. Creel, *What Is Taoism? And Other Studies in Chinese Cultural History*, Chicago, IL: University of Chicago Press, 1970; *Complete Works of Chuang Tzu*, transl. Burton Watson, New York: Columbia University Press, 1968, pp. 240–1. Rinzai quoted in Austin, *Selfless Insight*, p. 199.
31. Huxley, *The Perennial Philosophy*, pp. 2–7; Evans, 'Perennial Philosophy'.
32. Pollan, *How to Change Your Mind*, pp. 11–12, 42.
33. For a prime example of a perennialist arguing for a separate transcendent reality inaccessible to science, see Huston Smith, *Beyond the Postmodern Mind: The Place of Meaning in a Global Civilization*, Wheaton, IL: Quest Books, 2003; for a valuable critique of Smith's position, see Ursula Goodenough, 'Engaging Huston Smith's *Why Religion Matters*', *Zygon* 36:2, 2001, pp. 201–6.
34. Stanislav Grof, 'The Great Awakening: Psychology, Philosophy, and Spirituality in LSD Psychotherapy' in *Higher Wisdom: Eminent Elders Explore the Continuing Impact of Psychedelics*, ed. Roger Walsh and Charles S. Grob, Albany, NY: SUNY Press, 2005; Carhart-Harris et al., 'The Entropic Brain'; Pollan, *How to Change Your Mind*, p. 162.
35. Chapter 7, 'Attractors of consciousness'.
36. G. Petri et al., 'Homological Scaffolds of Brain Functional Networks', *Journal of the Royal Society Interface* 11, 2014, 20140873.
37. Huxley quoted in Pollan, *How to Change Your Mind*, p. 161; Robin L. Carhart-Harris et al., 'Neural Correlates of the LSD Experience Revealed by Multimodal Neuroimaging', *PNAS* 113:17, 2016, pp. 4853–8; Robin L. Carhart-Harris et al., 'Neural Correlates of the Psychedelic State as Determined by fMRI Studies with Psilocybin', *PNAS* 109:6, 2012, pp. 2138–43.
38. Alison Gopnik, 'How Babies Think', *Scientific American*, July 2010; Pollan, *How to Change Your Mind*, pp. 323–8.
39. Lent, *The Patterning Instinct*, pp. 84–8; Chapter 2, 'Toward an integrative intelligence'; Chapter 7, 'Cultural attractors and archetypes'.
40. Andreas Weber, *The Biology of Wonder: Aliveness, Feeling, and the*

Metamorphosis of Science, Gabriola Island, BC, Canada: New Society Publishers, 2016, pp. 287–9; Chapter 5, 'Better together'; Chapter 6, 'The wisdom of the crowd', 'The deep learning of the ecosystem'.

41. Daniel J. Siegel, *Mind: A Journey to the Heart of Being Human*, New York: W. W. Norton, 2017, p. 157.
42. Steven H. Strogatz, *Sync: How Order Emerges from Chaos in the Universe, Nature, and Daily Life*, New York: Hachette Books, 2003, pp. 106–9; Steve Nadis, 'All Together Now', *Nature* 421, 2003, pp. 780–2.
43. Strogatz, *Sync*, p. 14; J. A. Scott Kelso, *Dynamic Patterns: The Self-Organization of Brain and Behavior*, Cambridge, MA: MIT Press, 1995, p. 100; James L. Oschman, *Energy Medicine: The Scientific Basis*, Philadelphia, PA: Churchill Livingstone, 2000, p. 121.
44. Denis Noble, *The Music of Life: Biology Beyond Genes*, Oxford: Oxford University Press, 2006, p. 68; Henry P. Mirsky et al., 'A Model of the Cell-Autonomous Mammalian Circadian Clock', *PNAS* 106:27, 2009, pp. 11107–12; Oschman, *Energy Medicine*, p. 85.
45. Mae-Wan Ho, *The Rainbow and the Worm: The Physics of Organisms*, Singapore: World Scientific Publishing, 2008, iBook edn, Chapter 12; Arthur T. Winfree, 'On Emerging Coherence', *Science* 298, 2002, pp. 2336–7; Strogatz, *Sync*, p. 72; Oschman, *Energy Medicine*, pp. 48–67. The findings on women's menstrual synchrony have been challenged by studies that didn't find such synchronous behavior; however, Strogatz reports (pp. 36–7) that follow-up studies have, at a deeper level, shown complex pheromonal communication between women living together, which can sometimes nudge cycles together or (like Huygens' pendulums) push them apart.
46. György Buzsáki, *Rhythms of the Brain*, New York: Oxford University Press, 2006; György Buzsáki and Andreas Draguhn, 'Neuronal Oscillations in Cortical Networks', *Science* 304, 2004, pp. 1926–29; Andreas K. Engel, Pascal Fries and Wolf Singer, 'Dynamic Predictions: Oscillations and Synchrony in Top-Down Processing', *Nature Reviews: Neuroscience* 2:10, 2001, pp. 704–16; Joerg F. Hipp, Andreas K. Engel and Markus Siegel, 'Oscillatory Synchronization in Large-Scale Cortical Networks Predicts Perception', *Neuron* 69, 2011, pp. 387–96; Chapter 7, 'A crystal in a trillion dimensions'.
47. Vittorio Gallese, 'The Manifold Nature of Interpersonal Relations: The Quest for a Common Mechanism', *Philosophical Transactions of the Royal Society* B 358, 2003, pp. 517–28; Vittorio Gallese, Christian Keysers and Giacomo Rizzolatti, 'A Unifying View of the Basis of Social Cognition', *Trends in Cognitive Sciences* 8:9, 2004, pp. 396–403.
48. Ruth Feldman, Linda C. Mayes and James E. Swain, 'Interaction Synchrony and Neural Circuits Contribute to Shared Intentionality', *Behavioral and Brain Sciences* 28:5, 2005, pp. 697–8; Steven Mithen, *The Singing Neanderthals: The Origins of Music, Language, Mind, and Body*, Cambridge, MA: Harvard University Press, 2006, p. 81.
49. Greg J. Stephens, Lauren J. Silbert and Uri Hasson, 'Speaker–Listener Neural Coupling Underlies Successful Communication', *PNAS* 107:32, 2010,

pp. 14425–30; Marleen B. Schippers et al., 'Mapping the Information Flow from One Brain to Another During Gestural Communication', *PNAS* 107:20, 2010, pp. 9388–93; Piercarlo Valdesolo and David DeSteno, 'Synchrony and the Social Tuning of Compassion', *Emotion* 11:2, 2011, pp. 262–6; Uri Hasson, 'Brain-to-Brain Coupling: A Mechanism for Creating and Sharing a Social World', *Trends in Cognitive Sciences* 16:2, 2012, pp. 114–21; Lauri Nummenmaa et al., 'Emotions Promote Social Interaction by Synchronizing Brain Activity across Individuals', *PNAS* 109:24, 2012, pp. 9599–604; Paula M. Niedenthal, 'Embodying Emotion', *Science* 316, 2007, pp. 1002–5; Peter E. Keller, Giacomo Novembre and Michael J. Hove, 'Rhythm in Joint Action: Psychological and Neurophysiological Mechanisms for Real-Time Interpersonal Coordination', *Philosophical Transactions of the Royal Society* B 369, 2014, 20130394; Guy Claxton, *Intelligence in the Flesh: Why Your Mind Needs Your Body Much More Than It Thinks*, New Haven: Yale University Press, 2015, pp. 125–6.

50. Edward Hall, *The Dance of Life: The Other Dimension of Time*, New York: Anchor Books, 1989, p. 168; Sandra E. Trehub, Judith Becker and Iain Morley, 'Cross-Cultural Perspectives on Music and Musicality', *Philosophical Transactions of the Royal Society* B 370, 2015, 20140096; Beau Sievers et al., 'Music and Movement Share a Dynamic Structure That Supports Universal Expressions of Emotion', *PNAS* 110:1, 2013, pp. 70–5; Thomas Fritz et al., 'Universal Recognition of Three Basic Emotions in Music', *Current Biology* 19, 2009, pp. 573–6; Mithen, *The Singing Neanderthals.*

51. Merlin Donald, *A Mind So Rare: The Evolution of Human Consciousness*, New York: W. W. Norton, 2001, p. 272; Elizabeth Tolbert, 'Music and Meaning: An Evolutionary Story', *Psychology of Music* 29, 2001, pp. 84–94; William L. Benzon, *Beethoven's Anvil: Music in Mind and Culture*, New York: Basic Books, 2001, pp. 42–51; Oliver Sacks, 'The Power of Music', *Brain* 129:10, 2006, pp. 2528–32; Michael Winkelman, 'Shamanism and Cognitive Evolution', *Cambridge Archaeological Journal* 12:1, 2002, pp. 71–101; Sievers et al., 'Music and Movement'.

52. Christiane L. Joost-Gaugier, *Measuring Heaven: Pythagoras and His Influence on Thought and Art in Antiquity and the Middle Ages*, New York: Cornell University Press, 2006, p. 109; Thomas McEvilley, *The Shape of Ancient Thought: Comparative Studies in Greek and Indian Philosophies*, New York: Allworth Press, 2002, p. 48; Philip Ball. 'Facing the Music', *Nature* 453, 2008, pp. 160–2; Ching, *The Religious Thought of Chu Hsi*; Chapter 4, 'Ignoring the gorilla'.

53. Evan Thompson, 'Empathy and Consciousness', *Journal of Consciousness Studies* 8:5–7, 2001, pp. 1–32; Evan Thompson, *Why I Am Not a Buddhist*, New Haven: Yale University Press, 2020, Kindle edn, location 1760; Daniel Siegel, *Pocket Guide to Interpersonal Neurobiology: An Integrative Handbook of the Mind*, New York: W. W. Norton, 2012, pp. 5–6, 194; Evan Thompson and Mog Stapleton, 'Making Sense of Sense-Making: Reflections on Enactive and Extended Mind Theories', *Topoi* 28:1, 2009, pp. 23–30.

54. There is an interesting online debate on this topic entitled 'Do rainbows

exist objectively?' in which about one third of respondents deny the rainbow's objective existence, arguing from the pure reductionist standpoint discussed in this chapter. See: https://www.debate.org/opinions/do-rainbows-exist-objectively

55. Ferrer, *Revisioning Transpersonal Theory*, pp. 2–3, 12, 115–16; Thompson and Stapleton, 'Making Sense of Sense-Making'.
56. While this way of defining meaning is not in common usage, a similar viewpoint can be found in the work of British philosopher Mary Midgley, who wrote, 'Meaning is perhaps best thought of as the way in which facts connect to form what I have called world-pictures ... A meaningless "brute" fact is one which we cannot fit into this system. And, if the system itself falls apart, that is when we say that our life has become meaningless ... The more light [any particular fact] throws on the interconnections of the whole, the more meaning, significance or importance it has.' (Mary Midgley, *Evolution as a Religion: Strange Hopes and Stranger Fears*, London: Routledge, 2002, p. 15.) Prominent systems thinker Fritjof Capra similarly states, 'To understand the meaning of anything we need to relate it to other things in its environment, in its past, or in its future. Nothing is meaningful in itself.' (Fritjof Capra and Pier Luigi Luisi, *The Systems View of Life: A Unifying Vision*, New York: Cambridge University Press, 2014.)
57. Philosopher Jules Evans refers to a database that has been collected on over 6,000 'mystical experiences' recorded by ordinary people in the UK, as follows: 'The most common word used when describing such experiences is "connection" – we briefly shift beyond our separate self-absorbed egos, and feel deeply connected to other beings, or to all things.' See Evans, 'Dissolving the Ego'. In a similar vein, Michael Pollan speculates on the correlation between the increase in the brain's connectivity and the gain in meaning from psychedelic experiences: 'Is it possible that some of these new connections in the brain manifest in the mind as new meanings or perspectives? The connecting of formerly far-flung dots? ... These medicines may help us construct meaning, if not discover it.' (Pollan, *How to Change Your Mind*, pp. 353–4.)
58. Lent, *The Patterning Instinct*, pp. 30–32, 59–62; Chapter 1, 'The interpreter and the mystic'.
59. Watts, Gandy and Evans, 'The Whole-Planet View'; Pollan, *How to Change Your Mind*, pp. 377–9.
60. Chapter 4, 'A "pointless" universe'.
61. Ferrer, *Revisioning Transpersonal Theory*; Bache, *LSD and the Mind of the Universe*, Kindle edn, location 5960.
62. Terminal cancer study patients Patrick Mettes and Richard Boothby cited in Pollan, *How to Change Your Mind*, pp. 70, 342–3; Richards, *Sacred Knowledge*, p. 209.
63. The conception of love as connectedness is laid out persuasively by psychologist Barbara Fredrickson in *Love 2.0: How Our Supreme Emotion Affects Everything We Feel, Think, Do, and Become*, New York: Hudson Street Press, 2013. I am indebted to her for the reference to the song 'What a Wonderful World'.

64. A. N. Marlow, 'Hinduism and Buddhism in Greek Philosophy', *Philosophy East and West* 4, 1954, pp. 35–45; Ursula Goodenough, 'Gravity Is Love, and Other Astounding Metaphors', *NPR: 13.7 Cosmos & Culture*, 21 October 2010; Chapter 6, 'What does life want?'
65. Chapter 5, 'Cooperation, competition and harmony'; Patrick Mettes quoted in Pollan, *How to Change Your Mind*, pp. 342–3; Richards, *Sacred Knowledge*, p. 65.
66. Siegel, *Mind: A Journey*, p. 210.
67. Bache, *LSD and the Mind of the Universe*, Kindle edn, locations 3082–6.
68. Chapter 4, 'The pattern that connects'.
69. Stephen C. Angle, *Sagehood: The Contemporary Significance of Neo-Confucian Philosophy*, New York: Oxford University Press, 2009, pp. 44–9, 122–3; Siu-chi Huang, *Essentials of Neo-Confucianism: Eight Major Philosophers of the Song and Ming Periods*, Westport, CT: Greenwood Press, 1999, pp. 86–8; Zemian Zheng, 'Two Kinds of Oneness: Cheng Hao's Letter on Calming Nature in Contrast with Zhang Zai's Monism', *Philosophy East and West* 65:4, 2015, pp. 1253–72.
70. Ching, *The Religious Thought of Chu Hsi*; Wing-tsit Chan, 'The Evolution of the Confucian Concept Jên', *Philosophy East and West* 4:4, 1955, pp. 295–319; Angle, *Sagehood*, p. 68.

Chapter 12: From Fixed Self to Infinite Li: The Fractal Nature of Identity

1. https://en.wikipedia.org/wiki/We_Are_the_World; Kristi York Wooten, 'The Legacy of Live Aid, 30 Years Later', *Atlantic*, 13 July 2015.
2. https://en.wikipedia.org/wiki/Highwayman_(song)
3. Jeremy Lent, *The Patterning Instinct: A Cultural History of Humanity's Search for Meaning*, Amherst, NY: Prometheus, 2017, pp. 113–14, 227–38.
4. Ibid. pp. 279–85, 344–52.
5. Jacques Monod, *Chance and Necessity*, quoted in Freeman J. Dyson, 'Time without End: Physics and Biology in an Open Universe', *Reviews of Modern Physics* 51:3, 1979; Stephen Jay Gould, *Rocks of Ages: Science and Religion in the Fullness of Life*, quoted in Jerry A. Coyne, 'Science, Religion, and Society: The Problem of Evolution in America', *Evolution* 66:8, 2012, pp. 2654–63.
6. Chapter 4, 'A "pointless" universe'.
7. Steven Weinberg, 'Reductionism Redux', *New York Review of Books* 42:15, 1995; Chapter 5, 'Decoding the "book of life"', 'The language of the gene'; Chapter 7, 'A crystal in a trillion dimensions'.
8. Pascal cited in Karen Armstrong, *A Short History of Myth*, Edinburgh: Canongate Books, 2005, pp. 127–8; Monod cited in Fritjof Capra and Pier Luigi Luisi, *The Systems View of Life: A Unifying Vision*, New York: Cambridge University Press, 2014, p. 214; Russell quoted in E. A. Burtt, *The Metaphysical Foundations of Modern Science*, New York: Dover Publications, 2003, p. 23. For detailed critiques of ontological reductionism and the closely related doctrine of determinism, see Stuart Kauffman, *Reinventing the Sacred: A New View of Science, Reason, and Religion*, New York: Basic Books, 2008, pp. 10–15; Carl

R. Woese, 'A New Biology for a New Century', *Microbiology and Molecular Biology Reviews* 68, 2004, pp. 173–86; Paul Davies, *The Cosmic Blueprint: New Discoveries in Nature's Creative Ability to Order the Universe*, Philadelphia, PA: Templeton Foundation Press, 2004, pp. 139–40; E. Brian Davies, *Why Beliefs Matter: Reflections on the Nature of Science*, Oxford: Oxford University Press, 2010, pp. 61–2.

9. Michael Lipka and Claire Gecewicz, 'More Americans Now Say They're Spiritual but Not Religious' in *Factank: News in the Numbers*, Pew Research Center, 2017.
10. Stephen Gaukroger, *The Emergence of a Scientific Culture*, New York: Oxford University Press, 2006, pp. 16–43; Michael Silberstein and John McGeever, 'The Search for Ontological Emergence', *Philosophical Quarterly* 49:195, 1999, pp. 182–200.
11. For examples of both sides of the debate conflating 'scientism' or 'scientific materialism' with ontological reductionism, see Huston Smith, *Beyond the Postmodern Mind: The Place of Meaning in a Global Civilization*, Wheaton, IL: Quest Books, 2003; the Dalai Lama quoted in Owen Flanagan, *The Really Hard Problem: Meaning in a Material World*, Cambridge, MA: MIT Press, 2007; and Alex Rosenberg's *The Atheist's Guide to Reality*, discussed in Christopher R. Beha, 'Reason for Living: The Good Life without God', *Harper's*, July 2012.
12. Poincaré quoted in J. A. Scott Kelso, *Dynamic Patterns: The Self-Organization of Brain and Behavior*, Cambridge, MA: MIT Press, 1995, p. 97; Bang Wong, 'Points of View: Gestalt Principles (Part 1)', *Nature Methods* 7:11, 2010, p. 863; Capra and Luisi, *The Systems View of Life*, pp. 66–8; Davies, *Why Beliefs Matter*, pp. 61–2.
13. James Gleick, *Chaos: Making a New Science*, New York: Penguin, 1987, pp. 11–31; Edward Ott, 'Edward N. Lorenz (1917–2008)', *Nature* 453, 2008, p. 300; Chapter 4, 'The flap of a butterfly's wings'.
14. Thomas S. Kuhn, *The Structure of Scientific Revolutions*, Chicago, IL: University of Chicago Press, 1996, pp. 151–2; Davies, *The Cosmic Blueprint*, pp. 145, 198–9; Roger W. Sperry, 'Changing Priorities', *Annual Review of Neuroscience* 4, 1981, pp. 1–15; Chapter 4, '*Gewu*: the investigation of things'.
15. Brian Goodwin, *How the Leopard Changed Its Spots: The Evolution of Complexity*, Princeton: Princeton University Press, 2001, p. x.
16. Ricard Solé and Brian Goodwin, *Signs of Life: How Complexity Pervades Biology*, New York: Basic Books, 2000, p. 28.
17. Ibid.; Evan Thompson, *Mind in Life: Biology, Phenomenology, and the Sciences of Mind*, Cambridge, MA: Harvard University Press, 2007, pp. 163–5; Dyson, 'Time without End'.
18. Albert Einstein, 'What I Believe', *Forum and Century* 84:4, 1930, pp. 193–4.
19. Stuart Kauffman, *At Home in the Universe: The Search for Laws of Self-Organization and Complexity*, New York: Oxford University Press, 1995, pp. 185–6.
20. Heraclitus quoted in A. N. Marlow, 'Hinduism and Buddhism in Greek Philosophy', *Philosophy East and West* 4, 1954, pp. 35–45; Charles Freeman,

The Closing of the Western Mind: The Rise of Faith and the Fall of Reason, New York: Vintage Books, 2005, p. 44; David C. Lindberg, *The Beginnings of Western Science: The European Scientific Tradition in Philosophical, Religious, and Institutional Context, Prehistory to A.D. 1450*, Chicago, IL: University of Chicago Press, 2007, p. 80. As mentioned in Chapter 4, note 23, although dualism gained ascendancy in Western thought, a distinguished group of thinkers, incorporating what I have called the Moonlight Tradition, maintained a lineage of systems thinking throughout the Western tradition. Likewise, there has been a rich alternative spiritual tradition within Christianity that emphasizes a more panentheistic reverence for the divinity existing throughout the cosmos. This approach, which has been termed Creation Spirituality by theologian Matthew Fox, includes such luminaries as Hildegard of Bingen, Thomas Aquinas, Meister Eckhart, Julian of Norwich, Nicolas of Cusa, and Thomas Merton among others. See *Original Blessing: A Primer in Creation Spirituality Presented in Four Paths, Twenty-Six Themes, and Two Questions*, New York: Tarcher/Putnam, 2000.

21. David L. Hall and Roger T. Ames, *Thinking from the Han: Self, Truth, and Transcendence in Chinese and Western Culture*, Albany, NY: SUNY Press, 1998, p. 242; Ellen M. Chen, 'Is There a Doctrine of Physical Immortality in the Tao Te Ching?' *History of Religions* 12:3, 1973, pp. 231–49; Sōiku Shigematsu, ed., *A Zen Harvest: Japanese Folk Zen Sayings*, Berkeley, CA: North Point Press, 1988, p. 39.
22. David Hinton, *Existence: A Story*, Boulder, CO: Shambhala, 2016, pp. 1–14, 89–91.
23. Francis H. Cook, *Hua-Yen Buddhism: The Jewel Net of Indra*, University Park, PA: Pennsylvania State University Press, 1977, p. 4; Alan Fox, 'The Practice of Huayan Buddhism' in *Proceedings of 'The Past, Present and Future of Chinese Buddhist Studies'*, Yilan County, Taiwan: Fo Guang University Buddhist Research Center, 2015, pp. 259–86.
24. Lent, *The Patterning Instinct*, pp. 251–73.
25. Ibid.; Stephen C. Angle, *Sagehood: The Contemporary Significance of Neo-Confucian Philosophy*, New York: Oxford University Press, 2009, pp. 44–5; Julia Ching, *The Religious Thought of Chu Hsi*, New York: Oxford University Press, 2000, p. 130.
26. Paul Harrison, *Elements of Pantheism: A Spirituality of Nature and the Universe*, Shaftesbury, Dorset: Element Books, 2013; John W. Grula, 'Pantheism Reconstructed: Ecotheology as a Successor to the Judeo-Christian, Enlightenment, and Postmodernist Paradigms', *Zygon* 43:1, 2008, pp. 159–80.
27. Kauffman, *Reinventing the Sacred*, p. 71; Kauffman, *At Home in the Universe*, pp. 4–5; Ursula Goodenough, *The Sacred Depths of Nature*, New York: Oxford University Press, 1998; Brian Thomas Swimme and Mary Evelyn Tucker, *The Journey of the Universe*, New Haven: Yale University Press, 2011; Davies, *The Cosmic Blueprint*, p. 5; Sperry, 'Changing Priorities'.
28. Chapter 4, 'Emergent life'; Chapter 7, 'Attractors of consciousness'; Alan

Watts quoted in Lynn Margulis and Dorion Sagan, *What Is Life?* Berkeley/Los Angeles: University of California Press, 2000, p. 43.

29. Chapter 4, 'The pattern that connects'; Ursula Goodenough and Terrence W. Deacon, 'The Sacred Emergence of Nature' in *The Oxford Handbook of Religion and Science*, ed. Philip Clayton, New York: Oxford University Press, 2006; Charles Eisenstein, *The Ascent of Humanity*, Harrisburg, PA: Panenthea Press, 2007, p. 412.
30. Douglas R. Hofstadter, *I Am a Strange Loop*, New York: Basic Books, 2007, p. 228; Daniel J. Siegel, *Mind: A Journey to the Heart of Being Human*, New York: W. W. Norton, 2017, p. 262; Robert Pirsig, *Zen and the Art of Motorcycle Maintenance*, New York: HarperCollins, 1999, Afterword.
31. Hofstadter, *I Am a Strange Loop*, pp. 9–10, 23, 228–74.
32. Chapter 7, 'Cultural attractors and archetypes'.
33. Halifax quoted in Jorge N. Ferrer, *Revisioning Transpersonal Theory: A Participatory Vision of Human Spirituality*, Albany, NY: SUNY Press, 2002, p. 120.
34. Chapter 3, '"I think, therefore I am"'.
35. Zhuangzi quoted in Cook, *Hua-Yen Buddhism*, p. 27; Wai Wai Chiu, 'Zhuangzi's Idea of "Spirit": Acting and "Thinging Things" without Self-Assertion', *Asian Philosophy* 26:1, 2016, pp. 38–51; Chapter 1, 'Going with the flow'.
36. Glenn Wallis, *Basic Teachings of the Buddha: A New Translation and Compilation, with a Guide to Reading the Texts*, New York: Random House, 2007, pp. 31–2; Nyanaponika Thera, *The Heart of Buddhist Meditation*, San Francisco, CA: Red Wheel/Weiser, 1965, p. 38; Michaël Dambrun and Matthieu Ricard, 'Self-Centeredness and Selflessness: A Theory of Self-Based Psychological Functioning and Its Consequences for Happiness', *Review of General Psychology* 15:2, 2011, pp. 138–57.
37. Wallis, *Basic Teachings of the Buddha*, p. 145; Dambrun and Ricard, 'Self-Centeredness and Selflessness'; Chapter 8, 'Eudaimonia: fulfilling your true nature'; Chapter 9, 'The moral species'.
38. Samuel Scheffler, *Death and the Afterlife*, New York: Oxford University Press, 2013, pp. 15–79; Samuel Scheffler, 'The Importance of the Afterlife. Seriously', *New York Times*, 21 September 2013.
39. Margulis and Sagan, *What Is Life?*, p. 81; Chen, 'Is There a Doctrine of Physical Immortality in the Tao Te Ching?'. It is noteworthy that Bertrand Russell, quoted earlier as building his philosophy on reductionist 'despair', nonetheless found solace in transcending the boundaries of self, writing, 'An individual human existence should be like a river: small at first, narrowly contained within its banks, and rushing passionately past rocks and over waterfalls. Gradually, the river grows wider, the banks recede, the waters flow more quietly, and in the end, without any visible break, they become merged in the sea, and painlessly lose their individual being.' (Quoted in Michael Pollan, *How to Change Your Mind: What the New Science of Psychedelics Teaches Us About Consciousness,*

Dying, Addiction, Depression, and Transcendence, New York: Penguin, 2018, p. 355.)

40. Zhuangzi quoted in Chen, 'Is There a Doctrine of Physical Immortality in the Tao Te Ching?'.
41. Dogen quoted in David P. Barash, *Buddhist Biology: Ancient Eastern Wisdom Meets Modern Western Science*, New York: Oxford University Press, 2014, p. 129; Cheng Yi quoted in Donald J. Munro, *A Chinese Ethics for the New Century: The Ch'ien Mu Lectures in History and Culture, and Other Essays on Science and Confucian Ethics*, Hong Kong: Chinese University Press, 2005, pp. 24–5.
42. Chapter 9, '"I am life, in the midst of life"'.
43. Chapter 11, 'Opening our eyes to the rainbow'; Zhang Zai quoted in Angle, *Sagehood*.
44. Thích Nhât Hanh, *Call Me by My True Names*, Berkeley, CA: Parallax Press, 1999, p. 73.
45. Chapter 10, 'The ecological self'; Chapter 2, 'Toward an integrative intelligence'.
46. Chapter 9, '"One body with Heaven and Earth"'.
47. Lent, *The Patterning Instinct*, pp. 405–42; Duane Elgin, 'Collective Consciousness and Cultural Healing', San Anselmo, CA: Fetzer Institute, 1997; Michael Chorost, *World Wide Mind: The Coming Integration of Humanity, Machines, and the Internet*, New York: Free Press, 2011; Thích Nhât Hanh, 'The Next Buddha May Be a Sangha', *Inquiring Mind* 10:2, 1994.
48. David Grinspoon, 'Welcome to Terra Sapiens', *Aeon*, 20 December 2016; David Grinspoon, *Earth in Human Hands: Shaping Our Planet's Future*, New York: Grand Central Publishing, 2016, pp. 82–3, 115, 142.
49. The universe reflecting on itself is a concept proposed by Nancy Ellen Abrams and Joel Primack, quoted in David R. Loy, *A New Buddhist Path: Enlightenment, Evolution, and Ethics in the Modern World*, Somerville, MA: Wisdom Publications, 2015, p. 100.
50. Grinspoon, *Earth in Human Hands*, pp. 324–6, 475. See also Robin Hanson, 'The Great Filter – Are We Almost Past It?' http://mason.gmu.edu/~rhanson/greatfilter.html
51. Chapter 10, 'Toward the Symbiocene'.
52. Thomas Berry, *The Great Work: Our Way into the Future*, New York: Three Rivers Press, 1999.

Chapter 13: Weaving a New Story of Meaning

1. Robin Wall Kimmerer, *Braiding Sweetgrass: Indigenous Wisdom, Scientific Knowledge and the Teachings of Plants*, Minneapolis: Milkweed Editions, 2013, pp. 304–9.
2. Ibid. The Windigo is also known as Wendigo or Wetiko, and is part of the broader mythical tradition of other Algonquin-speaking tribes, including the Cree. A significant modern work linking Windigo to the Western culture of exploitation is Jack D. Forbes, *Columbus and Other Cannibals: The Wétiko Disease of Exploitation, Imperialism, and Terrorism*, New York: Seven Stories

Press, 2011. See also: Alnoor Ladha and Martin Kirk, 'Seeing Wetiko: On Capitalism, Mind Viruses, and Antidotes for a World in Transition', *Kosmos*, spring/summer 2016; Jeremy Lent, *The Patterning Instinct: A Cultural History of Humanity's Search for Meaning*, Amherst, NY: Prometheus, 2017, pp. 309–15.

3. Michael J. Sandel, *What Money Can't Buy: The Moral Limits of Markets*, New York: Farrar, Straus and Giroux, 2013; Naomi Klein, *This Changes Everything: Capitalism Vs. The Climate*, New York: Simon & Schuster, 2014, iBook edn, Chapter 6; Chapter 10, 'Making nature earn her living'.
4. United Nations, 'Twentieth-Century Model "a Global Suicide Pact", Secretary-General Tells World Economic Forum Session on Redefining Sustainable Development', *UN Department of Public Information*, 2011.
5. Some of the leading spokespersons for Uncle Bob's soundbites are Steven Pinker, Hans Rosling, Matt Ridley, Brendan O'Neill, Johan Norberg (Cato Institute), Nicholas Kristof, Max Roser and Michael Shermer. For a brief summary of their position, see Oliver Burkeman, 'Is the World Really Better Than Ever?' *Guardian*, 28 July 2017. For an in-depth polemic stating their position, see Steven Pinker, *Enlightenment Now: The Case for Reason, Science, Humanism, and Progress*, New York: Viking, 2018. For critiques of Pinker's book, see John Gray, 'Unenlightened Thinking: Steven Pinker's Embarrassing New Book Is a Feeble Sermon for Rattled Liberals', *New Statesman*, 22 February 2018; David A. Bell, 'The PowerPoint Philosophe', *Nation*, 7 March 2018; George Monbiot, 'You Can Deny Environmental Calamity – Until You Check the Facts', *Guardian*, 7 March 2018; and my own 'Steven Pinker's Ideas About Progress Are Fatally Flawed. These Eight Graphs Show Why', Patterns of Meaning blog, 17 May 2018.
6. Ida Kubiszewski et al., 'Beyond GDP: Measuring and Achieving Global Genuine Progress', *Ecological Economics* 93, 2013, pp. 57–68; Lent, *The Patterning Instinct*, pp. 398–400; Chapter 8, 'Cultivating societal well-being'.
7. Jason Hickel, *The Divide: Global Inequality from Conquest to Free Markets*, New York: W. W. Norton, 2017, pp. 82–8; Lent, *The Patterning Instinct*, pp. 309–10.
8. Carla Shedd, 'How the School-to-Prison Pipeline Is Created', *Atlantic*, 27 October 2015; Sentencing Project, 'Trends in U.S. Corrections', Washington DC: Sentencing Project, 2019.
9. Hickel, *The Divide*, pp. 16–17; Jason Hickel, 'Bill Gates Says Poverty Is Decreasing. He Couldn't Be More Wrong', *Guardian*, 29 January 2019; Larry Elliott, 'World's 26 Richest People Own as Much as Poorest 50%, Says Oxfam', *Guardian*, 20 January 2019. One scholar has attempted to quantify the moral egregiousness of the situation by considering how much it would cost the segment of humanity with more resources (more than double the poverty line) to raise the impoverished majority above the poverty line. Back in 1990, it would have cost 12.9 percent of their total income. However, by 2013 it would only have cost 3.9 percent, because of the widening gap between the haves and the have-nots. By that measure, the world's capacity to end global poverty has more than tripled in the past three decades, and yet nothing has been done to move the needle. One way of interpreting this is a tripling in the moral

egregiousness of global poverty. See Jason Hickel, 'The Moral Egregiousness of Poverty Is Worse Than Ever before in History', *Resilience*, 30 August 2018.

10. Chapter 10, 'The Great Dying'.
11. Anders Wijkman and Johan Rockström, *Bankrupting Nature: Denying Our Planetary Boundaries*, New York: Routledge, 2012; Mathis Wackernagel and Bert Beyers, *Ecological Footprint: Managing Our Biocapacity Budget*, Gabriola Island, BC, Canada: New Society Publishers, 2019.
12. Jeremy Lent, 'AI Has Already Taken Over. It's Called the Corporation', Patterns of Meaning blog, 30 November 2017; Hannah Osborne, 'Stephen Hawking AI Warning: Artificial Intelligence Could Destroy Civilization', *Newsweek*, 7 November 2017; Nick Bostrom, 'Ethical Issues in Advanced Artificial Intelligence' in *Cognitive, Emotive and Ethical Aspects of Decision Making in Humans and in Artificial Intelligence*, ed. I. Smit et al., International Institute of Advanced Studies in Systems Research and Cybernetics, 2003.
13. David C. Korten, *When Corporations Rule the World*, Sterling, VA: Kumarian Press/Berrett-Koehler, 2001; Al Gore, *The Future: Six Drivers of Global Change*, New York: Random House, 2013, iBook edn, Chapter 3; Richard H. Robbins, *Global Problems and the Culture of Capitalism*, Boston: Pearson Education, 2008, pp. 94–5.
14. Peter Dauvergne, *Will Big Business Destroy the Planet?* Medford, MA: Polity Press, 2018, pp. 51–2; John McMurtry, 'Behind Global System Collapse: The Life-Blind Structure of Economic Rationality', *Journal of Business Ethics* 108, 2012, pp. 49–60; Joe Myers, 'How Do the World's Biggest Companies Compare to the Biggest Economies?' *World Economic Forum Agenda*, 19 October 2016; Michael Slezak, 'Fossil Fuel Companies Undermining Paris Agreement Negotiations – Report', *Guardian*, 1 November 2017; Klein, *This Changes Everything*, Chapter 2.
15. Joel Bakan, 'Charming Psychopaths: The Modern Corporation', *Resilience*, 14 February 2020; Stephen Bainbridge, 'A Duty to Shareholder Value', *New York Times*, 16 April 2015; Chapter 9, 'The individual pursuit of happiness'.
16. Chris Hamby, 'The Secret Threat That Makes Corporations More Powerful Than Countries', *BuzzFeed*, 30 August 2016; Saeed Kamali Dehghan, 'Coke, Crisps, Convenience: How Ads Created a Global Junk Food Generation', *Guardian*, 26 December 2019; Chapter 8, 'Weaponizing *dukkha* for profit'.
17. Kate Raworth, *Doughnut Economics: Seven Ways to Think Like a 21st-Century Economist*, White River Junction, VT: Chelsea Green, 2017, pp. 50, 86, 102–3.
18. Yvan Guillemette and David Turner, 'The Long View: Scenarios for the World Economy to 2060', *OECD Economic Policy Paper* 22, 2018; Nick Kilvert, 'How Many Humans Can Earth Sustain? And What Does It Mean If We've Already Passed It?' *ABC News*, 25 July 2019; Johan Rockström et al., 'A Safe Operating Space for Humanity', *Nature* 461, 2009, pp. 472–5; Will Steffen et al., 'Planetary Boundaries: Guiding Human Development on a Changing Planet', *Science* 347:6223, 2015, 1259855.
19. Jason Hickel and Giorgos Kallis, 'Is Green Growth Possible?' *New Political Economy* 25:4, 2019, pp. 469–86; Timothée Parrique, 'Decoupling Debunked:

Evidence and Arguments against Green Growth as a Sole Strategy for Sustainability', *European Environmental Bureau*, July 2019.

20. Jonathan Watts, 'We Have 12 Years to Limit Climate Change Catastrophe, Warns UN', *Guardian*, 8 October 2018; Timothy M. Lenton et al., 'Climate Tipping Points – Too Risky to Bet Against', *Nature* 575, 2019, pp. 592–5; Asher Moses, '"Collapse of Civilisation Is the Most Likely Outcome": Top Climate Scientists', *Voice of Action*, 5 June 2020.
21. Mark Lynas, *Our Final Warning: Six Degrees of Climate Emergency*, London: HarperCollins, 2020; Nafeez Ahmed, 'The Collapse of Civilization May Have Already Begun', *Vice*, 22 November 2019; David Roberts, 'The World's Bleak Climate Situation, in 3 Charts', *Vox*, 1 May 2018.
22. Lynas, *Our Final Warning*; Ahmed, 'The Collapse of Civilization'; Bill McKibben, 'This Is How Human Extinction Could Play Out', *Rolling Stone*, 9 April 2019; Santa Fe Institute, 'Study: "Near-Unliveable" Heat for One-Third of Humans within 50 Years If Greenhouse Gas Emissions Are Not Cut', Santa Fe Institute, 5 May 2020.
23. Chapter 7, 'The Adaptive Cycle'; Rachel Nuwer, 'How Western Civilisation Could Collapse', *BBC Future*, 18 April 2017; Moses, '"Collapse of Civilisation Is the Most Likely Outcome"'; Ahmed, 'The Collapse of Civilization'.
24. Thomas Homer-Dixon et al., 'Synchronous Failure: The Emerging Causal Architecture of Global Crisis', *Ecology and Society* 20:3, 2015, p. 6; Marten Scheffer, 'Anticipating Societal Collapse; Hints from the Stone Age', *PNAS* 113:39, 2016, pp. 10733–5; Marten Scheffer et al., 'Anticipating Critical Transitions', *Science* 338:6105, 2012, pp. 344–8; C. S. Holling, 'Understanding the Complexity of Economic, Ecological, and Social Systems', *Ecosystems* 4, 2001, pp. 390–405.
25. Paul Raskin et al., *Great Transition: The Promise and Lure of the Times Ahead*, Boston, MA: Stockholm Environment Institute, 2002; Jeremy Lent, 'The Cruel, Topsy-Turvy Economics of Collapse', Patterns of Meaning blog, 31 October 2017.
26. Lent, *The Patterning Instinct*, pp. 428–33. Because of its blatant moral reprehensibility, the lifeboat strategy generally remains implicit or privately discussed, and is rarely expressed in public. However, one stunningly egregious exception was published by the influential neoliberal economist Garrett Harding in a 1974 paper entitled 'Lifeboat Ethics'. See Garrett Hardin, 'Lifeboat Ethics: The Case against Helping the Poor', *Psychology Today*, September 1974.
27. See Jonas Salk and Jonathan Salk, *A New Reality: Human Evolution for a Sustainable Future*, Stratford, CT: City Point Press, 2018, for a valuable perspective on the required shift in paradigm at this transitional point in history.
28. Freya Mathews, 'Biomimicry and the Problem of Praxis', *Environmental Values* 28:5, 2019, pp. 573–99.
29. Chapter 5, 'Better together'.
30. Chapter 5, 'Cooperation, competition and harmony'.
31. Chapter 6, 'The deep learning of the ecosystem'; John Fullerton, *Regenerative*

Capitalism: How Universal Principles and Patterns Will Shape Our New Economy, Capital Institute, 2015.

32. Ibid.
33. Many of the underlying principles and values for an ecological civilization may be found in the traditions of Indigenous communities throughout the world. In China the concept of 'ecological civilization' has been used as a platform by the Chinese Communist Party, but so far has not fully materialized in major policy priorities. In modern Western society the idea of an ecological civilization has been developed among a select group of visionary thinkers over decades, and is gaining increased traction. Early pioneers in developing the philosophical framework for a life-affirming civilization were Freya Mathews in *The Ecological Self*, 1991, and John B. Cobb Jr, who integrated this idea with the process philosophy of Alfred North Whitehead. More recently, leading thinkers on the topic, in addition to Mathews and Cobb, include Eileen Crist, Arran Gare, Fred Magdoff, David Korten and John Fullerton. The Institute for Ecological Civilization, based in California, works to disseminate these ideas and helped publish a recent book on the topic: Philip Clayton and Wm. Andrew Schwartz, *What Is Ecological Civilization? Crisis, Hope, and the Future of the Planet*, Anoka, MN: Process Century Press, 2019. I am indebted to all of the aforementioned thinkers, among others, for my own description of the vision of an ecological civilization.
34. Chapter 8, 'Eudaimonia: fulfilling your true nature'.
35. Chapter 8, 'Achieving fractal flourishing'.
36. Fred Magdoff, 'Ecological Civilization', *Monthly Review*, 1 January 2011.
37. Fred Magdoff, 'Harmony and Ecological Civilization', *Monthly Review*, 1 June 2012.
38. Fullerton, *Regenerative Capitalism*.
39. Chapter 10, 'Toward the Symbiocene'; Freya Mathews, 'Ecological Civilization: A Premise, a Promise and Perhaps a Prospect', *Ecological Citizen* 3, 2020, pp. 47–54; David Grinspoon, *Earth in Human Hands: Shaping Our Planet's Future*, New York: Grand Central Publishing, 2016.
40. Raworth, *Doughnut Economics*, pp. 70, 101–5. For a comprehensive analysis of how markets tend to corrode human values, see Sandel, *What Money Can't Buy*. Beyond Kate Raworth's *Doughnut Economics*, other leading books laying out a life-affirming framework for economics include: David C. Korten, *Change the Story, Change the Future: A Living Economy for a Living Earth*, Oakland, CA: Berrett-Koehler, 2015; Clair Brown, *Buddhist Economics: An Enlightened Approach to the Dismal Science*, New York: Bloomsbury Press, 2017; Tim Jackson, *Prosperity without Growth: Foundations for the Economy of Tomorrow*, New York: Routledge, 2017; Herman E. Daly and Joshua Farley, *Ecological Economics: Principles and Applications*, Washington DC: Island Press, 2011.
41. Raworth, *Doughnut Economics*, pp. 62–80.
42. Jonathan Rowe and David Bollier, 'It's Time to Replace the Economics of "Me" with the Economics of "We"', *Evonomics*, 30 January 2016; George Monbiot, 'Why Common Ownership Is a Route to Social Transformation', *Evonomics*,

11 March 2017; Michel Bauwens and Jose Ramos, 'Awakening to an Ecology of the Commons' in *The Great Awakening: New Modes of Life Amidst Capitalist Ruins*, ed. Anna Grear and David Bollier, Santa Barbara, CA: Punctum Books, 2020.

43. Ryan Avent, 'You Might Have Earned It, but Don't Forget That Your Wealth Came from Society', *Evonomics*, 2016; Roope Mokka and Katariina Rantanen, 'Basic Income and the New Universalism', *Resilience*, 15 February 2017.
44. Gar Alperovitz, 'Technological Inheritance and the Case for a Basic Income', *Medium*, 16 December 2016; Jeremy Lent, 'Five Ways to Curb the Power of Corporations and Billionaires', Patterns of Meaning blog, 12 July 2018.
45. Rutger Bregman, *Utopia for Realists: How We Can Build the Ideal World*, transl. Elizabeth Manton, New York: Little, Brown & Co., 2017, pp. 30–4; Alperovitz, 'Technological Inheritance'; Mokka and Rantanen, 'Basic Income and the New Universalism'.
46. Lent, 'Five Ways to Curb the Power of Corporations and Billionaires'; https://benefitcorp.net/; https://bcorporation.net/. It should be emphasized that strict enforcement procedures – including the threat of losing the charter – would be necessary to ensure all three bottom lines were optimized, with regular assessments by panels composed of representatives of the communities and ecosystems covered in the company's scope of operations.
47. Fritjof Capra and Ove Daniel Jakobsen, 'A Conceptual Framework for Ecological Economics Based on Systemic Principles of Life', *International Journal of Social Economics* 44:6, 2017, pp. 831–44; E. Dinerstein et al., 'A Global Deal for Nature: Guiding Principles, Milestones, and Targets', *Science Advances* 5, 2019, eaaw2869; Eckart Wintzen, 'Re-Engineering the Planet: Three Steps to a Sustainable Free-Market Economy' in *Creating a Sustainable and Desirable Future: Insights from 45 Global Thought Leaders*, ed. Robert Costanza and Ida Kubiszewski, Singapore: World Scientific, 2014; Chapter 10, 'Tending Mother Earth'. There is a common misconception, aggressively propagated by transnational corporations, that industrial agriculture is required to 'feed the world'. However, studies have shown that, when adopted properly, regenerative agriculture (also known as agroecology) can be as efficient or more efficient in productivity. See Maywa Montenegro, 'Agroecology Can Help Fix Our Broken Food System. Here's How', *Ensia*, 17 June 2015; Miguel A. Altieri et al., 'The Scaling up of Agroecology: Spreading the Hope for Food Sovereignty and Resiliency', ed. Sociedad Científica Latinoamericana de Agroecología, 2012.
48. Robert Costanza et al., 'What Would a Sustainable and Desirable Economy-in-Society-in-Nature Look Like?' and Peter Senge, 'Creating the Schools of the Future: Education for a Sustainable Society' in *Creating a Sustainable and Desirable Future*, ed. Costanza and Kubiszewski; Riane Eisler, 'Whole Systems Change: A Framework & First Steps for Social/Economic Transformation', *Next System Project*, 1 March 2016; Zachary Stein, 'Education in the Anthropocene: Futures Beyond Schooling', *Institute for Interdisciplinary Research into the Anthropocene*, 2018; Owen Flanagan, *The Geography of Morals: Varieties of Moral Possibility*, New York: Oxford University Press, 2017,

pp. 278–80; Daniel Goleman and Richard J. Davidson, *Altered Traits: Science Reveals How Meditation Changes Your Mind, Brain, and Body*, New York: Penguin, 2017, pp. 279–80; Chapter 9, '"I am life, in the midst of life"', 'The cultural evolution of values'.

49. Dipayan Ghosh, 'Don't Break up Facebook – Treat It Like a Utility', *Harvard Business Review*, 30 May 2019; Michael Onyebuchi Eze, 'I Am Because You Are: Cosmopolitanism in the Age of Xenophobia', *Philosophical Papers* 46:1, 2017, pp. 85–109; Massimo Pigliucci, *How to Be a Stoic: Using Ancient Philosophy to Live a Modern Life*, New York: Basic Books, 2017, p. 62; Evan Thompson, *Why I Am Not a Buddhist*, New Haven: Yale University Press, 2020, Kindle edn, locations 2300–540; Edgar Morin and Anne Brigitte Kern, *Homeland Earth: A Manifesto For the New Millennium*, transl. Sean M. Kelly and Roger LaPointe, Cresskill, NJ: Hampton Press, 1999.
50. Paul Raskin, *Journey to Earthland: The Great Transition to Planetary Civilization*, Boston, MA: Tellus Institute, 2016, pp. 84–7; Elinor Ostrom, 'A Polycentric Approach for Coping with Climate Change', *World Bank Development Economics Policy Research Working Papers* 5095, 2009; Alain de Vulpian and Irène Dupoux-Couturier, *Homo Sapiens: Collapse or Fulfillment*, transl. Richard Maxwell, Paris: Happymorphose, 2019, Kindle edn, location 1882; Morin and Kern, *Homeland Earth*; Polly Higgins and Cormac Cullinan, 'Towards a Universal Declaration of Planetary Rights' in *EnAct International London*, Cape Town, 2009; Stop Ecocide movement: https://www.stopecocide.earth/
51. Jem Bendell, 'Deep Adaptation: A Map for Navigating Climate Tragedy', *IFLAS Occasional Paper* 2, 2018.
52. Lent, *The Patterning Instinct*, pp. 405–42; Raskin et al., *Great Transition*.
53. Rebecca Solnit, *Hope in the Dark: Untold Histories, Wild Possibilities*, Chicago, IL: Haymarket Books, 2016, pp. 27–8; Paul Hawken, *Blessed Unrest: How the Largest Social Movement in History Is Restoring Grace, Justice, and Beauty to the World*, New York: Penguin, 2007, pp. 28–9; https://en.wikipedia.org/wiki/Emmeline_Pankhurst
54. Martin Luther King, Jr., *The Autobiography of Martin Luther King, Jr.*, New York: Warner Books, 1998, ed. Clayborne Carson; https://en.wikipedia.org/wiki/Tarana_Burke
55. Climate Justice Alliance, 'Just Transition Principles', ed. Climate Justice Alliance, 2020, https://climatejusticealliance.org/; Eduardo Gudynas, 'Buen Vivir: Today's Tomorrow', *Society for International Development* 54:4, 2011, pp. 441–7; Georgia Kelly, 'The Mondragón Report', *Praxis Peace Institute*, 2017.
56. Earth Charter, 'The Earth Charter', The Hague, 2000; Tu Weiming, 'Beyond the Enlightenment Mentality: An Anthropocosmic Vision' in *Civilizations and World Orders*, Istanbul: Foundation for Sciences and Arts, 2006; Chengzhou He, 'New Confucianism, Science and the Future of the Environment', *European Review* 26:2, 2018, pp. 368–80; Pope Francis, *Laudato Si': On Care for Our Common Home*, Huntington, IN: Our Sunday Visitor, 2015, 2015. It should be noted that, while the Chinese Communist Party officially

espouses an 'ecological civilization' as one of its policy platforms, its growth-oriented economy and grossly anti-democratic human rights abuses are in direct contravention of some of the key ecological principles described earlier. See Jeremy Lent, 'What Does China's "Ecological Civilization" Mean for Humanity's Future?' Patterns of Meaning blog, 8 February 2018.

57. Matthew Taylor, 'Schoolchildren Go on Strike across World over Climate Crisis', *Guardian*, 24 May 2019; Chaitanya Kumar, 'Britain Just Declared a Climate Emergency. What Happens Next?' *Open Democracy*, 7 May 2019; Climate Academy, 'This Movement Wants to Make Harming the Planet an International Crime', *Guardian*, 16 September 2020.

    Among a multitude of transformative organizations, here is a brief selection. The Wellbeing Economy Alliance is an international collaboration of changemakers working to transform the economic system into one that delivers human and ecological well-being. The Global Commons Alliance is similarly developing an international platform for regenerating the Earth's natural systems. Organizations such as the Next System Project and the Global Citizens Initiative are laying down parameters for the political, economic and social organization of an ecological civilization, while the P2P Foundation is building a commons-based infrastructure for societal change, and an international movement of 'transition towns' is transforming communities from the grassroots up. See Giorgos Kallis, 'In Defence of Degrowth', *Ecological Economics* 70, 2011, pp. 873–80; https://wellbeingeconomy.org/; http://globalcommonsalliance.org/; https://thenextsystem.org/; https://www.globalci.org/; https://p2pfoundation.net/; https://transitionnetwork.org/; https://www.stopecocide.earth/

58. Homer-Dixon et al., 'Synchronous Failure'.
59. Hawken, *Blessed Unrest*, pp. 18, 198; Jeremy Lent, 'As Society Unravels, the Future Is up for Grabs', Patterns of Meaning blog, 12 September 2019.
60. Solnit, *Hope in the Dark*, p. 11.
61. Douglas Rushkoff, *Team Human*, New York: W. W. Norton, 2019, p. 191.
62. Chapter 11, 'Opening our eyes to the rainbow'.
63. The term 'consensus trance' was first coined by Charles Tart; see Terry Patten, *A New Republic of the Heart: An Ethos for Revolutionaries*, Berkeley, CA: North Atlantic Books, 2018, pp. 35–7.
64. Joanna Macy and Molly Brown, *Coming Back to Life*, Gabriola Island, BC, Canada: New Society Publishers, 2014.
65. Stephen C. Angle, *Sagehood: The Contemporary Significance of Neo-Confucian Philosophy*, New York: Oxford University Press, 2009, pp. 118–19.
66. In Patten, *A New Republic of the Heart*, this phrase is ascribed to spiritual activist Andrew Harvey.
67. adrienne maree brown, *Emergent Strategy: Shaping Change, Changing Worlds*, Chico, CA: AK Press, 2017.
68. George Monbiot, *Out of the Wreckage: A New Politics for an Age of Crisis*, New York: Verso, 2017; Hawken, *Blessed Unrest*; Rushkoff, *Team Human*; Chapter 5, 'Better together'.

69. Frank Forencich, *New Old Way: Ancestral Health and Sapience for the Modern World*, Exuberant Animal, 2018, cites Mahatma Gandhi on this topic: 'Realization of the goal is in exact proportion to that of the means ... As the means, so the end.' (Kindle edn, location 4408.) See also Rushkoff, *Team Human*, p. 155.
70. David R. Loy, *A New Buddhist Path: Enlightenment, Evolution, and Ethics in the Modern World*, Somerville, MA: Wisdom Publications, 2015, pp. 129–31; First Nations Development Institute, 'Reclaiming Native Truth: Lessons Learned from Standing Rock', 2018.
71. Chapter 12, '"Call me by my true names"'.
72. Rabbi Michael Lerner, *Revolutionary Love: A Political Manifesto to Heal and Transform the World*, Oakland, CA: University of California Press, 2019, pp. 60–1; https://radicaldiscipleship.net/2020/10/30/4-thoughts-on-hope-and-resistance/
73. Chapter 3, 'The democracy of consciousness'.
74. Aurora Levins Morales, 'V'ahavta', 2016. See also Patten, *A New Republic of the Heart*, and Otto Scharmer and Katrin Kaufer, *Leading from the Emerging Future: From Ego-System to Eco-System Economies*, San Francisco: Berrett-Koehler, 2013.
75. Hawken, *Blessed Unrest*, pp. 155–6; Rushkoff, *Team Human*, p. 177.
76. Per Bak, *How Nature Works: The Science of Self-Organized Criticality*, New York: Springer-Verlag, 1996, pp. 69–75.

PERMISSIONS

— Excerpt from *Wall Street*. Copyright © 1987. Courtesy of Twentieth Century Fox. Written by Stanley Weiser and Oliver Stone. All rights reserved.

— Oodgeroo Noonuccal, excerpt from *We Are Going*, Jacaranda Press. Copyright © 1964. Reproduced with permission of John Wiley & Sons Ltd.

— 'Highwayman'. Words and music by Jimmy Webb. Copyright © 1977 White Oak Songs. Copyright renewed. All rights controlled and administered by Universal – Polygram International Publishing, Inc. All rights reserved. Used by permission. Reprinted by permission of Hal Leonard LLC.

— Excerpt from *Call Me By My True Names* by Thích Nhât Hanh, Parallax Press, 2001, parallax.org.

— Excerpt from *Catch-22* by Joseph Heller. Copyright © 1955, 1961 by Joseph Heller. Copyright renewed © 1989 by Joseph Heller. Reprinted with the permission of Simon & Schuster, Inc. All rights reserved.

— Excerpt from *V'ahavta* by Aurora Levins Morales. Copyright © 2016 by Aurora Levins Morales. Used with the permission of the Permissions Company, LLC on behalf of Aurora Levins Morales, www.auroralevinsmorales.com.

ILLUSTRATIONS

Figure 1 Oscillating patterns in biology and chemistry. Slime mold aggregation by permission of Peter C. Newell; Belousov–Zhabotinsky reaction © Michael C. Rogers and Stephen W. Morris, Nonlinear Physics, University of Toronto.

Figure 2 Spiraling patterns in nature. Paggi Eleanor; Zenobillis; Natalia van D; Insolite; Waroranger; Artsiom Petrushenka/Shutterstock.

Figure 3 Fractal patterns in nature. Eltaj Zeynalov; Breaking the Walls; hareluya; Viacheslav Lopatin/Shutterstock.

Figure 4 A murmuration of starlings. PA Images/Alamy Stock Photo.

Figure 5 Lévy flight path of an albatross near the Southern Indian Ocean, at three different scales. Nuno Queiroz/Nicolas E. Humphries et al., *PNAS*, 8 May 2012, 109:19, pp. 7169–74.

Figure 6 The Adaptive Cycle model of change. Amalesh Dhar et al., *Forests* 7:8, p. 171, adapted from L. H. Gunderson and C. S. Holling, *Panarchy: Understanding Transformations in Human and Natural Systems*, Washington DC: Island Press, 2002.

Figure 7 Comparison of income inequality and overall income levels in relation to health and social problems. Richard Wilkinson and Kate Pickett, *The Spirit Level: Why Greater Equality Makes Societies Stronger*, New York: Bloomsbury Press, 2009.

Figure 8 The Great Acceleration. Will Steffen et al., 'The Trajectory of the Anthropocene: The Great Acceleration', *Anthropocene Review* 2:1, 2015, pp. 1–18.

Figure 9 Simplified visualization of brain network changes on psilocybin. G. Petri et al., 'Homological Scaffolds of Brain Functional Networks', *Journal of the Royal Society Interface* 11, 2014, 20140873.

Figure 10 Shih T'ao, 'Broad-Distance Pavilion', *Illustrations to the Poems of Huang Yan-lü (1701–1702)*, Palace Museum, Beijing.

Figure 11 Chief Joseph, photographed by Edward Curtis (Library of Congress).

Figure 12 Comparing gross domestic product (GDP) per capita with genuine progress indicator (GPI) per capita. Maddison Project Database/All of Our World in Data; Ida Kubiszewski et al., 'Beyond GDP: Measuring and Achieving Global Genuine Progress', *Ecological Economics* 93, 2013, pp. 57–68.

Figure 13 The planetary boundaries defining humanity's safe operating space. Will Steffen et al., 'Planetary Boundaries: Guiding Human Development on a Changing Planet', *Science* 347:6223, 2015, 1259855. Design: F. Pharand-Deschênes/Globaïa.

INDEX

Note: references to endnotes are denoted by n.; references to the Glossary are denoted by g.

D

T

JEREMY LENT is an author and speaker whose work investigates the underlying causes of our civilisation's existential crisis, and explores pathways towards a life-affirming future. His award-winning book, *The Patterning Instinct: A Cultural History of Humanity's Search for Meaning*, examines the way humans have made meaning from the cosmos from hunter-gatherer times to the present day. A former internet company CEO, he is founder of the non-profit Liology Institute dedicated to fostering an integrated worldview in support of a flourishing future on a regenerated Earth. He lives with his partner in Berkeley, California.

www.jeremylent.com